Lecture Notes in Computer Science   9746

Commenced Publication in 1973
Founding and Former Series Editors:
Gerhard Goos, Juris Hartmanis, and Jan van Leeuwen

Aaron Marcus (Ed.)

Design, User Experience, and Usability

Design Thinking and Methods

5th International Conference, DUXU 2016
Held as Part of HCI International 2016
Toronto, Canada, July 17–22, 2016
Proceedings, Part I

 Springer

Editor
Aaron Marcus
Aaron Marcus and Associates
Berkeley, CA
USA

ISSN 0302-9743   ISSN 1611-3349   (electronic)
Lecture Notes in Computer Science
ISBN 978-3-319-40408-0   ISBN 978-3-319-40409-7   (eBook)
DOI 10.1007/978-3-319-40409-7

Library of Congress Control Number: 2016940889

LNCS Sublibrary: SL3 – Information Systems and Applications, incl. Internet/Web, and HCI

Printed on acid-free paper

This Springer imprint is published by Springer Nature
The registered company is Springer International Publishing AG Switzerland

Foreword

The 18th International Conference on Human-Computer Interaction, HCI International 2016, was held in Toronto, Canada, during July 17–22, 2016. The event incorporated the 15 conferences/thematic areas listed on the following page.

A total of 4,354 individuals from academia, research institutes, industry, and governmental agencies from 74 countries submitted contributions, and 1,287 papers and 186 posters have been included in the proceedings. These papers address the latest research and development efforts and highlight the human aspects of the design and use of computing systems. The papers thoroughly cover the entire field of human-computer interaction, addressing major advances in knowledge and effective use of computers in a variety of application areas. The volumes constituting the full 27-volume set of the conference proceedings are listed on pages IX and X.

I would like to thank the program board chairs and the members of the program boards of all thematic areas and affiliated conferences for their contribution to the highest scientific quality and the overall success of the HCI International 2016 conference.

This conference would not have been possible without the continuous and unwavering support and advice of the founder, Conference General Chair Emeritus and Conference Scientific Advisor Prof. Gavriel Salvendy. For his outstanding efforts, I would like to express my appreciation to the communications chair and editor of *HCI International News*, Dr. Abbas Moallem.

April 2016   Constantine Stephanidis

HCI International 2016 Thematic Areas and Affiliated Conferences

Thematic areas:

- Human-Computer Interaction (HCI 2016)
- Human Interface and the Management of Information (HIMI 2016)

Affiliated conferences:

- 13th International Conference on Engineering Psychology and Cognitive Ergonomics (EPCE 2016)
- 10th International Conference on Universal Access in Human-Computer Interaction (UAHCI 2016)
- 8th International Conference on Virtual, Augmented and Mixed Reality (VAMR 2016)
- 8th International Conference on Cross-Cultural Design (CCD 2016)
- 8th International Conference on Social Computing and Social Media (SCSM 2016)
- 10th International Conference on Augmented Cognition (AC 2016)
- 7th International Conference on Digital Human Modeling and Applications in Health, Safety, Ergonomics and Risk Management (DHM 2016)
- 5th International Conference on Design, User Experience and Usability (DUXU 2016)
- 4th International Conference on Distributed, Ambient and Pervasive Interactions (DAPI 2016)
- 4th International Conference on Human Aspects of Information Security, Privacy and Trust (HAS 2016)
- Third International Conference on HCI in Business, Government, and Organizations (HCIBGO 2016)
- Third International Conference on Learning and Collaboration Technologies (LCT 2016)
- Second International Conference on Human Aspects of IT for the Aged Population (ITAP 2016)

Conference Proceedings Volumes Full List

1. LNCS 9731, Human-Computer Interaction: Theory, Design, Development and Practice (Part I), edited by Masaaki Kurosu
2. LNCS 9732, Human-Computer Interaction: Interaction Platforms and Techniques (Part II), edited by Masaaki Kurosu
3. LNCS 9733, Human-Computer Interaction: Novel User Experiences (Part III), edited by Masaaki Kurosu
4. LNCS 9734, Human Interface and the Management of Information: Information, Design and Interaction (Part I), edited by Sakae Yamamoto
5. LNCS 9735, Human Interface and the Management of Information: Applications and Services (Part II), edited by Sakae Yamamoto
6. LNAI 9736, Engineering Psychology and Cognitive Ergonomics, edited by Don Harris
7. LNCS 9737, Universal Access in Human-Computer Interaction: Methods, Techniques, and Best Practices (Part I), edited by Margherita Antona and Constantine Stephanidis
8. LNCS 9738, Universal Access in Human-Computer Interaction: Interaction Techniques and Environments (Part II), edited by Margherita Antona and Constantine Stephanidis
9. LNCS 9739, Universal Access in Human-Computer Interaction: Users and Context Diversity (Part III), edited by Margherita Antona and Constantine Stephanidis
10. LNCS 9740, Virtual, Augmented and Mixed Reality, edited by Stephanie Lackey and Randall Shumaker
11. LNCS 9741, Cross-Cultural Design, edited by Pei-Luen Patrick Rau
12. LNCS 9742, Social Computing and Social Media, edited by Gabriele Meiselwitz
13. LNAI 9743, Foundations of Augmented Cognition: Neuroergonomics and Operational Neuroscience (Part I), edited by Dylan D. Schmorrow and Cali M. Fidopiastis
14. LNAI 9744, Foundations of Augmented Cognition: Neuroergonomics and Operational Neuroscience (Part II), edited by Dylan D. Schmorrow and Cali M. Fidopiastis
15. LNCS 9745, Digital Human Modeling and Applications in Health, Safety, Ergonomics and Risk Management, edited by Vincent G. Duffy
16. LNCS 9746, Design, User Experience, and Usability: Design Thinking and Methods (Part I), edited by Aaron Marcus
17. LNCS 9747, Design, User Experience, and Usability: Novel User Experiences (Part II), edited by Aaron Marcus
18. LNCS 9748, Design, User Experience, and Usability: Technological Contexts (Part III), edited by Aaron Marcus
19. LNCS 9749, Distributed, Ambient and Pervasive Interactions, edited by Norbert Streitz and Panos Markopoulos
20. LNCS 9750, Human Aspects of Information Security, Privacy and Trust, edited by Theo Tryfonas

Design, User Experience and Usability

Program Board Chair: **Aaron Marcus, USA**

- Sisira Adikari, Australia
- Claire Ancient, UK
- Arne Berger, Germany
- Jan Brejcha, Czech Republic
- Hashim Chunpir, Germany
- Silvia de los Rios Perez, Spain
- Marc Fabri, UK
- Tineke (Christina) Fitch, UK
- Patricia Flanagan, Australia
- Steffen Hess, Germany
- Long Jiao, P.R. China
- Nouf Khashman, Canada
- Khalil R. Laghari, Canada
- Tom MacTavish, USA
- Judith A. Moldenhauer, USA
- Francisco Rebelo, Portugal
- Kerem Rızvanoğlu, Turkey
- Christine Riedmann-Streitz, Germany
- Patricia Search, USA
- Marcelo Soares, Brazil
- Carla Spinillo, Brazil
- Virginia Tiradentes Souto, Brazil
- Manfred Tscheligi, Austria
- Ryan Wynia, USA

The full list with the program board chairs and the members of the program boards of all thematic areas and affiliated conferences is available online at:

http://www.hci.international/2016/

HCI International 2017

The 19th International Conference on Human-Computer Interaction, HCI International 2017, will be held jointly with the affiliated conferences in Vancouver, Canada, at the Vancouver Convention Centre, July 9–14, 2017. It will cover a broad spectrum of themes related to human-computer interaction, including theoretical issues, methods, tools, processes, and case studies in HCI design, as well as novel interaction techniques, interfaces, and applications. The proceedings will be published by Springer. More information will be available on the conference website: http://2017. hci.international/.

General Chair
Prof. Constantine Stephanidis
University of Crete and ICS-FORTH
Heraklion, Crete, Greece
E-mail: general_chair@hcii2017.org

http://2017.hci.international/

Contents – Part I

Usability and User Experience Evaluation Methods and Tools

Contents – Part II

DUXU in Learning and Education

Games and Gamification

Culture, Language and DUXU

DUXU for Social Innovation and Sustainability

Usability and User Experience Studies

Contents – Part III

DUXU in Virtual and Augmented Reality

DUXU for Smart Objects and Environments

Design Thinking and Design Philosophy

Embed Design Thinking in Co-Design
for Rapid Innovation of Design Solutions

Sisira Adikari[1(✉)], Heath Keighran[2], and Hamed Sarbazhosseini[1]

[1] School of Information Systems and Accounting,
University of Canberra, Canberra, ACT 2601, Australia
{Sisira.adikari,Hamed.Sarbazhosseini}@canberra.edu.au
[2] Business Design, Crooked Fox, Canberra, ACT 2601, Australia
Heath@crookedfox.com.au

Abstract. This paper presents a detailed research study that explores how a design thinking inspired co-design approach was applied to creating and evaluating design artifacts of an intended system. A prototype system so called Art Lab was created for the use of an art community for online engagement and collaborative decision-making. The prototype system was designed based on selective user community ideas picked up using an integrated idea generation and prototyping process. The results of this study suggest that the integrated ideation governance process and an active end-user involvement in idea generation and prototyping deliver effective human-centered, and user agreed design solutions. The significance of the paper is that it presents a well-detailed Ideation Governance process and a prototyping approach designated as the Idea Lab process for effective idea generation, idea selection, and prototyping.

Keywords: Creativity · Design thinking · Ideation · Innovation

1 Introduction

The design driven by user needs is termed as "Human-Centred" [1], and it aims to gain a deeper understanding of all stakeholders, context of use, and to involve users throughout the design process, development, and long-term monitoring of the artifact (product, system or service) [2]. Accordingly, Human-Centred Design (HCD) shows a direct relevance to the sustainability of information systems. HCD is constrained by many challenges, and one of the important issues is how to gain sufficient knowledge of the users, and all contextual requirements. Design Thinking (DT) is an approach that can be applied effectively to gaining a deeper knowledge of users and the context. Such knowledge is beneficial for HCD in creating user agreed design solutions. Moreover, DT blends an end-user focus with multidisciplinary collaboration and iterative improvements in creating artifacts [3]. DT has been recognized as an iterative process consists of five key activities [4]: 1. (re) Define the problem, 2. Need finding and benchmarking (understand the users, design space), 3. Brainstorm (ideate), 4. Prototype (build), 5. Test (learn). The success of all these activities is dependent on the extent to which users are involved in each activity with their ideas and idea-oriented tasks. Accordingly, ideas and idea management are important for DT.

© Springer International Publishing Switzerland 2016
A. Marcus (Ed.): DUXU 2016, Part I, LNCS 9746, pp. 3–14, 2016.
DOI: 10.1007/978-3-319-40409-7_1

In recent years, the idea management for innovation has become prominent and significant [4–7]. Ideation is referred as the process of creating new concepts or ideas and develops them further [8]; hence ideation is fundamental to the innovation. Ideation is significant for imposing business value and competitive advantage. Ideation makes an important contribution to the successful and constructive design of business processes and systems. The distinction between innovation and creativity has been highlighted by many authors [9–11] where creativity is identified as producing novel and useful ideas that can be used to develop processes, products, systems, or services [12, 13]. On the otherhand, the innovation is defined as the successful implementation of artifacts developed on creative ideas within an organization [14]. These definitions emphasize the relationship between ideas, and creativity and innovation showing that ideas are the primary source of innovation. According to Sawyer and Bunderson [15], creativity is the ideas or products generated by individuals and innovation is the successful execution of a new product or service by an entire organization. Accordingly, creativity can be viewed as the ability of people to generate useful ideas that exhibit business value and great promise. On the other hand, innovation is concerned with the successful implementation of those useful ideas to create business artifacts such as products, systems, and services. Figure 1 presents an abstract view of the innovation process that highlights the relationship between ideas (creativity) and implementation of ideas (innovation).

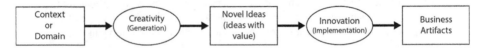

Fig. 1. Innovation process – relationship between ideas and innovation

In an enterprise, ideas from different sources help to form knowledge constructs that can be useful for creating new business artifacts or improving existing ones. In this respect, it is beneficial for the enterprise to collect and preserve useful ideas that show business value as they can be significant for developing new opportunities. However, every idea deemed useful for the enterprise may not have the potential to be invested in with financial or human resources. Accordingly, those ideas identified as the useful need to be investigated beforehand to determine the suitability in terms of business value, feasibility, viability, and desirability to ensure: (a). Efficient utilization of resources, (b). Providing a satisfactory return on investment, (c). Sufficient buy-in or adoption by stakeholders in the enterprise. Idea management systems and its relevance to the innovation management have been widely discussed in the recent literature [16–18] with a variety of models and frameworks in support of innovation management [19–21]. However, a literature review published in 2012 concluded that there was not much research conducted on how people interact with idea management in their daily work practices [22].

The aim of this paper is twofold: first, to present an ideation governance process model intended to generating and capturing ideas to explore and redevelop selected ideas in a type of incubator. Second, to show an effective ideation management process to collect ideas from different sources and reviewing them for a shared and agreed decision for further redevelopment and implementation through redesign, prototyping, and evaluation.

2   Ideation Governance Process

In an enterprise, there are many sources for idea generation such as internal employees, research and development staff, customers, suppliers, competitors, etc. Idea generation is an iterative cycle of idea production, reflection, and building new ideas on existing ideas or those ideas being discovered. Figure 2 shows the proposed Ideation Governance Process Model consists of three main functionalities: (a). Idea Generation and Collection, (b). Idea Selection, (c). Idea Lab.

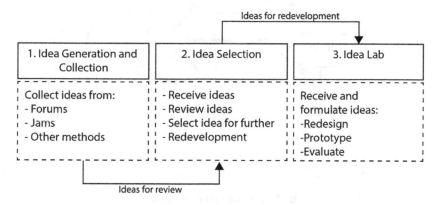

Fig. 2. Ideation governance system

The Idea Generation and Collection functionality is operated by skilled facilitators for effective idea generation, where idea based concepts are created as potentials for various design solutions. The user participants engaged in idea generation sessions are from different backgrounds. Accordingly, the diversity of the knowledge and experiences of the user participants helps to foster creativity in design. During the Idea Generation and Collection process, the ideas that show significant business value are sent to the Idea Selection where ideas are reviewed, selected and prioritized for further redevelopment. The prioritized ideas are received by the Idea Lab where those ideas are redesigned, prototyped and evaluated in collaboration with end-users to create agreed design solutions. The Idea Lab aims to create a minimum viable solution that addresses essential elements of the overall design challenge or problem.

2.1   The Idea Lab Process Model

The Idea Lab embraces collaborative and co-design approach and uses a collection of techniques, tools and a range of business design activities. The co-design approach is aimed at generating collective creativity by engaging designers and user participants together in the design process where user participants become a partner in the design. The primary objective of the Idea Lab is to evaluate ideas for creating agreed design solutions for the implementation in the organizational context. The main functionalities of the Idea Lab are: (a). Receive and formulate ideas, (b). Redesign ideas, (c). Prototype ideas, and (d). Evaluate ideas. The Agreed Design Solutions are the final output of the Idea Lab. The process model of the Idea Lab is shown in Fig. 3.

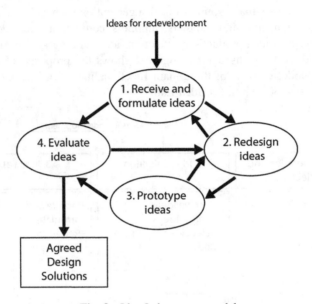

Fig. 3. Idea Lab process model

Close collaboration, active engagement of user participants with designers, rapid prototyping, and evaluations during the co-design help gain a deeper understanding of users, user and system requirements, and the context of use. Accordingly, the co-design approach is significant in providing the guidance to create and evaluate business artifacts towards Agreed Design Solutions. Idea Lab provides a test environment for evaluating prototypes of ideas to determine the usefulness and business value for the enterprise. Prototyping allows designers to work with user participants to test and improve ideas rapidly through an iterative process. Hence, prototyping helps designers and user participants to discover new knowledge and to identify potential design issues early and provide effective solutions through experimentation. Accordingly, Idea Lab provides the means to test ideas effectively to determine which ideas are best for the enterprise to invest in for further development.

3   Experimental Study

This section presents the details of a Human-Centred experimental study conducted over five weeks in designing an Information System for the use of artist community. The study aimed to design an Information System that encourages artists and art enthusiasts of all level of knowledge to learn, share and further enhance their knowledge, skills and expertise of art through online collaboration in a safe environment. This study was motivated by the need for the artist community to learn and share art, but their needs and expectations were restrained by (a). Lack of time, (b). Cost, and (c). Lack of knowledge on how to collaborate, and share art among peers.

3.1   The Idea Generation and Collection

The engagement of cross-functional team consists of user participants from different backgrounds with designers benefits the design of innovative systems. The diversity of a cross-functional team gives many different, useful ideas, hence, the facilitation and capturing information effectively is vital to realizing the contextual needs and wants accurately. The Idea Generation and Collection functionality of the Ideation Governance Process Model was operated by a management team consists of a skillful facilitator and an information designer. A group of people consists of artists, art students, parents of students, art teachers, a User Interface (UI) designer, a business analyst, and a software developer attended the idea generation sessions.

For this study, only one idea generation session was held. The aim of the idea generation session was to uncover good ideas that support delivering a learnable, enjoyable, and safe sharing platform that help artist people improve socialization, collaboration, and interaction with others. The facilitator led the idea generation session, and the group engaged in collaborative discussions to generate design ideas based on following key points:

- What do you see as ART and not ART?
- How do you categorize ART?
- What are your top three favorite forms of art?
- What is your art experience - e.g. artist, interest, learner, etc.?
- What are the significant limitations that prevent you from enjoying ART more?
- How would you like to share your art and art experience with peers?
- What do you suggest how to promote ART?
- How would you like to showcase your artwork? If not, what are the reasons?
- What do you enjoy most about your chosen art form(s)?
- Do you like to teach others what you know about art? Why and why not?

During the session, participants engaged in a brainstorming activity and proposed a variety of ideas based on the key topics given by the facilitator. The management team also uncovered other participant attributes such as group dynamics, behaviors, knowledge, experience, and attitudes. In agreement with participants, the management team then grouped ideas into logical categories and each category was given a theme name. These Themes represented some intended functionality by participants. The management team administered a voting among participants and selected following themes (functionalities) that had most votes.

- Registration (registration of artist users)
- User Profiling (setting up artist user profiles)
- Sign-in (logging into the system)

- Register Events (registration of new events by users)
- Find Events (finding the desired events by users)
- Book Events (registration of participants for events)
- Log-out (signing out of the system)
- Feedback (Providing feedback by users about the system at any time)

Participants emphasized that their passion for art inspired them to use the Internet to find better ways to make it easier for people to connect with others who have similar interests. One of their commonly agreed preference was to have a collaborative space that provides a safe environment for people to learn and share, ranging from intimate concert halls through to people's very own music rooms. All design ideas generated by participants were captured by the management team to be passed over to the Idea Selection functionality.

3.2 Idea Selection

The Idea Selection functionality was managed by a committee (called as the Management Committee) consists of a Senior User (a representative of the artist community), and an Executive (who represents the business interests of the proposed system and who has the authority to make decisions). The primary role of the Management Committee was to record and assess all ideas received from the Idea Generation and Collection functionality to determine the suitability of each idea for further development. Ideas are evaluated based on their business value, feasibility, desirability, and viability and the selected ideas that deemed promising enough for prototyping are then passed over to the Idea Lab for further development.

3.3 Idea Lab Process

The iterative Idea Lab process is shown in Fig. 3. The Idea Lab was led by a design team consists of a design facilitator, a business designer, and an Information Designer. In this study, the Idea Lab sessions were attended by a group of artists (three female artists, and three male artists who had over three years of professional art experience), and they actively participated in prototyping, redevelopment and evaluation activities. The processes Redesign ideas, Prototype ideas, and Evaluate ideas were conducted iteratively in consultation and collaboration with participants until they are agreed on the design solutions. The active engagement of participants in the whole design process gave them the opportunity to experience the prototypes, react to the design and task flows, and finally to provide a feedback of their interactive experience to the designers in the Idea Lab. The first step of the Idea Lab was to formulate the received ideas to match the order of the intended system task flows. The second step was to redesign ideas to improve idea clarity and relevance to the system task flows. During the third step Prototyping, all ideas were realized into low-fidelity artifacts such as rich pictures, post-it notes, storyboards, and the participants and designers developed a shared understanding of selected ideas.

4 Results

The evaluations of the prototypes during the Idea Lab produced a number of agreed design solutions for the intended system, which was designated as Art Lab. The participatory discussions during the idea lab process also led to an agreed end-to-end user pathway that represents the each user task of the overall design. User tasks are represented in prototype screens, and collectively these prototype screens form the minimum viable solution for the Art Lab. Figure 4 shows the end-to-end process view of the Art Lab from the first process Registration to the last process Log-out. For simplicity, Fig. 4 shows a sequential user pathway of the Art Lab. In practical terms, there are many non-sequential or alternative paths a user can follow to navigate through the system such as a user can provide Feedback immediately after the Registration, or Log-out from the system at any time after Sign-in.

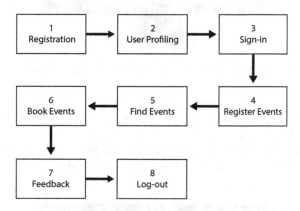

Fig. 4. End-to-end user pathway of the proposed system (Art Lab)

Figure 5 shows the prototype screen of the first process of the Art Lab: Registration. It shows different main menu options that were discussed and agreed in unison by the user participants during the prototyping sessions.

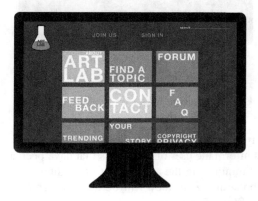

Fig. 5. Prototype screen for the registration process

The first screen also shows navigational paths to additional resources such as Copyright and Privacy, Frequently Asked Questions (FAQ), Forum, Contact, etc.

Figure 6 shows the prototype screen of the second process: User Profiling where a user registers their personal details and interests in the system.

Fig. 6. Prototype screen for the User Profiling process

This screen also provides a statement that describes how the system handle user provided information. The intention of such a statement is to ensure trust and confidence among users of the system about privacy and protection of user data.

Figure 7 shows the prototype screen of the third process: Sign-in where the user enters an email address and a password to login to the system.

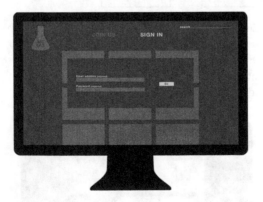

Fig. 7. Prototype screen for the Sign-in process

Figure 8 shows two prototype screens for the fourth process: Find Events. By default, these screens inform the user of the events that have been already booked in by the user. This aims at minimizing the effort spent on finding an event already booked in. If users wish to book an event, they will be able to search by Art Sector, Music Instruments, Country, State, Town, etc.

Fig. 8. Prototype screens for the Find Events process

Figure 9 shows two prototyping screens for the fifth process: Book Events. The first screen shows the prototype for booking events and the second screen shows the prototype where a user confirms the booking.

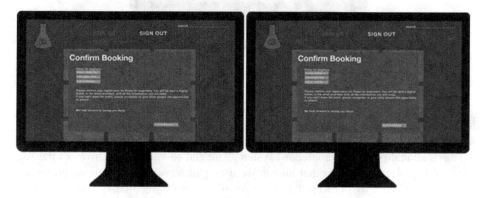

Fig. 9. Prototype screens for the Book Events process

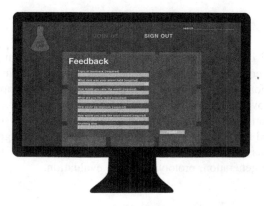

Fig. 10. Prototype screen for the Feedback process

Figure 10 shows the prototyping screen for the sixth process: Feedback where a user can provide a feedback of the system. The need for an effective Feedback process was agreed upon by participants as crucial to improving the system continuously.

Figure 11 shows the prototype screen for the last process of the system: Signing-out. Importantly, during the signing-out, the user is prompted with the message "Before sign out, would you like to provide any feedback?" This allows user another opportunity to provide a feedback of the system.

Fig. 11. Prototype screen for the Sign-out process

In summary, the active user engagement in idea generation and throughout the design process was significant in generating useful ideas and concepts with greater business value. These ideas and concepts were fundamental in forming new user tasks and navigational paths of the intended system. The end-to-end user pathway of the Art Lab (see Fig. 4) along with other alternative user pathways, and associated prototype screens (see Figs. 5 to 11) were the outcome of the user agreed design solutions that emerged from the idea generation sessions, and subsequent prototyping and evaluation sessions.

5   Conclusions

The main objective of this paper was to explore how the design thinking inspired co-design approach could be used for idea generation, and prototyping for creating user agreed design solutions for an intended information system. The paper reported a well detailed Ideation Governance process and an Idea Lab process for effective idea generation, idea selection, and subsequent prototyping to create design solutions agreed by users of the intended information system. Results of this study suggest that prototypes and design solutions provide more human-centeredness as a result of active user engagement in idea generation, prototyping, and evaluation.

References

1. Niemelä, M., Ikonen, V., Leikas, J., Kantola, K., Kulju, M., Tammela, A., Ylikauppila, M.: Human-driven design: a human-driven approach to the design of technology. In: Kimppa, K., Whitehouse, D., Kuusela, T., Phahlamohlaka, J. (eds.) HCC11 2014. IFIP AICT, vol. 431, pp. 78–91. Springer, Heidelberg (2014)
2. Johnson, M.: Towards human-centred requirements management in distributed design. In: Smith, M.J., Salvendy, G. (eds) Systems, Social and Internationalization Design Aspects of Human-Computer Interaction, vol. 2, pp. 642–646 (2001)
3. Gabrysiak, G., Giese, H., Seibel, A.: Towards next-generation design thinking II: virtual multi-user software prototypes. In: Plattner, H., Meinel, C., Leifer, L. (eds.) Design Thinking Research: Studying Co-Creation in Practice. Understanding Innovation, pp. 107–126. Springer, Heidelberg (2012)
4. Meinel, C., Leifer, L.: Design thinking research. In: Plattner, H., Meinel, C., Leifer, L. (eds.) Design Thinking Research: Understand – Improve – Apply. Understanding Innovation, p. xiv. Springer, Heidelberg (2011)
5. Alessi, M., Camillò, A., Chetta, V., Giangreco, E., Soufivand, M., Storelli, D.: Applying Idea Management System (IMS) approach to design and implement a collaborative environment in public service related open Innovation processes. Complex Syst. Inf. Model. Q. 5, 26–38 (2015)
6. Westerski, A., Dalamagas, T., Iglesias, C.A.: Classifying and comparing community innovation in Idea Management Systems. Decis. Support Syst. 54(3), 1316–1326 (2013)
7. Sadriev, A.R., Pratchenko, O.V.: Idea management in the system of innovative management. Mediterranean J. Soc. Sci. 5(12), 155–158 (2014)
8. Yock, P.G., Zenios, S., Makower, J., Brinton, T.J., Krummel, T.M., Kumar, U.N., Denend, L.: Biodesign, p. 176. Cambridge University Press (2015)
9. Bilton, C., Cummings, S.: Creative Strategy: Reconnecting Business and Innovation, p. 16. Wiley, Chichester (2010)
10. Cropley, D.H., Cropley, A.J.: The Psychology of Innovation in Organizations, p. 14. Cambridge University Press, New York (2015)
11. Shalley, C.E., Gilson, L.L.: What leaders need to know: A review of social and contextual factors that can foster or hinder creativity. Leadersh. Quart. 15(1), 33–53 (2004)
12. Shalley, C.E.: Effects of coaction, expected evaluation, and goal setting on creativity and productivity. Acad. Manag. J. 38, 483–503 (1995)
13. Woodman, R.W., Sawyer, J.E., Griffin, R.W.: Toward a theory of organizational creativity. Acad. Manag. Rev. 18, 293–321 (1993)
14. Amabile, T.M.: A model of creativity and innovation in organizations. Res. Organ. Behav. 10(1), 123–167 (2004)
15. Sawyer, R.K., Bunderson, S.: Innovation: A review of research in organizational behavior. In: Thakor, A. (ed.) Innovation and Growth: What Do We Know?, pp. 13–55. World Scientific Press, Singapore (2013)
16. Boeddrich, H.: Ideas in the Workplace: A New Approach Towards Organizing the Fuzzy Front End of the Innovation Process. Creativity Innov. Manag. 13(4), 274–285 (2004)
17. Flynn, M., Dooley, L., O'Sullivan, D.: Idea management for organizational innovation. Int. J. Innov. Manag. 7(4), 417–442 (2003)
18. Nilsson, L., Elg, M.: Secure spread-spectrum watermarking for multimedia. IEEE Trans. Image Process. 6(12), 64–69 (1997)

19. Brem, A., Voigt, K.: Integration of market pull and technology push in the corporate front end and innovation management - Insights from the German software industry. Technovation **29**(5), 351–367 (2009)
20. Hrastinski, S., Kviselius, N.Z., Ozan, H., Edenius, M.: A review of technologies for open innovation: characteristics and future trends. In: Proceedings of the Annual Hawaii International Conference on System Sciences (2010)
21. Xie, L., Zhang, P.: Idea management system for team creation. J. Softw. **5**(11), 1187–1194 (2010)
22. Jensen, A.R.V.: A literature review of idea management. In: Proceedings of the 9th NordDesign Conference, NordDesign 2012, Aalborg University, Denmark, 22–24 August 2012

The X Factor
Defining the Concept of Experience

Stefano Bussolon[✉]

Department of Psychology and Cognitive Science, University of Trento, Trento, Italy
stefano.bussolon@unitn.it

Abstract. The term User Experience has become mainstream. But what is an experience? In this paper I will give a definition of the concept, explaining it within the paradigm of evolutionary psychology. I will briefly describe its main components (executive functions, episodic and semantic memory), mechanisms (learning, reinforcement, evaluation), and goals (the motivational system and the inclusive fitness). Finally, I will provide some reasons of the usefulness of an explicit definition of experience, both within an academic context and the design and business practice.

We use our own experience and memory and wisdom and art Anaxagoras - Fragment 21b.

1 Introduction

The term user experience is 30 years old [26]. It has an official definition (ISO 9241-210), and is gaining momentum: a growing number of professionals define themselves as user experience designers, and the importance of the uxd is increasingly recognized by the industry.

Nonetheless, the concept remains elusive: Hassenzahl [20] calls it an *evasive beast*, Law et al. [27] gave five different definitions, the site All About UX cites 27 different *user experience definitions*.

Though some common elements recur, the concept seems more a family resemblance than a core concept: ux is seen as a holistic, multidisciplinary approach to design, where information architecture, interaction design, information design, graphic design, usability, accessibility, content management converge to the final product or service.

The concept of experience is usually only implicitly defined, and different aspects of it are usually reported: the needs; the perceptions and responses of the user to the product; how a person feels; the experiential, affective, meaningful and valuable aspects; the result of motivated action; the past experiences and the expectations; the interaction of internal states, a system, and a context; a momentary, primarily evaluative feeling.

Even when explicit definitions of experience are proposed [13,16], the authors are usually "not interested in experience per se but in experience in relation to interactive products" [21].

© Springer International Publishing Switzerland 2016
A. Marcus (Ed.): DUXU 2016, Part I, LNCS 9746, pp. 15–24, 2016.
DOI: 10.1007/978-3-319-40409-7_2

If, in the last 30 years, a formal definition of the x of ux is still not emerged, is it really necessary? As a teacher in a course of human computer interaction I find the lack of an explicit and comprehensive definition of the concept particularly frustrating. Furthermore, I believe that a *working* conceptualization of experience could help the community to identify a shared methodology of research, analysis, design and evaluation of a product or service.

2   The Definition of the Concept

The Oxford dictionary defines the noun experience as

- Practical contact with and observation of facts or events
- The knowledge or skill acquired by experience over a period of time, especially that gained in a particular profession by someone at work
- An event or occurrence that leaves an impression on someone

The three meanings refer to 3 related but different things:

- the phenomenological experience of the conscious *me-here-now*
- the episodic memory of *memorable* experiences [28]
- the process of abstraction of a number of experiential episodes in a pattern/scheme/script [37]

The first meaning represents *what I'm experiencing right now, here.* If I'm mindless of what is happening, and if what is happening is nothing new (for example, I'm reading a book while I'm commuting, and nothing unusual happens) this event will somehow reinforce my scheme of that kind of event (the scheme of commuting) and I will forget the specific event [38]. If I'm living something new, or if something unexpected and worth noting happens, however, I will remember the most salient events of the episode.

To identify the commonalities of the different meanings of the term experience, I propose a definition of the concept based on its main attributes.

In my definition, a **prototypical** experience is the subjective, conscious, intentional representation of an episodic autobiographical event:

- it has a strong phenomenological grounding, and is lived as a non mediated, immersive flow of consciousness;
- is usually triggered by a motivation
- can be imagined, and therefore mentally anticipated
- can be the result of a decisional process, a choice
- can be planned, at different levels of detail
- can be remembered
- is usually subject of evaluations: before, during and after
- can trigger a learning process
- can become a habit

The episodic and semantic memory and the executive functions are at the basis of the experiences. From a phenomenological perspective, an experience is a temporal window of the salient events that happened, are happening or are expected or planned to happen. From the past, present or future experiences we can build mental representations. Those representations integrate a causal and motivational dimension (why), a temporal dimension (when), a spatial dimension (where), and are formed by instances of conceptual classes (what) and possibly other people (who).

Concepts are organized in semantic networks and in hierarchies (taxonomies). The temporal, causal and spatial dimensions are hierarchically organized as well. The causal dimension is organized in goals and task hierarchies.

3 An Evolutionary Perspective

To understand the role and the functions carried out by the experiences, it is useful to adopt an evolutionary perspective [9]. The evolutionary psychology is based on the assumption (shared with the evolutionary biology) that the purpose of all living beings is their inclusive fitness [29].

In a complex environment, the inclusive fitness can be better achieved trough the cultivation of a number of material and non material goods. An individual with good skills, a solid social network, living in a favorable environment and owning some material goods has greater chances to maximize her inclusive fitness. Following this reasoning, it is assumed that the basic needs (living in a safe environment, physical and mental health, good relationships, material and economic resources, autonomy, competence, identity, meaning [11,12,15] are assets that increase the odds to maximize the inclusive fitness of the individual [18,25]. Humans, therefore, evolved the drive to satisfy those basic needs, because this enhanced their inclusive fitness. This hypothesis extends the results of the use of an intrinsically motivated reinforcement learning system of an artificial agent [34].

Affective and cognitive functions are seen as *adaptations*: "mechanisms or systems of properties crafted by natural selection to solve the specific problems posed by the regularities of the physical, chemical, developmental, ecological, demographic, social, and informational environments encountered by ancestral populations during the course of a species' or population's evolution" [41].

The satisfaction of the basic needs becomes the *ultimate goal* [33]. The cognitive an affective systems evolved to orient the individual to identify and fulfill both the ultimate and the proximate goals, to explore and to exploit the environment.

3.1 Learning

Knowledge transforms information into decision making to increase the inclusive fitness trough the satisfaction of the basic needs and proximate goals. Learning is, in the evolutionary perspective, a form of adaptation.

From the evolutionary perspective, the function of the learning mechanisms is to improve the fitness, by mapping the environment and the behaviors that decrease the risk of dangers and increase the odds to fulfill one's needs.

Humans (and other animals) use two different strategies to learn to choose actions that lead to positive and prevent negative outcomes [2]: model based and model free (or value based). Model based strategies involve an internal representation of the environment, whereas model free ones associate a behavior within a context and it's *reward history* [42].

The model-based mechanism consists in the ability of the agent (biological or artificial) to build an internal, dynamic representation of a physical or conceptual environment. The main advantage is that a *journey* within a model is much more economical and less risk prone.

Some nodes and paths of the conceptual space have an affective valence, because they represent dangers or aversive situations (negative valence) or the satisfaction of goals, subgoals or basic needs (positive valence).

Trough the simulation it is possible to identify - and memorize - some paths; this corresponds to the planning process. Every choice we make at any junction corresponds to a decision making process.

The main disadvantage of this mechanism is that a systematic, brute force exploration of the conceptual space is prone to a combinatorial explosion, and it becomes necessary to employ some heuristics. The process of generalization of experiences in schemas constitute the main heuristic: every time an individual encounters a situation that is similar to a known pattern, she uses the schema as the model, and tends to adopt those behavioral paths that correspond to the past experiences [36] and reinforcements [7], therefore using the model-free mechanism of habits as well [10].

3.2   Planning

Szpunar [39] define planning as a multicomponent process that operates at various levels of abstraction and serves as a predetermined course of action aimed at achieving some goal. It involves defining a variety of goals and subgoals, prioritizing those goals, monitoring one's progress, and reevaluating the original plan. Planning is the process of identification and memorization of a path in a conceptual space. The process implies the identification of the goal and of the possible routes. The representation is hierarchical: the main goal is subdivided in subgoals, in a recursive way. The agent estimates the value of the main goal, the cost of the tasks (in terms of resources, time, physical and psychological fatigue) and their possible intrinsic value.

This metaphor is a spatial one: the navigation of a conceptual space, the identification of a path, the journey. What individuals plan is, however, a sequence of behaviors and actions. [31] use the theater metaphor: the agent is a director that images a plot, trough the recombination of episodic elements within the structure of schemas and scripts (episodic simulation). Both the planning and the evaluation assume the form of mental travels, away from the egocentric *me-here-now*, in space, in time - toward the future for the planning, toward the past for the evaluation of past or ongoing experiences - and in the mind of other agents (theory of mind) [1,19,35].

The ability to simulate specific future events plays an important role in the planning process. The constructive episodic simulation hypothesis contends that episodic memory provides a source of details for (future) event simulations [1]. The constructive nature of episodic memory allows the flexible recombination of such details into a coherent simulation.

Episodic simulation supports autobiographical planning, trough the cooperation between the episodic memory system, that provides the content, and executive control processes, that allows the buffering and co-ordination of information [4].

3.3   Executive Functions

Executive functions play a fundamental role in devising, implementing, updating and evaluating plans and goal directed behaviors [5,14,22]. Inhibitory control, working memory and cognitive flexibility are the three main components of the executive functions. The working memory has the role to integrate temporally separate units of perception, action, and cognition into a sequence toward a goal [24], and to actively *play* with the representation. Inhibitory control allows us to avoid the distraction of salient internal or external stimuli that are in conflict with the plan and the goal. Cognitive flexibility allows to shift between subgoals (for instance, when a task is over), to identify creative and innovative ways to behave, and to adapt to unforeseen circumstances.

The dialog between executive functions, episodic and semantic memory allow the agent to:

- identify and represent the goal, map the goal hierarchy
- identify the *path*: the sequence of actions to reach the goal, and the sub-goals
- keep the goal and the path in mind
- at any juncture, start the appropriate action
- inhibit the alternative actions and the cognitive processes that can interfere
- monitor the action and detect any significant mismatch between the plan and the execution
- when required, update the plan; when opportune, modify the goal.

3.4   Evaluation

An important component of both learning mechanisms is the evaluation of the outcome and of the process that lead to it: only what *works* is reinforced. The evaluation, in the model-free mechanism, is mainly based on the dopaminergic liking-wanting system. The evaluation process of the model-based system, on the other hand, is much more complex, and is based on different mechanisms:

- the dopaminergic system, that is able to reinforce even the anticipation and the simulation of the experience;

- the cognitive evaluation of the process and the outcomes;
- the affective, emotional evaluation, both before, during and after the experience.

The evaluation of an experience depends also on its motivations: when extrinsic, goal oriented, the evaluation is mainly cognitive; when intrinsic, experience oriented, the evaluation is more emotional.

The Affective System. Within the perspective of evolutionary psychology, the main functions of the affective system are focused on:

- affective forecasting: the emotional anticipation of a simulated experience [17]
- the orientation of the behavior [40]
- the emotional evaluation of an ongoing or past experience [32].

3.5   Motivations

From a motivational perspective, it is possible to differentiate intentional experiences (those events we choose to live) and unintentional ones (events that happens but are not the result of any sort of decision from the subject). Intentional experiences can be differentiated between habits (model-free), goal oriented (model-based) extrinsically motivated experiences, and intrinsically motivated experiences. Among intrinsically motivated experiences, it could be useful to differentiate hedonic and eudaimonic motives.

It is important to observe that such categories are not mutually exclusive. Experiences are very often a mix of non intentional events, habits, goals and intrinsic motivations. Image a lunch with your colleagues; the lunch is a habit (every working day, at 1 pm, usually at the same restaurant), it is goal oriented (eating some food), it has some hedonic (that delicious dessert) and some eudaimonic aspects (spending time with the colleagues). If the restaurant is closed, and you are forced to take something at the fast-food nearby, the experience has an unintentional component.

In differentiating between hedonic and eudaimonic motives I will adopt the distinction made by Huta and Ryan [23]: the main function of hedonia is the self-regulation of emotions, and it's effect is strongest at the immediate or short-term time scale. The function of the eudaimonic motivated experiences is to fulfill at least one of the basic human needs (relationship, competency, autonomy, identity, self esteem, meaning). The two motivations tend to overlap (eudaimonic experiences tend to be associated by positive affect and emotions).

4   The Functions of Experiences

Experiences play a central role in both model-free and model based systems. The model-free learning mechanism requires the direct experience, and can not be mediated. It does not necessarily require, however, the full phenomenological consciousness of the individual, and therefore does not always represent the typical experience.

The model-based system is more complex, and it allows different types of learning. A direct experience is not always required in the learning and decision making processes: cultural, mediated learning has an important role in both semantic acquisition and models building. Its most important way of learning, however, is trough direct, conscious experiences: they are by far the most important sources of the internal representations. The schemas that are formed by the generalization of recurrent experiences [8] are one of the models of internal representation upon which the goal oriented behavior is based. Episodic details - memorable experiences [3] - are another essential source for planning and decision making.

The model-based system uses all the three main ingredients of what we consider experience.

1. The schemata and the scripts that arise from the process of generalization of the experiences are at the basis of the internal representation of the model. The schemata build upon recurrent experiences constitute the building blocks for the model based reasoning.
2. The memorization of the most salient features and gestalts of an episode [3] allow to represent the outliers of the schema, and to give phenomenological color to the model. The specific episodic memories are necessary for:
   - identify specific environmental patterns (special cases)
   - estimate both the plausibility and the expected value of simulated scenarios
   - keeping track of the ongoing plans
3. The dialog between the executive functions, the episodic and the semantic memory allows the system to generate the representation, identify the goal, the plan, the tasks and actions, monitor the execution and the events, and correct the action or adapt the plan.

4.1   The Role of Products and Services

People can have experiences without products and services. Technology, tools and cooperative behaviors, however, are part of the material and non-material culture that co-evolved with the humankind, shaping our environment, our genes and our brain. Within the metaphor of planning as a journey towards a goal, artifacts and services constitute bridges that enable a path, or make it more convenient, easier, smoother, or pleasurable. In the evolutionary perspective, artifacts and services are *adaptations* in the same definition we cited in the previous paragraphs. The product-as-bridge can be seen as the basis of the design as problem solving, and constitutes a proximate explanation [33]. The product-as-adaptation constitutes an ultimate explanation, and is compatible with the iterative view of design as a dialog.

Technology can have an important role in helping people to fulfill their goals and satisfy their needs [20], and in the most recent drafts of the ISO 9241-11 revision it is recognized that products, systems and services can help a person to satisfy a wide range of goals [6]: output related outcomes, personal outcomes, usability outcomes, and safety goals like security and privacy.

5 The Utility of the Definition

I felt the urge to identify a definition of experience when, as a teacher of a HCI course, I attempted to explain what the user experience is. My feeling was that the main differences between the many definitions of ux were attributable to different, implicit concepts of experience and that, therefore, an explicit definition would have been a useful basis of explanation.

A second reason that motivated me to seek a founding definition was the observation that my syllabus was a list of topics and methods without a systematic organization; the definition justify the study those topics as the building blocks of experiences: the motivations, the definition of knowledge, the episodic and semantic memory, the executive functions, and the mental models.

Third, this perspective can help students (and practitioners and stakeholders) to resist the temptation to begin designing without a research phase. The experience perspective induces the designer to start a project by trying to identify the needs, attitudes, internal schemes and mental models, to produce experience maps and customer journeys, using tools and elicitation methods like interviews, laddering, task analysis, experience journey mapping, free listing, triadic sorting, and repertory grid.

Finally, it can have the strategic function to help an organization to find a competitive advantage trough positioning.

In his classic *What is strategy*, Porter [30] defines strategy as competitive advantage, that can be reached by strategic positioning or by improving the value chain. There are three ways to acquire a competitive advantage: doing something that is cheaper, or better, or different. Improvements in the value chain can guarantee a cheaper or a better product. Strategic positioning is oriented at creating a different product.

Studying the individuals' experiences, their motivations, their attitudes helps to identify unfulfilled needs, encouraging the exploration of spaces and opportunities of strategic positioning.

The user experience design, with his emphasis on the usability and the experiential components, can have a dramatic impact on the value chain of a product, or system, or service. The combination of experience research and ux design can become a central asset in the definition of the strategy and in reaching a sustainable competitive advantage.

References

1. Addis, D.R., et al.: Hippocampal contributions to the episodic simulation of specific and general future events. Hippocampus **21**(10), 1045–1052 (2011)
2. Akam, T., Costa, R., Dayan, P.: Simple plans or sophisticated habits? State, transition and learning interactions in the two-step task. In: bioRxiv, p. 021428 (2015). doi:10.1101/021428

3. Ariely, D., Carmon, Z.: Gestalt characteristics of experiences: the defining features of summarized events. J. Behav. Decis. Making **201**, 191–201 (2000)
4. Baird, B., Smallwood, J., Schooler, J.W.: Back to the future: autobiographical planning and the functionality of mind-wandering. Conscious. Cogn. **20**(4), 1604–1611 (2011). doi:10.1016/j.concog.2011.08.007
5. Banich, M.T.: Executive function: the search for an integrated account. Curr. Dir. Psychol. Sci. **18**(2), 89–94 (2009). doi:10.1111/j.1467-8721.2009.01615.x
6. Bevan, N., Carter, J., Harker, S.: ISO 9241-11 Revised: What Have We Learnt About Usability Since 1998?, pp. 143–151 (2015). doi:10.1007/978-3-319-20901-2_13. ISBN: 9783319209005
7. Bulganin, L., Wittmann, B.C.: Reward and novelty enhance imagination of future events in a motivational-episodic network. PloS One **10**(11), e0143477 (2015)
8. Conway, M.A.: Episodic memories. Neuropsychologia **47**(11), 2305–2313 (2009). doi:10.1016/j.neuropsychologia.2009.02.003
9. Cosmides, L., Tooby, J.: Better than rational: evolutionary psychology and the invisible hand. Am. Econ. Rev. **84**, 327–332 (1994)
10. Daw, N.D., et al.: Model-based influences on humans' choices and striatal prediction errors. Neuron **69**(6), 1204–1215 (2011). doi:10.1016/j.neuron.2011.02.027
11. Deaton, A.: Income, health and wellbeing around the world: evidence from the Gallup World Poll. J. Econ. Perspect. J. Am. Econ. Assoc. **22**(2), 53 (2008)
12. Deci, E.L., Ryan, R.M.: The what and why of goal pursuits: human needs and the self-determination of behavior. Psychol. Inq. **11**(4), 227–268 (2000)
13. Desmet, P., Hekkert, P.: Framework of product experience. Int. J. Des. **1**(1), 57–66 (2007). doi:10.1162/074793602320827406. eprint: z0024
14. Diamond, A.: Executive functions. Ann. Rev. **64**(1), 135–168 (2013). doi:10.1146/annurev-psych-113011-143750. eprint: NIHMS150003
15. Diener, E., et al.: Wealth and happiness across the world: material prosperity predicts life evaluation, whereas psychosocial prosperity predicts positive feeling. J. Pers. Soc. Psychol. **99**(1), 52 (2010)
16. Forlizzi, J., Battarbee, K.: Understanding experience in interactive systems. Hum. Comput. Interact. Inst. **37**(2), 261–268 (2004). doi:10.1145/1013115.1013152
17. Gilbert, D.T.: Prospection: experiencing the future. Science **317**, 1351–1354 (2007). doi:10.1126/science.1144161
18. Griskevicius, V., Kenrick, D.T.: Fundamental motives: how evolutionary needs in uence consumer behavior. J. Consum. Psychol. **23**(3), 372–386 (2013). doi:10.1016/j.jcps.2013.03.003
19. Hassabis, D., Maguire, E.A.: Deconstructing episodic memory with construction. Trends Cogn. Sci. **11**(7), 299–306 (2007). doi:10.1016/j.tics.2007.05.001
20. Hassenzahl, M.: User experience and experience design. In: The Encyclopedia of Human-Computer Interaction, 2nd edn. (2013)
21. Hassenzahl, M.: User experience (UX). In: Proceedings of the 20th International Conference of the Association Francophone d'Interaction Homme-Machine - IHM 2008, p. 11. ACM Press, New York (2008). doi:10.1145/1512714.1512717. ISBN: 9781605582856
22. Hofmann, W., Schmeichel, B.J., Baddeley, A.D.: Executive functions and self-regulation. Trends Cogn. Sci. **16**(3), 174–180 (2012). doi:10.1016/j.tics.2012.01.006
23. Huta, V., Ryan, R.M.: Pursuing pleasure or virtue: the differential and overlapping well-being benefits of hedonic and eudaimonic motives. J. Happiness Stud. **11**(6), 735–762 (2010). doi:10.1007/s10902-009-9171-4

24. Jurado, M.B., Rosselli, M.: The elusive nature of executive functions: a review of our current understanding. Neuropsychol. Rev. **17**(3), 213–233 (2007). doi:10. 1007/s11065-007-9040-z

25. Kenrick, D.T., et al.: Renovating the pyramid of needs contemporary extensions built upon ancient foundations. Perspect. Psychol. Sci. **5**(3), 292–314 (2010)

26. Laurel, B.: Interface as mimesis. In: Norman, D.A., Draper, S.W. (eds.) Chap. 4, pp. 67–85. Lawrence Erlbaum Associates (1986)

27. Law, E.L.-C., et al.: Understanding, scoping and defining user experience. In: Proceedings of the 27th International Conference on Human Factors in Computing Systems - CHI 2009, p. 719 (2009). doi:10.1145/1518701.1518813

28. Pine, B.J., Gilmore, J.H.: Welcome to the experience economy. Harvard Bus. Rev. **76**(4), 97–105 (1998)

29. Ploeger, A.: Evolutionary psychology as a metatheory for the social sciences. Integr. Rev. **6**, 164–174 (2010)

30. Porter, M.E.: What is strategy? Harvard Bus. Rev. **74**(1645), 61–78 (1996). doi:10. 1098/rspb.2008.0355. eprint: z0022

31. Schacter, D.L., Addis, D.R., Buckner, R.L.: Episodic simulation of future events: concepts, data, and applications. Ann. NY Acad. Sci. **1124**, 39–60 (2008). doi:10. 1196/annals.1440.001

32. Schwarz, N.: Feelings-as-information theory. Handb. Theor. Soc. Psychol. **1**, 289–308 (2011)

33. Scott-Phillips, T.C., Dickins, T.E., West, S.A.: Evolutionary theory and the ultimate-proximate distinction in the human behavioral sciences. Perspect. Psychol. Sci. **6**(1), 38–47 (2011). doi:10.1177/1745691610393528

34. Singh, S., Barto, A.C., Chentanez, N.: Intrinsically motivated reinforcement learning. In: 18th Annual Conference on Neural Information Processing Systems (NIPS), vol. 17(2), pp. 1281–1288, June 2004. doi:10.1109/TAMD.2010.2051031

35. Spreng, R.N., Mar, R.A., Kim, A.S.: The common neural basis of autobiographical memory, prospection, navigation, theory of mind, and the default mode: a quantitative meta-analysis. J. Cogn. Neurosci. **21**(3), 489–510 (2009)

36. Suddendorf, T., Addis, D.R., Corballis, M.C.: Mental time travel and the shaping of the human mind. Philos. Trans. R. Soc. B Biol. Sci. **364**(1521), 1317–1324 (2009). doi:10.1098/rstb.2008.0301

37. Sweegers, C.C.G., et al.: Neural mechanisms supporting the extraction of general knowledge across episodic memories. NeuroImage **87**, 138–146 (2014). doi:10.1016/ j.neuroimage.2013.10.063

38. Sweegers, C.C.G., et al.: Mental schemas hamper memory storage of goal-irrelevant information. Front. Hum. Neurosci. **9**, 629 (2015). doi:10.3389/fnhum.2015.00629

39. Szpunar, K.K.: Episodic future thought: an emerging concept. Perspect. Psychol. Sci. **5**(2), 142–162 (2010). doi:10.1177/1745691610362350

40. Tamir, M.: What do people want to feel and why?: Pleasure and utility in emotion regulation. Curr. Dir. Psychol. Sci. **18**(2), 101–105 (2009). doi:10.1111/j.1467-8721. 2009.01617.x

41. Tooby, J., Cosmides, L.: The psychological foundations of culture. In: The Adapted Mind: Evolutionary Psychology and the Generation of Culture. Routledge, August 1992. doi:10.4324/9781410608994. ISBN: 1135648158

42. Wunderlich, K., Smittenaar, P., Dolan, R.J.: Dopamine enhances model-based over model-free choice behavior. Neuron **75**(3), 418–424 (2012). doi:10.1016/j.neuron. 2012.03.042

Lean but not Mean UX: Towards a Spiral UX Design Model

Hang Guo[✉]

SAP Singapore, Singapore, Singapore
hang.guo01@sap.com

Abstract. A new user experience design model was proposed and evaluated through a case study of a new product development project within a multinational software organization. Strengths and weaknesses in existing and proposed user experience design models were discussed based on how the following three challenges to user experience design – co-evolution of design problem and solution, organizational silos, conceptual integrity in design – affected user experience design quality and productivity through their impact on nature of design tasks and the social context of design activities.

Keywords: User experience design · Design models

1 Introduction

Competition in software market is intense. The best organizations have realized that differentiation through the quality of user experience design is a key component to a product's success [9]. Meanwhile, rapid product release strategy demands even higher productivity from the product organization's user experience design process. How can a user experience design process sustainably create product with great user experience quality in an increasingly fast paced product development environment?

Design process models provide guidance on the order in which a design project carry out its major tasks. The waterfall design model [15] is one of the first widely adopted design models in user experience design. The waterfall model imposes disciplines on design activities by dividing design task into separate design stages with clear transition criteria in and out of each stage. In contrast to the waterfall model's stepwise progression view of design, the iterative design model [11] emphasizes on continuous improvement of design outcome through repeated design iterations. The lean user experience (UX) design model [7] further situates iterative design into a collaborative organizational process.

The need to simultaneously promote user experience design quality and productivity suggests structural changes to today's design process in organizations. A new design model should be in place to redefine the working consensus between designers and others involved in the design process. This article opens with current UX design models and the issues they address. Subsequent sections discuss the process steps involved in the proposed UX design model; illustrate the application of the new UX design model to software projects using one new concept product design in a multinational software organization as case study; summarize the primary advantages and implications

© Springer International Publishing Switzerland 2016
A. Marcus (Ed.): DUXU 2016, Part I, LNCS 9746, pp. 25–33, 2016.
DOI: 10.1007/978-3-319-40409-7_3

involved in using the proposed UX design model and the primary challenges in using it at its current incomplete level of elaboration; and present resulting conclusions.

2 UX Design Models

The primary function of a UX design model is to bring order out of the natural chaos of developing new designs and to establish the transition criteria for progressing from one design stage to next. These include readjustment of design milestones to changing requirements, knowledge dissemination among design team members and assessment of design quality as entrance criteria for the next design stage. Thus, a UX design model addresses the following questions in user experience design:

- What shall design team do next to accommodate newly acquired information of user needs or business requirements?
- How to facilitate knowledge dissemination among interdisciplinary team members, and thus improve design process productivity?
- How shall design team ensure conceptual integrity of the design while promoting shared understanding in the team?

Ways to organize user experience design embody our fundamental views toward nature of design activities and the contexts of their happening. Following its legacy, the waterfall model is the first widely adopted user experience design model for enterprise products [4, 14]. Similar to the requirement–analysis–implementation stepwise procedure in information systems design, waterfall model imposes disciplines on user experience design activities by dividing design task into separate design stages with clear transition criteria in and out of each stage. The waterfall design model resembles Simon's rational problem-solving approach to design [18]. The problem of what to be designed is first rationally conceived and consolidated into requirement documentations such as user personas and usage scenarios, solutions to the problem definition are then explored in the design and prototyping stages.

However, a search problem requires a well-defined problem space whereas a design problem is often described as 'ill-structured' or even 'wicked' [6]. Furthermore, compared to fast-moving consumer products, enterprise products often have longer product design cycle, which means a longer 'requirement freeze' time from problem definition to final solution. For this reason, enterprise products are more prone to experience co-evolution characters of design [10] that design is an iterative interplay to "fix" a problem from the problem space and to "search" plausible solutions from the corresponding solution space.

Practitioners and researchers turned to iterative design method for a better design solution. In his reflection of product design for New Relic [8], Eton Lightstone highlighted the need to balance designer and engineer perspectives in the iterative design process – "A designer without an engineer is an art gallery, and an engineer without a designer is a parking lot." He also pointed out the importance of prototyping and evaluating design with real data. Arnowitz et al. [1] described their experience designing an enterprise expense reporting system. Their study identified internal politics as the most challenging aspect of design process highlighting complex stakeholder needs in enterprise software design. The iterative design model emphasizes on continuous improvement of design outcome through repeated design iterations. This approach exemplifies Schön's phenomenological thinking of design as a reflective practice [17], where design excellence can only be achieved through repeated practices.

Despite their conceptual differences, views of Simon and Schön center on the dialectic relationships between problem and solution of a given design space. Since design activities increasingly happen in complex organizational environments, sociality of design exerts a stronger influence on the design process. Oehlberg et al. discussed the importance of shared understanding in human-centered design teams [12]. Their study reckons Orlikowski's classic investigation of organizational issue in groupware implementation: effective utilization of technology in organization depends on people's mental model about the technology and their work, and the structural properties of their organizations [13].

Lean UX seeks to improve design quality by looking inward into the internal working of design team. It promotes a collaborative design and user research approach to create shared understanding among design team members. Still, the lean UX model has various challenges. Shared understanding in user experience design demands consensus by many people, but consensus making stifles great design work in many ways. Collaborative problem solving in user interface design often turns out to become adding more and more features to the user interface. Because each team member has incentive to have own ideas adopted, consensus-making process inevitably creates a union of many wish lists that result in bloated requirements for a product. Even when requirements proliferation is missing, consensus mechanisms often force compromise in design by taking off its most innovative parts.

3   Spiral UX Design Model

The spiral UX design model is an adaptation of spiral software development model [2] to user experience design process. As shown in Fig. 1, the radial dimension of the spiral UX design model corresponds to the cumulative cost of the iteration step, or the fidelity of design. As prototypes in early iterations might be simple paper sketches, after the design has been evaluated and redesigned several times, prototypes of higher fidelity get produced to embody refined learning. The angular dimension represents the progress made in completing each iteration of design, in which each iteration involves the same sequence of steps.

3.1   A Typical Cycle of the Spiral UX Design Model

Starting from lower left quadrant of Fig. 1, each cycle of the spiral UX design model begins with refinement of user needs. This involves two distinctive phases: a divergent phase where insights of user needs are shared freely by every team member, followed by a convergent phase where diverse opinions are weighted and taken into design by the lead designer.

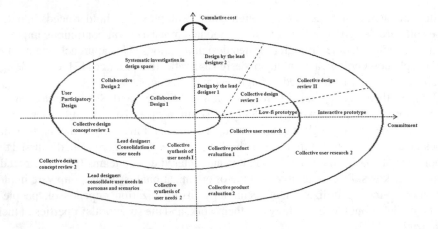

Fig. 1. The spiral UX design model

The next step is for the design team to review consolidated user needs. This may involve the lead designer sharing design rationales, results from competitive analysis, interpretation of user research findings and the team members sharing their critiques on the consolidated user needs. Frequently, this process will identify areas of uncertainty in personas and scenarios. If so, the lead designer should incorporate such critiques into the deliverable in the next step.

Once the user needs are consolidated and reviewed. The actual design should follow. Again, in the divergent phase of design, product team members brainstorm on alternative design solutions based on the shared understanding of requirements specified in personas and scenarios. Although we recognize the problem of co-evolution of problem-solution in user experience design, within each individual design cycle, it is still necessary to assume a relatively stable problem definition, such that systematic exploration of solution space becomes possible.

One important feature of the spiral UX design model is the collaborative open-ended brainstorming in design and interpretation of user needs. Open-ended brainstorming encourages sharing of diverse opinions, and affords debates about contradicting viewpoints. Conflict of opinions is the mechanism for facilitating knowledge acquisition in a productive design process. It is not a debilitating factor needing to be suppressed in the software design team. In user experience design, group brainstorming leads to the integration of the various knowledge domains owned by individual team members. This integration leads to shared understanding of the problem under consideration and potential solutions. A design team seldom starts with shared understanding of what to be designed. Instead, the shared understanding develops over time as team members learn from one another about the expected behavior of the design and the ways to produce such behavior.

The focus of design team should always be set on the final user appreciation of the product rather than on the acceptance of individual's idea into the product specification. The lead designer works in collaboration with other product team members. However, at the same time, the lead designer enjoys autonomy in the work designing both overall conceptual framework as well as finer details of the product.

In the spiral UX design model, a design review and critique stage follows each design stage. The lead designer invites the entire product team to critique on the design concepts and other contract objects created. This step also plays a counterbalancing role to entrusting product design to a single lead designer, as even the most established designers may make mistakes.

4 Case Study: Using the Spiral UX Design Model

The various rounds and activities involved in the spiral UX design model are best understood through user of an example. This design model was used in the design and development of a mobile application project for professional athlete coaches by a large enterprise software organization. The following text summarizes the application of the spiral UX design model to the first two rounds. The major features of each round are also discussed.

4.1 Round 0: Feasibility Study

Feasibility study involved participatory design sessions with professional coaches as well as ethnographic field studies observing their work in multiple training sessions. The design problems were expressed at a very high level and in qualitative terms like "increase training data collection efficiency," "improve coach and athlete communication," etc.

Some of the alternatives considered, primarily those in the solution domain, could lead to development of mobile application toolkit, but the possible attractiveness of a number of alternatives in wearable devices, data management software running on desktop, web based applications for coaching activities management could have led to a conclusion not to embark on a mobile application development.

The primary design decisions involved considerations of felt pains in coaches' work, conformity to the product organization's existing product portfolio and product strategies, technical feasibility and resource constraints. The user research activities undertaken in Round 0 were primarily participatory design to solicit implicit user needs; surveys and stakeholder interviews of software developers, sales and marketing professionals; competitive analysis of current products in the market with similar target user group.

Product team conducted user research activities collaboratively with help from a user researcher. In the following brainstorming sessions, each team member shared his/her understanding of the meaning of data collected through user research activities. The team developed shared understanding that significant efficiency gains in coaches' daily work could be achieved at a reasonable cost by pursuing a mobile toolkit application initiative. However, some necessary parts in the candidate solution, such as analysis of time series data to infer athlete gestures, were found to be difficult to be fitted into standard development 2-week sprint. Separate research track was created in parallel with development, design and user research. Thus, even at a very high level of generality of design objective, Round 0 was able to answer basic feasibility questions and also help to structure project progress roadmap.

4.2 Round 1: Concept Development

The design objectives and understanding of user needs evolved into more specificity in Round 1. Compared to Round 0, the current iteration had significantly greater investment from the product team; the product team collaboratively described more specific user personas and usage scenarios; concept prototypes were created by the lead designer in the convergent phase of design to convey team's shared understanding of what to be created; regular user evaluation was determined to happen in the second week of 2-week sprint.

The user interface design phase focused on systematic exploration of design space through rapid prototyping. The product team collaboratively proposed multiple design ideas based on shared understanding of user needs and project constraints. The lead designer then summarized such ideas into concrete low-fi prototypes and brought such prototypes to concept and design review sessions with product team.

4.3 Succeeding Rounds

It will be useful to illustrate some examples of how the spiral UX design model is used to handle situations arising in the subsequent design process, primarily, the interplay with software development.

Shared understanding among product team members means little design documentation is required as a part of official handoff procedure from design to development. In fact, the spiral UX design model requires no such official handoff between design and development teams. User experience designers are expected to have continuous involvement in development process. By working closely with developers during software development, designers have the opportunity to make timely responses to the numerous micro design decisions arising from the implementation of design, which are vital to the overall look and feel of the final product.

In a few occasions, development work outpaced design by implementing new features or making user interface design decisions that will influence the user experience of the product. Shared understanding among product team ensures there is no major deviation from the prescribed product user experience. However, it is important for the lead designer to guide the creation of the final product user experience, instead of letting the product grows organically in the design and development processes.

5 Discussion

The experimentation with spiral UX design model convinced us this design model has potential to be applied in other design situations. However, some difficulties must be addressed before it becomes a mature UX design model for enterprise products.

5.1   Design for Micro-interactions

Concept integrity – the consistency of a design's concept is a quality not only delights its users, but also yields ease of learning and ease of use in great design works. Many great designs with conceptual integrity are principally the work of one mind [3]. The solo designer usually produces work with this quality subconsciously by making each micro decision the same way each time he or she encounters it.

In user experience design, such micro decisions boils down to the elementary details of a user interface, such as a single user interaction with a UI control or color gradient chosen by the designer to perfect the visual representation of a screen element. Details matter in design, as famously put by industrial designer Charles Eames – "The details are not the details, they make the design". If the details are delightful and effective, then their success accretes up into the overall user experience, making the product more delightful and humane as a whole [16].

5.2   Reflections on UX Design Model

Great designs come from great designers, not from great design processes [3]. Although this article concerns primarily with the refinement of design models for user experience design process, the role of design model in creating products with great user experience design quality should be considered with sufficient nuance for the following reasons:

First, by its very nature, a design process is conservative. Much like other process models, a design process focuses on replicating past success rather than producing new ones. Design process model aims at reducing risks involved in the product design, build and go-to-market processes by blocking 'bad' ideas and catching oversights. Hence the design process following any model has the natural tendency to smooth out highly innovative designs, and as an outcome, regress the overall design quality to the average level commanded by cost estimation; sales forecast and scheduled delivery date etc.

Second, one of the major challenges to user experience team to adopt a particular UX design model is that we become dogmatic in what we do, apply what worked last time and avoid what didn't work. As with any process or tool, appropriate use yields superior results. Each project comes with unique goals and constraints, there is no single design model the design team could follow to repeatedly accomplish great designs. Within each design situation, there is opportunity to analyze the needs based on current context, and make choice of appropriate design approaches and method.

Third, because of the engineering culture of product development, user experience design is usually approached as an exercise of problem solving. A typical design might start with Step 1: problem definition, followed by Step 2: solution generation. This also has something in common with software engineering tradition of requirement collection and implementation. But what if some of the challenges facing user experience design are not best described as problems to be solved? Not all design is about solving problems. User experience designers may revisit a UI control, an interaction, or a workflow that has already been successfully designed many times before. In this case, the value does not lie in solving an unsolved problem. Designers return to ubiquitous designs in much the same way that musicians revisit and reinterpret old tunes. The results of these open-endedly explorations often embody a distillation of their own design philosophy. Similarly, designers distill an element of art in user interface design beyond fulfillment of user needs. Outside a design culture, within the dominantly problem-solving environment of Agile software engineering, this artistic exploration maybe misinterpreted. User experience design may benefit from a more balanced view between problem-solving approach and more open-ended, artistic exploration in design. The diversity of design exploration may serve as a powerful counterbalancing force to the conservative nature of design models.

6 Conclusion

This paper has defined the spiral UX design model as an inclusive and collaborative design process model centered on a lead designer. The definition was sharpened by presenting key design and organizational factors influencing the productivity and quality of user experience design work, and illustrating how the spiral UX design model incorporate their solutions compared to other available design models.

The spiral UX design model has been quite successful in its application of developing a mobile toolkit for professional coaches. Overall, it achieved a high level of user satisfaction in a very short time and provided the extensibility necessary to accommodate higher volume of requirements to incorporate the mobile app into wider product family. The model is not yet as fully elaborated as the more establish models. It needs further elaboration in areas such as supporting open-ended creative exploration in a dominantly problem-solving product culture; counterbalancing conservative nature of design process to allow more radical designs to be fully usable in all situations.

References

1. Arnowitz, J., Monica, H., Diana, G., Michael, A., Naomi, D.: The stakeholder forest: designing an expenses application for the enterprise. In: CHI 2005 Extended Abstracts on Human Factors in Computing Systems, pp. 941–956. ACM, New York (2005)
2. Boehm, B.W.: A spiral model of software development and enhancement. Computer 21, 61–72 (1988)
3. Brooks, F.P.: The mythical man-month. Addison-Wesley, Reading (1975)
4. Coble, J.M., Karat, J., Kahn, M.G.: Maintaining a focus on user requirements throughout the development of clinical workstation software. In: Proceedings of the ACM SIGCHI Conference on Human Factors in computing Systems, pp. 170–177. ACM (1997)
5. Curtis, B., Krasner, H., Iscoe, N.: A field study of the software design process for large systems. Commun. ACM 31, 1268–1287 (1988). ACM
6. Dorst, K., Cross, N.: Creativity in the design process: co-evolution of problem–solution. Des. Stud. 22, 425–437 (2001)
7. Gothelf, J., Seiden, J.: Lean UX: Applying Lean Principles to Improve User Experience. O'Reilly Media, Sebastopol (2013)

8. Lightstone, E.: Lessons In Designing Great Enterprise Software (2015). http://techcrunch.com/2015/03/31/lessons-in-designing-great-enterprise-software/. Accessed 11 Dec 2015
9. Lorenzo, D.: Even business brands need effective UX. http://fortune.com/2013/06/18/even-business-brands-need-effective-ux/
10. Maher, M.L., Poon, J., Boulanger, S.: Formalising design exploration as co-evolution. In: Gero, J.S., Sudweeks, F. (eds.) Advances in Formal Design Methods for CAD. IFIP–The International Federation for Information Processing, pp. 3–30. Springer, Dordrecht (1996)
11. Nielsen, J.: Iterative user-interface design. Computer **26**, 32–41 (1993)
12. Oehlberg, L., Kyu, S., Jasmine, J., Alice, A., Björn, H.: Showing is sharing: building shared understanding in human-centered design teams with dazzle. In: Proceedings of the Designing Interactive Systems Conference (DIS 2012), pp. 669–678. ACM, New York (2012)
13. Orlikowski, W.J.: Learning from notes: organizational issues in groupware implementation. In: Proceedings of the 1992 ACM Conference on Computer-Supported Cooperative Work (CSCW 1992), pp. 362–369. ACM, New York (1992)
14. Peffers, K., Tuure, T., Marcus, A.R., Samir, C.: A design science research methodology for information systems research. J. Manag. Inf. Syst. **24**, 45–77 (2002)
15. Royce, W.W.: Managing the development of large software systems, Los Angeles (1970)
16. Saffer, D.: Microinteractions: Designing with Details. O'Reilly Media Inc., Sebastopol (2013)
17. Schön, D.: Educating the reflective practitioner (1987)
18. Simon, H.A.: The Sciences of the Artificial. MIT Press, Cambridge (1996)

An Integrated Framework for Design Thinking and Agile Methods for Digital Transformation

Kavitha Gurusamy[1], Narayanan Srinivasaraghavan[1(✉)], and Sisira Adikari[2]

[1] Australian Public Service, Canberra, ACT, Australia
Kavitha_rkumar@yahoo.com.au, sangeethaandnarayanan@gmail.com
[2] University of Canberra, Bruce, ACT 2601, Australia
Sisira.Adikari@canberra.edu.au

Abstract. This paper proposes a framework to deliver a faster workable project module in an innovative, dynamic environment. The increased demand in mobile and internet applications drive businesses to rethink their customer needs to a greater extent and undertake digital transformation to compete in the marketplace. The agile methods as an approach is gaining popularity to develop innovative solutions while Design Thinking leads to transformation, evolution and innovation, and to form new ways of managing current and future business opportunities. The proposed framework supports the evolving Digital Transformation by combining the benefits of Agile methods and Design Thinking. This paper contributes to the body of knowledge on Design Thinking and Agile methodology by providing a framework which integrates the core processes of Agile methods and Design Thinking.

Keywords: Digital transformation · Design thinking · Agile methodology

1 Introduction

In this digital era, consumers are highly reliant on mobile applications for their day to day activities. This drives businesses to rethink their changing customer needs and undertake digital transformation to compete with their business competitors. Most of the organizations have undergone Digital Transformation in some way to provide improved customer service and experience. This revolution attracted researchers around the world. Researchers created new business models for Digital Transformation [1] and implemented Digital Transformation using Agile methodology [2]. One of the key aspects of Digital Transformation is creativity and is based on networking ideas and mindset. The success of Digital Transformation relies largely on organisational, technical, strategic planning and a team with high competence, high commitment that respond well to delegation [3]. One of the biggest barriers to implementing the Digital Transformation is the confabulation and co-mixing of operations, corporate IT, product development & technical, strategic planning functionality [14]. Both iterative and agile methods were developed to overcome the various obstacles faced in sequential forms of project organization. As technology projects grow in complexity, it is difficult for users to define the long-term requirements. Projects developed by constant iterations

© Springer International Publishing Switzerland 2016
A. Marcus (Ed.): DUXU 2016, Part I, LNCS 9746, pp. 34–42, 2016.
DOI: 10.1007/978-3-319-40409-7_4

(agile) can provide an opportunity for clients/users to provide feedback to help refine their requirements [2, 3]. However, integrating Design Thinking into the agile iterations overcome the challenges posed by Agile methodology and can contribute to deliver constant continuous deliveries to the customers faster than the traditional approach.

1.1 Design Thinking

Design Thinking (DT) is the catalyst for innovative development or transformation. DT is a human-centric approach and defined in many ways by different authors. For example, Tschimmel [4] defined Design Thinking as a way of thinking which leads to transformation, evolution and innovation, to a new form of living and to new ways of managing business. DT is emerged from Cognitive Process. However, DT today is not only a cognitive process or a mindset but has become an effective toolkit for any innovation process, connecting the creative design approach to traditional business thinking, based on planning and problem solving [4]. DT integrates human, business, and technological factors in problem forming, solving, and design. Its human-centric methodology integrates expertise from design, social sciences, engineering, and business [5].

The understanding and acceptance of failures and mistakes are important elements of DT, which differentiates DT from the traditional way of thinking business [4]. Three major constraints of DT are desirability, feasibility and viability. The first stage of the design process is often about discovering which constraints are important and establishing a framework for evaluating them. Design thinker brings the constraints into a harmonious balance rather than a competent designer resolving the issue [6]. According to Brown [6] Designers are different to Design Thinkers. Designers have learned to excel at resolving one or two or even all three of the DT constraints. Design Thinkers, by contrast, are learning to navigate between and among them in a creative way. Design Thinkers shifted their thinking from problem to project [6]. Images play an important role in DT. Design thinkers usually apply sketches, drawings and material models to explore project problems and solutions [4].

Design thinking is an interplay between diverging exploration of problem and solution space and converging processes of synthesizing and selecting. Plattner et al. [5] related design thinking to the structures, cultures and processes of IT development – in particular with regard to the following aspects: • Building on Diversity, Exploring the Problem Space, Exploring the Solution Space, Iterative Alignment of Both Spaces (Fig. 1).

Building on Diversity: Having a team of individuals with diverse skills and communicating frequently and closely collaborating during the design phase.

Exploring the Problem Space: Developing a comprehensive understanding of the problem before the actual development process starts, by exploring various scenarios and important use cases by learning about the users and their specific needs.

Exploring the Solution Space: Promoting creative ideation and conceptualization process by considering a number of options and choosing a solution that best meets the needs of the users.

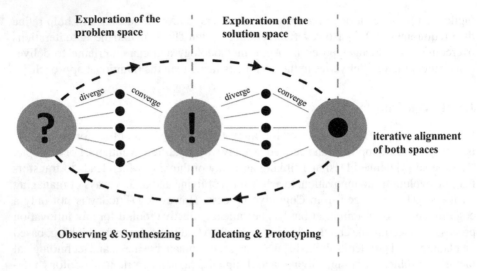

Fig. 1. Problem and solution space in design thinking [7]

Iterative Alignment of Both Spaces: Enabling a highly iterative development process by seeking and integrating feedback from within the team, users and experts throughout the development phase.

In both problem and solution space, there is room to explore multiple options through the divergent phase. The convergent space allows concentrating on one solution amongst many that drives to project solution.

1.2 Agile Methodology

Over the last decade, agile development approach has received much attention from researchers and practitioners as an approach to deal with project development in an innovative and dynamic environment. A core principle of Agile development is to satisfy the customer by providing valuable product on an early and continuous basis. The agile method aims to deliver a small set of features/working modules to the customers as quickly as possible in short iterations. This reduces much of upfront research and analysis required by traditional methodologies. However, in some cases, these fast deliveries do not necessarily need to satisfy user requirements in the end [8] due to lack of prior architectural design, research and poor documentation [9].

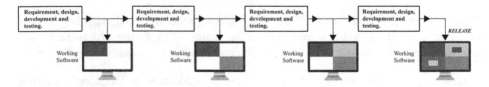

Fig. 2. Agile iterations [12]

Agile development processes are people and code-centric approach [10]. Agile development processes do not follow rigid milestone roadmaps, but instead by a set of rules that the team can easily act flexibly to adapt to unexpected events [5].

Agile methodologies such as Scrum and Extreme Programming (XP) advocates iterative development processes with the frequent communication with the customers in order to release a piece of workable module frequently. XP heavily focuses on development techniques whilst Scrum focuses on roles, processes and project management. In scrum project development, a scrum team consists of analysts, developers and testers work together in a centralized environment. All development processes and activities are transparent and visible. Scrum development activities are structured through a project backlog that consists a list of prioritized development activities [11, 12]. XP advocate continuously refactoring code to improve code quality and system architecture [13].

1.3 Research Motivation

This research focuses on helping business to take advantage of Digital Transformation in a cost effective manner. The aim is to produce an integrated framework using Design Thinking and Agile methodology to address the challenges posed by Digital Transformation. This research aims to deliver a better framework to produce a product that best meets customer needs with minimum costs, waste and time, and enables the business to achieve bottom line gains earlier than via traditional sequential approaches.

The rest of the paper is organized in the following order. Following the introduction, Sect. 2 provides commonality between the DT and Agile methodology whilst Sect. 3 reports the existing research on DT and Agile approach. Section 4 discusses the challenges posed by the Agile and DT methods. The proposed framework is discussed in Sect. 5. Finally, limitations of this research and future work are addressed with the conclusion.

2   Design Thinking vs. Agile Methodology

There are commonalities between DT and Agile methodologies. Hirschfeld et al., [10] identified commonalities with respect to DT and Agile methodologies which includes Wicked Problems: refers to problems that are not well understood and thus difficult to describe, becomes clearer when moving closer to the solution of the problem; Close Interactions: people interact closely with each other, exchange a lot of knowledge and opinions, which in turn supports making progress; Go for Feedback: iterative and incremental development is fundamental to agile approach [10]. Similar iteration is used in DT's problem and solution exploration [5]. Plattner et al. [5] discussed existing IT development approaches and their relation to DT in the context of agility. Their comparison with design thinking and agile shows some strong parallels: core features like "user-centricity", "iterative learning and development processes", and "extensive team communication" and identified that design thinking methodology has been already introduced to IT development [5].

3   Research on Design Thinking and Agile Approach

For all entrepreneurs, it is useful to apply DT when moving through a creative process of problem solving or when looking for opportunities and when facing challenges [4]. DT could be used in a range of fields. For example Simons et al. [14] adapted design thinking approach on Biotechnology Research and Development, which helped them to create innovative content repeatedly at a fast pace.

Simons et al. [14] adopted DT concepts in many ways. They used new perspectives from outside to gain an understanding of the problem and unexpected connections. Through radical collaboration, collected richest insights from team members. Further explored options and ideas early to reveal unexpected insights and gained evidence quickly to improve the decision making. Some research successfully integrated Agile approach with other research methodologies to enhance the power of the agile method. For example Hirschfeld et al., [10] Integrated Design Thinking methodology in Agile development process, and developed a model and used it to develop software in Virtual collaborated environment; Ferreira et al. [15], introduced User Interface Design in Agile software development; Fox et al. [8] analysed prior research that integrated User-Centric approach in Agile software development process, and identified that the integration added value to the software development process. Based on their findings, Fox et al. [8] tried to identify a common model with the integration of agile and user-centered approach and named them as Generalist, Specialist, and the Hybrid approach. The introduction of User-Centered Design specialists along with agile developers in each iteration improved the usability of the products. This confirms integration of agile and user-centered approach adds value to the innovative developments.

4   Challenges on DT and Agile Approach on Software Development

Agile breaks down the problem into small chunks that people can deal with and stay on track which removes options from the table. But DT tries to keep options on the table for as long as possible [5]. Agile reduces much of upfront research and analysis required by traditional methodologies. However, in some cases, this fast delivery doesn't satisfy user needs in the end. On the other hand, User-Centric approach spends a considerable amount of time for research and analysis prior to development, and takes longer to deliver the product [8].

Cao et al. [9] identified some of the challenges posed by the agile approach. During the development process, more emphasis is given on workable systems than documentation. This poses lack of formal architectural design and leads to irrecoverable architectural mistakes. Agile methods heavily rely on on-site customer input rather than predefined requirements documentation. This poses customer-related challenges as the customer's knowledge of the requirement for larger complex project is limited. Further, Agile methods heavily rely on tacit knowledge amongst the team members, so critical decisions may not be documented. This leads to developer related challenges. Agile works well for flat organizational structure but not for hierarchical structure. This introduces organizational challenges.

On a theoretical level, we have seen that design thinking can make valuable contributions to IT development and enhance the innovativeness of IT development. However, there are still unresolved challenges in applying DT successfully to IT development [5, 7]. The general concern about DT is too much time is spent on understanding the problem before actual development process starts. This reduces DT's viability when the project is under time pressure. Especially people reporting to higher hierarchy perceive DT as a risk and prefer secured milestone-based development process [7]. The proposed framework tries to address some of these challenges.

5   Proposed Framework

The proposed framework integrates DT and agile methodology for digital transformation. This framework extracts the benefits from both the methods and compliments the challenges posed by the methods. Adapting the DT concept on Agile transformation opens enhancement and can be applied in agile iterations.

The DT model shown above (Fig. 3) is from Hasso-Plattner Institute and is adapted for this research. The first phase *understand*, collects information about the topic or problem to be solved. *Observe* phase collects insights about the user needs by conducting interviews with the clients and research. The information collected from the first two phases are shared amongst the group and converted into a visual framework called *PointOfView*. In the *Ideate* phase an interdisciplinary team goes through the processes they have observed so far and design a solution with opportunities to change during the implementation. The core phase in the DT is the *Prototype,* and it turns ideas into an action. The last phase Test evaluates the requirements and user needs. All these processes are highly iterative and can be iterated from any phase a satisfactory product is delivered.

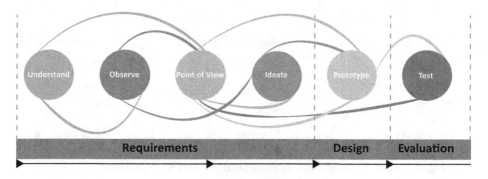

Fig. 3.   Adapted design thinking process model [4]

In the proposed framework, the six DT processes are adapted into 3 phases called *Requirements, Design* and *Evaluation*. As the first 4 phases of the original DT model focuses on collecting information required starting an actual implementation, it is named as *Requirements* phase. In this phase, information is collected from different experts including but not limited to technical experts, engineers, end users and business analysts. The *Prototype* phase from original model is termed as Design because in this phase a design prototype is created for real action. In the *Evaluation* phase the developed design will be evaluated to ensure it is ready to build the system. The adapted DT phases are going to be incorporated in proposed agile iterations.

Agile is a mindset; this can be applied to different situations as they arise. In Agile development, business representatives and developers work together daily throughout the project to produce workable modules. They prioritize the work and create backlogs for ongoing development. Agile development supports the practice of delivering a smaller workable product rather than delivering one product at the end of the project. The short deliveries and iterations allow the small chunks to tested and improved during development.

The Agile Framework shown in Fig. 2 consists of 4 phases and these phases are iterated to produce small Workable Module (WM). Agile *Requirements* encompasses the task information that goes into determining the needs or conditions to meet for a new or altered product or project. In this phase the features that need to be build are defined, the quality measures are also defined to validate the workable modules. *Design* phase includes but is not limited to solution design, user interface design, and architecture design to build the system. In *Development* phase the development team splits the work between the developers and selects the prioritized jobs from the backlogs [8]. On completion, the workable module is sent to the next phase *Test*. Once implementation features are verified in the test phase, then the finished product is released to customers.

In the proposed framework (Fig. 4) the adapted 3 phase DT concepts *Requirements*, *Design* and *Evaluation* are applied in Agile's *Requirements* and *Design* phase. DT's divergent thinking is applied to identify multiple options to solve a problem while the convergent thinking provides a practical way of deciding among existing alternatives. The divergent phase explores the problem and solution space. The convergent phase drives us towards the solution.

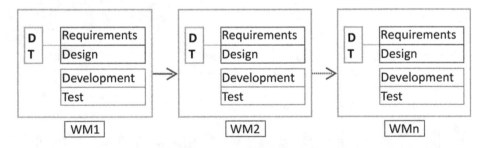

Fig. 4. Integrated design thinking and agile framework for digital transformation

The completed Requirements and Design phase outcomes will flow through to the agile Development and Test phases.

The challenges posed by the agile method such as lack of prior research are addressed in the proposed framework. In each agile phase, DT's exploration and convergent principles are applied which brings ideas from the multi-disciplinary expertise and provide room for prior research and analysis. Further, it provides the basis for envisioning and evaluating possible solutions. As these iterations are applied to the small module of the project, the case of failure is taken as an advantage to improve it in the consecutive iterations. This concept is similar to Brown's [6] "Fail early to succeed sooner". As the proposed framework is highly iterative and the incremental process is driven by people with diverse background and expertise, the frequent deliverables are more likely to satisfy user needs.

6   Limitations and Future Work

This framework was developed based on existing theory and literature on DT and agile methodologies. Attention was given to prior research and findings were considered while developing the framework. However, the framework hasn't been tested in the real environment yet. A dedicated transformation team is important for long term success. However, the research hasn't focused on team management or how to improve the coordination amongst the team members and across various levels of the projects. Future research can address these issues. This research framework can be extended/adapted to any type and/or size of the organisation. This research is not focused on a specific Agile method to follow. Future research may focus on the type of organisations and specific Agile methods for Digital Transformation.

7   Conclusion

In this paper, we presented an enhanced framework based on Design Thinking and Agile concepts in the context of Digital Transformation. The main contribution of this paper is highlighted in the new approach in Digital Transformation and addressed the challenges posed by traditional approaches. This paper contributes the knowledge on DT research, Agile development and Digital Transformation.

References

1. Berman, J.S.: Digital transformation: opportunities to create new business models. Strategy Leadersh. **40**(2), 16–24 (2012)
2. Sriram, N.: Agile IT organization design - for digital transformation and continuous delivery. Addison Wesley, Reading (2015)
3. Baker, M.: Digital Transformation - 4th Edition. Buckingham Monographs (2014)
4. Tschimmel, K.: Design thinking as an effective toolkit for innovation. In: Proceedings of the XXIII ISPIM Conference: Action for Innovation: Innovation from Experience, Barcelona, pp. 1–20 (2012). ISBN 978-952-265-243-0
5. Meinel, C., Leifer, L.: Design thinking research. In: Plattner, H., Meinel, C., Leifer, L. (eds.) Design Thinking: Understand - Improve – Apply, pp. xiii–xxii. Springer, Heidelberg (2011)
6. Brown, T.: Change By Design – How Design Thinking Transforms Organizations and Inspires Innovation. HarperBusiness, New York (2009)
7. Lindberg, T., Meinel, C., Wagner, R.: Design thinking: a fruitful concept for IT development? In: Plattner, H., Meinel, C., Leifer, L. (eds.) Design Thinking: Understand - Improve – Apply, pp. 1–20. Springer, Berlin (2011)

8. Fox, D., Sillito, J., Maurer, F.: Agile methods and user-centered design: how these two methodologies are being successfully integrated in industry. In: AGILE 2008, Conference, pp. 63–72. IEEE Computer Society (2008). ieeexplore.ieee.org

9. Cao, L., Mohan, K., Peng, X., Peng, X., Ramesh, B.: A framework for adapting agile development methodologies. Eur. J. Inf. Syst. **18**(4), 332–343 (2009)

10. Hirschfeld, R., Steinert, B., Lincke, J.: Agile software development in virtual collaboration environments. In: Plattner, H., Meinel, C., Leifer, L. (eds.) Design Thinking Understand-Improve-Apply, pp. 197–218. Springer, Berlin (2011). ISBN 978-3-642-13756-3

11. Kautz, K., Johansen, T.H., Uldahl, A.: The perceived impact of the agile development and project management method scrum on information systems and software development productivity. Australas. J. Inf. Syst. **18**(3), 303–315 (2014)

12. GAO: Effective Practices and Federal Challenges in Applying Agile Methods GAO Reports. 7/27/2012, preceding, pp. 1–34 (2012)

13. Beck, K.: Extreme Programming Explained: Embrace Change. Addison-Wesley, Boston (2000)

14. Simons, T., Gupta, A., Buchanan, M.: Innovation in R&D: using design thinking to develop new models of inventiveness, productivity and collaboration. J. Commercial Biotechnol. **17**(4), 301–307 (2011)

15. Ferreira, J., Noble, J., Biddle, R.: Agile development iterations and UI design. In: Agile Conference (AGILE), pp. 50–58. IEEE Computer Society (2007). ieeexplore.ieee.org

An Interactive Model of Creative Design Behavior with 3D Optical Technology

Hao Jiang[1], Xiao-li Liu[1(✉)], Xiang Peng[1], and Ming-xi Tang[2]

[1] Key Laboratory of Optoelectronic Devices and Systems of Ministry
of Education and Guangdong Province College of Optoelectronics Engineering,
Shenzhen University, Shenzhen 518060, People's Republic of China
lxl@szu.edu.cn
[2] School of Design, The Hong Kong Polytechnic University, Hong Kong, China

Abstract. The research is based on the design computer technique and optical 3D scanning technology, which integrated with cloud data, human engineering and surface simulation and reconstruction technology. In addition, a web based design education prototype with 3D scanning and printing technique will be created by researcher as well, in order to verify the results of the research in the actual application environment. It will allows us to refine our system and propose more subjects under with similar technologies to help to develop creative skills of students who are often got stuck with 3D modeling which are not helpful for those who wish to study design without sketching and modeling skill.

Keywords: 3D imaging · 3D scanning and printing · Creative design · Interactive design

1 Introduction

Digital media are increasingly collaborated with culture, design, and education fields. An increasing number of number of institutions and other heritage museums are now undertaking 3D digitisation as normal part of their activities [1]. The 3D model always created by a computer-aided design software or a scan an existing object [2].

The technologies of 3D scanning and printing are generally considered as one of the important symbols of the third industrial revolution, and apply into different type of industries. 3D technologies are able to generate the products with complex structures, high accuracy, and particular features. Therefore, such strengths lead 3D technologies used into various areas, which include industrial manufacture, biomedical engineering, construction engineering, and culture creativity. Besides, many companies around the world have launched the 3D scanners and personal 3D printers. Thus, 3D scanning and printing technique will be collaborated with digital producing mode to promote industrial development. According to the development of 3D technology, the application of 3D scanning and printing in education has been concerned by many researchers. As recorded in Horizon Report: 2013 higher education edition., the new technology of scanning and printing in the next four to five years brings innovation of teaching, learning and research. And in the next three years, 3D technique will become a major direction in educational technology [3]. The application of 3D technology

© Springer International Publishing Switzerland 2016
A. Marcus (Ed.): DUXU 2016, Part I, LNCS 9746, pp. 43–52, 2016.
DOI: 10.1007/978-3-319-40409-7_5

education helps students to enhance their interactive ability, innovative thinking, and creative thinking in classroom which compared to the traditional teaching scheme. In this paper, researcher proposed an interactive design model to analyze how 3D optical technology to improve creative skill of students.

Over the past decade, advanced 3D optical scanning technology developed into a widely used tool and medium in various enterprises and educational fields. Although the 3D scan process is not a new research topic, the integration of 3D scanning and printing in education has been paid a great attention to by many researchers and experts. High speed and accuracy of 3D optical scanning technology makes the productivity efficiency, and capturing point-cloud data in 3D modeling and animation will be a huge potential of ascension [4]. 3D application software for modeling, rendering, and animation has become an essential part of the industrial design [5, 6]. However, the 3D modeling based on 3D optical measurements data has not widely used in the field of education. In the case of design studies, the integration of 3D scan data and technology provides the unlimited potential for complex modeling. The students in design major still rely on 3D modeling software to produce complex surface model [7]. As we know, most of students need to spend amount of time to build a three-dimensional models [8], such as gloves, shoes, and face. Even those of them master the modeling skill and software, there are still many limitations in the application of surface modeling. In this paper, the 3D optical scanner used to capture the basic 3D modeling data, students able to choose existing output models for their own design requirement and re-creation without basic modeling process. This interactive model integrates cognitive, creative, collaborative and pedagogical representations of user behavior and creative skill that enable better understanding of students and their intents through a theoretical framework.

2 Background of Design Education

Design is the arrangement of forms and colours of an artefact or natural form. The word "design" is from the Latin designare, meaning to mark out, trace out, contrive, or arrange [9]. In The Oxford Dictionary, the explanation for the word "design" is a plan or drawing produced to show the look and function or workings of a building, garment, or other object before it is made. It is the creation of a plan and convention for the construction of an object or system. There are countless philosophies for guiding design as the design values and accompanying aspects of modern design vary, both between different schools of thought and among practising designers. Design, so construed, is the core of all professional training. It is the principal mark that distinguishes the professions from the sciences. Thus, design education forms an important part of the whole design research and practice.

Design education is the teaching of the theory and application of the design of products, services, and environments. It encompasses various disciplines of design, such as graphic design, user interface design, web design, packaging design, industrial design, fashion design, information design, interior design, sustainable design, and universal design. However, design education is also concerned with the training of theoretical thinking or practical skills in a process that can be mapped out to other areas of applications, while theoretical thinking is often provided at the postgraduate level and practical skills can be given to students at the undergraduate level or high-school level.

Throughout the history of Western civilization, education was limited to the children of families with wealth or social power [10]. Educational matters have been the subjects of earnest discussions by philosophers and statesmen. As we know, Western culture dawned in Greece, where two great philosophers, Plato and Aristotle, wrote not only about education but also about the place of the arts within it [9]. The concept of art education as distinct from craft training was realized in Italy in the sixteenth century due to the recognition of art as a product of the intellect rather than skilful hands, and a "scienza studiosa" investigated the principles of design of natural phenomena [9]. On the contrary, for many decades design studio pedagogy continued to be taboo, undebatable and untouchable. Until the late 1970s, few scholars discussed design education [11].

With the development of the world and artistic forms, art and design education as it stands today has been greatly influenced by the Bauhaus school (Bauhaus meaning house of building). Most consider it to be the first formal design school. The origins of Bauhaus can obviously be traced back to Kindergarten, the school system for educating young children perfected by Friedrich Froebel. Friedrich Froebel was a German pedagogue who created the concept of the "kindergarten" and also coined the word now used in German and English.

In Norman Brosterrman's book "Inventing kindergarten", the series of "gifts" used by children at kindergarten are very much what young designers were taught to experiment and to "play" with as they were learning about formal principles and relationships. The gifts stimulated imagination and creativity while teaching the designers to think about formal principles in two dimensions and in three dimensions. In 1919, a German architect named Walter Gropius was appointed as head of the Bauhaus in Weimar. He came from the Werkbund movement, which sought to integrate art and economics and to add an element of engineering to art [12]. Students at this new school were trained by both an artist and a master craftsman. Gropius thought that modern artists familiar with science and economics need to unite the creative imagination with practical knowledge of craftsmanship, and thus to develop a new sense of functional design [12].

The first aim of the school was to rescue all of the arts from the isolation in which each then found itself to encourage individual artisans and craftsmen to work cooperatively and combine all of their skills [13]. The school also set out to elevate the status of crafts to the same level enjoyed by fine arts such as painting and sculpting. Another important aspect is to maintain contact with the leaders of industry and craft in an attempt eventually to gain independence from government support by selling designs to industry.

In 1937, the stars of the Bauhaus fled to the United States in the wake of the Nazis' rise to power. At that time, the United States welcomed them with open arms. Gropius was made the head of the school of architecture at Harvard. One of the most versatile artists of the twentieth century, named Laszlo Moholy-Nagy, opened the new Bauhaus, which evolved into the Chicago Institute of Design ("Illinois Institute of Technology" today). Mies van der Rohe, who was a great architect of the time, became the head of the Bauhaus in 1930, and was installed as the Dean of Architecture at the Armour Institute in Chicago. Bauhaus is still a very important part of today's design education scene. Its effect stretches beyond product design into the realms of architecture, theatre, and typography, in which the designs and style of Bauhaus also occupy a significant position.

3   The 3D Optical Technology

3D scanning integrated light, machine, electricity and computer technology in order to obtain the spatial coordinates of the object surface. It mainly used to scan the object space shape and structure. As an important technical support in manufacturing, the technology plays an indispensable role in its development, research and application has become a new subject. The significant of this technology is able to convert the solid information of object into digital signal which is provide a convenient and efficient method of digitization with computer. There are two kinds of digitizing techniques for capturing 3D data, mechanical which uses contact sensors, and the optical/laser which processes by non-contact sensors. 3D optical scanning technology can realize the non-contact measurement with white light in high speed and accuracy. Besides, the measurements results are able to connect with wide variety of software, which makes it becoming popular in CAD, CAM, and CIMS application. The different subject fields 3D scanning is application into are RE [14], 3D modelling and visualisation, point cloud data comparison, prototyping, analysis, digital archiving, inspection and quality control requirements [15]. With 3D optical scanning technology for plants, samples, and models to obtain the steric size data. The data can adjust and repair in CAD system before sent final results to manufacturing center or prototyping equipment to reduce the product manufacturing cycle in efficiency.

3.1   The 3D Optical Scanner in Research

The 3D scanner used in this paper is a desktop 3D optical colour scanner, this basic structure of three-dimensional sensor based on the phase mapping of the structure light illumination. It mainly composed of binocular stereo vision camera and structure light illumination device, and the core technology of the sensor is phase assisted active stereo (PAAS) (Fig. 1). The working principle is the structure light illumination device projected sinusoidal fringe sequences to the object to be measured with variable frequency and phase shifting. The ideal stripe is modulated by the height of the object surface, and the deformation fringe pattern is processes by the phase recovery technique to reduce the absolute phase distribution on the surface of object. To be the only feature, absolute phase can be used to establish homonymy point matching of the right and left camera, and then reconstruct the 3D geometry of the object surface by binocular stereo vision theory.

At the same time, to construct multisensory measurements networks which uses of high pixel SLR camera and binocular stereo vision system not only capture geometry stereo structure data, also collects the colour texture information by SLR camera. The system matches geometric data and colour texture with internal and external parameters after obtain high quality colour texture from single vision through SLR camera (Fig. 2).

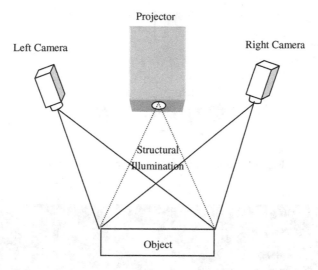

Fig. 1. Binocular stereo vision camera and structure light illumination device

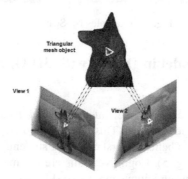

Fig. 2. Colour texture corresponded 3D geometric data

The obtained colour texture information need to establish one to one correspondence relationship with 3D geometric data. Then obtains the final 3D data model with real colour texture data through a variety of mechanisms of weighted coefficient algorithm and fusion processing of colour texture (Fig. 3). Researcher intend to apply 3D optical scanning technology on design education in order to improve the creative behaviour in design subject.

The 3D optical technology is able to measure and record the complex interface of the products (Fig. 4). There are lots of 3D basic models captured by 3D optical scanner, then designers and students could recreate the new shape on the basis of existing models.

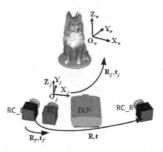

Fig. 3. Example texture geometric measurements

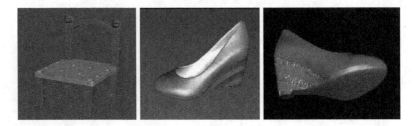

Fig. 4. Examples by Scanner

4 An Interactive Model in Design with 3D Optical Technology

Researcher creates an interactive model integrated four factors which are cognitive, creative, collaborative and pedagogical. This model proposed to improve user behavior and creative skill that enable better understanding of students and their intents through a theoretical framework (Fig. 5). Cognitive skills are the mental mechanisms that are used in the process of acquiring knowledge; these skills include reasoning, perception, and intuition. Reading and writing rely on a specific set of cognitive skills, such as attention, memory, symbolic thinking, and self-regulation. For example, when children learn to read and write, they continue to improve these skills, making them more purposeful and deliberate. Deliberate attention is required to differentiate between letters, even if they look alike, and to isolate specific portions of a word for encoding to decode it. Children must remember the previous words as they decode the subsequent words in a sentence. A teenager's cognitive skill set is made up of several mental skills, including auditory and visual processing, short- and long-term memory, comprehension, logic and reasoning, and attention skills. Most college prep courses focus on academic materials and study habits. Meta-cognition allows teens to think about how they feel and what they are thinking. It involves being able to think about how one is perceived by others. It can also be used to develop strategies, also known as mnemonic devices, for improving learning.

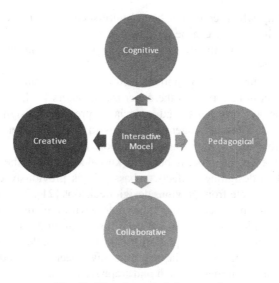

Fig. 5. The theoretical framework

Cognitive skills are also considered when designing an integrated interactive model. In this case, the cognitive model works in contrast to another element of artificial intelligence study, the cognitive architecture. The cognitive model attempts to recreate how the brain can carry out a particular task, such as design learning or making decisions. Cognitive design has been considered by many researcher in design fields. Cognition is the scientific term of "the process of thought" to knowing. Cognitive artefacts (CA) are acknowledged as important for individual cognition [16], but their function in design group work also has largely potential. In this paper, researcher inherent 3D optical technical hardware with design process in order to improve the creative ability. By advancing the science of design, and by creating a broad computer based methodology for automating the design of artifacts and of industrial processes, researchers can attain dramatic improvements in productivity [17]. The 3D optical technology introduced in this research to allow students and designers to perform how this technique impact the design cognition. A design project would be conducted in two groups, one group need to complete the product design in traditional process which include brainstorm, prototype, and modelling. Another group Finish the design project with existing 3D models captured by the 3D optical scanner. Researcher needs to observe the two groups, and record the whole design process to prove the achievement of this model.

Design in many settings is an inherently collective and creative undertaking, with phenomena of emergence at the heart of the activity [18]. Complex design problems require more knowledge than any single person possesses because the knowledge relevant to a problem is usually distributed among stakeholders [19]. Bringing different and often controversial points of view together to create a shared understanding among these stakeholders can lead to new insights, new ideas, and new artifacts [19]. Collaborative success can therefore be said to be achieved when we have accomplished something in a group which could not be accomplished by an individual. The representation available in the CA can be an effective means of passing this information between stakeholders. This theory supported designers are faced with distribute, ill-structures problems.

Shared Understanding is the important factor affect the collaborative design. In designing artifacts, designers rely on the expertise of others [20], by referring to text book, standards, legal constraints, and especially previous design efforts. Project complexity forces large and heterogeneous groups to work together on projects over long periods of time. Knowledge bases to support design should include not only knowledge about the design process but also knowledge about the artifacts of that process-parts used in designing artifacts, subassemblies previously created by other design efforts, and rationale from previous design decisions [21]. The interactive model is the basis for conducting research and experiments with the students.

In this research, a platform (Fig. 6) has been built based on this theoretical model. With this computational interactive platform, it is then possible to test and evaluate whether the original objectives of the research have been achieved or not, and to identify the direction for further research and improvements.

Fig. 6. The prototype of the online design platform

5 Conclusion

This paper aim to use 3D optical scanner to capture the basic 3D modeling data, students allowed to choose existing output models for requirement of design project and recreation without basic modeling process. The advanced 3D optical technology able to improve the speed for modeling especially for the students and designers without background of 3D software modeling. The integration interactive model includes four factors: cognitive, creative, collaborative and pedagogical representations of user behavior and creative skill that enable better understanding of students and their intents through a theoretical framework. The online platform as a medium for this interactive model to prove the proposition of researcher.

The research supports by Shenzhen University and Esun. Corporation Shenzhen.

References

1. Younan, S., Treadaway, C.: Digital 3D models of heritage artefacts: towards a digital dream space. Digit. Appl. Archaeol. Cult. Herit. **2**(4), 240–247 (2015)
2. Kostakis, V., et al.: Open source 3D printing as a means of learning: an educational experiment in two high schools in Greece. Telematics Inform. **32**(1), 118–128 (2015)
3. Johnson, L., Adams Becker, S., Cummins, M., Estrada, V., Freeman, A., Ludgate, H.: NMCHorizon Report: 2013 Higher, Education edn. The New Media Consortium, Austin (2013)
4. McCallum, B., Nixon, M., Price, B., Fright, R.: Hand-held laser scanning. In: Practice. Applied Research Associates NZ Ltd, 47 Hereford St, PO Box 3894, Christchurch, New Zealand
5. Monti, C., Fregonese, L., Achille, C.: Laser application on complex shapes of architecture profiles extraction processing and 3D modelling. Int. Arch. Photogramm. Remote Sens. Spat. Inf. Sci. xxxiv: 5/W10
6. Tovey, M.: Styling and design: intuition and analysis in industrial design. Des. Stud. **18**, 5–31 (1997)
7. Tovey, M., Owen, J.: Sketching and direct CAD modelling in automotive design. Des. Stud. **21**, 569–588 (2000)
8. Tovey, M., Porter, S., Newman, R.: Sketching, concept development and automotive design. Des. Stud. **24**, 135–153 (2003)
9. Macdonald, Stuart: The History and Philosophy of Art Education. University of London Press Ltd., London (1970)
10. Efland, Arthur D.: A History of Art Education: Intellectual and Social Currents in Teaching the Visual Arts. Teacher College Press, New York (1990)
11. Salama, M.A., Nicholas, W.: Introduction: critical thinking and decision making in studio pedagogy. In: Salama, M.A., Nicholas, W. (eds.) Design Studio Pedagogy: Horizons for the Future, pp. 125–129. Urban International Press, Gateshead (2007)
12. Bayer, H.: Bauhaus 1919–1928. Museum of Modern Art (1938)
13. Whitford, F.: Bauhaus. Thames & Hudson, London (1984)
14. Kus, A., et al.: A comparative study of 3D scanning in engineering, product and transport design and fashion design education. Comput. Appl. Eng. Educ. **17**(3), 263–271 (2009)

15. Slob, S., Hack, R.: 3D terrestrial laser scanning as a new field measurement and monitoring technique. In: Hack, R., Azzam, R., Charlier, R. (eds.) Engineering Geology for Infrastructure Planning in Europe, vol. 104, pp. 179–189. Springer, Heidelberg (2004)
16. Perry, M.: Cognitive artefacts and collaborative design. In: Colloquium Digest-IEE (1995)
17. Amarel, S.: Artificial intelligence and design. Information technology, 1990 'next decade in information technology'. In: Proceedings of the 5th Jerusalem Conference, pp. 315–333 (1990)
18. Benjamin G.S.: A cognitive account of collective emergence in design. In: Proceeding of 7th ACM Conference on Creativity and Cognition (2009)
19. Arias, E., Eden, H., Fisher, G., Gorman, A., Scharff, E.: Transcending the individual human mindcreating shared understanding through collaborative design. ACM Trans. Comput.-Hum. Interact. 7(1), 84–113 (2000)
20. Hornby, G.S., Lioson, H., Pollack, J.B.: Evolution of generative design systems for modular physical robots. In: Proceedings 2001 ICRA. IEEE International Conference on Robotics and Automation, vol. 4, pp. 4146–4151 (2001)
21. Sagheb-Tehrani, M.: Expert systems development: some issues of design process. ACM Sigsoft Eng. Notes 30(2), 1–5 (2005)

Developing High-Performing Teams:
A Design Thinking Led Approach

Heath Keighran[1](✉) and Sisira Adikari[2]

[1] Business Design, Crooked Fox, Canberra, ACT 2601, Australia
Heath@crookedfox.com.au
[2] School of Information Systems and Accounting, University of Canberra,
Canberra, ACT 2601, Australia
Sisira.adikari@canberra.edu.au

Abstract. A highly functional team is fundamental to the ongoing business success, and organizations spend a significant amount of resources on improving team performance. Creating a high-performing team is far more challenging than imagined in an enterprise with continuously changing business demands. This paper examines how the application of design thinking can lead to developing highly functional teams that deliver effective team performance and outcomes. This study involved embedding design thinking into co-design as an approach to develop and implement strategies that satisfy a high-performing team structure. Four dynamic teams of total seven team members actively engaged with two business designers in co-design. Upon the setting up, all team members worked with the new team structure for seven weeks. A questionnaire was administered to team members to assess their new experience, perceptions on performance and outcomes in the new team structure followed by a focus group workshop. The results of the subsequent data analysis indicate that team members performed significantly better in the new team structure and delivered higher levels of team outcomes.

Keywords: Co-design · Design thinking · High-performing teams

1 Introduction

The dynamic nature of today's enterprise is complex and faced with many challenges such as resource limitations, increased competition between similar enterprises, and continuously changing business demands. The primary goal of an enterprise is to maintain a sustainable development and meet business objectives effectively. The people factor is the main driving force in the business where teamwork has become an essential element. It has been identified that highly functional teams are fundamental to the ongoing business success of organizations [1]. Organizations recognize the importance of the higher level of performance and spend a significant amount of resources on programs that aimed at improving team performance [2]. A high-performing team is an asset to the enterprise and contributes significantly to make it successful. Organizations continuously explore new ways and methods that can improve the team performance for a higher level of organizational outcomes.

© Springer International Publishing Switzerland 2016
A. Marcus (Ed.): DUXU 2016, Part I, LNCS 9746, pp. 53–64, 2016.
DOI: 10.1007/978-3-319-40409-7_6

Accordingly, it is worthwhile to investigate novel approaches that significantly speed-up the team performance. Many methods are suitable for exploratory investigations such as interviewing, focus groups and brainstorming. Design Thinking has been recognized as one of the most effective means to discover deeper insights and empathy of users and context of use to develop a greater understanding [3]. Accordingly, design thinking led exploratory studies to benefit from the use of design thinking methodology to uncover a deeper contextual understanding of solution design.

Human-Centered Design (HCD) methodologies and principles underpin the necessary design practices to understand the needs of the end-user and to deliver user-focused design solutions [4]. One of the primary purposes of HCD is to gain a profound insight to develop proper understanding and needs of all users and the context. User-Centered Design (UCD) is an approach of Human-Centered Design [5]. Design Thinking (DT) is another approach of HCD that can be used to gain a real knowledge of all users and the context. From the perspectives of socio-technical aspects, a design team engaged in solution design can be considered as a Problem-Solving System. For the purpose of creating high-performing teams, we treat design teams as a Problem-Solving system. We have used design thinking as the primary HCD approach to gain a deeper knowledge of design teams and to improve the current situation to a desirable future state by designing with all users (team members).

The rest of the paper is organized as follows. Section 2 presents an overview of design thinking as a human-centered approach. Section 3 explains the research design of this investigation. Section 4 illustrates how the research was conducted. Section 5 describes the team ideation as a concept. Section 6 reports the results of the research study. Section 7 briefly discusses the usefulness of this study and concludes the paper.

2 Design Thinking as an HCD Approach

In recent years, 'design thinking' has gained a wider popularity in many disciplines as an approach to solving socially ambiguous design problems [6]. According to Dunne and Martin [7], design thinking is the way designers think and apply their mental processes to design objects, services or systems, as distinct from the end result of elegant and useful products. Design Thinking is an approach of Human-Centered Design.

According to Brown [8], design thinking is an approach of human-centered innovation that uses the designer's sensibility and methods to match people's needs with what is technologically feasible and what a viable business strategy can convert into customer value and market opportunity. Brown's definition of design thinking highlights three important points. First, design thinking is an approach of human-centered design. Second, design thinking is an approach to creating feasible design solutions that meet customer needs with added value. Third, design thinking is an approach to designing artifacts; hence design is an integral part of design thinking. Accordingly, the main idea behind design thinking is how designers progress the design process with a creative mind to discover new opportunities and to create design solutions.

The primary focus of design thinking is to gain a deeper understanding of the system under study. It uses an extended holistic view of the system under study and other associated interacting systems to capture relevant contextual information to identify system issues, constraints, system goals, and requirements. This emphasis is further elaborated in the design thinking capability framework [8] presented with five specific focus areas namely: 1. Empathy (view contexts holistically from multiple human perspectives), 2. Integrative thinking (see all of the aspects of a situation for creative solutions), 3. Optimism (optimize one potential solution over other alternatives), 4. Experimentalism (explore the situations in creative ways towards new directions), 5. Collaboration (collaborate with interdisciplinary actors for innovative solutions). There are many design thinking process models reported by many authors [7–11].

This research study was based on the iterative design thinking process model presented by Meinel and Leifer [11], which is shown in Fig. 1.

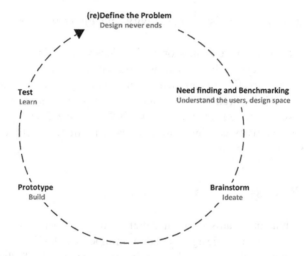

Fig. 1. Design thinking process model [10]

It consists of five main activities: 1. (re)Define the problem, 2. Need finding and Benchmarking, 3. Brainstorm, 4. Prototype, 5. Test. According to Meinel and Leifer [11], design thinking is a human-centric methodology that integrates expertise from different disciplines such as design, social sciences, engineering, and business for problem forming, solving and design. Importantly, it emphasizes an end-user focus with multidisciplinary collaboration and iterative improvement to produce innovative products, systems, and services.

3   Research Design

This section describes the research design used in this research study which comprised of two main qualitative steps namely, Creativity and Innovation. Figure 2 shows the research design to illustrate the relationship between the Team (problem-solving

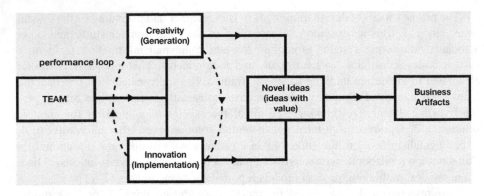

Fig. 2. Performance loop – relationship between ideas and innovation and output

system) and the two qualitative steps (Creativity and Innovation) towards producing business artifacts.

Creativity is the ability to create new or useful ideas with business value that can be used to implement business artifacts such as products, systems, or services [12, 13]. The primary aim of the creativity is an idea generation process. Idea generation is also known as Ideation [14]. Innovation is the successful implementation of those creative ideas to realize business artifacts [15]. As shown in Fig. 2, the Team (problem-solving system) engages in Creativity and Innovation steps to produce novel ideas to generate business artifacts.

4 Research Process

There were four dynamic teams of total seven team members participated in this research study. Two business designers led a number of design thinking-oriented co-design sessions where all team members actively engaged in for both creativity and innovation steps (activities). For team members, at one instance, one team member can be active only in one team, and also, a team member can be active in many teams in different instances. The research process is governed by a conceptual system called Idea Hub which is central to Team, Creativity, and Innovation. The Idea Hub functionality was managed by business designers who led the design workshops. The primary aim of the idea hub functionality was to record and assess all ideas received from the Idea Generation and Collection functionality to determine the suitability of each idea for further development. Ideas are evaluated based on their business value, feasibility, desirability, and viability and the selected ideas that deemed promising enough for prototyping are then passed over for further development and redevelopment towards business solutions and artifacts. All activities between Team, Innovation, and Creativity are iterative. The schematic view of the research process is shown in Fig. 3.

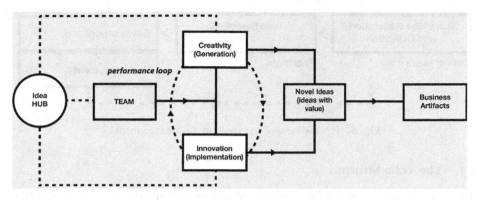

Fig. 3. Idea Hub– relationship between innovation and creativity

5   Team Ideation

A team in many ways is self-sustained, and team members provide many leads of information for idea generation sourced from their backgrounds, and personal and business experience. Team idea generation (team ideation) is a combination of consistent information flows from areas such as collaboration, production, team members, building, discovery, reflection. Figure 4 shows the Team Ideation Model.

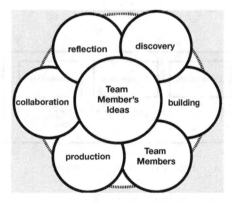

Fig. 4. Team Ideation model

With the strong emphasis on human-centered design and design thinking orientation, all members of the team participated in idea generation and collection process. All members of the team engaged in this process on a day-to-day basis. Team members come from different backgrounds and their engagement in each idea generation sessions helped to enhance the collaboration and to produce shared and agreed ideas that support creativity and innovation. The team idea generation was governed by an Ideation Governance Model that showcase how ideas are moved through and are prioritized for development or moved back for further redevelopment in collaboration with the team. The process view of the ideation governance model is shown in Fig. 5.

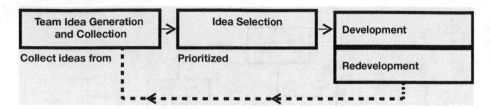

Fig. 5. Process view of the ideation governance model

5.1   The Team Structure

The team structure uses a suite of techniques, tools, and an array of design activities based on a collaborative and co-design approach. The co-design approach was used to create an open and collective team with access to creativity and innovation; this process puts the most suitable team members together for the most appropriate task. The purpose of an open and collaborative team was to utilize design thinking to increase performance. The main functionalities of the Team were to generate ideas, explore ideas, develop ideas, implement ideas and evaluate ideas. The Design Solutions were created based on the evaluated ideas. The team structure model is shown in Fig. 6.

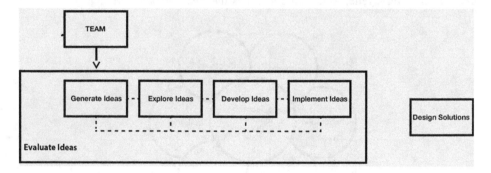

Fig. 6. Team structure model

6   Experimental Study

This section presents the details of embedding design thinking into co-design as an approach to developing and implements strategies that satisfy a high-performing team structure. The aim of co-design activity is to generate collective creativity of designer and participants who are actively engaged in the design process where participant becomes a partner of the design [16]. The study aimed to create a high performing team structure that promotes creativity and innovation through the use of an ideas management system. This research study was conducted to assess if the application of design thinking can lead to developing highly functional teams that deliver effective team performance and outcomes.

Two business designers led design workshops to unpack the tasks and requirements for a suite of given business problems. The requirements then determined team structures, and the team of seven discussed and agreed on who was best suited to the task, taking into accountability, individual skills, current workloads and willingness to learn. During the workshop, team members engaged in design activities and offered a number of creative ideas based on the key topics outlined by the Business Designers. Some of the topics discussed were:

- Business challenge
- Current state
- Desired state
- How to go to the desired state and what need to be done
- Achieving results
- Team collaboration
- Team environment
- Team direction
- Team responsibilities
- Team goals
- Individual skills and talents
- Team commitments
- Values and rewards
- Continuous improvements
- Skillful communication
- Team consultation
- Team spirit
- Trust and respect
- Innovation
- Creativity
- Co-design

Moreover, the design workshops uncovered other participant attributes such as group dynamics, behaviors, knowledge, experience, attitudes, likes, dislikes and how team members see themselves, the team and the enterprise. The workshops allowed team members to develop a shared knowledge of the context, efficient means for how they would work together, how to utilize the idea managements system and what design principles and methodologies they would adopt.

6.1 Design Thinking Teams

Design thinking teams are based on collaborative, and cross-functional principles that allow members with different experiences work to realize design benefits in their day to day job activities. The fundamental orientation of teams is strongly linked to design thinking principles, methods, techniques, and tools. Teamwork primarily involves design thinking-oriented tasks aimed at devising design solutions. Moreover, having an open and cross-functional team provides the opportunity to generate purposeful creative and innovative ideas towards effective design solutions. The Team Ideation, Hub, and Structure are collaboratively managed, developed and reviewed by the team, which is multidisciplinary with different skills sets.

For this study, four dynamic teams of total seven team members were set up as shown in Table 1. As its name suggests, a dynamic team is not static or permanent, and team structures can be short lived. Dynamic teams are set up and disband based on business needs of the enterprise. The team structures were such that one team member can take part in one-to-many teams in a given day. As shown in Table 1, seven team members are represented by alphabetic characters A to G. Team leads are a part of the seven-member team, and a team can be led by more than one team member.

Table 1. Dynamic team structures

Team leads	Team members	Design thinking teams
A, B, C	D, E, F, G	Main team
C	E, F	Sub-team one
F	B, G	Sub-team two
A, B	C, D	Sub-team three

For example, the Main Team is led by three team leads A, B, and C and the team members of the team are D, E, F, and G. Similarly, the sub-team two is directed by a single team member F, and the team members are B and G.

Unnecessary redundancies in teams affect the performance [17]. This research study also paid attention to optimizing teams by removing duplications or unnecessary redundancies of resources in teams. One possible approach is to apply relational database normalization principles considering teams as relations, and team leads define rest of the team (team members are functionally dependent on team lead or leads). However, further discussion on team optimization using relational database normalization principles is out of scope for this paper due to space limitations.

6.2   Data Collection and Analysis

Upon the setting up, all team members worked with the new team structures for seven weeks. A questionnaire was administered to all seven team members to assess their new experience, perceptions on performance and outcomes in their new team structures followed by a focus group. The aim of the questionnaire was to uncover perceptions to support better delivering an open, enjoyable, and cross-functional team that helps improve output and collaboration. The questionnaire was a cut-down version of the team building questionnaire by Warrick [18], and it contained following questionnaire items with Likert-scales 1 to 7 (1 = very low and 7 = very high):

- The team leader provides vision, direction, and inspiration
- The team has a clear mission
- The responsibilities of the team and each team member are clear
- The team has clear goals

- The potential of the team and each team member is fully utilized
- The team is flexible and responds quickly to needed changes
- The team leader encourages participation and involvement
- All team members are committed team players
- Team members feel free to be candid and communicate openly
- Ideas are critiqued in a positive way by attacking problems and not people
- Team members are valued and rewarded for their efforts
- The time is taken periodically to evaluate and improve the team.
- The team has a sense of vitality, enthusiasm, and team spirit
- Team members work well together and support and encourage each other
- An atmosphere of trust exists among the team members
- The team has an environment that encourages innovative ideas and constant improvements
- The team has an environment that is warm, friendly, and fun
- The team fully utilizes the talents of each team member
- The team is very successful at achieving the desired results

The focus group discussed similar topics in the questionnaire and aimed at capturing collective voice from the team more of the qualitative nature. The questionnaire data were analyzed to identify which Likert scale categories for which questionnaire items were preferred by the majority of team members. The captured focus group data were analyzed to determine recurring themes relevant to the new team structures. The details of data analysis and results are presented in Sect. 6.3.

6.3 The Results of Data Analysis

Table 2 illustrates the results of the questionnaire data analysis showing a total number of responses by team members for each questionnaire item. The quantitative data from Likert scales were analyzed by calculating a total number of responses received for each Likert score value for each questionnaire item. Seven point Likert scales were used, ranging from 1 = Very Low, 2 = Low, 3 = Somewhat Low (SWL), 4 = Average (AVE), 5 = Somewhat High (SWH), 6 = High, 7 = Very High.

As shown in Table 2, there are four *total of seven* responses, and ten *total of six* responses for Very High Likert score and these have been highlighted by dark green and light green colors. Based on Likert scale ranges, a *total of seven* response and a *total of six* response are treated as *very high* and *high* respectively. Accordingly, a *total of seven* responses means all team members agree with the relevant questionnaire item for a *very high* score, and a *total of six* responses means six team members agree with the corresponding questionnaire item for a *high* score. These total scores altogether amount to 4 + 10 = 14 questionnaire items for which participants agree that they are *very high* or *high*-performance indicators.

Two business designers led the focus group workshop, and all team members attended it. Discussions were based indicators of high-performance and how to achieve best results in a team environment. Eleven themes were identified during the focus group workshop by team members namely: 1. Business change, 2. Requirements, 3.

Table 2. Results of questionnaire data analysis

Questionnaire Items	Very Low	Low	SWL	Ave	SWH	High	Very High
	1	2	3	4	5	6	7
The team leader provides vision, direction, and inspiration						1	6
The team has a clear mission					1	2	4
The responsibilities of the team and each team member are clear						1	6
The team has clear goals						1	6
The potential of the team and each team member is fully utilized							7
The team is flexible and responds quickly to needed changes						5	2
The team leader encourages participation and involvement							7
All team members are committed team players						4	3
Team members feel free to be candid and communicate openly						1	6
Ideas are critiqued in a positive way by attacking problems and not people						1	6
Team members are valued and rewarded for their efforts						4	3
The time is taken periodically to evaluate and improve the team.							7
The team has a sense of vitality, enthusiasm, and team spirit					1		6
Team members work well together and support and encourage each other						1	6
An atmosphere of trust exists among the team members						1	6
The team has an environment that encourages innovative ideas and constant improvements						1	6
The team has an environment that is warm, friendly, and fun					1	1	5
The team fully utilizes the talents of each team member						1	6
The team is very successful at achieving the desired results							7

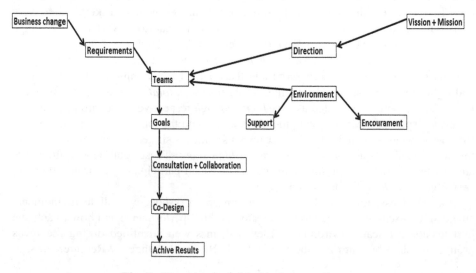

Fig. 7. The agreed relationship between themes

Vision and mission, 4. Direction, 5. Environment, 6. Support, 7. Encouragement, 8. Goals, 9. Consultation and collaboration, 10. Co-design, 11. Achieving results. The relationship between these themes was discussed and agreed by team members as shown in Fig. 7.

Figure 7 is an indication of the team perceptions on themes and how they specifically should relate in order to achieve best results and deliver high-performance.

7 Conclusions

In this paper, we presented three ideation models: Idea Hub, Team Ideation Model, and Ideation Governance Model along with a design thinking-oriented co-design approach to design high-performing teams. These models and the embed co-design approach applied to create four dynamic teams in an enterprise. After seven weeks of working on new team structures, a questionnaire was administered to all team members to assess their new experience in the new team structures. The results of the subsequent data analysis indicate that team members positively expressed their opinions to suggest that they performed significantly better in the new team structures and achieved higher levels of team outcomes.

The main contribution of the paper comes from the design, implementation, and validation of three ideation models used in a design thinking led co-design space. We are confident that these models and the co-design approach can be applied in wider academic and industrial settings to derive effective human-centred design solutions.

References

1. Woodcock, M., Francis, D.: Team Metrics: Resources for Measuring and Improving Team Performance, p. 303. HRD Press, Amherst (2008)
2. Donaldson, S.I., Berger, D.E., Pezdek, K.: Rewarding careers applying positive psychological science to improve quality of work life and organizational effectiveness. In: Donaldson, S.I., Berger, D.E., Pezdek, K. (eds.) Applied Psychology: New Frontiers and Rewarding Careers, p. 238. Psychology Press, Abingdon (2012)
3. Weigel, L.: Design thinking to bridge research and concept design. In: Luchs, M.G., Swan, K.S., Griffin, A. (eds.) Design Thinking: New Product Development Essentials from the PDMA, pp. 59–70. Wiley, New York (2015)
4. Johnson, M.: Towards human-centered requirements management in distributed design. In: Smith, M.J., Salvendy, G. (eds.) Systems, Social and Internationalization Design Aspects of Human-Computer Interaction, vol. 2, pp. 642–646. CRC Press, Boca Raton (2001)
5. Adikari, S., McDonald, C., Campbell, J.: Little design up-front: a design science approach to integrating usability into agile requirements engineering. In: Jacko, J.A. (ed.) HCI International 2009, Part I. LNCS, vol. 5610, pp. 549–558. Springer, Heidelberg (2009)
6. Tilmann, L., Raja, G., Birgit, J., Christoph, M.: Is there a need for a design thinking process? In: Proceedings of 8th Design Thinking Research Symposium, pp. 243–254 (2010)
7. Dunne, D., Martin, R.: Design thinking and how it will change management education: an interview and discussion. Acad. Manag. Learn. Educ. 5(4), 512–523 (2006)
8. Brown, T.: Design thinking. Harvard Bus. Rev. 86(6), 85–92 (2008)

9. Eris, O.: Insisting on truth at the expense of conceptualization: can engineering portfolios help? Int. J. Eng. Educ. **22**(3), 551–559 (2006)
10. D.School – Stanford University. https://dschool.stanford.edu
11. Meinel, C., Leifer, L.: Design thinking. Understand – improve – apply. In: Plattner, H., Meinel, C., Leifer, L. (eds.) Design Thinking Research, p. xiv. Springer, Heidelberg (2011)
12. Shalley, C.E.: Effects of coaction, expected evaluation, and goal setting on creativity and productivity. Acad. Manag. J. **38**, 483–503 (1995)
13. Woodman, R.W., Sawyer, J.E., Griffin, R.W.: Toward a theory of organizational creativity. Acad. Manag. Rev. **18**, 293–321 (1993)
14. Yock, P.G., Zenios, S., Makower, J., Brinton, T.J., Krummel, T.M., Kumar, U.N., Denend, L.: Biodesign. Cambridge University Press, Cambridge (2015)
15. Amabile, T.M.: A model of creativity and innovation in organizations. Res. Organ. Behav. **10**(1), 123–167 (2004)
16. Sanders, E., Stappers, P.J.: Co-creation and the new landscapes of design. CoDesign **4**(1), 5–18 (2008)
17. Hanlan, M.: High-Performance Teams: How to Make Them Work, p. 17. Greenwood Publishing Group, Santa Barbara (2004)
18. Warrick, D.D.: What leaders can learn about teamwork and developing high-performance teams from organization development practitioners. OD Pract. **46**(3), 68–75 (2014)

Empathy at Work

Using the Power of Empathy to Deliver Delightful Enterprise Experiences

Janaki Kumar[✉], Eliad Goldwasser, and Prerna Seth

3410 Hillview Ave., Palo Alto, CA 94304, USA
{janaki.kumar,eliad.goldwasser}@sap.com,
prernaseth@gmail.com

Abstract. To deliver best in class user experiences, design practitioners have to create the end to end experience based on a solid understanding of the target user's needs. In the case of consumer products, this task is made somewhat easier by the fact that the designer can "imagine" themselves as the potential user of the product. This strategy is rendered ineffective in an enterprise context since the designer is most likely not the end user they are designing for. To overcome this hurdle, designers can use the power of empathy to understand their user's needs and design delightful experiences for them.

In this paper, we will share a case study from SAP's Design and Co-Innovation Center that illustrates the power of empathy to understand a complex domain and design experiences that delight.

Keywords: User experience · UX · Strategy · UX management · UX leadership · Customer experience · Human centered design · Information technology

1 Introduction

Scientists discovered special neurons called "mirror neurons" that fire when we watch another person do something. Neuroscientist Giacomo Rizzolatti and his colleagues made this accidental discovery while testing a motor neuron in a monkey's brain that fired every time the monkey grabbed a peanut. They were surprised to find that the same neuron fired when the monkey watched a human researcher reach for a peanut. It was as if the monkey's brain could not tell the difference between seeing and doing – watching somebody do something was just like doing it yourself! They soon found that this was true for the human brain as well, and named these set of neurons mirror neurons.

This research on mirror neurons is relevant for enterprise software designers, and it offers a powerful tool they can leverage. This tool is empathy. Designers of consumer products have a slight advantage in that they can imagine themselves as users of the product they are designing. For example, when designing a social networking site, the designer and his or her team could be the potential users. Hence, they can design based on their preferences and usage of the site, and have a good chance of being on the right track.

Enterprise software designers do not have this advantage. They are unlikely to be the CFO managing financials through a dashboard, the sales representative generating

© Springer International Publishing Switzerland 2016
A. Marcus (Ed.): DUXU 2016, Part I, LNCS 9746, pp. 65–72, 2016.
DOI: 10.1007/978-3-319-40409-7_7

customer leads, or the warehouse worker managing inventory and fulfilling customer orders. To overcome this challenge, designers need to build empathy with their target users and watch them in action. This fires their mirror neurons and gives them a better chance of designing an experience that will delight the end user.

We start this paper with an analysis of the unique challenges faced by an enterprise software designer in an increasingly complex IT and business environment. We then go on to share a case study of Vilore Foods, an importer and distributor of food products. They brought us, the Design and Co-Innovation Center (DCC) at SAP, in to improve their warehouse operations and increase productivity. The case study highlights how we, as enterprise software designers, use empathy as a tool to understand our end user and create technological tools that delight them and simplify their work.

2 Unique Challenges for Enterprise Software Designers

Enterprise software vendors such as SAP are committed to meeting and exceeding their users' expectations. This implies designing experiences for our enterprise customers that delight them and simplify their work at the same time. However, to be able to do so, our design and development teams need to overcome certain challenges that are unique to the enterprise software industry.

2.1 Complexity of Technological Landscapes

According to CIO Magazine[1], technology landscapes in organizations are increasing in complexity. This is primarily due to the heterogeneous and distributed nature of IT systems, which are facing increased pressure to adopt consumer technologies, support a mobile workforce, manage technical architectures, govern this workforce and ensure security in a distributed environment.

According to Mark McDonald, Gartner's vice president of executive programs[2], "the challenge of (IT) complexity is exacerbated by the fact that many organizations have technology systems built over time, or acquired through acquisitions or complicated by many waves of vendor consolidations. For these companies, moving forward requires an almost archaeological effort to unearth, understand and work with all these layers of sedimentary technology".

Therefore, even a simple upgrade to business software has a ripple effect on an already complex landscape. Enterprise software companies need to go through a rigorous process of planning, implementing and testing such software upgrades, to ensure that integration between systems is intact, and business reporting is still accurate.

From a user experience perspective, enterprise software designers face the challenge of considering not only the efficacy of the user interface, but also the cost of adoption, and the additional technical complexity it introduces into the landscape.

---

[1] http://www.cio.com/article/158250/Consumer_Tech_The_New_Complexity_Add.

[2] http://cxo-talk.com/mark-p-mcdonald-group-vp-gartner/.

2.2   Business Complexity

Businesses are becoming more complex, and the rate of change is faster than ever. Due to increasing globalization, a company's customers, suppliers, manufacturers, and distributors may span the world. With this comes increased regulatory pressure and penalties of non-compliance.

While enterprise software is delivered to fit standard business processes, each company may have unique workflows. Business software designers are faced with the task of recognizing these unique needs of the customer, while enabling a simple, easy-to use experience for end users (Fig. 1).

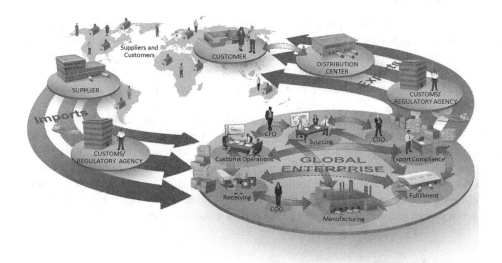

Fig. 1. Complex business environments

2.3   Lack of Design Skills in IT Organizations

To address the technical and business complexity, enterprise software is customized and configured by teams of consultants and IT staff. While these teams are typically comprised of people with technical and business skills, they usually lack design skills. Therefore, they consider the technical and business requirements of the organization, but ignore the overall user experience. This leads to software that may be functionally complete, but does not take into consideration the human being who needs to use it to get their job done.

3   Case Study: Vilore Foods

In June 2014, we engaged in a project with Vilore Foods – a leading importer, distributor, and marketer of Mexican food products and beverages in the United States and Canada. Vilore uses SAP Enterprise Resource System (ERP) to run their operations.

With offices across the U.S. and warehouses in Imperial, California and Laredo, Texas, Vilore's mission is to create "best-in-class" selling strategies that satisfy the hunger for real Hispanic food from coast-to-coast.

Vilore Foods and their implementation partner ElementFive asked our team to analyze and improve their visibility into operations and inventory levels, and streamline communication between the sales and warehouse teams. The engagement was extremely fast paced, spanning two weeks, with three days spent on site at Vilore's warehouse and regional office in Texas.

3.1   The Problem

Vilore's trucks carry food products like refried beans, pickled jalapenos and canned juices across the border from Mexico to the U.S. every day. On average, a warehouse receives over 30 trucks daily. The "Inbound Delivery Process" for trucks, was complex and took over 50 steps to complete. This process resulted in the creation of a "Good Receipt," a receipt confirming the amount and types of goods received from a particular truck.

Only once a Good Receipt has been created can Vilore take orders from wholesalers and retailers against the incoming stock. This implies that the longer it takes to create a Good Receipt for a truck, the longer it takes to accept orders against those items. Vilore recognized that by optimizing the process, they could accept orders on a more real-time basis and increase profits. They asked the DCC to analyze their Inbound Delivery Process, and reduce the amount of time it takes from when a truck arrives at the warehouse security gates to the creation of a Good Receipt.

3.2   The Approach

At the Design and Co-Innovation Center, we believe that empathy is the heartbeat of every project. Find the heart beat early and it will guide your decisions in the right direction, leading to a delightful customer experience. To find the heartbeat of the project, we began with the discovery phase, wherein we observed and interviewed stakeholders to build empathy, understand the challenge at-hand and create a problem definition. We used this research to define personas and derive insights and principles that guided us through the design phase.

During the design phase we generated ideas to address the design challenge and started building prototypes that were continually validated and iterated on with the end users. This was followed by the delivery phase, when we started implementing functional prototypes by applying technology. We explored what was technically feasible to address the design challenge, and continued to test and iterate with users before deploying a new solution.

Integral to our approach and success was a multi disciplinary team. In addition to designers from the DCC team, we had a technical expert from ElementFive who was very familiar with both Vilore Foods and SAP solutions, a business expert, and an analyst from Vilore's IT department.

3.3   Discovery Phase

We started our research at Vilore Food's warehouse in Laredo, Texas. As it was essential for us to meet with and observe end users, we asked the management to ensure access to warehouse workers and other employees involved in the Inbound Delivery and Good Receipt Process. This took the management by surprise initially – they were unsure of the value of this step, and were hesitant that we would have limited time with users as they were tied up with quarter end reporting activities.

This is a challenge our team has faced in the past and we tend to be very flexible when asking for people's time. Once meeting timelines were agreed upon, we started the day with a tour of the facility by Luis Garza, the Receiving Director at the site. To understand the entire process, starting with trucks arriving at the warehouse gate, we decided to follow people performing the different tasks sequentially.

Our first stop was with the security guard, the first person to interact with the trucks once they arrived at the warehouse gates. The guard explained the process she follows step-by-step. Her two main activities were to inspect the truck and initiate the correct paperwork. We observed that the guard manually records all the trucks that come through on paper. She inspects the container and makes photo copies of the documents provided by the driver (Fig. 2).

Fig. 2. Security guard inspecting trucks at the warehouse

Once the truck is cleared and the driver is authorized to enter the warehouse and unload the trailer, the security guard goes to her booth and copies the information into an excel file manually for the night shift guard. The night shift guard enters this

Fig. 3. Observing data entry process

information from the excel file into the company's ERP system, which runs on SAP. This allows the forklift driver to proceed with docking the truck staging the goods for inspection the next day (Fig. 3).

Through the next day and a half, we continued to observe and interview individuals involved in the process. The empathy we built by observing end users allowed us to develop a deep understanding of their day-to-day activities and pain points. With this information, we created a journey map of the existing process, color coding the manual steps, electronic touch points and points of hand off between different roles. Six distinct roles were identified, and it was visually apparent that the process was very manual (Fig. 4).

3.4 Design Phase

During the discovery phase, we heard some key opinions and aspirations from users that can be summarized into the following product requirements –

- Accurate and data driven information about the goods coming into the warehouse
- Better overview of inventory levels, and improved communication between the sales and warehouse teams about committed stock
- Optimization of off-loading process based on stock requirement priorities
- Electronic record of incoming and outgoing stock, allowing for better audit compliance.

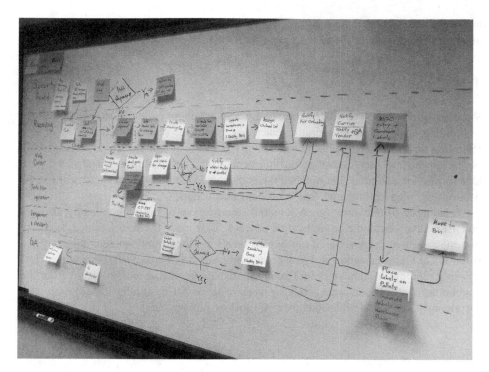

Fig. 4. Journey map used to design application prototype

We started by creating a quick prototype of an application for security guards using the existing design stencils in SAP Fiori. This prototype was validated with managers, security guards, and others involved in the process, and further developed based on their feedback.

Ready access to end users and technical resources allowed us to rapidly iterate and validate potential solutions, much to the customer's delight. The security guards were excited to be involved in shaping a solution meant for their daily use, and commented on the fact that no one had asked them what they wanted or needed to assist with their job till now.

3.5 Delivery Phase

We closed the project by providing both technical and non-technical solutions to the customer. On the technical front, we provided a functional prototype of the application for security guards, along with a roadmap to develop six additional applications covering the entire Inbound Delivery Process. On the non-technical side, we identified simple solutions like adding a printer in the inspection area to reduce the amount of time spent collecting print outs.

Building empathy for the end user played a significant role here. Observing them in their workspace implied we were able to recognize their technical as well as non-technical pain points and suggest solutions accordingly. Had only technical answers been provided, the users' pain would only be partially alleviated.

4 Conclusion

We often site our project with Vilore Foods as an excellent example on the importance of building empathy when designing enterprise software. While nobody on the design team had direct experience in the roles involved in the Inbound Delivery Process, by observing the end user, activating our mirror neurons, and building empathy, we were able to provide solutions that satisfied the end users, Vilore Foods management and IT department, ElementFive and SAP's account executives.

In addition to delivering great solutions, the process of building empathy also got end users involved in the co-innovation process. This made them feel valued, and they became excellent proponents of our work, conveying their confidence in our proposed solutions to their management. Upon completing our warehouse visit, once we reached Vilore's regional headquarters in Texas, the management had already heard from the warehouse workers and were ready to work with us on designing the solution. Not surprisingly, we see similar outcomes on most of our projects!

High Fives to the Avant-Garde

Kurtis Lesick[✉]

Alberta College of Art and Design, Calgary, Canada
kurtis.lesick@acad.ca

Abstract. This essay both explores and rationalises the role of the avant-garde in visceral design and Human-Computer Interaction by comparing the Digital and Industrial Revolutions and situating the role of 'counter-culture' practitioners as early expressers of both new cultural paradigms and new social ontologies.

Keywords: Visceral design · Experience design · Philosophy · Ontology · Emotion · Historiography · Critical history · Art · Avant-garde · Interfaces · Praxis · Design fiction · Innovation · Expressionism · Situationism · Fluxus · Subjectivity

1 I Am Not a Developer, a Computer Scientist, or an HCI Specialist

I do, however, have a very particular relationship with electronic technology and computing: I hate it. Don't get me wrong, it's not like I have some deep seeded luddite compulsions (at least I don't think I do). My strained relationship with technology is born out of inadequacy: I'm crap at it. Perhaps it is karma, but despite this fact, since my childhood I've found myself consistently drawn into the world of computing and digital technologies—a world in which I should only ever really reside on the fringes. As if to remind me of my questionable abilities, I've also consistently been surrounded by people who are brilliant at it.

To counter this I developed three strong survival mechanisms: (1) I could always pull off an analogue version of whatever they were doing on the computer; (2) By necessity I watched from the sidelines and absorbed what was going on; (3) I equalised the situation by analysing, critiquing (and often criticising), and asking the right questions. In short, I survived by evolving into kind of a know-it-all jerk. So, my challenge in the next 12 pages is to figure out why a know-it-all jerk who hates technology constantly gets pulled into the discussion. How and why are us jerks necessary?

2 This Essay Is About the Avant-Garde

You'll notice that there are no capital letters on that. Here I am not talking about a particular movement (though I shall introduce one or two for discussion), rather the avant-garde I wish to explore is established around a condition of inquiry, or a particular

A. Marcus (Ed.): DUXU 2016, Part I, LNCS 9746, pp. 73–84, 2016.
DOI: 10.1007/978-3-319-40409-7_8

relationship to naturalised paradigms. The avant-garde in this respect are the vanguard of praxis-based criticism and socio-cultural experimentation. As such, they are responsible for exploring the boundaries of socio-cultural taken-for-granteds, and defining new standards of knowledge, expression, and being. In the contemporary world where both thinking and culture (each now largely driven through relationships to media and technology) have outgrown the evaporating edifice of modernism (and arguably post-modernism) the need for the avant-garde is as strong now as any time in the past.

3 Our Story Begins in the 19th Century

Both the ethos and the mythos under which we work as contemporary academics, artists, designers, and inventors are inextricably tied to this era. This is not only the story of the avant-garde, but the story of "industry", the story of the "market economy", the story of "progress", and the story of the "future". Everything that defines the multi-billion dollar computing industry in the present, all of these related trajectories, began with the Industrial Revolution and all are re-converging at this particular point in history.

Arguably, not since the Industrial Revolution have we seen such a palpable and impactful technological shift. There is a key difference, however, between that technological revolution and this one: the currency has changed. During the Industrial Revolution the currency was "efficiency" and "intensification". Success was measured in terms of these two tangible, quantifiable variables. The Digital Revolution (within which we are still fully submerged) is driven by a different measure of success. True to digital form (or the lack thereof) there is nothing tangible here. The new currency is formless and unquantifiable. Here the world unites under a single mantra. The word we all chant is "innovation".

INNOVATION: noun in·no·va·tion \ i-nə- 'vā-shən

- *A new idea, device, or method;*
- *The act or process of introducing new ideas, devices, or methods;*
- *The introduction of something new* [1].

Of course the concept of innovation is, in itself, nothing new. Humanity is built upon innovation. Our evolution as a species is dependent upon it. The issue at the present time, however, is that the word "innovation" has no qualifier. We are no longer innovating for the sake of efficiency or intensification. We are not trying to be faster, less destructive, more destructive, or any other variable of impact. Innovation for us has no meaning. It is merely a measure of newness and newness is now the only standard of contemporary market relevance.

The market demand for innovation today is a pressure that even the most robust companies are finding difficult to navigate. Apple, for instance, having been one of the instigators of this perennial "culture of the new" dropped $200 billion in value in 2013, despite increasing its revenues, merely because it was turning out fewer "new" products. [2] Tangible metrics such as revenue, holdings, and liquidity have lost their measuring power. "Innovation is a wild card that trumps everything else, and it is making these old metrics obsolete" [3].

We have somehow found ourselves in the midst of a dominant cultural paradigm that has no definition. We are now expected to innovate without direction, without intention, and without cause. The action of innovation itself, or the guise thereof, is enough to both justify and signify our dedication to the pursuit. So we rally with all great enthusiasm to the battle cry of this new crusade: "Innovation today is worth more than cash—so get out there and innovate!" [4].

I'm going to take a moment to stop rolling my eyes, and ask "are we just too deep into the Digital Revolution to truly understand what's going on?" During the industrial feeding frenzy that was the 19th century was there an awareness of the significance of the paradigmatic shift that was occurring, or, like the 21st century were the stake-holders merely patting themselves on the back for their ingenuity and their penchant for progress and innovation? The answer in both cases is most certainly yes. As McLuhan [3] quipped "A wit has said we don't know who discovered water, but we're pretty sure it wasn't a fish." It would seem that we are unable to objectively scrutinise systems and environments within which we are ourselves immersed. Ironically, the sort of pre-science it takes to understand what is happening at a significant cultural moment more often requires hindsight.

With hindsight, for instance, we can see through the mythology of progress pervasive during the Industrial Revolution. Polanyi [4] made this succinct distillation of the 19th century socio-economic metamorphosis:

> [19th] century civilisation alone was economic in a different and distinctive sense, for it chose to base itself on a motive only rarely acknowledged as valid in the history of human societies, and certainly never before raised to the level of a justification of action and behaviour in everyday life, namely, gain.

The 19th century gospel of "progress" is thus exposed as mere packaging which helps facilitate the paradigmatic shift to a value of individual wealth. The question is, however, is our current day mythology of innovation any different from the 19th century rationalisation of progress? More importantly, what underlying motivations will expose themselves as the impetus of the ongoing Digital Revolution? Are we still motivated only by gain (how horrifically derivative if that is the case), or is there some other fundamental cultural value at play that we have yet to recognise?

4 This Value Is the Future

For the masses in the eighteenth century who knew little outside of their agrarian lifestyles few could imagine a situation any different, let alone anticipate a world on the verge of the most rapid change in all of human (pre)history. In the present world we are hard pressed to conceive of the shear amount of change that might occur even within the next five years. While the future was a concept of little consequence in the pre-industrial world, now there are few concepts which can rival its importance. The idea of the "future" that now pervades our collective consciousness existed largely only in the heads of exceptionally visionary individuals: Leonardo da Vinci and Francis Bacon come to mind. With the advent of the Industrial Revolution the spark of "the future" was ignited and thus began its incursion into the popular psyche.

Changes in technology bring about changes in society. "It's translation. It's a loop. You shape your tools in your own image and, in their turn, they shape you." [5] The Industrial Revolution, for the first time on a widespread scale, saw a change in technology bring about more than just a change in regime. Cultures morphed and societies shifted. The cause and effect was obvious, and the potential impact human technological agency could make on the world was transparent. What does it mean when popular consciousness swaps the assumption that cultural life will remain essentially the same in perpetuity for the assumption that cultural life will and must change, even substantially, in one's own lifetime? Suddenly an imagined future is born; implicit within this is imagined technological advancement. By the turn of the century artists were conjecturing about and visualising a future world of dressing machines and automated tailors a hundred years hence [6].

The impact of an imagined future is profound. I will posit here that this is one substantial departure the Digital Revolution takes from the Industrial one: while efficiency and intensification brought about progress and gain in the 19th century, now in the 21st innovation not only results in gain, more importantly it substantiates our abilities to manifest our imagined futures or imagine "better" ones. Hence, deep down, we measure our successes in how closely we approximate our science fictions—right down to our Jetson's inspired videophones. When revenues go up, but Apple stocks go down the market is signaling that gain is not the measurement of worth, rather it is the ability of companies to deliver the future.

5   There Is One Last Invention of the Industrial Revolution to Discuss

The sweeping social and cultural consequences of industrialisation took many guises. Populations shifted to urban centres, cultural life and occupations became more compartmentalised and specialised, money flooded into the new middle classes and an emerging class of labourers (as opposed to peasants) was being born. Most importantly, people were discovering that the future could change. Technology was opening up an unimaginable expression of agency. If people could now envision new technological futures, people could also imagine new social ones. As such, the avant-garde was coming into play.

The avant-garde is first and foremost a military term alluding to those at the front lines of battle. The term materialises with strong political connotations after the French Revolution pre-anticipating the emerging proletarian consciousness of the 19th century. By 1825 the term is used as an intellectual and artistic call to arms:

> It is we, artists, that will serve as your avant-garde; the power of the arts is indeed the most immediate and the fastest. We have weapons of all sorts: when we want to spread new ideas among the people, we carve them in marble or paint them on canvas; we popularise them by means of poetry and music [7].

Artists, writers, and musicians, were already held in close association with the intelligentsia of the time. Those who were not directly radicalised through republican and socialist politics, were still caught at the forefront of negotiating the host of new cultural influences. Pre-industrial artistic fixations on representation and realism segued to a new experimentalism in form, function, and material. The pressure to balance the wholesale adoption of technologies and commodities by the masses with a critical artistic engagement that questioned the impact of these new cultural phenomena often placed the artist in contrast and opposition to the mainstream.

> *An avant-garde is a concrete cultural phenomenon that is realised in terms of identifiable (though never predetermined) practices and representations through which it constitutes for itself a relationship to, and a distance from, the overall cultural patterns of the time* [8].

6   Focus 1: Expressionism

The avant-garde spawned a long pedigree of such movements throughout the late 19th and early 20th centuries. I will forego the Art History lecture at this time and focus instead on three examples through which we can explore the historical avant-garde as well as contemporary analogues relevant to visceral design. Expressionism, as a for instance, privileges the emotional expression, subjectivity, and individual condition of the artist rather than realism or form. Matisse, for instance, chose his colour palette, gestures, and stroke style not to capture a particular scene, but to emote a particular sentiment. "My choice of colors is based on observation, on feeling, on the very nature of each experience... [I] merely try to find a color that will fit my sensation" [9].

Art is no longer merely representative, narrative, nor necessarily tied reverentially to religion or hierarchy. It is, instead, interpretive, expressive, experimental, and increasingly visceral. It flies directly in contrast to what we may observe objectively in our day-to-day lives; it begins to endorse a sentiment of affective, emotional, and individualised experience. Art becomes a device for manifesting alternate realities, states of being, states of feeling, first on behalf of the artist, but then, by implication, for the audience. This is significant at the time because art controlled the image, and image, being the only representation outside of an objective material reality, controlled popular imagination.

The Case Study: Blinklifier | Tricia Flanagan [10]. *Blinklifier* is a wearable technology headdress that converts eye gestures, through conductive inks or stickers in the user's eye makeup, into data driving LED visualisations that amplify non-verbal communication. Imagine a fashionable, futuristic, Princess Leia-type character. Her eyes are accentuated with dark pigments harkening to ancient Egypt; her head adorned with a large loop of what looks at the same time like woven textile and metal. Visually the loop extends the face doubling or tripling the radius of the face's presence. It intersects with the head just above the cheekbones drawing the eye of the viewer to the face's most expressive features. The dark electro-conductive eye makeup closes the circle. Even before the device has fully engaged with its full technological capacity it is already multiplying the body's expressive proportions. When fully implemented the headdress illuminates according to the blinking and other eye gestures of the wearer.

> *Blinklifier enriches our emotional dialogues and manages our social relations through blink-ing. It follows the natural eye muscles contraction and extends the motion into a visible light array. It responds to the specific eye movement patterns of the wearer and amplifies emotions that the wearer wants to communicate by presenting noticeable, exaggerated visual compo-sitions* [11].

Blinklifier transcends the boundaries of traditional wearable technology. The emphasis is not on coupling the user to information input or output systems like a computer or a monitor. On the contrary, *Blinklifier* is an expressive system that con-nects the internal state of the user, through an embodied experience, with the outside world. It is not adornment, but an expression or translation of the inner state of its now 'cyborg' companion. The technology only has meaning within its articulation with the body and the subjective and/or unconscious desires of its wearer.

In the same way as the Expressionists of the early twentieth century, rejected the literal constraints of form and narrative *Blinklifier* dismisses the universal objectivity of data systems in favour of a subjective and affective exchange between user (performer) and audience. The project anticipates through design fiction a day where technology must compensate for the alienation of the constant flow of neutral and meaningless data.

7 Focus 2: The Situationists

The example of Expressionism also serves to underline the fact that the art historical pigeon-hole of the "Avant-Garde" was by no means prescribed, cohesive, nor monolithic. Individual movements coexisted, contradicted, supported, and contested one another. Expressionism was heavily criticised for focussing the gaze upon the "interiorization of reality," [12] both obscuring and mystifying contemporary social issues and therefore laying a foundation for a right-wing propagandist appropriation of the image. [13] The concern was that rather than keeping vigilant of shifting socio-political power relations the proletariat were increasingly distracted with internalised emotional engagements.

We see this focus on the distraction of the image becoming a growing preoccu-pation in Marxist critique. While Expressionism was being normalised through its adoption by a variety of social institutions, be they governments, popular media, and a burgeoning marketing industry, a new avant-garde, the Situationist International, was defining itself in opposition to a rapidly developing culture fixated on the image and the commodified object. Guy Debord, one of the movement's *de facto* spokespeople sig-nals the shift in the human experience from being, to possessing, and then from possessing to appearing. Life, once grounded in lived (visceral) experience, then mediated through the physical object, was now merely a performance of shifting identities and deeply subjective, individualised knowledge.

> *The whole life of those societies in which modern conditions of production prevail presents itself as an immense accumulation of spectacles. All that once was directly lived has become mere representation.... The spectacle is not a collection of images; rather, it is a social relationship between people that is mediated by images* [14].

With a sort of McLuhanian prescience, Debord's words foretell and perhaps describe our current cultural climate more accurately than the world of 1967, when his article was first published in French. There is no denying the impacts of pervasive media and technology, nor the dual, mutually embedded existence we now live between material and virtual environments. Harris [15] underlines this observation with a snapshot of contemporary culture that would surely make Guy Debord shudder:

> *I always picture the archetypal modern crowd: squeezed up against each other, but all looking intently at the blinking screens they hold in their hands, while their thumbs punch out an imitation of life that surely proves Debord's point ten thousand times over.*

The strategy adopted by the Situationists was the deployment of "situations". By this they meant a sort of authentic experience, an intervention in which the audience was located in a material, sensory engagement with their physical environment. The emphasis was on embodiment, presence, and phenomenology. In Debord's [16] own words:

> *Our central idea is the construction of situations, that is to say, the concrete construction of momentary ambiences of life and their transformation into a superior passional quality. We must develop a systematic intervention based on the complex factors of two components in perpetual interaction: the material environment of life and the behaviors which that environment gives rise to and which radically transform it.*

The Case Study: The Agora | Kurtis Lesick, Paul Robert, Craig Fahner, and Angus Leach [17]. If *Blinklifier* can be seen as an analogue of Expressionism liberating the body from the alienation of data and re-forging a connection between the individualised, subjective, and emotional worlds of social agents, the *Agora* harkens to the Situationists grounding social media not as a performance of identity, but as a negotiation of community dynamics located in a physical, experiential space. The *Agora* is a critical making project deconstructing both social and news media under the premise that the current social media paradigm encourages a detachment from a critical and negotiated social engagement. Society is therefore a performance of "social acting" rather than "social action". The project takes as its foundation five observations of mediated life:

- *It rests on the ability to be seen or heard, not to be understood;*
- *It is predicated on the ability to have an opinion at any time, in any place;*
- *It privileges opinions based on "likes," trends, and popularity rather than the negotiation of the common good;*
- *It revolves around the performance of individual identities, rather than the negotiation of social consensus;*
- *Thus it is not embedded in discourse, but in* consumption [18].

The project responded by creating a mediated social exchange that reversed all of these assertions. Rather than ubiquitous access communication was located in time and space; rather than a performance of identity contributions were anonymous; rather than talking about yourself, you talked about shared issues and common identities. The project was paper-tested over six months on a large 9 foot × 6 foot mobile wall and a seemingly endless supply of sticky notes in the main mall of the Alberta College of Art and Design (ACAD). With the simple call to action, "What should ACAD be talking about," participants were invited to submit comments simply by writing them on a sticky note and placing them on the wall.

After the six month trial the paper-test was adapted for digital deployment using a screen-wall accessed wirelessly through any networked device over a local area network. We repurposed twitter colonising their short message system for use as digital sticky notes. Rather than sending messages out into the digital aether, however, we closed the feedback loop. A single twitter account, @acadagora, sent messages only to itself. In the *Agora*, there is only one identity being negotiated, that of the community. All individual opinions are digested into the system and equalised. Those "healthy" conversations with deep and sustained discussion endured, whereas the noise of performative chatter quickly dissipated.

The *Agora*, in itself, is not visceral computing. There are no sensors, no haptics, no body interaction. By locating it firmly in the social geography of ACAD and removing the distraction of identity performance, however, we transform what was once a virtualised data repository into a fully materialised and meaningful social engagement. The system becomes more than a computer interface, it becomes a lived situation bounded firmly in time and space and mediated only by praxis.

8   Focus 3: Fluxus

Rather than explaining what Fluxus is, it is easier to understand what Fluxus was a response to. Fluxus grew out of the same cultural trajectories as Situationism, a world in which identity and social knowledge were increasingly reliant on the image and the commodified object rather than authentic lived experiences. This was especially true in relation to Art (with a capital 'A'). Now, itself, an institution and an industry, Art in its post war context, was seen as having fallen victim to the pressures of commodification and commercialisation. Fluxus was to bring (A)rt back to the people grounding it in the concrete experiences of daily life. "Coffee cups are no less beautiful than the most exalted of sculptures, a kiss as dramatic as the Liebestod, the slosh of water in wet boots is not to be invidiously distinguished from organ music." [19] Fluxists drew their audiences into their work through, events (happenings), performances, interactions, improvisation, "do-it-yourself" aesthetics, and "kits" that implicated engaged social action. Objects derived value through their use, not through their implicit commercial value.

There are several implications of Fluxus for HCI and visceral design besides this lesson on use over commodity. Artist and "play-theorist," Flanagan [20] notes that "play and 'the joke' evolved as a methodology, bringing a level of interaction and audience participation away from the galleries and traditional theatre environments and creating for the first time multi-user artistic environments." O'Neill and Benyon [21] likewise note that Fluxus artists were playing with semiotic and rule-based systems to help guide participants through happenings and intermedia events while still providing for an open-ended, subjective, and even non-prescriptive experience. This emphasis on meaning-play, subjective and affective experience, and embodied, material interactions makes Fluxus a productive metaphor for visceral, qualitative explorations in computing.

The Case Study: A Machine to See with | Blast Theory [22]. *A Machine to See With* blurs the line between theatre, cinema, and games. While being defined as a media project, the piece actually serves to invert the traditional relationship between the viewer/consumer of media and the media being consumed. Rather than producing a single linear narrative property that is then distributed to multiple passive audience members, the project creates a framework for an experience that is enacted by the audience in the "real" world. The authority and objectivity of "the screen" thus fades away. Instead, the medium through which the audience sees the story is their own eyes; each version of this cinematic piece is completely idiosyncratic to each audience member. Thus, not only is each "screening" of the piece different, so is each individual viewing.

In *A Machine to See With* each audience member opts-in through their cellular phone to a participatory narrative about an impending bank robbery. They are given an address at which to rendezvous. When they arrive their phone rings; they receive their first set of auditory director's notes:

> By taking part in 'A Machine to See With' you agree to take responsibility for your own safety. If the police are called they will not take any notice of your excuses. Everything around you is just pretend. It's all made up [23].

The piece is augmented reality in its truest affective form. Rather than relying on technology for the augmentation, however, Blast Theory overlays an open ended contextual narrative. Both the visual and experiential environments are real; the characters are real people making real decisions in real time. The only fiction is the context through which they are all brought together into this modern day happening. With *A Machine to See With,* rather than mediating the narrative, the mere suggestion of mediation has the audience questioning how much of their "authentic" lives is now a performance lived through a frame of reference to the ubiquitous media screen. The actions of the everyday not only take on new meaning and a cinematic significance through this contextual sleight of hand, they necessitate a whole new and original phenomenology for each participant.

What is the interface in this project? Is it the user's phone through which she or he receives the contextual narrative? Is it the physical environment through which the audience navigates and defines the flesh and bones of the experience? Is it the other participants, embedded in their own experiences, who in their interaction with other audience members bring this piece of cinema to life? Is it the uninformed bystanders unwittingly playing extras in this lived fiction as their real lives cross over in time and space with the narrative? I would contend, that perhaps in this case the interface is dead. The lines have been so blurred between mediated and lived reality, body and interface, that all become one. Hence, truly visceral design is not about interface at all, it is about deployment. The measure of affective quality is not in terms of an embodied interaction with the interface, it is in the embodied interaction with the experience as a whole. The lesson here is not a technological one, it is an experiential one.

9   I Apologise: This Essay Was Supposed to Be About You

This essay was written for the HCI International Conference, for a session on Visceral Design, and I made it all about myself. I told you about my dysfunctional relationship with computing; I got on a rant about the strange socio-economic pressures that I see affecting research and design in computational systems; I had to go back to the Industrial Revolution and rationalise that while we've been through much of this before, there are critical contexts that make the Digital Revolution something significantly new; I had to draw parallels between the (r)evolution of industry, technology, the market economy, ideology, art, and the nature of how we experience, perform, and understand our lives; and, worst of all, instead of talking about technological interfaces that physically connect with the body I've focused on projects that are more systemic in nature, where the meaning doesn't come from our interactions with an interface, but how technology blurs with both the body and the physical engagement with lived experience. The interface might be a red herring: maybe visceral design is about facilitating embodied social engagements, not technological interactions. Maybe I really am a jerk.

10   Are Us Jerks Really Necessary?

In a nutshell, no, I don't think jerks are necessary. It doesn't take me to push the boundaries of HCI and computing. Is the avant-garde necessary? The answer is ABSOLUTELY. As we've seen above in the examples of avant-garde movements in art and analogous practices in contemporary technology and experience design, the avant-garde is not merely difference for difference sake; practitioners are not merely swapping variables to achieve the much valued and much illusive "innovation" prize. The avant-garde disrupts epistemological conventions and ontological assumptions. Without them we remain in a self-referential loop incapable of thinking through boundaries and barriers. Avant-garde thinking, while having the appearance of originating from the fringes or outside the system in question, actually develops as a first response to cultural pressures already at play. The Expressionists weren't concerned with the "new". They were responding to individualising pressures that needed to be rationalised in artistic praxis in order to be made sense of. The Situationists were grounding ontology back into social action not just to be contrary and counter-cultural. They were exposing a theorised growing sense of alienation by offering an effective experiential alternative. Fluxus didn't deviate from the institution of Art to forge a new sense of fashionable authenticity. It was the natural progression and natural expression of changing paradigms of the subjective and individual construction of reality. To sum up, the avant-garde is not defined by the invention of different ideas, it is the early expression of new systems of being. As such, the identification and exploration of new avant-garde trends is essential for rationalising socio-cultural pressures and changes within which we are so immersed that they are hard to identify.

We don't just wake up and decide to be avant-garde. We bring baggage into our practice as a form of response to these socio-cultural pressures requiring rationalisation. By implementing these in our practice we begin to test and manifest ideological and theoretical changes at an ontological level. Hence the hallmark of avant-garde practice is experimentation and rationalisation through praxis. As we have seen in our examples, both old and new, the avant-garde doesn't introduce new thinking, they are merely the first wave to manifest changes in their culture through their work. I shall leave you with the words of Mathews and Wacker [24] who sum up the old and new condition of the avant-garde:

> If you're a deviant you're in luck! The market has decided to look on you with favor-you actually have a chance to cash in on your weirdness. In slightly less forgiving times, deviants didn't make vice president. Instead, they were exiled, stoned to death, imprisoned in cold dark dungeons, or burned at the stake. So things could be a lot worse.

References

1. http://www.merriam-webster.com/dictionary/innovation
2. Popelka, L.: What We Learned From Twitter's IPO: The Value of Innovation Is at an All-Time High, 18 November 2013. http://www.bloomberg.com/bw/articles/2013-11-18/what-we-learned-from-twitter-s-ipo-the-value-of-innovation-is-at-an-all-time-high
3. McLuhan, H.M.: Understanding Me: Lectures and Interviews. In: McLuhan, S., Staines, D. (eds.) (Two part Marfleet Lectureship delivered at the Convocation Hall at the University of Toronto by Marshall McLuhan on March 16 and 17, 1967), "Canada, The Borderline Case", Start Page 105, Quote Page 106, McClelland & Stewart Ltd., Toronto, Ontario. (Google Books Preview)
4. Polanyi, K.: The Great Transformation: The Political and Economic Origins of Our Time. Beacon Press, Boston (1944). P. 30
5. Anderson, L.: McLuhan's Wake. Directors: Sobelman, D., McMahon, K. Primitive Entertainment, 94 minutes (2002). https://www.youtube.com/watch?v=A9y-ZAIdxrE (00:16:41)
6. http://publicdomainreview.org/collections/france-in-the-year-2000-1899-1910/
7. Saint-Simon, H.: Opinions Litteraires, Philosophiques et Industrielles. Galerie de Bossange Pere, Paris (1825). L'Artiste, le Savant et l'Industriel. Dialogue appears as the Conclusion of the volume, pp. 331. In: Oeuvres de Saint-Simon et d'Enfantin, Reimpression photomecanique de L'edition de 1865–79 (Aalen: Otto Zeller, 1964), Rodrigues's dialogue is published, under its author's name in volume XXXIX of the general collection (volume X of Saint-Simon's works), pp. 210–11. Cited in Calinescu, M.: The Five Faces of Modernity: Modernism, Avant-Garde, Decadence, Kitsch, Postmodernism, p. 103. Duke University Press (1987)
8. Orton, F., Pollock, G.: Avant-gardes and partisans reviewed. In: Avant-Gardes and Partisans Reviewed, p. 141. Manchester University Press (1996)
9. Matisse, H.: Notes d'un peintre', La Grande Revue 52 (24), pp. 731–45, 25 December 1908, as quoted in: Barr, A.H. Jr.: Matisse: His Art and His Public, p. 552, New York 1951, as cited in Gordon, D.E.: On the Origin of the Word expressionism. J. Warburg Courtauld Inst. 29, pp. 368–385 (1966)
10. http://triciaflanagan.com/blinklifier/
11. Vega, K.F.C., Flanagan, P.J., Fuks, H.: Blinklifier: a case study for prototyping wearable computers in technology and visual arts. In: Marcus, A. (ed.) DUXU 2013, Part III. LNCS, vol. 8014, pp. 439–445. Springer, Heidelberg (2013)

12. Gordon, D.E.: Expressionism: Art and Idea, pp. 178–181. Yale University Press, New Haven (1987)
13. Braun, E.: Expressionism as fascist aesthetic. J. Contemp. Hist. **31**(2), 273–292 (1996). Web
14. Debord, G.: The Society of the Spectacle, p. 5. Zone Books, New York (1994). http://www.antiworld.se/project/references/texts/The_Society%20_Of%20_The%20_Spectacle.pdf
15. Harris, J.: Guy debord predicted our distracted society. In: The Guardian (2012). http://www.theguardian.com/commentisfree/2012/mar/30/guy-debord-society-spectacle
16. Debord, G.: Report on the construction of situations. In: Knabb, K. (ed.) Situationist International Anthology, p. 38. Bureau of Public Secrets, Berkeley (2002). Location 881, Kindle File
17. Lesick, K., Robert, P., Fahner, C., All teach and research at the Alberta College of Art and Design (ACAD), Leach, A., is an Independent Researcher in Calgary, Canada, and a Researcher with ACAD's CE3C Lab
18. Lesick, K.: Twerking it! disruptive strategies against (anti) social media, Talk presented at TALKXTALK, OCAD University, Digital Futures Lecture Series, Toronto, Canada, 17 October 2013
19. Danto, A.C.: The world as warehouse: fluxus and philosophy. In: Hendricks, J. (ed.) What's Fluxus? What's Not! Why. (O que é Fluxus? O que não é! O porquê). Exhibition catalogue, p. 25. Centro Cultural Banco do Brasil, Rio de Janeiro; The Gilbert and Lila Silverman Fluxus Collection, Detroit, Mich (2002)
20. Flanagan, M.: Play, participation, and art: blurring the edges. In: Lovejoy, M., Paul, C., Bulajić, V.V. (eds.) Context Providers: Conditions of Meaning in Media Arts, p. 92. Intellect, Bristol (2011). Print
21. Benyon, D., O'Neill, S.: Semiotics, HCI and the avant-garde. In: Proceedings of Reflective HCI: Towards a Critical Technical Practice, A Workshop at CHI 2004. SIGCHI (2004)
22. http://www.blasttheory.co.uk
23. Blast Theory: A Machine to See with. https://vimeo.com/29157478
24. Mathews, R., Wacker, W.: Deviants, Inc. In: Fast Company Magazine, pp. 70–80, March 2002

Applying Matterology in Internet Product Design

Hongrong Luo[✉]

Baidu, Beijing, People's Republic of China
luohongrong@baidu.com

Abstract. The article is exploring the relationships between Chinese Internet product display and the needs of Chinese users by the design research methodology named Matterology. There is a new way for designers, only six steps of Matterology, to find out some creative methods of Internet product design.

Keywords: Matterology · User experience · Internet product design · Design psychology

1 Introduction

Matterology is a kind of design research methodology created by Liu Guanzhong, who is the professor of Tsinghua University. Matterology is a useful theory for designers, in areas such as graphic design, industrial design, and even environmental design, to clarify their minds and perceive the essence from clear and creative thinking. In recent years, the rapid development of information technology has changed the way of obtaining information and service. All walks of life are inseparable from the Internet, which is the reason why Internet products are emerging all the time. Therefore Internet product design, which is a newborn design area, becomes the focus of attention. This article will help Internet product designers to understand matterology and find out a new way to create life-changing Internet products.

2 Design Models of Matterology

2.1 Evolution Principles of History

Throughout history of creation, there is a positive correlation between the developments of created objects and human desires. Take hunting for example. Primitive men would be able to prey on the weak by fist and teeth, but might lose their lives when encountering fierce animals. With the evolution, human had learned to hit animals by rough objects like stones, branches and wooden sticks to avoid injury, but still were easily attacked by wild beasts. And then, for protecting better, human would tie a stone in front of a wooden stick, and created the first tools named stone axe and stone hammer. By using the principle of elastic potential energy, human combined their own strength and elastic force of objects to create bows and arrows, so they would be able to

© Springer International Publishing Switzerland 2016
A. Marcus (Ed.): DUXU 2016, Part I, LNCS 9746, pp. 85–93, 2016.
DOI: 10.1007/978-3-319-40409-7_9

kill prey from far away. During the Iron Age, the material iron was widely used. Human decorated iron tools with plants patterns or totem. Tools were more durable and beautiful. Until Firearms Age, guns and cannons had taken place of bows, arrows and catapults.

There is something could be seen from the evolution of hunting tools. Human desires have been developing. They killed prey for survival at first, and then they wanted to prey without hurt, even improved the efficiency of catching prey. They decorated tools to express individuality. And with the development of technology, they designed much more efficient tools to work. At the same time, the evolution of created objects has been developing, from natural things, primary processed products, to complex processed products, decorated objects, and finally efficient and practical products with technical innovation.

Matterology created by Professor Liu Guanzhong has summarize the relationships in the evolution of product design and the interaction among environment, human emotion and product appearance: human emotion and desires improve the development and the perfection of product appearance (Fig. 1).

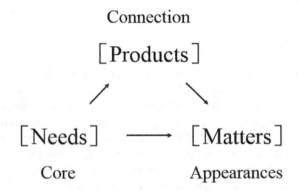

Fig. 1. Basic model of Matterology

2.2 Relationships Between Emotion and Internet Product Display in China

From the example of hunting, we can see that the evolution of human emotion coincides with the Maslow-Need-hierarchy theory: levels of need are physical, security, social, self-esteem, and self-fulfilment. Similar to the theory, the rules and the development of Internet product display in China are related to human needs (Fig. 2).

The products of the first level satisfy basic biological and psychological needs, such as those products about searching, e-mall, takeaway food, and travel. Those products are necessary for everyone and closely related with everyday life, so they will be frequently used for quite a long time. The representatives are Baidu Search, Taobao, Baidu Takeaway, Ctrip Travel.

The products of the second level satisfy emotional appeal. Family and friends need to care for each other at any time and anywhere by communication. With the

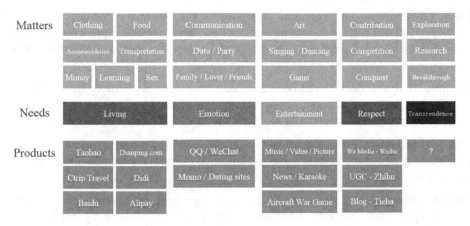

Fig. 2. Relationships between emotion and internet product display in China

development of the Internet, products about communication like QQ, WeChat, and kinds of dating apps emerging in recent years like Momo, are being used for high frequency and long time.

The products of the third level satisfy demand of entertainment. People would like to live a happier life, appreciate better tastes, and relax themselves more. Content products and entertainment products, such as products of news, pictures, videos, games, are belonging to this level.

The products of the fourth level satisfy the need of self-esteem and respects from society. After the satisfaction of survival, emotion and entertainment, people attempt to get social recognition. Interest-oriented products like Tieba, Zhihu, Douban, can assemble people who have similar tastes. Users can contribute their knowledge to gain more recognition from particular circles and themselves.

And the final level is to satisfy the need of self-transcendence. This kind of products hasn't been found until now. It will be the next direction in the future.

Living standards are improving and technology is developing. Internet products are also developing from satisfying physical needs to get love and entertainment, and many products help people to gain recognition have achieved success. In the next three years, the amount of products in the second level to the fourth level will make a rapid growth.

3   Design Methods of Matterology

3.1   Six Steps to Apply Matterology

As emotion promotes the development of products, the emotional appeal behind behaviors should be properly read and turned into the power of products. There are six steps for designers to apply Matterology into Internet product design.

First, Observation. Observe users' behavior in the whole environment carefully, including different roles, contexts, motives, action, language, and capture motions like eye contact and shiver. Sort out these observations, and then they will be the behavior data.

Second, Analysis. Base on the behavior data, designers must analyze the emotional goals behind every users' behaviors: for survival, emotional bonding, or respect. Read the hidden emotional appeals from the data.

Third, Conclusion. Make a conclusion in depth after understanding users' behavior and emotion. Designers need to solve and improve the pain points, and make them as design goals.

Fourth, Divergence. When having a definite design goal, designers need to analyze competing products, make brainstorming in group discussions and try out kinds of design plans, to design creatively and calculate reasonably by scientific methods, until finding the most effective and most sensible solution.

Fifth, Creation. After determining the final plan, more departments such as development, operation, marketing, are involved into the plan, to create and promote the product. The design plan will finally turn to a practical product.

Sixth, Evaluation. Launching does not mean the end of the product but the beginning. Feedback and comments will be received. Data of function and experience will be collected by use tests. All above will upgrade the product better.

3.2 WeChat Lucky Money: Thinking and Practice

When WeChat designs one of Chinese characteristic articles Lucky Money, it applies Matterology by six steps.

Fist, designers need to observe the scenes when people use lucky money. For example, to wish elders and children for health and happy in festivals, to encourage employees to work hard in the next year, to be sorry for someone's lose, are the most familiar ones.

Then designers should analyze and conclude the pain points behind sending luck money. People have their own purpose to send luck money, but there is only one pain point: it is a hard time to decide the particular amount of lucky money. Chinese society has its way of doing things. People receiving more money will make them under pressure, on the other side, they will feel upset when they get less money. And also, there are no fresh words for sending lucky money every year. So the next step is to transfer the pain point into the Internet and choose the proper scenes. The Internet has the spatial scale effect, which can eliminate the influence of distance. And there is no size limitation for sending lucky money at the same time. So WeChat Lucky Money has its unique advantages for the scenes such as boss to employees or star to fans.

When having determined the scenes and the pain points, it is the time to discuss the topic "How to send lucky money without losing face" carefully. Through brainstorming, the product is combined with game mechanics about entertainment and randomness. At last, WeChat Lucky Money has several interesting functions, like random lucky money for happy new year, group lucky money, happy new year money from stars, and so on. People can use lucky money politely and even gracefully. Because the simple and interesting design, everyone can give best wishes to their friends with the best cost-controlled solution. Therefore many users activate the function in payment by WeChat Lucky Money and at the same time the number of WeChat Lucky Money users is increasing. Of course, the feedback received from marketing is beyond the imagination of designers (Fig. 3).

Simple Interface and Easy Usage

Fig. 3. Interface of WeChat Lucky Money

4   Design Applications of Matterology: Weather APPs

Let us see the applications of Matterology in other Internet products, such as weather APPs, and find out how they apply the six steps - observation, analysis, conclusion, divergence, creation, and evaluation - into the product design:

Observation and Analysis. There is a natural link between weather and everyone's life. Every day when we wake up in the morning, the first thing is to observe the weather condition to decide which kinds of clothes to wear. Cool clothes are worn in hot days and umbrella is prepared for rainy days. If we plan to have a trip at the weekend, we should read the weather forecast in the following days to make the proper arrangement. Weather is a kind of guide books for life, whether we plan to wash cars, do sports, wear a dust mask, have a barbecue, or not. Those above are the basic needs for living. We tend to protect ourselves from rains, freezing air and other bad weathers, so we need accurate weather forecast to help us.

If we continue to make a deep observation, we will find some other interesting things occurs. When we have to live apart from parents or lover, weather is usually the most familiar topic between us. "I heard it snows these days there. Be carefully to drive, honey." "Bundle yourself up before you go outside, or you will be catch a cold in such freezing weather." If there is a long geographic distance between parents and children, lovers, or friends, weather is a good topic to show concern for or take care of family and friends. This is the second level of emotional needs. We need to care about who we love, and on the other hand, we need to receive their love messages too. So we need to know the weather in their cities.

There are some special situations as well. The weather condition is not good in China these years. The pollution of fog and haze is a big problem in cities like Beijing. When a clear blue sky appears, many people will take a picture of the fine weather and show it in the Moments of WeChat. They have a strong desire to express the feeling of having an incredible nice day. It is the same reason that someone meet special weather like aurora, rainbow and tornado, they will share their happiness of discovery to others. This is the third level of needs, which is self-esteem and respects from society (Fig. 4).

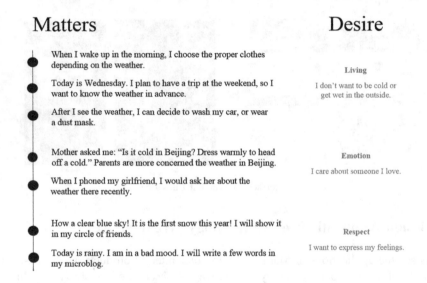

Fig. 4. The link between people and weather

Conclusion. Based on the observation and analysis, if we try to make a weather APP, we will focus three key points to solve problems. First, the weather forecast should be accurate and help people to make a decision. Second, the APP should allow users to know the weather of cities their loved ones live in. Third, people could use the APP to express themselves if possible (Fig. 5).

Divergence, Creation, and Evaluation. Now we can make the functional design on the basis of users' needs. When designing the weather APP, we should define the layout with satisfying the needs from level to level. First, users could see today's weather condition, especially the next few hours. Next, they would be given some suggestions to make quick decisions, like dresses, car wash and sports. Also they could see the weather going to be like in the following days to make a short-term plan easily. Then they could select other cities to show their concern to their loved ones. So some

Products

Provide accurate weather forecast:

- Provide weather report as accurate as possible.
- Forecast today's weather as well as that in the next few days.
- It is better to forecast the weather in the next six hours.
- Provide some other information related with weather.
- ......

Be an accurate weather APP.

Allow to know particular cities' weather:

- If apart from parents, know the weather conditions there as well.
- If friends or lover lives in another place, know the weather conditions there as well.
- Inform users and send love message when weather changes.
- ......

Design a function to care for beloveds.

Combine weather with emotion:

- Recommend sad songs in the rainy days and delightful melodies in the sunny days.
- Show the pictures of peculiar weather and get a view of other places.
- ......

Put some social elements in the weather APP

Fig. 5. Key points to satisfy users' needs in weather APPs

intimate functions should be design, such as automatic weather reminder of particular cities. As well, weather could be one of the social elements. For example, different kinds of weather could have their own unique reminder music; there would be an individual activity list according to the different weather; and users could communicate with different people from different cities in different weather conditions.

There are several popular weather APPs in China. We can find that their product functional design is in basic agreement with Matterology, that satisfying users' different levels of needs and promoting the user experience of products step by step (Figs. 6, 7 and 8).

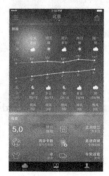

Fig. 6. Interface of MoWeather

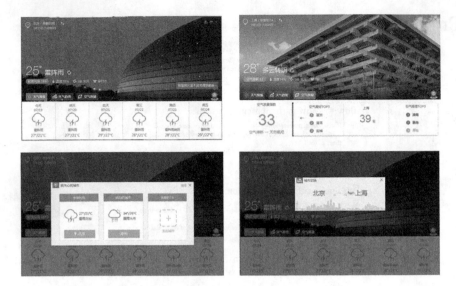

Fig. 7. Interface of Kingsoft weather

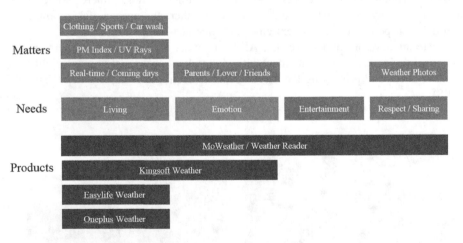

Fig. 8. Weather products to satisfy users' needs

5 Summary

Get a thorough understanding of products about weather, university students and other outstanding Internet product design, it can be found that those getting good word-of-mouth ones have applied the six steps precisely: deep observing, pain points analyzing, concluding and focusing, designing and diverging, rapid creating, and finally evaluating and upgrading. Hoping that Matterology could be used by more designers and product managers to create more and better products.

Acknowledgements. Thanks again to design methodology Matterology created by Professor Liu Guanzhong, which gives me deep thinking of Internet product design.

References

1. Liu, G.: Science of Human Affairs. Central South University Press, Changsha (2006)
2. Maslow, A.: A theory of human motivation. Psychol. Rev. **50**(4), 370–396 (1943)

User Experience Design
of User Generated Content Products

Hongyuan Ma[✉]

Beijing Baidu Netcom Science Technology Co., Ltd., Beijing, China
mahongyuan@baidu.com

Abstract. Currently UGC model has been widely concerned in the Internet field. In China, Baidu is a technology-based Internet search engine company. However, in the process of development, Baidu hasn't been only helping the Chinese users to search for the content that already exists, but also encourage them to create and post content to users who are using the search engine. Based on that principle, a few of excellent and widely known products have been created, such as Baidu Post Bar (Baidu Tieba), Baidu Pedia (Baidu Baike), Baidu Knows (Baidu Zhidao), Baidu Travel (Baidu Lvyou), etc. By analyzing these UGC mainstream products, we will summarize the key design points and experience design rules of UGC products.

Keywords: User experience design · User generated content · User analysis · Baidu · China

1 Introduction

UGC (User Generated Content) means that users create original content by their own, which is followed by the rise of personalization characteristics of Web 2.0. It is not a specific business, but a new user behavior model on the internet. That is, users change their behavior from the original generating to both generating and consuming. With the development of the internet application, the interaction of network users is reflected, and the user is not only the browser of the web content, but also the creator of the content. Currently, UGC has been widely used in various types of websites, such as Wikipedia, blogs, microblog (Weibo), community networks, video sharing sites, etc.

According to data released by CNNIC (China National Network Information Center), on December 31, 2015, the number for SNS (Social Network Site) users reached 530 million the number of Online Video users reached 504 million, the number for forum and BBS users reached 119 million, and the number for online education users reached 110 million, all of which obviously reveals the great influence of UGC [3].

On February 2005, with the launch of video sharing site YouTube, UGC mode flourished and came into rapid development. In fact, most of current internet products more or less contain the UGC elements. For instance, replying and commenting can be considered as a relatively simple form of UGC. UGC products also bring high commercial value and user stickiness. Therefore, more and more internet products add UGC, so they can develop their own user groups, create high-quality content and build their brand by creating original content.

A. Marcus (Ed.): DUXU 2016, Part I, LNCS 9746, pp. 94–104, 2016.
DOI: 10.1007/978-3-319-40409-7_10

2 UGC Product and User Analysis

Before talking about UGC user experience, we need to analyze the users who use UGC products. In Baidu, what we are mainly doing in the very early stages of the PC era is UGC, which is about how users generated content. Different from Google, it does not index content that is already there, but let Chinese internet users create content. Therefore, this chapter will analyze how users participate in and use UGC Products by focusing on four Baidu's representative UGC products, such as Baidu Travel (Baidu Lvyou), Baidu Library (Baidu Wenku), Baidu Post Bar (Baidu Tieba), Baidu Knows (Baidu Zhidao).

2.1 User Behavior Analysis of Baidu Travel

Baidu Travel is a tourism information service platform, designed to help the people make travel decisions and satisfy the user with all kinds of requirements about tourism [7].

Creating content: users who love to travel, want to find friends who have the same interests or want to express themselves. For example, writing travel notes, writing travel tips, making comments on scenic spots (user A in Fig. 1).

Browsing the content, replying and commenting: when users want to travel, they need to know more information about the travel city and how to make more fun of it. They browse other users' travel notes and ask them for advice. If satisfied with the content, the users can share and copy the useful content so they can plan their travels in accordance (user B in Fig. 1).

Browsing the whole content: users can browse the high-quality part of the whole content created by users A and B (user C in Fig. 1).

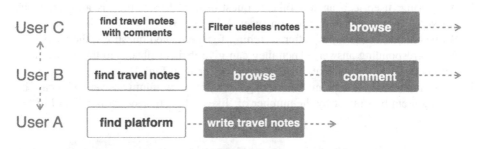

Fig. 1. User behavior of Baidu travel

2.2 User Behavior Analysis of Baidu Library

Baidu Library is an online platform to share documents. The document of Baidu library is uploaded by users, users can also read online and download these documents [8].

1. Uploading: users upload the documents (user A in Fig. 2).

2. Browsing, downloading and commenting: the users discover documents by typing keywords, they can preview, download, save as favorite, rate, purchase and other related actions (user B in Fig. 2).
3. Browsing the whole content: With the increase in the number of documents, users can find useful documentation directly via the keywords, ratings, favorites, and the amount of downloads. One of pretty things Baidu Library has done is that users are allowed to download documents by using the payment what called 'virtual property'. You can obtain virtual property by uploading documents, which results in forming a closed-loop of UGC and consequently drive a huge commercial value (user C in Fig. 2).

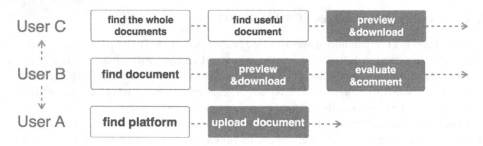

Fig. 2. User behavior of Baidu library

2.3 User Behavior Analysis of Baidu Knows

Baidu Knows is a question and answer platform, combining with search engines to let users learn knowledge efficiently [10].

1. Answering: users can answer others' questions, each of which is allowed to be answered by more than one person (user A in Fig. 3).
2. Browsing and commenting: after searching for the related questions, the users may find corresponding answers. Then they can give their feedbacks to the answer they are interested in, or evaluate its usefulness (user B in Fig. 3).
3. Browsing the whole content: users can gain the more premium answers with ease by sorting them by time or by the number of 'likes' of each answer (user C in Fig. 3).

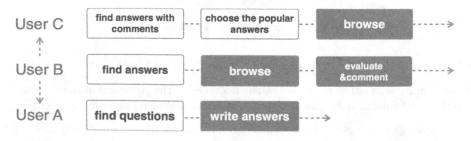

Fig. 3. User behavior of Baidu knows

2.4 User Behavior Analysis of Baidu Post Bar

Baidu Post Bar is an online communication platform, let those who interested in the same topic together to share and help each other easily [9].

1. Posting: users find whichever of the specific post bars they would like to follow, and post whatever topics they are glad to talk about, which is the main action in the post bar (user A in Fig. 4).
2. Browsing and replying: users can review and comment what other people have posted (user B in Fig. 4).
3. Browsing: users browse the whole content created by users A and B, they can read it in accordance with the high-quality posts and recent post, and a proper noun what is use to describe the users who only read posts and refuse to reply is a diver (user C in Fig. 4).
4. Creating a bar: in order to assemble the partners and share the same interests, the user can create a post bar and post some specific topics to attract them. The creator of the post bar becomes the master who can appoint administrators to manage and operate the post bar (user D in Fig. 4).

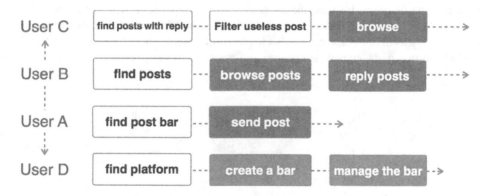

Fig. 4. User behavior of Baidu post bar

2.5 User Models of UGC Products

The users of Mainstream UGC products as the four cases above can be divided into three groups:

- Content creators: in addition to social identity, self-worth and motivated by altruism, social interaction is their main motivation. They contribute in providing quality content, show themselves, get respected by others and derive self-satisfaction from these achievements.
- Content respondents: their behavior is influenced by others or by the surrounding communities. They are active consumers and respondents of content. By consuming the content of UGC, they not only satisfy their individual mental needs, but also meet the demand of communicating with others.

- Content browsers: although they rarely generate content, they still have a strong desire for social interaction. The reason is that they have not yet been embraced into a community with a sense of belonging [2].

Therefore, in order to improve the UGC Product, it is essential for designers to pay attention to the touch points of all the above three kinds of users' behavior.

3 How to Design UGC Products

During the design process of UGC products, in addition to focusing on designing experience around the three kinds of users (content creators, content respondents and content browsers) as above, we still need to consider the relationship and interaction between 'user-platform' and 'user-user' [1].

As shown in Fig. 5, what content creator has created on the platform is the main source of the UGC platform. In response, the platform returns creator with positive feedback. Content respondent consumes the content created by content creator and then replies and rates. Content browser consumes the creator's product and the content respondent's feedback. During this process, there is a close interaction between the users and the platform. Besides, the users can also communicate with each other, the roles can be reversed smoothly. However, all the relationships and interactions between users and platform are content, so this chapter will describe how to design the UGC products in two parts, content generation and content consumption.

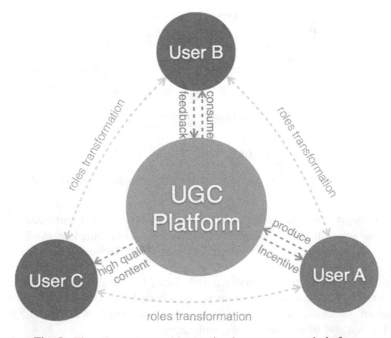

Fig. 5. The relationship and interaction between user and platform

3.1 Experience Design of Content Generation

(1) The content entry of scenario-based production
In UGC products, we often see a lot of buttons and information which direct users to produce content. Although this approach can be temporary to increase the amount of content, in the long run it is a kind of interference to the users through my observation of long-term data.
The most correct way is to allow users to produce content according to the user scenarios. If a travel app wants to let users contribute to content, it prompts the users to keep track of their travel itineraries by detecting where they have traveled. A Q&A product can put the input box of answer at the bottom instead of putting it after a question, so that users will be able to browse other users' answers and won't produce a repeating answer, which improves the quality of UGC.

(2) Easy-to-use tools for content production
Easy-to-use tools for content creators can reduce the maximum cost of contribution of content. So in the design process, designers need to pay attention to the three points as below:

- Reduce the users' learning costs as much as possible. As shown in Fig. 6, Baidu Pedia content editing tool is very familiar with some common office software like 'Word' in layout and operations. Users with Word experience can easily get started without learning costs.
- Provide users with the help and editing norm, and solve problems that users may have during the editing process. If possible, prepare the basic material for users, allow them to select directly instead of typing. As shown in Fig. 7, users can simply choose content rather than fill in a blank when editing their travel plans.
- Try to keep the consistency of content structure in both editing status and browsing status. If it cannot maintain consistency, we need to add the preview button, and allow the content creators to enter the editing mode smoothly at any time.

(3) User incentive
A platform can stimulate users to contribute on the content with both spiritual and material incentives. Spiritual incentives can be divided into several points:

- Offer users with the levels, the user medals and other encouraging labels.
- Give a positive feedback or praise according to the content of the users' production, especially when the user has just contributed to new content, which as a result makes them feel the popularity and love.
- Set up honor list, rank list, or recommend good content to the home page or other important position. Users care about whether their production will be recommended to the homepage.

On material incentives, monetary System can be implanted. For example, Baidu Literary requires mutual benefits from the mechanism, that is to say, only the users who have contributed to some content are qualified for having access to the content from others.
Users can also generate content to gain points to redeem gifts, or received gifts in the holidays, which reveals the importance of material incentives.

Fig. 6. The editing page of Baidu Pedia

Fig. 7. The editing page of Baidu travel

In addition, the platform needs to show respect for original content and enhance copyright consciousness of Chinese users in order to encourage users to contribute more content. When other users want to copy, forward, or take advantage of it for other purposes, they have to quote the subsidiary author's name, source, and copyright information [4].

3.2   Experience Design of Content Consumption

(1) Low-cost of receiving information

In terms of the user group who is consuming content, designers need to reduce the effort cost of having access to information. If the page navigation is clear, the user who is not logged in can still browse it. By using the searching engine, users can obtain different forms of content such as pictures, texts, videos, etc. If failed to retrieve relevant information, they can get timely feedbacks, related recommendations, manual or other relevant content from the platform. When users are browsing content, more content can be recommended based on the user's behavior or users other attribute. For instance, on China National Day holiday (7 days), some long journeys are recommended, and some short trips are recommended on other holidays such as Qingming Festival holiday, Labor Day holiday which last generally 3 days.

(2) High quality content presentation

- Prioritize the second level pages. For the most users who use UGC products, the content pages are viewed for the most amount of times instead of viewing homepages. So designers need to focus on the design of them. With a clear navigation for users to understand the content, we can have the users quickly browse the content and modules which attract them enough (Figs. 8, 9 and 10).

Fig. 8. The content page of Baidu Chuanke

Fig. 9. The content page of Baidu travel

Fig. 10. The content page of Baidu Pedia

- Regular summary of content. To many users, the first glance at the website content determines the first impression of these users. Based on that, the website regularly needs the arrangement and summary of the content. The website can send emails to the users regularly by summarizing and recommending high quality content, in order to keep the user viscosity and activity.

(3) Personalized customization

In the UGC products, since the content can be created by any user, there is a risk in the failure of ensuring the quality and credibility. Thus, we need tools to filter content to ensure credibility and higher quality content in terms of user needs.

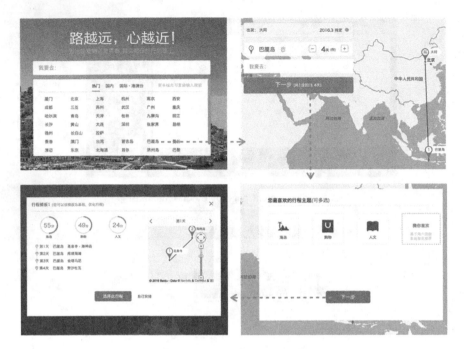

Fig. 11. Making Trip Plan in Baidu Travel

Among those tools, big data is a powerful one. First, through data mining, we are capable of integrating the UGC content fragments into a useful and complete content so that the platform can supply high quality contents to users. As shown in Fig. 11 (making the user's trip plan in Baidu Travel), through the users input the information which they want to go to the city and date, we have dug out the quality content of the city at the time. This kind of service makes the information more efficient and effective to show. As a result, this feature which has been online for one year, has become the most popular function for users.

(4) Reasonable design of evaluation

It is necessary to design the evaluation system for UGC product, it can help users to find some good content to browse and block some useless content.

- For feedbacks that consist of negative criticism and positive praise: It applies the product which content is low-cost to produce and has the quality which varies considerably (Fig. 12 left).
- For feedbacks that only consist of positive praising. It applies the product which content is high-cost to produce and has the high quality (Fig. 12 middle).
- For feedbacks that only consist of scoring. It applies the product which content is high-cost to produce and multi-dimensional. The scoring is more objective and real (Fig. 12 right).

Fig. 12. The feedbacks of UGC products

3.3 Design Considerations

In China, in order to do the UGC experience design, in addition to the design rules of content generation and content consumption as above, we also need to pay attention to the following two points:

(1) The more, the better? Not really.

If a UGC product has a large amount of users, it may possibly be likely to become a bad product. In order to ensure the quality of content, designers should focus on the shape of the product to better prevent the user from generating a lot of invalid content.

Here comes the most typical example: every Baidu post bar has its own theme that assembles the users who's in tune. The conflict of different cultures often directs users burst into 'Post War' [5] spontaneously. 'Post War' means that a large number of users constantly post tons of topics that nothing short of spams, which makes the normal posters behind the spam posters by several pages and those posters cannot be viewed by users. Post War prevents users from normally browsing, posting, and commenting. The most serious result of Post War may crush the whole bar. So that's why a lot of relatively large post bar set limits of posting for users who are not 'fans' of the bar, as shown in Fig. 13, before posting, the users must submit a Chinese character verification code. After launching the verification feature, if there are still many spam posters, the post bar may stop the posting feature, users can only use the feature of browsing.

(2) Design for different devices

If the users are using a mobile device, we should reduce the times users need to type. When the users are browsing content, they prefer scanning the QR code and locating than inputting.

During the progress of content production, designers should design UGC content presentation styles based on the characteristics of mobile devices. For example, with the live feature of Baidu Travel app, users are allowed to publish current positional information with interested photos that have other users know the views of the city at the particular moment.

Fig. 13. Chinese character verification code in Baidu post bar

4 Conclusion

To sum up, the content is the most important in the UGC product design. Also, generating content needs users' active participation. As mentioned earlier, users are both suppliers and consumers of the content. Thus, the most core objective for designers is all about users' generating content and consuming content. Designers must ensure the efficiency of outputting and displaying content, which finally deposits the value of the user needs into the product value.

References

1. Burgess, S., Sellitto, C., Cox, C., Buultjens, J.: Trust perceptions of online travel information by different content creators. Inf. Syst. Front. **13**, 221–235 (2011)
2. Zhang, S.: Motivation analysis and research on quality evaluation of generated content of mobile internet users [EB/OL]. University of Jilin (2014)
3. China Internet development statistics report by China National Network Information Center [EB/OL] (2016). http://cnnic.net/hlwfzyj/hlwxzbg/201601/P020160122469130059846.pdf
4. Chinese UGC report by Iresearch [EB/OL] (2013). http://www.iresearch.com.cn/report/1872.html
5. Baidu Pedia: Post War [EB/OL]. http://baike.baidu.com/link?url=ODHkkYxtrq4ZLzg57 VdgXtMHhI9Q5qDozuoq6mIlGW1bS50okyHYFQ7og2cxOI0a5Wr7-nxTEpW0UR_r14kbfK
6. Baidu Chuanke [EB/OL]. http://chuanke.baidu.com
7. Baidu Travel [EB/OL]. http://lvyou.baidu.com
8. Baidu Library [EB/OL]. http://wenku.baidu.com
9. Baidu Post Bar [EB/OL]. http://tieba.baidu.com
10. Baidu Knows [EB/OL]. http://zhidao.baidu.com

Clichés vs. Ingenuity for a Success Design

Oksana Orlenko[(✉)]

KWENDI Impact Studies, Kiev, Ukraine
orlenko@kwendi.net

Abstract. Human perception of visual objects in adults is on the most part grounded in cliché expectations based on previous experiences and knowledge. Hence, any visual object within a cultural context represents for a viewer rather a representation concept than a visual concept. That is, it is primarily interpreted for what it represents and only then for what it stands for – a singular set of meanings and connotations. In the consumer goods realm, even more so, the impact from designs is about conveying successfully the optimum balance between two distinct sets of codes - familiarization codes and de-familiarization codes. Familiarization codes are the set of category clichés that are activated at the first automatic 'scanning for safety' phase of visual assessment of any given design. These comprise category benchmark codes, important repetitive navigation codes, codes conveying important category anchorage territories. Visual codes of any design when interpreted by the consumer perception have primarily to satisfy the familiarization bias as a representation concept in order that ingenuity visual concept of such design be successfully accepted and perceived to have the desired impact. Understanding of the balance between familiarization and de-familiarization codes active in product categories is essential in order to develop success design launches. New Design Activation Mapping is suggested as a practical solution to pinpoint the potential impact of new design routes and timely introduce needed modifications at early stages of development prior to costly consumer research assessments.

Keywords: Semiotics · Design impact · Visual perception · Perception bias · Frame of reference · Visual concepts · Representation concepts · Familiarization codes · De-familiarization codes · Category anchorage · Design activation codes · Design activation context · New design activation mapping

1 Introduction

Multiple market research results on testing impact from designs across diverse categories show important tendencies. Whereas most of the creative effort often aims at originality, uniqueness and differentiation, that is, ingenuity, the research shows with remarkable consistency that when it comes to consumer response, in fact, the importance of ingenuity is over-rated, or at least its role and balance is not fully captured in many creative developments.

There is obviously a clear understanding that any visual object is perceived and assessed based on a certain frame of reference based on previous experiences and knowledge of similar objects. When it comes to perception and assessment of

© Springer International Publishing Switzerland 2016
A. Marcus (Ed.): DUXU 2016, Part I, LNCS 9746, pp. 105–113, 2016.
DOI: 10.1007/978-3-319-40409-7_11

consumer goods designs, market research comes into play to gather data on what and how potentially effects consumers, what is their perception bias in relation to certain products, visual stimuli, sets of codes. All the above is supposed to bring the needed alignment between creative effort, which in semiotic terms is about coding visually the intended meanings, on the one hand, and, on the other, successful de-coding of the latter by the intended consumer audience for the desired impact.

Furthermore, the research is often there to obtain the snapshot and understanding of the most recent totality of visual codes as perceived by consumers and to trace less cluttered and fresh territories that could serve as the springboard for the new offer, in particular, new designs that could better capture attention of potential target audience.

At the stage of construing new concepts, perception bias of the consumer is well accounted for. However, at the stage of new developments, specifically developments of visual representations of the products and packaging the focus is often shifted towards developing ingenuity design solutions, that would have most potential in capturing consumer attention. Whereas consumer aesthetic preferences are often taken into consideration at the stage of design creation, the product category context is often treated rather superficially, again, most frequently through the prism of general consumer perceptions and expectations.

Starting as far off as when it comes to pieces of art that are mostly about ingenuity, it is known that adult human perception would treat those as 'representation' concepts and not purely 'visual' concepts [1]. Visual concepts would be the perception type characteristic of children and of adults in some earlier human cultures. In contrast, people of normal socialization in any given modern culture starting with life stages of active socialization from school years and on, will have representation concepts as their major perception mechanism. That is, they would always have pre-conceptions about any visual object they are confronted with, with no exception. "Our experiences and ideas tend to be common but not deep, or deep but not common. We have neglected the gift of comprehending things through our senses. Concept is divorced from percept, and thought moves among abstractions. Our eyes have been reduced to instruments with which to identify and to measure; hence we suffer a paucity of ideas that can be expressed in images and an incapacity to discover meaning in what we see. Naturally we feel lost in the presence of objects that make sense only to undiluted vision, and we seek refuge in the more familiar medium." [1].

More so, when it comes to impact from designs in product categories that have rather pragmatic primary appeal to consumers, these are definitely perceived primarily as representation concepts. When treated by human perception as s a representation concept, designs would first automatically be scanned for familiar codes to get the clear unambiguous understanding what this object represents. Only after the 'safety control' scan results in clear categorization of the design codes as corresponding to the essential expectations of the product designs in the given category, the ingenuity codes are given a play to convey image-driven meanings and connotations that could differentiate the given product from the competitive offer.

In other words, in order to avoid subsequent fiascos at design tests at market research stage, new designs could incorporate a proper balance of 'hot'/'cold' stimulation [3] or proper balance between ingenuity and clichés at the stage of their developments for a desired impact. Along with incorporating aesthetic preferences of the potential audience, novel trendy visual solutions, ingenuity differentiating codes when creating a new design, semiotic approach could help to pinpoint the codes that constitute the important frame of reference for the target audience in perceiving designs in the given product category. Luckily enough, when it comes to product categories, the representation concepts are quite predictable, as the perceptive bias is distinctly coded through category clichés that can be observed, categorized and taken into account as early as developing or fine-tuning the design prior to costly consumer research.

2   Category Clichés and Anchorage

Consumer frame of reference or representation concepts comes into play with regards to response to existing visual stimuli. Category designs undergo certain evolution in consumer perception, where benchmark designs and popular design codes of the past and the present of the category existence activate certain visual codes as having unified unambiguous meanings and triggering rather concrete expectation towards the product thus forming category clichés. The most obvious examples of category cliché codes would be category recognition codes, SKU navigation codes, etc.

Furthermore, category usage experience, certain category benchmarks, culturally specific biases with regards to the product category form in consumer mind certain understanding and expectations of the category that correspond to certain semantic clusters, meanings closely related to the category in the perception of most active consumers. These semantic territories that correspond to the most basic generic aspirational attributes related to a particular product category constitute category anchorage. Category anchorage speaks directly to important consumer expectations about such category, often regardless of particular price segments. Among most frequent and clear examples are expectations of 'naturalness' with regards to most dairy categories and juices or 'outspoken masculinity' with regards to most spirits and men's care, though quality understanding requires closer focus with regards to culture, market saturation and price segments.

Examples of possible miss-outs are not rare [2]. Consider a youth targeted juice brand aimed at presenting consumers with fun images, contrasting fluorescent colors to meet the consumer at their aesthetic territory. Yet, for juice category context in the given culture the essential category anchorage would be 'naturalness' - where 'aggressive' fluorescent colors obviously completely violated the essential connotation for codes and resulted in very lukewarm response to the appeal of new designs. If it was about energy drinks or party beverages, the needed clichés and anchorage would be in a very different place.

Many big-scale companies when confronted with an objective to introduce singular design at different markets will often see the need to pinpoint the hazards, which are directly linked to differences in category anchorage in different market cultures [2]. Beer and cigarettes are among the categories that could provide many examples of this kind, where anchorage territories of 'masculinity', 'authenticity', 'cosmopolitan vibe' along with some others would often come to the surface in different proportion and in relation to different sets of clichés in different markets.

On the one hand, cliché codes would convey momentarily the messages of comfort, trust, safety, ensuring at the automated perception level that the overall first impression of the product would fit the important 'safety' profile – 'This product is OK, reliable, I can use it'. Hence, by function category clichés would form the basis of familiarization [4] codes. As the above 'familiarization' scanning for safety occurs within first few seconds of design observation and its mechanics often cannot be fully rationalized and articulated by the perceiving party, it is rather important that these codes are well selected and are the ones that are activated instantaneously in consumer perception, convey clear uniform meaning, trigger minimum or no connotations and obviously convey the right and precise messages about the product.

Focus on daring stand-out and being original if combined with low attention to the above aspects of 'grounding' new designs with respect to 'automatic' consumer expectations could result in missing on important charge of the intended design impact.

3   Preconditions for Design Activation – Codes and Context

Analyzing across best impact designs an important tendency comes to the foreground that could be considered prior to creative developments and subsequent testing of new designs. For any new design, the desired impact would source from proper balancing of two quite different sets of culturally conditioned codes (Cf. Table 1).

There are obviously different categories of products with different needs in and potential for stand-out that are image-driven to different degrees, yet, for any given category product designs need to integrate the proper balance of familiarization and de-familiarization codes.

Codes of familiarization are the grounding codes based on category clichés and anchorage, that have the primacy in that they provide clarity and acceptance needed at the very first instants in the process of design perception, those are the gateway for further differentiating assessment. The correct familiarization codes, that are in essence 'safety' codes, need to be in place in order to keep the attention further for the 'fun ride' in perceiving and appreciating the ingenuity part of the design. In fact, when the 'normalcy' and 'safety' foundation is well laid with familiarization codes, the 'stand-out' or de-familiarization codes can play their fullest [4]. Balanced familiarization and de-familiarization codes make for stronger more consolidated design impact and the intended competitive advantage.

The analysis of the balance between the familiarization set of codes that speak of important category expectations and de-familiarization codes of self-image that consumers derive from design stand-out and ingenuity could be further explored through cross-analysis of design impacts in different categories. Such analysis brings about further understanding of how the interplay between two sets of codes works in different categories.

As most of research results reveal, there are gratification biased categories that would primarily require stronger accent on familiarization codes as well as self-image biased product categories where designs need to be considerably stronger in de-familiarization codes. Mineral water and perfume would be the categories that are

Table 1. Preconditions for design impact - activation codes

DESIGN IMPACT = activating in proper balance 2 sets of codes	
FAMILARIZATION CODES	DEFAMILARIZATION CODES
Product Gratification Codes	**Self-Image Upgrade Codes**
'Product is OK, reliable, I can use it'	*'Product offers added value, RW to buy it'*
Stricter, clearer codes	Less predictable, innovative
Simplistic	Elaborate
Based on popular category clichés – i.e. repeated through designs by different brands, often based on benchmark designs across segments	Ingenuity – fresh, new in the category, differentiated from the competitive offer, also those sourced from new trends, TA aesthetics
Interpreted by consumers momentarily (triggering minimum connotations)	Enigmatic, intriguing, offering richer associative interpretations
Conveying meanings on important generic product features – format, taste or flavor, etc.	Conveying meaning on image and product distinction – special quality, added-value attributes, emotive appeal, etc.
Category & Segment Clichés **SKU Navigation Codes**	**Unique, Symbolic** **Brand Differentiaton Codes**

rather conspicuous in many cultures as being gratification biased and self-image biased respectively [2].

Obviously, concrete focus and expert opinion is needed for any category in any given culture for proper understanding, but having the general initial guidance in place in the right time saves much effort. Most of FMCG categories in many markets would be very close to rather even proportion in terms of balance requirements between the two sets of codes [2].

Signs are interpreted based on context. Semiotics always relates any impact from visual stimuli back to the very concrete context where these visual stimuli are originated from and/or will need to function. The interplay between familiarization and de-familiarization codes of product/pack designs is understood when analyzed in context of concrete markets, categories and segments.

Hence, it is further important to consider that perception and streamline impact from product designs much depend on their standing vs. the whole of the shelf and consumer experience context (Cf. Table 2). This context visually is represented by: (1) visual identity of direct competition products, (2) visual identity of 'clutter' competition – i.e., designs by similarly priced or next-choice segment propositions, (3) benchmark designs and designs by more expensive and aspirational offer that form new noticeable tendencies and clichés within the category.

The above categories of visual stimuli that create the background for new design perception and impact are the most direct and essential context to consider for the preliminary analysis of potential impact from the new design launches.

Table 2. Preconditions for design impact - activation context

DESIGN IMPACT is activated vs.:		
Direct competition	Clutter competition	Benchmarks and Out-of-segment
Visual identity of direct competitor products as reflected by actual market situation of date	Designs of similarly priced or next-choice segment propositions on the market – regardless of their actual sales and market standing – that adopt noticeable tendencies and clichés and thus create the visual 'clutter' for certain codes	Designs of more expensive and aspirational offer that are noticeable and form new, noticeable tendencies and clichés or are early followers of such noticeable tendencies and clichés

4   Design Impact Pre-test Analysis

The interplay of design impact activation context and relevant active codes could be taken into consideration at the stage of new design development and prior to costly market research tests. As a means of offering a practical solution for the preliminary analysis of new designs for comparative impact within the given category, there could be applied a mapping that will take into consideration the above need in balance between sets of familiarization and de-familiarization codes.

The semiotic square that has been in use for some time across research and showcase studies in one of its variations could represent the primary grid for such pre-test analysis of new design impact potential and the basis for the design context activation mapping. A version of the semiotic square with basic descriptive attributes per quadrants is provided in Fig. 1.

Fig. 1. Semiotic square as the basis for design activation impact pre-test mapping

The quadrants of semiotic square serve as the basis to cluster visual codes and related senses for a particular product category in a given market. Further on, the visual objects that form the context for activation of a new design are placed following a distinct layout that reflects key parameters that provide the needed precise reference to pinpoint the potential position and corresponding potential impact of a new design route (Fig. 2). The Design Activation mapping shows the position of new designs with respect to balance of two sets of codes – familiarization and de-familiarization codes to ensure that the prospective launch is neither perceived as 'too strange' by using to maximum differentiation codes, nor as 'too blank' by following closely the existing category clichés.

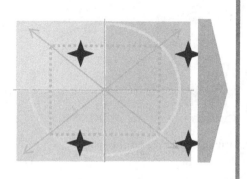

In the frame to the left:

—Position closer to punctured line would mean more balanced designs with respect to familiarization/de-familiarization codes interplay

—Position closer to diagonal axes → signifies more consolidated codes relevant to quadrant connotations and senses

—Distance from the center → signifies differentiation level

—✦ Marks benchmark positions that in part form active category and segment clichés

Fig. 2. Basic grid for new design activation impact pre-test mapping.

The Design Activation Map as suggested above allows to clearly position and identify for further usage in relation to prospective design launches the following aspects of design activation context:

– zones of active code clusters (e.g. category variations of traditional 'quadrant' of perspective | multi-perspective | positional | causal codes);
– clichés /benchmark designs;
– strong positions of properly balanced designs;
– 'weak' designs of lower stand-out;
– designs with overly 'bright' stand out that disrupt important category codes to the extent when consumers do not have sufficient trust towards tangible category attributes being present in the product.

The full mapping would incorporate all of the essential elements of the category context: (1) designs by direct competition; (2) designs by clutter competition; (3) category benchmarks positioned with respect to the role they play in the new design activation context (Fig. 3). The new designs are placed in relation to the active category context, where it becomes visible how well the balance of familiarization/de-familiarization codes is respected by the new design, where its standing is vs. the direct competition and the whole of the category offer, as well as prospective better-off positions for the new designs in the category.

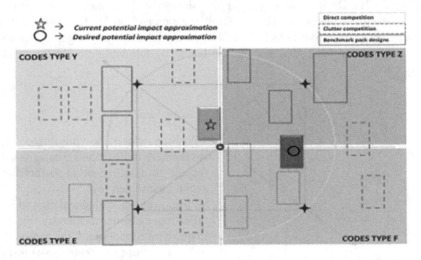

Fig. 3. A sample of new design activation impact pre-test mapping

The above example suggests that the standing of the new design (marked with the star symbol) in its current execution shows insufficient de-familiarization codes strength for the category (placed below punctured line) and hence is not differentiated enough, it is furthermore stands further off from essential clichés and codes of benchmark designs if compared to the standing of direct competition, thus it could easily trigger confused perception as out-of-segment offer and could remain unnoticed mixed in clutter competition perception cluster field, in this way, conveying at perceptive representation level senses and connotations that are not relevant for the active consumers in the intended segment.

It is also important to observe that clutter designs, which are primarily designs by brands that do not show considerable sales within a market often find themselves at the positions of 'extreme' expression of de-familiarization codes, showing minimum or none continuity with familiarization category clichés. This repeated practical observation across research in different categories and markets [2] once again suggests the primacy of familiarization codes in conveying the overall sensation of 'safety' and 'quality' that are essential pre-requisites for choosing a product. Respect to familiarization codes also creates the proper foundation for the de-familiarization codes to have their full play and intended impact.

The suggested mapping for pre-test design impact activation allows for clear vision of new design potential, it also shows the directions to reconsider design modifications with reference to existing codes, clichés, clutter, benchmarks and 'fresh' territories for better differentiation.

Certain universality of the suggested map distribution principle aids to extrapolate similar mapping to further assess the consolidated impact from advertisement and other related new launch activity. It helps to extend the strong impact from well balanced visual identity further to ensure maximum impact from the whole of the brand DNA.

References

1. Arnheim, R.: Art and Visual Perception. A Psychology of the Creative Eye. The New Version, University of California Press, Berkley, Los Angeles, London (1954). 10974 expanded and revised edition of the original publication. https://books.google.co.in/books?id=9RktoatXGQ0C&pg=PP1&ots=NQNkFVJni5&dq=arnheim&redir_esc=y&hl=en
2. Market Ad Hoc Research results by IPSOS Ukraine and KWENDI Impact Studies, Ukraine (2012–2015)
3. Hongwanishkul, D., Happaney, K.R., Lee, W.S.C., Zelazo, P.D.: Assessment of hot and cool executive function in young children: age-related changes and individual differences. Dev. Neuropsychol. **28**(2), 617–644W (2005)
4. Wittgenstein, L.: Tractatus Logico-Philosophicus. https://books.google.com.ua/books?id=FQCCAAAAQBAJ&pg=PR14&dq=wittgenstein+tractatus

Enhancing User Experience Design with an Integrated Storytelling Method

Qiong Peng[1,2(✉)] and Jean-Bernard Matterns[2]

[1] Department of Culture and Art, Chengdu University
of Information Technology, Chengdu, China
[2] Department of Industrial Design, Eindhoven University of Technology,
Eindhoven, The Netherlands
Q.Peng@tue.nl

Abstract. Storytelling has been known as a service design method and been used broadly not only in service design but also in the context of user experience design. However, practitioners cannot yet fully appreciate the benefits of story-telling, and often confuse storytelling with storyboarding and scenarios. The digital storytelling emerged in recent years mostly focused on digital and inter-active technology for new expression of stories as a tool, not pay much attention to improve user experience from the story and storytelling itself. This paper provides an integrated storytelling method consisting of three parts: Constructing Story—Inspiring Images—Visually Storytelling. Constructing Story is based on two principles to construct a story focusing on user's needs conflict. Inspiring Images means using a set of frames to express the story based on the techniques of film to express more details about emotion and value. Visually Storytelling means visualize the story in sketching or photo storyboard. The aim is to promote discussion and communication to share insights and concepts during the whole storytelling process at the early stage of the design to enhance user experience design. The research grounds on a literature study and exemplary application of the support. This method is also a quick start for a storytelling tool design.

Keywords: Storytelling · User experience · Conflicts

1 Introduction

Since the role of design has shifted from designing objects towards designing for experience, there have been many different kinds of methods and successful design cases for user experience design. However, it's a big challenge to design for experience, as Hassenzahl describes experience is subjective, context-dependent and dynamic [1]. He also explains that experience as an episode that one went through. It emerges from the interwined works of perception, action, motivation, emotion and cognition in dialogue with the world, so that an experience is a story [1]. In order to craft user experience, it calls for the designers to understand the users and the special using context deeply. Storytelling, known as a service design method, has been used broadly in design management, advertisement design, product design, and in the context of user experience design as well. While many practitioners cannot yet fully appreciate the benefits of

© Springer International Publishing Switzerland 2016
A. Marcus (Ed.): DUXU 2016, Part I, LNCS 9746, pp. 114–123, 2016.
DOI: 10.1007/978-3-319-40409-7_12

storytelling and often confuse storytelling with storyboarding and scenarios. The digital storytelling emerged in recent years mostly focused on digital and interactive technology for new expression of stories as a tool, not pay much attention to improve user experience from the story and storytelling itself. The motivation is to help designers to obtain deep understanding of users, and also get more possible creative ideas from storytelling.

2 Methodology

The similarity between stories and experience is so evident that in this research, our purpose is to make research of storytelling in order to get deep understanding of users and the context to enhance user experience in design and establish an integrated storytelling method. This research is based on the design thinking combination of design guided by research and research through design, the methodology includes storytelling-UX literature research, storytelling design, the integrated storytelling method establishing and workshop verification.

3 Research Process

3.1 Storytelling-UX Literature Research

3.1.1 Story and Storytelling

Stories expressed in text, images, sounds etc. are understandable, and can be used across the different cultures and languages to create a shared vision. In most cases, people tell stories in their own way, even in movie and drama. There are some essential elements in stories, such as detailed characters, rich plot development, contextual settings, clear causality or conflicts and specific goal. A story should be constructed based on structural framework which determines the presented story's order and fashion [2] and links all the elements as a whole. A plot is the storyteller's pick of event and their arrangement in time from numerous interrelated possibilities of how things could unfold [3]. They are used as a strategic guide to pull the audience emotionally and hold their attention [4]. Literatures show that there is a common structure in stories so that they can be transcend through time without the problem of language and cultural differences. In Freytag's Curve (see Fig. 1), he pointed out Five Act Structure: Exposition which the context, Rising Action where the tension increase through complications and uncertainties towards an identified goal, Climax which is the key point pulling up the audience engagement to the maximum, Falling Action which unravels the conflict and the Denudement 1 the conclusion [5].

In Field's Paradigm, the three-act structure include Act 1 is Beginning (Setup), Act 2 is Middle (Confrontation) and Act 3 is End (Resolution) (see Fig. 2). These plot points are definitive moments where an event happens that changes the direction of the story [6].

In Freeman's Aristotle's Plot Curve, the relationship between the horizontal (time) and vertical (dramatic intensity) is visually presented (see Fig. 3) [7].

In Quesenbery and Brooks' research, they suggested that a well-structured story with appropriate plot points can provide a storyline with qualities such as coverage, fit,

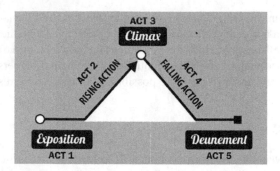

Fig. 1. Freytag's five-act structure curve

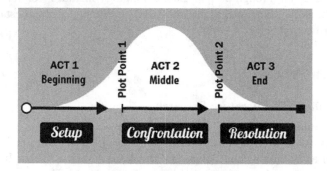

Fig. 2. Field's Three-Act

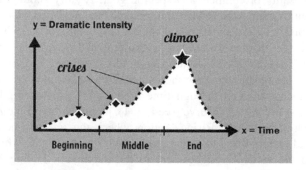

Fig. 3. Freeman's Aristotle's Plot curve

coherence, plausibility, uniqueness and audience imagination [8]. Coverage means that the story addresses all the necessary facts. Coherence and Plausibility assure that the story makes sense. Uniqueness is used to intrigue the audience for imagination [8].

The structure of a story serves as the guideline to construct a good story and think in a structured way. Designers of movies or animation usually craft stories visually with storyboard which are easy to understand and convenient for communication.

3.1.2 Storytelling and User Experience Design

As Hassenzahl (2010) described experience is stories [1], Gruen et al. (2002) said that story is a key mechanism through which human experience has been shared for generations [9]. He also pointed out that stories are powerful tools not only for capturing the situations in which technologies will be used, but also for encouraging other to recall relevant situations from their own experience [10]. Shank (1990) pointed out that stories represent event and experiences in a coherent way through schemas that capture the relations and structures connecting individual detail [10]. Storytelling and user experience share the similarity: they are made up with people, places, activities and emerging over time. Both of them have a sequential structure including beginning, middle and the end. They evoke and influence the emotions of people. Thus user experience is very closely related to storytelling.

Since stories can focus on users' experience and prompt more, accurate, honest and detailed feedback, storytelling is valuable tool which can be used to tell some personal or cultural stories in user research and user experience design to uncover the potential problems and possible solutions. Storytelling has the advantage of describing the problem, narrating the process, implying emotions and value in user experience design. That's why storytelling is a technique that user experience designers should do their best to leverage [11]. The story-based method takes the users and their needs, goals as reference throughout the whole user experience design, not only in the early stage of user experience design. The motivation of storytelling is to help designers to get deep understanding of users in a logical and coherent way.

Fictional stories and user stories [10] are the main two stories in user experience design. Fictional stories, normally based on understanding of the goals for a solution, are effective for eliciting feedback from potential users and benefit all the stakeholders of the stories to review their activities [10]. While user stories (customer stories), based on user experience, are usually real stories and anecdotes created by field research of users to help designers to understand the user needs and generate design solutions from individual details [10].

Sometimes, user experience designers cannot fully appreciate the benefits of storytelling due to confusing it with storyboarding and scenarios. Though they serve as tools for communication for design, they are different in essence. Storyboarding is a sequence of images to show a moment of time or an interface state [12] and a scenario generally focuses on developing the right sequence of actions needed to capture and convey an activity, often lacking the plot development and drama integral to a compelling story [10]. While storytelling uses specific stories including necessary story elements and implying the emotions, ensuing the overall value and positive user experience of design system [13]. In many ways, storytelling means doing the same work of designing a compelling solution [10].

Giving to the relationship between storytelling and user experience, in this paper, we tried to integrate the related story theories, and the support from the research of Storyply by Atasoy and Martens [14] to provide a storytelling method to enhance user experience especially in the early stage of design process. This is also a pilot research beginning with storytelling design aiming to establish the storytelling method.

Fig. 4. Storytelling designing examples

3.2 Storytelling Design

Storytelling design including both the story constructing and the storytelling, is made in this phrase to support the method (see Fig. 4).

The story constructing was not strictly differentiated by fictional story and user story, because our purpose is to using storytelling to improve user experience in the early stage of design, which means that the stories usually are the mixture of both. All the stories were organized in a structured way including clear storylines and essential elements of who (character), when and where (setting), what and how (plot). The plots were developed based on the typical story arch [15] of Beginning (Setting) – Middle (Climax) — End (Resolution), and guided by the character-driven [16] and conflict-focus storytelling thinking. In the Beginning, it introduces who, where, when and implied the beginning of the conflict, so that the plot can be developed. In the Middle, the conflict is developed into climax. In the Middle—End stage, the conflict is developed to resolution. The process of storytelling design is iterative, and several rounds of improvement was made. For the storytelling itself, nearly all of the possible medias including sketching-storyboard, photo-storyboard, video and animation were used for expression.

3.3 The Integrated Storytelling Method

The integrated storytelling method includes three parts: Story Constructing—Inspiring Images—Visually Storytelling (see Fig. 5).

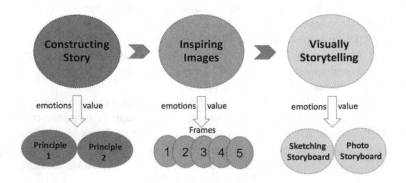

Fig. 5. The integrated storytelling method

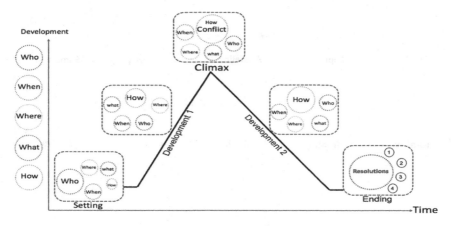

Fig. 6. Constructing story principle

The principle of story constructing is concluded into five stages (see Fig. 6): Setting—Development 1—Climax—Development 2—Ending. A story module moves and elements of the story in the module changes as the story plot develops based on storyline (time). The story can be a real user story as well as a fictional story or the mixture of both, for our purpose is not only getting UX information from a story, but also using it as discussion for a design. It is suggested to be finished as a story scrip for making any change conveniently.

Stage 1: Setting. A story module is designed which contains the elements of a story including Who (character), Where, When, What and How. How means the activities the character will do implying the conflict. In different stage along the timeline, the elements change their importance in the story module.

Stage 2: The story plot development 1. Elements in the story module will change as the activities of the character does, and the conflict becomes more and more obvious. That means in the story the character has some conflicts in his/her need and reality which implying the problems in user experience. In this phrase, the conflict is analysed based on the conflict-analysing principle (see Fig. 7). It's a principle is character-driven, based on Hassenzahl's selection of psychological needs [17]. Through analysing of the conflict of the five needs (competence, relatedness, popularity, stimulation and security [17]) and the reality, the conflict of the story can be constructed logically and rationally. Competence means felling capable and effective in the actions. Relatedness means feeling regular intimate contact with people who care about you. Popularity means feeling you are liked, respected and have influence over others. Stimulation means feeling that you get plenty of enjoyment and pleasure. Security means feeling safe and in control of your life [17]. The analyse of the need conflict is not so strict as qualitative or quantitative analyse. Usually, the analyse of need conflict is so simple and obvious that the story constructor or storyteller can figure it out very easily and quickly. The emotion and value of the characters in the story as well as the one from the other stakeholders of the story can be taken into account.

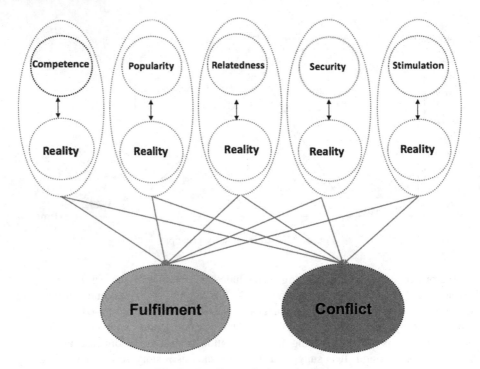

Fig. 7. Conflict-analysing principle

Stage 3: Climax. The plot develops to the climax attracting people to explore and the main conflict implying the emotion and value of the character in the story becomes the focus.

Stage 4: Development. In this phrase, the activities of the character means how to deal with the conflict, and it becomes a discussion for any possible resolutions. However, it also implies the emotion and value of all the stakeholders of the story.

Stage 5: Ending. Discussion results in the many concrete resolutions which means the story is broken into smaller one and can be developed into different possible design concepts in the early stage of design process.

Based on this structure, the problems of user experience are obvious through the expression of the conflict and the discussion of resolutions. The whole process of story constructing can be organized by script to make sure it can be complete and make sense.

In the Inspiring Images part, the reason why images are chosen for storytelling is that there won't be problems in the language and cultural difference. Images like silent movies can be understood easily by all the people. In the storytelling, images should be constructed follow the story script and usually one simple activities should be explained by many different frames which should be guided by the techniques of film such as long shot, close-up so that the emotions and value can be implied through all the images flexibly and clearly. It can also promote discussion for how many frames and how to inspire images and sharing insights during this phrase.

In the third part of visually storytelling, the story can be visualized by sketching – storyboard or photo-storyboard by choosing the right and appropriate images and arranging them in a reasonable sequence. However, discussion for the change of the sequence, adding or deleting of some images in the sequence may have different resolutions of the conflict. This is why we stress the use of storytelling in user experience, because discussion for conflicts resolution in storytelling can trigger the discussion. So that different possible resolutions result in different design concepts.

3.4 Workshop Verification

There were workshops with both the master students and bachelor students in the university to provide exemplary application and verification of this integrated storytelling method.

In the workshop with students, 40 students mixed with master students of Industrial design and Interaction design were separated into ten groups to make storytelling guided by this method. The story constructing principle was introduced firstly and story scrip was asked to finish by each group as team work. Then images and visual storytelling were made according to the script. Most of the discussions for the resolutions of the conflict were made in the story constructing, and some were also made during the other phrases. Different stories of each group resulted in many different possible resolutions which mean various creative concepts for design and more possibilities to improve need fulfilment and enhance user experience. After the workshop, the interview with the participants shows that more than 80 % of the participants gave positive feedback to this integrated storytelling method. At the same time, researchers and some of the master participants have tried to finish some of the design work based on the workshop results as a complete project. The user experience tests planned after the design work gave the similar positive feedback as well.

4 Conclusions

In this research, we tried to integrate the related story theory and experience from our storytelling design to come up with a new integrated storytelling method. The process of this storytelling method can trigger a discussion for conflict resolution, which can result in different design concepts. It can express the emotions and value of characters in the story which imply the scenarios in real social life. User experience can be enhanced not only by providing deep understanding of the needs, conflicts and emotional aspects of the users from the storytelling process, but also by more possible design concepts for story conflict resolutions resulted from the discussion during the storytelling process. It has been used in some workshop and creative design practice and has been proved effective to improve user experience because it has a clear story structure method, and take emotions and value of the stakeholders of a story into account.

5 Discussion and Limitation

There are some limitations of the research. Firstly, it's a pilot of exploring how to enhance user experience through storytelling method. Though there have been many cases by using user stories based on persona and storyboarding construction, the role of the stories is limited to be used as examples not considering the emotional aspects. It's challenging to make storytelling without differentiating user story and fictional story to discussion how to improve user experience.

Secondly, the samples of experiment for verification are limited. Students of design gave their feedback based on their limited experience. More designers with rich experience in UX design should be included in order to get comprehensive and objective evaluation.

Thirdly, how to assess the level of improvement for user experience is still a problem. Understanding of users may not lead into enhancing user experience. More possible resolution may not mean good user experience. So that the assessment still need to be optimized.

In any case, it provides a method for supporting story constructing and storytelling. It has been proved that it can be used to support sharing insights and concepts to promote discussion between designers and users to enhance user experience. It is also a quick start for a storytelling tool design in the next research stage.

Acknowledgements. The research reported in this paper was a part of the Ph.D.'s research project, and also supported by the 2014 project (13SB0109) and 2016 project (16ZB 0217) of Sichuan Province Department of Education and CSC. Thanks to all who were involved in this research.

References

1. Hassenzahl, M.: Experience Design. Technology for all the Right Reasons. Morgan & Claypool, San Rafael (2010)
2. Atasoy, B., Martens, J.-B.,: Crafting user experience by incorporating dramaturgical techniques of storytelling. In: DESIRE 2011 Conference (2011)
3. McKee, R.: STORY: Substance, Structure, Style, and the Principles of Screen- Writing. HarperCollins, New York (2010)
4. Inchauste, F.: Better User Experience With Storytelling-Part One. http://www. Smashingmagazing.Com/2010/01/29/better-user-experience–using-storytelling-part-one/. Accessed 30 Jan 2009
5. Wheeler, K.: Freytag's Pyramid (2004) adapted from Gustav Freytag's Technik des Dramas (1863). The Structure of Tragedy. http://web.cn.edu/kwheeler/documents/Freytag.pdf
6. Duarte, N.: Resonate: Present Visual Stories that Transform Audiences. Wiley, Hoboken (2011)
7. Tassi, R.: Moodboard: Service Design Tools. http://servicedesigntools.org/tools/17. Accessed 16 Mar 2010
8. Quesenber, W., Brooks, K.: Storytelling for User Experience: Crafting Stories for Better Design. Rosenfeld Media, New York

9. Ozcelik, D., Buskermolen, J.T.: Co-constructing stories: a participatory design technique to elicit in-depth user feedback and suggestions about design concepts. In: PDC 2012, Roskide, Denmark, 12–16 August 2012
10. Gruen, D., Rauch, T., Redpath, S., Ruettinger, S.: The use of stories in user experience design. Int. J. Hum.-Comput. Interact. **14**(3&4), 503–534 (2002)
11. The Power of Story in UX Design. http://ninampolson.com/new-page/
12. Greeberg, S., Carpendale, S., Nicolai, M.: Bill Buxton, Sketching user experiences
13. Fritsch, J., Judice, A., Soini, K., Tretten, P.: Storytelling and repetitive narratives for design empathy: case Suomenlinna. In: Proceedings of Design Inquiries (2007)
14. Atasoy, B., Martens, J.-B.: Storyply - a tool to assist design teams in envisioning and discussing user experience. In: CHI 2011, 7–12 May 2011
15. Francisco Inchauste: Better User Experience with Storytelling (2010). https://www.smashingmagazine.com/2010/01/better-user-experience-using-storytelling-part-one/
16. Glebas, F.: Directing the Story, Professional Storytelling and Storyboarding Techniques for Live Action and Animation. Elsevier Inc., Philadelphia (2009)
17. Hassenzahl, M., Diefenbach, S.: Well-being, need fulfilment, and experience design. In: DIS 2012 Workshop Designing Wellbeing (2012)

Accessible Icons for Deaf: An UX Approach

Armando Cardoso Ribas, Luciane Maria Fadel[(⊠)], Tarcísio Vanzin,
and Vania Ribas Ulbricht

Postgraduate Program in Knowledge Engineering and Management,
Federal University of Santa Catarina (UFSC),
Florianópolis, Santa Catarina, Brazil
mandorgr@gmail.com, liefadel@gmail.com,
tvanzin@gmail.com, vrulbricht@gmail.com

Abstract. Considering that deaf people have their own culture based upon their unique manners and characteristics this paper investigates the criteria for development of accessible icons, which are easily recognized by deaf. Thus, this paper starts with a brief description of the deaf culture and reviews related research. Finally, a systematic review of literature was carried out in order to describe the state of the art on the criteria to develop icons.

Keywords: Criteria · Icon design · Deft

1 Introduction

Technology is intended to enhance or facilitate human actions, as well as improve communication, leveraging the economy, politics, culture and dissemination and absorption of knowledge. In this respect, all technology is considered a social device, because it is about products, techniques and methods developed to benefit society [1, 2]. Castells [3] argued that: "… society shapes technology according to the needs, values and interests of persons who use these technologies […] technologies of information and communications are particularly sensitive to the effects of the social use of the technology itself. […]".

Cerezo [4] added that people must also have conditions to assess the impacts of information brought by the technologies, which tend to influence their surroundings. Castells [3] corroborates with Cerezo [4] by arguing that the knowledge generated by these technologies, is directly connected to the ability of organization of the society, capturing the benefits and excluding irrelevant information. Thus, all individuals of this society should have access to information, which leads to the problem of enhancing accessibility of technology.

Accessibility aims to make digital systems accessible to all people, with or without disabilities [5]. According to the W3C [6], Web accessibility means that people with disabilities "can perceive, understand, navigate, interact and contribute to the web". Pupo et al. [7] corroborate with ABRA [5] stating that the accessibility also benefits those who do not have disabilities, because a digital accessible system is designed to facilitate learning and use to improve the overall user experience.

© Springer International Publishing Switzerland 2016
A. Marcus (Ed.): DUXU 2016, Part I, LNCS 9746, pp. 124–132, 2016.
DOI: 10.1007/978-3-319-40409-7_13

Despite many Information and Communication Technologies (ICT) assist people with disabilities these technologies can also introduce limitation. That might happen because the information is designed focusing on satisfy the senses of vision and hearing. Therefore, those users with vision or hearing loss may have difficulty in perceiving information.

Perception results from what individuals capture with their senses. Senses can be divided into introspective and non-introspective senses. The former refers to the perception of the body, such as pain and movement of internal organs. The later is what we apprehend from the surroundings, captured by the senses of sight, sound, smell, taste and touch [8]. But, it's in the mind that occurs the perception from the information collected by the senses. According to Santaella [9] the perception results of referencing prior knowledge, which is necessary to an understanding of the facts presented [10]. In addition, the perception differs from one individual to another and from one culture to another, because each person has a singular experience of life. Therefore, each person has a unique perception of an artifact observed [8]. Then, designing for all is the topic of many researches. This paper discusses the user experience design approach that might ensure that most users experience the object as intended. This approach aims to design artifacts qualities that are recognized by most people, which means design for experience.

This means to create conditions so that people with a similar cultural perspective like deaf people who share a sociocultural background, will perceive and interpret a product in an intended way. Ribeiro [11] puts that there is little production of accessible material, and there is too much text in written form and with low production of images, icons, pictures, or videos to this public.

Considering that deaf people have their own culture based upon their unique manners and characteristics this paper investigate the criteria for development of accessible icons, which are easily recognized by deaf. Therefore, this papers starts with a brief description of the deaf culture and reviews related research. Finally, a systematic review of literature was carried out in order to describe the state of the art on the criteria to develop icons.

2   Deaf Culture

The history of deaf education presents a continuous evolution despite several significant impacts [12]. One of the most outstanding and impactful crises in the history of the deaf was in education. Deaf people "were subdued to non-deaf practices, having to abandon their culture, their identity as deaf and have undergone a 'ethnocentric hearing', having to imitate them for over 100 years" [12]. According to Quadros [12] this crises occurred after 1880 when the International Conference of Teachers of the Deaf in Milan discussed and analyzed the importance of the three rival methods of teaching: sign language, oral and mixed (sign language and oral). Most of the countries of Europe quickly adopted the oral method in schools for deaf, forbidding sign language. That was the beginning of the fight for deaf people's cultural linguistic right [12]. Perlin [13] affirms that this prejudice against the deaf culture still occurs today. Many countries allow sign language only if students fail with the oralization of spoken and written language.

Sá [14] argues that the deaf culture wants to be recognized as culture in a social context. But being minority it is dominated by the dominant culture (culture of listeners). For this reason, deaf culture is recreated almost every day. Therefore, Sá [14] understands that deaf people do not have a culture of their own. They interact among each other but tend to turn away from listeners by lack of understanding, which creates the illusion of a real culture of their own. Even though, they insist on demonstrating that they have their culture and that will not change because of the prejudice of the listeners.

Deaf culture is constructed by society as a subculture, as it aims to make the deaf accepted in society. This subculture is not formed by a minority, but by the minority of the minority [15]. And, according to Jeff McWhinney, Executive Director of the British Association of the Deaf in the year 2001, deaf community is a community proud of itself. They are proud of their culture, proud of its history and proud of its language.

Perlin [13] argues that deaf children should have, from an early age, contact with deaf adults, because at the same time that they learn sign language, they also create a psychosocial and cultural identity with the deaf community. Another important part of the deaf culture consists in writing-signal or Signwriting. This is the result of the search for a system of sign language representation. The development of this writing system was interrupted for several years due to foreclosure and the non-recognition of deaf culture. The Signwriting was created in the 90's by Valerie Sutton of the Deaf Action Committee (DAC), California, USA. It is based on a system that Sutton created to write down the dancers moves. The Signwriting is composed of symbols that represent the sign language both schematic and graphically. It works as an alphabetic writing system, in which the fundamental graphic units represent fundamental gestures units, their properties and relationships. The author states that the Signwriting can register any sign language in the world without passing through the translation of the spoken language. Each language of signs needs to adapt it to their own spelling system [16].

There are also institutions that are helping deaf culture with technology. The Board of Directors of the National Education Development Fund (FNDE) is one of them, and since September 8 2003, by resolution n° 26, is investing financial resources for the development of software to translate texts from Portuguese to LIBRAS.

3   Related Research

Deaf develop their own culture based primarily on the visual channel to acquire information because they have unique manners and characteristics. However, as stated by Moura [17], it is through language that people give meaning to the world in which they live. Thus, not only the understanding of each word influences the simple act of browsing at a web page for example, but also the shape of cognitive organization regarding the information in the long-term memory [18]. According to Fajardo [18] listeners and deaf adopt different forms of scanning information available on an interface. The former seek semantic hypertext standards, which means that they seek meaningful words. While the latter almost never use semantic patterns but they perform a random search of all visual information on the screen. The deaf has a more accurate visual language and they read images as listeners read a text o [9, 19]. Fajardo [18] had experimented using images as hyperlinks in order to verify how navigation for deaf users would be like on the Web. They concluded that these users found more easily the information and took less time scanning the pages than on verbal interfaces. In addition, they concluded that if a page has many subpages (which might increase the semantic process) the performance on graphic interface was compromised. This happened because images with similar features have similar meanings, which makes it difficult to distinguish between the two, hindering navigation.

For this reason Reitsma, Galen [20] and Fajardo [18] point out that icons can be used to represent certain actions, because an icon is likely to be easier understood by a deaf. However, icons may be misunderstood when they portrait words with abstract meaning. In this case signs are usually a better choice. A sign is an image that does not have any semblance with the real object or information, such as transit signs.

In addition, iconic signs based on metaphor, which are icons that represent real objects, are usually pertinent for the deaf. These icons are meaningful to the user because they represent an object with quality. But this representation can be subjective, because the icons are designed to a specific culture or users. That is to say that icons are created based on real elements, which are part of the culture of the selected users, but also depend on the perception of the user and the representativeness of the icon design.

In this sense, the designers of visual elements (designers, painters, sculptors and others), in many cases, are unaware of the characteristics and culture of the deaf, not taking into consideration many aspects, which are only perceived by the deaf. For this reason the UX approach highlights the importance to involve the user in order to develop or evaluate a visual element in accessibility issues. Formiga [21] and Fekete [22] argue that a graphic symbol used in the Web, has advantage over texts, because the signs have free language and a single sign is enough to present information accessible to most people because it does not require the knowledge of the written language.

Next section discusses the findings of a systematic literature review on criteria to develop icons accessible to deaf.

4 Accessible Icons for Deaf

The systematic literature review was conducted based on Scopus (www.scopus.com), CAPES journals and Web of Science (webofknowledge.com). The papers analyzed bring relevant information about deaf accessibility and deafness, but none include the topic icon + deaf. The search was restricted to full papers, published in the last five years that had in the title one of the following keywords: information visualization, deaf, visual perception, icons, information display and visual sense. These keywords were chosen prioritizing those with a higher frequency on a preliminary search. These keywords were combined to perform the search, such as: "Information visualization and deaf"; "visual perception of the deaf"; "visual perception of deaf" and icons; "deaf information display" and icons e "visual sense" and deaf.

Table 1 shows the final combination of keywords and the number of documents found on Scopus, CAPES and Web of science.

After the selection of all 64 papers, their abstracts were analysed. The analysis chose 5 papers from Scopus, 5 papers from Capes and 3 from Web of science.

Table 1. Keywords and number of documents found on Scopus, CAPES and Web of Science data base.

Keywords	Scopus	CAPES	Web of science
"Information visualization" + deaf	2	0	3
"visual perception" + deaf	2	46	2
"visual perception of deaf" + icons	0	0	0
"Deaf information display" + icons	0	0	0
"Visual sense" + deaf	3	1	4
Final selected papers	5	3	3

This final selection was based on the pertinence of the content and excluded all repetitions. The analysis of the 11 papers follows.

The paper "Universal Use of Information Delivery and Display System using Ad hoc Network for Deaf People in Times of Disaster" [23] discuss visual messages to alert deaf people about risk activity, such as earthquake, flood and storm. The authors concluded that the system is useful to support both the elderly and hearing impaired in disaster. However, it would be important to make some changes in the size of the characters and its brightness.

The paper "Visual impairment in the hearing impaired students" [24], discusses occurrences of vision problems in children with hearing disabilities. The author concluded that there is no difference when compared with children without disabilities. These deficiencies, if detected belatedly, could aggravate the educational and social disability.

The other paper analyzed was "The study of the tactual and visual reception of fingerspelling" [25]. The author demonstrates the interaction and communication of deaf-blind student, which uses the reception of tactile fingerspelling (also knowledge as the finger alphabet or hand alphabet) to communicate and acquire knowledge. In this method, the hands of people who are deaf-blind are placed on the sender's side to monitor the hand shapes and movements associated with the letters of the hand alphabet.

The paper "The exchangeability of speech by cognitive metaphors" [26] deals with issues such as information visualization of deaf people using symbolic systems. Burmeister used metaphors as the background for the semantic of symbol systems, which is based on Piaget's work. The author states that metaphor represents a type of prelingual thinking.

In another paper Burmeister [27] intends to generalize given techniques in modeling semantic content. The paper "A semantic approach for user depending information visualization" Burmeister [27] discusses these techniques to the purpose of transferring them from industrial application scenarios and apply into projects for everyone's needs. The author found that deaf people assimilate information differently than hearing ones and he seeks for methods to map semantic roles with their situation dependent usage to proper metaphors. He explains that the sign language of deaf people may be a rich field to extract such metaphors, because gestures encode not only intentional aspects of information but are situation dependent visualizations of content. Thus, Burmeister proposes to rely on linguistic research concerning the decomposition of sign language in basic semantic units.

Another relevant work is a dissertation entitled the "Visuality of the deaf in the context of audio-visual education" [28]. In this work the author addressed themes focusing on audio-visual narratives for deaf people who are beginning on academia. One aspect that drew attention was the lack of importance the deaf community give to produce audio-visual products. Most productions are adapted for subtitles or windows with LIBRAS interpreter.

The paper "Perception of temporal patterns by deaf and hearing adults" [29] compared performance of under-graduate deaf students and listeners. Both had the same performance when it comes to simple activities, but when activities were more complex the deaf student had a disadvantage over the listener, because the temporal perception model of the deaf is different. This was already evident in the work written by Templin [30] entitled "A comparison of the spelling achievement of normal and defective hearing subjects". Templin [30] analyzed errors of spelling among three groups: 78 participants were deaf, 78 had hearing disabilities (listen something) and 78 children whose hearing was normal. Templin concluded that deaf students have more difficulty in writing and misspelled more than students with hearing impairments. In addition, those with hearing disabilities misspelled more than the non-disabled. This might happened because the perception of groups differs with respect to their culture (American Psychological Association).

The paper "Making Sense of an Unexpected Detrimental Effect of Sign Language Use in a Visual Task" [31] discusses a survey conducted in Italy to check the deaf visuospatial performance. They compared performance between those use sign language to those who do not use (nonsigners). They concluded that students who use sign language have a higher spatial information visualization compared to nonsigners students.

The paper entitled "Requirements of deaf user of information visualization an interdisciplinary approach" [32] deals with matters of avatar and viewing knowledge. Burmeister [32] highlights the importance of a good visualization of information in order to obtain a correct mental model. The author believes that the union of the gestural movements of the avatars to visually complement information considered abstract to the deaf user helps in the understanding of past information.

Another important work about accessible icons is a master dissertation [33] that discusses a learning environment prototype where all hypertexts are icons. The author states, "The icons were created by a deaf designer, who accepted to volunteer in this research. He used his creativity and then applied the technique of creativity Icon Sorting[1]". But no further research about icon design was carried out.

5 Conclusion

Considering that designers have few principles to guide icon design [34] designing accessible icons becomes a challenging task. In addition, Zender [34] reports depressingly results about icon understanding and highlights the need for researches about how visual symbols work or how they might be made to work better. Hence, this

---

[1] Icon Sorting a technique for development of icons using correlated systems to everyday life.

paper is a first step toward understanding accessible icons that might contribute to create accessible interfaces. In addition, the knowledge involved in this task might benefit designing accessible visual-based elements. Therefore, this paper investigated criteria for development of accessible icons, which are easily recognized by deaf. A systematic review of literature was carried out in order to describe the state of the art on the criteria to develop icons.

The systematic literature review used six keywords to select 30 articles from three databases. The analysis of the abstracts resulted on eleven papers selected. None of these papers describes criteria, guidelines or recommendations for the development of icons, which are accessible to the deaf. Nonetheless, the papers analyzed bring relevant information about accessibility for deaf.

Zender argues that the interaction of the right number of symbols and a more apt combination of individual symbols for the referent, can improve the construction of an icon that communicates what was intended. Zender sees icon as a combination of symbols. In fact the icon "Paste" in Microsoft Word, for example, is a combination of paper sheet and a clipboard. Burmeister supports the quality part of this argument when he states that the importance of a good visualization of information in order to obtain a correct mental model.

In a previous work Zender [35] argued that context is the key concept for decoding the meaning of symbols. Once more, Burmeister findings may enrich this statement because he suggests that gestures encode not only intentional aspects of information but are situation dependent visualizations of content. Zender envisions three levels of context for a given icon: the Immediate, the Proximate and the Environment Context. Environment Context refers to the environment in which the images function, such as an airport. Proximate Context is an icon combination in a system relating to another to clarify meaning. For example, elevator icon next to escalator icon helps to clarify meaning of each. The Immediate Context refers to icons combined in the same space to clarify meaning. For example, man + bed = hotel. Therefore, the Proximate Context perception for deaf people might differ from hearing ones because deaf almost never use semantic patterns but they perform a random search of all visual information on the screen [18]. In addition, the Immediate Context might have a strong influence on the understanding of an icon by the deaf because images with similar features have similar meanings, which makes it difficult to distinguish between the two [18].

Kosslyn et al. [36] explored how the brain uses, stores, manipulates and processes mental visual representations to think and solve problems. They found that the brain holds simple representations of familiar objects in a specific region, which can be recalled into visual working memory to think and solve problems. This opens the possibility that people share a similar image for common objects.

Based on his studies Zender [34] proposes 3 rules of thumb for icon design:

1. Match symbols to definition: individual symbols should match to definitions of the referents. This means that the designers need to understand how deaf people define the referent
2. Add symbols to narrow focus: a symbol for each referent concept is necessary
3. Create symbol hierarchy: in some icons a sequence of concepts is an important feature of the referent definition

In addition to these rules Zender calls attention for the importance of study failure to improve success. Further studies will be carried out to investigate how influence of the context and these three rules on accessible icon design.

Acknowledgement. The author Luciane Maria Fadel is sponsored by CAPES Foundation, Ministry of Education of Brazil.

References

1. Fernandes, E.: Problema linguísticos e cognitivos do surdo. Agir, Rio de Janeiro (1990)
2. Feenberg, A.: Racionalização democrática, poder e tecnologia. In: Nerder, R.T. (org.) Construção Crítica da Tecnologia e Sustentabilidade, vol. 1(3), Brasilia (2010)
3. Castells, M.A.: Sociedade em rede. Paz e Terra, São Paulo (2009)
4. Cerezo, J.A.L.: Ciência, Técnica e Sociedade. In: Ibarra, A., Olivé, L. (eds.) Questiones Éticas de la Ciência y de la Tecnologia en el siglo XXI, OEI y Biblioteca Nueva, Madri (2003)
5. ABRA- Associação Brasileira de Acessibilidade. http://www.acessibilidade.org.br
6. W3C. www.w3c.org.com
7. Pupo, D.T., Melo, A.M., Pérez Ferrés, S.: Acessibilidade: discurso e prática no cotidiano das bibliotecas, pp. 62–70. UNICAMP, Campinas (2006). http://www.ic.unicamp.br/~melo/livro_acessibilidade_bibliotecas.pdf
8. Wolfe, J.M., Kluender, K.R., Levi, D.M.: Sensation and Perception. Sinauer Associates, Sunderland (2009)
9. Santaella, L.: Percepção. Fenomenologia, Ecologia, Semiótica. Cengage Learning, São Paulo (2012)
10. Ribeiro, J.P.: Gestalt-terapia: Refazendo um caminho. Summus, São Paulo (1985)
11. Guimarães, A.D.S.: Leitores surdos e acessibilidade virtual mediada por Tecnologias de Informação e Comunicação Chaves. IFECTMT, Cuiabá (2009)
12. Quadros, R.M.: O contexto escolar do aluno surdo e o papel das línguas (2010)
13. Perlin, G.: O lugar da cultura surda. In da S. Thoma, A., Lopes, M.C. (orgs.) A Invenção da Surdez: Cultura, Alteridade, Identidade e Diferença no Campo da Educação. EDUNISC, Santa Cruz do Sul (2004)
14. Sá, N.L.: Cultura, poder e educação de surdos (2006)
15. Wrigley, O.: The politics of deafness. Gallaudet University Press, Washington (1996)
16. Stumpf, M.R.: Aprendizagem de Escrita de Lingua de Sinais pelo Sistema SignWriting: Linguas de sinais no papel e no computador. UFSC, Florianópolis (2005)
17. Moura, M.C.: Surdez e Linguagem. In: Lacerda, C., Santos, I.F. (orgs.) Tenho um aluno surdo e agora. Edufscar (2013)
18. Fajardo, I., Abascal, J., Cañas, J.J.: Bridging the digital divide for deaf signer users. In: 15th European Conference on Cognitive Ergonomics: The Ergonomics of Cool Interaction, ECCE 2008, pp. 1–37. ACM, New York (2008)
19. Botelho, P.: Segredos e silêncios na interpretação dos surdos. Autêntica, Belo Horizonte (1998)
20. Reitsma, P., Galen, M.S.: Developing access to number magnitude: A study of SNARC effect in 7- to 9-year-olds. J. Exp. Child Psychol. **101**, 99–113 (2008)
21. Formiga, E.: Símbolos gráficos: métodos de avaliação de compreensão. Blucher, São Paulo (2011)

22. Fekete, J.D., et al.: O valor de visualização de informação. In: Visualização de Informação: Questões centrado no ser humano e Perspectivas, pp. 1–18. Springer, Berlim (2008)
23. Ito, A., Murakami, H., Watanabe, Y., Fujii, M., Yabe, T., Haraguchi, Y., Tomoyasu, Y., Kakuda, Y., Ohta, T., Hiramatsu, Y.: Universal use of information delivery and display system using ad hoc network for deaf people in times of disaster, Tokyo (2008)
24. Gogate, P., Rishikeshi, N., Mehata, R., Ranade, S., Kharat, J., Deshpande, M.: Visual impairment in the hearing impaired students. Indian J. Ophthalmol. 57(6), 451 (2009)
25. Reed, C.M., Delhorne, L.A., Durlach, N.I., Fischer, S.D.: A study of the tactual and visual reception of fingerspelling. J. Speech Hear. Res. 33, 786–797 (1991)
26. Burmeister, D.: The exchangeability of speech by cognitive metaphors. In: 9th International Conference on Information Visualization. IEEE (2005)
27. Burmeister, D.: A semantic approach for user depending information visualization In: 8th International Conference on Information Visualization. IEEE (2004)
28. Gutierrez, E.O.: A visualidade dos sujeitos surdos no contexto da educação audiovisual. Universidade de Brasília, Brasília (2011)
29. Mills, B.C.: Perception of visual temporal patterns by deaf and hearing adult (1985)
30. Templin, M.C.: A comparison of the spelling achievement of normal and defective hearing subjects. J. Educ. Psychol. 39, 337–346 (1948)
31. Lauro, R., Leonor, J., Crespi, M., Papagno, C., Cecchetto, C.: Making sense of an unexpected detrimental effect of sign language use in a visual task. J. Deaf Stud. Deaf Educ. 19, 358–365 (2015)
32. Burmeister, D.: Requirements of deaf user of information visualization an interdisciplinary approach In: 7th International Conference on Information Visualization. IEEE (2003)
33. Amorim, M.L.C.: Estilos de Interação Web de Navegação e Ajuda Contextual para Usuários Surdos em Plataformas de Gestão da Aprendizagem. Recife (2012)
34. Zender, M., Mejía, M.: Improving icon design: through focus on the role of individual symbols in the construction of meaning. Visible Lang. 47(1), 66–89 (2013)
35. Zender, M.: Advancing icon design for global non verbal communication: or what does the word bow mean? Visible Lang. 40(2), 177–206 (2006)
36. Kosslyn, S.M., Thompson, W.L., Ganis, G.: The Case for Mental Imagery. Oxford University Press, Oxford (2006)

Design Thinking Framework for Project Portfolio Management

Hamed Sarbazhosseini[1(✉)], Sisira Adikari[1], and Heath Keighran[2]

[1] School of Information Systems & Accounting,
University of Canberra, Canberra, ACT 2601, Australia
{Hamed.Sarbazhosseini,
Sisira.Adikardi}@Canberra.edu.au
[2] Business Design, Crooked Fox, Canberra, ACT 2601, Australia
Heath@crookedfox.com.au

Abstract. Project Portfolio Management has been introduced as a strategy to manage multiple projects at the same time. To stay ahead of the competition, organisations require PPM approach to achieve results. PPM is an area of organisational activity that helps organisations to govern the selection of projects and/or programs and management of organisations. The PPM discussed as an area that requires conceptualisation to give meaning to it and make it usable for organisations. This paper applies design thinking framework to conceptualise PPM and to investigate what Australian Government Organisations wish to achieve through the PPM. Findings of the study are important in better understanding the complexities of PPM.

Keywords: Project Portfolio Management · Design thinking framework

1 Introduction

Project Portfolio Management has been recognised as one of the information systems areas that require further research and frameworks to better understand its effectiveness for academics and practitioners. The research study presented in this paper was motivated by the need to develop a design-oriented conceptual framework to conduct research in a domain that has a little academic foundation.

A design thinking framework has been applied to PPM theory to conceptualise its meaning and to better understand what Australian Government Organisations (AGOs) wishing to achieve.

A summary of PPM's literature has been discussed in this paper in terms of three main sources; academic, industry and software. The design thinking framework of PPM has been introduced to comprehend how the data can be collected and analysed. The finding of this paper has a significant contribution to PPM and design thinking framework of PPM.

© Springer International Publishing Switzerland 2016
A. Marcus (Ed.): DUXU 2016, Part I, LNCS 9746, pp. 133–140, 2016.
DOI: 10.1007/978-3-319-40409-7_14

2 The Project Portfolio Management

For organisations to deliver better outcomes, managing multiple concurrent projects "an endeavour (temporary [1]) in which human, (or machine) material and financial resources are organised in a novel way to undertake a unique scope of work, of given specification, within the constraints of cost, quality and time, so as to deliver beneficial change defined by quantitative or qualitative objectives [2] " and programs "a group of projects that are managed in a coordinated way to gain benefits that would not be possible were the projects to be managed independently [3] " is essential.

PPM is a dynamic decision-making process in which new projects and/or programs are evaluated, selected and prioritised and balanced in the context of the existing projects and programs within the portfolio [4].

Organisations are attracted to PPM because of the claims made for it. Kersten and Verhoef [5] and Verhoef [6] argue that firms reduce IT (Information Technology) spending by 10 to 40 percent using PPM. Laslo [7] claims that PPM allows an organisation to maintain agility while avoiding wasteful investments and Thorp [8] argues PPM techniques are fundamental to getting value from IT projects. According to Rongzeng et al. [9], banks look for ways to cut costs and eliminate waste in IT expenditure and such approaches are advised to taking a portfolio management approach.

2.1 Academic Literature

Portfolio management has been introduced as a theory in 1952 from financial investments [10]. The purpose of the initial theory of portfolio was aimed at determining the particular combination of investments to maximise returns for the owners at a given level of risk [11]. The theory was used as a mathematical solution for the selection of research and development projects [12].

Portfolio management has been adopted in the ICT (Information and Communication Technologies) management domain from the finance sector in 1981 [13]. On 1988, the theory was applied as a mathematical solution to the selection of research and development projects [12].

Based on Michael [14] most of the portfolio management articles were published from the mid-1990 s onwards. Numbers of published journals articles increased "from two in 2000 to 35 in 2004" [15]. As such, the study suggested that there was a significant development of standards in the domain of portfolio management. PPM has been investigated from different aspects such as potential resource shortages [16]; Management of interdependencies [17]; right number of projects [18, 19]; PPM and program Management [20, 21] and strategic alignment [22].

2.2 Industry Standards

Industry standards seem to offer reliable information to the field. Currently, there are two main standards identified in PPM published by the Project Management Institute [23], and the UK's Office of Government Commerce [24]. While there are two standards available, the correct implementation of PPM and its attributes are not defined clearly.

2.3 PPM Software

In a comparative study of PPM software and PPM theory, Sarbazhosseini and Young [25] found that PPM vendors aim to achieve strategic alignment, balanced portfolios, maximised value of portfolios and a centralised source of information. However, the software did not seem to address issues such as selecting the right number of projects, or ensuring portfolio sufficiency versus overall product innovation goals. The software did; however, seem to have attributes that were not considered in the research literature.

3 Design Thinking Framework for PPM

There are number of definitions for information system design which considers the use of computer systems, human activity system, the people and technological system, the environment and context, and organisational context [26].

In the perspective of information systems, this study considered levels of environment namely, real-world, organisational context, and the context of use to present a global view of information system and the user interaction. The Design thinking is the way designers think and apply their mental processes to design objects, services or systems, as distinct from the result of elegant and useful products [27].

The Design Thinking is "a methodology used by designers to solve complex problems and find desirable solutions for clients" [28]. It is also mentioned that "design is the action of bringing something new and desired into existence- a proactive stance that resolves or dissolves problematic situations by design. It is a compound of routine, adaptive and design expertise brought to bear on complex by dynamic situations [29]."

The Design Thinking process "defines the problem first and then implements the solution, always with the needs of the user demographic at the core of concept development [28]." These processes consist of five steps; Empathize, Define, Ideate, Prototype, and Test [28]. Within these steps, problems can be framed, the right questions can be asked, more ideas can be created, and the best answers can be chosen [30].

PPM in this research has been conceptualised based on design thinking method, and State-Transition Model (STM) has been offered as a conceptualisation approach to PPM.

The STM is being used in Clinical [31] and Ecological [32] applications in order to evaluate the state of the ecosystem and evaluate patient's status in different medical time frames. It also has applications in software engineering, being used in UML (Unified Modelling Language) and state-charts [33].

It is the on-going, continuous nature of PPM that makes the STM useful in looking at organisational state, change and responsiveness as by its definition that PPM is the dynamic and on-going environment and context. The developed framework has been updated from a previous approach discussed [34]. The design thinking framework for PPM based on organisational approach in Business World consists of four elements of

(1) initiation of projects and/or programs; (2) identification of actions, tools and techniques; (3) clarification of desired goals for organisations; and (4) learning from organisational changes and overall system, to improve its performance (See Fig. 1).

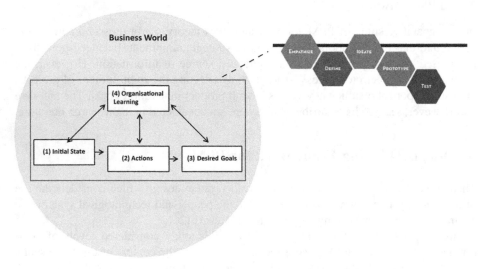

Fig. 1. Design Thinking PPM Framework

This framework works circular meaning that in each state of Business World, the organisation would learn from its performance, and that can enhance the same state as well as updates the other states to improve the overall performance of the organisation.

While there is a little clarification in the PPM literature about each state, it is assumed that this framework would assist to better investigate and better understand the PPM in government organisations as well as theory.

Recently, Sarbazhosseini et al. [35] discussed the organisational issues involved in project portfolio management. In addition, an evaluation of Business World of the STM has been discussed in [36] to better understand similarities and differences in each state. This paper aims to investigate desired goals and outcomes from the framework in AGOs.

4   Data Collection Methods and Analyses

To investigate the developed framework in the PPM field, we conducted a set of interviews with directors of portfolio management offices in AGOs. Data was also gathered from documents provided such as P3M3 reports, roadmaps, strategic plans, capability improvement plans, annual reports, and portfolio statements.

The interview protocol followed a set of procedures and instruments used to specify interactions between researchers and study participants including designs for participant contact, the interview data collection instrument, the interview script and analysis techniques as suggested in [36]. The interview notes included items from the proposed framework.

Interview questions were developed based on four states of the developed framework. The data collection was conducted using interviews and document reviews. Then data were analysed based on structural coding and thematic analysis.

Structural coding applies a content-based or conceptual phrase representing a topic of inquiry to a segment of data that relates to a specific research question used to frame an interview [37]. It is also explained that structural coding is a question-based code. During the structural coding of data, it was discovered that there were possible new categories other than the categories developed in the framework.

Based on Saldana [38, p. 139], a theme is an outcome of coding, categorisation, and analytic reflection, not something that is, in itself, coded. Boyatzis [39] explains that a theme "at a minimum describes and organises possible observations or at the maximum interprets an aspect of the phenomenon." Thematic analysis and the search for themes in the data are a strategic choice and part of the research design that includes the primary objectives, goals, conceptual framework and literature review [38, p. 139].

In this paper, the data analysis includes findings of desired goals for AGOs. The summary of findings would be represented based on themes which were discovered for each state of the framework. In the next section, the discovered themes would be discussed.

5 Findings and Discussion

The analysis of data represented some themes which were identified for the desired goal of organisations. As it is represented in Table 1, seven themes were discovered for PPM's desired goals. The description of each desired goals represents that what state organisations wished to be in each of the themes.

Table 1. Themes in Desired Goals

Themes in Desired Goals	Description
1. Visibility 2. Transparency 3. Accountability 4. Consistency	To improve the state to Higher; e.g. higher visibility.
5. Strategic goals	To deliver government initiatives
6. Doing the Right Projects	To make right decisions and deliver goals
7. P3M3	Case 1: Maintain level 2, focus on Benefit Management
	Case 2: Target level 4, focus on Stakeholder Management and Risk Management
	Case 3: Target Level 3, focus on Risk Management
	Case 4: Target Level 3, Focus on Improving Consistency and developing standard portfolio processes
	Case 5: Target level 3, focus on Benefit Management
	Case 6: Target level 3, Focus on Benefit and Stakeholder Management
	Case 7: Target Maintain level 3, Focus on Resource and Benefit Management

According to Table 1, organisations wish to achieve higher visibility, transparency, accountability and consistency. The organisations believed that with the use of PPM, they will have consistent decision-making processes because PPM frames their actions and processes. For the same reason, PPM helps them to increase the level of visibility, transparency, accountability and consistency in organisations.

Also, it shows that organisations desired to achieve strategic goals in order to deliver what they have been asked. The P3M3 reports indicated that organisations, in order to target a new level, need bigger budgets, however, they wish to improve their levels by considering different issues.

This research from a desired state perspective showed agencies are striving to achieve organisational goals and government initiatives which also called as strategic goals. To achieve this they recognise that improving the portfolio level of Benefit Management and Risk Management in P3M3 assessment is essential. This concept links the desired state mentioned in the literature [36]. Literature demonstrated organisations are wishing to achieve "linking portfolio to the strategy and maximising the value of portfolios." This could be seen to have links to Benefit Management. In addition, "achieving the balanced portfolio" can be seen as Risk Management.

6   Conclusion

In this paper, we developed a design thinking framework for PPM, to investigate what organisations desire to achieve. The designed framework was helpful in developing the interview questions and data collection instruments. The set of interviews were conducted with seven organisations to collect the required data. Data was analysed based on structural coding and thematic analysis which considered four main states of the framework. Themes from the analysis were identified and discussed in this paper. The findings of the paper represented that organisations wished to achieve higher Visibility, Transparency, Accountability and Consistency in their organisations.

Organisations also apply PPM to have a better framework for the entire organisation to communicate better and better control management of the resources and projects/programs. Organisations wish to achieve strategic goals by prioritisations and balancing their portfolios to do the right projects. The analysis of P3M3 reports indicated that organisations are mainly focusing on improving their benefit and resource management to have a better performance in their organisations and achieve their organisational goals.

The proposed designed-oriented framework assisted to better capture PPM theory in organisations and to better understand the goals they are aiming to achieve. The framework clarifies the current use of PPM in AGOs. It is suggested that organisations and researchers investigate this framework in a different places and evaluate other states to identify if their initial state and actions lead to desired goals. It also can be suggested to compare this framework with other designed thinking frameworks.

Acknowledgment. This paper is part of a larger research project, and is an extension of previous research works.

References

1. Project Management Institute Global Standard.: A Guide to the Project Management Body of Knowledge: PMBOK® Guide. Fourth Edition, An American National Standard (2008)
2. Turner, J.R.: The Handbook of Project-Based Management, vol. 92. McGraw-Hill, New York (2009)
3. Ferns, D.: Developments in programme management. Int. J. Proj. Manag. **9**(3), 148–156 (1991)
4. Cooper, R., Edgett, S., Kleinschmidt, E.: New product portfolio management: practices and performance. J. Prod. Innov. Manag. **16**, 333–351 (1999)
5. Kersten, B., Verhoef, C.: IT portfolio management: a banker's perspective on IT. Cutter IT J. **16**(4), 27–33 (2003)
6. Verhoef, C.: Quantitative IT portfolio management. Sci. Comput. Program. **45**(1), 1–96 (2002)
7. Laslo, Z.: Project portfolio management: an integrated method for resource planning and scheduling to minimize planning/scheduling-dependent expenses. Int. J. Proj. Manag. **28**(6), 609–618 (2010)
8. Thorp, J.: The Information Paradox: Realizing the Business Benefits of Information Technology. McGraw-Hill, New York (1999)
9. Rongzeng, C., Wei, D., Chunhua, T.: Using resource and portfolio management solution to align IT investment with business. In: IEEE International Conference on e-Business Engineering, 2005. ICEBE 2005 (2005)
10. Markowitz, H.: Portfolio selection. J. Finance **7**(1), 77–91 (1952)
11. Reyck, B.D., Grushka-Cockayne, Y., Lockett, M., Calderini, S.R., Moura, M., Sloper, A.: The impact of project portfolio management on information technology projects. Int. J. Proj. Manag. **23**(7), 524–537 (2005)
12. Bard, J.F., Balachandra, R., Kaufmann, P.E.: An interactive approach to R&D project selection and termination. IEEE Trans. Eng. Manag. **35**(3), 139–146 (1988)
13. McFarlan, F.W.: Portfolio Approach to Information Systems. IEEE Press, Piscataway (1989)
14. Michael, P.: IT project portfolio management-a matter of organizational culture? In: PACIS Proceedings (2010)
15. Killen, C.P, Hunt, R.A, Kleinschmidt, E.J.: Managing the new product development project portfolio: a review of the literature and empirical evidence (2007)
16. Padovani, M., Carvalho, M.M., Muscat, A.R.N.: Critical Gaps in Portfolio Management Implementation: A Brazilian Case Study. In: Paper presented at the Technology Management for the Global Future, PICMET (2006)
17. Maio, A.D., Verganti, R., Corso, M.: A multi-project management framework for new product development. Eur. J. Oper. Res. **78**(2), 178–191 (1994)
18. Cooper, R., Edgett, S.: Portfolio management for new products: picking the winners. Product Development Institute, Ancaster (2001)
19. Cooper, R., Edgett, S., Kleinschmidt, E.: Optimizing the stage-gate process: What best-practice companies do-II. Res.-Technol. Manag. **45**, 43–49 (2002)
20. Gareis, R.: Program management and project portfolio management: new competences of project-oriented organizations. In: Proceedings of the Project Management Institute Annual Seminars & Symposium (2000)
21. Zhu, Y., Pan, Q., Guo, P.: Research on the application of project portfolio management (PPM), program management (PM) and project management in enterprise strategic management. In: International Conference on Wireless Communications, Networking and Mobile Computing, WiCom (2007)

22. Iamratanakul, S., Shankar, R., Dimmitt, N.J.: Improving project portfolio management with strategic alignment. In: Portland International Conference on Paper presented at the Management of Engineering & Technology, PICMET 2009 (2009)
23. PMI.: The Standard for Portfolio Management, Project Management Institute, In: Filipov, S., Mooi, H., van der Weg, R. 2012: Stratetic Project Portfolio Management an Empirical Investigation, Journal on Innovation and Sustainability (2006)
24. OGC. http://www.p3m3-officialsite.com/P3M3Model/Model_mhtry.aspx
25. Sarbazhosseini, H., Young, M.: Mind the gap: exploring the divergence between PPM software and PPM theory. In: Paper Presented at Australian Institute of Project Management Conference, 7–10 October, Melbourne, Australia (2012)
26. Adikari, S.: Use Experience Modelling for Agile Software Development, Ph.D. thesis, University of Canberra, Australia (2015)
27. Dunne, D., Martin, R.: Design thinking and how it will change management education: an interview and discussion. Acad. Manag. Learn. Educ. 5(4), 512–523 (2006)
28. d.school. http://dschool.stanford.edu/redesigningtheater/the-design-thinking-process/
29. Design Thinking: A Unified Framework for Innovation. http://www.forbes.com/sites/reuvencohen/2014/03/31/design-thinking-a-unified-framework-for-innovation/#6ee66f9d56fc
30. Institute of Design dschool Stanford. https://dschool.stanford.edu/sandbox/groups/designresources/wiki/36873/attachments/74b3d/ModeGuideBOOTCAMP2010L.pdf?sessionID=2f58897684fb982484d0df8fbb73761194ef1158
31. Siebert, U., Alagoz, O., Bayoumi, A.M., Jahn, B., Owens, D.K., Cohen, D.J., Kuntz, K.M.: State-transition modeling a report of the ISPOR-SMDM modeling good research practices task force–3. Med. Decis. Making 32(5), 690–700 (2012)
32. Stringham, T.K., Krueger, W.C., Shaver, P.L.: State and transition modeling: an ecological process approach. J. Range Manag. 56, 106–113 (2003)
33. UML. http://www.uml.org/
34. McDonald, C., Sarbazhosseini, H.: A state transition approach to conceptualising research: the project portfolio management domain. In: Published at 24th Australian Conference on Information Systems, Melbourne (2013)
35. Sarbazhosseini, H., Hart, A.:. Organisational issues involved in project portfolio management in terms of organisational state-transition approach. In: European, Mediterranean & Middle Eastern Conference on Information Systems (EMCIS), Athens, Greece (2015)
36. Sarbazhosseini, H., McDonald, C., Saifullah, D.: An evaluation of organisational state-transition approach in project portfolio management: results from five government cases. In: AIPM National Conference Proceedings, pp. 24–34 (2014)
37. MacQueen, K.M.: Team-based codebook development: structure, process, and agreement. In: Guest, G., MacQueen, K.M. (eds.) Handbook for Team-Based Qualitative Research, pp. 119–135. AltaMira Press, Lanham (2008)
38. Saldaña, J.: The Coding Manual for Qualitative Researchers. Sage Publications Ltd, London (2012)
39. Boyatzis, R.E.: Transforming Qualitative Information: Thematic Analysis and Code Development. Sage Publications, Inc, Thousand Oaks (1998)

Forward Thinking: An Integrated Framework for Formulating Vision, Strategy and Implementation

Narayanan Srinivasaraghavan[1(✉)], Kavitha Gurusamy[1], and Heath Keighran[2]

[1] Australian Public Service, Canberra, ACT, Australia
sangeethaandnarayanan@gmail.com,
Kavitha_rkumar@yahoo.com.au
[2] Business Design, Crooked Fox, Canberra, ACT 2601, Australia
Heath@crookedfox.com.au

Abstract. Predicting and shaping future for better human experience, has been the core aim of design methodologies. Design Thinking aims to integrate human, technology and business factors together to solve problems. Design Thinking is largely focused on the 'now' (current state) and 'short term'. This paper proposes a framework that integrates Design Thinking with a complementary thinking approach called the Futuristic Thinking and Scenario Modelling approach. The proposed framework, when applied covers the end-to-end temporal lifecycle of strategy formulation, current project delivery through to implementation. The approach is necessitated by the need for Design Thinking inputs to be based on a long term vision. The article explores a sample case study based on the proposed approach.

Keywords: Design thinking · Futuristic thinking · Scenario modelling

1 Introduction

1.1 Background

Vision and strategy setting for organizations is a core challenge. This involves assessing the organizational direction in the context of upcoming challenges, including short term and longer term ones. Design Thinking addresses the strategic challenge through human centric experience design and solves problems faced in the short term. However, setting vision and strategy in the context of a longer term challenge, involves futuristic thinking. This article reconciles the two and integrates them.

The article first explores the concepts of design thinking and futuristic thinking and compares them. A reconciled Forward Thinking framework is then proposed and explored through a case study example, to provide benefits for organizations.

© Springer International Publishing Switzerland 2016
A. Marcus (Ed.): DUXU 2016, Part I, LNCS 9746, pp. 141–149, 2016.
DOI: 10.1007/978-3-319-40409-7_15

1.2   Design Thinking

Design thinking is about new ideas. Design Thinking is an effective toolkit for any innovation process, connecting the creative design approach to traditional business thinking, based on planning and problem solving [1]. It integrates human, business, and technological factors in problem forming, solving, and design. Its human-centric methodology integrates expertise from design, social sciences, engineering, and business.

Stanford University Design School [2] outlines a five mode approach to design thinking. (Figs. 1 and 2)

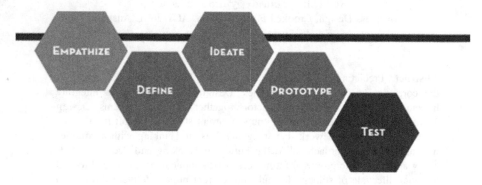

Fig. 1. Design thinking phases [2]

- Empathy mode illustrates the human-centered approach to the overall design process and considers the context, including physical, emotional needs, intent, motivations and environmental considerations that surround [2].
- The goal of the Define mode is to craft a meaningful and actionable problem statement that is formulated through an insightful discovery process [2].
- Ideate is the mode of the design process in which you concentrate on idea generation and innovative solutions that solve problems for the users [2].
- The Prototype mode is the iterative generation of artifacts intended to answer questions that get you closer to your final solution [2].
- The Test mode is when you solicit feedback, about the prototypes you have created, from your users and have another opportunity to gain empathy for the people you are designing for [2].

Design thinking has been heavily used across various domains in industry to produce notable outcomes. Examples: (a) Success of Pepsi Co in using design thinking for improving strategy formulation [3], (b) Kaiser Permanente (a health care organization in the USA) using DT for nursing shift changes to improve patient care [4, 5].

1.3 Futuristic Thinking

While design thinking is focused on identifying problems or requirements at hand, through a human centric approach, futuristic methods aim to predict future in a medium to longer term perspective. Futurology has been defined as the "the scientific study of possible, probable and desirable future developments, the options for shaping them, and their roots in past and present" [6].

According to a futurist practitioner, the future thinking is an iterative process which helps consider a range of possible, probably, and preferable outcomes. It's not predicting the future, but rather taking a structured approach to understanding the potential impacts of today's decisions and actions [7]. Scenario Analysis is one of the leading methods of futuristic thinking methods.

Scenario Analysis methods have been used across various domains of industry. For example, statistical modelling of futuristic scenarios is quite common through sophisticated analytical modelling. Climate change modelling done by International Panel on Climate Change [8] is a widely debated example for this.

A scenario can be defined as a description of a possible future situation, including the path of development leading to that situation. These are generally hypothetical and are intended to highlight central elements of a possible future and to draw attention to key factors [9]. Scenarios help to communicate, generate ideas, generate knowledge about past, present and future and aid as a strategy and decision making tool.

A typical scenario analysis technique goes through following phases [9].

- Identification of the scenario field by establishing the scope of the study.
- Researchers identify key factors that will have strong influence over how future will unfold.
- A range of outcomes are then formulated.
- Based on these a relatively small number of meaningfully distinguishable scenarios are produced
- Application of the finished scenarios for purposes such as strategy assessment.

Scenarios analysis can be for normative or exploratory. They can be either qualitative or quantitative. Scenarios can be judged by their plausibility, internal consistency, comprehensibility and traceability, distinctness and transparency [9].

1.4 Comparison Between Design Thinking and Futuristic Thinking

While reconciling the two concepts of futuristic scenario analysis and design thinking, one could get a view that both have similar intent and purpose, but for the focus on the tenure. Design Thinking focusses on now and problems at hand. While futuristic scenario analysis is aimed at a longer term view. A normative scenario analysis, where the path to a defined future state is worked through, appears as a close cousin of design thinking. An explorative scenario analysis, on the other hand, is more open ended, the results of which are still used for strategy formulation or decision making.

The Design Thinking methodologies have evolved over time and have incorporated prototyping and testing as phases in the pathway. But, in case of a futuristic scenario analysis technique, due to the uncertainties with timeframes and complexities of predicting future, it may not be possible to prototype and test holistic scenarios. The other difference lies on the emphasis on human centric nature of design thinking. This would need to be incorporated into a normative scenario analysis method.

By its very nature, futuristic scenario analysis focusses on an aero-plane view of the problem and may not necessarily incorporate all factors into consideration.

The Table 1 shows the summary of this reconciliation.

Table 1. Design Thinking and Futuristic thinking comparison

No	Factor	Design Thinking	Normative scenario modelling	Exploratory scenario modelling
1.	Tenure	Now to short term	Longer term	Longer term
2.	Outcome	Defined	Defined	Open ended
3.	Human-centric Approach	Uses a Human-centric approach	Not a focus	Not a focus
4.	Level of detail	Detail required to solve the problem	High level birds eye-view	High level birds eye-view
5.	Prototype/Test	Prototype and test asap.	May not be possible	May not be possible
6.	Uses/Applications	Problem solving, Strategy formulation	Strategy Implementation and Decision-making	Strategy formulation and Decision making
7.	Core Method	Thinking and Ideation	Thinking and Ideation	Thinking and Ideation

2 A Reconciled Framework for Vision, Strategy and Problem Solving

It is proposed that by combining both the futuristic thinking and design thinking methods into a single framework and them working in tandem, it is possible for organizations to formulate vision, strategy and solve problems and address the entire end to end temporal life cycle. Organizations have a fundamental interest in their survival and to be the best amongst its peers. A continuous process of strategy formulation, design and implementation is required to achieve this intent, as shown below.

Fig. 2. A Forward Thinking framework

3   A Case Study: Internet of Things and Its Impacts to Public Sector

The Internet of Things (IoT) is an emerging concept that is intended to connect the unconnected [10]. Theoretically, every object could be connected to the internet, via sensors and small computer modules. These objects will be able to collect information, communicate with services that capture and analyses the data and reach decisions autonomously. Gartner [11] estimates 25 Billion objects connected by 2020.

Number of Iota use cases is already in action in society today. For example, household items such as fridges, security alarms, ovens and lights can be connected to the internet and remote management possible through applications on smart phones.

It is estimated that IoE is poised to generate $4.6 trillion in Value at Stake for the public sector over the next decade (compared with $14.4 trillion for the private sector over the same period) [12].

When a need was recognized to formulate strategic and operational directions on IoT for public sector organizations, a framework was required. The span of IoT vision setting and strategy planning ranged from short term to a much longer period of more than 10 years. Future could be abstracted through Scenario Analysis techniques. However, the short term scenarios require much higher level of concreteness, testing and implementation. Design Thinking was found to be suitable, for the 'now' and short-term requirements.

3.1   Forward Thinking Framework

The Forward Thinking framework (Fig. 3) was used to ideate future for short, medium and longer term.

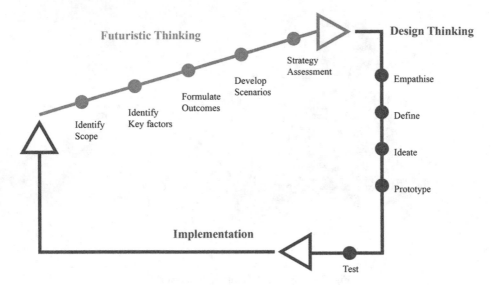

Fig. 3. Forward Thinking framework – with phases

The intent of this case study example with IoT, is only to highlight that it is possible to use the Forward Thinking framework for vision setting, strategy formulation for both longer term and short term requirements. The following case study does not go at length into the actual factors considered, scenarios and details of the plan.

Scope. The implications of Internet of Things to Public Sector organizations have been defined as the scope of this Forward Thinking process.

Key Factors. A literature review shows that significant work has been completed on various scenarios for public sector agencies by number of commercial organizations. Key factors can be gathered based on these and also qualitative research with Subject Matter Experts.

Outcomes. The Public sector organizations have been in existence, since governments. The outcomes expected of public sector organizations remain the same. For example, the mission statement of USA Inland Revenue Service (IRS) remained the same for tens of hundreds of years, as below:

"Provide America's taxpayers top quality service by helping them understand and meet their tax responsibilities and enforce the law with integrity and fairness to all" [13].

This mission is expected to remain the same further into the future, irrespective of IoT and emerging technologies. It was identified that what is important, for IRS, is the contemporary practices are incorporated in achieving this mission statement.

Scenarios. Various scenarios on implications to public sector administrations were formulated. These were largely categorized into following themes.

- Improvements in internal administration of revenue collection
  - Smart Cars
  - Smart buildings
  - Smart Computers
- Improvements to service delivery for public sector clients
  - Fully Automated End to End Interactions for tax and transfer systems
  - Customized Interactions using Big Data Analytics
- Legal implications
  - Law Implications due to IoT and Big Data
  - Privacy and Security Implications for citizens
- Need for client engagement and compliance mechanisms.
  - Data collection using sensors for various government services
  - Proactive engagement through Big Data Analytics
  - Compliance and Law enforcement through Big Data Analytics
- Need for a Technology platform for Internet of Things connectivity

Example scenarios from best practices in other places were included. These best-practices evidences from elsewhere and hence could only be considered for the short-term. Some scenarios considered were as follows:

- South Korea has embarked on a broad program to introduce and lead the world in embedded RFID and USN (ubiquitous sensor network) in manufactured goods [14]
- The company 3 M is marketing a blue tooth enabled digital stethoscope, allow applications to view the heart movement signal and introducing the ability to record, store, manage and analyses an individual's heart beat and compare and pattern match against the other stored heart beats [15].

These sorts of scenarios help the Design team, to look at forwarding scenarios for the public sector.

Strategy Assessment. As part of the strategy assessment process, each of the scenarios were prioritized into specific usable scenarios and prioritized with a tenure (short, medium to long term). For example, based on literature review and expert interviews, the customized interactions using technology platform for IoT, big data analytics and smart buildings were identified as short term scenarios that could be implemented and design process initiated for them.

Design Process. The design process is proposed for short-term scope items, with specific goals created for each of the Agile Program Epics (Epics are large, Program like initiatives that provide business benefits [16]). For example, smart buildings and a Proof of Concept for IoT Technology platform were identified as Epics, to provide benefit to the organization at the same time prepare for the ongoing vision achievement.

Empathise. The human centric nature of the design experience and empathizing with client is a step that would need to happen throughout the design process.

Define. Based on the SAFe framework [16], the outcomes for Program Epics are defined in this phase. The Smart buildings outcomes and IoT Technology Platforms are intended to be defined as Epics at this stage and detailed Agile Release Trains (ART) could be initiated. Features and relevant user stories could be developed for these Epics, as requirements are much more clear for these Epics.

Ideate. A human centric design ideate phase, that looks at the core requirements to come up with ideas and user stories that can be implemented as a prototype is planned at this phase.

Prototype. Prototypes for Smart building ideas and IoT Technology platform Proof of Concept (PoC) are to be developed in this stage.

Test. Testing and validation of the prototype occurs for the identified user-stories. The ultimate aim of the testing is to test whether the original intended outcome is reached.

4 Limitations

While the framework was ideated out of necessity, for understanding the implications of IoT in different temporal life cycles, the framework is still speculative in nature. Full testing of the entire lifecycle needs to be performed to confirm benefits. The framework is a conceptual stage framework only and details require to be enhanced with more guidelines, templates and further testing.

5 Conclusion

This paper presented an over-arching framework based on forward thinking, incorporating Futuristic Thinking, Design Thinking and Implementation (either Agile or Waterfall) concepts in the context of long term potential domain/industry disruptor. This framework contributes to the overall Strategic Planning and Implementation lifecycles of organizations and associated literature.

References

1. Tschimmel, K.: Design thinking as an effective toolkit for innovation. In: Proceedings of the XXIII ISPIM Conference: Action for Innovation: Innovation from experience. Barcelona, pp. 1–20 (2012). ISBN: 978-952-265-243-0
2. An Introduction to Design Thinking Process guide. Stanford University Design School. https://dschool.stanford.edu/sandbox/groups/designresources/wiki/36873/attachments/74b3-d/ModeGuideBOOTCAMP2010L.pdf?sessionID=e29682c7569e583344b123a7116d9172e-65e8531
3. Ignatius, A.: How Indra Nooyi Turned Design Thinking Into Strategy: An Interview with PepsiCo's CEO. Harvard Business Review, September 2015. https://hbr.org/2015/09/how-indra-nooyi-turned-design-thinking-into-strategy
4. Brown, T.: Change By Design – How Design Thinking Transforms Organizations and Inspires Innovation. HarperBusiness, New York (2009)

5. Kaiser Permanente. Kaiser Permanente Innovation consultancy. Kaiser Permanete, http://share.kaiserpermanente.org/article/kaiser-permanentes-innovation-consultancy-featured-in-harvard-business-review/

6. Kreibich.: Handwörterbuch des Marketing. s.l. : Stuttgart:Schaef - fer-Poeschel, 2814–2834 (2007)

7. Cascio, J.: Futures-Thinking-Basics. (2016). http://www.fastcompany.com/1362037/

8. International Panel on Climate Change. IPCC Guidelines for climate change modelling data. http://www.ipcc-data.org/guidelines/dgm_no2_v1_09_2004.pdf

9. Gabner, K.: Methods of Future and Scenario Analysis. https://www.die-gdi.de/uploads/media/Studies_39.2008.pdf

10. Internet of Things Council. Internet of Things. http://www.theinternetofthings.eu/

11. Gartner. Digital Business' Reports. http://www.gartner.com/technology/research/digital-business/

12. Cisco. IOE Public sector white paper. http://internetofeverything.cisco.com/sites/default/files/docs/en/ioe_public_sector_vas_white%20paper_121913final.pdf

13. Inland Revenue Service, IRS. https://www.irs.gov/uac/The-Agency,-its-Mission-and-Statutory-Authority

14. National IT Industry Promotion Agency. ICT Promotion policy and R & D in Korea. AOS Korea. https://www.itu.int/osg/spu/ni/ubiquitous/Presentations/2_oh_RFID.pdf

15. M. Littmann. 3 M Littmann Telescopes. http://www.littmann.com/wps/portal/3M/en_US/3M-Littmann/stethoscope/telemedicine/

16. Scaled Agile. SAFe 4.0 for Lean software and systems engineering. www.scaledagileframework.com/

The Epidemiology of Innovation

Tim Stock[1,2(✉)]

[1] scenarioDNA, New York, USA
timstock@scenariodna.com
[2] Parsons School of Design, New York, USA
stockt@newschool.edu

Abstract. To better match the complex challenges innovation presents, it is critical to consider an approach and methodology more akin to epidemiology – a method that accounts for the full picture of how trends in culture are evolving. A process rich with layers. One that recognizes often overlooked triggers to new behaviors. One that is exploratory, yet grounded by real data and structured by cultural parameters. An approach that unites consumer anthropology with data science.

Keywords: Anthropology and ethnography · Branding · Design thinking, Design philosophy, and Design patterns · Marketing · Semiotics: sign/symbol/icon design · Data science

1 That's Funny…

Scan the headlines of business journals and you might believe everyone is deeply invested in a transformative and dynamic long view of the markets they serve. The measure of a great company today is how innovative it is. Over $650 billion is spent on innovation efforts globally. But what do we really mean when we use this term? The efforts do not reflect the outcome. Scratch the surface of research and a dismal picture emerges. A recent McKinsey poll revealed that 94 % of managers are dissatisfied with their company's innovation performance [1]. One of the key factors appears to be a persistent corporate mindset that rewards conclusions over evolving intelligence.

Technology has fundamentally transformed how trends and product adoption work. In order to be innovative, innovation requires the cultivation of inductive practices over deductive practices. Practices that encourage risk and experimentation in a framework of ongoing nuanced insight into how the complex markets are processing the world around them. As Isaac Asimov put it: *"The most exciting phrase to hear in science, the one that heralds new discoveries, is not 'Eureka!' but 'That's funny…'"* [2]. This is the framework we need to embrace if we are to tackle the complex challenges of 21st century markets. Our pursuit of innovation needs to embrace the *process of uncovering knowledge* more than *confirming what we think we might know*. There is a unique complexity and speed to how markets function today. The people are way ahead of our traditional research practices.

© Springer International Publishing Switzerland 2016
A. Marcus (Ed.): DUXU 2016, Part I, LNCS 9746, pp. 150–160, 2016.
DOI: 10.1007/978-3-319-40409-7_16

2 An Epidemiological Approach

To better match the complex challenges that innovation presents, it is critical to consider an approach and methodology more akin to epidemiology – a method that accounts for the full picture of how trends in culture are evolving. A process rich with layers that unfold over time. One that recognizes often overlooked triggers to new behaviors. Processes can be exploratory, yet simultaneously be grounded by real data and structured by cultural parameters. The ideal approach unites consumer anthropology with data science. Why? Because we need the human in the picture, and our own biases out of the frame. Innovation stagnates when our understanding of how the world works gets stuck in ineffective models of insight.

Without the guidance of culture, it is easy to get lost in the influx of information. And without a meaningful measurement of this flow of important cultural data, we will miss the next transformative idea. W. Lee Howell of World Economic Forum writes *"Over the past three decades, value creation has shifted from the efficient production of goods and services globally to generating greater shareholder returns financially – both approaches are proving to be outdated and unsustainable. Today long-term success rests on two pillars: Creativity and Society"* [3]. Today, people shape our products more than our products shape our people. It is the serendipity found in the human shaping that needs to be captured.

3 The Challenges of Hidden Biases

A great quote from Michael Lewis's book *The Big Short* is "Truth is like poetry. And most people fucking hate poetry" [4]. The true value of insight is only as strong as the actionable truth it empowers. The reality is that truth becomes dangerous when organizations do not have the materials and techniques to execute on that truth. This is typically where bias slips in. We begin to see the insight as consisting of stuff we currently understand and know how to implement. It simplifies our task and makes our goals concrete. Unfortunately, our insight then becomes a reflection of our current state of literacy rather than a way to challenge and expand that literacy. Equally worse is when we invest heavily in a new idea without any ongoing validation. Bubbles are a product of bias. Our approach to research must encourage an *always on* and *always connected* mode of engagement. Lest we throw the proverbial baby out with the bathwater.

These biases are a cognitive deficit. We assume we know. Or if we see something we don't know we block it out. The greatest obstacle of innovation is how these biases keep our cycle of ideas in a loop of existing preconceptions. That cascade of assumptions infects the ideation process and stagnates transformative ideas. Confirmation bias and the bandwagon effect can pollute the process of innovation in different ways. Both in curbing the application of new ideas as well as blindly supporting ideas that we become convinced in groupthink are innovative. The true test of innovation must always be made in relationship with the social and cultural context. Our methods should help us see what is actually working in culture. It should train the process in an inductive visual literacy that curbs quick conclusions and keeps the ideation in sync with nuances and fluctuations as they evolve.

The potential for bias increases as the size of the data increases, like a large pool of nothingness that we are burdened to make sense of. A key feature of epidemiology is measurement in relation to a population at risk. Not the entire population. And so this follows suit with tracking trends that drive innovation. In order to see where human desire might take us next, a smaller tighter universe must be decided upon. Innovation can thrive if we are better tuned to these small early signals and are able to track how they migrate and adapt over time. If the universe is too broad, the trends that seemingly appear are vague and meaningless. In such cases, what presents itself as trend is the lowest common denominator of ideas. Those kind of ideas thrive only within the confines of our existing vocabulary. This does not lead to innovation. It leads to more stuff, but never propels forward thinking.

Studying smaller groups of people and being able to extract important insights is the foundation of effective epidemiology. We don't cure disease by sampling the entire population. We find cures by being able to see the parts of the population that are behaving in unique ways. We can then use methods to extrapolate that insight into what it means in relation to the whole population. It is a systems thinking approach to how things play out in the world. Similarly to understand an emerging trend you must be able to tune your research to find the signals that are only visible in a smaller part of the population but will be impacting the overall population in time.

4   A System and Method of Culture Mapping

We developed a semiotic methodology called Culture Mapping to make the nuanced and evolving dynamics of culture easier to track and pattern. We first used this method as part of our ethnographies to structure linguistic patterns in the data gathered in field work. We wondered what if we added new technologies such as natural language processing and machine learning to transform the consulting method into a scalable software tool. This has resulted in a patented method of cultural analysis that feeds

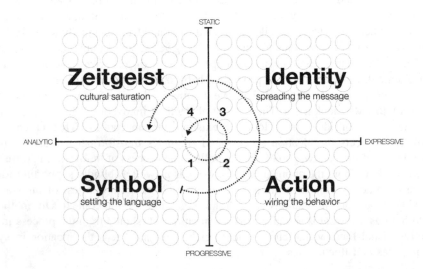

software that allows us to track emerging signals and patterns over time [5]. It has become a tool that works alongside the creative process to keep ideas grounded in how culture might respond. Much like how human populations respond to new vaccines.

5 Visualizing and Patterning Cultural Data

We developed Culture Mapping into a patented semiotic algorithm for analyzing the patterns and migration of culture and trends. The result is a functioning API that collects and structures semiotic data from both open and closed data sources. This semiotic data consists of the signs and symbols put out into the world (online and offline), knowingly or not, by human beings. These signs are both words and images. And they come from diverse sources of both closed and open data. A closed data set could be books, magazines, songs and fanzines. Open data would be social media and other linguistic corpora. They all can be processed for key cultural signifiers using systems of natural language processing informed by analysts with expertise in unique subject matter areas.

It's a balance from human to machine and back again. Our algorithms, based on our matrix structure, are intended to learn from the data collected, and query back to us. The process is akin to gardening. Cultivating and propagating to understand the relationship between unique strains. The process is repeatable and scalable. Is it an empirical technique? Is it quant? It's a new gray area. We are quantifying language by plotting cultural language at data points. The task is not categorically sorting, but truly mapping the coordinates of cultural signs and symbols. Once we map and visualize the data, we can step back from it and begin to analyze and consider connections. This mapping keeps the creative process engaged in signals as they emerge and migrate over time. We become invested in a living system that we are designing to. This method affords us a way to shape our empathy to consider a variety of potential scenarios that may arise from the products and services we design. We can confidently consider a segmentation that is grounded in the reality and patterns of culture.

Current methods of data analysis are flawed because they allow bias to enter unexpectedly. It happens because we are too quick to look for finality in the data. When we look at information in pie-charts and table graphs these visualizations impose an implied conclusion to the analysis. We think if it looks right, it must be right. It is only human to seek a single clear action from the information. But we need to build confidence in thinking deeper. The data masks the physics that shape these recorded outcomes. Methods such as sentiment analysis over-simplify the results to a binary of positive or negative and is recorded only if the signal becomes loud enough. These loud signals are muddied with cultural noise that is not taken enough into account. If we are not considering the triggers of the response, we are not considering the empirical truth of the data at all. Our methods must help us stay engaged with the data in creative ways. Our methods must help us be brave in our quest for innovation.

When visualizations gloss over important nuances that might lead to critical behavioral shifts, we all lose. It leads to findings that are impossible to integrate into the creative side of the innovation process. It leaves no room for inspiration. It dictates.

Potential viability of product is interwoven with potential desirability of product. The only way of seeing that vision is to use a cognitive framework. We need our insight into culture to be fused with our way of imagining and making new things. As we create, we must be able to connect ideas to a living and evolving system that contours future potential.

Visualizing expressive linguistic data offers an inductive process of mapping cultural patterns, migrations and evolution across genres. This inductive process is what separates semiotic thinking from design thinking, which follows a more deductive approach. Whereas design thinking lands on a new concept, semiotic thinking allows clients to see the cultural system unfold over time. Our empathy drives great ideas, but it cannot live in isolation. Ideas must stay connected to the way culture continuously works through its cognitive frameworks. The reality is that the successful products we design are made in the minds of the culture that consumes them. That consumption constantly adapts and integrates what is made, the way a human being sees as appropriate. That is the necessary living state of innovation, and our technology has to synchronize with that reality. Our ability to pattern the linguistic parts of the whole will better assure that products and ideas have long term health in the culture they seek to impact.

6   Connecting with the Human Genome

Seeing synergy, tension, diversity and void gives us places to start asking questions, probe and think: "What don't we know?," "What might happen next?" and "Why?" We need to get to the point where we know all that we could. The goal of a visualization should be to flush out and conjure up all the things in our power to know. The ability to see how meaning is being created, cultivated and shared over time. We must cultivate an approach that allows to see the system of culture. We have to get the nuances of the humane genome onto our radar as they evolve, adapt and mutate over time and under changing conditions.

Our implementation of effective and sustainable innovation requires that we deepen our understanding of these cultural signals to empathize opportunities and anticipate evolving conditions. The context of human events determines how stories develop. Culture emerges as reinforcement of ideology. Our cultural traits, values, and beliefs are different and diverse. That is the power of human beings. Our constant expressive ability in making our world is powerful and not to be underestimated. We shape the culture of our world. That is incredible.

Everything we consume is rooted in a system of meaning creation. The choices we make are connected to a network of language that we tap into cognitively to make decisions for ourselves and other people we are responsible for. That first time we purchase a product is predetermined by information we have been subconsciously collecting that makes it permissible. We tap into meaning already cultivated by social networks engaged more intimately in the symbolic value of these attributes. The same brand attribute has unique meaning depending on the context shaping that meaning. We can see that unique expression of meaning in context and understand more clearly how motivation and behavior are linked. The same signifier may imply personal knowledge to some while to others it implies its value as social currency.

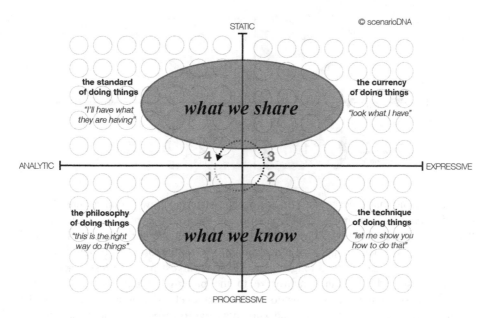

By structuring the language of the products we consume we can see two key patterns that shape the evolution of meaning. First, the networks that shape *what we know*. These networks determine *the philosophy of doing things* as well as *the techniques of doing things*. It is the symbolic starting point of all product attributes. The right way of doing things is a cultural response in opposition to currently accepted methods of production that have become diluted of their original meaning. A pattern of dissent that emerges to resolve the weakness of the meaning as it is more broadly adopted. This process of dissent and creation of new symbolic value moves through culture and eventually reaches a tipping point of adoption where the symbolic becomes the new badge of social currency. The hipster moment for all things is the moment of broader adoption. And it is important to note the cycle moves faster and faster the more connected the consumers are. The moment of *being cool* is fleeting. It's the time for companies to start prepping for decline and oversaturation, not latch on to more of the same.

Consider, luxury. Concepts such as luxury require a cultural context of what we value as indulgent. However, for its symbolic meaning to be further cultivated and integrated into the cultural genome it must be wired to the cultivation of technique. The symbolic needs to be made physical. Indulgence needs to demonstrate its physical state of being. An expressive extension of that philosophical starting point. Then it can manifest as a physical and emotional experience, encompassing everything from sources of materials to techniques of making. The expressed language of these cultural narratives serves to wire the value of the new language as repeated and ritualized behavior. We can't frame something like luxury unless there is a symbolic root of cultural meaning. That root begins long before the market consumes and shares more broadly the product attributes. And the knowledge must be first understood culturally through smaller tighter networks before social sharing can work effectively.

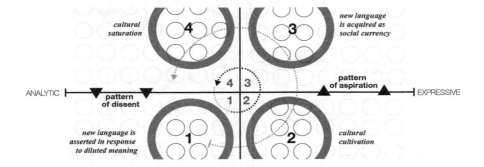

The patterns that emerge are critical to understanding how social groups directly shape the product's meaning. These patterns are the living experience of the design attributes of the products we develop. Recognizing that phenomenon can help feed incremental investment in layers of innovation. Some with short-term benefit and other that must be cultivated over a longer term. How we invest must be less reactive and more responsive. If we can synchronize to the patterns of culture we can better encourage an ongoing state of innovation at different levels. The organization should be picking up on the smallest signals and knowing how to respond to those patterns.

7   Diversity Is Critical

A lack of diversity is the enemy of innovation. If you want to increase the creative potential of your innovation efforts it is important to understand how diversity works as a critical ingredient. That diversity includes not only how we gain the knowledge and insight for product innovation, but also the mindfulness of keeping a healthy diversity in the markets we serve. In the natural world, genetic diversity holds the key to the ability of populations and species to persist over evolutionary time through changing environments. Homogeneity weakens us. It's foolhardy to be homogenous. The simple process of interacting with people who are different forces us to prepare and adapt better for what comes next.

Markets share these same conditions. Markets become weak from lack of diversity. We recognize the signals of this commoditization too late as existing methods of tracking dilution often register only once the information cascade has caught critical mass. A better method of tracking is to be able to visualize the signifiers that emerge in response to the over saturation. There is a built-in cultural mechanism that resists this dilution. Seeing this as a living system of language can have a powerful impact on how ideas emerge and are propagated within the company.

Critical themes emerge when we begin to track the narrative of products. It makes the importance of sustainability more obvious. We can see the ways short-term techniques can actually erode the system of meaning currently working in culture and work against long-term goals of the company and society. Our idea that once we find something working well in a market, we invest our attention to moving everyone to that way of seeing things. The imperialist point of view. The reality is that there is a built in trigger to dilution of meaning. Once certain product attributes are overtly marketed, they immediately begin to lose their original value. Like a cultural immune system to uniformity.

Patterns of aspiration and dissent are in constant motion. We can see as language migrates that meaning changes and that change becomes a good indicator of future sustainability. The fact is that sustainability is dependent on seeing this pattern of meaning adoption so as to understand how erosion of meaning will manifest and what language emerges to inoculate the cultural system in response to the dilution. Companies are faced with upsetting the continuity when confronted with mandates for innovation. Seeing the pattern of dilution early can help us invest in innovation platforms that integrate gradually and help evolve the DNA of existing methods and techniques.

8 A Living Research Framework for Innovation

Our goal should be to create a living prototype of innovation platforms. The process of ideation should continue as products and services are introduced into the marketplace. The way we develop new platforms must leave room for ongoing adaptation. It should not end from project to project, quarter to quarter. Different clusters will hone unique attributes of the product through their own social mechanism of kinship. Archetypes emerge as models of perception and behavior can be structured according to the language. These archetypes establish the parameters for the future state of our product. Visualizing that process helps translate the specific action the organization can take in the form of innovation platforms.

When we conduct ethnography, we seek a picture of what is going on. The problem is that the structure of that research is often only a snapshot. Living archetypes, on the other hand, serve as physical manifestations of taxonomies. We can dynamically riff off of them. We can conduct field research and match the signifiers in research to ongoing

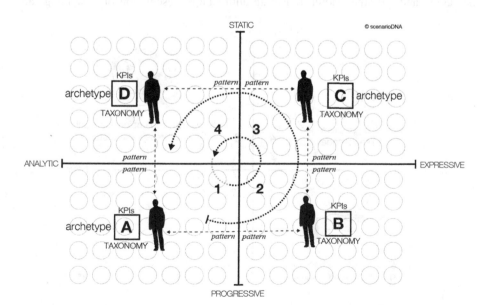

tracking of how these archetypes continue to evolve past the point of the fieldwork. We can correlate fieldwork to open data sources and other cultural corpora. This elevates fieldwork to a new plateau to see more nuance in how ritual and behavior is working and probe on elements that we can see from other data we are collecting simultaneously.

9   Developing a Practice of Synchronized Innovation

In the case of a global food and beverage company, culture mapping helped visualize how consumer knowledge of certain product attributes was evolving. The critical benefit is to understand how each attribute works at different levels of resonance. Some are more pronounced and obvious in the cultural chatter, others are still taking shape in the context of evolving social phenomenon. Shaping a sustainable food portfolio requires working on a number of different levels the same time. Solidifying existing authenticity while also investing early in new ways of doing things so these new methods integrate and continue to evolve believably as an expression of the organization. An example of this would be to begin using language such as organic without investing in what that means as a ongoing cultural discourse tested by parts of the social organism.

The standard trendspotting approach is to scan for new signals and work to integrate those that are working into the product, to cosmetically badge a new language on top of the existing product rather than grow new authentic value. This does little for the sustainable meaning of the portfolio. It also accelerates the dilution by commoditizing its meaning. The system of culture immediately begins to work to inoculate against such manufactured authenticity. Every piece of language from packaging to product to messaging and narrative should reflect an authentic representation of how things are

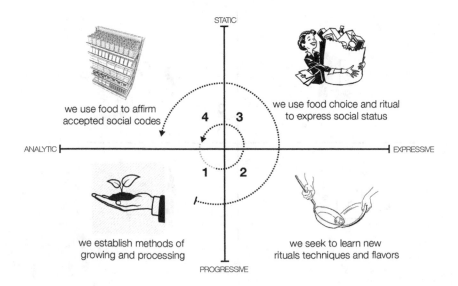

made and done by the brand. Consumer shift to local producers is a signal of the expectation for that transparency. Localism is a cultural system response to the mistrust of commoditization. Innovation platforms have the opportunity to engage culturally with consumers at every point in the value chain. Understanding how that cultural exchange works will make the connection both authentic as well as an ongoing learning opportunity for the brand. The cultural response can help us tune platforms as they evolve in their integration with the company.

Visualizing the way product attributes are being cognitively processed in the context of culture helps the company invest in smaller details that have much greater impact. When we can see these emerging signals in the context of a broader system, it helps bolster investment in nascent areas for the category. Being first is good. Being first with a vision for how that can evolve and change over time is real innovation. We should assume there are different levels of engagement going on in the culture that consumes our product. What we want is symbiotic relationship with investment that makes for healthier and sustainable brands.

If you look at the evolution of organic over the last ten years, we can see that organic had been a food subculture for decades as industrial methods were subsidized by government programs. Our supermarket shelves were reflections of an affirmation of this cultural zeitgeist. To a consumer, organic before the 1980s would be subversive. But as organic methods are wired into recipes, cookbooks, food co-ops and restaurants, organic becomes the cultural elixir for currently imposed concepts of what food means. As yuppies seek new consumption to demonstrate social currency, these subculture rituals get picked up and recast as badge. We see organic taking over more than 80 % of supermarket shelves today. This story evolved over time. And with the wide acceptance of organic as cultural zeitgeist today, there is new language being formed in dissent of that dilution. Organic becomes meaningless to the subcultures that formed its original value. They now move further to deepen the symbolic value in response to the co-option and dilution. It is a genetic process of counteracting cultural homogeneity. We see new language like "raw" and "biodynamic" emerge as a response to the broader adoption of organic throughout the population.

10   Global Diversity as Engine for Sustainable Health

Another example of culture mapping's practical value is looking at how brand value evolves from region to region. The assumption is that if a product is doing well in one country that we simply need to build awareness to make it work similarly in a new market. This does not hold true. Innovation is served by reframing our approach to be more in tune with the unique dynamics of the new market and pattern those attributes to how perception is uniquely evolving there. If we force the new product, it may appear stable, but under the surface it is eroding the sustainability of its value. We don't see this erosion unless we are tuned to these patterns. These new markets can also have immense value beyond their own borders in developing new narrative strains. Our approach should recognize each market's unique value in helping more mature markets regain health. Again, the goal should be a diverse system of healthy sustainability.

11   Conclusion

Change is inevitable. The question is what we do about it along the way. Our participation in the world must evolve to sustain and cultivate the kinds of change that will help us. Conversely, we must also catch the kinds of change that will undermine our long-term health. The hardest part of this evolution is to recognize innovative as learning more than knowing. If we can open ourselves to this new literacy, we can help shape a truly dynamic and participatory relationship to innovation.

References

1. McKinsey & Company 2014
2. Wainer, H.: Chapter 3: That's Funny. Medical Illuminations: Using Evidence, Visualization, and Statistical Thinking to Improve Healthcare, 1st edn., pp. 50–57. Oxford University Press, Oxford (2014). Print
3. Howell, L.: What Does Innovation Mean in Today's World? Agenda. World Economic Forum, 15 March 2014. Web
4. Lewis, M.: The Big Short: Inside the Doomsday Machine. W.W. Norton, New York (2010). Print
5. Timothy J., Stock, M.L.: System and Method for Culture Mapping. ScenarioDNA, assignee. Patent 9002755. 7 April 2015. Print

User Interface and Interaction Design in Future Auto-Mobility

Hendrik Wahl[1](✉) and Rainer Groh[2]

[1] American University in Dubai, Dubai, United Arab Emirates
hendrik@optio-n.com
[2] Technische Universität Dresden, Dresden, Germany
rainer.groh@tu-dresden.de

Abstract. This paper focuses tendencies and developments in HMI design in regard of automotive and human mobility in general. By providing two perspectives, one design theoretical oriented one system development related, we want to contribute to a systematic mapping this particular field of Human Machine Interaction.

Keywords: User Interface Design · Auto-Mobility · Human-Machine-Interaction · Layer-Like Boundary · Individual transportation · Dashboard · Adventure of driving · Augmentation · Manual gear shifting · Automotive "toys" · Targeted to a smaller group of enthusiast · 3D look · Tracking · Gesture based interaction

1 Context and Tendencies

Considering the term interface today, evokes the idea of a layer-like-boundary between areas governed by varying principals. Supplemented with the image of the iconic wipe on the ultra smooth surface of a touchscreen, the leading metaphor of the interface becomes condensed in a planner stratification, orthogonal oriented to the direction the interaction is pervading it. Relating this Information-Industrial-Age concept to user interfaces within contemporary cars evokes a contradiction. Identifying steering-wheel, gearstick, levers, pedals, various types of switches and analog gauges as the location where the Human-Machine-Interaction takes places while driving, renders this setup in an odd picture. Asking further about the interaction basically needed to achieve a satisfactory performance in the vast majority of individual transportation tasks (e.g. the daily drive to work and back home) reveals at once, how obsolete actually this setup is and how more interesting the resilience of the design concepts applied to individual mobility today. Simply the facts: that after a century of automotive development no consensus about the best position of the steering wheel (left over right) could be achieved, that the dashboards are still dominated by circular analog gauges (physical or nowadays even more bewildering as screen-graphics) insinuates, how retrogressively and sentimentality are about to suppress substantial innovation in this domain. Providing an USB-port underneath the dashboard, a touchscreen operated navigation or a homelike entrainment system does not contribute to a forward oriented mindset ether.

© Springer International Publishing Switzerland 2016
A. Marcus (Ed.): DUXU 2016, Part I, LNCS 9746, pp. 161–171, 2016.
DOI: 10.1007/978-3-319-40409-7_17

Actually at this edge, where two generations, two doctrine in User Interface Design meet each other, the underlying dilemma becomes even more evident.

The following explanation is based on the outcome of a summer school conducted 2015 at the Technische Universität Dresden (TUD, Faculties of Mechanical Science and Engineering and Computer Science) in cooperation with the American University in Dubai (AUD, Department of Visual Communication). The summer school was supported by AUDI AG.

2   Methodical Approach

Originating from this position we want to conduct deliberations about varying aspects of User Interface and Interaction Design in regard to future mobility and transportation. By creating distinctions along boundaries defined: by objective needs in individual and commercial mobility, by emotional and esteem correlated facets of the Auto, by the disintegration of monolithic design paradigms, by modern tendencies in urban design and sustainable thinking, by implications due to fundamental changes in the industrial production to come and more aspects, we want to create a framework where in a variety of approaches can be related each other in order to gain momentum for demand driven thinking and innovation.

2.1   Analysis 1

The fist distinction we want to undertake focuses the actual motivation of mobility and driving. Recalling the contemporary claims the automotive industry uses to emphasise their core values e.g. BMW: "Freude am Fahren" / "Enjoying Driving", Audi: "Vorsprung durch Technik" / "Advantage through Technology", Mercedes Benz: "Das Beste oder nichts" / "The Best or Nothing", VW: "Das Auto"/"The Auto" it becomes conspicuous, that nothing of this is a need related argument. Refereeing to American or Asian automotive bands from Chrysler over Tesla to Kia Motors no claims at all are used, Lamborghini (belonging to Audi) on the other side talks about "Enjoyable Technology". If we wouldn't know it better, the automotive industry under the aspects could be seen as a peripheral matter, meant to content ephemera desires of a smaller peer-group of enthusiasts and not as a major factor in national economies. The ambiance which is to perceive through this wording appears to be from the very past, when driving a car was an adventure, which only could be mastered by having the best possible equipment, when the advantage through technology was a essential e.g. round the globe by car as Clärenore Stinnes did in 1927/29.

Thinking about key technologies today, engineering only becomes eminent, when the iPhone tends to bend in the back pocket or when a product cycle is about to end, in order to prevent buying an outdated model. We expect contemporary technology just to work and if it crashes we want to be able to solve the problem with a reboot not with a wrench or a wrecker. This difference in the appreciation of technology becoming evident here helps us to understand why the HMI's in the automotive sector are still so strongly committed to the past. Yes, to drive on an empty mountain-road in Haute-Savoie, in an autumnal forest is an experience, which hardly can be exceeded by anything else and it is legit to have such a paradigm in mind while thinking about user interfaces in the automotive domain. This backdrop of course delivers sentimentality at it's best, if any possible one would like to drive this scenario in a classic Gran Turismo car, chrome rimmed instruments, veneers from most precious woods, hand stitched upholstery form noblest Italian lather, manual gear shifting … a scenic route during the blue hour before sunset. But while this metaphors echoing away, I'm almost afraid to say, this is barely the situation what Automobile User Interfaces are made for. They are or they should be designed to help people to master their tasks under worst case conditions such as a rain covered highway, jammed with commuter traffic or driving under time pressure in a convoy while a snowstorm hits the road.

Comparing the HMI's of ordinary private owned automobiles with trucks, forklifts, and busses, with vehicles where the driver-seat is considered to be a working area - the situation becomes significantly different. Here it is much more likely to encounter more contemporary user interfaces (touch-screens, communication and observation devices) meant to help the driver in a sublime manner to do the job. This situation gives us cause draw the first line to map the cosmos of Automotive Interaction Design. By separating the concept of the workplace from experience-oriented design, the widespread conviction in automotive marketing, that the customer would not accept more contemporary solutions in HMI Design is forfeiting its paradigmatic charter. Moreover it becomes clear on one side, that this reminiscence centred approach gets even more emphasised in regard to the domain of expensive automotive "toys", targeted to a smaller group of enthusiasts who are able and willing to spend "comprehensive" expenses. On the other hand it becomes evident, that this doctrine is not universal and does not suit the contemporary appreciation of technology in general. Yes, to create a screen-graphic of a tacho- or rev-meter in a circular layout is au fond nothing to criticise. It is obvious, that depicting a rotation related value in a circular form helps to establish a sublime dispatching [1], helping the person in front of the instrument to interact highly efficiently due to a subconscious cohesion. But actually why do digital gauges need to have a 3D look, why it seems to be necessary to ad drop-shadows, highlights and reflections to create a "realistic" look, despite all the efforts done in the past to suppress precise this kind of distractive influences form the automotive HMI's?

2.2 Analysis 2

But this is not the main direction this article is aiming to. After distinguishing the experience form workspace related domain in automotive HMI-Design we now can go the next step in mapping this territory. Seeing the drivers seat as a workstation and understanding the efforts in HMI-Design done her as mostly need driven, as aiming to provide the best possible interaction between human and technology, while waiving unnecessary narratives and connotations we can extrapolate this thoughts further.

This will lead us to the glass-cockpits, head up and helmet mounted displays, pragmatic for military and increasingly also in commercial aviation. Here the basic concept is to understand the human as the supervising instance, controlling and managing complex streams of varying information. The human as seen an Inter-agent, is part of an highly integrated system, working together with air traffic control, weather forecast, ground handling and so on. Despite it being probably possible to operate the commercial air traffic fully automatically, the human factor still matters here. Not at first for sentimental reasons, but in order to sustain mastership upon technical installations (whether and how to adhere this concepts is apparently more a cultural problem then a question of HMI-Design). Turning the attention further to the field of military aviation we are confronted with a much more serious situation. Flying an airplane into hostile air-space is without question a highly risky undertaking for the pilot. Within the economics of war therefor it is apparently reasonable to separate the pilot from the warhead. Instead of equipping the airplanes with armour plating, life supporting systems and emergency equipment to increasing the pilot's survival odds and in the light of the performance provide by contemporary information technology, the use of the UAV, seems to be increasingly the mean of choice in modern air combat. Although we should denial the application of violence in any means, the example leads us further. By establishing a remote-relation between the human being and the area were the actual mobility takes place another distinction can be made.

2.3   Analysis

By dividing the field of commercial mobility into one which is related to transportation and delivery of goods and payloads and one other oriented to the mobility of persons we can describe another differentia specifica, helping us organising our thoughts more. Thinking the transportation of materials one step forward gives cause to sees this as a entire system of remote operating trains, trucks, parcel delivers and drones. All of these units will be supervised by a smaller group of traffic managers, using standardised stationary computers interfaces. None of the mobile units will be equipped with any individual user-interface meant to serve a driver, pilot or a captain. But of course, at least in the first instance HMI's used wile service and maintenance will give need for related design solutions. Thinking the next step in this direction, we will have to question the need of transported goods itself. Extrapolating the progress of the Internet of Things and the Maker Culture leads us to a thought experiment, wherein all or at least most of the things needed (e.g. furniture, foot or action hero figures) can be made at home or at a "Making-Centre" in the vicinity of the actual living place. In conjunct with the tendency of urbanisation, the incasing desire of the human beings to live in cities, now only blueprints, schematics and assembly instructions need to be transmitted by already to day existing, largely proven technology. Using recyclable filaments and renewable energy in the "Making-Process" - a new level of a sustainable society can be achieved, counteracting the threat the humans civilisation is exposing to our planet right now.

Thinking about the mobility of persons under the paradigm of business needs delivers in the first instance a similar picture of a highly diversified public transport system. Only the "payload" is less predictable, needs much more attention and safety precautions and is able to move shorter distances autonomous, seen from a system overlooking point of view. Due to presence of human beings with in the system the scope of needs and possibilities in HMI-Design is of course much wider. People who need to spend time in travel and whom attention is not drained by dealing with stressful driving situation are interested in accessing entrainment and communication networks using various types of interfaces (cellphone, tablets, AR-Devices, holograms…). Whereby the spectrum of ideas can range for an individual solitude providing media-cocoon to wall covering digital signage and further.

Thinking the second stage of peoples need driven transportation delivers a picture, which renders the paradigm of mobility as imperative to meet the needs of the post industrial job market as going astray. Looking along the axis constituted by the development of telecommunication and telepresence systems shows how rapidly the things are about to change in this domain. Was video telephony in the past (as we can see in respective Si-Fi-movies) only revered to a very elite of global leaders and only worthy to be used in the instance of e.g. Godzilla doing weird things with styrofoam buildings in Japan, a world without Skype, FaceTime and co. today would deliver much more serious problems. How would my mother be able to finish the puzzle in the newspaper without asking me over 3 timezones distance for help?

Relating this to the needs of peoples future mobility, it becomes clear, that people who are flying half around the globe, just to attend a business meeting are less to admire, possessing less prestige then those who get the same task done without leaving the building. So, thinking the aspects to the extend; an end or a serious decent of need driven travel and transportation is to be on the cards. But how does this match with the numbers provided by the IATA, expecting a annual grow of passengers of 5.3 % [6]?

3   First Summary

Indeed, mobility is apparently for the most of us more than moving from A to B in order to achieve the thing that needs to be done. The human being is and has forever been on a journey, urged to approach the world out there and speed is a appropriate means in doing so. From Exploring the vicinity of the cave to the moons of saturn and beyond - our curiosity compels us at first to a movement within a simultaneous existence of the spatial extend and only then by assigning the concept of duration to an intellectual journey into the mind [2].

Opposite this egocentric first person point of view we need to recognise, that the extended world is about to shrink due to our obsession with speed and mobility. Since continents are only hours apart from each other the space in-between becomes congested with air traffic - in the same manner our urban environments are getting obstructed by automobility. But in comparison to the public transportation in the air the system of individual mobility on the ground operates even more far below its optimum. Considering the fact, that the wast majority of the private owned cars (this ones with the most sentimental HMI's) are only in use for a fraction of the day and if used then almost in the same time (generating rush hour traffic jam), while otherwise occupying extended parking lots; makes it eminent to rethink this situation on a systemic level. Doing this reveals the digressiveness of the idea of growing numbers, which was and still is paradigmatic for the industrial age and leads our attention to smarter solutions.

In the domain of individuals mobility this can only mean to develop an system of autonomous cabins, instantly accessible by a smartphone app, able to reach any location during an optimal timespan. This will lead to a much more optimised situation, requesting less resources, space, energy and a drivers attention. The only argument against this, might be the esteem and prestige related idea of having an individual environment while traveling (from precious woods or in carbon fibre optic). Reconsidering the contemporary resilience of major players automotive industry against progressive, need oriented developments (thinking about the diesel emission scandal) it becomes clear, that this is last line of defence in order obtain outdated structures. Thinking forward, it would be easy to develop a scenario where the interior of the autonomous cabin, the human oriented side of this technology can be designed to be a multimodal interface, the coauthor of the article is researching on. Having a individual mobility system, which operates accordantly contemporary paradigms in regard to technology, the hardware of the multimodal interface can be also separated from the individual demands of the passenger, who can create or purchase her/his individual user experience and submit this to the system with the same device she or he orders the cabin to the desired location, using the mobile phone.

4   Practical Approach

Following this philosophical introduction the question of practical and methodical consequences must be asked. For answering this question a look at the history of human machine interaction (HMI) might be useful, cause new concepts of designing and planning are based on specific tools. The term tool covers a wide range of meaning: Tools can be understood as software products as well as classical physical objects. In case of interacting with computer systems an interface is the general tool. The interface is placed between reality (R) and user (U), who wants to change his relationship with reality. This user-reality relation changes throughout technical history in terms of space and time depending on the tools used. The following graphic overview (see Fig. 1) shows the changing relation.

The development of HMI is performed in four steps. In the pre-industrial age the user is physical coupled to reality. Tools are just extensions of human physical possibilities and are handled in a direct way (e.g. on a bogie). In the age of industrialization the user is decoupled from energetic aspects of the machine (R). He is now free for control tasks by gear lever, button or signalling element. In the computer age user gains a large autarchy in space and time. He changes reality via the computer in indirect ways. The interface (understood as an interactive image, GUI) currently represents the reality (e.g. with a dashboard). Presently great efforts are made to control the created data flood. The domination of the visual moment turns out to be a problem. Therefor planar representations based on a static and one-eyed user, developed as standards and cultural techniques. The user's dynamic and body-based potential lies unaddressed. His inhered space-time behavior is not relevant.

This leads to deformation. McLuhan (cited by Culcin) notes: "We become what we behold. We shape our tools and then our tools shape us." [3] The new subject area »Behavior Design« promises support. A special design of interfaces is intended to change, develop or optimize the user's behavior, respectively behavior patterns. This method is based on a limited term of behavior, which is focused on control and

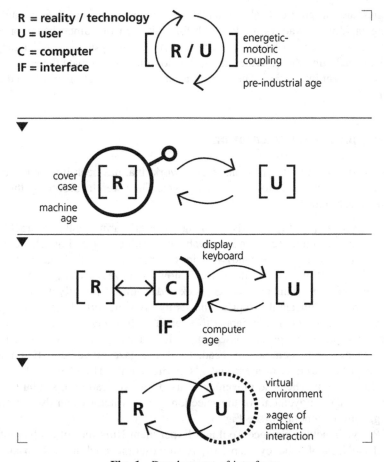

Fig. 1. Development of interfaces

guidance of interaction. [4] The short term change of behavior in this method is the main problem. The purpose of behavior patterns are, of course, based on their steadiness. They are part of the conditio humana. Within this mind, it is right to research behavioral techniques, by giving attention to the acting and exploring user. At this point it's possible to find hope. Driven by gaming and movie industry more and more techniques for tracking and visualization of the spatial behaving user are explored:

- Motion Capture Systems (body-, head- and eye-tracking)
- Kinect
- Leap Motion
- Oculus Rift.

These mostly inexpensive gadgets are equipped with a rich and disposable arsenal of software, frameworks and application programming interfaces permitting inclusion of game engines and other virtual scenarios. But not only tracking and recording technologies are in progress, also qualitative data analysis and interpretation are developing rapidly. Nowadays modelling a formalization of human behavior is possible. The gap between behavior patterns and notation systems and languages is bridgeable. Concluding the described facts, it is possible to designate the emerging age as an age of ambient interaction. The user (as a car resident) is acting »unshaped« in his own environment.

5   Prototypical Implementation

Four projects (research prototypes and student work, that has been implemented at the summer-school) are intended to serve as examples. They were achieved by the further up described techniques.

1. *Aughanded Virtuality* [5] embeds the image of user's arms (real time track) into a virtual scene. The entire scenario is viewable by Oculus rift (see Fig. 2). Aughanded Virtuality (Augmentation + hand) provides experience of real hands (gestures, motion) in virtuality. The handling area is now »vitalized«. The felt and observed movements of user's hand provide feedback and scaling. Currently it is necessary to make efforts to duplicate the depicted hands by invisible virtual hands. Cause only these virtual hand models are »able« to interact with virtual objects.
2. Under the heading of gesture based interaction a concept was developed [7] to interact with virtual scenarios by head, hand and gaze movement (Example scenario: learn how to control a car and it's environment). The Oculus rift serves as visualizing system. The head movement is used for exploration of spatial structures and the eye/hand movement for the selection of menu items (after dwell time) and for triggering of functions (see Fig. 3).
3. *ESTER* (Eye-Tracking Science Tool and Experiment Runtime) offers the option to expand the idea of saliency maps. [9] A stereoscopic tracking system allows to

Fig. 2. Aughanded Virtuality (Photography: Franke, I. S.)

Fig. 3. Gesture based interaction (Photography: Müller, M.)

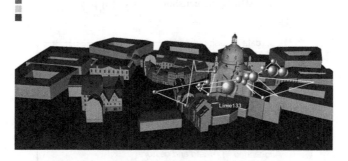

Fig. 4. ESTER (Screenshot, Source: [9] p. 382)

transform the eye gaze movements (gaze behavior, saccades, fixations) to a 3D diagram. ESTER can easily track and show the user's trails of observing in a sculptural way. In the end the student (user U) can be watched during gazing by the teacher (supervisor S) (see Fig. 6). An abundance of applications for training is imaginable (see Fig. 4).

4. The research framework *BiLL* (BildspracheLiveLab) enables the interlinking of powerful tools for creating, editing and presenting graphic information. [8] This is the condition to research and develop novel depiction principles. In particular new methods of perceptually realistic visualization (non-photorealistic projection) have been investigated (see Fig. 5).

The projects - although the topical focus is different – can be allocated to the diagram in Fig. 6. It's a positive impact that working on such projects only can succeed with an interdisciplinary approach. For example interpretation and analysis of tracking data is impossible without cognitive psychology. Interlinking of hardware components fails without knowledge on electrical engineering.

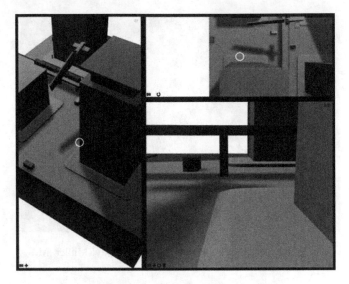

Fig. 5. BiLL (Screenshot, Source: [8] p. 71)

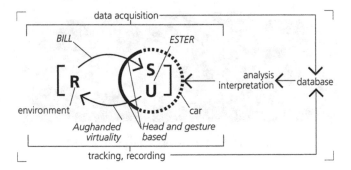

Fig. 6. Order of prototypes

6 Last Conclusion

Even if the contour of the field of research develops stepwise it is necessary to define the lines of research to overcome the period of experiment. Possibly a generalizing discipline should take the lead: anthropology or ethology? Finally you will notice: »First we define our behavior patterns, thereafter they shape our tools.«

References

1. Barthes, R.: The Rhetoric of the Image. Oxford University Press, Oxford (1964)
2. Bergson, H.: Matière et mémoire. Essai sur la relation du corps à l'esprit. Alcan, Paris (German: Materie und Gedächtnis. Eine Abhandlung über die Beziehung zwischen Körper und Geist. translated by Julius Frankenberger. Diederichs, Jena 1908, Hamburg 1991) (1896)

3. Culkin, J.M.: A schoolman's guide to Marshall McLuhan. Saturday Rev., 51–53, 71–72 (1967)
4. Fogg, B.J.: Persuasive Technology: Using Computers to Change What We Think and Do (Interactive Technologies). Morgan Kaufmann, San Francisco (2003)
5. Günther, T., Franke I.S., Groh, R.: Aughanded Virtuality – The Hands in the Virtual Environment. Research Demo and Poster IEEE VR 2015, Arles (2015)
6. http://www.iata.org/pressroom/pr/pages/2012-12-06-01.aspx
7. Schulze, E.: Virtuelle Realität - Kopfbasierte Navigation und Interaktion. Diplomarbeit. TU Dresden, Fakultät Informatik (2015)
8. Starke, M., et al.: Interactive panels - a tool for structured three-dimensional scene exploration and visualisation. In: Proceedings 3D-NordOst 2011, pp. 67–75 (2011)
9. Wojdziak, J., Kammer, D., Stahl, A., Groh, R.: ESTER - eye-tracking science tool and experiment runtime. In: Stephanidis, C. (ed.) HCII 2014, Part I. CCIS, vol. 434, pp. 379–383. Springer, Heidelberg (2014)

User Experience Design in "Internet Plus" Era

Wentao Wang[✉], Shiqi Liu, and Yang Zhang

Baidu, Beijing, People's Republic of China
{wangwentao,liushiqi,zhangyang22}@baidu.com

Abstract. As the internet plus strategy stated by Chinese government, more and more internet companies, and traditional companies are taking actions to adopt internet as an engine to boost development or even revolutions on various domains. Industry focus and resource concentration set unprecedented opportunity for internet plus business. At the same time, user experience design is under high expectation in this new form of business trend. This article will use real design cases in Baidu, such as Baidu Stock project, Baidu Education project, Baidu Lottery project, and etc. to share experience of designing for internet plus business, and to conclude some design rules for user experience professionals in internet plus era.

Keywords: User experience design · Internet plus · Big data · China

1 Introduction

2015-3-5, in government work report, Chinese Prime Minister Li Keqiang released national strategy of "internet plus" action. In the report, He said Chinese government would implement policy benefits, resource concentration, and etc. to support the combination of internet service (mobile internet, cloud computing, big data, and etc.) and tradition business (manufacture business, education, healthcare, finance, and etc.).

Hence, the year of 2015 is also regarded as first year for Chinese internet plusera.

2 Why Internet Plus

According to our research and understanding, this strategy is beneficial for both internet business and traditional business in China.

We can first take a look at internet business. The following chart shows internet users was increasing rapidly from 2011 to 2014, and was expected to keep increasing, which shows a huge market potential for internet service in upcoming years.

© Springer International Publishing Switzerland 2016
A. Marcus (Ed.): DUXU 2016, Part I, LNCS 9746, pp. 172–183, 2016.
DOI: 10.1007/978-3-319-40409-7_18

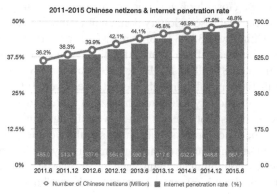

China internet user scale [1]

However, there are still blemish behind these shining figures. Along with the upper chart, government also released another chart as the following.

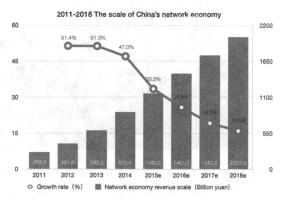

China network economy trend [2]

This chart report is done in the year 2014, before internet plus strategy was formed. From the chart we can see that even though internet users were increasing sharply, network economy was not increasing in the same proportion. And network economy increase rate was expected to slow down from year 2014. The major reason for this is that internet service was connected to traditional business in a superficial way. In other words, internet only connect people with information before year 2014, and internet can do much more if it can connect people with service in internet plus era.

After looking at internet service, we can take a look at traditional business now. Pain points for it are also obvious, such as high operation cost, high logistic cost, information asymmetry, and etc. Luckily, the advantage of internet service is a decent supplement for these drawbacks for traditional business.

We can take a closer look at the power of combining internet service and traditional business from the real case in lottery domain in China. In the year of 2014, the total sale of lottery in China was 382.378 billion RMB (or 58.1979 billion US dollars), which was 23.6 % of increase from year 2013. [3] Within this total sale, lottery sale over internet contributed 85 billion RMB (or 12.937 billion US dollars). [4] This number not only means that lottery sale through internet takes over 20 % of the total sale of lottery, but also means that lottery sale through internet increased 104 % from it was in 2013. [4] This result shows that internet is a powerful engine in lottery domain.

As user experience professionals, how should we interpret these numbers? Before internet started serving lottery domain, the major way for lottery users to buy lottery, to check result, to communicate with each other was at lottery booth. The following picture is a typical environment of lottery booth in China.

Therefore, this messy, crowded, and uncomfortable environment stops so many potential users from entering into lottery booth. And running a lottery booth requires pretty high fix cost. Lottery service through internet means that users can enjoy time flexibility and space flexibility neatly.

From UX design's perspective, internet is not only a new channel for lottery, but also introduces numerous lottery potential user cases. Taking Baidu lottery service as an example, you can buy lottery, check result, chat with lottery friends, read lottery news and etc. in Baidu lottery mobile application. With mobile application, users can fully take advantage of any small time fractions, such as in the metro, in the elevator, short break time and etc. to pull out their mobile phone and do something about lottery whenever they think about it in their minds.

On the other hand, dating back to two years ago, when internet did not closely collaborate with lottery domain, users can only search for previous lottery result. Other lottery related services were not available at that point.

This Baidu lottery case shows that the significance of internet plus strategy is to develop internet service from "linking people with information" to "linking people with service". With this development, on one hand traditional business can take advantage of internet specialty to provide concrete service through internet. On the other hand, internet service can step forward from being superficial information communication connecter to service providing channel.

3   How Internet Plus Serves Traditional Business

These years, traditional business has encountered many problems in information acquisition, processing, analysis and etc. At the same time it brings much inconvenience to users. This is exactly what internet plus service is good at and very likely to bring in to improve user experience, so as to boost traditional business' development.

3.1   Information Acquisition

In traditional business, information acquisition often comes together with high time cost and high money cost for users, because traditional business model use this information asymmetry to make money. Taking user experience designers' education and training as an example in China, a college student wants to be an entry level designer at work. Right now user experience design is a fast blooming domain in China, but education-wise it is still in its early stage. Because not over 20 % of universities provides systemic UX design program to students, most of them are providing industry design, environmental design, graphic design, and other design programs that are not targeting user experience design industry directly. Therefore, students still have to take extra courses after graduation which costs extra time and money, before they can finally become a competent UX designer. This following chart shows this dilemma:

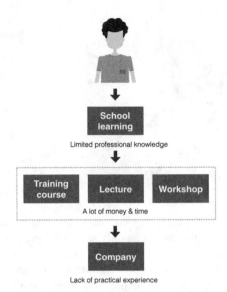

Under the trend of internet plus strategy, Baidu is providing "UX lecture" education both online and offline to teach students systemic UX design knowledge and design experience that Baidu learnt from real internet design projects. In this new model, we are trying to create a win-win balance to both companies and students. For students, they can learn real hands-on knowledge from designers in big internet companies; even communicate with these experienced designers directly. For companies, students who received these trainings carry good skills and are ready to join companies to start work.

This projects' significance is even more notable under internet plus era in China. Internet plus era requires more designers to design more services and products. Therefore, in our Baidu "UX lecture" service, Baidu does not only provide knowledge to students, but also contributes designer levels and evaluation system to these students. Along learning from Baidu "UX lecture" students can also test for certificates which can represent their design capability.

The certificate provided by Baidu UX lecture, is not a certificate with no standards. Baidu adopts designer evaluation levels which have accumulated in Baidu for over 10 years. Hundreds and thousands of designers are evaluated or used to be evaluated under this evaluation levels. What is more, this evaluation levels and standards are not only valid in Baidu, but also cross checked by many internet companies' UX design department, such as Tencent, Alibaba, and etc. Therefore, students holding this certificate are more likely to join companies to start UX career smoothly. At the same time, companies like Baidu can save significant amount of time in interviewing candidate designers, since the certificate speaks for itself. This model can be extracted in the following chart.

In conclusion, when internet plus works together with traditional industry, UX designers are supposed to streamline users' pain points caused by information asymmetry, and tried to solve this problem in real user cases in all domains.

3.2   Information Processing and Analysis

The second way of improving user experience for traditional business is to apply internet's information processing capability. We can take stock market as an example. The goal of stock investors is monetary payback. Therefore, in traditional stock market, these investors would delve into variety of data, such as buying "premium" services from securities traders, reading news in front of television screen, and then trying to make sense of all information from different channels in order to come up with their best transaction decision.

How can internet plus help these investors in this use case? Theoretically, all the before mentioned analysis can be done through big data analysis. And this is for sure a big advantage of internet service. Baidu as an internet company is delivering this service in its mobile stock application. Baidu utilizes big data capability to extract transaction suggestions to investors from analyzing news, companies' achievements, governments' strategy and etc. which are primary influence factors in Chinese stock market. For doing this, Baidu stock application helps users in two ways. First, it collects related data into sense making topics for users. Second, it gives users a way to deliberate reasons behind big data's suggestions.

However, this is much easier said than done. What does big data look like? It is very unlikely for users to understand big data format from our machine learning research. As user experience designers, we have to translate machine-readable information into human-readable information to our users.

For example, the following is the "hot concept" interface design from Baidu Stock. This page tells users that what the latest hot concepts are. The hotness of these concepts is presented in different colors. From yellow to orange, to red it means hotter the concepts.

If users want to see what the stories behind these concepts are, what transaction should be done at this point, and which stocks should pay attention to. Users can click on one concept they are interested in, and application will navigate users to detailed page as the following.

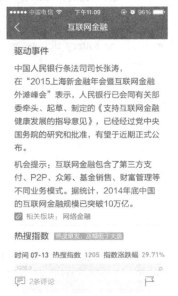

Concept detail page first screen

Concept detail page second screen

In the detail page, it shows users the background story, why this concept is enlisted as a hot concept for today, the hotness trend of this concept during the last several days, and which stocks are related to this hot concept for users to delve into. With this information and suggestions, we are happy to see that investors can reach right transaction decision easier than before.

In conclusion, as user experience designers, we are supposed to translate advanced technology such as big data, cloud computing, semantic web, and etc. into designs that users can make sense of. This is an essential step to take advantage of internet information processing and analysis capability to help us in real time use case.

4 Warning for Internet Plus Design When Serving Traditional Business

Comparing to traditional business, internet plus business is for sure delivering more usability and convenience. But when it comes to merging these two, we should be careful from running into problems as well. The following are lessons that we learned and would like every designers to pay attention to when designing for internet plus business.

4.1   Respect Users' Cognition and Habits from Traditional Business Time

Internet plus can improve user experience for traditional business, but it does not mean creativity is necessary everywhere. Internet plus design should pay respect to traditional business rules, and users' cognition.

For example, before internet marched into lottery domain. Lottery buyers used tickets like the following to buy lottery for over 10 years. And they were familiar with picking numbers like this. Therefore, when we design it on internet interface, designers are supposed to design in continuation as a metaphor to offline lottery tickets.

Offline lottery ticket   Online lottery ticket

It is same story in designing for stock market. When designers in Baidu first encountered the chance to design Baidu Stock application, designers were excited and

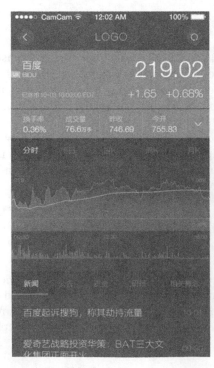

wanted to revolute the traditional design in our first brainstorming session. One designer adopted purple as theme color for Baidu Stock, and also some fashion visual elements in interface design as the following.

However, in usability test result, most stock investors did not like this kind of innovation, and could not perceive much benefit from design like this. From our study, we found out that there were two reasons behind this test result. First, this design was far away from user' expectation and different from their offline cognition, so they had to learn all over again about how to use this application. Second, color-wise it was too much. In stock market some color carries special meaning, such as red/green means rise/fall. Purple as theme color attracted too much attention and set a negative effect on users' reading of interface contents.

4.2   Pay Special Attention to Internet Safety Related Design

These years, words as internet hacker, personal information leakage, and etc. sounded pretty rapidly around internet users. These problems might get more and more exaggerated in internet plus era, since internet plus business is connecting users to service, and payment is usually part of it. We can take a closer look at the following interface design.

Some design from other mobile applications

With design like this, designers for them should be blamed for not delivering professional, and safety design.

Hence internet plus design should adopt various design skills to improve service safety cognition. In wording design, designer should use more clear-cut wordings to present your service's professional spirit. In visual design, designers are supposed to use more stable and safe visual elements, such as extracting more shapes, colors, and styles from traditional business visual work. In interaction design, designers should imbed more safety related interactions helping users to feel that they are in control of their service, personal information, and etc.

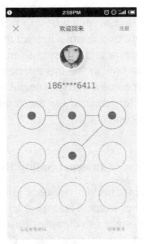

Example: finger gesture check before personal account page

And finally in branding design, designers should pay extra attention to create a unified visual identity throughout your service. From one hand, professional branding design will give your users more confidence to trust your service. On the other hand, unified style can help your users to remember your brand, and easier for your business to scale up.

Baidu Stock Visual Identity Design

5 Conclusion

2015 is internet plus strategy and implementation's first year in China. More and more industry domains will collaborate with internet service to boost industry development. As user experience professions, it is our obligation to make use of our design skills, thinking, and strategies in the right way, so as to maximize internet services advantage.

References

1. [1] Data resource: Chine internet user scale by CNNIC. http://cnnic.cn/hlwfzyj/hlwxzbg/hlwtjbg/201507/P020150723549500667087.pdf
2. Data source: 2015 China network economy annual supervision report. http://report.iresearch.cn/report/201506/2405.shtml
3. Chinese Lottery Sale Report. http://sports.qq.com/a/20150112/050028.html
4. Chinese Internet Lottery Sale Report. http://sports.qq.com/a/20150122/012251.htm

User Experience Design Methods
and Tools

Prototyping Complex Systems: A Diary Study Approach to Understand the Design Process

Jumana Almahmoud[1(✉)], Almaha Almalki[1], Tarfah Alrashed[1],
and Areej Alwabil[1,2]

[1] Center for Complex Engineering Systems (CCES),
King Abdulaziz City for Science and Technology (KACST),
Riyadh, Saudi Arabia
{jalmahmoud,aasalmalki,talrashed}@kacst.edu.sa
[2] Ideation Lab, Massachusetts Institute of Technology (MIT),
Cambridge, MA, USA
areej@mit.edu

Abstract. Diary studies in human-computer interaction (HCI) design are qualitative methods for collecting data about users' behavior and insights while going through an experience or interacting with a certain system. This paper examines the efficacy of using this method in exploring the design process for complex engineering systems. An online diary study was conducted to capture data from designers working on an interactive visualization platform for large-scale data sets. Design implications and insights for practitioners and developers are discussed.

Keywords: Diary study · Complex systems · Artifacts · UX · HCI

1 Introduction

Developing new systems requires deep understanding of the context and expectations of the intended users. In HCI research, a diary study is a qualitative technique for collecting data about the user experience (UX) or behavior when interacting with a system or within a certain context [4]. A UX diary study often contains a log of the participants' experience with an interactive system or during a specific incident, which could serve as a quality-assurance tool to verify that the system is what the users want and is fulfilling their needs [5, 6].

What makes diary studies stand out when compared to other HCI tools/methods is that they offer insight into the UX through temporal and longitudinal information about the users, products and contexts of use in a natural context of interaction [1, 3–5]. Participants in a diary study log data immediately at the occurrence of the event by answering a set of questions to help researchers get feedback about a certain experience. Alternatively, some other diary studies ask participants to capture momentary data with minimum logging and use the artifact collected to trigger participants' memory when interviewed later on by the researchers [2].

© Springer International Publishing Switzerland 2016
A. Marcus (Ed.): DUXU 2016, Part I, LNCS 9746, pp. 187–196, 2016.
DOI: 10.1007/978-3-319-40409-7_19

2 Background

Complex systems are systems that involve large numbers of components and inter-connect multiple interfaces together, such as real-time embedded systems and inter-active platforms [8]. They do not follow a linear progress in which the output of one system is the input of another; they require an interdependent mode interaction between the different subsystems [9]. Designing user interfaces (UIs) for such systems can be a complex process for developers and designers. The literature shows different design processes followed by designers to produce prototypes for the UI of complex systems [10–12]. For example, Bonnie E. John suggested following the GOMS model for UI design and evaluation, which is a widely known theoretical concept in HCI that predicts user interaction behavior with proposed UI designs for complex systems and it stands for Goals, Operators, Methods and Selection rules [11].

Interconnected engineering systems require a special consideration when designing the interfaces given the specificity of the information displayed to the user and the level of accuracy. Using social-science concepts in HCI provides a systematic framework for the UI design of complex systems. In [10], the author provided a set of five questions related to UI design challenges that the designer should answer during the design process. These questions are based on classic graphic user interface (GUI) conventions and recent research into innovative interaction techniques to provide general design accomplishments for different interaction machines.

Researchers have used diary studies as a method to elicit requirements and insights by exploring processes and observing workflows. For instance, in [4], the authors were trying to understand the different activities conducted by information workers and the different complexities and variations of those activities. Specifically, they were using a diary study to observe how interruptions affect those activities and how office workers switch between tasks. In [5], the authors explored using a diary study as an evaluation tool to capture the system-design process and UX. It was used as a communication tool to validate users' needs and communicate them to the designers and the researchers.

Previous work used diary study to understand the behavior and interactions of end-users interacting with a complex system. However, considering the designers of complex systems as the main focus of study, and capturing their experiences while prototyping and logging their process is the gap we have found in the literature. In our paper, we are evaluating the use of diary studies as a tool to explore the creative process in designing complex engineering systems. In addition to the diary-study logs, the participants were interviewed and asked about their insights regarding their experience prototyping each artifact. The following sections will present the methodology and the insights gathered from the study.

3 Diary Study in Complex Systems

3.1 Method

To understand the added value of diary studies in the context of interaction design for complex systems, a diary study was conducted to gather insights from the designers and developers. In this study, an online diary tool was used to collect instant data from designers involved in the design of a complex system in the form of an interactive visualization platform. Given the nature of this agile development environment, the diary approach allowed us to overcome the issue of interrupting the natural flow of work for our users (designers). The use of an online diary to capture snippets of the prototyping experience provided more flexibility by allowing more logs and a greater number of designers to join the study when the project required [7]. This flexibility would have not been possible if the study facilitator had to be physically present in each design feedback session.

The diary study was applied to explore the design process within the development of a Web-based interactive visualization platform, which is in its early stages of development as part of a project at the Center for Complex Engineering Systems[1]. The project's team consisted of engineers who were developing the mathematical models behind the engine, and the platform's designers and developers who were developing the interactive visualization platform. Three designers of this platform participated in the study, which spanned a time frame of four months. In the following subsections, we provide an overview explaining the diary process, the artifacts as communication tools, and the analysis that was conducted as part of this study.

3.2 Process

At the beginning of the diary-study process, the facilitator briefed the designers on the tasks required and how to use the diary-logging tool. The tool used was Dscout[2], an app for moment-based research to collect quantifiable data from users. The app allowed collecting photos, text and numbers momentarily from the designers after each design feedback session. In this study, the goal was to integrate the diary-logging task seamlessly into the design process without causing an interruption to the workflow of the designer. As depicted in Fig. 1, the process started with the designer sharing a prototype

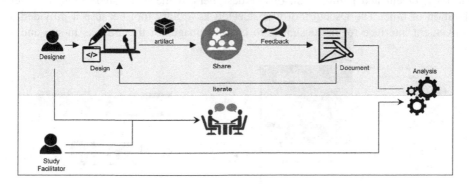

Fig. 1. The framework of the diary study

---

[1] http://www.cces-kacst-mit.org.

[2] https://dscout.com.

with the team to gain feedback. The designer then logged the feedback in the diary tool. The tool collected the data and provided insights for the study facilitator. An interview was conducted when the designers indicated that they faced a problem in the design of the artifact or if the type of artifact has changed from the last feedback session.

Each time the designers logged in their artifact; the diary asked them a set of questions regarding the feedback session. The questions were defined to help the researchers understand the design process for this specific project, and were general enough to accommodate other projects. The questions were chosen to minimize the effort of logging by limiting the number of text inputs and instead giving the participant options and lists to choose from. Figure 2 shows some of these questions.

Fig. 2. Examples of the questions we have specified through the Dscout tool

The interface was designed to capture media files in the form of images or videos of the prototype that show the context in which the artifact was shared, whether it was through a Web conference or an in-person feedback session. This approach supported the engagement and participation of our designers in the diary study over a longer duration of time. The Dscout tool was selected as a diary tool because it provided a convenient interface for the designers to capture images of the artifacts in-situ and a

Fig. 3. Diary study tool and the designer/facilitator interfaces

streamlined process for creating diary entries and aligning them in a storyboard across the project's timeline. Figure 3 shows the diary tool's interfaces from the perspective of the designer and the study facilitator. The app logs the data and sends them to the website on which the facilitator could access all the logs and conduct further analysis.

There are several time spans of UX with prototypes depending on the moment of usage in the design process for complex systems, as depicted in Fig. 4. While some methods for studying the UX shed light on one or more phases of the UX (e.g., user testing provides an insight in the "during usage" time span, focus groups can elicit insights before, during or after usage, SUS surveys provide an insight in the "after usage" time span), the diary-study method provides longitudinal information on UX that spans these four time frames [6, 7].

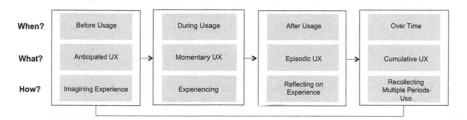

Fig. 4. Time spans of UX

In addition to reporting activities and documenting experiences with artifacts used in the design process, the UX diary in this study was also used by the participants (designers) to discuss design issues or information about the front end of the complex systems' interfaces. The type of artifact often impacts the participants' experience while logging data or being interviewed and the researcher's ability to analyze the data [2]. In this study, there were three types of artifacts used in the design process: sketches, digital prototypes (Axure and Illustrator) and coded prototypes (HTML5/D3.js). Table 1 shows how different types of artifacts (Fig. 5) were used to communicate the designs to the developer teams through the different UX time spans.

Sketch   Digital Prototype   Coded Prototype

Fig. 5. Examples of collected artifacts

Table 1. Artifacts during different UX time spans

Artifacts	Sketches	Digital Prototype	Coded Prototype
Before Usage Anticipated UX Imagining Experience	Wanted to use a simple tool to show the layout and the flow of the design. No skills needed	Use an intuitive prototype to communicate the vision of the prototype to the users. UX design skills needed	Coded prototype takes more time and effort than digital ones. Programming skills needed
During Usage Momentary UX Experiencing (perspective of designers)	It was easy to use, but the challenge was converting the ideas to sketches in an understandable form	It takes more time than the sketches. It reflects the real 'look & feel' of the platform's front-end more than sketches. (high fidelity)	Implementing and coding the visualizations was a complex process, dealing with both different data sets and visualizations types
After Usage Episodic UX Experiencing (perspective of target users and developers)	Challenge was to explain to the audience the designs and the flow of the prototype	Feedback that designers received was more meaningful than with sketches. Challenge was that editing the digital prototypes requires more time, skill and effort	The feedback was even more meaningful than low-fidelity artifacts since it was interactive. Changes to the coded prototype require more time and effort
Over Time Cumulative UX Recollecting Multiple Periods of Use	The same sketches were shared with engineers and designers on the team. The effectiveness of communication varied based on the background of the participant giving feedback	Getting more feedback by showing the same prototype to other participants who are not part of the team to elicits insights from different perspectives on the designs	The deployed version of the platform facilitated more Feedback from team members and others designers and developers who are working on similar platforms

4   Analysis

To capture the design process and the role of artifacts used to communicate ideas during design sessions, the researchers went through the collected diary logs periodically to identify patterns. The diary study was supported with feedback interviews conducted with the participants (designers and developers) when the log of the participant indicated a noticeable pattern. These interviews were triggered based on two different incidents that were noticed: first, when designers indicated that they had faced a problem in designing a certain artifact and second, when designers changed the artifact they were using from one logged session to another.

For every feedback session logged, the type of artifact, the experience of the designer using that artifact and the number of designers participating in the session and with whom the designers shared their designs all were captured in the diary. In addition to that, the feedback that they received during each session was documented. Figure 6 shows some quantified data on these metrics from the study. The analysis revealed the variation in the number of participants in the feedback sessions, as they varied from few to many members. It also provided insights into the prototyping process, the issues that the designers face temporal dynamics of perceived usability of the system during the design process. Finally, the study also shows the variation in frequency of usage of artefacts (e.g. digital prototyping was the type of artifact that was mostly used to communicate the designs).

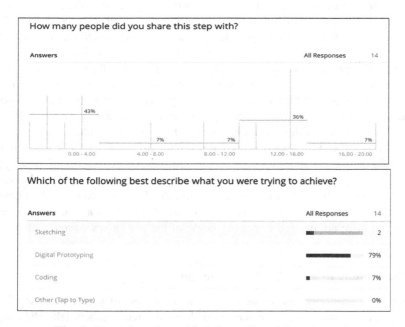

Fig. 6. Examples of quantified data collected from the study

5   Reflection

Through this work, the goal was to explore the benefits of using digital diaries as user research tools in complex engineering systems. The objective of the diary study was twofold: first, to capture the design process of complex systems and the use of artifacts as communication tools using a diary study and second, to understand the influence of the diary study on the designer's flow and designs. The insights we gathered were from two different perspectives: the perspective of the designer and the perspective of the researcher observing the design process. The data collected and the interviews provided insights into the early stage prototyping process and the exploratory phases in which the researcher observed the design process for complex systems. On the other hand, the diary study was used as a method to improve the user experience of communication artifacts (low-high fidelity) that are often considered by designers in prototyping complex systems.

5.1   The Design Process for Complex Systems

When designing for complex systems, the design process tends to adapt to accommodate the complexity of the product to be delivered. Within the interactive visualization platform observed in this study, an interesting pattern emerged during the design process. At the early stage, the designers started by sketching the layout of the tool and when more iterations were required for the digital prototype, the designers worked on the process in parallel. A design workflow was established to build the layout, and another workflow branched to prototype the visualization components. The visualization prototyping relied on producing coded prototypes, and the reason for this, according to the feedback interviews conducted, is that the design team wanted to speed up the design process to show a working mockup. Thus, the visualization section had to represent real data. The diary-study was effective in understanding why coding was perceived to be the best option to prototype the visualization in this specific context, since sketches or digital prototypes were not sufficient to display the complexity and interaction with such components. Other insights gathered from the data collected were related to temporal dynamics with different artefacts (e.g. findings indicated that designers spent most of the design time producing digital prototypes). After interviewing the designers to check on their progress and get their feedback, they indicated that using digital prototypes gave them more flexibility to share their designs, apply feedback and then update their designs and share them again, as opposed to sketches that were not enough to convey some of the platform's complex elements.

5.2   Diary Study as a UX Method in Design

Designers and developers go through an iterative process of prototyping and implementation. In this study, the designers used three different artifacts (sketches, digital prototypes and coded prototypes), and for each artifact, the designers made several versions or drafts to communicate the concept and ideas to the team. As mentioned in the methods section, designers shared their designs with the project's team members and principal investigators in co-located and remote communication settings. After every session, the designers documented or logged the designs they shared (sketches, prototypes or codes) and their perceived efficacy of the feedback they got in the diary-study's tool. Based on the interviews we conducted with the designers, we found that this study helped them categorize their design process by going through different types of artifacts and documenting each session they conducted with their team and the feedback they received. The study asked designers to go through different steps, which helped them reflect on key design issues:

1. The type of feedback they got from sharing their design using different artifacts, which had a considerable impact on the next design decision they made and the artifact that they would consider in the prototyping process.
2. The importance of artifacts as a communication tool between designers and other stakeholders in the project.
3. The design considerations that the designers can gain from low-fidelity designs (e.g., sketches) and high fidelity (e.g., Azure prototype and coding).

The designers indicated in the interviews that logging their design process, the artifacts they have to create their designs, the people they shared these designs with and the feedback they received helped them in their next designs. Knowing how different artifacts worked as a communication tool between the designers and the stakeholders, the kind of feedback they received, and logging how difficult each step was, provided the designers with insights regarding what type of artifact could be used to convey their vision and communicate ideas. In addition to planning and communicating, going through the diary-study process helped the designers better understand the time requirements for each task, based on the feedback they received. Based on that, critical decisions were made regarding the artifact type they needed to use next. Going from low-fidelity prototypes to an interactive high-fidelity one was based on evaluating how challenging it was to communicate the designer's idea to the stakeholders to elicit their feedback.

6 Conclusion

The use of an online diary for data collection from designers proved successful in the context of complex-engineering systems; its design was effective in providing a contextual understanding of artifacts and prototypes as communication tools, and its flexibility met users' needs for minimal interruption in their workflow. Insights into patterns of feedback elicited from different types of artifacts allowed monitoring of the communication between the designers and other stakeholders within the project. In addition to the observations that the researchers gathered from the diary study, this approach also served as a documentation tool, helping the designers to track the contexts of use for their prototypes and plan the next artifact to be shared.

Nevertheless, there were also some challenges associated with using a diary approach in the context of agile development in complex-systems design. Although the tool provided a convenient way to capture and log data, designers had to be reminded several times to log their experiences with using artifacts in communicating ideas and conceptual designs. Given the nature of the agile development process, the designers could seek feedback during multiple events throughout the day, which made it challenging to select a feedback session to be logged in the diary study. The diary-study is ongoing and more insights are being collected on later stages of the design process for complex systems.

References

1. Johnson, B.T., Eagly, A.H., Reis, H.T., Judd, C.M.: Handbook of Research Methods in Social and Personality Psychology (2000)
2. Carter, S., Mankoff, J.: When participants do the capturing: the role of media in diary studies. In: Proceedings of the SIGCHI Conference on Human Factors in Computing Systems, pp. 899–908. ACM, April 2005
3. Singh, A., Malhotra, S.: A researcher's guide to running diary studies. In: Proceedings of the 11th Asia Pacific Conference on Computer Human Interaction, pp. 296–300. ACM, September 2013
4. Czerwinski, M., Horvitz, E., Wilhite, S.: A diary study of task switching and interruptions. In Proceedings of the SIGCHI Conference on Human Factors in Computing Systems, pp. 175–182. ACM, April 2004
5. Lichtner, V., Kounkou, A.P., Dotan, A., Kooken, J.P., Maiden, N.A.: An online forum as a user diary for remote workplace evaluation of a work-integrated learning system. In CHI 2009 Extended Abstracts on Human Factors in Computing Systems, pp. 2955–2970. ACM, April 2009
6. Tomitsch, M., Singh, N., Javadian, G.: Using diaries for evaluating interactive products: the relevance of form and context. In: Proceedings of the 22nd Conference of the Computer-Human Interaction Special Interest Group of Australia on Computer-Human Interaction, pp. 204–207. ACM, November 2010
7. Brandt, J., Weiss, N., Klemmer, S.R.: txt 4 l8r: lowering the burden for diary studies under mobile conditions. In: CHI 2007 Extended Abstracts on Human Factors in Computing Systems, pp. 2303–2308. ACM, April 2007
8. Ladyman, J., Lambert, J., Wiesner, K.: What is a complex system? Eur. J. Philos. Sci. 3(1), 33–67 (2013)
9. Harel, D., Lachover, H., Naamad, A., Pnueli, A., Politi, M., Sherman, R., Shtull-Trauring, A., Trakhtenbrot, M.: Statemate: A working environment for the development of complex reactive systems. IEEE Trans. Softw. Eng. 16(4), 403–414 (1990)
10. Bellotti, V., Back, M., Edwards, W.K., Grinter, R.E., Henderson, A., Lopes, C.: Making sense of sensing systems: five questions for designers and researchers. In: Proceedings of the SIGCHI Conference on Human Factors in Computing Systems, pp. 415–422. ACM, April 2002
11. John, B.E., Kieras, D.E.: Using GOMS for user interface design and evaluation: Which technique? ACM Trans. Comput. Hum. Interact. (TOCHI) 3(4), 287–319 (1996)
12. Olson, J.R., Olson, G.M.: The growth of cognitive modeling in human-computer interaction since GOMS. Hum. Comput. Interact. 5(2–3), 221–265 (1990)

Usability Engineering of Agile Software Project Management Tools

Noura Alomar[(⊠)], Nouf Almobarak, Sarah Alkoblan,
Sarah Alhozaimy, and Shahad Alharbi

Software Engineering Department, College of Computer and Information
Sciences, King Saud University, Riyadh, Saudi Arabia
{nnalomar, nmalmobarak, salkoblan,
salhozaimy, saalharbi}@ksu. edu. sa

Abstract. The successful management of software projects requires taking human and managerial factors into consideration. Agile software project management methodologies have made their way into the mainstream culture of software development and have gotten the attention of software engineers and researchers due to their rapid growth. The aim of this research effort is to comprehensively evaluate the usability of four software project management tools based on experimental findings as well as heuristic assessment. We focus on evaluating widely known tools based on rigorous usability assessment criteria and subjective and objective evaluation techniques. By utilizing the capabilities of a usability testing software solution, Morea, and considering the subjective views of five Human Computer Interaction experts, we believe that our findings can inspire the design of more effective agile software project management tools that allow development teams to manage their work efficiently while helping decision makers to base their tool selection on a trusted usability evaluation approach that addresses the needs of software development teams. We also believe that our findings will have promising implications for task management activities performed throughout all the phases of the software development lifecycle.

Keywords: Agile · Usability · Software engineering · Software project management · User experience

1 Introduction

With the growing demand for streamlining software project management activities by increasing the level of collaboration between individuals who work in software development teams, many agile software project management tools have been introduced. These software solutions offer a variety of features that mainly help software engineers distribute and prioritize development tasks and manage the overall progress of their projects. When deciding which software project management tool would better fulfill the needs of a given organization and help in achieving its business goals, looking for a complete solution that gives each member the ability to efficiently plan, track, and manage each iteration of the project is of extreme importance. Usability focuses on how end users will work with the software, and agile development processes focus on how software developers can flexibly deliver their assigned tasks.

© Springer International Publishing Switzerland 2016
A. Marcus (Ed.): DUXU 2016, Part I, LNCS 9746, pp. 197–208, 2016.
DOI: 10.1007/978-3-319-40409-7_20

Once a specific software project management tool is chosen by a team, the software analysts, designers, developers and testers are supposed to use the selected tool to track the progress of other members and collaborate to achieve the objectives of their project and thus contribute to satisfying their business goals. Therefore, although team members are assumed to have the technical expertise to use these software solutions, agile software project management tools that suffer from usability shortcomings might discourage team members from using the chosen tools and thus negatively affect the progress of their teams. For globally distributed teams, the lack of transparent and visible progress of all team members might lead to these teams' resources being wasted. For instance, some members might start working on work items that were already completed by other members. This in turn might complicate the integration of the development work done by distributed teams and increase inconsistencies between the work items completed by different teams, leading to cost and schedule overruns.

In this study, practical research is conducted on widely adopted tools and their features that are widely demanded in the software industry are explored. These tools are JIRA, AgileZen, VersionOne and ZebraPlan. The tool selection process was based on the support of the essential features that agile software development teams demand in practice, such as visibility of progress, communication, task prioritization and time management features. Before evaluating the usability of the chosen tools, we define comprehensive evaluation criteria covering elements chosen specifically to evaluate our participants' confidence with the tools' user interfaces, such as the readability of the written texts, the applicability of the presented icons and the overall user-friendliness of the evaluated tool. Further, because our participants are software engineers who have experience dealing with software development, analysis and testing tools and techniques, we give special attention to evaluating the features that are related to agile management methodologies and the ability to track progress at project and iteration levels. The results of our study can help the designers of these tools to identify the usability drawbacks of their systems and adjust them to fulfill the demands of the target users by highlighting the strengths and weaknesses of each tool from a usability engineering perspective. To the best of our knowledge, we have conducted the first research study that focuses on addressing the usability limitations of agile software project management tools based on a systematic approach that takes the subjective views of HCI experts and software engineers into consideration while utilizing the capabilities of a widely known usability assessment tool.

2 Literature Review

While taking into account the specific characteristics of software systems and the expectations of their users, many usability evaluation frameworks have been proposed to address the usability shortcomings of software applications in domains including banking, educational and gaming contexts [1–6]. While there are many usability parameters that could be considered for developing comprehensive usability evaluation criteria and frameworks, which might be related to either the properties of user interfaces or the cognitive abilities of target users, we believe that these parameters should not be considered equally important for all application types; some of them could be valued over others depending on the domain requirements of target systems. In [1], for instance, the factors that increase learners' motivation to learn, the properties of instructional material and the subjective opinions of academics were utilized to develop a usability evaluation method for e-learning software systems. Similarly, researchers in [2] based the categorization of usability evaluation metrics specifically developed for massively multi-player online role-playing games on game-specific properties.

Prior studies have also highlighted the importance of reducing the development time of software systems, increasing the level of collaboration between members of development teams and achieving optimal allocation of product resources [7–10].

For globally distributed and co-located teams, the results presented in [8, 11] have shown that most of these teams use traditional communication, monitoring and task tracking tools (e.g., wikis, e-mails and instant messaging applications) instead of utilizing the software project management tools that were specifically designed to facilitate the coordination of distributed development work. Azizyan et al. found that the ease of use of agile project management tools is the most important factor impacting the adoption of these tools [12]. Silva et al. recommended studying the factors that would strengthen these tools and thus encourage software developers to take advantage of them [11]. In agile software project management contexts, after evaluating the ease of use of a number of software project management tools in [13], researchers have correlated the number of features provided by the evaluated tools with their ease of use and found that the tools with fewer features received higher ratings. However, the literature lacks comprehensive and systematic empirical evaluations of the usability of agile software project management solutions. There is also a lack of comprehensive usability evaluation criteria that could be taken as a basis for assessing the usability of these solutions from a project management perspective.

3   Research Methodology

We utilized a usability testing software called Morea to conduct a task-based usability analysis. We defined an evaluation checklist that was specifically developed for measuring the usability of software project management tools. We also used a pre-session questionnaire designed to help us understand our participants' experience in the software industry and their overall familiarity with our chosen tools. We also took advantage of the System Usability Scale (SUS) questionnaire to understand the overall usability of each tool included in our study. Each participant was also asked to answer a 5-point Likert scale questionnaire that was specifically developed to measure the usability of each tool from a software project management perspective. The statements included in this questionnaire are: to what extent do you agree that the use of the tool would help your development team to achieve its goals? (**Q1**); to what extent do you agree that the use of the tool would increase the level of collaboration between your team members? (**Q2**); to what extent do you agree that the usability problems that you observed would not have negative effects on the overall workflow within your team? (**Q3**); to what extent do you agree that the tool is easy to use? (**Q4**); to what extent do you agree that the tool would help in improving the productivity levels of your team members? (**Q5**); to what extent do you think that the tool would help distributed teams to coordinate their work? (**Q6**); and to what extent do you agree that the tool would help in managing complex and large software systems? (**Q7**). Figure 1 summarizes our research methodology.

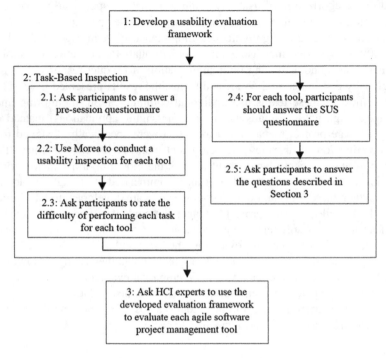

Fig. 1. Our research methodology

4   Usability Evaluation Criteria

The interface of each of the four selected agile project management tools was examined using Neilsen's heuristics. From a project management perspective, some other heuristics were defined and have been mapped to the different project management-specific tasks. Each agile project management tool was examined by selecting its key tasks and examining its interface using the specified heuristics. This framework has grouped 41 defined metrics into different categories. These metrics were used by the five HCI experts to evaluate the different tools and their interfaces as shown in Table 5 which illustrates the overall heuristic evaluation of the four selected tools.

1. *Immediate Feedback:* The ability to provide appropriate feedback in the different cases while performing different tasks within a reasonable time. Two metrics were defined under this category: displaying error messages at the right time (**A1**) and presenting appropriate feedback based on explicit user actions (**A2**).
2. *Real-world mapping:* The ability of the tool to map and reflect real-world project management and development workflow. For this category, five metrics were

defined: the elimination of information irrelevant to software project management (**B1**), the usage of software project management metaphors (**B2**), the usage of user-oriented terms in the interface (**B3**), the usage of agile terminologies (**B4**) and the appropriate reflection of real-world software development workflow (**B5**).

3. *Consistency and standardization:* The ability to use standard terminologies and organization to avoid confusing the users with different terms and actions. Four metrics were defined under this category: the use of consistent in-tool and across-tools naming (**C1**), the use of consistent layout of interface elements (**C2**), the use of consistent colors across the user interface (**C3**) and the consistent alignment between user interface elements and documentation/help (**C4**).

4. *Ease of use and learnability:* The degree to which a tool can be used by the intended users to effectively achieve the required task with fewer errors/failures. Eight metrics are grouped under this category: the ease of mastering the software project management tool (**D1**), the ease of learning by different classes of users (e.g., project managers vs. team members) (**D2**), the ease of tracking the progress of other members (**D3**), the ease of task distribution (**D4**), the ease of changing the status of created tasks (e.g., from "in progress" to "completed") (**D5**), the ease of locating burndown charts (**D6**), the ease of involving customers or clients in the development process (**D7**), the ease of specifying the complexity of each work item (**D8**) and the ease of navigating between different software project artefacts (**D9**).

5. *Layout and organization:* The ability to use a reasonable layout and logical grouping of the different project artefacts, which can help different users to navigate easily between different options and pages. Six metrics are defined under this category: the existence of reasonable grouping of project related artefacts (**E1**), reasonable grouping of sprint related artefacts (**E2**), reasonable grouping of team related artefacts (**E3**), logical grouping of menu options (**E4**), logical ordering of menu options (**E5**) and logical depth of menu options (**E6**).

6. *Flexibility:* Providing different options that allow users to handle and preform a given task easily. We consider whether the tool allows for a flexible arrangement of teams (**F1**), flexible reassignments of roles within and across projects (**F2**), flexible adjustment of the status of tasks (e.g., in progress or completed) (**F3**), flexible prioritization of software requirements according to their importance (**F4**) and flexible management of time (**F5**).

7. *Streamlining the experience and visibility:* The ability of a tool to match real-world scenarios and communicate the context of the situation. We consider the support for user-customized profiles (**G1**), the appropriate support for recognition rather than recall (**G2**), the efficiency of task completion (**G3**), the availability of visually appealing user interface designs (**G4**), the visibility of visual interface elements (**G5**) and the visibility of the roles of different team members (**G6**).

8. *Clarity:* Enabling users to interact with the tool and distinguish its tasks easily without causing confusion. Under this category, we examine whether there is a clear distinction between the tasks and user stories throughout the user interface (**H1**), a clear distinction between bugs, epics and defects (**H2**), a clear distinction between the roles of software-development team members (**H3**) and clear navigation options throughout the software project management tool (**H4**).

5 Experimental Evaluation: Task-Oriented Usability Inspection

Eight participants were recruited to perform 17 tasks on the four chosen agile software project management tools (JIRA, VersionOne, AgileZen and ZebraPlan). Although agile software project management tools differ in the services they offer and have many features, we chose tasks that we believe most software engineers who work in development teams would utilize. Verifying admin home pages (**T1**), creating a project (**T2**), creating a member (**T3**), creating a user story (**T4**) and creating a task (**T5**) were the first five tasks that we asked our participants to perform. Our participants also tried creating sprints (**T6**), creating releases or versions (**T7**), assigning team members to tasks (**T8**), customizing the settings of their profile pages (**T9**) and viewing burndown charts (**T10**). They were also asked to specify the length of sprints in days or weeks (**T11**), access project conversation rooms (**T12**), mark tasks as completed (**T13**), change the priority of a task (**T14**), track the progress of team members (**T15**), place a comment on someone's work (**T16**) and log in as clients and give feedback (**T17**). During each session, two observers were taking notes and tracking the progress of the participants. To identify usability problems and report users' concerns while they were experimenting with the tools, the think-aloud protocol was utilized. Further, we intentionally decided not to ask participants to follow a particular order while performing the required tasks to avoid the effect resulting from using a difficult tool on an easier one. Participants were also asked to rate the difficulty of each task using a 5-point Likert scale.

6 Results

Pre-session Questionnaire. At the start of each session, the participants were asked to complete a short pre-session questionnaire so we could assess their familiarity with the software engineering domain and software project management tools. The questionnaire was composed of six closed-format questions. Most of the participants have worked as software engineering practitioners in the software industry. Six of our participants had worked in the industry for a couple of months and two of them had worked for one to three years. All the participants who had worked in software engineering domains were responsible for programming and writing software codes, while only one participant was responsible for testing. In addition, four participants worked as requirement analysts, designers and project managers. Most of the participants have used software project management tools to coordinate their development work; however, most of them indicated that they used Microsoft Project and web-based tools (e.g., Google spreadsheets and wikis) to coordinate their work. Of the eight participants, two had used VersionOne whereas only one participant indicated that she had used JIRA, AgileZen and ZebraPlan.

Task Completion. For all 17 of the above-mentioned tasks, Table 1 illustrates the task success rates among the participants for the four agile software project management tools. For JIRA, for instance, all of the participants successfully completed four tasks out of seventeen without facing any difficulty. All participants were able to figure out how to

Table 1. Task completion rates among our eight participants

	JIRA	VersionOne	AgileZen	ZebraPlan
T1	8/8	7/8	8/8	8/8
T2	8/8	5/8	8/8	8/8
T3	7/8	8/8	8/8	8/8
T4	4/8	0/8	8/8	7/8
T5	7/8	6/8	6/8	8/8
T6	7/8	6/8	7/8	7/8
T7	5/8	5/8	1/8	0/8
T8	7/8	8/8	5/8	7/8
T9	8/8	8/8	8/8	8/8
T10	7/8	6/8	7/8	8/8
T11	6/8	8/8	1/8	7/8
T12	1/8	8/8	2/8	0/8
T13	6/8	5/8	8/8	8/8
T14	7/8	7/8	7/8	8/8
T15	5/8	7/8	6/8	7/8
T16	8/8	6/8	7/8	3/8
T17	1/8	4/8	3/8	1/8

Table 2. The average numbers of mouse clicks and time our participants required to complete the tasks

	JIRA		VersionOne		AgileZen		ZebraPlan	
Task	TT	NMC	TT	NMC	TT	NMC	TT	NMC
T1	13.2	1.43	13.6	1.25	8	1	22.8	3.88
T2	34.5	5.71	112	22.1	10.7	1.38	45.1	10.6
T3	62.4	8.86	40.5	7.25	31.5	6	53.7	7.5
T4	116	20	124	22.5	54	10.1	58.9	8.38
T5	47.3	11.6	98.2	18.1	106	19.6	16.2	3.38
T6	69.8	11.6	82.9	11.4	88.4	18	45.3	11.9
T7	85.2	15.6	89.2	14.9	93.8	23.5	69.3	13.9
T8	28.2	6.13	52.9	10.3	46.2	12.8	47.5	13.7
T9	32.3	6.5	35.9	5.63	21.2	3.25	18.7	3.75
T10	58.1	12.9	54.5	10.8	65.5	19.6	15.4	3.75
T11	122	27.3	39.4	6.88	43.2	9.38	31.9	9.88
T12	84	16.3	25.4	4.13	55.7	11.4	51.1	10.4
T13	89.5	23.3	143	28.6	52.8	12.4	60.1	13.6
T14	51.3	10.8	59	11.9	38.4	8.38	21.6	6
T15	71.6	14.5	81.5	12.4	41.7	8	54.4	9.63
T16	15.5	3.38	44.	7.57	30	7.75	39.8	9.13
T17	55.4	9.38	72.1	8.25	48.8	9.63	34.2	6.38
Mean	61	12	68	11.9	49.2	10.7	40.4	8.58

complete the third, eighth, ninth, eleventh and twelfth tasks using VersionOne. Agile-Zen showed a better success distribution in comparison with JIRA and VersionOne in that six out of the 17 tasks were completed successfully by all eight participants. ZebraPlan obtained the greatest success distribution among the four project management tools as all participants were able to successfully complete 10 out of the 17 tasks.

Time on Task (TT). For the four software project management tools evaluated in this paper, Table 2 shows the average time spent by our participants to complete each task (in seconds).

Number of Mouse Clicks (NMC). We use this metric to help us determine how easily a user can accomplish a basic task the first time they use the tool. We measured navigability by calculating the number of mouse clicks required to complete each task using each of the four evaluated tools (see Table 2). Depending on the difficulty of the task and how easily a user could navigate through the user interface of each tool, we observed variations in the average numbers of mouse clicks our users needed to complete each task using the four tools.

System Usability Scale (SUS). This questionnaire is composed of ten statements that are scored on a 5-point Likert scale ranging from 1(strongly disagree) to 5 (strongly agree). In SUS, the statements cover a variety of aspects of system usability such as learnability, reliability and validity, thus providing us with high-level measurement of the usability of each tool. According to [14], the average SUS score is 68 %.Table 3 demonstrates the average SUS scores for the four tools. AgileZen and ZebraPlan achieved very high average SUS scores of 70.63 % and 80.31 %, respectively. These results suggest positive perceptions of the usability of the two systems. On the other hands, the average SUS scores for JIRA and VersionOne were similar (44.69 % for JIRA and 42.19 % for VersionOne). The SUS scores for both JIRA and VersionOne were below the average acceptable SUS score.

Second Post-session Questionnaire. We included questions to indicate whether the use of each of the four evaluated tools would help streamline development and management activities in agile teams (see Sect. 3). Using 5-point Likert scale questions, we asked our participants to rate the extent to which the utilization of each of the four software project management tools would help fulfill the objectives of development teams, facilitating discussions and interactions between team members and managing large and complex software systems. Our questions also addressed the applicability of using each tool to coordinate distributed development projects and reflect the overall workflow of development teams in real-world scenarios. After mapping each answer to a score (e.g., *strongly agree* answers worth 5 points, *strongly disagree* answers worth 1 points, etc.) and calculating the means of these scores, we were able to measure the degrees of satisfaction of our participants for each agile management tool (see Table 4).

For ZebraPlan, all of our participants agreed that it is easy to use and expected it to help development teams achieve their goals. On the contrary, our results show that JIRA and VersionOne were more complex to use compared with ZebraPlan and AgileZen. When asked about the positive effects the tools would have on the productivity levels of team members, our results show that there were slight differences between the calculated

Table 3. Results of the SUS questionnaire

	JIRA	VersionOne	AgileZen	ZebraPlan
Minimum	25.00	17.50	22.50	50.00
Maximum	70.00	70.00	97.50	97.50
Mean	44.69	42.19	70.63	80.31
Standard Dev.	16.12	17.50	23.37	16.17

Table 4. Results of our second post-session questionnaire

	JIRA	VersionOne	AgileZen	ZebraPlan
Q1	3.25	3.25	3.75	4.5
Q2	3.75	3.88	2.88	3.63
Q3	2.75	2.63	4.13	3.63
Q4	2.75	2.63	3.88	4
Q5	3.38	3.63	3.75	4
Q6	3.25	3.25	3	3.63
Q7	2.88	3.38	2.63	3.5

means for all the tools although ZebraPlan and AgileZen took the first and second positions, respectively. By linking this finding with the level of complexity reported for each tool, we note that the tools that were observed as easiest to use were expected to have the greatest positive effects on the productivity levels of software engineers.

From the results presented in Table 4, we can also observe that JIRA and VersionOne obtained the lowest average scores for the third question, indicating that most participants expected the usability problems they faced to have negative effects on the overall workflow of development work in agile teams. For managing large and complex systems, most of the participants preferred using VersionOne or ZebraPlan. Our findings also show that participants found VersionOne to be helpful in managing communications and discussions between team members in development teams. Considering that ZebraPlan obtained the highest mean scores for five of the seven questions and was reported the easiest to use, our results suggest that the usability of this software project management tool would have significant impact on the overall progress and coordination of development work in teams that follow agile methodologies.

Observed Usability Problems. Generally, due to the variety of artefacts used among developers who work in agile teams, we note that the four tools differ in the ways they present and organize the functions that each user can take advantage of. For instance, when adding a task, not all of the tools ask users to specify the user story to which the task belongs. Further, when specifying a type of task, some of the tools present the user with a list of options to choose from whereas others ask the user to type in the details of each backlog item that he/she would like to add. To prioritize user stories or development tasks, some of the tools ask the user to choose whether the priority of a task is low, medium or high, while others ask users to either type in the priorities that they want to specify or employ drag-and-drop features. Thus, by considering the fact that numbers can also be used for specifying task priorities, we note that typing the values of these priorities could lead to team members inconsistently specifying these values, which might slow the overall progress of development works. To change the status of task, we observed that some tools allow users to indicate whether a task has started, is in progress or has been completed, whereas others present checkboxes to allow users to indicate the percentage of completion of a given task as either 0 % or 100 %. We also observed that due to inconsistencies in the presentation and structure of functions inside some of the evaluated tools, some participants struggled to find the appropriate button and/or link to perform some of the tasks. For example, although each project has a set of sprints with some user stories that might be further divided into tasks, some of the evaluated tools do not clearly organize these pieces of information based on this hierarchy or do not present users with clear indications to allow them to find the required information easily. After spending a while trying to add a backlog item, one of the participants said, "The navigation menus are not helpful, I remember I saw the button I need but I have no idea where it is" (P4). Other participants also indicated that they had to remember so much information or practice and learn how to use some of the functions many times in order to efficiently perform the required tasks. Therefore, we recommend attaching all the artefacts related to a specific project consistently throughout agile software project management tools. We note that participants faced problems related to the visibility and placement of interface elements (e.g., some tools use grey to color clickable URLs). Furthermore, some participants failed to complete certain tasks because some hyperlinks

Table 5. Ratings reported by our HCI experts based on our defined criteria (see Sect. 4)

	S1	S2	S3	S4		S1	S2	S3	S4
A1	5	5	5	4	E1	3	4	4	2
A2	5	1	1	1	E2	4	4	1	3
B1	5	5	5	5	E3	3	3	4	2
B2	5	5	5	4	E4	4	2	4	3
B3	5	5	5	5	E5	4	4	4	3
B4	5	5	5	4	E6	4	4	4	4
B5	4	4	5	4	F1	5	5	3	4
C1	4	3	4	3	F2	4	5	3	5
C2	4	3	3	3	F3	5	5	3	5
C3	5	5	5	5	F4	5	5	2	5
C4	5	5	5	5	F5	4	5	3	5
D1	2	3	5	4	G1	5	5	4	3
D2	2	3	5	4	G2	4	3	4	5
D3	4	4	5	5	G3	3	3	4	5
D4	5	4	4	5	G4	5	5	3	5
D5	5	5	5	5	G5	3	3	2	5
D6	5	5	4	2	G6	3	4	4	5
D7	5	5	2	5	H1	4	4	5	4
D8	1	1	1	1	H2	5	3	1	4
D9	2	2	5	2	H3	3	3	2	5
–	–	–	–	–	H4	3	2	4	5

did not appear as clickable. In some of the evaluated tools, our participants also faced difficulty in tracking the progress of team members or previously created tasks, either because they could not find the task boards or product backlogs in the corresponding tools or forgot where to find them. It is also worth mentioning that some participants queried search engines to figure out where to find burndown charts, add members to their teams and specify the start and end dates of sprints.

Heuristics Evaluation. Table 5 presents the results of the usability ratings reported by five HCI experts. The evaluation is based on the criteria define in Sect. 4. In this table S1, S2, S3 and S4 represent JIRA, VersionOne, AgileZen and ZebraPlan, respectively.

7 Conclusion

In agile project management contexts, the involvement of human, time, financial and organization-specific factors increases the burden on usability practitioners to study the factors that could improve the workflow of agile teams in software project management tools without increasing the complexity of these tools. In this research effort, we utilize a number of qualitative and quantitative usability engineering methods to identify the major and minor drawbacks of four widely used agile software project management tools. We believe that the experimental findings and the usability evaluation framework presented in this paper can help software development companies to select their tools. We also expect our results to help designers of agile project management tools to identify the shortcomings of their solutions and improve them to suit the requirements of co-located and distributed teams that follow agile software development methodologies.

References

1. Zaharias, P.: A usability evaluation method for e-learning: focus on motivation to learn. In: CHI 2006 Extended Abstracts on Human Factors in Computing Systems, pp. 1571–1576. ACM (2006)
2. Song, S., Lee, J.-H., Hwang, I.: A new framework of usability evaluation for massively multi-player online game: case study of "world of warcraft" game. In: Jacko, J.A. (ed.) HCI 2007. LNCS, vol. 4553, pp. 341–350. Springer, Heidelberg (2007)
3. Lettner, F., Holzmann, C.: Usability evaluation framework. In: Moreno-Díaz, R., Pichler, F., Quesada-Arencibia, A. (eds.) EUROCAST 2011, Part II. LNCS, vol. 6928, pp. 560–567. Springer, Heidelberg (2012)
4. Chen, S.Y., Macredie, R.D.: The assessment of usability of electronic shopping: A heuristic evaluation. Int. J. Inf. Manage. **25**(6), 516–532 (2005)
5. Dybkjær, L., Bernsen, N.O.: Usability evaluation in spoken language dialogue systems. In: Proceedings of the workshop on Evaluation for Language and Dialogue Systems, vol. 9, p. 3, Association for Computational Linguistics (2001)
6. Alhumoud, S., Alabdulkarim, L., Almobarak, N., Al-Wabil, A.: Socio-cultural aspects in the design of multilingual banking interfaces in the arab region. In: Kurosu, M. (ed.) Human-Computer Interaction. LNCS, vol. 9171, pp. 269–280. Springer, Heidelberg (2015)

7. Sathi, A., Morton, T.E., Roth, S.F.: Callisto: An intelligent project management system. AI Mag. **7**(5), 34 (1986)
8. Katsma, C., Amrit, C., van Hillegersberg, J., Sikkel, K.: Can agile software tools bring the benefits of a task board to globally distributed teams? In: Oshri, I., Kotlarsky, J., Willcocks, L.P. (eds.) Global Sourcing 2013. LNBIP, vol. 163, pp. 163–179. Springer, Heidelberg (2013)
9. Manifesto for Agile Software Development. http://www.agilemanifesto.org/. Accessed 2 March 2016
10. Al-Ani, B., Wang, Y., Marczak, S., Trainer, E., Redmiles, D.: Distributed developers and the non-use of web 2.0 technologies: a proclivity model. In: 2012 IEEE Seventh International Conference on Global Software Engineering (ICGSE), pp. 104–113. IEEE (2012)
11. da Silva, F.Q.B., Costa, C., Franca, A.C.C., Prikladinicki, R.: Challenges and solutions in distributed software development project management: a systematic literature review. In: 2010 5th IEEE International Conference on Global Software Engineering (ICGSE), pp. 87–96. IEEE (2010)
12. Azizyan, G., Magarian, M.K., Kajko-Matsson, M.: Survey of agile tool usage and needs. In: Agile Conference (AGILE), 2011, pp. 29–38. IEEE (2011)
13. Azizyan, G., Magarian, M., Kajko-Mattson, M.: The dilemma of tool selection for agile project management. In: 7th International Conference on Software Engineering Advances (ICSEA 2012), pp. 605–614 (2012)
14. Sauro, J.: Measuring usability with the system usability scale (sus). http://www.measuringusability.com/sus.php. Accessed 5 March 2016

Exploring the Role of Adults in Participatory Design for Children on the Autism Spectrum

Bryan Boyle[✉] and Inmaculada Arnedillo-Sánchez

School of Computer Science and Statistics,
Trinity College Dublin, Dublin, Ireland
{boyleb5,Macu.Arnedillo}@scss.tcd.ie

Abstract. The use of participatory design for the development of technology for children with Autism Spectrum Disorder is highlighted for its importance in ensuring a successful outcome and empowering participating children and their families. To date, research has focused on the role the child with autism can play within the design process. This qualitative study examines the contribution adult stakeholders can bring to such participatory design processes.

Our results suggest that parents and professionals have contributions to make in terms of: (1.) supporting the participation of children; (2.) bringing their own experience to bear on the process. Nonetheless, their inclusion requires a more supportive infrastructure that encourages and assists their participation. Overcoming the reluctance of parents and professionals to partake in research and development processes could be facilitated by the provision of awareness, training and education activities that would allow them to contribute more and better prepare their children to engage in the process.

Keywords: Autism spectrum disorder · Participatory design

1 Introduction

Autism spectrum disorder (ASD) and autism are both general terms for a group of complex disorders of brain development. It is considered a lifelong, neuro developmental disability and it's characterized by the presence of persistent deficits in two core areas of functioning. Namely, social interaction and communication skills and the presence of fixed or repetitive behaviours [1]. As interventions increasingly look to technology to provide novel and innovative approaches to support education and treatment of children with ASD, there is a need to ensure best practice in research and development is used to underpin future developments [2].

This paper explores challenges to employing participatory design (PD) methodologies to the process of designing technology for children with ASD, who present with significant cognitive, behavioural and communication difficulties. First recognising the reluctance of many adults to partipate in design processes that are of direct relevance to their children, a discussion of the role of the adult within PD projects is presented. Second the proactive inclusion of adults in terms of their unique contribution and their role as proxy participants, ensuring the meaningful inclusion of the children with ASD, is explored. Third the design of a study examining the self-perceptions of

© Springer International Publishing Switzerland 2016
A. Marcus (Ed.): DUXU 2016, Part I, LNCS 9746, pp. 209–218, 2016.
DOI: 10.1007/978-3-319-40409-7_21

adults and their roles within a technology design process and its findings are described. The paper concludes presenting a set of contributions defined by participant adults in the study which could form the basis for providing more effective structure for collaborative PD workshops with children on the ASP and adult stakeholders.

1.1 Participatory Design (PD)

PD is a design approach that actively involves multiple stakeholders (children, parents, teachers, therapists and others) as participants throughout the design process. It differs from traditional user centred approaches to design insofar as the user is not only a source of information or evaluator but, also plays a decision making role acting as a "co-designer" [3]. To this end the levels of engagement with users which characterizes a PD process is not only more appropriate for groups of people that are margnizalized, such as those with ASD [4, 5], but in fact yields higher quality outcome [6]. Notwithstanding the previous, there are significant challenges for designers with ambitions to engage children with ASD in a PD process. This paper explores the benefits for designers, people with a disability and other stakeholders when PD is implemented within the context of a technology design process. In particular, it examines the contribution adult stakeholders can bring to it.

1.2 Challenges of Designing for Children with Autism

Autism is referred to as a "spectrum disorder", reflecting the high degree of variability of presentation between those diagnosed, with symptoms displayed across a broad range of severity. This heterogeneity of presentation complicates the study of its diagnosis, prognosis and treatment interventions [7] and, it challenges technology designers to create solutions that can match a diverse range of needs and preferences. As many as 50–70 % of children with ASD also have intellectual disabilities, compromising their social, cognitive, and adaptive skills [8] and impacting upon their abilities to participate in collaborative design [9]. Furthermore, one of the core features of ASD: impairment of communication; has a significant effect on a child's ability to partake in activities requiring face-to-face collaboration with others. Although deficits in language skills are by no means universal in autism, they are found in the majority of children with the disorder [10]. Nonetheless, there are benefits to placing the child with ASD at the centre of the design process. For instance, the children's perspective of the world can differ significantly from that of adults [11] and hence, their perceptions of the outcome of the design process may be at odds. Againsts this background, the question remains how can we best facilitate the inclusion of children with ASD in PD processes.

1.3 Inclusion in Design: The Role of the Adult as Inclusion Partnerß

As the complexity of the disability increases so do the requirements for support to ensure that the inclusion of children with ASD in PD is meaningful and adds value. Children with more significant disabilities often require prompting, encouragement and support from adults and peers to effectively use technology. To date, research has focused on the role of the child within the design process rather than that of the adult. However identifying more explicitly the role of the adult within a PD process, translates into a tangible framework to maximise their own participation and the participation of the children they represent or support. Thus the responsibilities of adults in technology PD projects for children with special needs, extend beyond contributing to the design process and the designed artefact. They provide support and encouragement for the child and create an environment that supports the child's active participation [12]. Given that many designers and researchers may have limited experience of working with children with disabilities, the role of the adult also extends to acting as a communication partner for the child; assisting in the interpretation of language between the designer and the user in the conveyance of meaningful responses [13]. The current study explores the role adults can play within a PD process, in terms of: 1. bringing to bear their own experience and skills; and 2. ensuring the participation of children with more significant cognitive, social and language disabilities is maximised.

2   Method

A qualitative study, within the context of an on-going PD project to develop a collaborative game to facilitate the development of social interaction skills for children with ASD, was conducted with a group of 27 adult stakeholders. The study employed an interpretive phenomenological analysis approach, previously used to underpin similar research [14], within which the participant is considered an expert of their own experience [15].

2.1   Objectives of the Research

The study aimed to increase understanding of:

1. The contribution adults can make within the process of designing technology for children on the autism spectrum.
2. The challenges and barriers to ensuring the active engagement of adults within a technology development process.

2.2   Description of the Study Process

A workshop, part of an elective session in a national conference on autism and technology in the state of Qatar, was conducted. Potential participants were asked to attend if they had direct experience of working with or caring for a person with autism and if they had an interest in critiquing an educational game developed for children with autism. The workshop comprised two parts: (1) a demonstration of a design workshop providing participants with experience of a simulated design workshop involving an educational game for children on the autism spectrum; (2) a reflective exercise involving participation in a facilitated focus group and a face-to-face interview with a researcher.

2.3 Data Collection and Analysis

Data was collected via two interconnected mechanisms: focus groups and individual questionnaries. Firstly, participants were organized into 5 focus groups comprising 5-6 participants each. Every group was facilitated by a member of the research team and was given a list of specific tasks to complete during the assigned timeframe. Each group had an appointed, non-participant researcher to record the discussions and interactions of group members and to transcribe these afterwards. Data gathered was analysed using procedures guided by constant-comparative methods. This method compares and contrasts data gathered during interviews or other qualitative methods, forming data categories, assigning content to categories, seeking negative evidence so as to identify conceptual similarities in gathered data and to discover patterns [16].

Focus Group Task Assignment: The focus groups provided a platform to discuss the roles and responsibilities for the participation of adults in design projects. They were structured to discuss and report on the following discussion tasks:

- Please identify and provide a brief description of the contributions adult stakeholders can make within the process of design of technology for children with autism.
- Identify challenges to adult participation in design projects.
- In what ways are children on the autism spectrum best utilized within a typical technology design process?

Facilitators ensured discussions stayed on topic, answered specific questions and queries about the tasks and monitored the progress of each group.

Questionnaire: Further data was gathered using a face-to-face interview with each participant.

The principal data gathering tool for this interview was a three part questionnaire focussed on: 1. the participants' experience of children with ASD; 2. their experience of using technology; and 3. their perception of themselves as contributors to technology design projects. The interview aimed to obtain the views of participants regarding the role they felt that they could play within the context of the design of educational games for children with autism and to gain a measure of their perceived confidence in their role. Responses were recorded by the researcher and transcribed alongside each participant's completed questionnaire.

2.4 Participants

Participants fell into two categories: (1) those describing themselves as Health, Education or Social Care professionals (n = 12); (2) those describing themselves as parents of children with autism (n = 15). The majority of participants were female and collectively represented a broad range of nationalities (Table 1).

Table 1. Participant's (n = 27) description

Gender:	Age:		Role:	
Male: 8	18 – 25 years:	3	Parent (Male)	2
Female: 19	25 – 35 years	16	Parent (Female)	13
	36 – 45 years	7	Professional (Male)	6
	>45 years	1	Professional (Female)	6

3   Findings

This section presents findings in relation to the five roles: *Advocate*, *Teacher*, *Technology Enabler*, *Autism Expert* and *Communication Parter*; adults perceive they can play as active contributors to the design of technology for children with ASD. The perspective of *Parents* and *Professionals*, in terms of how their skills and experiences contribute to their abilities as co-designers, are also provided. While the roles emerged from the analysis of the focus group discussions, the.

3.1   Perceived Adult Contribution

The From the facilitated focus group discussion emerged a total of five specific contributions adults of children with ASD could make in a design project. During follow up interview, each participant was asked to identify the areas that best described their own contribution to a design process. The roles and the discussions regarding their contribution to a design process are elaborated upon and discussed below.

1. Advocate

Parents in particular as a group suggested that the primary responsibility for adults in a technology design process was to advocate for the needs of their own child. Ensuring the function of new technology matches the perceived needs of the children they represented is the primary purpose of their involvement in design. Thus, the design processes and technology should reflect the interests, needs and abilities of each child. The *Advocate* role also highlights the importance of the adult, and in particular the *Parent*, in ensuring the safety and well-being of children when they participate in design projects.

2. Teacher

The role of *Teacher* involves identifying and articulating how the technology can best contribute to each child reaching his/her educational potential. Therapists and specialist teachers of children with autism emphasize their personal responsibility to ensure the design of new technology reflects this and has authentic educational value. All the *Professionals* participating in this study felt that this role was critical in terms of defining the success of the process and identified it as their primary role within a design process. For *Professionals* the value of new technology resides squarely with its overall impact on either educational provision or learning outcomes for children on the spectrum.

3. Technology Enabler

The role *Parents* and *Professionals* play as enablers of technology use for children with ASD was highlighted in discussions. Several parents mentioned that children on the autism spectrum will often not seek out new technology to use and may not have the initiative or motivation to explore new technology alone. As such, the role of the parent becomes that of introducing the technology, creating the context for its use and encouraging and motivating the child. This role is often overlooked in many design processes or is relegated to the margins of the development cycle. *Parents* and *Professionals* have a unique insight of the additional human supports required to enable children with disabilities to use technology.

4. Autism Expert

A common theme emerging from the focus group discussion was the need for domain expertise to influence the direction of design processes. The consensus amongst study participants was that everyone brought a degree of this expertise based on their own experience, but in general, *Professionals* felt that they were in a better position to bring this particular quality to bear on the design process.

5. Communication Partner

Parents in particular struggled during the focus group to find a short description of what they felt was a very important role they could potentially play. Supporting a child's ability to communicate and represent themselves in a collaborative workshop with other adults was highlighted as a potentially stressful situation for many children on the spectrum. Parents spoke about the need to prepare children for participation well ahead, through mechanisms such as Social Stories [17] or other cognitive behavioural interventions. For children that are non-verbal, the parent's role as communication proxy is a determining factor in their inclusion in design. An additional factor emerging from discussions, particularly for parents of older children or those with more significant presentations of their disability was of motivating the children. Firstly to participate and secondly to maintain their participation throughout what is often a time consuming process.

The lack of distinction and the blurring and overlapping of the above roles and contributions was a theme that extended through the discussions on this task. This possibly reflected the breadth of contributions that adult stakeholders could in fact present if included more comprehensively in PD processes. When asked to choose one or more role that described their potential contribution to a design project the entire sample of *Professionals* (n = 12) and the majority of the *Parents* (n = 13) chose two or more roles (Table 2).

3.2 Perceived Challenges to Active Adult Inclusion in Design

Overwhelmingly both *Parents* and *Professionals* pointed to several issues they consider impair the participation of adults in design processes. The more salient ones were the lack of previous experience, skills or knowledge of what constitutes a "design process", as articulated in a statement by the mother of a 14 year-old boy with autism:

Table 2. Parents & Professionals views of their contributions to a technology design process

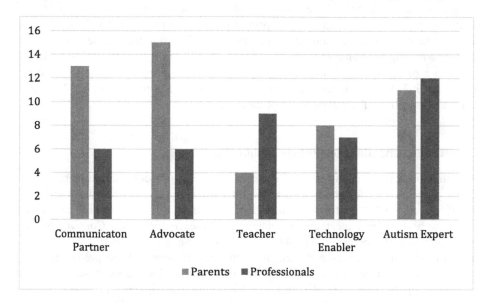

"I would think it natural that those who design the technology know best, better that I let them get on with their job"

Another, impairment for their participation was the lack of clarity regarding the expectations of them and their contributions to a design process. In particular statements by the parents within the group suggested that their experience as parents of children with disabilities was such that their general engagement with service providers was fraught with a lack of clarity of purpose. *Parents* reported that as their children grew older engaging with services or supports for their children required a clear and tangible benefit for their children and their families in the short-term, due to demands on their time.

3.3   Determining Objectives for Technology Design

Determining the objective of a new technology, whether from a therapeutic or a learning perspective, is often the first step within the design process. Inclusion in design from the earliest stage emerged as an important consideration for adults. In particular, the participation of children at the outset of a design process is crucial for adults in order to establish technology that is meaningful for children, and ensuring that the outcome can provide some degree of intrinsic motivation for use by its intended audience.

Collectively, *Parents* and *Professionals* expressed the belief that PD practices should focus on collaboratively defining the objectives of the proposed technology. *Parents* in particular, expressed the view that they are not often aware what the purpose of using specific technology is and hence are not in a position to attribute value to its use. Furthermore, *Parents* suggested that the emphasis on learning and therapeutic objectives for technology often disenfranchises them as parents. Parental feedback was that they do not have the skills required to evaluate the learning or therapeutic progress a child may experience when using a specific piece of technology. The lack of technology designed for leisure and fun was highlighted alongside the unique role parents have determining the value of technology for their children's pleasure. These findings echo those of Frauenberger and his colleagues where the focus on design for people with disabilities tends to follow a deficit model focused on "repairing" rather than on a holistic perspective of the experience of disability [18].

3.4 Recommendations for Future Design Workshops

Our study indicates benefits from the active inclusion of adult stakeholders in the design of technology for children with ASD. However, challenges remain in order to identify, exactly what contribution individual parents and/or professionals can make and, how best to facilitate their articulation of these contributions. Contrary to the suggestion that PD processes should be entirely self-managing [19], it appears the inclusion of adults requires a degree of scaffolding in terms of the preparation for participation and tools to be used during the project. Increasing awareness and knowledge of the anticipated design process amongst participants and a clear articulation of the expectations of those about to engage in collaborative PD are desirable. In preparation for this study an effort was made to identify relevant and appropriate training packages for parents and professionals who are recruited in participatory design processes. It would appear however, that there is a need for those involved technology design to pro-actively seek to develop training and support packages to support the inclusion of not only potential end-users of technology but other stakeholders. The effective use of structured training for participants could ensure that research and design endeavours are truly collaborative and more reflective of participatory processes rather than user-centred design processes.

Utilising the experience and expertise of parents in particular to structure the timing, duration and demands of children's inclusion in the process are practical suggestion to incorporate in PD projects.

Moving forward, the five contribution roles identified here can form the basis for the development of a range of tools for PD workshops. The development and field testing of a range of supports, including training and information packages, role guidance for participants and decision making would appear to be the next step necessary in creating a structure of support for designers that ensure that they can maximise the participation of parents and professional stakeholders.

4 Conclusion

Adults participating in the design of technology tend to be employed to support the inclusion of their children or those they work with [12]. This would appear to be a missed opportunity for designers, considering that there are unique contributions they can offer based on their experience with children and technology. The focus of this study was to begin to investigate the contribution adults can make through their participatory engagement in technology design for children with ASD. Their unique role reflects not just that they are supporters, enablers and facilitators of their children as technology users, but that they have the additional responsibility of representing and articulating the beliefs and experiences of their children or those they work with.

One of the defining differences between user-centred design and PD is in relation to how decision-making is devolved from designers to participants. For truly PD there is a need for designers to not just gather data that will inform the design process, but to create the conditions necessary and the tools required to proffer upon participants the opportunity to be articulate and creative. Designers must also be cognisant of the need to facilitate adult participants both in terms of determining their own values and opinions but also, their responsibilities to represent children who do not have the skills to fully articulate their own experiences and beliefs. In fact, there is an expectation upon designers to ensure that they as a community create the tools and infrastructure required to support and facilitate continued resonance with user experiences [20].

The final arbiter of the success or otherwise of PD must be the eventual outcome of the process. For technology designers the additional burden involved in creating a participatory process is of value only if the final product is enriched and improved by the participation of other stakeholders. To justify the on-going efforts to promote PD processes it is imperative that a body of evidence emerges articulating the value to be accrued through inclusive, participatory design practices. Echoing the recent work by Benton and Johnson [12] determining the impact of the inclusion of adults in the design process should lead to a better understanding of the value of their contribution to the outcomes of design.

Acknowledgements. The authors would like to extend their gratitude to the Mada Qatar Assistive Technology Center for their support for this study and to members of the Autism Parents Group in Doha, Qatar that contributed to this research.

This research has received funding from the charity RESPECT and the People Programme (Marie Curie Actions) of the European Union's Seventh Framework Programme (FP7/2007-2013) under REA grant agreement no. PCOFUND-GA-2013-608728'.

References

1. Jo, H., Schieve, L.A., Rice, C.E., Yeargin-Allsopp, M., Tian, L.H., Blumberg, S.J., Kogan, M.D., Boyle, C.A.: Age at Autism Spectrum Disorder (ASD) diagnosis by race, ethnicity, and primary household language among children with special health care needs, United States, 2009-2010. Matern. Child Health J. **19**(8), 1687–1697 (2015)
2. Rajendran, G.: Virtual environments and autism: a developmental psychopathological approach. J. Comput. Assist. Learn. **29**(4), 334–347 (2013)
3. Loup-Escande, E., Burkhardt, J.M., Christmann, O., Richir, S.: Needs' elaboration between users, designers and project leaders: analysis of a design process of a virtual reality-based software. Inf. Softw. Technol. **56**(8), 1049–1061 (2014)

4. Parsons, S., Millen, L., Garib-Penna, S., Cobb, S.: Participatory design in the development of innovative technologies for children and young people on the autism spectrum: the COSPATIAL project. J. Assist. Technol. **5**(1), 29–34 (2011)

5. Guha, M.L., Druin, A., Fails, J.A.: Cooperative Inquiry revisited: Reflections of the past and guidelines for the future of intergenerational co-design. Int. J. Child-Comput. Interact. **1**(1), 14–23 (2013)

6. Fletcher-Watson, S.: Evidence-based technology design and commercialisation: recommendations derived from research in education and autism. TechTrends **59**(1), 84–88 (2014)

7. Georgiades, S., Szatmari, P., Boyle, M., Hanna, S., Duku, E., Zwaigenbaum, L., Bryson, S., Fombonne, E., Volden, J., Mirenda, P., Smith, I., Roberts, W., Vaillancourt, T., Waddell, C., Bennett, T., Thompson, A.: Investigating phenotypic heterogeneity in children with autism spectrum disorder: a factor mixture modeling approach. J. Child Psychol. Psychiatry Allied Discip. **54**(2), 206–215 (2013)

8. Matson, J.L., Shoemaker, M.: Intellectual disability and its relationship to autism spectrum disorders. Res. Dev. Disabil. **30**(6), 1107–1114 (2009)

9. Coons, K., Watson, S.: Conducting research with individuals who have intellectual disabilities: ethical and practical implications for qualitative research. J. Dev. Disabil. **19**(2), 14–22 (2013)

10. Kjelgaard, M.M., Tager-Flusberg, H.: An investigation of language impairment in autism: implications for genetic subgroups. Lang. Cogn. Process. **16**(2–3), 287–308 (2001)

11. Frauenberger, C., Good, J., Keay-Bright, W.: Designing technology for children with special needs - bridging perspectives through participatory design. CoDesign **7**(2015), 1–28 (2011)

12. Benton, L., Johnson, H.: Widening participation in technology design: a review of the involvement of children with special educational needs and disabilities. Int. J. Child-Comput. Interact. **3–4**, 23–40 (2015)

13. Irvine, A.: Conducting qualitative research with individuals with developmental disabilities: methodological and ethical considerations. Dev. Disabil. Bull. **38**(1–2), 21–34 (2010)

14. MacLeod, A.G., Lewis, A., Robertson, C.: 'CHARLIE: PLEASE RESPOND!' using a participatory methodology with individuals on the autism spectrum. Int. J. Res. Method Educ. **37**(4), 407–420 (2014)

15. Smith, J.A.: Evaluating the contribution of interpretative phenomenological analysis. Health Psychol. Rev. **5**(1), 9–27 (2011)

16. Boeije, H.: A purposeful approach to the constant comparative method in the analysis of qualitative interviews. Qual. Quant. **36**(4), 391–409 (2002)

17. Gray, C.A., Garand, J.D.: Social stories: improving responses of students with autism with accurate social information. Focus Autism Other Dev. Disabl. **8**(1), 1–10 (1993)

18. Frauenberger, C., Good, J., Alcorn, A.: Challenges, opportunities and future perspectives in including children with disabilities in the design of interactive technology. In: Proceedings of the 11th International Conference on Interaction Design and Children, IDC 2012, pp. 367–370 (2012)

19. Curzon, J.: With hindsight: an overview of the autism spectrum disorder participatory action research project. Kairaranga **9**, 3–8 (2008)

20. Sanders, E.B.: From user-centered to participatory design approaches. In: Design and the Social Sciences: Making Connections, pp. 1–8. CRC Press (2002)

Usability Pattern Identification Through Heuristic Walkthroughs

Manuel Burghardt[✉]

Media Informatics Group, Institute for Information and Media,
Language and Culture, University of Regensburg, Regensburg, Germany
manuel.burghardt@ur.de

Abstract. Patterns are a popular means to document design knowledge in different fields of application, including HCI. Accordingly, a large number of different HCI pattern formats have been suggested. However, relatively little is said about how to systematically identify such patterns. In order to make the process of identifying patterns more transparent and comprehensible, I apply a usability inspection method to generate data that can be used as input for the systematic creation of usability patterns. This article describes the basic idea of identifying usability patterns through a series of heuristic walkthroughs and illustrates the approach by means of a case study in the field of "linguistic annotation tools".

1 Introduction

During the 1970s, Christopher Alexander observed that in architecture there seems to be a "timeless way of building" (Alexander 1979) in which certain successful – yet rather implicit – design solutions for towns appear over and over again. Accordingly, Alexander suggests to capture such implicit design knowledge, which implements a certain "quality without a name", in the form of what he calls *patterns*

1.1 Usability Patterns

Patterns are a useful format to capture design knowledge, and thus have quickly found their way into the HCI community (Borchers 2001). The main advantage of usability patterns is that they express "a relation between a certain context, a problem, and a solution" (Alexander 1979: 247), i.e. they do not solely describe an isolated solution, but also document for what kind of problem and in what kind of context the pattern can be used successfully. The benefits of patterns as a means to document design knowledge are also underlined by a survey (Kruschitz and Hitz 2010), indicating that the majority (approx. 71 %) of those who are using patterns during the design process feel it improves the overall process.

The work described in this paper is part of a PhD project finished in 2014 (cf. Burghardt 2014).

A. Marcus (Ed.): DUXU 2016, Part I, LNCS 9746, pp. 219–230, 2016.
DOI: 10.1007/978-3-319-40409-7_22

1.2   Pattern Identification

When it comes to the creation of design pattern, two aspects are to be considered: First, patterns have to be identified, and second, they have to be written down in a generic pattern format. While there exists a plethora of different pattern formats in the area of HCI, (cf. for instance Borchers 2001; Obrist 2010; Tidwell 2011; Van Welie and Trætteberg 2000)[1] as well as guides on how to write down patterns (Wellhausen and Fiesser 2012), Martin et al. (2001) note that little is said about how to systematically identify patterns. Alexander (1979: 258ff.) describes three basic approaches for the identification of patterns, that may be characterized as being more inductive or more deductive, or a mix of both modes of reasoning. In software engineering and HCI, the inductive approach, which is oftentimes referred to as *pattern mining*, seems to be particularly popular, following the assumption that patterns are present in the artifacts that already exist (DeLano 1998). In practice, however, such inductive pattern mining approaches remain rather vague. As a matter of fact, very little is known about a structured process for pattern creation in the field of HCI, as it mostly relies on the implicit knowledge of experienced designers (Krischkowsky et al. 2013). This notion seems to be conflicting with the fundamental idea that usability is not a vague criterion, but rather can be tested and engineered systematically, by applying a large set of available methods.

In order to close this gap, and to make the process of identifying patterns more transparent and comprehensible, I apply a usability inspection method to generate data that can be used as input for the systematic creation of usability patterns.

2   A Systematic Approach to the Identification of Usability Patterns

The basic idea of the approach is to apply a usability inspection method to evaluate several competing products in one common domain of application (e.g. linguistic annotation tools), assuming that the solution to usability problems identified for one product is possibly present in a competing product. These problems (weaknesses) and solutions (strengths) can then be used to generate usability patterns for that very domain of application.

2.1   Description of Evaluation Method

As it is crucial for the pattern identification process to analyze multiple competing products, a large-scale user study would be too laborious and costly; that is why I decided to use an expert-based inspection method. While inspection methods typically recommend the use of multiple evaluators, I suggest a single evaluator approach, which is more likely to produce consistent results that in

---

[1] For a short review of different pattern formats (not only for HCI) cf. Kruschitz and Hitz (2009).

turn can be used as appropriate input for generic design patterns. Furthermore, the involvement of multiple evaluators is more prone to produce rather heterogeneous results with regard to the form, description and severity of identified usability problems.

From the broad spectrum of available inspection methods, I have chosen the popular *heuristic walkthrough* method (Sears 1997). The heuristic walkthrough is a hybrid approach that borrows ideas from *heuristic evaluation, cognitive walkthrough*, and *usability walkthroughs*, to make up for the specific drawbacks of each single method (Sears 1997). As I am interested not only in usability problems, the heuristic walkthrough was extended to also document good designs and potential solutions for previously identified problems. For both, usability problems and strengths, a short *ID* (for easy referencing later on), a *title*, a short *problem description* and the *heuristic* (Nielsen 1994a) that – in case of a problem – was violated, or – in case of a strength – was obeyed, are documented.

2.2 Usability Pattern Structure

Van Welie (2001) describes a usability pattern structure that seems to integrate particularly well with data gathered from a heuristic walkthrough (cf. Sect. 2.3). The following list shows the complete template with abbreviated descriptions taken from Van Welie (2001: 102ff.).

Name – short, catchy name that either relates to the problem or the solution
Problem – user problem the pattern is trying to solve, and the objectives it is trying to achieve
Usability principle – higher-level usability principle the solution is based on
Context – contextual information on when a certain pattern can be applied successfully
Forces – trade-offs that have to be made in order to find a solution
Solution – formulated in a rather abstract, generic way, so it can be applied and implemented for various different scenarios
Rationale – makes clear why a pattern works; this argumentation can be based on aspects of usability such as *performance speed, learnability, memorability, satisfaction, task completion* and *errors*
Example – concrete examples (typically a screenshot) help to understand the pattern and underline that the solution has been proven to work in existing applications
Counterexample – optional section with examples of applications that do not use the pattern
Known uses – further examples of applications that implement the pattern
Related patterns – other patterns that address related problems may be referenced.

2.3 Integrating the Heuristic Walkthrough Results with the Pattern Structure

As was mentioned before, usability problems and strengths were documented – together with one or more associated heuristics – during the heuristic evaluation.

These sources of input can be translated step-by-step into Van Welie's pattern structure.

Heuristics. While heuristics on the one hand facilitate the systematic discovery of usability problems, they can also be used as positive usability principles that help to formulate a solution for the problem. For this reason, heuristics are used as an explicit reference in the *usability principle* section, but also as implicit input in the *solution* section of a design pattern.

Usability Problems. Usability problems that were identified during the heuristic walkthroughs are an essential input for several fields of the pattern: First of all, a problem can be used to find an adequate *name* for a pattern, as the name should always relate to the problem or the solution. Second, one or more problems will be paraphrased in the *problem* section. Additionally, all associated usability problems are listed alphabetically by means of their ID at the end of the problem section, to make the process more transparent. Third, usability problems can be used to describe the *context* in which the patterns can be used. They can also serve as input for the extended context section, the *forces*. As "many usability problems have fairly obvious fixes as soon as they have been identified" (Nielsen 1994b: 31), they may also be used as input for the formulation of an adequate *solution*. Finally, usability problems can help to describe tools that qualify as a *counterexample* for the respective pattern.

Strengths. Similar to the usability problems, the identified strengths can be used as input to formulate an adequate *name* for the pattern. Much like the usability problems, specific strengths can help to elaborate the context of application, which is documented in the *context* and *forces* sections. Furthermore, strengths of a product can be generalized in the *solution* section of a pattern. If appropriate, they can also be documented in the *example* (screenshot and short description) or *known uses* (mention of tool name) section.

2.4   Pattern Identification Process

The systematic identification of usability patterns starts by examining the results of the previously conducted series of heuristic walkthroughs for a number of competing products in one common domain of application. As was described before, the heuristic walkthrough method allows the evaluator to reveal usability problems as well as particularly good solutions for certain problems. Conducting an evaluation of several competing products, however, leads to a large number of identical or at least thematically similar problems and strengths. Accordingly, an important prerequisite for the pattern identification process is to create clusters of similar problems and strengths that recur for different evaluation objects. During this clustering phase, three basic scenarios may occur:

1. Existence of problems and appropriate solutions – Ideally, a solution to a recurring problem can be identified in one of the test objects, which may then be used to relate both, the problem categories and the good solutions in one common usability pattern.
2. Existence of solutions without concrete problems – Some patterns may also be created merely on the basis of good solutions, without explicitly documented usability problems. Note that with a single-evaluator approach, not all potential usability problems might be identified. It is, however, easy to derive the problem situation that is improved by those strengths retrospectively.
3. Existence of problems without concrete solution – In a number of cases, a group of similar problems could be identified without having a concrete solution in the heuristic walkthrough data. In these cases, new solutions were created based on the usability problems and the heuristics that are violated when the problem occurs.

Also note, that not all of the identified problems and strengths will qualify for the derivation of a specific usability pattern. Typically this is the case whenever the identified problems are not domain-specific, but rather general usability problems (e.g. bad menu structuring, bad use of typography, etc.).

3   Case Study with Step-by-Step Guide

This section describes all the steps that are necessary to translate results from a series of heuristic walkthroughs into the usability pattern format. The approach is illustrated by means of a case study, in which 11 tools from the application domain "linguistic annotation" were evaluated to discover a total of 207 problems and 84 strengths. From this data, 82 problems and 62 strengths were used to derive a total of 26 usability patterns, which are publicly available in a pattern wiki (www.annotation-usability.net). The systematic creation of one of these patterns is described in the following step-by-step guide.

3.1   Clustering According to Similar Content (Step 1)

Analyzing the problems according to their description content, one cluster of problems emerged that was concerned with the issue that the "annotation scheme" cannot be created inside the annotation tool, but rather has to be created in an external code editor, by means of XML markup. At the same time, there are several tools that implement an integrated annotation scheme editor, which seems to be a good solution for that problem. After the clustering, seven usability problems (cf. Table 1 for an example) were identified that are concerned with this issue, but also six strengths (cf. Table 2 for an example) could be interpreted as partial solutions for the issue. The cluster of problems and strengths that all address the issue of "annotation scheme creation" is then used as input for the different sections of the pattern structure.

Table 1. Example usability problem for the issue "annotation scheme creation".

Tool	Brat
Problem	Annotation scheme cannot be created/edited inside the tool (ID: BRA10)
Description	The annotation scheme needs to be created outside of the tool, in a code editor. If the user changes the scheme outside of the tool, the browser needs to be refreshed to apply the changes.
Heuristics	Error prevention, flexibility and efficiency of use

Table 2. Example strength for the issue "annotation scheme creation".

Tool	CATMA
Strength	Annotation scheme creation and modification via GUI (ID: CAT03)
Description	The annotation scheme can be created and edited directly in the tool, by means of graphical elements and a simple form window.
Heuristics	Flexibility and efficiency of use

3.2 Pattern Name (Step 2)

In this case, the name of the pattern is closely related to the solution of the problem, which, in short, is to provide an integrated annotation scheme editor. Accordingly, the pattern is named as follows:

Name: P4.1 - Integrated annotation scheme editor

Note: The pattern ID "P4.1" indicates that this is the first pattern in the fourth category ("Annotation scheme"), as the 26 patterns identified for linguistic annotation tools were eventually categorized according to six main groups of patterns. This grouping of patterns is optional, but recommended for larger pattern collections, as it facilitates the navigation in the collection.

3.3 Problem Description (Step 3)

In the problem description section, the seven previously identified problems are paraphrased and summarized. In addition, all related problems are listed by means of their ID (alphabetic order). The respective *problem description* section for pattern P4.1 looks like this:

Problem description: The creation of an annotation scheme that defines different levels of annotation as well as concrete annotation items on each level is a crucial task in any annotation project. Typically, annotation schemes are defined by means of document grammars known from markup languages like XML or SGML. Users without technical knowledge about markup languages will have difficulties in creating a scheme in XML syntax. At the same time, many tools require to define an annotation scheme outside the annotation tool, which makes the task even more challenging for markup novices.

Related problems: BRA10, [...]

3.4   Usability Principle (Step 4)

Nielsen's (1994a) heuristics cannot only be used to discover usability problems, but also to derive fixes for identified problems. As the heuristics were already used during the heuristic walkthrough, it suggests itself to use the same set of heuristics to describe the usability principles the solution of the pattern is based on. If the heuristics documented for the problems and strengths of the respective cluster are very heterogeneous, only the most important, predominant heuristics are mentioned in the pattern section. In this example, the two predominant heuristics that are violated by the identified usability problems, and that in turn can be used to fix these problems, are "error prevention" and "flexibility and efficiency of use": Markup novices, who have to create and modify an annotation scheme in an external XML editor are likely to produce errors during this process. At the same time, having to switch between the actual annotation tool and an external editor slows down the user and thus reduces his flexibility and efficiency.

Usability principle: Error prevention, flexibility and efficiency of use.

3.5   Context (Step 5)

The context of a pattern describes in which scenarios and under which conditions it can be used. The usability problems, as well as concrete strengths, help to derive a more specific context of use. The context for this example is to provide users who are markup novices with an intuitive and efficient way to formulate annotation schemes.

Context: This pattern can be used to facilitate the creation of annotation schemes for users without technical knowledge about markup languages and document grammars.

3.6   Forces (Step 6)

This section of the pattern structure can be seen as an extension of the previous context section, as it describes some conflicting forces that may require trade-offs when the pattern is applied. The sources of input are the same as in the context section, but they are interpreted in a way that reveals potential conflicts and helps to balance existing contradictions. In this example, the main conflict is that on the technical side, annotation schemes are typically realized by means of a markup language, which is the ideal instrument for this kind of task, as it can be easily processed by machines. On the side of the user, who may not be familiar with the concept of markup languages, this may be a rather irritating and cumbersome way to create an annotation scheme.

Forces
- Annotation schemes are typically defined by means of document grammars (DTDs or XML Schemas).
- Annotation schemes are typically defined outside of the annotation tool, in a text editor that facilitates the creation of document grammars.
- For editing existing schemes during the annotation process, it is impractical to switch between the annotation tool and an external text editor.

3.7 Solution (Step 7)

This is an integral part of the pattern, as it describes a solution to the previously introduced problem. In this exemplary pattern it is possible to derive a solution from many positive examples (strengths) of other annotation tools. Essentially, the solution is to provide an integrated annotation scheme editor that allows the user to create schemes without having to use XML or some other markup syntax.

> **Solution:** The tool integrates a scheme editor that allows the user to define and edit annotation schemes inside the annotation tool. By providing a graphical user interface for the scheme editor it is also possible to hide technical details of the storage format from the user. Such an interface should utilize well-known metaphors for the creation of hierarchical structures, such as file-trees or ordered lists. It can also make use of established input elements, such as forms and input fields. It must be made clear via the interface which annotation items belong to which level of annotation, i.e. typically the annotation levels are at the highest hierarchical level of the scheme, while concrete annotation items can be subordinate to those different levels.

3.8 Rationale (Step 8)

The rationale section does not use input from the heuristic walkthrough data, but rather relies on a set of usability aspects that help to explain why and how the pattern improves the usability of an annotation tool. The five usability aspects that are used in this pattern collection were introduced by Nielsen (1993: 26ff.): *learnability, efficiency, memorability, error rate,* and *satisfaction.* In this example the suggested solution improves the usability of an annotation tool as it helps to increase the overall performance speed (*efficiency*), but also helps to quicker learn (*learnability*) the tool and to avoid errors (*error rate*) when using it productively.

> **Rationale:** As ad hoc modifications of the annotation scheme are part of the typical annotation process, an integrated editor for annotation schemes speeds up the overall annotation process (*efficiency of use*). At the same

time, the availability of a GUI for the creation and modification of annotation schemes increases the *learnability* of the annotation tool and decreases the number of potential *errors* that may occur when novices are forced to translate linguistic annotation schemes into formal markup languages.

3.9 Examples and Prototypes (Step 9)

This section of the pattern contains screenshots that illustrate the solution as a concrete example in an existing tool. It is important to note that these examples do not present the pattern's solution in an isolated way, but rather as part of the overall tool interface. Therefore, an example that illustrates a good solution may, nevertheless, be accompanied by usability problems that are related to other interface aspects.

In the few cases where there is no positive example available in the tested tools, an interactive prototype that implements the proposed solution and that may serve as an example will be provided. For this example pattern, a number of tools can be identified that implement the suggested solution of an integrated, non-XML annotation scheme editor (cf. Figure 1)

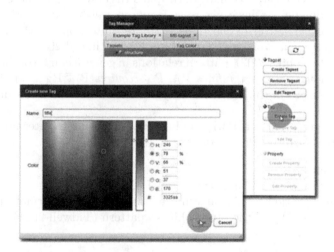

Fig. 1. CATMA – Integrated annotation scheme editor.

3.10 Optional Counterexamples (Step 10)

The optional section counterexamples was left out in most patterns, as the information is largely redundant with the alphabetic list of concrete usability problems that is provided in the problem description section: All tools that are documented with a usability problem for a specific pattern may as well serve as a counterexample.

3.11   Known Uses (Step 11)

This section can be seen as an extension of the *examples* category, as it lists all tools that implement the solution of the pattern, but have not been mentioned in the examples section for means of reduced redundancy. In some cases – though not in this example pattern – the *known uses* section may also contain examples for tools that have not been part of the heuristic walkthrough evaluation, but that are known from previous studies or from hints in related literature.

Known uses: *GATE, Knowtator.*

3.12   Related Patterns (Step 12)

One of the strengths of the pattern format is the possibility to relate different patterns to each other, and thus create an interconnected repository for design knowledge. Relations may either point to a pattern from an external collection of HCI patterns, or to other patterns in the same collection.

In the domain of HCI, there are numerous pattern collections[2] that describe good design on various levels of abstraction, e.g. concrete interaction elements, general user behaviors, etc. As many of the patterns described in these collections are either redundant, or have a strong focus on web-based interfaces, I only relate to two other pattern collections that are quite popular throughout the HCI community (Van Welie and Trætteberg 2000; Tidwell 2011).

According to Conte (2002), pattern relations in general can be of the following four types: P_A *uses* P_B, P_A *refines* P_B, P_A *requires* P_B, P_A is an *alternative* for P_B. All relations in the pattern collection will be created according to these basic types.

For the example pattern P4.1, the following relations to internal as well as external patterns can be identified:

Related patterns
   - Internal relations: This pattern uses P4.2
   - External relations: This pattern uses the "Structured format" pattern (Tidwell 2011) and the "Input hints" pattern (Tidwell 2011).

4   Discussion

While patterns provide a detailed description of a problem and its solution in a generic form that can be understood by tool developers as well as tool users, it must be noted that the systematic identification of such patterns is far more time-consuming than the creation of a traditional usability report. It has also shown that not all problems and strengths are appropriate as input for a usability pattern. De facto, many of the observed problems are either too specific or too general to be suitable for the derivation of a pattern.

---

[2] On his website, Van Welie gives an overview of many other collections of HCI patterns (cf. http://www.welie.com/index.php).

In a follow up-study, the pattern identification process was applied to the domain of "graph visualization tools", with a smaller number of evaluation objects: The evaluation of 3 different graph visualization tools (*Tulip*, *Cytoscape* and *Gephi*) by means of a heuristic walkthrough led to a total of 79 usability problems and 24 strengths. 43 problems and 14 strengths qualified as input for a total of 14 patterns. The results of this study indicate, that a decent amount of patterns can also be identified with a smaller number of evaluation objects.

Another point of discussion is the validity and applicability of the patterns. Van Welie and Van der Veer (2003) point out that pattern languages are always subjective to a certain degree, as they reflect the mental model of the designer who created it. For a discussion of the validity and applicability of a pattern collection, it is important to comprehend the creation of design patterns as an iterative process. This process starts with a first (subjective) suggestion of a "pattern candidate" (Ratzka 2008) and is successively refined afterwards. In the software engineering and HCI communities, the successive refinement has been formalized as the so called shepherding process, which is essentially a reviewing process where the shepherds (experienced pattern authors) help to improve the pattern candidates of novice patterns authors (Harrison 1999). The approach suggested in this article is well suited for the identification of pattern candidates that can be further refined in a subsequent shepherding process.

References

Alexander, C.: The Timeless Way of Building. Oxford University Press, New York (1979)

Borchers, J.O.: A Pattern Approach to Interaction Design. Wiley, Chichester (2001)

Burghardt, M.: Engineering annotation usability - toward usability patterns for linguistic annotation tools. Doctoral dissertation, University of Regensburg, urn:nbn:de:bvb:355-epub-307682 (2014). http://epub.uni-regensburg.de/30768/. Accessed on 28 Feb 2016

Conte, A., Fredj, M., Hassine, I., Giraudin, J.-P., Gui, J.: A tool and a formalism to design and apply patterns. In: Bellahsène, Z., Patel, D., Rolland, C. (eds.) OOIS 2002. LNCS, vol. 2425, pp. 135–146. Springer, Heidelberg (2002)

DeLano, D.E.: Patterns mining. In: Rising, L. (ed.) The Patterns Handbook: Techniques, Strategies, and Applications, pp. 87–95. Press Syndicate of the University of Cambridge, Cambridge (1998)

Harrison, N.B.: The language of shepherding - a pattern language for shepherds and sheep (1999). http://hillside.net/index.php/the-language-of-shepherding

Krischkowsky, A., Wurhofer, D., Perterer, N., Tscheligi, M.: Developing patterns step-by-step a pattern generation guidance for HCI researchers. In: Zimmermann, A. (ed.) Proceedings of the 5th International Conferences on Pervasive Patterns and Applications, PATTERNS 2013, pp. 66–72. ThinkMind (2013)

Kruschitz, C., Hitz, M.: The anatomy of HCI design patterns. In: Dini, P., Gentzsch, W., Geraci, P., Lorenz, P., Singh, K. (eds.) Proceedings of Computation World 2009: Future Computing, Service Computation, Cognitive, Adaptive, Content, Patterns, pp. 202–207. IEEE, Los Alamitos (2009)

Kruschitz, C., Hitz, M.: Are human-computer interaction design patterns really used? In: Proceedings of the 6th Nordic Conference on Human-Computer Interaction Extending Boundaries, NordiCHI 2010, pp. 711–714. ACM, New York (2010)

Martin, D., Rodden, T., Rouncefield, M., Sommerville, I., Viller, S.: Finding patterns in the fieldwork. In: Prinz, W., Jarke, M., Rogers, Y., Schmidt, K., Wulf, V. (eds.) Proceedings of the Seventh Conference on European Conference on Computer Supported Cooperative Work, ECSCW 2001, pp. 39–58. Kluwer Academic Publishing, Norwell (2001)

Nielsen, J.: Usability Engineering. Morgan Kaufman, Amsterdam (1993)

Nielsen, J. (1994a). Enhancing the explanatory power of usability heuristics. In: Plaisant, C. (ed.) Conference Companion on Human Factors in Computing Systems, CHI 1994, pp. 152–158. ACM, New York

Nielsen, J.: Heuristic evaluation. In: Nielsen, J., Mack, R. (eds.) Usability Inspection Methods, pp. 25–62. Wiley, New York (1994b)

Obrist, M., Wurhofer, D., Beck, E., Tscheligi, M.: Towards contextual user experience patterns. In: Proceedings of the 2nd International Conferences on Pervasive Patterns and Applications, PATTERNS 2010, pp. 60–65. ThinkMind (2010)

ratzka, A.: Steps in identifying interaction design patterns for multimodal systems. In: Fobrig, P., Patern, F. (eds.) HCSE/TAMODIA 2008. LNCS, vol. 5247, pp. 58–71. Springer, Heidelberg (2008)

Sears, A.: Heuristic walkthroughs: finding the problems without the noise. Int. J. Hum. Comput. Interact. 9(3), 213–234 (1997)

Tidwell, J.: Designing Interfaces, 2nd edn. OReilly Media, Sebastopol (2011)

Van Welie, M., Trætteberg, H.: Interaction patterns in user interfaces (2000). http://hillside.net/plop/plop/plop2k/proceedings/Welie/Welie.pdf. Accessed on 28 Feb 2016

Van Welie, M.: Task-based user interface design. Doctoral dissertation, Vrije Universiteit Amsterdam, SIKS Dissertation Series No. 2001-6(2001)

Van Welie, M., Van der Veer, G.C.: Structure and organization (2003). http://www.idemployee.id.tue.nl/g.w.m.rauterberg/conferences/interact2003/INTERACT2003-p527.pdf. Accessed on 12 June 2013

Wellhausen, T., Fiesser, A.: How to write a pattern? A rough guide for first-time pattern authors. In: Proceedings of the 16th European Conference on Pattern Languages of Programs, EuroPLoP 2011 (Article No. 5). ACM, New York (2012)

User Methods and Approaches
to Design Cognitive Systems

Heloisa Candello[⊠]

IBM Research, Rua Tutóia 1157, São Paulo, SP, Brazil
hcandello@br.ibm.com

Abstract. This paper presents the results of a review of existing literature on user research practices for designing cognitive systems. Three databases were analyzed to review the user methods and approaches researchers apply in this field. It was considered methods and approaches aimed to gather user information and provide insights to design systems that augment human knowledge. As a result 82 papers were examined. It was clear the design process of Cognitive systems depends of user input and interaction to be successful; therefore new research methods are necessary to investigate how design artifacts might influence in decision-making, considering user interpretation, trust and confidence.

Keywords: Design process · Design methods · Cognitive systems · User experience

1 Introduction

The objective of this literature review is an attempt to identify user approaches and research methods to unveil cognitive computing practices to develop Cognitive-computing systems. As machines start to enhance human cognition and help people make better decisions, new issues arise for research. For instance, which actions can we transpose to cognitive systems? How to design information for cognitive systems dialogue with humans? What are the design methods available to investigate the main everyday practices and cognitive human process to make decisions? It is important to understand how research in the design research field may serve as a contribution to develop cognitive systems. It is important to point out the meaning to develop for cognitive systems applying design research. In Design Research area, methods, theories and better development of certain artificial and interactive products are carefully studied to improve the design process, solve problems and extend the knowledge generated to other similar artifacts (Zimmerman 2007). Design methods are tools to help to unveil main practices, cognitive processes and user understanding of information sources available in certain contexts. Collect, organize and present information sources in a way humans will grasp is a challenge for cognitive systems, as those systems may be dialogue based. In order to have a big picture of user research for cognitive systems we propose a literature review. 225 papers available were analyzed in three search databases. The papers were published between 2010 and 2015. The review identified recurring themes and patterns of the most common activities and beneficial user methods for designing future Cognitive Systems. This paper is organized as follows.

© Springer International Publishing Switzerland 2016
A. Marcus (Ed.): DUXU 2016, Part I, LNCS 9746, pp. 231–242, 2016.
DOI: 10.1007/978-3-319-40409-7_23

First a brief overview of Cognitive systems is given. Second, we explain how this review was conducted. Third, we discuss the main results of the review. The limitation of this work and further research was highlighted.

2 Cognitive Systems

Cognitive Computing is the use of computational learning systems to augment cognitive capabilities in solving real world problems. According to Kelly and Hamm (2013:8):

> Tomorrow's cognitive systems will be fundamentally different from the machines that preceded them. While traditional computers must be programmed by humans to perform specific tasks, cognitive systems will learn from their interactions with data and humans and be able to, in a sense, program themselves to perform new tasks. Traditional computers are designed to calculate rapidly; cognitive systems will be designed to draw inferences from data and pursue the objectives they were given. […]. In the cognitive era, computers will adapt to people. They'll interact with us in ways that are natural to us.

Kelly and Hamm (2013) also emphasize that Cognitive systems will help us to be smarter offering effectiveness processing large amount of information, dealing with complexity; expertise to help see the overall picture to make better decisions; objectivity avoiding bias; imagination helping us explore a broad range of choices to generate ideas; sense using sensors and analytics software to grasp also physical information. Not only is Cognitive computing a fundamentally new computing paradigm for tackling real world problems, exploiting enormous amounts of data using massively parallel machines, but also it engenders a new form of interaction between humans and computers. Cognitive systems bring human-like reasoning to the problems of Big Data, and also permit us to expand into the white space of domains that require human-like cognition but that either exceed human capacity or are impossible for a live human presence (Nahamoo 2014). Noor (2015) explains that computer essentially process a series of conditional equations and suggest answers. Therefore, it has consequences for user decision-making, since probability can be taken in consideration when making choices. Cognitive systems are able to infer information usually based on parameters that use data captured by sensors or/and user input and interaction. According to Lintern (2011) the robustness of a cognitive system is due to the manner in which the human participants in the system integrate their activities. For instance, those systems may learn more user behavior patterns and provide more assertive inferences. In this context, humans collaborate with machines to create knowledge, and issues of trust and collaboration are topics that are being considered to design those new kinds of systems (Baillieul et al. 2012). In this context, the present review emphasizes research methods to design systems aimed to augment human knowledge and enhance user experience. Additionally, papers that present research methods to acquire contextual information to provide a better user experience were selected.

3   Literature Review

The research papers summarized in the review are referred to as primary studies, while the review itself is a secondary study. The accumulation of evidence through secondary studies can be very valuable in offering new insights or in identifying where an issue might be clarified by this review (Brereton 2007). This paper is a first attempt to identify main design processes (methodologies, methods and approaches) to assist and design future cognitive systems. It was a challenge to choose suitable terms to cover the main design practices applied in the Cognitive systems domain. Words such as: intelligent, smart, wise are used in the cognitive systems context. Not always those terms refer only to computer systems, but also interchangeable with human machine interfaces, integrated systems or human robot/agent cooperation. Additionally, terms as advisor, recommender and tailor define technologies based on human preferences and needs. The diversity of terms is also noted in papers referring to user-centered design processes of interactive technologies, such as: human-centered design; user experience, human computer interaction, user research and so on. In this paper we use the term Cognitive system to refer to technologies that learn and/or dialogue with humans and augment their sense of making decisions. The term User-centered design refers to all the design activities involving users during the Design research process.

3.1   Research Questions and Search Strategy

The main research question is: What are the common user research methods and approaches to design Cognitive Computing systems? The research question guided the selection of keywords for the search. The search keywords were (Table 1):

Table 1. Keywords

Category	Keywords
Cognitive systems	Cognitive systems, Intelligent systems, Cognitive Computing, Cognitive psychology, Smart machines, Advisor, Recommender, Decision support, Uncertainty, Dialogue, User research
User centered design	Human centered design, Human-computer interaction, User experience, User-centered design, Design methods, Design Research, Design methods, Design process

The sources selected for the systematic review were: IEEExplore Digital Library, Elsevier ScienceDirect and ACM Digital Library Each digital library has its own query rules for advanced search tasks, hence, the search strings and operators had to fit in each library. In the ACM digital Library, a general automatic search and a hand search was made of the last 5 years of well-known conference proceedings: UIST - ACM User Interface Software and Technology Symposium, IUI – ACM Conference on Intelligent User Interfaces, CHI - ACM Conference on Computer Human Interaction, DIS – ACM Conference on Designing Interactive Systems. A general search was also conducted in

Elsevier Science Direct, although special attention was given to papers published on the Design Studies Journal, with a hand-searched review. This publication is a rich resource of papers relying on design process, design cognition and design research.

3.2 Criteria Strategy

The search string was adapted according to each data source engine. To be included in the analysis, a paper must have been peer reviewed, available online, written in English, and reported on the confluence of cognitive computing, qualitative methods, design process and human computer interaction. The search criteria were focused on the last five years of available knowledge (2010 to 2015). Selected papers should have a user research approach (field study, evaluation study with users) and systems described in the paper should have one or more highlighted characteristics of our adopted definition of Cognitive Systems: Complexity; Expertise; Objectivity; Imaginations and Sense (Kelly 2013). The papers were classified following a two-fold approach. Firstly, the titles and abstracts were analyzed. The papers were included or excluded according to the protocol criteria. Firstly, the researcher applied the search strategy to have a preliminary list, and filtered the papers by abstracts' content, following by reading the full text and filtering the relevant papers. This preliminary filter was analyzed by the database. In sequence, the papers were categorized based on their relevance of methods described to inform the design process and to evaluate the design process of cognitive systems.

4   Results

The literature review was conducted between June 2015 and January 2016. A total of 225 papers were selected for the first inclusion and **93** were selected for the second inclusion and 82 papers selected for being classified into the Design process phases (methods to inform and methods to evaluate).

Papers were excluded based on their relevance to the criteria. Most of the papers excluded were experiments to validate algorithms or did not have a Cognitive system component (support decision making, provide learnability, augment human reasoning). Additionally, some of the works excluded were technical simulations not described as inspired by user studies. Others were technical descriptions of prototypes with no users involved. Three papers described relevant methods for informing the design process and evaluating cognitive systems (Table 2).

Table 2. Inclusion process

Digital Library	Inclusion (1st)	Inclusion (2nd)	Inclusion (3rd)
IEE explore	53	25	20
ACM	62	27	26
Science Direct	110	41	36
Total:	**225**	**93**	**82**

4.1   Methods to Inform the Design Process

Over all 31 papers were selected, 18 were Journal Articles and 13 were conference papers. Usually the preliminary research stage combines projects that apply diverse methods to inform the design process and data acquisition applied to understand human reasoning. Papers that include a Participatory design approach were also included in this phase. Those selected papers describe studies with users and project teams before and during the process of developing cognitive systems.

The use of material artifacts to elucidate human thinking was a common trend since obtaining requirements with only user research to design cognitive systems is not a fixed starting phase. Usually those systems use human parameters and users inputs into technological artifacts for self-improvements, applying machine-learning algorithms. Therefore, some papers described prototypes that were used with the intent to gather parameters for the future systems, as experimental investigations, and not to evaluate a prototype that represents a system. Robins et al. (2010) investigated how robotic toys could be used as a play tool to assist in the children's development. Experimental investigations with artifacts (field trails with children), expert panels and questionnaires (with caretakers) help to develop scenarios for robots to give stimulus for autistic children that may promote further learning. Scenarios to illustrate context to field trails (Chatley et al. 2010) and to envision future use of Cognitive systems was also a common method applied with Protocol analysis and Think aloud techniques (Wilkinson and De Angeli 2014). Some of the projects used a mixed method approach with qualitative data from interviews (Li and Mao 2015) and quantitative data from surveys and questionnaires (Antoniou and Lepouras 2010). Some projects aimed to understand users visual preferences applying quantitative techniques such as the study proposed by Yang et al. (2014). In their research, authors used the Amazon Mechanical Turk to understand users comprehension and preferences to composite visualizations under different condition. As a result, they developed taxonomy of participants' difficulties in understanding the graphics. Liu et al. (2015) describes two cases that use behavioral data to drive requirements to design new services. Although, this data is helpful to generate design insights, still the space of design alternatives is complex, according to the authors, and more knowledge based approaches with their proposal method can improve system design. Therefore, with those methods to gather user information is possible to know WHAT is wrong or not working effectively but its not usually possible to know WHY those behaviors happen without user research methods (contextual inquiry, observation studies). Group interviews, focus groups (Xu 2011) were also a method applied to understand better user reasoning in this preliminary stage. Additionally, knowledge acquisition from multiple experts in a meeting helped to create domain knowledge for cognitive systems in Vivacqua et al. (2011). The authors created an ontology to understand participant's behaviors in collaborative design meetings that may be applied to create intelligent systems. The researchers used design sessions videos to understand behaviors also giving attention to non-verbal messages. Methodologies and approaches were also used to investigate problems that Cognitive systems might help to solve. For instance, Distributed cognition with Collaborative learning approach was applied with students to change the perspectives of public transport (Vasiliou et al. 2014). Grounded theory was conducted to understand the application field and improvisational practices in crisis management followed by field observation, group discussions, and individual interviews (e.g. police, fire department, red cross). Authors suggest recommendations to support aggregation and visualization of information for this sector (Ley et al. 2012).

This review also included user studies that helped collect insights of users' cognitive processes to facilitate new concept generation. Participatory design was a common approach to understand users in the design process. For instance, the work described by Wilkinson and De Angeli (2014) applied participatory design approach to generate new ideas for a new intelligent mobility app for older people. The authors investigated users with simulated observation cases, questionnaires regarding their shopping behavior, user focus groups with lead users, survey of past experiences, semi-structured interviews and cognitive walkthroughs. They found evidences of the psychological impact design has upon self-esteem that might affect product adoption. These results helped designers to choose the tone and information design for the intelligent system that would not stigmatize their users. A participatory design approach and the use of data captured by sensors were illustrated in Lundberg and Gustavsson (2011). Users with cognitive impairments participated in the design process; researchers illustrated two cases with scenarios of people with special needs in their day-today living. Researchers used sensors to infer context and provide semantic information to potential users, showing information through representations (icons, signals) that help in interpretation. Additionally, participatory design was applied with a group of users with dementia and stakeholders to enhance empathy and involvement in the design process of a Dementia care app (Slegers et al. 2013). Care should be taken when considering users with impairments, in this case dementia, researchers found it difficult to keep potential users active in the participatory design activities in the later stages of the design process, since cognitive declines typical for dementia. New methods should be created to involve people with impaired abilities in design activities.

Studies in the area of Affective Computing, understanding user's emotion, might help to evaluate human perception when interacting with cognitive systems. Zhou et al. (2013) affirms that cognitive and affective factors may influence user experience (UX) design in the decision-making process. The same authors present a case study of aircraft cabin design, it aims create positive UX in the cabin, including a healthier and more comfortable cabin environment. Overall, 20 participants were recruited. Half of them watched a video to elicit fear and the other half watched a video to elicit amusement. The UX outcome was measured on a scale between 100 (extremely unpleasant) and 100 extremely pleasant. Subsequently, participants were required to make decisions between two design profiles. This study helped to create an improved user experience model for decision-making. Behoora et al. (2015) use non-wearable sensors and machine learning algorithms to identify emotions in team meetings. Understanding emotional states of the design team members helps quantify interpersonal interactions and how those interactions might affect resulting design solutions. Participants were invited to a scenario based design meeting and a catalogue of 8 body language poses relevant to emotional states was used as data. Their machine learning algorithms identify individual's body language and relates to emotional states to quantify design team interactions.

Since cognitive systems aim to augment human reasoning, some of the projects did not consider at first ordinary user knowledge but expert knowledge to acquire enough information to make the system available for future use. 12 papers focused on experts in the domain of the projects. Likewise in the project (Oliver et al. 2012) that involved stakeholders and local farmers in the design process to understand on the ground decisions that can impact on environmental quality and rural economy. Based on a survey questionnaire with 77 farmers they choose 10 farmers to engage and validate answers from the questionnaire and deeper understanding of farmer's knowledge. Authors present a protocol with seven iterative stages. An interesting phase was the first one, in which researchers established relationships with farmers distributing a leaflet explaining about the project before the farm visit. Researchers also applied survey questionnaires, face-to-face interviews, a paper map based approach to understand user's farm area and techniques applied in the farm and qualitative validation of findings with farmers and a community of farmers. In those stages, they built a trusting relationship with the farming community and they acquired farmer's knowledge to develop a graphic user interface for a Decision support system for land and water management.

Qualitative methods were applied in most of the studies selected for this session. Usually quantitative methods were used with qualitative methods in the design process. Nine papers reported work aimed at special requirements audiences (seniors, impaired users, dementia and disadvantaged people). Most of those papers applied Participatory design as the main approach. Three were focused on children. The predominant areas of the studies were Healthcare and Education.

4.2 Methods to Evaluate Cognitive Systems

In this Assessment phase we selected 43 papers concerned with user evaluation methods of cognitive systems. 19 were papers published in conferences and 20 were published in journals. Papers that discuss the assessment methods selected for this session rely on three groups: Dialogue and/or speech based interfaces; Agent based interfaces and Information Visualization.

Papers discussed dialogue and speech based interfaces which usually use comparative studies, to understand different conditions. The aim to understand uncertainty was also a trend in those papers. Piccardi et al. (2014) apply a mixed-initiative user interface that follows the human-in-the-loop perspective, where the algorithm generates solutions and the role of the human is to select what solution to use. A Q&A system calculates the probabilities which questions will be answered by a crowd; the user assesses the system's output and makes a decision. 20 crowd-managers had to dispatch questions that they believe unlikely to be resolved by a crowd, they performed this task under two conditions in a web-based simulated tool: visualizing the system prediction and without this information. Participants should drag and drop questions selected to operators into the system. In this lab-experiment participants also did a pre-test questionnaire, then participated in a brief training session and filled out the NASA task load questionnaire. As a result, they found that the visualization of the predictor reduced the participant's workload. A Wizard of OZ technique, where a human (wizard) simulates the intelligent system tasks such as natural language understanding without user awareness, was perceived as one of the main approaches to evaluate cognitive dialogue systems. Forbes-Riley and Litman (2011) applied the Wizard of Oz technique. The system was a spoken language tutoring system in which the wizard performed speech recognition, natural language understanding, and uncertainty annotation, for each student to answer. 81 students participated in the study. The authors also claim it was the first study to show that dynamic responding to student uncertainty can significantly improve learning during computer tutoring. Rieser et al. 2014 applied the Wizard of Oz tool to improve information presentation in natural language generation dialogues; humans simulated the intelligent system that provided recommendations of restaurants to other humans. Their aim was to present enough information to users while keeping the utterances short and understandable. Authors identified the adaptive natural language generation, as well the information presentation, affects perceived or objective task success of the system.

Agent-based system projects were evaluated mostly by simulations and usability and/or user experience questionnaires. The evaluation study proposed by D'Mello (2012) was a within-subjects design where 48 undergraduates completed four biologic lectures in an intelligent (agent) tutor. Half of the lectures were evaluated with a gaze-reactive tutor and the remaining with a non-gaze-reactive version tutor. They evaluate students' boredom and disengagement by asking students to report their affective state in the Affect Grid (evaluates pleasant and unpleasant feelings) and filling out an engagement questionnaire after each lecture. As a result, students that used the gaze sensitive dialogues reoriented their attention to patterns of the important areas of the interface, was effective in promoting learning gains for questions that require deep reasoning and minimal impact on the students' motivation and engagement. Some works described systems that combines the use of human and computer agent simulation. For instance Tremblay et al. (2011) evaluated a system with those mixed characteristics (human and agent) for tactical commander. Overall 10 subject matter experts participated in the study four helped create scenarios for user tests and six evaluated the system. The system was designed to improve Situation awareness to help in accuracy and fast decision-making. Participants tested the simulated system in two different scenarios, answered usability questions and a semi-structured interview. The study provides insights into the design process adopted and other findings for designing situation awareness intelligent systems.

Information visualization tools may serve as a platform for data manipulation and exploration, those representations complement and enhance mental abilities (Meirelles 2013). Designing information that unveils data patterns to help in decision-making is not a trivial task. Since the number of variables, parameters and information links are typically large, and, well-chosen representations are needed (distinct colors, shapes, contrasts) to facilitate interpretation. Insights and new relationships may emerge from diverse ways to display the same dataset. Research in the field tries to understand how users interpret those representations of uncertainties based on probabilistic data. Daradkeh (2015) conducted a user qualitative evaluation of an information visualization (RiDeViz) that shows investment alternatives. The aim was to understand the user awareness of risk and uncertainty with bar charts. Observation approach using the think aloud protocol and content analysis were the methods applied with 10 subjects. Participants were asked to choose one investment choice evaluating risk and uncertainty in a bar chat visualization with limited range and a risk explorer table. The system provided different types of information, although participants did not use all for investment decision-making, they focused on small number of salient pieces and concentrated in the perceived consequences of undesirable outcomes. Additional work using bar charts with samples shows charts representing uncertainty that help understand risk in decision-making (Ferreira et al. 2014). In an initial user evaluation, with 7 users authors wanted to know how accurate and confident users would answer to 5 different types of questions to analyze three visual conditions. The study used a repeated measures design that showed 75 questions in random order. Users also rated confidence/certainty in a Likert scale for each question they answered, after that they answered a questionnaire about the overall experience. Authors also measured accuracy by a quantitative analysis of the questions answered right. The authors identified that participants were more confident in their accurate responses. Baur et al. (2010) evaluates visualization techniques with large datasets and recommended-based systems on mobile phones. They evaluated the visualization technique for repeated item selection in the context of music playlist creation. They considered the particularities of the mobile phone devices (orientation) with 12 users to do a user trail. Users selected options and for each option five suggestions were given out, and one should be right selected. Authors measured completion times and error rates. They found that the vertical orientation and interface was faster to interact and had less error rate than the horizontal one. Arshad (2015) compared the confidence of expert users and non-expert users varying level of uncertainty presented on a prediction case study of water-pipe failure. Participants did three groups of tasks and received a viewgraph of overlapping and non-overlapping uncertainty presentations as supplementary material for decision-making. Showing this supplementary material improved user confidence and uncertainty with unknown probabilities decreasing user confidence, although uncertainty with known probabilities can increase expert user confidence but the same is not true for non-experts.

A mix of qualitative and quantitative approaches was identified in this session. The number of participants were more variable in evaluation studies, most of them had less than 30 participants per study, the reason for that might be the kind of evaluation authors needed to perform, with more details about user experience, and also insights and parameters that should be included to improve current systems. Attention was given to user interpretation of cognitive interfaces. The subjects in the studies reviewed were most adults and from variable domain Education, Healthcare, Military, Management, Finance.

5 Limitations of This Review and Further Work

The result of this review should be used carefully, since the keyword string was limited and a new choice of keywords may retrieve different results. Additionally, this review was a first attempt; an exploratory study, to identify design methods for designing Cognitive systems, for this reason only one author reviewed and selected the data. However, in the future investigations and reviews the importance of inter coder reliability would be emphasized to methodological rigor. (Tinsley and Weiss 2000).

6 Conclusion

Methods for designing cognitive systems did not differ hugely from traditional design processes. Although a significant change found in the review is the consideration of expert domain to design intelligent systems. Care should be taken when narrowing down the types of users to consider as informants. For example in the health care area or designing systems for children, the final user is not always the expert, e.g. caretaker, so the final user should also be included in the user research process as informant and testers. When designing new traditional systems designers usually consider the mental maps of users and their cognitive constraints. The difference when designing cognitive system relies on the number of choices that those system present to users and how those choices are represented to influence in decision-making. In spite of applying traditional evaluation methods to assess user understanding of system outputs (e.g. uncertainties) still new methods are needed to refine those interpretations. Cognitive systems use human data input with the intent to improve and learn in an iterative process. Context is crucial and changes over time. Therefore, design process phases are not linear. As seen in this review, several times prototypes are crucial to gather data and inform the design, and many times prototypes are used as experiments to develop the real system. Primary research focuses on context and assembles the basis for the design process, it is not a phase that is isolated as in some traditional design processes were ethnography work can be the first phase and enough to inform the overall design process, it is an iterative process. Evaluation methods are applied in several stages of the design process and not only as the final phase. The evaluation phase never ends, because those systems as much as they learn and are assessed using user information they become more intelligent and user friendly. More studies such as the one reported by Gustavsson (2011) are necessary to understand the suitable tone cognitive systems should use with humans. Matters of trust, confidence and transparence might be related to visual and verbal representation of information. Showing uncertainty and risk, as Arshad (2015) identified, it is not always beneficial to non-expert users. New methods to understand how ordinary people interpret risk and uncertainty should be created. Current methods evaluate presentation studies showing or not showing if prediction and uncertainties is beneficial for users. It would be interesting to understand which kind of interfaces; shapes and color saturations attend this purpose more and are better understood by users.

In short, methods to inform and methods to evaluate cognitive systems were reviewed. The main methods and approaches applied were: interviews, questionnaires, scenarios to test current abilities of future prototypes, and field observations. Moreover, semantic scales were common in comparative studies. Dialogue based systems were usually evaluated applying the Wizard of OZ technique. In the future, a new category of design methods also should be investigated. It is the category of validating output information; the kind of feedback (visual, verbal haptic) cognitive systems should give to help in more informed decision-making.

References

Antoniou, A., et al.: Modeling visitors' profiles: a study to investigate adaptation aspects for museum learning technologies. J. Comput. Cult. Herit. **3**(2), 1–19 (2010)

Arshad, S.Z., et al.: Investigating user confidence for uncertainty presentation in predictive decision making. In: Proceedings of the Annual Meeting of the Australian Special Interest Group for Computer Human Interaction. Parkville, VIC, Australia, ACM, pp. 352–360 (2015)

Baillieul, J., et al.: Interaction dynamics: the interface of humans and smart machines. Proc. IEEE **100**(3), 567–570 (2012)

Baur, D. et al.: Rush: repeated recommendations on mobile devices. In: Proceedings of the 15th International Conference on Intelligent User Interfaces. Hong Kong, China, ACM, pp. 91–100 (2010)

Behoora, I., Tucker, C.S.: Machine learning classification of design team members' body language patterns for real time emotional state detection. Des. Stud. **39**, 100–127 (2015)

-Brereton, P., et al.: Lessons from applying the systematic literature review process within the software engineering domain. J. Syst. Softw. 80(4) 571–583 (2007)

Chatley, A.R., et al.: Theatre as a discussion tool in human-robot interaction experiments - a pilot study. In: Third International Conference on Advances in Computer-Human Interactions, ACHI 2010 (2010)

Daradkeh, M.: Exploring the use of an information visualization tool for decision support under uncertainty and risk. In: Proceedings of the International Conference on Engineering & MIS 2015, Istanbul, Turkey, pp. 1–7. ACM (2015)

D'Mello, S., et al.: Gaze tutor: A gaze-reactive intelligent tutoring system. Int. J. Hum. Comput. Stud. 70(5) 377–398 (2012)

Ferreira, N., et al.: Sample-oriented task-driven visualizations: allowing users to make better, more confident decisions. In: Proceedings of the SIGCHI Conference on Human Factors in Computing Systems, Toronto, Ontario, Canada, pp. 571–580. ACM (2014)

Forbes-Riley, K., Litman, D.: Designing and evaluating a wizarded uncertainty-adaptive spoken dialogue tutoring system. Comput. Speech Lang. **25**(1), 105–126 (2011)

Gustavsson, R., Lundberg, J.: Challenges and opportunities of sensor based user empowerment. In: IEEE International Conference on Networking, Sensing and Control (ICNSC) (2011)

Kelly, J.E., Hamm, S.: Smart Machines: IBM's Watson and the Era of Cognitive Computing. Columbia Business School Publishing (2013)

Kelly III, J., Hamm, S.: Smart Machines: IBM Watson and the Era of Cognitive Computing. Columbia University Press (2013)

Ley, B., et al.: Supporting improvisation work in inter-organizational crisis management. In: Proceedings of the SIGCHI Conference on Human Factors in Computing Systems. Austin, Texas, USA, ACM, pp. 1529–1538 (2012)

Li, M., Mao, J.: Hedonic or utilitarian? Exploring the impact of communication style alignment on user's perception of virtual health advisory services. Int. J. Inf. Manag. **35**(2), 229–243 (2015)

Lintern, G.: Cognitive systems and communication. Lang. Sci. **33**(4), 708–712 (2011)

Liu, L., et al.: Requirements cybernetics: elicitation based on user behavioral data. J. Syst. Softw. (2015)

Lundberg, J., Gustavsson, R.: Challenges and opportunities of sensor based user empowerment. In: Networking, Sensing and Control (ICNSC) (2011)

Meirelles, I.: Design for Information: An Introduction to the Histories, Theories, and Best Practices Behind Effective Information Visualizations. Rockport Publishers, Gloucester (2013)

Nahamoo, D.: Cognitive computing journey. In: Proceedings of the First Workshop on Parallel Programming for Analytics Applications. ACM, pp. 63–64 (2014)

Noor, A.K.: Potential of cognitive computing and cognitive systems. Open Eng. **5**(1), 75–88 (2015)

Oliver, D.M., et al.: Valuing local knowledge as a source of expert data: Farmer engagement and the design of decision support systems. Environ. Model Softw. **36**, 76–85 (2012)

Piccardi, T., et al.: Towards crowd-based customer service: a mixed-initiative tool for managing Q&A sites. In: Proceedings of the SIGCHI Conference on Human Factors in Computing Systems. Toronto, Ontario, Canada, ACM, pp. 2725–2734 (2014)

Rieser, V., et al.: Natural language generation as incremental planning under uncertainty: adaptive information presentation for statistical dialogue systems. IEEE/ACM Trans. Audio, Speech, Lang. Process. **22**(5), 979–994 (2014)

Robins, B., et al.: Human-centred design methods: Developing scenarios for robot assisted play informed by user panels and field trials. Int. J. Hum Comput Stud. **68**(12), 873–898 (2010)

Slegers, K., et al.: EXC-Active collaboration in healthcare design: participatory design to develop a dementia care app. In: CHI 2013 Extended Abstracts on Human Factors in Computing Systems, Paris, France, 475–480. ACM (2013)

Tinsley, H.E.A., Weiss, D.J.: Interrater reliability and agreement. In: Tinsley, H.E.A., Brown, S. D. (eds.) Handbook of Applied Multivariate Statistics and Mathematical Modeling, pp. 94–124. Academic Press, New York (2000)

Tremblay, S., et al.: A multi-perspective approach to the evaluation of a portable situation awareness support system in a simulated infantry operation. In: Cognitive Methods in Situation Awareness and Decision Support (CogSIMA) (2011)

Vasiliou, C., et al.: Understanding collaborative learning activities in an information ecology: A distributed cognition account. Comput. Hum. Behav. **41**, 544–553 (2014)

Vivacqua, A.S., et al.: BOO: Behavior-oriented ontology to describe participant dynamics in collocated design meetings. Expert Syst. Appl. **38**(2), 1139–1147 (2011)

Wilkinson, C.R., De Angeli, A.: Applying user centred and participatory design approaches to commercial product development. Des. Stud. **35**(6), 614–631 (2014)

Xu, M., et al.: Intelligent agent systems for executive information scanning, filtering and interpretation: perceptions and challenges. Inf. Process. Manag. **47**(2), 186–201 (2011)

Yang, H., et al.: Understand users' comprehension and preferences for composing information visualizations. ACM Trans. Comput.-Hum. Interact. **21**(1), 1–30 (2014)

Zhou, F., Jiao, R.J.: An improved user experience model with cumulative prospect theory. Proc. Comput. Sci. **16**, 870–877 (2013)

Zimmerman, Z.: Research through design as a method for interaction design research in HCI (2007)

Preliminary Studies on Exploring Autistic Sensory Perception with Sensory Ethnography and Biosensors

Doğa Çorlu and Asım Evren Yantaç[(⊠)]

KUAR - Koç University Arçelik Research Center
for Creative Industries, Istanbul, Turkey
{dcorlu14, eyantac}@ku.edu.tr

Abstract. More than anybody else, individuals with Autism Spectrum Disorder (ASD) easily suffer from environmental stimuli and sensory overloads due to their particular sensory perceptual systems which also cause attention related problems as well as communication difficulties in everyday lives. In our previous interaction design explorations for augmenting attention of autistics, we suggested that it would be beneficial to keep track of autistics' individual differences and needs, and provide information accordingly [1]. Even though the existing methods that examine autistic sensory perception provide extensive knowledge, they are insufficient to provide in-depth user specific live data for a learning and a sensory-aware system which satisfy such particular differences. Thus, as we carry on ideating attentive user interfaces for autistics, our current studies focus on possible research methods which can access sensory perceptual data in individual levels. Here in this paper, we share our preliminary insights from the studies on exploring sensory ethnography and, depending on our three ongoing and interconnected prototypical studies, we suggest that this can reveal and represent novel ways of seeing the already known information of how autistics perceive the world and insights for the design of a sensory ethnography tool.

Keywords: Autistic spectrum disorder (ASD) · Mediated reality · Sensory perception · Sensory ethnography · Design research · Biosensors · Attentive user interfaces

1 Introduction

Autism spectrum disorder (ASD) is clinically defined as a neurodevelopmental disorder manifesting itself during early developmental period of life and it is characterized by impairments in social interaction and communication, repetitive behaviors and restricted interests. These characteristics vary in severity from person to person and this is why it is called spectrum. With the DSM-5 (The Diagnostic and Statistical Manual of Mental Disorders - 5th Edition) definition [2] sensory aspects of the disorder appears among other characteristics and current studies [3] suggest that sensory perceptual experiences (SPEs) underlie these characteristics.

SPEs cover the symptoms such as hypo- and hypersensitivity to environmental stimuli, distorted and fragmented perception, sensory overloads, difficulty in interpreting

© Springer International Publishing Switzerland 2016
A. Marcus (Ed.): DUXU 2016, Part I, LNCS 9746, pp. 243–254, 2016.
DOI: 10.1007/978-3-319-40409-7_24

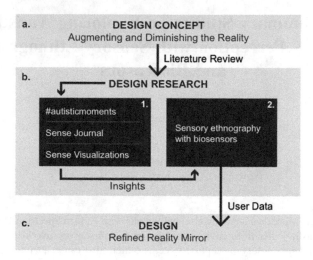

Fig. 1. Exploration methodology: (a) conceptualization and literature review (b) design research with the insights from our preliminary studies (c) designing the system with the user data collected from sensory ethnography study with biosensors.

the stimuli, fascination with or inability to tolerate certain colors, objects, textures etc. [4]. These symptoms are prominently reported in autistic accounts such as autobiographies [5–7] as well as in clinical studies. Due to such conditions, ASD individuals often suffer from attention problems and tantrums particularly while socializing, learning and working.

In order to provide less challenging spaces for autistics, we are exploring the design space of novel user interfaces and/or interactive spaces that refine autistic sensory perception by means of augmented and diminished reality (Fig. 1). Deriving from the discussions of our previous studies [1] on such solutions for autistics, we now explore the world of autistics' SPEs. Our explorations are based on ethnographic studies which lead us to search for new data collection methods grounding themselves to ethnographic research. At the end of this study, we discuss the possible scenarios when we use biosensors to track SPEs of ASD individuals and combining the data with sensory ethnography studies in order to inform design processes.

2   Background

With the main aim of developing learning and sensory-aware interaction design solutions for refining autistic sensory perception in everyday life situations, we suggest to use sensory ethnography and biosensors. Here, we briefly go through significant and recent literature on these two concentrations.

2.1   Autistic Sensory Perception

In film and TV, most of the autism representations invite non-autistics to understand autism only by looking at it [8] from a non-autistic perspective. Thus, existing media representations are lacking in conveying the ASD perception to non-autistic audiences, even if they are based on real stories and consulted by domain experts as well as ASD individuals [9]. Even though there are simulation examples of SPEs such as the performative show in the theater adaptation of Mark Haddon's fictional book [10] on autistic traits, these examples can only cover a limited part of autistic SPEs and they are not adaptive. Such absence motivated us to go deeper in this relevant research question of how to visually represent, illustrate the autistic perception, or in other words, create a live, learning autistic reality.

On the other hand, autobiographies and novels written by autistics are of high importance in terms of sampling SPEs through autistics' eyes. Bogdashina [3] revealed the patterns of SPEs in autism by analyzing sensory descriptions and related behaviors in such accounts. She examines these experiences in four different aspects: (a) possible sensory experiences; (b) perceptual styles; (c) cognitive styles; (d) other sensory conditions. In possible sensory experiences, she explains how the real world, the raw stimuli (as non-autistics sense), such as colors, tastes, sounds etc. Sensed differently by autistics due to their particular sensitivities and processing styles such as fragmented, distorted or delayed. In perceptual styles, she lists autistic's coping strategies against the sensory experiences. As information processing, memory and attention in autism is examined in cognitive styles, in the last part she explains unusual SPEs such as resonance and daydreaming [4]. Categorization of SPEs is underpinned by qualitative and quantitative studies with autistics as well [11, 12]. These studies also show that each autistic person has unique combinations of perceptual and behavioral traits that we can not be fully covered with categorizations.

Since each autistic is uniquely affected from different types of environmental stimuli, and preferences and SPEs change over time, we need profound user data when developing interactive solutions for autistics. However, existing studies and categories are insufficient to base our user research on. Additionally, collecting data from autistic individuals is a challenging task due to the differences in their perception, cognition and communication abilities, particularly of those who are on the severe points of the spectrum. Mostly because they don't communicate how they sense the world. We are in need of adaptive, aware and learning environments to keep track of and deal with SPE related problems.

2.2   Sensory Ethnography and Biosensors

Sensory ethnography is where the researcher engages with interconnected senses (i.e. multisensory), uses different media together and goes beyond textual representations by engaging with art practice [13]. It covers the activities that researcher does with the participant in order to sense together. Walking, eating or dancing with the participant (mobile methods) are examples of such activities. During these activities, sensory ethnographer creates evocative material such as photos or videos in order to re-sense and represent the participant's encounter with the environment.

In this regard, sensory ethnography is a fruitful method which can inform the design process by providing knowledge about how the participant (user in design context) senses the environment. For example, in LEEDR (Lower Effort Energy Demand Reduction) Project, sensory ethnography is applied in order to reveal how participants interact with sensory (e.g. temperature, lightings, coziness) and digital (usage of control devices) aspects of home [14]. This enables redefining the energy consumption problem and developing new Human-Computer Interaction (HCI) design solutions for domestic usage [15].

Besides its outcomes for design practices, O'Dell and William suggest that sensory ethnography can provide better 'sensory understanding' when it is represented with drawings, cartoons or sculptures as well as photos and videos [16]. They also propose that such representations are more 'evocative and convincing' comparing to textual transcriptions. This is where sensory ethnography meets with art practice in order to convey the ethnographic content to related audiences.

Spinney [17] brings sensory ethnography one step forward: He claims that mobile methods are reductive due to participants' verbalizations and unintentional filterings, thus, these methods don't profoundly reveal how the participants are affected by the environment. According to his theoretical suggestion, 'unfiltered' data collection is possible by combining these methods with biosensors. Based on the studies of Aspinall et al. [18] and Nold [19], he suggests that, doing mobile ethnography, with the support of biosensors such as EEG and GSR, provides quantitative data as much as qualitative.

As ethnographic research methods are shifting from conventional observations into engagements with the research subject by adapting multiple media and methods [20], autism, as one of the most unlocked realms of qualitative research [21], needs new methods that can reveal individual differences profoundly. Herein, combination of sensory ethnography and biosensors as a research method [17] sounds promising to build a learning and aware system for ASD individuals. However this combination was used in different contexts in previous studies [18, 19], ASD is not included in these contexts yet.

3   Method

When doing design research for autistics, perceptual, cognitive and social autistic traits hinder conventional ethnographic methods such as interviews and observations. In order to design for autistics, we believe that our design research should be constructed upon unconventional ethnographic methods which can help us going beyond these barriers by probing how each autistic individual senses and perceives environmental stimuli. Drawing on our literature review on autistic sensory perception and sensory ethnography, we are conducting three preliminary, interconnected and life-long ethnographic studies. We hope these studies will inform our next steps in design research.

3.1   #Autisticmoments

We started shaping our ethnographic research on Instagram since it's a suitable platform to access numerous users, observe and archive the way they see the world as well as to

 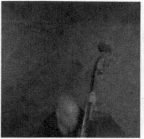 

Fig. 2. #autisticmoments photo examples by which we reflect possible SPEs

reflect how we engage with the sensoriality of our surroundings. We created a hashtag called #autisticmoments on Instagram and, based on our literature review, we try to see the world through autistic eyes. We take and upload photos and videos that can represent autistic sensory perception. We search for irregular patterns, flickering color combinations, fragmented images etc. Particularly based on the sensory experiences categorized in Bogdashina's study [4]. This hashtag has lately turned into a participatory study with the contribution of people who are interested in the topic. We and many other users we don't know, still upload new photos on this hashtag and invite participants to represent their sensory perceptions regardless of being autistics or not (Fig. 2). Additionally, we try to spread this hashtag among ASD individuals to represent their SPEs.

3.2 Sense Journal

In order to collect autistic sensory perceptual data, we designed a 'Sense Journal' which is an A5-size notebook that allows participants to carry around and record their sensory perceptual preferences and experiences based on time, location (Fig. 3a) and six senses (vision, hearing, touch, smell, taste and proprioception).

After publishing an announcement of this study on various social media channels, we reached 12 autistic participants through their parents who responded to the announcement. Based on their level of ability to read and write (which was reported by their parents), we selected 5 autistics who are older than 18 years and sent them the

 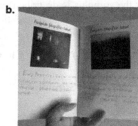 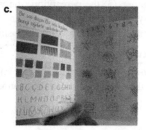

Fig. 3. Sense Journal: (a) chart for recording the SPEs based on time and location (b) #autisticmoments photos to evoke expressive descriptions of SPEs (c) matching a stimulus with visual elements.

journals. In order to reveal the differences between articulations of SPEs between autistics and non-autistics, we sent the journals to 5 non-autistics, who are older than 18 years and willing to participate in this study, as well.

The open-ended questions about different senses in the journal invited participants to describe their perceptions of different stimuli. We supported these questions with visual elements and photos from #autisticmoments in order to reveal expressions that are descriptive of experiences (Fig. 3b). Moreover, some questions are designed to provide associations between senses. For example, a question requires describing a taste with selecting the most associative visual elements among others on the page (Fig. 3c). Ultimately, in case of inability to describe experiences verbally, we introduce #autisticmoments hashtag to participants so that they can upload photos or videos of their SPEs and preferences.

3.3 Sense Visualizations

In addition to the #autisticmoments study, we started to visualize autistics' own accounts on their SPEs in order to make an archive of evoking and communicating ethnographic material. We chose the autobiographical novel Nobody Nowhere [5], written by an autistic writer, Donna Williams, due to the diversity of descriptions of her SPEs in the book.

First, two research assistants, who are psychologists, read the book and decided work on the first 76 pages, that cover the first 15 years of Donna Williams' life, since the way she described her experiences in this part was more detailed and fruitful compared to the rest of the book. After an iterative reading process, they created a guideline for picking the descriptive sentences in the book. In this step, we included an illustrator in the study. Based on the guideline, the research assistants and the illustrator individually picked the sentences which include at least one description of an environmental stimulus. Secondly, the picked sentences were extracted to their components according to four characteristics in the guideline (sensory channel, stimulus, perception and description style; Table 1). The ones that cover all these characteristics were listed

Table 1. The guideline for culling out the descriptive sentences. (1) The sensory channel (the modality the stimulus is sensed), (2) the stimulus (the environmental input described by the author), (3) the perception (the way the stimulus is described) and (4) the description style (the way the relationship between the stimulus and the perception is described by the author: metaphorical, personification, simile or basic description).

Sentence	(1) Sensory Channel: Auditory		
Their words became a mumbling jumble, their voices a pattern of sounds.	(2) **Stimulus**	(3) **Perception**	(4) **Description Style**
	Their words	A mumbling jumble	Metaphorical
	Their voices	A pattern of sounds	Metaphorical

by the research assistants and the illustrator. When these three individually created lists were brought together, out of 162 sentences in total, 52 sentences fully matched. Finally, the illustrator started visualizing the 52 significantly descriptive sentences in an abstract style so as to communicate how Donna Williams perceive the world without showing the stimulus itself (Fig. 4).

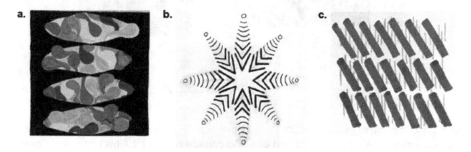

Fig. 4. Sense Visualization examples of descriptive sentences in the book Nobody Nowhere: (a) "(…) proper school uniform (…), always buttoned to keep me in." (b) "All touching was pain." (c) "Their words became a mumbling jumble, their voices a pattern of sounds."

4   Insights and Discussions

Our ethnographic research is an ongoing project. We are still collecting user data through #autisticmoments and the Sense Journal, thus we have not analyzed the full data yet. However, during our research process, we gain insights on how to bring our research a step forward and we will now use these insights for the conceptualization of sensory ethnography with biosensors idea.

4.1   #Autisticmoments

We started taking photos of SPEs such as fragmented perception, hyper-or-hyposensitivity and delayed perception. In the process of seeking for these experiences wherever we go, we realized that we are actually surrounded by flashy lights, bright surfaces, irritating patterns or unexpected movements. We became more aware of possible distractions around us and how frequently and easily an autistic could be overloaded by such environmental stimuli. Moreover, the pictures we took revealed our individual differences in terms of sensory experiences. All of us focused on different aspects of environmental stimuli even though we were looking for the same SPE categories [4] This study also showed us how often we face which kind of SPEs. Another outcome of this study was to see these pictures as captured autistic moments to be inspired during the ideation process of Refined Reality Mirror design.

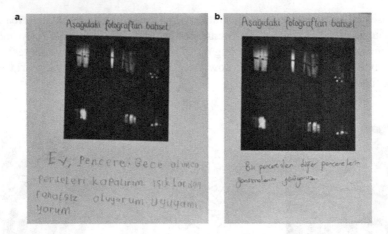

Fig. 5. A comperative example of autistic and non-autistic expression for the same evocative photo: (a) autistic: "A house, a window. I close the curtains by night. Lights bother me. I cannot sleep." (b) non-autistic: "We see window reflections on a window."

4.2   Sense Journal

Since the data collected from the journal is limited so far, comparisons we made between non-autistics and autistics are preliminary. However, here we share some patterns we observed in the collected journals.

First of all, autistics don't fulfill the tasks requiring a stimulus recalling and abstract item matching whereas non-autistics easily perform these tasks. Instead of recalling and matching a certain stimulus with various visual elements, autistics prefer to name each of these elements with various stimuli (Fig. 3c). For example, when they are asked to match a certain sound they recall with the given abstract patterns, textures, numbers, colors and letters on the page, they describe these items with different sounds. Evocative photos also help them recall their SPEs (Fig. 3b). They comment on these photos expressing their prior SPEs whereas non-autistics tend to describe what they see on the photos (Fig. 5). Based on this founding, using evocative visual materials seem appropriate for ethnographic data collection studies with autistics.

Secondly, the time-location based form (Fig. 3a) helps both groups to record their SPE patterns. They use this form to describe their frequent sensory experiences in all sensory channels (not just visual experiences) and in certain types of locations (at home, at work/school, on the road and in social places) on different times of the day. In order to collect specific SPEs, the time-location based form could be embedded particularly in autistics' lives as a part of their daily routines instead of suggesting them to use the journal whenever and wherever they want.

4.3   Sense Visualizations

After analyzing and visualizing the significantly descriptive sentences in Donna William's auto-biographical book Nobody Nowhere, we conducted a quick study with 31 non-autistic participants in order to collect basic qualitative feedback on how these visualizations communicate themselves with a non-autistic audience. When participants were asked to comment on these abstract visualizations via an online survey, which doesn't inform participants about the study, their accounts were mostly on what and how they felt when they looked at them. Moreover, the way they felt qualitatively overlapped with the sensory channel and sensory perceptual experiences described in the sentences as well as illustrator's intentions when visualizing them. Some examples of participants' accounts on the given visualizations are as follows: Fig. 4a: "I feel jammed but still hopeful, seems like I will be free soon." or "Vomiting. Something wants to come out or to be thrown up. Irritating." Figure 4b: "This is around me all the time. Looks nice from distance but inside it's just annoying." or "I feel my face is getting stretched. I am on a knife-edge." Figure 4c: "Something too obvious is purposely hiding the background. We know it is there but not focusing." or "This is the thing I don't know. I'm not sure if I'll encounter with them in my life ever. Maybe yes or not, it's neutral to me for now. I'm passing by them." Here, we see that abstract visualizations can be means of experiencing the autistic sensory perception.

These preliminary ethnographic studies help us to represent and engage with autistic perception. All in all, we gained four main insights:

1. Photos can help us reveal SPEs and visual preference patterns such as what kind of stimuli an autistic intentionally or unintentionally prefer (or not) to capture.
2. Abstract visualizations can be used as a tool by which non-autistics visually engage with autistic SPEs.
3. As insight 1 gives us hints about which moments to track or which stimuli to refine when designing an adaptive and attentive system, insight 2 helps us creating the interface through which autistics engage with their environments in such a system.
4. Evocative materials such as photos can help participants to recall and describe their prior SPEs, thus, such materials can benefit possible uses of sensory ethnography with biosensors.

4.4 Implications for Future Studies on Sensory Ethnography with Biosensors

With the preliminary insights we gain from these studies and literature, we suggest that, combining sensory ethnography and biosensors may provide profound data to build a learning and aware attentive interface making use of the mediated reality technologies to refine autistic sensory perception. The possible advantages of such combination are as follows:

1. Biosensors can collect different types of **bodily data** (e.g. heart rate, posture and muscle tracking, GSR, EEG) during daily encounters. These data provide **unfiltered, undistorted, pre-conscious aspects** of the encounters.
2. When embedded in wearable devices, biosensors become a part of the body and participant can **use it during daily tasks**. Participant becomes independent of the researcher or controlled settings. This can increase diversity of encounters and

provide more data. Moreover, this may decrease reinforcement of perceptual, cognitive and communicational differences in research participation of ASD.

3. The data collected by biosensors can be combined with **GPS data in order to locate encounters**. This forms a basis for both participant and researcher where participant reflects upon his/her own data and researcher re-sense the encounter with participant's reflections. This may reduce abstraction when researcher analyze encounters.

4. Rigorous analysis of sensory perception may become possible by measurable data. Additionally, **quantitative and qualitative** analysis can be made by **overlapping the data collected from both biosensors and sensory ethnography**. Matching the sensory input from the surrounding with bodily reactions might provide patterns to inform about autistic sensory perception or even non-autistic sensory perception in a broader sense.

5. It is possible to **diversify methods within sensory ethnography**. So different combinations of these methods can be used with biosensors in order to collect different types of data.

6. Being aware of own bodily data in sensory level may also contribute to Quantified Self movement where people **record their bodily data** through mobile applications and wearable devices.

We use these insights to design a learning and aware mediated reality, attentive interface for the use of autistics. Ethics and possible disadvantages of this method should be further discussed in future studies.

5   Conclusion

Our main ongoing research aims to design an attentive interface which can provide sideways for sensory perception related attention problems of autism in daily life. Our main aim is to refine external stimuli to augment attention of autistics when necessary so that they can be more involved in social daily life activities such as working in open offices, education in mixed classrooms or a social activity in a cafe. However, to design such an interface that can satisfy each autistic individual's needs is challenging. Because, first, each autistic is particularly affected by different external stimuli. Secondly, existing studies provide categories of SPEs in autism, yet are not sufficient to contribute to our user research since we don't create personas, but instead, we seek for tailor-cut solutions for each autistic separately. Third, due to their perceptual, cognitive and communicational differences, it may not be suitable to conduct some of the conventional user studies with those who has severe autism. Yet, to be able to build a real-time attentive interface, the system needs to be aware and learning. This paper shares our insights from a group of preliminary user studies where we explore sensory ethnography tools, before building bio-sensing solutions into our system (Fig. 6).

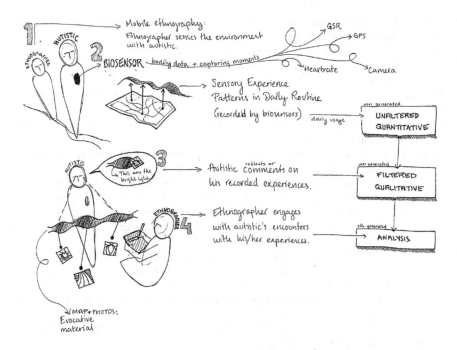

Fig. 6. Bio-Sensory Ethnography Concept

Acknowledgements. Our thanks to Pelin Karaturhan, Verda Seneor and Damla Yıldırım for their collaboration in description analysis and Sense Visualizations.

References

1. Yantac, A.E., Çorlu, D., Fjeld, M., Kunz, A.: Exploring diminished reality (DR) spaces to augment the attention of individuals with autism. In: 2015 International Symposium on Mixed and Augmented Reality Workshops (ISMARW), pp. 68–73. IEEE (2015)
2. American Psychiatric Association: Diagnostic and Statistical Manual of Mental Disorders:: DSM-5. ManMag (2003)
3. Horder, J., Wilson, C.E., Mendez, M.A., Murphy, D.G.: Autistic traits and abnormal sensory experiences in adults. J. Autism Dev. Disord. **44**(6), 1461–1469 (2014)
4. Bogdashina, O.: Sensory perceptual issues in autism and Asperger Syndrome: different sensory experiences, different perceptual worlds. Jessica Kingsley Publishers, London (2003)
5. Williams, D.: Nobody nowhere: The extraordinary autobiography of an autistic. Jessica Kingsley Publishers, London (2007)

6. Tammet, D.: Born on a blue day: Inside the extraordinary mind of an autistic savant. Simon and Schuster, New York (2007)
7. Grandin, T.: Thinking in pictures. Bloomsbury Publishing, London (2009)
8. Murray, S.: Representing autism: culture, narrative, fascination. Liverpool University Press, Liverpool (2008)
9. Draaisma, D.: Stereotypes of autism. Philos. Trans. R. Soc. Lond. B Biol. Sci. **364**(1522), 1475–1480 (2009)
10. Haddon, M.: The Curious Incident of the Dog in the Night-time. National Geographic Books, Washington, D.C. (2007)
11. Crane, L., Goddard, L., Pring, L.: Sensory processing in adults with autism spectrum disorders. Autism **13**(3), 215–228 (2009)
12. Kirby, A.V., Dickie, V.A., Baranek, G.T.: Sensory experiences of children with autism spectrum disorder: in their own words. Autism **19**(3), 316–326 (2015)
13. Pink, S.: Doing sensory ethnography. Sage Publications, Thousand Oaks (2009)
14. Pink, S.: Digital–visual–sensory-design anthropology: ethnography, imagination and intervention. Arts Humanit. High. Educ., 1474022214542353 (2014)
15. Mitchell, V., Mackley, K.L., Pink, S., Escobar-Tello, C., Wilson, G.T., Bhamra, T.: Situating digital interventions: mixed methods for HCI research in the home. Interact. Comput., iwu034 (2014)
16. O'Dell, T., Willim, R.: Transcription and the senses: cultural analysis when it entails more than words. Senses Soc. **8**(3), 314–334 (2013)
17. Spinney, J.: Close encounters? mobile methods, (post) phenomenology and affect. Cult. Geographies **22**(2), 231–246 (2015)
18. Aspinall, P., Mavros, P., Coyne, R., Roe, J.: The urban brain: analysing outdoor physical activity with mobile EEG. Br. J. Sports Med. **49**(4), 272–276 (2013). bjsports-2012
19. Nold, C.: Emotional cartography (2009). http://emotionalcartography.net/
20. Pink, S.: Multimodality, multisensoriality and ethnographic knowing: social semiotics and the phenomenology of perception. Qual. Res. **11**(3), 261–276 (2011)
21. Bölte, S.: The power of words: is qualitative research as important as quantitative research in the study of autism? Autism **18**(2), 67–68 (2014)

Evaluating the Expressiveness of MoLICC to Model the HCI of Collaborative Systems

Luiz Gustavo de Souza[1(✉)], Simone Diniz Junqueira Barbosa[2], and Hugo Fuks[2]

[1] Tecgraf Research Institute, PUC-Rio, Rio de Janeiro, Brazil
luiz@tecgraf.puc-rio.br
[2] Department of Informatics, PUC-Rio, Rio de Janeiro, Brazil
{simone,hugo}@inf.puc-rio.br

Abstract. In this paper we present an analysis on MoLICC, an interaction design language rooted in Semtiontic Engineering that perceives the user-system interaction as a conversation between designer (the system) and user, bringing focus to collaborative systems based on the 3C Model of Collaboration. In our analysis, we present the different aspects of collaboration as defined by the 3C Model of Collaboration, presenting case scenarios and using them to verify the language expressiveness.

Keywords: Interaction design · Semiotic engineering · MoLIC

1 Introduction

Collaborative systems go beyond user-system interaction as they must allow users to interact by cooperating, coordinating, and communicating with each other [1, 2]. These systems present issues and challenges in several research fields regarding the process of designing collaboration, especially considering the interaction design. The 3C Model of Collaboration was first proposed by [1], later improved by [2]. According to Fuks et al. [2], 3C stands for Communication, Coordination and Cooperation, which are the basic elements in collaborative systems, where they interact with one other in a cycle, allowing collaboration to occur. Later, Fuks et al. [3] presented an analysis of the various forms of relationship between each possible set of elements of the 3C model, highlighting the importance of the interplay between the different aspects of collaboration.

In previous works, we proposed MoLICC [4], an extension for the MoLIC language [5] based on the 3C Model of Collaboration. MoLIC [2] supports the designer in modeling the interaction, focusing on the users' goals and serving as an epistemic tool to help the designer understand the problem to be solved. Adopting an interaction-as-conversation metaphor, MoLIC allows designers to represent the interaction as a set of conversations that the user can have with the user interface to achieve his goals. MoLIC is rooted in Semiotic Engineering (SemEng) [6], a theory that considers the human-computer interaction to be a conversation between designer and user, and as such, represents all computational artifacts as a kind of computer-mediated

© Springer International Publishing Switzerland 2016
A. Marcus (Ed.): DUXU 2016, Part I, LNCS 9746, pp. 255–265, 2016.
DOI: 10.1007/978-3-319-40409-7_25

communication. According to SemEng, the user interface is the designer's deputy, conveying a one-shot message from the designer to the user. This message, called a metacommunication message, represents the solution proposed by the designer about her understanding of the users' problems, needs and preferences, thus representing how the user may interact with the system to achieve a range of anticipated (or unanticipated) goals.

In previous research, we studied the use of MoLICC in representative use cases [7, 8] and analyzed the language notation [9]. To address the challenge of representing the interaction of the different types of collaborative systems, we set out to answer the following research question: *How can MoLICC represent the collaborative interaction on different types of systems?*

In this paper, we present an analysis of the MoLICC language considering some prototypical collaborative systems: time scheduling, social networks, and crowdsourcing. We focus on the interaction aspects and on the MoLICC expressiveness, presenting possible interaction design solutions for each case and discussing how MoLICC supports the identification of design issues and the implications of certain HCI design decisions.

The next section presents the background of this research, the MoLICC language, its basis, the Semiotic Engineering and the 3C Model of Collaboration. Next, we present each case scenario considering the 3C Model with a representation using MoLICC, evaluating its efficacy. We conclude by discussing the language's potential and possible problems, pointing to future studies.

2 Background

In this section, we briefly present the SemEng and the 3C Model of Collaboration, followed by a description of MoLICC.

2.1 Semiotic Engineering

As mentioned, SemEng is based on communication, where the designer, using one or more sign systems codified in the user interface of interactive systems, communicates with the user. SemEng brings both designer and user together as interlocutors in the communicative process during user-system interaction. The user interface is the designer's deputy, representing the designer at interaction time. Through the user interface, the designer's deputy must inform the user about the meaning of the artifact (aka interface), expecting the user to understand and respond to it by interacting with him [6].

The metacommunication message from designer to user can be paraphrased as follows:

"Here is my understanding of who you are, what I've learned you want or need to do, in which preferred ways, and why. This is the system that I have therefore designed for you, and this is the way you can or should use it in order to fulfill a range of purposes that fall within this vision" [6, p. 84].

MoLIC was devised to encode the second part of the metacommunication message ("This is the system..."). As MoLICC aims to support modelling the collaboration aspects of interaction, the 3C Model of Collaboration was investigated to serve as a conceptual foundation for the MoLICC extensions to MoLIC. The next sub-section presents the 3C Model.

2.2   3C Model of Collaboration

Fuks et al. [2] proposed the 3C Model of Collaboration based on the work of Ellis, Gibs and Reins [1]. They defined that the collaboration process can be described by three elements: communication, coordination, and cooperation. The Model focused on groupware development, supporting the understanding of aspects involved in collaborative work.

Collaboration in the 3C Model occurs when the three elements work together as a cycle, where each element provides a bit of the collaboration and prepares the next element. One example of this application is the Conversation for Action, where members of a work group communicate, negotiating the work and making decisions, so they can coordinate their work in order to cooperate. This way, the communication element provides the communication process among members, allowing them to make commitments on the work to be performed. These commitments are then managed by a coordination process. In the end, the cooperation allows members to work together in a shared environment, where changes during the work take members to review their commitments and possibly renegotiate their work during communication again, thus restarting the cycle. Figure 1 shows how this configuration of the 3C Model works.

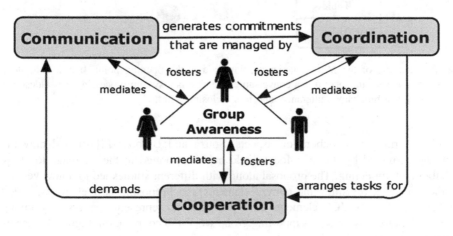

Fig. 1. The 3C model of collaboration for conversation for action

As Conversation for Action, there are other configurations that the 3C Model can achieve, grouping different kinds of collaborative systems, as previous studies have already shown [3]. Based on the 3C Model, the MoLIC language was extended to consider the collaboration aspects of interaction, resulting in a language called MoLICC, presented in the next sub-section.

2.3   MoLICC

MoLIC (Modeling Language for Interaction as Conversation) is an interaction design language based on SemEng, first proposed by Barbosa and Paula [5], later revised by Silva and Barbosa [10] and Souza and Barbosa [4, 9]. The language allows designers to represent the interaction as a set of possible conversations that the user can have with the user interface (considered by the theory to be the designer's deputy), expecting that it is clearly presenting the metacommunication message conceived by the designer. MoLIC serves as an epistemic tool, helping designers to improve their knowledge about the problem to be solved.

In a MoLIC diagram, the designer can define the different possible conversation topics, and the turn-taking utterances that users and designers can issue to advance the conversation towards a goal or to change topic to achieve another goal. Figure 2 presents the main elements of the MoLIC language.

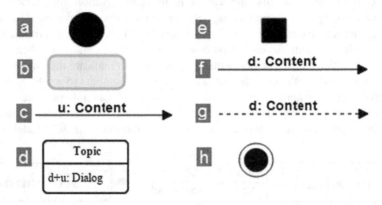

Fig. 2. Elements of the MoLIC language, where: **a** is the opening point; **b** is a ubiquitous access; **c** is a user utterance; **d** is a conversation scene; **e** is a system processing; **f** is a designer utterance; **g** is a breakdown utterance; and **h** is a closing point.

Considering the collaboration aspects, Souza and Barbosa [4] studied how the concepts provided by the 3C Model could be incorporated in the language to allow collaboration modeling. The proposal along with different studies led to a new version of the language, revisiting the current elements and proposing new elements, called MoLICC [7–9]. MoLICC elements allow designers to represent conversation among users and awareness aspects, supporting group work and cooperation. Figure 3 presents the new elements.

The next section presents the methodology we followed to study how collaboration can be represented with the language, analyzing its expressiveness based on the 3C Model of Collaboration.

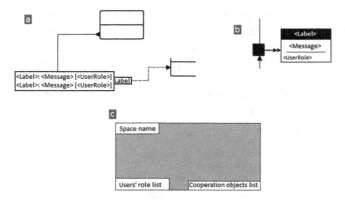

Fig. 3. Collaborative elements incorporated in MoLICC, where: **a** is the Incoming Message Indicator (IMI); **b** is the Outgoing Message Indicator (OMI); and **c** is the Shared Spaced Indicator (SSI).

3 Methodology

The MoLICC language evolved based on the 3C Model, and was tested with potential users [7, 8] and revised using a cognitive approach [9]. So far, we studied how well the interaction aspects are accomplished and how designers understand the new elements.

In this paper, we are interested in understanding how well the language can adapt considering the different kinds of collaboration, as the 3C Model shows. To verify the language usage, we considered three kinds of systems: Time Scheduling, Social Network, and Crowdsourcing.

For each kind of system, we described a practical case based on the 3C model, and proposed a solution using the MoLICC language.

In the next section, we present the results of the study, the proposed model and reflections on the collaboration aspects and how it is presented in the language.

4 Studied Cases and Analysis Results

In this section, we present each type of system studied and, based on the 3C Model, we present a discussion on the collaboration aspects and a possible solution using MoLICC.

4.1 Time Scheduling

Arranging meetings and events in general can be a challenge when having a reasonably large group. The scheduling system takes the 3C form Coordination → Communication → Cooperation, where coordination is the scheduling, communication allows users to negotiate and select dates, and during cooperation users select their available dates.

In Fig. 4 we present a possible solution, where a user can create schedules and share it with other users. When a new schedule is shared with the user (OMI M1: New Schedule invitation), he can then choose his preferred dates (scenes "View Appointment" and "Solve Scheduling"), and in the process see the other users' interaction with the schedule, and therefore their choices (within the SSI). The user who owns the schedule can finish the process by reviewing the selected dates and choosing the best option (scene "Solve Scheduling").

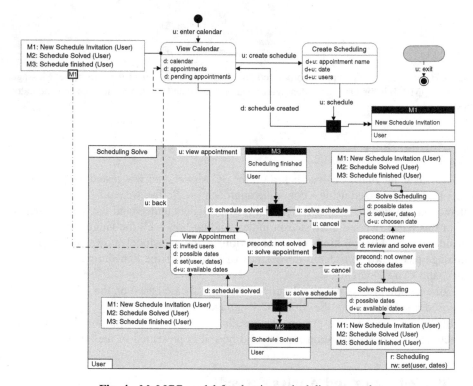

Fig. 4. MoLICC model for the time scheduling example

As the model shows, communication happens through the interaction of each user with the system, and not necessarily based on direct conversation such as chat or video conferencing. Decisions related to closing an event and choosing the best date is up to the users. This way, the interaction model focuses on providing the necessary tools to improve the process of scheduling an event collaboratively.

In conclusion, the SSI allow users to cooperate when choosing their best dates and finishing an schedule, as well as the OMI and IMI inform users about important decisions made for an specific schedule. On the other hand, as the cooperation relies on the users, it is not possible to represent the synchronization of the users (only between each user and the system), along with possible communication breakdown between them.

4.2 Social Network

Social Networks rely on more informal communication and interaction, where the users' main intention is to communicate with others. This way, this kind of system takes the configuration Cooperation → Communication → Coordination, where cooperation is the users' act of sharing their profiles with others, communication provides information exchange among users and coordination occurs when users add or invite others, so they can create and share their profiles.

In Fig. 5 we propose a model where the designers help the users to be aware of who is online and whether they can communicate, in this case using chat.

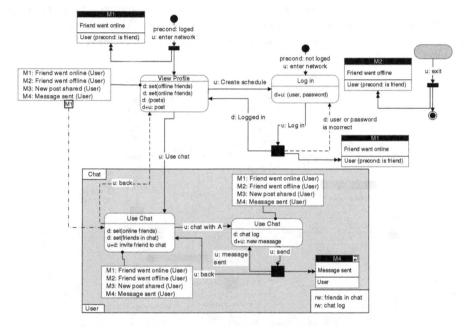

Fig. 5. MoLICC model for the social network example

As the model shows, the users are informed through the IMI and OMI elements when someone changes their status to online or offline (OMIs M1: Friend went online and M2: Friend went offline). There is no guarantee that the user will be aware during interaction and that the information is either enough or too much, but as we consider this as a concrete user interface (and not interaction) issue, it is out of the scope of MoLICC diagrams. In this example, we can consider MoLICC capable of representing what the system will present to the user, and that the user is able to receive and understand the message. On the other hand, the awareness that OMI and IMI provides with messages from other users, as well as the other users' status, is subjective and may distract the user. MoLICC does not provide an element to handle this kind of breakdown, different from communication breakdowns between user and designer's deputy [11].

4.3   Crowdsourcing

Crowdsourcing systems are more domain specific, focusing on cooperation, where users work together to create a product or knowledge based on this cooperation.

In this domain, the 3C Model takes the configuration Cooperation → Coordination → Communication, where cooperation provides ways to share an object with users, coordination guarantees that there is no conflict between different works, and communication contributes on planning and work division.

Let us consider the example of a translation-on-demand service, where users can find language specialists to request the translation of a document (scene "Request Translation" in Fig. 7). This way, translators share their profile and receive requests from users. During the translation work, the user who made the request can intervene in the translation process and be informed about its progress (SSI in Figs. 6 and 7). Figure 6 presents a model for the translator role, and Fig. 7 presents a model for the requester's role.

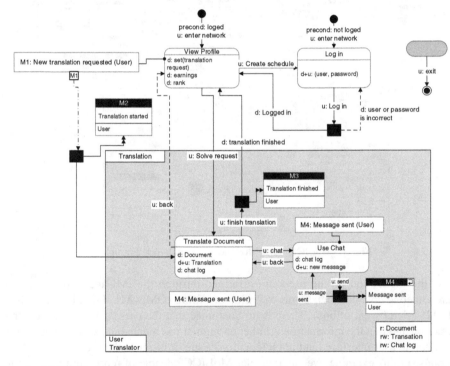

Fig. 6. MoLICC model for the crowdsourcing example of a translation request system, presenting the translator's role view

As Fig. 6 presents, the main feature of the system is related to cooperation, where the translator receives requests from users (OMI M1: New translation requested), and whose work can be observed during translation (OMI M2: Translation started, and both SSIs). In this scenario, the main object is shared (Object "Document" in SSI) (other examples include crowdfunding systems), but only one user has writing privileges during cooperation, avoiding any possible conflict.

In cases where one or more cooperation objects are shared with many users, such as coding, mapping or group translation, a design solution more oriented to concurrency is required, which we can somehow represent with MoLICC, due to the concurrent information propagation that the SSI provides.

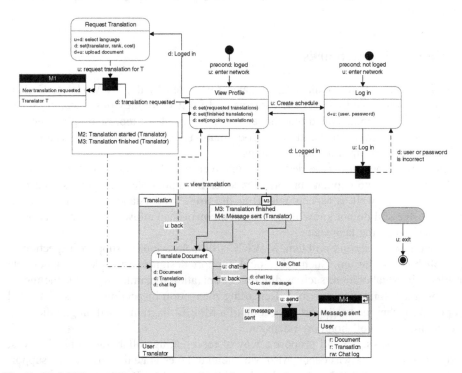

Fig. 7. MoLICC model for the crowdsourcing example of a translation request system, presenting the requester's view

MoLICC provides ways to represent concurrency with SSI, and information sharing with OMI and IMI, allowing an interaction model to focus on cooperation. Along with the previous cases, we can see that communication among users can be achieved by different alternatives, including interaction with OMI and IMI to share information a chatting. MoLICC can also represent video conferencing, providing the audio and video as shared object inside the SSI.

4.4   Conclusions

As we delved into the aspects of the 3C Model, collaborative use cases became more complex, pushing the MoLICC representation to its limits. As human factors are essential to collaboration, we are aware that MoLICCs' models, such as the ones we presented, cannot define or predict how the system will influence group work, or how the expected awareness can work. Moreover, cultural differences that cannot be modeled can also influence group work.

From the design point of view, the ability to conceive and model human interaction can shed some light on interaction problems earlier, as well as collaboration problems. Considering the intention of documentation and planning, MoLICC was shown to support modeling collaboration. The next section presents the concluding remarks of the research.

5　Concluding Remarks

Considering the different collaboration aspects provided by the 3C Model of Collaboration, we were able to depict use cases using MoLICC. In previous research, Souza and Barbosa [4] demonstrated that the language is capable of representing another 3C Model configuration, Cooperation $\rightarrow$ Coordination $\rightarrow$ Communication, designing a system for synchronized document editing.

Designing each use case led us to uncover two limitations of the language. MoLICC showed no explicit support to recover from possible breakdowns related to collaboration, as well as aspects related to the users' understanding and information overload. We still do not know if the current elements can allow this representation or the cost to adapt the language.

Regarding the second problem, MoLICC still lacks a tool to support inspection of the collaboration design. Such tool could support designers to understand possible problems in collaboration, such as different cooperation dynamics for the same model and possible information overload. Regarding interaction inspection, Lopes et al. [12] proposed a technique to support inspection of a MoLIC diagram based on gamification, not including the collaboration extension.

In future works, we will propose a way of representing collaboration breakdowns, studying how breakdowns occur. Also, we intend to investigate how to provide support to verify and locate collaboration-related problems in a MoLICC diagram.

References

1. Ellis, C.A., Gibbs, S.J., Rein, G.L.: Groupware - Some Issues and Experiences. Commun. ACM **34**(1), 38–58 (1991)
2. Fuks, H., Raposo, A.B., Gerosa, M.A., Lucena, C.J.P.: Applying the 3C model to groupware development. Int. J. Coop. Inf. Syst. **14**(2), 299–328 (2005)
3. Fuks, H., Raposo, A., Gerosa, M.A., Pimentel, M., Filippo, D., Lucena, C.J.P.: Inter- and intra-relationships between communication coordination and cooperation in the scope of the 3C collaboration model. In: Proceedings of the 2008 12th International Conference on Computer Supported Cooperative Work in Design, CSCWD, vol. 1, pp. 148–153 (2008)
4. Souza, L.G., Barbosa, S.D.J.: Extending MoLIC for collaborative systems design. In: Proceedings of the 17th HCI International Conference, Los Angeles, pp. 271–282 (2015)

5. Barbosa, S.D.J., de Paula, M.G.: Designing and evaluating interaction as conversation: a modeling language based on semiotic engineering. In: Jorge, J.A., Jardim Nunes, N., Falcão e Cunha, J. (eds.) DSV-IS 2003. LNCS, vol. 2844, pp. 16–33. Springer, Heidelberg (2003)
6. de Souza, C.S.: The Semiotic Engineering of Human-Computer Interaction. The MIT Press, Cambridge (2005)
7. Souza, L.G., Barbosa, S.D.J.: Evaluating a MoLIC extension for collaborative systems design. In: Proceedings of the 2015 IEEE Symposium on Visual Languages and Human-Centric Computing, Atlanta, USA (2015)
8. Souza, L.G., Barbosa, S.D.J.: An Empirical study of MoLICC: a MoLIC extension for collaborative systems design. In: Proceedings of the XIV Brazilian Symposium on Human Factors in Computer Systems, Salvador, Brazil (2015)
9. Souza, L.G., Barbosa, S.D.J.: Avaliando a notação da MoLICC utilizando o framework cognitive dimensions of notations. In: proceedings of the XIV Brazilian Symposium on Human Factors in Computer Systems, Salvador, Brazil (2015)
10. Silva, B.S.: MoLIC 2a Edição: Revisão de uma Linguagem para Modelagem da Interação Humano-Computador. Dissertation (Master's in Informatics). PUC-Rio (2005)
11. Silva, B.S., Barbosa, S.D.J.: Designing human-computer interaction with MoLIC diagrams - a practical guide. In: Monografias em Ciência da Computação. PUC-Rio, Rio de Janeiro (2007)
12. Lopes, A., Marques, A.B., Conte, T., Barbosa, S.D.J.: MoLVERIC: an inspection technique for MoLIC diagrams. In: Proceedings of SEKE (2015)

The Triad of Strengths: A Strengths-Based Approach for Designing with Autistic Adults with Additional Learning Disabilities

Katie Gaudion[1(⊠)] and Liz Pellicano[2]

[1] The Helen Hamlyn Centre for Design, Royal College of Art, London, UK
Katie.gaudion@network.rca.ac.uk
[2] Centre for Research in Autism and Education (CRAE), UCL Institute of
Education, University College London, London, UK
l.pellicano@ucl.ac.uk

Abstract. Autism is a condition that is often defined in terms of difficulties in social interaction, social communication, social understanding and imagination. Much existing research in autism and design is still framed around these so-called Triad of Impairments [1] the goal of which is to improve a person's deficits; for example, developing technologies and environments to enhance communication and social interaction. This paper supports and builds upon existing autism research that views autism through a person's strengths and abilities. This project aims to broaden this discussion into the field of design and turn the deficit-based framework on its head, through the development of a less generalized and more personalised design approach termed the Triad of Strengths, that views autism through a positive and enabling light. The paper describes how a strengths-based approach can support tangible design outcomes to create a positive impact on everyday life for autistic adults.

Keywords: Autism · Design · Strengths · Environment · Participation · Interests · Sensory preferences · Action capabilities

1 Introduction

Neurotypical (NT)[1] is a term coined by the autism community to describe the 99 % of the population who are not on the autism spectrum [3, 4]. It is short for neurologically typical and refers to a person who is within the typical range of human neurology that falls within the dominant societal standards of "normal." Some autistic people think of being neurotypical, rather than autism, as being the disorder. There is also a growing number of blogs, publications and websites that describe the neurotypical experience. 'A Field Guide to Earthlings' for example, presents 62 behaviour patterns used by neurotypical people and states that 'Neurotypical perception is restricted by their use of

---

[1] Throughout the thesis, the term neurotypical is used to describe people who are not autistic – a term widely used by the autism community. The term autistic person is the preferred language of many people with autism [2]. The designer uses this term as well as person-first language (such as 'adults with autism') to respect the wishes of all individuals on the autistic spectrum.

© Springer International Publishing Switzerland 2016
A. Marcus (Ed.): DUXU 2016, Part I, LNCS 9746, pp. 266–280, 2016.
DOI: 10.1007/978-3-319-40409-7_26

language and cultural symbols' [5]. Below is another description of neurotypicality by an autistic person.

Neurotypicality is a pervasive developmental condition, probably present since birth, in which the affected person sees the world in a very strange manner. It is a puzzle; an enigma that traps those so affected in a lifelong struggle for social status and recognition. Neurotypical individuals almost invariably show a triad of impairments, consisting of inability to think independently of the social group, marked impairment in the ability to think logically or critically, and inability to form special interests (other than in social activity) [6].

The extract above and others like it provide a useful starting point for this paper, as from the onset it helps to frame and adjust the neurotypical reader's perspective to the point of view of an autistic person. The extract is an empathic exercise; whilst it may not relate to the reader's understanding of who they are, this inadvertently highlights how an autistic person might feel when they are continuously being characterised through a deficit-based description that does not necessarily relate to or create a holistic impression of who they are.

2 Autism

Autism spectrum condition (ASC) is a lifelong complex neurodevelopmental condition, which affects the way that a person interacts with and experiences the world around them [7]. It is a spectrum condition that affects people in vastly different ways. Someone with autism might be sociable, while others find it difficult to sustain and initiate social relations. Some have learning disabilities while others possess high levels of intellectual ability. It is no longer considered rare: it is estimated that 1 in every 100 people is diagnosed with autism [8, 9]. Between 30–50 % of autistic people have an additional learning disability, that is, "a significantly reduced ability to understand new or complex information, to learn new skills and reduced ability to cope independently which starts before adulthood with lasting effects on development" [10].

Many of the theoretical accounts attempting to explain the behavioural manifestations of autism have largely focused on a person's deficits. For example, the theory of mind hypothesis [11] proposed that autistic people's social and communicative difficulties were fundamentally due to problems in appreciating the mental states of others. Similarly, the executive dysfunction account [12, 13] posited that the repetitive and restricted behaviours and interests resulted from a deficit in executive function – a set of higher-order functions (e.g., planning, working memory, inhibitory control, cognitive flexibility) necessary for flexible, goal-oriented behaviour, especially in novel circumstances. But the anecdotal and reported instances of skills and talents – sometimes of a savant nature – highlighted the need for researchers to go beyond a deficit-based model when explaining autism [14].

2.1 Autism and Strengths

Dr. Leo Kanner (1894–1981) and Dr. Hans Asperger (1906–1980) formed the basis for our understanding of autism today and the springboard from which research in autism has grown and evolved. In Kanner's seminal article 'Autistic Disturbances of Affective Contact' [15], he describes the patterns of behaviours and personalities of 11 children (eight boys and three girls). It is here – in the first description of autism –that made reference to the children's abilities and talents. The first child in Kanner's case series, Donald T., was reported to have a range of abilities; from humming and singing songs accurately, a great memory for names and faces, and knowing an "inordinate amount of pictures in a set of Compton's Encyclopaedia". Other children could recite many prayers, nursery rhymes and songs, "in different languages" and "discriminate between eighteen symphonies" Kanner explained that "almost all the parents reported, usually with much pride, that the children had learned at an early age to repeat an inordinate number of nursery rhymes, prayers, list of animals, the roster of presidents, the alphabet forward and backward, seven foreign – language (French lullabies)".

Whilst Kanner and Asperger had highlighted the strengths of the autistic children, it was not until 1983 that this area of enquiry was revitalized. Shah & Frith [16] asked groups of autistic and non-autistic children, as part of the Children's Embedded Figures Test [17], to find a triangle hidden in a larger, meaningful figure (e.g., a pram) as quickly as possible. They found that the autistic children performed significantly *better* than the non-autistic children, which they proposed was due to an enhanced ability for seeing the parts of the figure rather than the whole. This unique perceptual 'islet of ability' of autistic people was further explored by Frith's [14] notion of weak central coherence, which describes how autistic people have a bias for processing the parts of any stimulus at the expense of the global whole, unlike non-autistic people, who have a tendency to process stimuli for meaning. The following description by an autistic person illustrates this theory.

When I step into a room for the first time I often feel a kind of dizziness with all the bits of information my brain perceives swimming inside my head. Details precede their objects; I see scratches on a table's surface before seeing the entire table, the reflection of light on a window before I perceive the whole window, the patterns on a carpet before the whole carpet comes into view [18].

Mottron and Burack's [19] proposed an alternative competing theory to weak central coherence [14]. They suggested that global processing was not weakened in autism; rather, autistic people have enhanced perceptual functioning, including an excellent focus on details as well as superior abilities in various aspects of perception– recognising, remembering and detecting objects and patterns. From then on research that focuses on the strengths and talents of autistic people has slowly escalated, which has focused on an autistic person's strong systemizing skills and the ability to recognize repeated patterns in stimuli [20], savant abilities, [21, 22], excellent attention to detail [16, 23–26] and recently strengths in creativity through divergent thinking [27].

2.2 Strengths-Based Interventions

In 1971, 28 years after his seminal article, Kanner conducted a follow-up study of 11 autistic children originally reported in 1943 to determine how the children in the original study had progressed [28]. Four of the children had since spent most of their lives in institutional care with poor results. Kanner described "they all lost their lustre early after their admission". However two children, Donald T and Fredrick W, went on to work as a bank teller and duplicating machine operator, respectively. Kanner believed their success was thanks to family members who nurtured their strengths and interests to create new positive experience: Fredrick through his interest in music and photography, and Donald "…because of the intuitive wisdom of a tenant farmer couple, who knew how to make him utilize his futile preoccupation for practical purposes". The follow-up study revealed that to view a person's strengths and interests through a positive lens could be a good point of contact and a way to help transition a person into learning and experiencing new things. This sentiment had already been emphasised by Asperger who stated, "We see here something that we have come across in almost all autistic individuals, a special interest, which enables them to achieve quite extraordinary levels of performance in certain areas" [29].

Irrespective of Kanner and Asperger's articles and a more recent article Donvan and Zucker [30] which further describes Donald T's special-interest-led progress, it is only recently that a person's special interests has begun to be used as a positive way to help connect them with opportunities for social, emotional, academic and vocational growth. One of the earliest studies to examine special interests [31] examined autistic children's special interest in pinball machines. Since then, special interests have become a growing topic of conversation within blogs, forums and autobiographical accounts [32–35] and parent accounts [36].

There is a growing body of research exploring special interests and how they may influence social interaction [37–43]. Researchers have also begun looking at special interests as an important vehicle for learning and skills development [44–51]. Special interests amongst autistic people may be a valuable source when developing employment strategies for autistic people [52]. Most notably a strength-based model was developed by Winter-Messiers [46], which illustrates the strengths resulting from engagement of children and youths with autism in their special interest areas. Winter-Messiers defined special interests as, "those passions that capture the mind, heart, time, and attention of individuals with Asperger Syndrome, providing the lens through which they view the world" [47].

3 Design for Autism: Environment

One of the earliest design studies relating to autism and design involved the design of a playroom for autistic children and guidelines for staff to illustrate how it could be used [53]. Following on from this, in Holland in the early 1980's came the Snoezelen [54], also known as the multi-sensory environment, which is an environment designed to stimulate the primary senses for leisure and relaxation. The Snoezelen was one of the first 'environmental interventions' that considered the person in relation to their physical surroundings; this model has since expanded internationally, and can now be found in many schools and care homes.

Since the Snoezelen, the physical environment has continued to be an important point of intervention and the phrase 'autism friendly environment' has become a buzzword within the autism community – so much so that it fetches 5,360 results on Google (February 2015). Through online blogs, forums and social networks, autistic people and family members are sharing tips and ideas on how to make the domestic environment more autism friendly. Autism friendly environments have also extended into the wider community, several UK cinemas (Odeon, Cineworld) and theatres (such as The Lyceum) host autism friendly screenings and productions; this involves the lowering of lights and sound, freedom to move about and visitors can bring along their own food and drink. The airline JetBlue also offers autistic children a programme called Blue Horizons, which takes them through the process of taking a plane flight in preparation for a real flight, and the Royal Caribbean is the world's first autism friendly cruise line. For more everyday experiences, autistic charities such as The National Autistic Society provide support and advice for people on what to expect when visiting different environments, such as a dentist's surgery, hairdressers and the workplace.

With the increased awareness of the physical environment and its profound impact on an autistic person's everyday life, there are a growing number of designers working in this area within different environmental contexts, such as schools [55–62] multi-sensory environments [63] housing [64–67] and outdoor spaces ([68–73]. Inspired by her autistic brother Marc, Decker's urban design project used a theoretical urban systems toolkit to evaluate how inclusive the city of Nashville, Tennessee, was for autistic people [74]. The evaluation looked at services such as health, education and work, and the findings informed the design of a visual proposal that described how to make the city more inclusive for autistic adults.

Several of the design projects mentioned above took a top-down approach, starting with a pre-determined goal of how to fix or make the environment more functional for autistic people. While some researchers do assert that their design guidelines are not prescriptive and do not apply to everyone [64, 65] the majority of the projects are framed around the generalised classification of autism, that focuses on a person's deficits such as poor social interaction and communication [75, 76], thereby producing generic guidelines that are derived from and restricted to functional need such as safety, robustness, accessibility and durability [55, 56, 58, 60, 62, 77] with little consideration of a person's strengths, interests and aspirations.

4   A Strengths-Based Design Approach

Having looked at different design approaches, we come back to the way autism research is dominated by the medical model of disability. This looks at what a person cannot do rather than what they can do. It is concerned with the severity of the impairment, and looks for ways in which it can be cured or treated. This project supports the social model perspective [78, 79], which was created by disabled people themselves between the 1960s and 1970s. The social model is not concerned with individual deficit but believes disability is caused by the way society is organised rather than the person's impairment. It tries to remove physical, organisational and attitudinal barriers that restrict people to give them more choice and control over their life.

As discussed in the preceding sections autism is often described and generalised by a Triad of Impairments, which is commonly used to describe autistic people. In contrast to the Triad of Impairments and in support of the social model of disability, this study takes on board a strengths-based approach termed the 'Triad of Strengths', that views autism through a positive and enabling light. The Triad of Strengths is a framework that supports a less generalised and more individualised design approach, framed around three diagnostic components of autism presented in the fifth Diagnostic and Statistical Manual (DSM-5): (1) sensory preferences, (2) special interests and (3) action capabilities [7].

It is proposed that a person's Triad of Strengths can influence a person's actions and reactions to the environment. To put this idea into context, if we take the example of music being played at the top of a flight of stairs, if a person is interested in the music, this might motivate them to walk up the stairs to the source of the sound. Conversely, if a person is hypersensitive to sound they might choose to walk away from the music altogether. If a person likes the music but has limited mobility, then the affordance of the environment (the stairs) may not support their action capabilities, preventing them from going up the stairs. The example describes how an environment that complements a person's Triad of Strengths can create positive experiences, but highlights how the environment and what it affords (i.e. the music and stairs) in conjunction with how well it fits with a person's Triad of Strengths, is an important consideration to avoid negative experiences.

The three diagnostic components of autism are outlined below and inverted through a positive lens to create the Triad of Strengths, with a description of how a person's sensory preferences, special interests and action capabilities could inform the design process.

(1) DSM-5 states that autistic people may experience 'hyper- or hypo-activity to sensory input or unusual interests in sensory aspects of the environment'. It could be proposed that by exploring and identifying a person's sensory preferences, the quality of stimuli relating to the sensory elements of the environment can be modulated to suit a person's preferences and reduce or even eliminate their sensory dislikes, making the environment more relaxing and enjoyable to be in.

(2) DSM-5 states that an autistic person may 'experience highly restricted, fixated interests that are abnormal in intensity or focus.' It is possible that exploring and identifying a person's interests may help inform the design of personalised environments, which could greatly increase the likelihood of active engagement. The research also suggests that design can potentially harness a person's interests and connect that interest with opportunities for more meaningful social, emotional and vocational growth.

(3) DSM-5 states that autistic people may experience 'stereotyped or repetitive motor movements, use of objects, or speech.' We propose that affordances are the key mechanism that designers use to trigger understanding and action in others. Through exploring a person's action capabilities to a world predominantly designed for and by neurotypical people, tangible insights and clues can be unraveled, which enables designers to create flexible environments that also relate to the perceptual world and action capabilities of autistic people.

4.1 Design Study

Here, we provide a brief overview of a design study that used the Triad of Strengths approach. This were enabled by a long-term collaboration with the UK's Kingwood Trust, who provide support and accommodation for autistic adults with limited verbal speech and additional learning disabilities. We were interested in particular how these adults perceive and experience everyday activities and the domestic objects associated with them (e.g., vacuum cleaning and washing clothes). In contrast to most conventional design studies, the adults' limited verbal communication meant that the designer was unable to directly ask their views and perspectives on design issues. To ensure their needs, abilities and interests were considered, the designer used a variety of innovative tools that invited the autistic adults, their support staff and family members into the design process.

The following section describes a selection of design tools used to generate insights about a person's Triad of Strengths, and illustrates how the information derived from the tools helped to create a palette of ingredients to form specific design outcomes; a bubble blowing vacuum cleaner.

Objects of Everyday Use Cards. In this study, the designer built upon Lawton and Brody's [80] work on daily living activities to create a set of visual cards called Objects of Everyday Use. The cards photographically represent 43 everyday activities to create explicit visual prompts to help autistic participants conceptualise and process what the activity. This approach makes it more inclusive for the participants with the help of their support staff to take part in expressing the things they do or do not like to do around their home, with the opportunity to describe their reasons why and how much support (if any) they might need to perform certain activities.

Seventeen autistic adults participated with the Objects of Everyday Use cards.

The cards revealed that a person's motivation for doing an activity was often influenced by their sensory preferences and fuelled by the sensory feedback of the activities, rather than the intended affordance for doing the activity. For example, some participants enjoyed boiling eggs to watch the egg move around the pan, putting cutlery away to hear it chime, and pegging clothes on a washing line to watch them move in the breeze. Equally, some participants avoided certain activities due to their sensory sensitivities, for example avoiding vacuum cleaning or mowing the lawn because of the sound and washing up because of getting wet. In this way, the cards enabled the research team to explore patterns and correlations between the most popular and least popular activities, the amount of support required to perform an activity and the reasons, when possible, why the participants liked or disliked various activities. Most notably activities that involved bubbles i.e. washing up was a popular activity and washing clothes to watch the clothes spin.

Sensory Preference Cards. The next tool was the Sensory Preference Cards [81]: a physical and visual extension of the existing Adult/Adolescent Sensory Profile ® questionnaire [82]. The 72 cards are set within the context of the home, with each card showing a different type of sensory experience described in simple words and illustrated by photographed images. The cards act as visual prompts inviting the participant to express whether she/he likes, dislikes or is neutral about the subject of each card.

The activity aims to involve autistic people in the sensory profiling as active participants rather than relying on family members or support workers to express preferences on their behalf.

The reverse sides of the cards are colour-coded by the sensory systems – touch, sight, smell, auditory, vestibulation and proprioception – providing a quick-reference visual indication of the participant's preferred sensory system(s). Once categorised into groups of likes, dislikes and neutral, the cards create visual mood boards about a person's sensory profile and can be used to make decisions about the manner in which they are supported and the design of their home.

Sensory Activities. The designer facilitated sensory activities by way of exploring a person's sensory preferences and action capabilities through directly observing their reaction to and interaction with their home environment. The activities were structured around the designer's past experience of facilitating sensory sessions in multi-sensory environments. The designer and support staff were present but the activities were led by the autistic participants who were invited to engage with various props (rather than engaging with people and having to achieve specific tasks) to help them explore and test the boundaries of their sensory preferences in a safe, fun and relaxed manner. The props were chosen for their visceral and sensory properties in terms of touch, sound, sight, smell and movement. They were abstract in shape, stripped of social context with no intended affordance. The function and archetype of the props was deliberately undefined, which helped the designer to observe a person's interactions with them without being distracted by subjective prior knowledge about the intended affordance of the prop.

The designer looked for patterns of use and connections between the sensory characteristics of the props that the participant discarded, appeared indifferent to, or gravitated towards. To help this process the designer took note of a person's actions, contact and sensory engagement with each prop and afterwards created a compilation of the sensory props with which each participant engaged. The compilation of props highlighted for example how Matt enjoyed the props that made a sound or movement to his motion of tapping, Emily liked the props that changed shape in response to her interaction and Tom enjoyed the props that offered resistance that encouraged him to push and pull.

Interest and Hobbies. Given the designer's philosophy of designing around a person's interests, accurately diagnosing a genuine interest was vital, therefore an interest mapping tool was developed to record a person's more idiosyncratic interests (rather than timetabled activities). The designer drew upon research conducted by Baron-Cohen and Wheelwright [39], which invited 92 parents to complete a questionnaire, designed to determine the subject of their autistic child's special interests. The authors developed a taxonomy of interests found within autistic children, and this became a framework for the designer to create a visual Interests and Hobbies booklet. Each page in the booklet is dedicated to one of the 19 interests described by Baron-Cohen with ample room for the participant to expand upon through writing or drawing.

To visualise the wealth of information, a tree was used as a metaphor to represent the interests of each autistic participant. The branches on the each tree are colour-coded and represent an area of interest drawn from Baron-Cohen's taxonomy of interests. Leaves are then added to each branch to go into more detail about the particular interest of each person. Each branch therefore represents potential areas of growth. This lyrical way of representing the special interests of autistic adults, using a Tree of Opportunity, aimed to encourage the support staff to identify and create opportunities for growth based on a person's interests. As in the Objects of Everyday Use cards, bubbles and watching objects spin were a popular interest.

Doing Things with Things Booklets. A useful output of the Objects of Everyday Use cards was identifying the everyday tasks that the autistic participants found to be the most difficult. Vacuum cleaning, washing clothes and toasting bread in particular were reported as requiring the most support and therefore warranted further investigation. The designer began by breaking the tasks down into much smaller tasks, noting the challenges with each. Each of these sub-tasks could be the potential 'roadblock' that, if identified and removed, would make the overall task seem much more attractive to a person with autism. In response to these challenges and to help identify how each activity challenges or complements the participants' capabilities, the designer developed Doing Things with Things – a series of booklets that visually breaks down activities into manageable steps, to help guide the autistic participant through the actions required to perform the activity.

By taking a holistic view of one activity, the aim of the booklet is to encourage self-evaluation, identify opportunities for support and to record how a person has progressed over time. The designer distributed Doing Things with Things booklets to three autistic adults and their support staff, which they completed over a six-week period. The booklets were filled with descriptive observations made by staff, which helped to pinpoint what the autistic participants liked/disliked about each activity, how they chose to afford each activity and where the affordance of each activity did not complement a person's capabilities. For example, one participant enjoyed step eight in washing up (putting the soap power in the washing machine) because he liked the smell. Other participants disliked operating a toaster because of the unpredictability of the toast popping up, which might be prevented by adding an affordance (a visible timer) to enable a person to anticipate when this might happen to mitigate sensory discomfort.

4.2   Design Output: Hubble Bubble and Spinny Disc

The design tools described above revealed how some autistic participants responded to the visceral qualities of an activity and were motivated to perform an everyday activity due to the sensory feedback the activity gave them; two key themes that kept repeating were bubbles and spinning. Furthermore, the Objects of Everyday Use cards revealed that vacuum cleaning and washing clothes were activities many participants required more support, on this basis, the designer explored ways in which vacuum cleaning and washing clothes could become a more meaningful and enjoyable experience for the autistic participants.

1. Hubble Bubble; The design tools revealed activities such as washing up and making porridge were found to be a particularly popular largely due to the bubbles, equally a bubble wand was a popular prop used during the sensory activities. Having identified a particular interest and sensory preference for bubbles, the designer began to explore ways of extending bubbles into the activity of vacuum cleaning, thereby making the pleasurable element – in this case the bubbles – intrinsic to more than one activity. To achieve this, the designer designed and developed 'Hubble Bubble' – a bubble blowing vacuum cleaner. The designer proposes that by incorporating a person's interest and sensory preference into vacuum cleaning could intrinsically motivate a person to do the activity and enhance positive experiences.

2. Spinny Disc; The design tools revealed that some people might particularly enjoy the by-products of operating a washing machine; for example they might enjoy listening to the washing machine, or pleasure from pouring the washing powder because of the smell. The design tools also revealed that many of the participants also enjoyed spinning objects specifically watching the washing machine spin. To accentuate and celebrate the recurring preference for spinning, the designer developed 'Spinny Disc' which adds an extra – and pleasurable- fun step into the process of washing clothes. Spinny Disc is attached to the inside of the washing machine door and creates different visual effects as it spins with the washing. The designer proposes that by creating a new step in the act of washing clothes based on something identified as enjoyable, may encourage the autistic participants to master more difficult steps within this particular activity.

5 Conclusions

As identified in the literature review, the majority of existing research in design and autism focuses on a person's deficits, where the main goal is to overcome a person's impairments. This project has taken a novel approach that inverts a person's deficits to strengths by creating a design framework termed the Triad of Strengths, in which a person's sensory preferences, special interests and action capabilities can help guide the design process. This research revealed that the Triad of Strengths supported the design process in a variety of ways. Information about a person's interests helped the designer to connect and communicate with the autistic participants, and a person's sensory preferences and action capabilities helped the designer to anticipate and explain a person's motivations, interactions and reactions to the physical environment. Finally, a person's strengths provided an important palette of ingredients that triggered design ideas for two prototypes; Hubble Bubble and Spinny Disc.

Whilst an evaluation of Hubble Bubble was carried out, due to the word constraints of this paper it is impossible to describe in detail the outcome, but it is fair to say the evaluation process was difficult on many levels [83]. Importantly, the evaluation process highlighted the challenges involved with introducing a new design prototype into an autistic person's home, and more time needs to be spent exploring ways to introduce and integrate the evaluation process into the autistic participants daily life. This paper hopes to draw the readers' attention to this complex part of the design process and hopes to raise critical discussion around the ethical implication of the evaluation process and develop ideas on how it can be made more comfortable for those involved. This paper hopes to expand the field of inclusive design to consider neurodiveristy and encourage more designers to collaborate with people who are neurologically diverse who can offer unique ideas for innovation that are excluded from mainstream ways of thinking.

References

1. Wing, L., Gould, J.: Severe impairments of social interaction and associated abnormalities in children: epidemiology and classification. J. Autism Dev. Disord. **9**(1), 11–29 (1979)
2. Sinclair, J.: Why I dislike "person first" language (1999). http://www.autcom.org/articles/defeated.html. Accessed 24 September 2012
3. Sinclair, J.: A note about language and abbreviations used on this site. Jim Sinclair's website (1998). http://web.archive.org/web/20080606024118/http://web.syr.edu/~jisincla/language.htm. Accessed June 2012
4. Gray, C., Attwood, T.: The discovery of aspie criteria. Morning News **11**(3), 18–28 (1999)
5. Ford, I.: A Field Guide to Earthlings, p. 16. Ian Ford Software Corporation, Albuquerque (2010)
6. Human 19. Understanding neurotypicality. Politics.ie (2012). http://www.politics.ie/forum/culturecommunity/201954-would-you-laugh-3.html. Accessed 12 January 2013. American Psychiatric Association, 2013
7. American Psychiatric Association. Diagnostic and statistical manual of mental disorders: DSM 5 development (2013). http://www.dsm5.org/Pages/Default.aspx. Accessed 5 February 2014
8. Baird, G., Simonoff, E., Pickles, A., Chandler, S., Loucas, T., Meldrum, D., Charman, T.: Prevalence of disorders of the autism spectrum in a population cohort of children in South Thames: the special needs and autism project (SNAP). Lancet **368**(9531), 210–215 (2006)
9. Brugha, T., McManus, S., Meltzer, H., Smith, J., Scott, F.J., Purdon, S., Harris, J., Bankart, J.: Autism spectrum disorders in adults living in households throughout England: report from the Adult Psychiatric Morbidity Survey 2007. Leeds: The NHS Information Centre for Health and Social Care (2009)
10. The Department of Health: Valuing People: A New Strategy for Learning Disability for the 21st Century; a white paper, p. 14 (2001)
11. Baron-Cohen, S., Leslie, A.M., Frith, U.: Does the autistic child have a 'theory of mind'? Cognition **21**, 37–46 (1985)
12. Pennington, B.F., Ozonoff, S.: Executive functions and developmental psychopathology. J. Child. Psychol. Psychiatry **37**, 51–87 (1996)
13. Ozonoff, S., Bruce, F., Pennington, F., Rogers, S.J.: Executive function deficits in high-functioning autistic individuals: relationship to theory of mind. J. Child. Psychol. Psychiatry **32**, 1081–1105 (1991)
14. Frith, U.: Autism: Explaining the Enigma. Blackwell, Oxford (1989)
15. Kanner, L.: Autistic disturbances of affective contact. Nerv. Child **2**, 217–250 (1943). p x/238/236/243
16. Shah, A., Frith, U.: An islet of ability in autistic children: a research note. J. Child Psychol. **24**(4), 613–620 (1983)

17. Karp, S.A., Konstadt, N.L.: The children's embedded figures test (CEFT). In: Witkin, H.A., Oltman, P.K., Raskin, E., Karp, S.A. (eds.) A Manual for Embedded Figures Test, pp. 21–26. Consulting Psychologist Press, Palo Alto (1971)
18. Tammet, D.: Embracing the Wide Sky, p. 177. Hodder and Stoughton, New York (2009)
19. Mottron, L., Burack, J.: Enhanced perceptual functioning in the development of autism. In: Burack, J.A., Charman, T., Yirmiya, N., Zelazo, P.R. (eds.) The Development of Autism: Perspectives from Theory and Research, pp. 131–148. L. Erlbaum Press, Mahwah (2001)
20. Baron-Cohen, S.: Autism, hypersystemizing, and truth. Q. J. Exp. Psychol. 61(1), 64–75 (2008)
21. Howlin, P., Goode, S., Hutton, J., Rutter, M.: Savant skills in autism: psychometric approaches an parental reports. Philos. Trans. 364(1522), 1359–1367 (2009)
22. Hermelin, B.: Bright Splinters of the Mind: A Personal Story of Research with Autistic Savants. Jessican Kingsley, London (2002)
23. Shah, A., Frith, U.: Why do autistic individuals show superior performance on the block test design test? J. Child Psychol. 34, 1351–1364 (1993)
24. Jolliffe, T., Baron-Cohen, S.: A test of central coherence theory: can adults with high-functioning autism or Asperger Syndrome integrate fragments of an object? Cogn. Neuropsychiatry 6, 193–216 (2001)
25. O'Riordan, M., Plaisted, K., Driver, J., Baron-Cohen, S.: Superior visual search on autism. J. Exp. Psychol. Hum. Percept. Perform. 27(3), 719–730 (2001)
26. Mottron, L., Burack, J.A., Larocci, G., Belleville, S., Enns, J.T.: Locally orientated perception with intact global processing amond adolescents with high functioning autism: evidence from multiple paradigms. J. Child Psychol. 44, 904–913 (2003)
27. Best, C., Arora, S., Porter, F., Doherty, M.: The relationship between subthreshold autistic traits, ambiguous figure perception and divergent thinking. J. Autism Dev. Disord. 45(12), 4064–4073 (2015)
28. Kanner, L.: Follow-up study of eleven autistic children. J. Autism Child. Schizophr. 1(2), 119–142 (1971). p 143/
29. Asperger, H.: Autistic psychopathy in childhood. In: Frith, U. (ed.) Autism and Asperger syndrome, pp. 37–92. Cambridge University Press, Cambridge (1991). p. 45 (1944)
30. Donvan, J., Zucker, C.: Autism's first child. The Atlantic, article no. 308227 (2010). http://www.theatlantic.com/magazine/archive/2010/10/autisms-first-child/308227/. Accessed November 2012
31. Kerbeshian, J., Burd, L.: Asperger's syndrome and Tourette syndrome: the case of the pinball wizard. Br. J. Psychiatry 148, 731–736 (1986)
32. Welton, J.: Can I Tell You about Asperger's Syndrome? A Guide for Friends and Family. Jessica Kingsley, London (2003)
33. Grandin, T.: My experiences as an autistic child. J. Orthomolecular Psychiatry 13, 144–174 (1984)
34. Grandin, T.: The Way I See it: A Personal Look at Autism and Asperger's. Future Horizons, Texas (2008)
35. Trehin, G.: Urville. Jessica Kingsley, London (2006)
36. Fling, F.R.: Eating an Artichoke: A Mother's Perspective on Asperger Syndrome. Jessica Kingsley, London (2000)
37. Charlop-Christy, M.H., Haymes, L.K.: Using obsessions as reinforcers with and without mild reductive procedures to decrease inappropriate behaviours of children with autism. J. Autism Dev. Disord. 26(5), 527–546 (1996)
38. Charlop-Christy, M., Haymes, L.: Using objects of obsession as token reinforcers for children with autism. J. Autism Dev. Disord. 28(3), 189–198 (1998)

39. Baron-Cohen, S., Wheelwright, S.: 'Obsessions' in children with autism or Asperger syndrome: a content analysis in terms of core domains of cognition. Br. J. Psychiatry 175, 484–490 (1999)
40. Baker, M.J.: Incorporating the thematic ritualistic behaviours of children with autism into games. J. Positive Behav. Interv. 2, 66–84 (2000)
41. Attwood, T.: Understanding and managing circumscribed interests. In: Prior, M. (ed.) Learning and Behavior Problems in Asperger's Syndrome, pp. 126–147. Guilford Press, New York (2003)
42. Boyd, B.A., Conroy, M.A., Mancil, G.R., Nakao, T., Alter, P.J.: Effects of circumscribed interests on the social behaviours of children with autism spectrum disorders. J. Autism Dev. Disord. 27, 1550–1561 (2007)
43. Dunst, C.J., Trivette, C.M., Masiello, T.: Influence of the interests of children with autism on everyday learning opportunities. Psychol. Rep. 107(1), 281–288 (2010)
44. Vacca, J.J.: Incorporating interests and structure to improve participation of a child with autism in a standardized assessment: a case study analysis. Focus Autism Other Dev. Disabil. 22, 51–59 (2007)
45. Vismara, L.A., Lyons, G.L.: Using preservative interests to elicit joint attention behaviours in young children with autism. J. Positive Behav. Interv. 9, 214–228 (2007)
46. Winter-Messiers, M.A., Herr, C.M., Wood, C.E., Brooks, A.P., Gates, M.A.M., Houston, T. L., Tingstad, K.I.: How far can Brian ride the daylight 4449 express? a strength-based model of Asperger syndrome based on special interest areas. Focus Autism Other Dev. Disabil. 22 (2), 67–79 (2007)
47. Winter-Messiers, M.A.: Dinosaurs 24/7: understanding the special interests of children with Asperger's, 2 April 2007. http://iancommunity.org/cs/about_asds/the_special_interests_of_children_with_aspergers. Accessed 10 April 2012
48. Gagnon, E.: Power cards: using special interests to motivate children and youth with Asperger syndrome and autism. Autism Asperger Publishing Company, Shawnee Mission (2001)
49. Kluth, P., Schwarz, P.: Just give him the whale: 20 ways to use fascinations, areas of expertise, and strengths to support students with autism. Jessica Kingsley, London (2009)
50. Kluth, P., Schwarz, P.: Pedro's Whale. Jessica Kingsley, London (2010)
51. Kavan, S., Kavan, B.: Trainman: gaining acceptance and friends through special interests. AAPC Publishing, Kansas (2011)
52. Kirchner, J.C., Dziobek, I.: Toward the successful employment of adults with autism: a first analysis of special interests and factors deemed important for vocational performance. Scand. J. Child Adolesc. Psychiatry Psychol. 2(2), 77–85 (2014)
53. Richer, J.M., Nicoll, L.: A playroom for autistic children, and its companion therapy project. Br. J. Mental Subnormality 17, 132–143 (1971)
54. Hulsegge, J., Verheul, A.: Snoezelen: Another World. Rompa, Chesterfield (1987)
55. Beaver, C.: Breaking the mold. Communication 37(3), 40 (2003). 485
56. Beaver, C.: Designing environments for children and adults on the autism spectrum. Good Autism Pract. 12(1), 7–11 (2011)
57. Khare, R., Mullick, A.: Educational spaces for children with autism: design development process. In: Proceedings of CIB W 084: Building Comfortable and Liveable Environments for All, Atlanta, GA, 15–16 May 2008, pp. 66–75 (2008). http://www.irbnet.de/daten/iconda/CIB8861.pdf. Accessed 31 March 2015
58. Khare, R., Mullick, A.: Incorporating the behavioural dimension in designing inclusive learning environment for autism. Int. J. Architectural Res. 3(3), 45–64 (2009)
59. Mostafa, M.: An architecture for autism: concepts of design intervention for the autistic user. Int. J. Architectural Res. 2(1), 189–211 (2008)

60. Scott, I.: Designing learning spaces for children on the autism spectrum. Good Autism Pract. **10**(1), 36–51 (2009)
61. Tufvesson, C., Tufvesson, J.: The building process as a tool towards an all-inclusive school: a Swedish example focusing on children with defined concentration difficulties such as ADHD, autism and Down's syndrome. J. Hous. Built Environ. **24**(1), 47–66 (2009)
62. Vogel, C.L.: Classroom design for living and learning with autism. Autism Asperger's Digest **7** (2008)
63. Gumtau, S., Newland, P., Creed, C., Kunath, S.: MEDIATE: a responsive environment designed for children with autism. In: Accessible Design in the Digital World Conference, 23–25 August 2005, Dundee (2005). http://ewic.bcs.org/content/ConWebDoc/3805. Accessed 21 September 2013
64. Ahrentzen, S., Steele, K.: Advancing full spectrum housing: designing for adults with autism spectrum disorders: a technical report. Tempe, Arizona: The Herberger Institute School of Architecture and Landscape Architecture and the Stardust Center for Affordable Homes and the Family (2009)
65. Brand, A.: Living in the Community: Housing Design for Adults with Autism. Helen Hamlyn Centre for Design, Royal College of Art, London (2010)
66. Lopez, K., Gaines, K.: Environment and behavior: residential designs for autism. In: Proceedings of the 43rd Annual Conference of the Environmental Design Research Association, Seattle, OR, 30 May – 2 June 2012, pp. 265–266 (2012). http://www.edra.org/content/impact-acoustical-environmental-design-children-autism. Accessed 11 October 2013
67. Woodcock, A., Georgiou, D., Jackson, J., Woolner, A.: Designing a tailorable environment for children with autism spectrum disorders. In: Proceedings of the Triannual Conference of the International Ergonomics Association, 'TEC', Maastricht, 10–14 July 2006 (2013). http://www.iea.cc/ECEE/pdfs/art0228.pdf. Accessed 11 October 2013. The Design Institute, Coventry
68. Herbert, B.: Design guidelines of a therapeutic garden for autistic children. Ph.D. thesis, Louisiana State University (2003)
69. Hussein, H.: Using the sensory garden as a tool to enhance the educational development and social interaction of children with special needs. Support Learn. **25**(1), 25–31 (2010)
70. Linehan, J.: Landscapes for autism: guidelines and design of outdoor spaces for children with autism spectrum disorder. Ph.D. thesis, University of California (2008)
71. Menear, K.S., Smith, S.C., Lanier, S.: A multipurpose fitness playground for individuals with autism: ideas for design and use. J. Phys. Educ. Recreation Dance **77**(9), 20–25 (2006)
72. Sachs, N., Vincenta, T.: Outdoor environments for children with autism and special needs. Implications **9**(10), 1–7 (2011)
73. Yuill, N., Strieth, S., Roake, C., Aspden, R., Todd, B.: Brief report: designing a playground for children autistic spectrum disorder: effects on playful peer interactions. J. Autism Dev. Disord. **37**(6), 1192–1196 (2007)
74. Decker, E.: A city for Marc: an inclusive design approach to planning for adults with autism. Master's thesis, Kansas State University (2014)
75. Francis, P., Balbo, S., Frith, L.: Towards co-design with users who have autism spectrum disorders. Univ. Access Inf. Soc. **8**(3), 123–135 (2009)
76. Khare, R., Mullick, A.: Universally beneficial educational space design for children with autism. In: Designing for Children, IDC, IIT, Mumbai, India, 2–6 February 2010. http://www.designingforchildren.net/papers/r-khare-designingforchildren.pdf. Accessed 2 April 2015
77. Humphreys, S.: Autism and architecture. Autism Lond. Bull. **494**, 7–8 (2005). Jenkins, H.S.: Gibson's 'affordances': evolution of a pivotal concept. J. Sci. Psychol. **12**, 34–45 (2008)

78. Oliver, M.: A new model of the social work role in relation to disability. In: Campling, J. (ed.) The Handicapped Person: A New Perspective for Social Workers?. RADAR, London (1981)
79. Oliver, M.: The Politics of Disablement. Macmillan, Basingstoke (1990)
80. Lawton, M.P., Brody, E.M.: Assessment of older people: self-maintaining and instrumental activities of daily living. Gerontologist **9**, 179–186 (1969)
81. Brand, A., Gaudion, K.: Exploring Sensory Preferences, living environments for adults for autism. The Helen Hamlyn Centre for Design, Royal College of Art (2012)
82. Brown, C., Dunn, W.: Adult/Adolescent Sensory Profile: User's Manual. Psychological Corporation, San Antonio (2002)
83. Gaudion, K.: A designer's approach: Exploring how autistic adults with additional learning disabilites experience their home environment. Ph.D. thesis, Royal College of Art, London (2015)

Scaffolding a Methodology for Situating Cognitive Technology Within Everyday Contexts

Michael Heidt[1]($\boxtimes$), Madlen Wuttke[2], Peter Ohler[2], and Paul Rosenthal[1]

[1] Chemnitz University of Technology, Visual Computing Group,
Straße der Nationen 62, 09111 Chemnitz, Germany
{michael.heidt,paul.rosenthal}@informatik.tu-chemnitz.de
[2] Chemnitz University of Technology, Chair Media Psychology,
Thüringer Weg 11, 09126 Chemnitz, Germany
{madlen.wuttke,peter.ohler}@phil.tu-chemnitz.de

Abstract. Cognitive technology is leaving the lab and entering the world of the everyday. Systems such as knowledge navigators, conversational agents, and intelligent personal assistants are increasingly incorporated into real-world systems. This success of cognitive technologies poses novel methodological challenges for interdisciplinary teams tasked with their development. In order to behave successfully within the variegated conditions of the everyday, systems have to be developed within processes of continuous iterative evaluation and analysis. These development processes necessarily proceed in an interdisciplinary manner, combining the expertise of cognitive science and the productive know-how of interaction design. These disciplines operate within incompatible methodological and epistemological framings, complicating synthesis of their results. However, in order to situate cognitive technology productively within everyday situations their respective results have to be integrated into a single research process. We discuss a methodological framework facilitating this synthesis which was developed within concrete projects of interdisciplinary cooperation.

Keywords: HCI · Methodology · Practice based research · Cognitive science

1 Introduction

Technological artefacts such as intelligent personal assistants are increasingly employed within everyday contexts. Systems such as CALO [1] and its popular spin-off Siri accompany users throughout their daily lives, supporting a wide array of leisure activities and professional obligations. Consequently, they have to operate across a broad range of diverse, hardly predictable and sometimes chaotic contexts.

This diversification of contexts of use calls into question the utility of traditional patterns of lab-based research. Many of the classical tools used when evaluating and developing said technologies such as controlled lab studies or

© Springer International Publishing Switzerland 2016
A. Marcus (Ed.): DUXU 2016, Part I, LNCS 9746, pp. 281–292, 2016.
DOI: 10.1007/978-3-319-40409-7_27

evaluations relying on predetermined tasks do not fare well when faced with the uncertainties and ambiguities of the everyday [2,17,29,31,51].

When developing for everyday contexts, a methodological toolset is required that supports construction, description, and evaluation activities unfolding over extended periods of time within environments that we as researchers cannot control or design beforehand. The dynamic patterns of communication present within these contexts thus put a high strain on our capabilities both of scientific analysis and prospective design, challenging proven methods in respective fields.

Methodological Diversity

The field of human-computer-interaction (HCI) has acknowledged and responded to these novel challenges with a diversification of its methodological base, theoretical framings and epistemological groundings:

In-the-wild methods [30,40,44,46], methodologies informed by ethnomethodology [15,55], grounded theory [47], or ethnography [16], frameworks such as Embodied Interaction [18] and Thoughtful Design [39], have established themselves within the increasingly diverse methodological landscape of the field [45].

In reaction to challenges to the cognitive paradigm, researchers have sought to establish novel encompassing theoretical frameworks. Activity Theory (AT) was adopted as a promising candidate for informing development activities within rich real-world contexts [42].

A different approach lies in identification of incommensurable paradigms [22,33], waves [10], and thus different communities of academic practice. An especially well received and sophisticated approach of this kind is the concept of *Third paradigm HCI* developed by Harrison, Sengers, and Tatar [21]. Drawing on Kuhn [32], the authors argue for the presence of three distinct academic communities operating within individual systems of epistemological commitments and methodological procedures. Accordingly, knowledge claims remain partially incommensurable, allowing mutual respect and precluding unnecessary discussion between practitioners operating within differing paradigms.

Intra-Team Diversity

When building cognitive artefacts for everyday contexts, project teams frequently find themselves in situations where stakeholders are indepted to differing paradigms or perspectives. Media psychologists employ the cognitive paradigm, interaction designers subscribe to a practice paradigm, computer scientists exercise methodological indifference, while ethnographers champion a constructive construal of reality. Most of the approaches mentioned above leave the question open how methodological coordination within interdisciplinary teams is possible that operate *across* paradigms, or do not achieve consensus on one of the discussed theoretical umbrella frameworks.

We argue that an interesting candidate for coordination within interdisciplinary teams is provided by a theoretical vocabulary based on the notion of *complexity.* On the level of methods, appropriation of techniques used within *practice-based research* are proposed in order to contain development and evaluation complexities. Instead of proposing an integrated theoretical-methodological stance, that all participants have to agree on, or a compartmentalisation of researcher activity into distinct paradigms, we are formulating a set of concepts that allow for processes of ongoing conflictual negotiation during development projects.

2   Theoretical Framing

Choice of a theoretical base for an interdisciplinary framework is no easy endeavour. Often, academic communities of practice remain entrenched within idiosyncratic theoretical vocabularies, nurturing theories specific to their interests, while seeking to establish discourses of their own in order to differentiate and isolate themselves from bordering disciplines.

Contact areas between disciplines do exist, however, allowing for specification of theories intelligible to multiple communities. We have identified the notion of *complexity* as an intellectual 'plexus' of this kind, connecting various disciplines that otherwise remain weakly interlinked on the level of theoretical discourse. As a concept complexity stretches disciplinary boundaries; the signifier is known within the domains of psychology, computer-science, human-computer-interaction, sociology, science and technology studies, among others. As goes without saying, such a diverse pattern of intellectual proliferation does not reproduce without effecting equivocations and ambiguities in usage: Computational complexity theory [23,50] might understand the concept very differently from sociological systems theory [38], science and technology studies [35,37], or design theory [51].

However, as a conceptual starting point, the concept remains useful. Where it is not accompanied by clear or congruent concepts, it at least triggers associations relating to relevant notions, which subsequently can be employed in order to bootstrap a discussion process.

2.1   Everyday Complexity

In order to give an account of complexity within everyday situations conducible to the requirements of human-computer interaction, we discuss an approach developed by interaction designer Ron Wakkary. In his text *Framing complexity, design and experience: a reflective analysis* Wakkary frames the problematic of everyday situations within the theoretical vocabulary of complexity. In order to describe the specific requirements of addressing the everyday within HCI projects, Wakkary highlights the necessity of approaching rich interactional networks present within domestic, cultural, and leisure contexts through practice.

As is often the case, complexity is applied as qualification in order to signify the inability of achieving an analytic solution, of not being able to break up a problem into its constituent parts or variables. Building on HCI discourse and insights derived from his own projects, Wakkary identifies this quality within everyday situations.

Being faced with a complex problem has direct implications for possible design strategies: As comprehensive analysis is impossible, design actions must operate on the basis of imperfect, provisional, and ambiguous information. The resulting problem space has to be explored through practice in a situated manner.

In response to this necessity, Wakkary proposes an approach similar to *dead reckoning* in navigation [51, pp. 7, 10]. Thereby, he sketches an incremental design methodology responding to the problematic of complexity. It consists of setting a general direction for the design process, which is modified and corrected during every design decision. At every point within the design process, a course correction is performed, whose direction is marked in reference to the last.

Implications for Interdisciplinary Development of Cognitive Artefacts. The concept of *complexity* was introduced as a possible device for regulating interdisciplinary discourse. The detailed account Wakkary provides of everyday complexity facilitates a precise description of the necessities of adopting an iterative and practice-based approach towards interdisciplinary development of artefacts performing within everyday contexts.

There is an inherent conflict between a conception of complexity entailing non-representability and a construal of cognitive artefacts as providers of representations. As a consequence, cognitive science and interaction design strategies will at times be at odds: The former aims at generalisability beyond the exigencies of specific situations, while the latter wants to explore the particularities of said situations, moulding constructed artefacts into the interactional niches reproduced within users' life-worlds.

2.2 Complication

A further conceptual differentiation provides a positive account of the objects of cognitive and computer sciences. Science and technology studies scholar Bruno Latour proposes distinguishing between *complexity and complication*: Complicated phenomena can be analysed in the form of a countable set of variables, while complex phenomena either consist of non-countable sets of variables or resist description through variables altogether [35, 36].

Distinguishing complexity and complication in this fashion, allows for a characterisation of computing/cognitive level processes as well as social complexity, employing a theoretical vocabulary already received within the field of HCI [8, 14, 19, 20].

3 Boundary Objects

When operating across paradigms, discourse within a development team inevitably exhibits a high degree of diversity. Respective stakeholders frame their results within the languages of complexity or complication, construing relevant phenomena in a way specific to their perspectives. In the case of cognitive and computing artefacts, resulting systems can be highly formalised, while sociological analyses of complex phenomena entail a high amount of theoretical prerequisites. We discuss *boundary objects* as a conceptual aid for facilitating productive discussion among these diverse communities of practice.

Social scientist Susan Leigh Star and philosopher James R. Griesemer introduce the notion of *boundary objects* in their seminal study on institutional ecology [49]. They identify the boundary object as a conceptual phenomenon occurring within cooperative work contexts. Boundary objects present at least two instances of themselves, a well specified one, and a family of versions open to interpretation. Participants within a collaborative setting are able to alternate between both instances, There is a resulting discursive back-and-forth movement between well-specified and appropriated versions of the boundary object. As a result, disciplinary communities dependent on more formalised versions of the boundary object find requisite exactness within the object, while neighbouring communities can adapt and reconstruct it according to their respective disciplinary language games. The resulting communicative dynamic allows for cooperation to unfold in the *absence of consensus* [3].

The problematic can be exemplified with respect to the concept of *narration*. In "Storytelling as a Means to Transfer Knowledge via Narration" [53] Wuttke et. al. describe design elements of a cognitive agent capable of narration. The developed conception is quite different from conceptions formulated within the field of humanities [43], yet it provides a boundary object facilitating coordination. Consequently, it can be brought into productive yet conflictual discourse regarding the relationship of narration and interactive artefacts [27].

4   Methodological Framework

In response to the challenges posed by developing at the intersection of complexity and complication, we propose an iterative development methodology. It is based on the observation that fundamental differences concerning disciplinary methodological commitments usually cannot be overcome, but can be rendered productive by establishing an ongoing process of conflictual negotiation [25].

4.1   Development Context

Methodological building blocks outlined were developed in the course of interdisciplinary development projects, tasked with development of intelligent agents [52,54] and interactive installations for cultural education [24,26,27,41]. They aim at facilitating prototyping activities through provision of shared vocabularies [7] as well as providing incentives on the level of design methods [6]. Discursive devices developed are grounded within a conceptual analysis of disciplinary differences regarding the notions of *interaction* [9] and *materiality* [28].

During cooperation with qualitative social research huge obstacles had to be overcome on the levels of language and concept building [25]. On a superficial level, cooperation between media psychology and computer-science is faced with much lower obstacles. Both disciplines share a common paradigm, being centered on information processing, rooted within the traditions of science. Consequently, none of the misunderstandings between incommensurable language games occur.

However, comparing cooperation with cognitive science also foregrounds some of the similarities between computer-science and qualitative social research which were not apparent before. Cooperating social researchers were using grounded-theory methodology, thereby employing an iterative methodology. Consequently, it was possible to align iterative development methodologies within computer-science [12,13,34,48?] to those of social research.

4.2   Iterative Development Style

In order to facilitate artefact centric modes of cooperation and minimise the detrimental impact of misunderstandings, an iterative development style is adopted:

With respect to the interdisciplinary nature of developments it is important to adopt a shared practice of conducting iterations. While iterative modes of development are common within computer-science and HCI, they are less common within the domains of cognitive science and media psychology. Since extensive lab studies require a large amount of planning, supervision, and evaluation, proceeding within a large number of small iterations is not always an option.

Consequently, it is important to interleave the more waterfall-like structured aspects with practices of continuous iterative technology development. This entails acknowledging a difference in the mode of knowledge construction: while practice-based knowledge is constructed within an ongoing process of interpretation, Interaction-paradigm lab-study data arrives in larger chunks.

Irrespective of this acknowledgement, cognitive scientists play an integral continuous role throughout the practice-based design process. Their input is needed in order to continuously renegotiate the status of previously formulated theories. Since lab-based knowledge has to be situated within extensive processes of contextualisation and renegotiation [31], respective processes of situation proceed iteratively, even if hypothesis testing according to psychological protocol does not.

4.3   Switching Perspectives – Dialogue in Practice

Participants are encouraged to translate theoretical and empirical results into design. Computer-scientists are encouraged to design experiments and studies, psychologists are encouraged to specify technological prototypes.

4.4   Continuous Renegotiation

Drawing on Wakkary's approach concerning complexity [51], we adopt a methodological pattern, inspired by what he likens to 'dead reckoning': Instead of seeking agreement concerning a fixed stipulated endpoint in the form of a system or arte-fact, we agree on a general direction within the project. Development proceeds in this agreed direction, while future iterations perform 'course corrections' in reference to the outcome of the antecedent iteration.

This approach is necessary when targetting complex everyday situations: As Wakkary argues [51], the specifics of relevant problem descriptions themselves cannot be known in advance.

Accordingly, the status of produced artefacts and respective epistemological claims within the project remain the subject of continuous discussion and rene-gotiation. Not only do methods employed and designs constructed to reach a certain goal change during the course of a development project, the goals itself are subject to evolution and renegotiation.

When employing an iterative process such as this, it becomes especially important to impose limits on goal flexibility in order for the process not to devolve into a random free-for-all but instead retain structure and momentum. On the other hand, the need of fixing goals in advance does not do justice to the complex renegotiations necessary when adressing the problematic of every-day complexity: The dynamic of emerging design situations cannot be known in advance, relevant relationships are only discovered iteratively.

4.5   Theoretical Framing

Theoretical framings possess a special status within the methodology: No com-mon framing is aimed for, since the conflicting nature of respective disciplinary epistemological commitments and discourse practices have to be acknowledged. Instead, the methodology calls for individual readings of a shared theory, in order to provide a shared vocabulary for processes of conflict, negotiation, and development. All sides are familiar with a specific theory, though they need not subscribe to its claims within their own practice.

4.6   Process vs. Outcome

Even if the utility of lab-based studies is severely limited concerning the realm of everyday complexity, insights can still be wrested from participating in respective processes of complication. In order to create controlled environments conducible to hypothesis testing, psychologists have to perform requisite *complications*. They construct environments in which a large number of repeatable, homogeneous inter-actions can be observed.

Artefacts should be able to afford a wide range of diverse activities, not constricting users to repetitive or inflexible procedures. At the same time, dig-ital artefacts exhibit a specific coded mechanics, limiting their flexibility. They always act as complicating material frames. Accordingly, knowing the feasible and infeasible pathways for complication is necessary in order to successfully design digital artefacts for complex situations.

In this sense, observing the failures of cognitve-science complications tells constructive computer scientists as much as learning from knowledge derived from successful experiments and studies.

The insight just formulated has to be read against the backdrop of its practical conditions: it is valid only in relationship to everyday complexity. Within research focussing on inherently complicated processes, such as issues relating to perception and physiology, the *results* of quantitative research again become more central.

5   Discussion and Conclusion

We have provided an analysis of the status of cognitive artefacts within everyday contexts. There are considerable challenges when employing cognitive technology within everyday contexts, especially in non-work, non-task oriented ways. The dynamicity of everyday contexts necessitates novel ways of interrelating cognitive science, computer-science and design practices.

The field of cognitive theory itself provides interesting impulses to this effect in the form of ecological psychology and situated cognition approaches. The unfolding discussion need not devolve into a culture clash between disciplines, opposing scientific cognitive psychology and hermeneutic/constructive interaction design techniques. Psychological theory itself provides theoretical frameworks that go well beyond the simplistic focus on task times and error rates that Carroll and Kellog warned us from in the 1980s [11, p. 13].

We have tried to establish a discursive framework, able to bridge the disciplinary gap between cognitive science and practice-based researchers. Drawing on the concept of *complexity* we have outlined a methodology facilitating interdisciplinary development of cognitive artefacts for everyday contexts. In doing so, we have been consciously operating outside the epistemological safety margins afforded by respective theories.

Acknowledgements. This material is based partially upon work funded by the European Union with the European Social Fund (ESF) and by the state of Saxony.

References

1. Ambite, J.L., Chaudhri, V.K., Fikes, R., Jenkins, J., Mishra, S., Muslea, M., Uribe, T., Yang, G.: Design and implementation of the CALO query manager. In: Proceedings of the 18th Conference on Innovative Applications of Artificial Intelligence, IAAI 2006, vol. 2, pp. 1751–1758. AAAI Press, Boston (2006). http://dl.acm.org/citation.cfm?id=1597122.1597133
2. Bannon, L.: From human factors to human actors: The role of psychology and human-computer interaction studies in system design. Design at work: Cooperative design of computer systems, pp. 25–44 (1991). https://www.researchgate.net/profile/Liam_Bannon/publication/242569963_From_human_factors_to_human_actors_the_role_of_psychology_and_human-computer_interaction_studies_in_system_design/links/550616400cf24cee3a0509da.pdf

3. Bechky, B.A.: Sharing meaning across occupational communities: the transformation of understanding on a production floor. Organization Sci. **14**(3), 312–330 (2003). http://pubsonline.informs.org/doi/ref/10.1287/orsc.14.3.312.15162
4. Beck, K.: Embracing change with extreme programming. Computer **32**(10), 70–77 (1999). http://ieeexplore.ieee.org/xpls/abs_all.jsp?arnumber=796139
5. Beck, K., Beedle, M., Van Bennekum, A., Cockburn, A., Cunningham, W., Fowler, M., Grenning, J., Highsmith, J., Hunt, A., Jeffries, R., et al.: Manifesto for Agile Software Development (2001). http://academic.brooklyn.cuny.edu/cis/sfleisher/Chapter_03_sim.pdf
6. Berger, A., Heidt, M.: Exploring prototypes in interaction design – qualitative analysis and playful design method. In: Proceedings of the International Associationof Societies of Design Research Conference 2015 – Interplay, Brisbane, Australia (2015). http://iasdr2015.com/wp-content/uploads/2015/11/IASDR_Proceedings_Final_Reduced.pdf
7. Berger, A., Heidt, M., Eibl, M.: Towards a vocabulary of prototypes in interaction design – a criticism of current practice. In: Marcus, A. (ed.) DUXU 2014, Part I. LNCS, vol. 8517, pp. 25–32. Springer, Heidelberg (2014). http://link.springer.com/chapter/10.1007/978-3-319-07668-3_3
8. Berger, A., Heidt, M., Eibl, M.: Conduplicated symmetries: renegotiating the material basis of prototype research. In: Chakrabarti, A. (ed.) ICoRD 15 Research into Design Across Boundaries. Smart Innovation, Systems and Technologies, vol. 1, pp. 71–78. No. 34. Springer India. http://link.springer.com/chapter/10.1007/978-81-322-2232-3_7
9. Bischof, A., Obländer, V., Heidt, M., Kanellopoulos, K., Küszter, V., Liebold, B., Martin, K.U., Pietschmann, D., Storz, M., Tallig, A., Teichmann, M., Wuttke, M.: Interdisziplinäre Impulse für den Begriff "Interaktion". In: Hobohm, H.C. (ed.) Informationswissenschaft zwischen virtueller Infrastruktur und materiellen Lebenswelten. Tagungsband des 13. Internationalen Symposiums für Informationswissenschaft (ISI 2013), pp. 448–453. Hülsbusch, Glückstadt (2013)
10. Bødker, S.: When second wave HCI meets third wave challenges. In: Proceedings of the 4th Nordic Conference on Human-Computer Interaction: Changing Roles, pp. 1–8. NordiCHI 2006, NY, USA (2006). http://doi.acm.org/10.1145/1182475.1182476
11. Carroll, J.M., Kellogg, W.A.: Artifact as theory-nexus: hermeneutics meets theory-based design. In: Proceedings of the SIGCHI Conference on Human Factors in Computing Systems, CHI 1989, pp. 7–14, NY, USA (1989). http://doi.acm.org/10.1145/67449.67452
12. Cockburn, A.: Crystal Clear: A Human-Powered Methodology for Small Teams. Pearson Education (2004)
13. Cockburn, A.: Agile software development: the cooperative game. Pearson Education (2006). https://books.google.com/books?hl=de&lr=&id=i39yimbrzh4C&oi=fnd&pg=PT15&dq=agile+software&ots=Y6W_d2U-bY&sig=bjxtqfNxqcdwp-ATqXPghxteL58
14. Cordella, A., Shaikh, M.: Actor-network theory and after: what's new for IS research. Naples, Italy, June 2003. http://home.aisnet.org/associations/7499/files/Index_Markup.cfm
15. Crabtree, A., Rodden, T., Tolmie, P., Button, G.: Ethnography considered harmful. In: Proceedings of the SIGCHI Conference on Human Factors in Computing Systems, CHI 2009, pp. 879–888, NY, USA (2009). http://doi.acm.org/10.1145/1518701.1518835

16. Crabtree, A., Benford, S., Greenhalgh, C., Tennent, P., Chalmers, M., Brown, B.: Supporting ethnographic studies of ubiquitous computing in the wild. In: Proceedings of the 6th Conference on Designing Interactive Systems, DIS 2006, pp. 60–69, NY, USA (2006). http://doi.acm.org/10.1145/1142405.1142417

17. Dourish, P.: What we talk about when we talk about context. Pers. Ubiquitous Comput. **8**(1), 19–30 (2004). http://link.springer.com/article/10.1007/s00779-003-0253-8

18. Dourish, P.: Where the Action is: The Foundations of Embodied Interaction. MIT Press, Cambridge (2004)

19. Fuchsberger, V.: Generational divides in terms of actor-network theory: Potential crises and the potential of crises. In: Online Proceedings of the 7th Media in Transition Conference. MIT, Cambridge (2011). http://web.mit.edu/comm-forum/mit7/papers/Fuchsberger_MiT7.pdf

20. Fuchsberger, V., Murer, M., Tscheligi, M.: Human-computer non-interaction: the activity of non-use. In: Proceedings of the 2014 Companion Publication on Designing Interactive Systems, DIS Companion 2014, NY, USA, pp. 57–60 (2014). http://doi.acm.org/10.1145/2598784.2602781

21. Harrison, S., Sengers, P., Tatar, D.: Making epistemological trouble: Third-paradigm HCI as successor science. Interact. Comput. **23**(5), 385–392 (2011). http://iwc.oxfordjournals.org/content/23/5/385

22. Harrison, S., Tatar, D., Sengers, P.: The three paradigms of HCI. In: Alt. Chi. Session at the SIGCHI Conference on Human Factors in Computing Systems San Jose, California, USA, pp. 1–18 (2007). http://people.cs.vt.edu/~srh/Downloads/HCIJournalTheThreeParadigmsofHCI.pdf

23. Hartmanis, J., Stearns, R.E.: On the computational complexity of algorithms. Trans. Am. Math. Soc. **117**, 285–306 (1965). http://www.jstor.org/stable/1994208

24. Heidt, M.: Examining interdisciplinary prototyping in the context of cultural communication. In: Marcus, A. (ed.) DUXU 2013, Part II. LNCS, vol. 8013, pp. 54–61. Springer, Heidelberg (2013). http://link.springer.com/chapter/10.1007/978-3-642-39241-2_7

25. Heidt, M., Kanellopoulos, K., Pfeiffer, L., Rosenthal, P.: Diverse ecologies – interdisciplinary development for cultural education. In: Kotzé, P., Marsden, G., Lindgaard, G., Wesson, J., Winckler, M. (eds.) INTERACT 2013, Part IV. LNCS, vol. 8120, pp. 539–546. Springer, Heidelberg (2013). http://link.springer.com/chapter/10.1007/978-3-642-40498-6_43

26. Heidt, M., Moulder, V.: The aesthetics of activism. In: Proceedings of the 2015 ACM SIGCHI Conference on Creativity and Cognition, C&C 2015, NY, USA, pp. 155–156 (2015). http://dl.acm.org/citation.cfm?doid=2757226.2764550

27. Heidt, M., Pfeiffer, L., Berger, A., Rosenthal, P.: PRMD. In: Mensch & Computer 2014 - Workshopband, pp. 45–48. De Gruyter Oldenbourg (2014). http://dl.mensch-und-computer.de/handle/123456789/3908

28. Heidt, M., Pfeiffer, L., Bischof, A., Rosenthal, P.: Tangible disparity - different notions of the material as catalyst of interdisciplinary communication. In: Kurosu, M. (ed.) HCI 2014, Part I. LNCS, vol. 8510, pp. 199–206. Springer, Heidelberg (2014). http://link.springer.com/chapter/10.1007/978-3-319-07233-3_19

29. Henderson, A.: A development perspective on interface, design, and theory. In: Designing Interaction, pp. 254–268. Cambridge University Press, New York (1991). http://dl.acm.org/citation.cfm?id=120365

30. Hinrichs, U., Carpendale, S.: Gestures in the wild: studying multi-touch gesture sequences on interactive tabletop exhibits. In: Proceedings of the SIGCHI Conference on Human Factors in Computing Systems, CHI 2011, NY, USA, pp. 3023–3032 (2011). http://doi.acm.org/10.1145/1978942.1979391
31. Hornecker, E., Nicol, E.: What do lab-based user studies tell us about in-the-wild behavior? Insights from a study of museum interactives. In: Proceedings of the Designing Interactive Systems Conference, DIS 2012, NY, USA, pp. 358–367 (2012). http://doi.acm.org/10.1145/2317956.2318010
32. Kuhn, T.S.: The Structure of Scientific Revolutions. University of Chicago Press, Chicago (1962)
33. Kuutti, K., Bannon, L.J.: The turn to practice in HCI: towards a research agenda. In: Proceedings of the SIGCHI Conference on Human Factors in Computing Systems, CHI 2014, NY, USA, pp. 3543–3552 (2014). http://doi.acm.org/10.1145/2556288.2557111
34. Larman, C., Basili, V.R.: Iterative and incremental development: A brief history. Computer **36**(6), 47–56 (2003). http://www.computer.org/csdl/mags/co/2003/06/r6047.pdf
35. Latour, B.: On interobjectivity. Mind Cult. Act. **3**(4), 228–245 (1996). http://www.tandfonline.com/doi/pdf/10.1207/s15327884mca0304_2
36. Latour, B., Hermant, E.: Paris: invisible city (1998). http://web.mit.edu/uricchio/Public/television/documentary/Latour_ParisInvisibleCity.pdf
37. Law, J.: After ANT: complexity, naming and topology. In: Actor Network Theory and After, pp. 1–14. Oxford, Blackwall (1999)
38. Luhmann, N.: Social systems. Stanford University Press (1995). https://books.google.com/books?hl=de&lr=&id=zVZQW4gxXk4C&oi=fnd&pg=PR9&ots=7EHPl53KRO&sig=dwG3oQJSwtBtIukhPqVJqSiaSNc
39. Löwgren, J., Stolterman, E.: Thoughtful Interaction Design a Design Perspective on Information Technology. MIT Press, Cambridge (2004). http://site.ebrary.com/id/10405262
40. Marshall, P., Morris, R., Rogers, Y., Kreitmayer, S., Davies, M.: Rethinking 'Multi-user': an in-the-wild study of how groups approach a walk-up-and-use tabletop interface. In: Proceedings of the SIGCHI Conference on Human Factors in Computing Systems, CHI 2011, NY, USA, pp. 3033–3042 (2011). http://doi.acm.org/10.1145/1978942.1979392
41. Moulder, V., Heidt, M., Boschman, L.: Transcoding the aesthetics of activism. In: Proceedings of the 21st International Symposium on Electronic Art ISEA 2015 - Disruption, Vancouver, BC, Canada (2015). http://isea2015.org/proceeding/submissions/ISEA2015_submission_259.pdf
42. Nardi, B.A.: Context and consciousness: activity theory and human-computer interaction. MIT Press (1996). https://books.google.de/books?hl=en&lr=&id=JeqcgPlS2UAC&oi=fnd&pg=PR7&dq=Nardi,+B.+A.+(1996)+Context+and+consciousness:+activity+theory+and+human-computer+interaction&ots=e_ecZ-xCYCy&sig=vXj9utOXu4IUw5C4VHOeKqtO-Ds
43. Ricœur, P.: Time and Narrative. University of Chicago Press, Chicago (1984)
44. Rogers, Y.: Interaction design gone wild: striving for wild theory. Interactions **18**(4), 58–62 (2011).http://doi.acm.org/10.1145/1978822.1978834
45. Rogers, Y.: HCI theory: classical, modern, and contemporary. Synth. Lect. Hum. Centered Inf. **5**(2), 1–129 (2012).http://www.morganclaypool.com/doi/abs/10.2200/S00418ED1V01Y201205HCI014

46. Rogers, Y., Connelly, K.H., Tedesco, L., Hazlewood, W., Kurtz, A., Hall, R.E., Hursey, J., Toscos, T.: Why it's worth the hassle: the value of in-situ studies when designing ubicomp. In: Krumm, J., Abowd, G.D., Seneviratne, A., Strang, T. (eds.) UbiComp 2007. LNCS, vol. 4717, pp. 336–353. Springer, Heidelberg (2007). doi:10. 1007/978-3-540-74853-3_20. http://link.springer.com/chapter/10.1007/978-3-540-74853-3_20

47. Sarker, S., Lau, F., Sahay, S.: Using an adapted grounded theory approach for inductive theory building about virtual team development. SIGMIS Database **32**(1), 38–56 (2000). http://doi.acm.org/10.1145/506740.506745

48. Schwaber, K.: SCRUM development process. In: Sutherland, D.J., Casanave, C., Miller, J., Patel, D.P., Hollowell, G. (eds.) Business Object Design and Implementation, pp. 117–134. Springer, London (1997). doi:10.1007/978-1-4471-0947-1_1

49. Star, S.L., Griesemer, J.R.: Institutional ecology, 'translations' and boundary objects: amateurs and professionals in Berkeley's museum of vertebrate zoology, 1907–39. Soc. Stud. Sci. **19**(3), 387–420 (1989). http://sss.sagepub.com/content/19/3/387

50. Turing, A.M.: On Computable numbers, with an application to the entscheidungsproblem. Proc. Lond. Math. Soc. **s2–42**(1), 230–265 (1937). http://plms.oxfordjournals.org/cgi/doi/10.1112/plms/s2-42.1.230

51. Wakkary, R.: Framing complexity, design and experience: a reflective analysis. Digital Creativity **16**(2), 65–78 (2005). http://www.tandfonline.com/doi/abs/10.1080/14626260500173013

52. Wuttke, M.: Pro-active pedagogical agents. In: International Summerworkshop Computer Science 2013, vol. 17, p. 59 (2013). http://www.qucosa.de/fileadmin/data/qucosa/documents/11854/CSR-2013-04.pdf#page=61

53. Wuttke, M., Belentschikow, V., Müller, N.H.: Storytelling as a means to transfer knowledge via narration. i-com **14**(2), 155–160 (2015). http://www.degruyter.com/view/j/icom.2015.14.issue-2/icom-2015-0034/icom-2015-0034.xml

54. Wuttke, M., Heidt, M.: Beyond presentation - employing proactive intelligent agents as social catalysts. In: Kurosu, M. (ed.) HCI 2014, Part II. LNCS, vol. 8511, pp. 182–190. Springer, Heidelberg (2014)

55. Yamazaki, K., Yamazaki, A., Okada, M., Kuno, Y., Kobayashi, Y., Hoshi, Y., Pitsch, K., Luff, P., vom Lehn, D., Heath, C.: Revealing gauguin: engaging visitors in robot guide's explanation in an art museum. In: Proceedings of the SIGCHI Conference on Human Factors in Computing Systems, CHI 2009, NY, USA, pp. 1437–1446 (2009). http://doi.acm.org/10.1145/1518701.1518919

The Research on Elderly-Adaptive Interface Design Based on Choice-Oriented Attention Theory

Bin Jiang[✉] and Dan Deng

School of Design Arts and Media, Nanjing University of Science
and Technology, 200, Xiaolingwei Street, Nanjing 210094, Jiangsu, China
jb508@163.com, 772875982@qq.com

Abstract. Visual selective attention is a way of cognition processing which makes the limited mental resources focus on the most significant information during a specific period of time. The visual selection is introduced to the interface design research for the elderly in order to analyze the elderly's mental cognitive process and establish the relationship between the two from the perspective of selective attention. Two experimental methods are used: No.One, to compare and research the elderly group and the young one's visual preference through the extraction of interface's visual elements. No. Two, eye tracking experiment. Calculate the elderly group and young group's average fixation time and average fixation points, then validate the calculation data. Through coding the visual elements which are obtained from the two experiments, the visual element code sets are determined, which conforms to the elderly's visual selective attention on the interface, so as to guide the interface design practice for the elderly.

Keywords: Selective attention · Suitable for the elderly · Visual code set · Interface interaction

1 Introduction

As we known, China is the only country which has an aging population of more than 100 million. The elderly over the age of 60 usually regard the newspapers as the medium of "first contact". But the new medias like the internet have more and more information because of the arrival of information age. It is a huge challenge for them to transcend the traditional media and use the new media. The interaction interface of the new medias which are mainly made up of rich information has become complicated.

It is more difficult for older users to search for and find the information they need than young users. The old people will have some heavy psychological burden if the design form of the information can't attract their enough attention. And they can't use the new medias better.

It will become a very important part to introduce the visual selective attention to the interface interaction design for the elderly. On one hand, human's visual system is the most developed sensory systems and is also an important channel for the communication between human and electronic interface. On the other hand, the physical and

© Springer International Publishing Switzerland 2016
A. Marcus (Ed.): DUXU 2016, Part I, LNCS 9746, pp. 293–303, 2016.
DOI: 10.1007/978-3-319-40409-7_28

cognitive abilities of the elderly began to show different degrees of recession. They have the stronger requirement for the design for the elderly. Therefore the emphasis of our study is to explore how to use the new design standards to promote the elderly to interact with the interface of the new medias.

1.1 The Interface Interaction's Visual Elements

Humans have unusual prominent data screening ability. people always can quickly detect the important information which is closely related with them and respond in time. This selective and initiative psychological activity is known as attention mechanism. In humans' visual information processing, they always select a few significant objects to prioritize quickly, and ignore or abandon other non-significant objects, in order to improve greatly the work efficiency of information processing. The process is called visual attention.

The significant objects in the image information is called visual Focus (the Focus of Attention, short for FOA) [1]. Visual focus is likely to be a certain range humans are interested in, or a characteristic value of the interest. (As shown in Fig. 1), the stage model of Treisman's visual attention. At first, some basic properties of the visual scene (color, direction, size, and distance) are encoded in separate and parallel pathways, and generated into the characteristics map, then these maps are integrated into the images. After that, the focus of attention (FOA) extracts information from the images in order to get the detailed analysis about the related characteristics of the selected area in the graphics.

Psychology research found that those image areas which can produce the extraneous and stronger stimulus, and the stimulation that people expect are easy to attract the attention of the observers. Accordingly, the attention can be divided into two types: one is based on the primary visual sense, which is the attention from the bottom up driven by data, namely passive attention; Another is based on high-level vision, which is the top-down attention related to mission and knowledge and so on. It is called active attention.

To explore the factors of the visual selection in the elderly, this article extracts the layout, colors, shapes, materials of the interface interaction to do experiments..First of all, the means of the interface layout affect directly the convenience which the customers use interface information, reasonable interactive layout will help the users quickly find

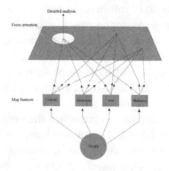

Fig. 1. The stage models of the visual attention

the core content and services. Second, in the interactive interface, colors are the first ones which users can feel, they can leave impression in your mind through the retina, and affect our mental activities and experience in the subconscious, the demand for color becomes the person's potential mental set. So colors of the interface suggest the users the direction and meaning that interface represents. Third, the main way the users recognize objects is through the silhouette of the objects, icon shape or framework used in the interface. They affect the property and definition defined by the users. Fourth, the materials themselves have the unique language, ideas and feelings. Different materials and textures can bring people different impressions and aesthetic feelings. In the interactive interface design, .the use of the materials should be fully considered. Therefore, the above four interactive interface visual elements should be extracted in preparation for the experiments.

1.2   Psychological Effect and Factor Extraction

Psychological cognition includes the perception process how to accept and understand the information from the environment through visual, auditory sense and so on, and the processes of memory, thinking, logic reasoning etc., through the humans' brains. According to five stage models about psychological cognition proposed by Edward·K·-strong in 1925, respectively, the first step: to attract and maintain the attention, the second step: to show an interest in, the third step: to strengthen the understanding, the fourth step: to strengthen the memory, the fifth step: the willingness of action. Therefore, the effect of visual elements to psychological effect should be studied from the five aspects.

1.3   Establish the Relations Between Visual Information
and Psychological Cognition

The important visual evaluation factors in the four interfaces like the layout, colors, shapes, materials can be got through the research of the interactive interface visual

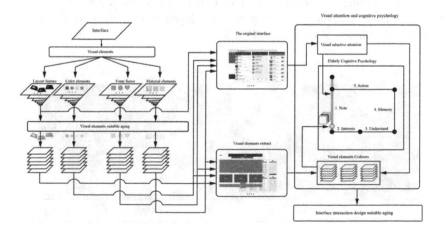

Fig. 2. The interface interaction evaluation models for the elderly

elements. and characteristics of these elements are obtained by the users through visual selective attention mechanism, and the psychological cognition is formed [2]. The interface interaction evaluation models (As shown in Fig. 2 for the elderly used in this article's study are set up, combining Treisman's stage models of visual attention and five stage models of psychological cognition proposed by Edward·K· strong.

2 Methods

Study was conducted on the basis of the data collection. 40 people are invited to participate two ways of experiments. They include subjective visual preference and objective tests, namely perceptual evaluation of visual elements and the analysis of eye tracking experiment.

They give some quantity analysis about the old people's attention, interest, understanding, memory and action, through the extraction testing experiment about the layout, colors, shapes, materials of the interactive interface, then compare with young people in all kinds of data, in order to extract visual selective attention preference elements of the elderly and the codes of the various visual elements. They will sum up the principles which can be regarded as a reference for the interface interaction design for the elderly.

VET. (visual elements test). VET is tested through a series of interactive interface visual elements, as shown in Fig. 3, the adaptability of the physiological function in the elderly are decaying, such as difficulty in vision, slow response, inattention, confusion, forgetfulness, getting tired easily etc. Therefore the number of tests should be minimized, in order to maximize the test stimulus and enable participants to recognize and understand easily, and make a choice in 15 min [3]. In this study, four kinds of visual elements are selected to collect the elderly and young people's subjective visual preference data. As shown in Fig. 3.

ET. (eye tracking experiment), Tobii Glasses eye movement device is used in this study in order to collect the elderly group and young group's eye movement data with it. Stimulation Settings is consistent with VET, but only combination images of visual elements are displayed. Each test category is displayed on the screen for 5 s to collect eye moving data index. As shown in Fig. 4.

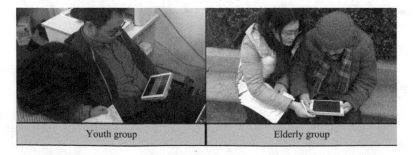

Fig. 3. Comparison test about group visual elements

Fig. 4. Comparison experiment of group eye tracking

3   Primary Studies

In order to explore the visual elements of the interface interaction for the elderly, in the process of study, the subjects were divided into the elderly group and young group. The two groups are used to do the comparison experiments. The elderly group is made up of 20 people (10 men and 10 women, 60-80 years old), the total of the young group is 20 people (10 men and 10 women, between 18 to 25 years old).

The test methods of visual elements can be divided into two, one is the test method of combination images, The research objects give the marks according to the scales of their love on each test project, "very good" is "5 " points, and "good" is "4", "general" is "3", "not good" is "2", and "very not good-looking" is "1". In the process, the test objects can put forward some perceptual words to describe the reasons they make a choice [4].

The other is the test method of a single image. When a single visual element is decomposed to test, the pictures which are used to test a single visual element will be made into slides, a tester ask the subjects, the other tester is responsible for recording the answers. The time is set within 5 s while they are played. the main questions involved in the test are: 1 what is the characteristic of the layout shown in the picture? 2 what color is shown in the picture? 3 what is the graphic shown in the pictures? 4 What material is shown in the picture? the top three of the single visual elements chosen are used to make answers from five dimensions, 1. attracting the visual attention, 2. showing interest, 3. easy to understand, 4. leaving deep Impression, 5. having the willingness to take action. Also the five-level Likert Scale is used to give scores, "strongly agree" is "5" points, "agree" is "4", "general" is "3", "do not agree with" is "2", and "strongly disagree" is "1" [5].

3.1   The Composition of the Test Set

The Method of the Automatic Generation of the Test Set. Because older people tend to some problems such as inattention and being tired easily, so the quantity and time of their test must be controlled. therefore we need to typify the test set. The so-called typical processing means to classify test sets which had the numerous test objects before, and extract the most representative of the test object in each type to form the new test set in order to simplify the test sets and not to lose their characteristics. Traditional typical operations for the test sets about layout, color, texture and shape are depended on experts. It means that we should invite a number of experts in related fields to classify and extract the test objects in the appropriate test sets. The operation method is involved in much subjective human trace, and tends to have a lot of uncertainty and replication. Therefore, this article adopts intelligent algorithm to give the automatic typical processing to the test sets. The advantages which the man-made operation practice is completely abandoned is not only to save a lot of manpower and time, but also to make each typical operating of the test set more objective and repeatable.

X - means algorithm [6] is the improved version of K-means [7], the famous clustering algorithm. K − means is one of the most widely used clustering algorithm. Its idea is to initialize K clusters heart randomly, to assign each sample which will be classified later to every cluster according to the most proximate principles, then redistribute repeatedly the classified samples by repeating calculation automatically and moving the heart of each cluster in order to get the largest similarity among the objects which are divided into the same cluster, and the minimal similarity among different clusters. X - means is regarded as the enhanced version of the K - means algorithm. Its biggest advantage is that it doesn't need to be specified by human the partition type or number K, and can automatically work out the clustering number which is the most suitable for the whole test sample set. That is to say, it can achieve full automation.

X - means algorithm process can be described like this :

1. Initialization: $K = K1$.
2. Random initialization cluster centers c_i', and generate K cluster C_i according to the K - means algorithm $1 \le i \le K$.
3. Do the following operations for each cluster Ci:
   ① calculate C_i about its Bayesian Information Criterion (BIC) [3]:

$$BIC(k{=}1)= -\frac{n_i \cdot d}{2}\log(2\pi)-\frac{n_i}{2}\log \sigma_i-\frac{n_i-1}{2}-\frac{1}{2}\log n_i \qquad (1)$$

n_i is the size of the cluster C_i, variables σ_i is calculated with the following formula:

$$\sigma_i=\frac{1}{n_i-1}\sum_{t=1}^{n_i}||x_t-c_i'||^2 \qquad (2)$$

   ② Cluster Ci is divided into two subclasses Cij (j = 1,2) according to 2 - means algorithm, and calculate the new BIC :

$$BIC(k{=}2)=\sum_{j=1}^{2}[n_j\log n_j-n_j\log n_i-\frac{n_j \cdot d}{2}\log(2\pi)-\frac{n_j}{2}\log \sigma_j-\frac{n_j-2}{2}]-\log n_i \qquad (3)$$

   ③ If BIC(k = 1) > BIC(k = 2), the cluster Ci remains unchanged; Otherwise, Ci will be divided into two subclasses.
4. record BIC got in Step 3.

5. If there is no cluster needed to be divided into in Step 3, we will output the current clustering model; Or judge whether K is greater than K2, namely when K > K2, the output will have the largest cluster model; When K < K2, K = K + 1, and jump to Step 2.

Among them, (K1, K2) is the possible scope of the cluster number. In the test set which is calculated by X-means clustering algorithm, the center of each cluster in every class is the typical sample of each class.

3.2   The Encoding of the Test Set

When using the X - means algorithm to do the typification processing automatically for the test set, the input data can't be the original shape sample, or the color sample. We must do the coding operation firstly on the shape, color, material texture, layout accordingly. Each kind of shape (color, texture, layout) corresponds to a kind of coding. The coding is used as the input of X – means to do the clustering operation.

Shape Coding and Clustering Results. This article selects 1000 shapes which are commonly used in the current page design. After coding the 1000 shape, we input X - means algorithm for automatic clustering. Through the iteration, the algorithm will divide the 1000 shapes into 14 classes. Each type is shown in Fig. 5 respectively.

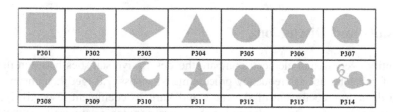

| P301 | P302 | P303 | P304 | P305 | P306 | P307 |
| P308 | P309 | P310 | P311 | P312 | P313 | P314 |

Fig. 5. Typical shapes worked out with X - means algorithm

Color Coding and Clustering Results. The method of color coding is simple. This article uses RGB, the color classification model. It inputs X - means algorithm with the (R, G, B) values of each color as the input values to do automatic clustering. After the iterations, we will get 12 types. They are shown respectively in Fig. 6. The 12 colors will be the last ones to be used in the visual elements test.

Material Texture Coding and Clustering Results. With material texture encoding, we select 100 material texture used commonly to do the clustering. As a result, 8 kinds of typical texture are worked out. As shown in Fig. 7.

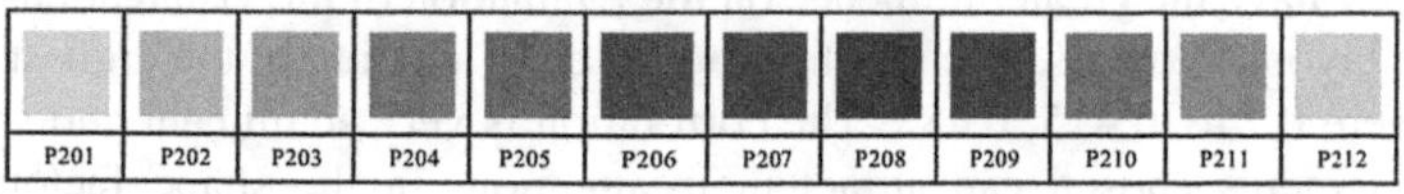

| P201 | P202 | P203 | P204 | P205 | P206 | P207 | P208 | P209 | P210 | P211 | P212 |

Fig. 6. Typical colors worked out with X - means algorithm

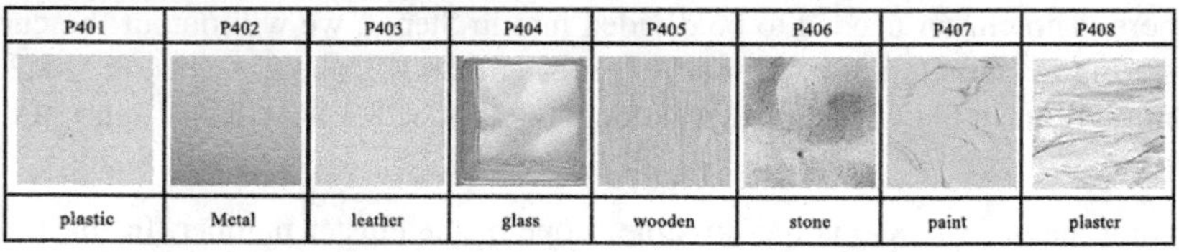

P401	P402	P403	P404	P405	P406	P407	P408
plastic	Metal	leather	glass	wooden	stone	paint	plaster

Fig. 7. Eight typical material texture worked out with X - means algorithm

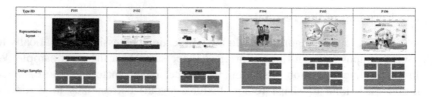

Fig. 8. Six typical layouts worked out with X - means algorithm

Because the code of the page layout is relatively complex, this article takes the related technologies about the eye movement identification to code. We select 69 interactive interface layouts used commonly, and work out 6 types of layouts with X - means algorithm at last. As shown in Fig. 8. Their own typical layouts are also in them.

4   Results and Discussions

We quantify every visual element, compare the descriptive statistics between the two groups of subjects, use as frequency processing with spss17.0, get their mean value, standard deviation, coefficient of skewness and kurtosis coefficient respectively, then analyze them. We will further determine the corresponding relationship between the elderly group's visual preference elements and psychological effect, and have some correlation analysis on the visual element evaluation and psychological effect to get the Pearson correlation coefficient.

According to the data, there are significant differences between the elderly group's visual preference and the young group's. The maximum of the scores' standard deviation about the elderly group's visual element choice is 1.09, the minimum is 0.92. They are not too small or too large, it proves that the evaluation of the objects is relatively concentrated and shows a strong identity. and the highest average value of the visual elements in each group were 3.94, 3.90, 3.59 and 3.68. The evaluation was relatively high. It proves that the visual elements selected were typical.

From the related data about the elderly group's visual elements and psychological cognition, they have the greater influence on the evaluation of the visual attention in the group of the layout elements. The top three attention evaluation of the highest selection frequency were 0.246, 0.415, 0.483. The correlation is very significant and shows that the layout elements chosen can attract their attention. In the shape factors, all the correlation is high on the evaluation of various psychological effect, and the correlation about attracting their attention is the highest, and the maximum of correlation coefficient was 0.622. In the group of material elements, the correlation of the psychological effect evaluation on material is lower than that of other visual elements. It shows the elderly pay more attention to the layout, colors, shapes than materials significantly. And the visual elements of colors and shapes and the correlation coefficient about the evaluation of strengthening memory are higher, they are 0.472 and 0.466, respectively. It shows the correct use of colors and shapes can evoke memories of the elderly.

Most subjects can have profound memory within 5 s according to the reaction of the tester and the effect of answering the questions in the decomposition test for single visual elements. It shows that the visual elements which are extracted have obvious characteristic memory for the elderly, and can attract visual attention in a short period of time. Especially color elements, 100 % of subjects could remember red correctly in the testing time, but the memory accuracy of blue, purple and orange were 98.72 %, 95.7 % and 94.35 %. In addition, the test results found that the differences of age have influence on the layout, colors, shapes and materials. There is a certain gap between old people and the young in cognitive time. For old people, the closer shapes and contours get to the specific objects, the faster the elderly have feedback.

They use the eye movement experiment to test the above testing results of visual elements. Each group of visual elements which are extracted in the visual testing experiment are made in a experiment picture. The purpose of this experiment is to reflect that the visual elements of the interaction interface have effect on the attention effects of the elderly through the eye movement experiment data index. In every group of visual elements, the two groups of subjects, the elderly and the young are regarded as independent variables, and the eye movement experiment index which gets the attention of the subjects is regarded as the dependent variable. keep the single variable and get the information of attention points and eye tracking data, compare and analyze respectively all the visual elements in view of the data index from the elderly group and young group, in order to get the average fixation time and the average fixation point which the two groups pay attention to the visual elements. As shown in Fig. 9.

Elderly group					Youth group		
		Average Fixation (ms)	Fixation count (n)			Average Fixation (ms)	Fixation count (n)
Layout feature	P106	220	7	Layout feature	P102	231	9
	P102	215	5		P101	227	7
	P101	201	2		P105	213	5
Color Elements	P205	225	13	Color Elements	P202	198	11
	P207	217	11		P210	191	9
	P209	209	9		P211	183	5
Form factor	P312	246	9	Form factor	P312	250	5
	P311	243	7		P311	243	3
	P310	230	5		P310	231	2
Material elements	P403	235	3	Material elements	P403	232	4
	P407	210	2		P407	225	4
	P406	197	1		P406	214	2

Fig. 9. The statistics about the fixation time and the fixation point of the subjects on each visual element

5   Conclusion and Recommendations

The old people's visual selective attention preferences can be get according to the comparing data of eye movement experiment and visual elements test. (As shown in Fig. 10). The design should meet the cognitive demand of the elderly on layout, colors, shapes and materials. otherwise visual coding will be imperfect and some memory will be lost, then the learning burden and anxiety will be produced, to form a vicious cycle of low visual cognitive efficiency.

- Layout Code. The elderly like No. P106 pop-up layout, No. P102 the layout without frames, and No. P101 the layout which the big frames encase the small ones. To a certain extent, it shows the elderly have visual preference about the traditional rules and symmetrical layout. The way of information architecture should be used, which has simple feature set, easy operation and takes short time. And the information which has fewer hierarchical levels and the smooth process should be used in the design of interface, combining with the behavior characteristic of older users.
- Color Coding. Red is the old people's favourite color according to the experimental results, purple and blue are also popular. The following principles of color design should be followed in the interface design: 1 using colors for visual reminder. The colors with high degree of attention and recognition should be used more in the interface design in order to have visual reminder on key content and area, and guide the elderly do manipulation and reading with targets. 2 making full use of the emotional attributes of colors. The emotional attributes of colours can produce psychological effects, such as associating, thinking and memorizing etc. It includes the transfer of color, associating of colors, the symbols of the colors and color preferences. Interface colors should evoke memories of old people, let them have a positive happy associating and explore common beautiful things in the old people's memory.
- Shape Coding. The shape coding encodes the message, based on geometry codes. The following principles of designing the interactive interface shape for the elderly are proposed according to the shape coding features: 1 using shapes which have better emotional attributes. From the shape and visual elements testing experiment in this article, the old people show some visual preference on No. P312 heart-shape, No. P311 pentagram. For the elderly, they have a lot of life experiences. The shapes which can conform to their living habits, have common memories and come from the real life have stronger emotional attributes. Each shape has different coding meaning and has a certain emotional color. So the emotional design should be considered when choosing the shapes. 2 choose the shape with high plumpness. The old people like the shapes with full outline, but the sharp structure can be easier to cause visual sensitivity of the elderly.
- The Material Coding. The elderly show the visual preference on No. P403 wood, No. P407 paint, No. P406 sand. Most of the feelings about different materials and crafts are directly from different visual stimulations which a variety of materials give people, and the skin texture effects of the materials' appearance, (such as sparse and dense, smooth and rough, soft and hard, random and neatly, etc.) impact the user's psychology through vision. The soft materials make the elderly relaxed,

comfortable and peaceful. They can be combined with mild colours in order to create quiet and comfortable atmosphere. The design of interface materials should follow this principle.

These Suggestions help further improve the interactive interface design for the elderly to a certain extent, and provide some valuable reference.

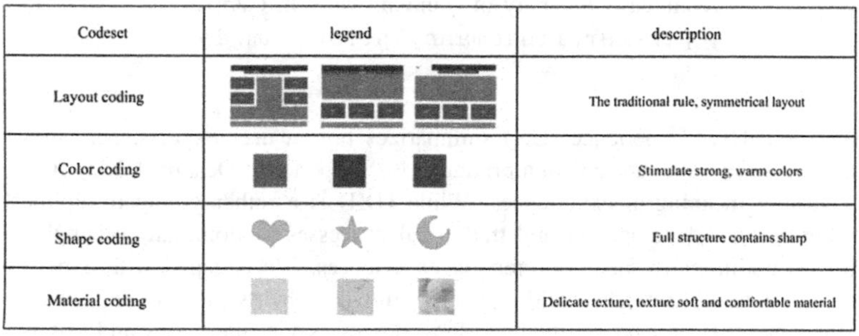

Codeset	legend	description
Layout coding		The traditional rule, symmetrical layout
Color coding		Stimulate strong, warm colors
Shape coding		Full structure contains sharp
Material coding		Delicate texture, texture soft and comfortable material

Fig. 10. Visual coding set

References

1. Luo, S.J., Fu, Y.T., Zhou, Y.X.: Perceptual matching of shape design style between wheel hub and car type. Int. J. Ind. Ergonomics **42**(1), 90–102 (2012)
2. Luo, S.J., Fu, Y.T., Korvenmaa, P.: A preliminary study of perceptual matching for the evaluation of beverage bottle design. Int. J. Ind. Ergonomics **42**(2), 219–232 (2012)
3. Leckart, B.T., Keeling, K.R., Bakan, P.: Sex differences in the duration of visual attention. Percept. Psychophysics **1**(11), 374–376 (1966)
4. Ballesteros, S., Reales, J.M., Mayas, J., et al.: Selective attention modulates visual and haptic repetition priming: effects in aging and Alzheimer's disease. Exp. Brain Res. **189**(4), 473–483 (2008)
5. Heinbuck, C.L., Hershberger, W.A.: Development of visual attention: a stereoscopic view. Percept. psychophysics **45**(5), 404–410 (1989)
6. Pelleg D, Moore A.W.: X-means: extending K-means with efficient estimation of the number of clusters. In: Proceedings of the Seventeenth International Conference on Machine Learning. pp. 727–734. Morgan Kaufmann Publishers Inc. (2000)
7. MacQueen, J.B.: Some methods for classification and analysis of multivariate observations. In: Le Cam, L.M., Neyman, J. (eds.) Proceedings of the Fifth Berkeley Symposium on Mathematical Statistics and Probability. vol. 1, pp. 281–297 University of California Press, California (1967)

Extracting Insights from Experience Designers to Enhance User Experience Design

Simon Kremer[✉] and Udo Lindemann

Institute of Product Development,
Technical University of Munich, Munich, Germany
{kremer,lindemann}@pe.me.tum.de

Abstract. User Experience (UX) summarizes how a user expects, perceives and assesses an encounter with a product. User Experience Design (UXD) aims at creating meaningful experiences. While UXD is a rather young discipline within product development and traditional processes predominate, other disciplines traditionally focus on creating experiences. We engaged with experience designers from the fields of arts, movies, sports, music and event management. By analyzing their working processes via interviews and observations we extracted triggers that can possibly lead to outstanding experiences in the original disciplines as well as in UXD: incorporating and shaping the atmosphere of interaction, balancing new and established aspects, connecting products with attributes of living beings, providing challenge and competition, enabling inductive and multifaceted learning and interaction processes, and using souvenir artifacts for connecting user and product after usage.

Keywords: Management of DUXU processes · User Experience · Emotional design · Product development

1 Introduction

1.1 Motivation

It is not a product in itself which is decisive for its success, but perception and assessment of the product by the user. Besides traditional product characteristics like speed of interaction, usability, etc. users assess products due to subjective feelings and complex criteria. The concept of User Experience (UX) incorporates these issues. UX describes how a user expects, perceives and evaluates a product in a certain context. User Experience Design (UXD) aims at enabling joy and fun [1], eliciting emotions [2] and satisfying psychological needs [3]. In other words: creating experiences. Yet, UXD is a rather young discipline within product development. Although new technologies enable more than mere functionality, differentiating products in one category and designing experiences is still often left to marketing. On the other hand, disciplines like arts, films, sports, etc. traditionally focus on creating experiences for their customers. It is an opportunity to learn from those disciplines for designing experiences with technical products [4].

© Springer International Publishing Switzerland 2016
A. Marcus (Ed.): DUXU 2016, Part I, LNCS 9746, pp. 304–313, 2016.
DOI: 10.1007/978-3-319-40409-7_29

1.2   Goal

The work presented in this paper is part of a broader research approach which aims at analyzing experience focused disciplines and transferring findings to product development in three categories [4]: characteristics of experience products (e.g. video game, sports event, movie), design processes which eventually lead to those products (e.g. game design process, film production process) as well as competences and tasks of experience designers involved (e.g. creative director, film producer). This paper focuses on characteristics of experience products, aiming at the question: Which triggers enable inspiring experiences in the areas of arts, movies, sports, concerts and events? The following aspects specify our goal:

Analysis of Experience Design Practice. In a previous study we performed a literature review and extracted factors that possibly lead to experiences in sports, gaming and tourism – according to theoretical experience models. According to the design thinking approach [5], we now engaged with experience designers and studied their design processes in practice: Which factors do experts in the analyzed disciplines design in order to enable inspiring experiences?

From "Mainstream" to "Avant-garde". The previous literature review was focused on mainstream experiences. We only considered those areas of life in which most people already have had experiences. Due to the importance of newness and relevance of going beyond traditional boundaries for the emergence of unique experiences, we conducted experience designers of so called sub cultures for the study presented in this paper (e.g. event manager for socio cultural activities for teenagers without prospects).

Insights for Subsequent Analysis. We want to extract insights as validation and confirmation for experience factors that we analyzed in the previous literature review. As well we aim at finding new insights to start consecutive deeper analysis. Our findings should be a starting point to finally transfer approaches for designing experiences to product development and more specifically to UXD.

2   Previous Work

Based on a literature review we analyzed a broad range of theoretical models from sports, gaming and tourism which explain the emergence of experiences in these fields. We joined the different approaches into the ExodUX model (from **Ex**perience **o**riented **d**isciplines to User **EX**perience) [6]. This model (see Fig. 1) presents factors that can possibly lead to experiences both in the original domains as well as in user product interaction. The ExodUX model splits 44 identified experience factors into 5 main categories (setting, aesthetics, interaction, user mind and technology), 5 subcategories (mechanics, user guidance, cognition, emotions and instincts) and 34 specific experience elements (e.g. environment, rules, story,…). 5 additional subcategories specify the aesthetics segment (visual, sound, feel, taste, smell).

The setting defines the overall topic for all other categories. Taking into account the environment of interaction this category defines an overarching theme, arranges the experience orchestration and finally aims at creating a certain atmosphere with the user product interaction.

The **aesthetics** category realizes experiences connected to all human senses – going beyond traditional focus on aspects like shape and size.

In the **Interaction** category, mechanics define rules and possibilities of action. E.g. experiences can arise due to precisely addressing and shaping skills of the user. The user guidance determines the interplay and timeline of the interaction.

User mind refers to the user's psychological characteristics. In the sub category cognition, e.g. experiences can arise when perfectly satisfying or even exceeding expectations. Furthermore, products can enable unique UX by evoking certain emotions (e.g. fun, fear,...) or addressing instincts (e.g. competition, greed,...).

The **technology** is the medium that realizes the intended experiences in the other categories. At the same time the application of outstanding technologies itself can enable the emergence of positive UX.

There are different possibilities how to apply the ExodUX model: applying the whole model in a top down or bottom up approach, using single elements as starting point for potential experience design or aiming at integration of existing experience ideas.

In ongoing research we specify the experience elements – analyzing characteristics of each factor and interrelations between certain elements and developing methods how to design experiences based on these experience factors with technical products.

3   Analysis Approach

Our methodology is based on the design thinking approach. It was split into two major parts. Firstly, we had to analyze in which areas experiences arise in the life of people and what the decisive aspects of these experiences are. Therefore, we performed an interview study with 7 persons between the age of 20 and 30. Also being called generation Y this group should have a high interest in innovative experiences. We collected experience stories and categorized them with respect to underlying psychological needs and connected experience disciplines.

After having analyzed the users we chose arts, movies, sports, music and event management as most promising for further research. In the second and main part of our study we engaged with 6 professional experience experts in these fields: an artist for abstract paintings, an arts curator for contemporary art, a director for political, social and philosophical documentary movies, a sports coach, a DJ and an event manager of a socio-cultural non-profit organization. As newness played an important role for the experiences in the first part of our approach we also chose experts outside the mainstream. According to the step "empathize" of the design thinking approach we observed, interacted and took part in the work of these persons and analyzed motivation, target group, methods used and the experience design processes. For each process we discussed which aspects can be transferred to UXD. We show our summarized results using the example of the arts curator.

- *Motivation:* The arts curator defined his motivation as critically scrutinizing society. He wants to make exhibits publically available – using existing knowledge of visitors, activating it towards new ways of thinking and creating new associations.
- *Target Group:* The interviewee described his target group as arts-related and interested in social-political topics. He defined two sub groups: the first one being impressed from previous exhibitions and wanting to experience something similar again; the second one wanting to experience newness and dynamics and striving for surprise.
- *Design Process:* 1. Inspection of potential exhibits; 2. Inspection of the exhibit environment; 3. Designing a story structured by drama theory; 4. Matching of exhibits and story; 5. Adapting exhibit environment according to story; 6. Guiding visitors through the exhibit environment; 7. Providing souvenir artifacts to visitors.
- *Insights for UXD (see Sect. 4):* Incorporating and shaping atmosphere. Balance between new and established aspects. Multifaceted and inductive learning processes. Using souvenir artifacts.

4   Insights

In the following we present experience principles which we extracted from all disciplines as main result of our study and which are worth transferring to UXD. We divide our insights from experience designers into two categories. Section 4.1 presents possible triggers for experiences. This is the main part of our analysis – highlighting characteristics of each trigger in the original disciplines and possibilities to transfer them to User Experience Design. Besides these factors that can shape experiences, Sect. 4.2 summarizes recommendations for design processes on the way to successful experience products.

4.1   Possible Triggers for Experiences

Incorporating and Shaping Atmosphere. Much more than already done in product development, the considered experience experts design with respect to context factors. Choosing the right atmosphere can be decisive for the generation of an experience. The arts curator, the film director, the DJ and the event manager highlighted the importance of the place and surrounding of their products' presentation. Particularly it is not the design of the art object, movie or music but the way they are presented in a museum, theatre or concert and the people taking part which count most for the users' evaluation. Figure 2 shows the example of a planned choreography at a football match of Germany against Italy in Munich. It is also possible to watch sports on TV – usability and comfort is even higher. But the atmosphere is what makes the difference and it is the reason why spectators visit the stadium. Product development should consider two aspects: Firstly, it is relevant to precisely analyze and incorporate all context factors that highly influence the product experience of a user. Secondly, product designers

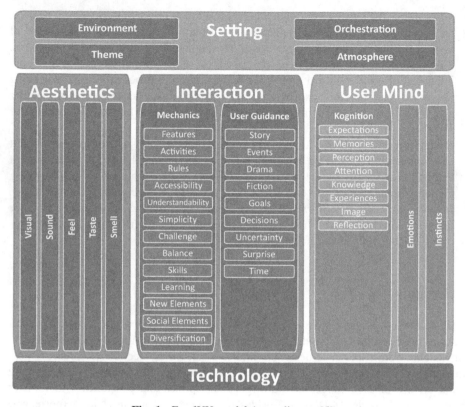

Fig. 1. ExodUX model (according to [6])

should aim at shaping an intended atmosphere rather than merely concentrating on the product itself.

Balance Between New and Established Aspects. Introducing new elements is a key factor for meaningful experiences in product development and all other disciplines which we examined. Yet, it is crucial for most users not to overexert newness but rather to keep them in a situation they are still comfortable in. The sports coach we interviewed organizes his sports events for teenagers in the following way: Activities stay more or less the same every year. But by changing certain factors like field size, group constellation etc. the game changes, adapts to the players' skills and provides new experiences. Similarly the arts curator provides a familiar environment in which it is then possible to challenge social norms and provoke experiences. These design processes are dynamic. Experiences in general as well as User Experience in interactions with technical products change over time [7]. This is a starting point for future research – analyzing how experience oriented disciplines shape this balance between new and established aspects. E.g. earworms in music have the exactly right balance between well-known and surprising aspects and are worth further investigation.

Fig. 2. Atmosphere in a football stadium (© by Simon Kremer)

Connecting Products with Attributes of Living Beings/Endorsement. It is a challenge to evoke meaningful emotions with technical products. Looking at other disciplines, experience designers work with connecting their "products" with attributes of living beings. The documentary film director stressed the possibility to win over his audience and to convince them of his concern by introducing animals or humans that represent the main topic. By identifying oneself with characters the viewer moves from passively watching towards taking a fictional experience role (e.g. Indiana Jones, Fig. 3).

Also in sports and event management building fictional relationships with the protagonists is a main source for experiences. Furthermore, endorsement is an established tool in marketing [8]. Companies use celebrities to promote intended values and characteristics of their products. We aim at adapting this approach by selecting a person with an intended image in an early analysis phase of product development, analyzing his characteristics and subsequently transferring these aspects into product properties.

Fig. 3. Identifying oneself with movie characters: e.g. Indiana Jones (© by Disney)

Inductive and Multifaceted Learning and Interaction Processes. This insight consists of two main aspects. Firstly, the experience designers plan step-by-step learning processes for their users. Letting the user solve unexpected and unknown problems and learn accordingly plays an important role in the processes we analyzed. The artist and arts curator take the visitors from their daily life step by step towards understanding complex contents and the underlying visions. In sports it is also essential to "feel" the learning progress on your own. Furthermore, behind movies theoretical models explain the process how viewers understand the presented fictional world: from perception of colors, shapes, etc. to recognizing objects, identifying characters, realizing events and timelines, summarizing contents and final interpretation [9].

Besides this step-by-step learning there is a second main point of this insight. Dramatic stories support learning and other interaction processes. The film director uses an arc of suspense to build his story and create an emotional experience bonding between user and movie.

Concluding, this insight can be transferred to User Experience Design by consciously developing strategies how to introduce new products at first time of usage and how to continuously convince the users with diversified interactions. It is crucial not to doubt the users' competence. Instead, the interaction should challenge the user but at the same time not overexert him. An underlying partly dramatic story can support a multifaceted product interaction.

Challenge and Competition. Competition is another factor that can enable meaningful experiences – originally coming out of sports. The sports coach uses challenge and competition as tool to motivate his participants. According to him, experiencing competition and coping with challenges in a group together with other people can even increase this kind of experience. Traditionally products should be designed to work without excessive effort of the user. But analyzing experiences, it is not the summary of only positive emotions which matters. An evenly positive emotional curve during interaction might lose its excitement. Positive could become normal. Meaningful experiences are highly related to the difference between negative and positive emotions. In sports, physical and mental effort and stress require a high amount of training. And still there is a chance of losing. It is very much this possibility to lose which facilitates the experience of winning to even exist. Losing and failure are not covered in product development so far and worth further research. Finding the right balance between easy to use and challenging usage is decisive.

Using Souvenir Artifacts. Physical artifacts coming out the process of experiencing connect users with temporary interactions and can help creating long lasting experiences. The arts curator mentioned interactive concepts where visitors take a physical object home to inspire them and to remember after visiting an exhibition. Figure 4 shows such a souvenir artifact from the German Pavilion at the universal exhibition EXPO 2015. When entering the pavilion every visitor received a specific card board with reflectors. Inside the exhibition you could place this cardboard at specified points of information. The cardboard served as screen, content was projected onto, as well as an interface for choosing the presented information (by moving and turning the cardboard). Afterwards it remained property of each visitor – reminding him or her of experiencing the technology and the exhibition. An example for a technical product that already serves as souvenir artifact is a car key which is used to unlock and start an automobile and which is carried around, maybe placed on a table, etc. by the driver. Transferring our insight to product development we could enable a User Experience by a smartphone which is used as an interface in an automobile. After driving the user takes the smartphone with him. It is a physical artifact connected to the experiences faced while driving and might even provide information about the experienced while apart from the car (e.g. at home).

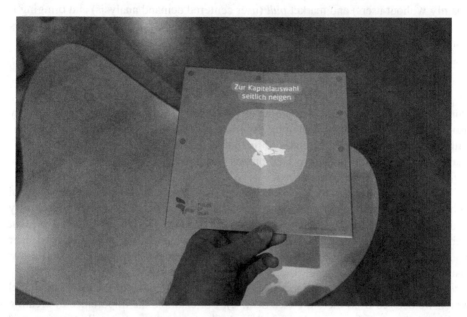

Fig. 4. Souvenir artifact from German Pavilion at EXPO 2015 (© by Simon Kremer)

4.2 Recommendations for Experience Design Processes

Open Development Goal. To create something really new (e.g. in arts) it is important to challenge norms and to keep the development goal changing dynamically. The artist who we interviewed emphasized the wish to create something unique. Instead of knowing what to paint in the beginning and focusing on a certain goal, he starts his design process with maximizing the influence of his environment. Starting with this inspiration, only in the iterative process of action and reflection the artist defines goal and meaning of his paintings. To transfer this recommendation to User Experience Design we have to define criteria in which situation the development goal should be kept open or focused.

Integrating and Excluding User Feedback. Integrating users is an important aspect of user centered design approaches. But e.g. in arts it is important to also exclude the users in order to go beyond obvious user motives. Our interview partner paid high intention to including dynamic influences of his environment. But no possible buyer was included in his creative process. Only after having finished a painting he confronted a customer with his piece of work. According to the demands of and interpretation by the customer, the artist named the painting. Similarly, theatre productions usually do not include spectators' feedback until the premiere. But during and after the performance there is an immediate and direct feedback from visitors to experience designers (e.g. actors, director,...). Therefore, it seems to be important not to include user feedback in general but in the right moment in the design process. Our approach for transfer to product development: Combining strength of both technology *push* (mainly without users) and market *pull* (user centered demand analysis) and bringing it to the next level of *excite* (by exceeding users expectations with experience triggers from this paper and previous work – see Sect. 2).

5   Discussion

Our study is not based on a representative survey. Much more we extracted key insights to work with when designing experiences both in the original disciplines and with technical products. This relates to the nature of User Experience which is hard to analyze and design in all details. But making the difference in one specific aspect can shape outstanding User Experience.

Moreover, the triggers for experiences are not fundamentally new and maybe seem to be obvious. Nevertheless, making researchers and experience designers consciously aware of these aspects can bring forth User Experience Design. We do not present elaborated design approaches but starting points which allow consecutive deeper analysis. Furthermore, this paper just presents an overview over main aspects of our insights and does not cover all details from the interviews.

Extracted triggers for experiences are often related to factors of the ExodUX model which we derived from literature (see Sect. 2). For example the importance of creating an intended atmosphere can be found in both approaches. As well, learning and challenge are experience factors in the ExodUX model which we also extracted from experience experts. This means similar factors lead to and influence experiences both in mainstream and avant-garde. Furthermore, many experience triggers are relevant in a broad range of analyzed disciplines.

6   Summary and Outlook

User Experience Design (UXD) aims at creating exciting experiences but is a rather young discipline within product development. On the other hand, other disciplines traditionally focus on creating experiences. We engaged with experience designers from the fields of arts, movies, sports, music and event management. By analyzing their working processes via interviews and observations we extracted triggers that can possibly lead to outstanding experiences in the original disciplines as well as in UXD: incorporating and shaping atmosphere, balance between new and established aspects, connecting products with attributes of living beings/endorsement, inductive and multifaceted learning and interaction processes, challenge and competition, and using souvenir artifacts.

Future work will focus on specifically analyzing the extracted insights. Our goal is to develop methods for addressing and implementing these experience triggers in product development and including them in the User Experience Design process [10].

References

1. Jordan, P.: Designing Pleasurable Products. An Introduction to the New Human Factors. Taylor & Francis, London (2000)
2. Norman, D.: Emotional Design – Why We Love (or hate) Everyday Things. Basic Books, New York (2005)
3. Kim, J., Park, S., Hassenzahl, M., Eckoldt, K.: The essence of enjoyable experiences: the human needs – A psychological needs-driven experience design approach. In: Marcus, A. (ed.) HCII 2011 and DUXU 2011, Part I. LNCS, vol. 6769, pp. 77–83. Springer, Heidelberg (2011)
4. Kremer, S., Lindemann, U.: Learning from experience oriented disciplines for user experience design. In: Marcus, A. (ed.) DUXU 2015, Part I. LNCS, vol. 9186, pp. 306–314. Springer, Heidelberg (2015)
5. Plattner, H., Mienel, C., Leifer, L. (eds.): Design Thinking: Understand – Improve – Apply. Springer, Heidelberg (2011)
6. Kremer, S., Hoffmann, A., Lindemann, U.: Transferring approaches from experience oriented disciplines to user experience design: the exodux model. In: Proceedings of the IASDR 2015 Interplay, pp. 1163–1175. International Association of Societies of Design Research (IASDR) (2015)
7. Roto, V., Law, E., Vermeeren, A., Hoonhout, J.: User experience white paper - Bringing clarity to the concept of user experience (2011).
http://www.allaboutux.org/files/UX-WhitePaper.pdf
8. Mc Cracker, G.: Who is the celebrity endorser? Cultural foundations of the endorsement process. J. Consum. Res. **16**(3), 310–321 (1989)
9. Persson, F.: Understanding Cinema. A Psychological Theory of Moving Imagery. Cambridge University Press, Cambridge (2003)
10. Bengler, K., Butz, A., Diwischek, L., Frenkler, F., Körber, M., Kremer, S., Landau, M., Loehmann, S., Lindemann, U., Michailidou, I., Norman, D., Pfalz, F., von Saucken, C., Schumann, J.: CAR@TUM: The Road to User Experience (2014).
www.designingexperiences.org

Developing a Lifestyle Design Approach in Brand Design Process Through UCD Methodology

Honghai Li[(✉)] and Jun Cai

Academy of Arts and Design, Tsinghua University, Beijing, China
lihonghai@vip.sina.com, caijun@mail.tsinghua.edu.cn

Abstract. This paper presents a lifestyle design approach in the design process of the QM (a local furniture manufacture in China) brand design project. The approach was developed to help designers efficiently understand segmented customers' profile based on market research. Designers can be inspired by lifestyle prototypes generated through the lifestyle design approach. This approach is developed based on three UCD methodology principles: user focus, using prototype and iteration with evaluation. The lifestyle design approach has three steps: concretizing customer profile, creating lifestyle prototype and evaluating lifestyle prototype. We implement the approach in the QM brand design project to deliver several lifestyle prototypes and evaluate them. This paper concludes that the lifestyle design approach can connect costumer research and creative design. It will be of interest to designers and market researchers.

Keywords: Lifestyle design approach · Brand design process · UCD methodology

1 Introduction

Increasing social media and e-commerce have changed the relationship between customers and the brand. Customers' value has become a significant factor in brand strategy design. Recent brand design studies have been focused on rearrangement of a brand design process and approach to apply in different circumstances. Some researchers have found that companies should co-create the brand strategy with their customers [1]. They have provided a series of tools to engage customers as participants in the band design process. Other brand design methods have been developed through an important design foundation theory that is the emotional design theory [2].

The co-creation method and the emotional approach could be categorized as a UCD (user centered design) methodology. UCD is a design process and philosophy in which the designer focuses on users' needs, wants, and limitations through the planning, design and development stages of a product (Usability Professionals Association, 2011). These UCD methods focus on the creation stage of design process. In this stage, studies of customers' need are the key issue. However, few attempts were made to build UCD approaches in the earlier stage of brand design. In this design, key issues of the study are customer classification, customer value definition, consumption view etc. In the traditional brand design process, these studies were included in lifestyle research

© Springer International Publishing Switzerland 2016
A. Marcus (Ed.): DUXU 2016, Part I, LNCS 9746, pp. 314–322, 2016.
DOI: 10.1007/978-3-319-40409-7_30

for marketing. It would be of interest to establish a lifestyle research approach from the UCD perspective in brand design.

The main purpose of this study is to build a UCD based lifestyle approach focused on the first stage of brand design process. The paper is organized as follows: Firstly, a review of the UCD methodology and lifestyle research is presented. Secondly, a framework of lifestyle research approach is proposed including purposes, methods, tools etc. Thirdly, we demonstrate this method with a case study of the lifestyle research approach in the QM furniture brand design project. Finally, we explain several future research opportunities of our work.

2   A Theoretical Framework

2.1   Lifestyle Research in Traditional Brand Design Process

Lifestyle is a series of consumer behavior patterns, which reflects consumer's choice to spend their time and money [3]. In most cases, marketers and designers use lifestyle research as a market segmentation method, such as VALS(Values and Lifestyles system). VALS method segments American adults into eight distinct types using a specific set of psychological traits and key demographics that drive consumer behavior. In China, researchers introduced a China-VALS system to segment Chinese consumers into 14 groups [4]. Marketers use these tools to define target market segmentation and transfer them to designers in the early stage of brand design. This stage is called design definition. The segmentation information including consumers' activities, opinion and interests is usually organized by demographic characteristics. In the next stage, creative design stage, designers develop brand design strategy on the basis of segmentation information. They use some UCD methods such as persona [5], co-work with consumers [1] to understand market segmentation clearly and use it efficiently (Fig. 1).

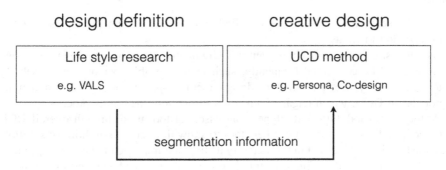

Fig. 1. Lifestyle research in design process

2.2   Insert a Lifestyle Design Stage into Brand Design Process

However, in this process designers always misunderstand segmentation information. Because most of lifestyle researches focus on consumers' general characteristics, they lost details of consumers' life style. Designers need these details to build an image of consumers' life when they generate a design strategy. Besides, the segmentation information is based on facts that occurred in the past. Designers prefer to be inspired by something new. To solve these problems, we insert a new stage named lifestyle design between design definition and creative design. In this stage, designers create some design themes from the result of lifestyle research, which show new lifestyles in a concretized way (Fig. 2).

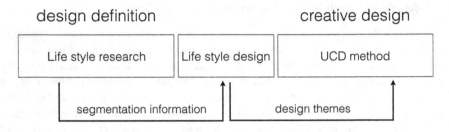

Fig. 2. Lifestyle design stage in design process

2.3   A Discussion of UCD Principles

UCD methodology was developed from computer engineering field (Nielsen), which includes a series of methods organized by a design process. Many researchers discussed the methods and process and some models can be categorized into a framework (Table 1).

- From these research results we can find out some common principles in UCD process and methods.
- User focus. Users are very important in UCD methodology because in every design stage users are concerned frequently, such as user profile, personas and usability test. And today user participatory design methods are becoming more and more popular in UCD, which engage with users throughout the whole process.
- Prototype methodology. Prototype is an essential tool used through overall UCD process. In the early stage it can be a tool to show different possibilities of solution; in the last, it can be tested in the usability testing and improved to be a final product.
- Evaluate and iteration. This principle is related to the user focus and prototype.

Users mean people who use the product in UCD method, and in our study, customer will replace users because they only touch the brand and have not used the product.

Table 1. A review of UCD methodology

Researchers	Process	Methods
Mark Ominsky [6]	Solution outline	user profile, solution modeling
	Macro design	low-fidelity prototyping, cognitive walkthrough
	Micro design	high-fidelity interaction prototyping, usability design walkthrough
Vredenburg, K [7]	•Market definition •Task analysis •Competitive evaluation •Design and walkthrough •Design evaluation and validation •Benchmark assessment	___
JAN GULLIKSEN [8]	Vision and plan	
	analyze requirements and user needs	Contextual inquiries, task analysis
	design for usability by prototyping	Low-fidelity prototyping
	Evaluate use in context	Usability test
	Construct and deploy	Usability test
	Feedback and plan the next iteration	___
Tomasz Miaskiewicz [5]	___	Personas
Wilkinson, C. R. [9]	Requirements analysis	Participatory design
	Prototypical design solutions	
	Finalist design solution	
	Evaluation and analysis	

3 Development of the LSD Approach Through UCD Principles

We define LSD (Lifestyle design) as a design inspiration mechanism that connects design definition and creative design. In LSD stage, the design purpose is to show customers' life style image and details. We deliver the outcome of LSD stage as a life style proposal or prototype including customers' aesthetic preferences, consumption motivation, social position and so on. In the next **creative** design stage, designers can use this lifestyle proposition as sources of creativity. We develop the LSD approach through the UCD principles discussed in the last paragraph into three steps, concretize customer profile, create lifestyle prototype and evaluate lifestyle prototype.

3.1 Concretize Customer Profile

In this step, we concretize customer profile into a concrete form, image boards. Every segmented customer profile information is including their life conditions, consumption views and brand views is collected using traditional marketing methods such as focus group and different customer segments categorize interview and this information. The image board is a tool for information visualization, which uses typical images to interpret abstract data. Except the photos we took from customers' daily life, we also use a customer participatory method to choose image in this step. In the focus group session, every participating customer was requested to pick out pictures that can show their life style from materials prepared for them. The pictures were collected from the popular life style magazines and websites about fashion, home furnishing, food, automobile and digital products. These pictures are the main references when we make the image boards.

3.2 Create Lifestyle Prototype

Prototype is a very important tool in UCD method, which transfers the concepts in designer's brain to real products. In the beginning of design process, Low-fidelity prototypes are made to show different possibilities of solution. With the deeply design on the prototypes, they approach to the final scheme and will be tested by users before the final product release. We use the prototype concept to build lifestyle design method. In LSD stage we create hypothetical lifestyle prototypes based on the customer profile, which shows different possibilities of target customers' life. Although lifestyle prototype is designed from real customers' life segments, it is a totally new scene differentiated from customers' real life. It is a hypothesis and prediction of a target customer segment, which can give inspirations to designers in the creative stage.

We create lifestyle prototype from customer profile in three steps as follows.

Step 1. Extract keywords from customer profiles.

In this step, we review every customer profile and select keywords that can describe their life style features. These keywords are abstract information from people's real life and will be the basis of lifestyle prototype design.

Step 2. Use images to define lifestyle characteristics.

According to the keywords extracted in last step, we search images to explain and describe the customers' life style features. We scan the popular media and leading company websites to find images that can show trends. The images may be product photos, color schemes, material samples, interior decoration, fashion shows and so on. The purpose of this step is to enlarge and enhance the lifestyle characteristics that keywords represented.

Step 3. Create lifestyle themes.

In this step, we give every image a keyword to define its style, just like Step1. The difference is that keywords represent the customer lifestyle features in Step1 while they represent the lifestyle trends in this step. We sort the image and keyword into different groups and give each group a style theme.

Step 4. Assemble themes into lifestyle prototype.

After step1-step3 finished, we can design several lifestyle themes for every customer segment, which show different aspects of people's life. These themes can be assembled into lifestyle prototype that is concrete, detailed and cutting edge. Lifestyle prototype can be different forms including image board, video, object and space. Different forms can inspirit designers for different purposes. For example, when a designer wants to advertise a brand, the target customers' lifestyle prototype he needs should be an image board or video.

This whole process of lifestyle prototype creating is a combination of logical thinking and image thinking. When we extract a keyword, we use logical thinking and when we choose an image to explain a style, we use image thinking. After several rounds of thinking combination, the prototype can be presented richly and accurately. Figure 3 describes the full view of lifestyle prototype creation.

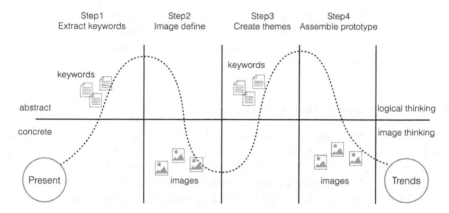

Fig. 3. Full view of lifestyle prototype creation

3.3 Evaluate Lifestyle Prototype

After lifestyle prototype design finished, we invite target customers to evaluate and improve it. We use usability test as a reference to build method in this part. Just like a usability test we observe customers when they review and experience the lifestyle prototype. Moreover we interview customers or make a survey after the test. Then we analyze customers' behaviors and options to support the improvement.

Through UCD principles, we build the LSD approach with three main parts, concretize customer profile, create lifestyle prototype and evaluate lifestyle prototype. As the result of the LSD stage, lifestyle prototypes can be a bridge to connect the customer research and creative design. Designers will have concrete and detailed customer lifestyle samples instead of the abstract text, number or chart, so they can understand the target customers' life more accurately and efficiently when they design the brand strategy.

4   Results and Discussion

We implemented the LSD approach in the QM brand strategy design project that aimed to help QM brand connecting with their target customers more tightly. We took a research roadmap from concretizing customer profile to lifestyle prototype creation and evaluation, and delivered a series of lifestyle prototypes to designers for QM advertising and flagship store design.

4.1   Concretize Targeted Customer Profiles

After early studies, targeted customer segments were defined for QM brand. In the early studies stage, we have taken some typical photos from customers' daily life and some costumers who participated in the focus group were asked to pick some pictures to represent their lifestyle. These pictures help us to make the customer profiles image board more accurately and efficiently. As a delivery of this step, we made image board for every customer segmentation that includes customer persona, interior decoration, consumption scenario and so on.

4.2   Lifestyle Prototype Design Workshops

We held several workshops in this step and invited some target customers and designers to work together to design lifestyle prototypes. Firstly, we extracted keywords from the profiles, which can describe customer lifestyle's characteristics. Then, we search images to concretize keywords, which are about cloth, food, car and so on (Fig. 4). All this images are found in leading company and top media and represent the newest trend.

In the next step, we gave every image a keyword to describe the lifestyle trends that they represent. The keywords in this step are an update of the keywords in the previous step. After a round of logical thinking mixed image thinking, we found the newest trend of target customers' lifestyle. In the following step, we mixed and matched some keywords to be some trend themes and visualization them.

Fig. 4. Extract lifestyle keywords

Every targeted customer segmentation has several trend themes that show different aspects of people's life. We assembled them together to build an overall perspective lifestyle prototype, which represents customer's value, consumption view, daily life scenario, aesthetic preference and so on.

4.3 Evaluate Lifestyle Prototype in QM Store

With the help of QM Company, we conducted a lifestyle prototype in QM store. This lifestyle prototype is a space based prototype and built in a QM flagship store in Beijing. We put some furniture and decorations in the store space depending on our LSD proposition (Fig. 5). The evaluate process is more like a usability test, which aimed to gather customer's option about our lifestyle prototype. We invited target customers to shop in the store wearing a headset eye tracker machine that can record people's sight. After analysis of customers' eye track data and opinions, we fixed and improved our lifestyle prototype.

Fig. 5. Lifestyle prototype in QM store

5 Conclusion

The purpose of our study is to build a method to connect design research stage and creative design stage. Mostly designers feel difficult and confused when they read a design research report full of abstract information. And what we study is to transfer the research result to be a form that designers can easily recognize. We redesign the abstract information to be a prototype that can be used as design inspiration resources. From this point of view, the design inspiration resources become a design object, so we can use a design methodology to create them.

In our study, we choose UCD methodology to design the research result, which is the most popular design method in this time. Through the essential principles of UCD method, we build the lifestyle design approach in the brand design process, which developed around the lifestyle prototype. Compared with the prototype in the creative design stage, lifestyle prototype is very special because it is not a real product or service. Lifestyle prototype is more like a prediction of customers' life status in the future.

At last, through this paper a lifestyle design approach in brand design process was presented and its instruction was made by a case study of QM brand design project. The approach can be divided into three steps. They are concretizing customer profile, creating lifestyle prototype and evaluating lifestyle prototype. Another feature of this approach is the mixed usage of logical thinking and image thinking. After several rounds of keywords-image interaction, the lifestyle can be described accurately.

In this study, the designers become the "customers" of our LSD approach. However, designers in the case study did not evaluate our approach. We will gather designers' options about our approach and improve it in the future.

References

1. GONZALEZ, S.J.: Consumer engagement in co-creation of contemporary brand design. In: Proceedings of the 19th DMI: Academic Design Management Conference: Design Management in an Era of Disruption, p. 323. Design Management Institute (2014)
2. Hwang, J., Baek, E.: Development of a retail brand enhancement tool through the use of emotional design theory. In: Leading Innovation Through Design, pp. 9–23 (2012)
3. Solomon, M.R.: Consumer Behavior: Buying, Having, and Being. Prentice Hall, Engelwood Cliffs (2014)
4. Yin, W.: The research towards model of China-Vals. Nankai Bus. Rev. 2, 2 (2005)
5. Miaskiewicz, T., Kozar, K.A.: Personas and user-centered design: how can personas benefit product design processes? Des. Stud. 32, 417–430 (2011)
6. Ominsky, M., Stern, K.R., Rudd, J.R.: User-centered design at IBM consulting. Int. J. Hum. Comput. Interact. 14, 349–368 (2002)
7. Vredenburg, K.: Building ease of use into the IBM user experience. IBM Syst. J. 42, 517–531 (2003)
8. Gulliksen, J., et al.: Key principles for user-centred systems design. Behav. Inf. Technol. 22, 397–409 (2003)
9. Wilkinson, C.R., De Angeli, A.: Applying user centred and participatory design approaches to commercial product development. Des. Stud. 35, 614–631 (2014)

Transdisciplinarity, Community-Based Participatory Research, and User-Based Information Design Research

The D•VERSE Group and Two Projects

Judith A. Moldenhauer[(⊠)] and Donnie Johnson Sackey

Wayne State University, Detroit, MI, USA
{judith.moldenhauer,donnie.sackey}@wayne.edu

Abstract. This paper will discuss how the confluence between community-based participatory research and user-based information design is an effective approach to researching science in the public interest as seen through their application to the conceptual and methodological frameworks of two projects by the transdisciplinary research team D•VERSE (Detroit Integrated Vision for Environmental Research through Science and Engagement). D•VERSE, an example of team science, tackles complex scientific issues with community residents working as "citizen scientists." One project assesses the health and environmental effects on residents of the southwest Detroit community of storing open piles of petcoke (a by-product of the shale oil fracking process) on the Detroit River; the second project focuses on the impact of air quality on asthmatic Detroit teenagers. This paper will also suggest a set of guidelines that other researchers might use to create research clusters similar to D•VERSE.

Keywords: Team science · Community-based participatory research · User-centered design · User-based design

1 Introduction

Communication – that is, how people interact with one another and exchange ideas, feelings, and facts – is at the heart of the disciplines of rhetoric and information design. These disciplines employ community-based participatory research (CBPR) and user-centered design (UCD) to explore the ways people interact with one another and use information. This exploration then shapes the development of materials that enable people to easily get and share information that is important and affects their lives. This focus on communication is especially important for the practice of team science where collaboration and community engagement are at the nexus of research efforts. This paper will discuss how community-based participatory research and user-centered (also known as user-based) design are working together to contribute to the conceptual and methodological frameworks of two research projects of a transdisciplinary research team in Detroit, Michigan.

© Springer International Publishing Switzerland 2016
A. Marcus (Ed.): DUXU 2016, Part I, LNCS 9746, pp. 323–332, 2016.
DOI: 10.1007/978-3-319-40409-7_31

2   Team Science

The science of team science (SciTS) is a transdisciplinary approach to research borne out of increased interest in the early 1990s toward understanding how the intersectionality of different disciplinary frameworks could enhance research outcomes. Team science (TS) as a practice of SciTS are research initiatives designed to answer research questions among a group of interested scholars. The concept of TS involves (1) tackling complex scientific issues, such as public health and environmental problems, (2) the collaboration of individuals from a variety of disciplinary backgrounds and (3) a commitment to cross-disciplinary research. Of the three kinds of cross-disciplinary approaches to TS – multidisciplinarity, interdisciplinarity, and transdisciplinarity – transdisciplinarity might be the best heuristic for engaging with the complexity of scientific issues, especially as they intersect with community engagement. Specifically, transdiciplinarity "is a process in which team members representing different fields work together over extended periods of time to develop shared conceptual and methodological frameworks that not only integrate but also transcend their respective disciplinary perspectives" [15, p. S79].

For two years, a group of researchers from divergent disciplinary backgrounds have organized into a research cluster based on the TS model. The work of the Detroit Integrated Vision for Environmental Research through Science and Engagement (D•VERSE) group at Wayne State University has been to engage in transdisciplinary research at the intersection of health, environmental, and communication sciences. Team members include an information designer, a rhetorician, a proteomics biological scientist, a civil and environmental engineer, and an environmental lawyer. What has held D•VERSE together as a research cluster is our embrace of community-based participatory research and user-centered design as a guides for how to approach scientific research about the environment.

Critiques of how to approach or "do" scientific research have been large and diffuse across the humanities and social sciences, particularly from feminism and theories of environmental justice. Much of these assessments have centered on issues of cognitive and participatory justice. Scholars have demurred both the primacy that scientific communities afford to certain methods and languages as means of making knowledge, and the purposes that drive scientific inquiry. For local communities residents impacted by decades of environmental injustice, scientific research follows a model of science for the sake of science or research for the sake of research. This means that most scientific research is not necessarily driven from the ground up, but instead from the perspective of businesses for the purpose of profit. While there are certainly spin-offs stemming from scientific research, science rarely runs on a non-profit model.

Feminist critics of science like Evelyn Fox Keller [4] and Vandana Shiva [12] have articulated that *doing science* necessitates adoption and implementation of disciplinary languages and syntactical structures in writing that disallow local communities to participate before, during, and after the conduction of scientific research. In this regard, feminist critiques of science have questioned access in scientific communities by pointing to either the relative absence of women and people of color scientists or the lack of interaction between scientific communities and residential communities. Genuine participation in science requires a mutual sharing of both a language and conceptual universe [4, p. 136]. This requires that researchers not only translate their research into forms that local communities can more readily understand but also make community members a part of the research planning, implementation, and dissemination phases. This follows closely with community activists' demands that the scientific epistemology of research projects be written within the vernacular of the people [18, p. 84]. Yet, it is not enough that science translate its work into local vernaculars. The largest problem with science and knowledge is the lack of collaboration between researchers and local communities. And any approach to research with the goal of reforming science must make people the center of research.

The D•VERSE team makes research decisions together with community residents. We are dedicated to a paradigm of scientific research that empowers people to make changes that can improve their health and environment; our choice of research projects reflects that commitment. This is a multifaceted goal that can only be tackled with researchers from a variety of disciplines from the sciences and humanities who are willing to create new ways to work together in addressing links between health and the environment. We approach research from the perspective of performing interwoven tasks – what each of us does, impacts the other's task – and this sense of operating via consensus and collaboration is at the heart of our work with our community partners to develop new ways of engaging with researchers that include successful communication materials. The trust between members of the research team extends to the trust we strive to engender with our research partners, an important aspect of CBPR as cited by Wallerstein and Duran in their paper, "Community-Based Participatory Research Contributions to Intervention Research: The Intersection of Science and Practice to Improve Health Equity" [19]. That we function as a transdisciplinary team aligns well with our use of the participatory design process, which, according to Henry Sanoff, "is an attitude about a force for change in the creation and management of environments for people" [11, p. 213].

3   CBPR and UCD Together: Similarities and Differences

The confluence of community-based participatory research and user-centered information design strategies is essential to our two concurrent projects in which community residents work as "citizen scientists" with our team. One project assesses the health and environmental effects on residents of the southwest Detroit community of storing open piles of petcoke (a by-product of the shale oil fracking process) on the banks of the Detroit River. The second project, in conjunction with asthma researchers from the Henry Ford Health System (HFHS), focuses on the impact of air quality on asthmatic Detroit teenagers. In the petcoke project, community-based research will guide the direction of the research – e.g., what are the concerns of the community about petcoke? what do they want to know and do about it? – and user-centered design will be central to developing communication materials/media used by these citizen scientists. For the air quality project, teens will volunteer to use a personal air monitor and keep an asthma symptom diary. We will then work with them to evaluate the data from the air monitors and the diaries and brainstorm ideas for developing a digital asthma symptom diary.

Through the development of their concepts and prototypes for the diary, the teens will be practicing participatory design or co-design (which embodies CBPR practice).

The value of user-centered design is summed up by Romedi Passini in his chapter for the book, *Information Design*, "design solutions can only be properly assessed by potential users – regardless of how confident the designer is about the proposed design" [9, p. 86]. The value of participatory design is summed by Henry Sanoff in the 2007 special issue on participatory design in the journal *Design Studies*:

> [Participatory design's] strength lies in being a movement that cuts across traditional professional boundaries and cultures. Its roots lie in the ideals of a participatory democracy where collective decision-making is highly decentralised throughout all sectors of society, so that all individuals learn participatory skills and can effectively participate in various ways in the making of all decisions that affect them... [It is] to engage people in meaningful and purposive adaptation and change to their daily environment... [and] refers to an approach that is rooted in trust, intimacy, and consensus [11, pp. 213–214].

Liem and Sanders [5] describe the difference between three perspectives of design research and practice – user-centered, design-led, and co-creation – in a map showing the intersecting axes of approach and mindset. The opposing approaches are research-led and design-led; the opposing mindsets are the "expert mindset where users are seen as subjects (reactive informers)" and the "participatory mindset where users are seen as partners (active co-creators)." User-centered design "should start from a deep analysis of users needs" – human factors and ergonomics, usability testing, etc. The design-led approach looks at the socio-cultural context to explore the values and interactive patterns of users' behavior. In both of these approaches exhibit the expert mindset, designers and research design *for* people. Co-creation, however, focuses on designing *with* people using the participatory mindset in which people are seen "as the experts in the domains of experience such as living, learning, working, etc." [5, pp. 74–75].

Our research utilizes both user-centered research and CBPR in the development of materials for and with the participants in our studies, but the sequence of emphasis in the use of each approach for each project is different. In the asthma study, the research focus is defined by the research team based on user-centered research but the result or "product" of the research is to be developed through CBPR and participatory design. The teens will be collecting and analyzing data, and then determining how (and what) to communicate about the data based their experiences as citizen scientists. In the petcoke study, the research focus is to be defined through CBPR so that the product can be developed to enable people to do their work as citizen scientists; their work as citizen scientists in turn will circle back to CBPR as their data will continue to redefine the research foci. In both projects, the intersection of knowledge of the participants and researchers is the key to the success of the projects – a merging of experiences and knowledge that negotiates the scale of co-creation to meet the information needs of the people in each situation.

For the asthma study, teens will be randomly given one of three different asthma diaries: two existing diaries and one designed by the research team, based on our HFHS colleagues' previous research experiences. The teens will keep their diaries for 2 weeks in conjunction with using their personal air monitor (PM). The study will enroll 60 teens, of which 10 will attend 2 special workshop sessions. In the first one, teens would provide researchers with an "ideal" sense of what a PM should be like and how best to use it (and incorporate into their lives) and in the second workshop, the teens would take the data from the PM and discuss how to best visualize the data and use their experiences with the PM and diaries to design a digital asthma diary. All 60 teens would complete their diary, use the PM, and turn in their diaries and PMs to provide the researchers with data for the project. Diary usage plus feedback from the teens on the pros and cons of these diaries can be applied to the design of the digital asthma diary.

For the petcoke study, the researchers are conducting focus groups to find out the environmental and health concerns of residents of the southwest Detroit neighbor nearest where the petcoke piles were stored. When we know the issues and information that the residents want addressed and how people in the neighborhood get and exchange information with one another, we will then design materials that match the residents' communication modes and their information needs. Using these materials, the residents can then collect data and decide how to visualize and disseminate the data.

In both projects, our research will involve what Maureen Mackenzie-Taylor refers to as participatory conversations "to explore the situation, to open up ways of moving forward, to test the way we present information" [7]. These conversations embody the generalized principles of respect and conversation listed by David Sless in his article, "Usable Medicines Information," [13]. These principles are essential to the information design process (as visualized by Sless in the Fig. 1 diagram) and will be central to the development of our materials, regardless of whether their emphasis is user-centered design or co-creation.

One of the important aspects of scoping focuses on learning about what people need or want to know or do and the tasks people perform to get that information; benchmarking evaluates their current means to get that information; prototyping produces new designs to accomplish the information tasks; testing/refining evaluates the success of the new designs.

> "...information design uses practices which both implicitly and explicitly grow out of respect of people in their own settings... The successful design comes through conversation. Indeed if one looks at exactly what is going on during most of these activities – scoping, benchmarking, etc. – then conversation is at its very heart." [13, pp. 67–68]

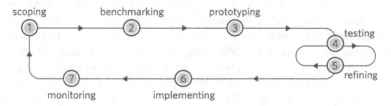

Fig. 1. Diagram of the information design process from "Measuring Information Design," by David Sless [14, p. 253]. Sless has subsequently changed the term "benchmarking" to "baseline measurement" in the diagram; see his article Design or "Design" – Envisioning a Future Design Education. Visible Language, vol. 4.6, no. 1/2, 54–65 (2012). Image courtesy of David Sless.

4 CBPR and UCD in Science and Design

The use of CBPR has been shown to be of value in the development of interventions to improve healthcare, especially as a way to meet the healthcare needs of underserved communities [2, 17, 19]. Wallerstein and Duran cite CBPR "as an orientation and overall approach, which equalizes power relationships between academic and community research partners" that "can create an environment that fosters trust more easily" in changing "the research discourse from 'research subject' to 'research participant,' of from 'targeting community members' to 'engaging community partners'" [19, p. S42]. They list six challenges to health interventions in translational research and discuss how CBPR can address those challenges:

- *External validity* – ask "for community health priorities" and collaborate on the development or adaption health initiatives.
- *Evidence* – integrate "culturally based evidence, practice-based evidence, and indigenous research methodologies, which support community knowledge."
- *Language* – change the "research discourse" by addressing participants as partners rather than subjects
- *Business as usual* – shift the research emphasis from university control of resources, budgets, and processes to one that focuses on "the participation of community-level investigators throughout all research process, with sufficient participatory structures and collaborative decision making."
- *Sustainability* – "strengthen the community ownership and the use of data."
- *Lack of trust* – create "policies that equalize power... [and understand that] trust is always dynamic and requires continual nurturing through dialogue and reflection." [19, pp. S40–S42]

Cashman et al. note the practice of "consensus decision-making" and the use and valuation of "experiential learning" to "support community-university engagement" especially to maintain the "commitment to the time and interactive process required... in arriving at outcomes" [2, p. 1414]. Trickett et al. advocates an "ecological/systems framework" for community interventions that see "health matters as embedded in a community ecology that includes local conditions, community history, relations among subgroups and groups external to the community (including relationships with community intervention researchers), local resources, networks and their social capital, and effects of macrosystem policies on community life" [17, p. 1411]. The result of this understanding is the "creation of empowering collaborative processes where by community members play key roles as members of the intervention team" [17, p. 1412].

The above research dovetails with the approaches of user-centered design and participatory design. Employing UCD and CBPR, especially within the same research project, have shown to be important tools in the development of healthcare information design. The April 2015 special issue of *Visible Language: The Journal of Visual Communication Research* was devoted to design and health. Of the ten articles in this issue, five discussed the use of both user-centered and participatory design/codesigning in the development of designs that addressed specific health issues. (The other five used UCD practices, although one focused on the experiences of physicians interacting with their patients.) In fact, Audrey Bennett's article credited the use of CBPR in healthcare communication in her decision to use CBPR in developing the visual identity (logo) for a HIV prevention program in Ghana that advocates the use of condoms [1]. Zender and Plate discussed the use of co-design in the development of a poster for the program, Hygiene Matters, to reduce infection by parasitic worms in the Central African Republic [20]. CBPR was also essential in the design work described in the other articles: hospice care in Glasgow, Scotland [16]; IT healthcare simulations for nursing students at the university of Tennessee, Knoxville [6]; and the "Daily Situational Awareness Brief" used by healthcare emergency managers in Indianapolis, Indiana [8]. In all these cases, the interaction with all stakeholders – but especially with those who would most directly be interacting with or affected by the designs – was essential for designs that are integral to researching science in the public interest.

5   CBPR and UCD in D•VERSE Research

Our projects incorporate Wallerstein and Duran's challenges, are built around community engagement, and see health issues within the context of the experience of life within the local community. They also bear hallmarks of the research documented in *Visible Language*. In both of our studies, we are working with underserved communities and see CBPR and UCD as keys to our research.

For the petcoke study, we worked with Wayne State University community relations representatives who guided us in how to best engage (and maintain engagement) with community members. By identifying and meeting first with community leaders in a focus group, we were able to get an initial sense of the community's immediate and future concerns about contact with petcoke dust and particles (e.g., breathing it, on skin, how to protect yourself, how to prevent additional open-air petcoke storage in the Detroit area, etc.) and of how community members think about the role of science in their lives and in society (e.g., their knowledge of the scientific process, how they view scientists). Community leaders then identified and invited residents to attend focus groups with us; these focus groups are in process. Our team has also tested the chemical "signature" of petcoke (i.e., what it is made of). The results of these focus groups will ultimately enable us to develop communication materials that enable researchers and community to (1) collaboratively decide on what aspect(s) of dealing with petcoke is most beneficial for residents and scientists and (2) collect and share data about the nature of petcoke and its impact on individuals and communities (Fig. 2).

For the Detroit teen asthma study, a university community relations representative is part of the research team as well as asthma researchers from the Henry Ford Health System (HFHS). Contact with the community for the recruitment of 60 teens for the study is being headed by the community relations representative and the HFHS researchers who have many community contacts through their previous asthma studies. The recruitment materials were designed with their input to meet both the content needs for IRB approval and to connect at the visual and verbal levels with the teens and their parents. We will be searching for any correlation between asthma symptoms experienced by the teens and the number and kind of particulates collected by their personal air monitors (PMs). We are stressing the collaborative nature of the teens participation in the

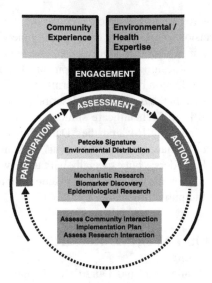

Fig. 2. Diagram from the petcoke grant application emphasizing the process and overriding framework of community engagement in the research project. Image courtesy of the D•VERSE group.

study, especially for the 10 who volunteer to participate in two workshops – one before and one after the data collection. In the first workshop, the teens will be asked to provide their ideas about the "ideal" PM (how and when to use it, what it might look like, etc.). In the second workshop, they will be asked to explore ways to visualize the data from the PMs, how to best distribute the data and to whom, and to develop concepts/prototypes for the design of a digital asthma symptom diary based on their experiences with the 3 different paper-based diaries used in the study. In this study, CBPR will lead directly to codesign. The teens' prototypes will reflect the important point by Sanders and Stappers in their article, "Probes, toolkits and prototypes: three approaches to making in codesigning" [10] that "making is a practice for participation" [10, p. 7].

In both projects, the design of the materials will be user-centered – incorporating the CBPR and continuing to engage the community in the testing the materials.

6   Conclusion

Brenda Dervin advocates that designers approach information from the "*communication perspective on information*" she calls *Sense-Making,* in which "information design is a "system to assist people in designing their own information... in effect, metadesign: design about design, design to assist people to make and unmake their own information, their own sense" [3, pp. 42–43]. She goes on to say that Sense-Making is based on "the assumption that humans *must* muddle through together" because we have "an incomplete understanding of reality (ontology) and an incomplete understanding of what it means to know something (epistemology)" [3, pp. 44–45].

It is this spirit of Sense-Making that we bring to our petcoke and Detroit teen asthma study in the belief that in muddling together through community-based participatory research and user-centered design will foster improvements in the health and environment of Detroit residents.

So it is with Dervin's comments in mind that we offer these guidelines for transdisciplinary team science:

- integrate CBPR and UCD into the whole research plan from start to finish;
- include at least one representative from the community be part of the team;
- make sure that dedicated time and funding be allotted to test any materials intended to be used by members of the community – and for at least one round of subsequent re-design and re-testing.

We look forward to hearing about other exciting transdisciplinary research using CBPR and UCD.

Acknowledgements. Funding for the petcoke project is provided by the U.S. National Institute of Environmental Health Sciences (NIEHS) via the Center for Urban Responses to Environmental Stressors (CURES) Core Center Grant (P30 ES020957). Funding for the Detroit teen asthma project is provided by the Institute for Population Sciences, Health Assessment, Administration, Services, and Economics (INPHAASE), a joint program of Wayne State University and the Henry Ford Health System.

References

1. Bennett, A.: Connotative localization of an HIV prevention image to promote safer sex practices in Ghana. Spec. Issue Visible Lang. **49**(1–2), 29–39 (2015)
2. Cashman, S., Adeky, S., Allen III, A., Coburn, J., Israel, B., Montaño, J., Rafelito, A., Rhodes, S., Swanston, S., Wallerstein, N., Eng, E.: The power and the promise: working with communities to analyze data, interpret findings, and get to outcomes. Am. J. Public Health **98**(8), 1407–1417 (2008). doi:10.2105/AJPH.2007.113571. Accessed 31 October 2015. http://www.ncbi.nlm.nih.gov/pmc/articles/PMC2446454/?tool=pmcentrez
3. Dervin, B.: Chaos, order, and sense-making: a proposed theory for information design. In: Jacobson, R. (ed.) Information Design, pp. 35–57. MIT Press, Cambridge (2000)
4. Keller, E.F.: Gender and science: an update. In: Wyer, M., Barbercheck, M., Geisman, D., Öztürk, H., Wayne, M. (eds.) Women, Science and Technology: A Reader in Feminist Science Studies, pp. 132–142. Routledge, New York (2001)
5. Liem, A., Sanders, E.: Human-centred design workshops in collaborative strategic design projects: an educational and professional comparison. Des. Tech. Educ. Int. J. **18**(1), 72–86 (2013). Accessed 30 January 2016. http://www.maketools.com/articles-papers/Liem Sanders2013.pdf
6. Lowe, S., Wyatt, T., Li, X., Fancher, S.: Trans-disciplinary partnerships in IT health software development: the benefits of learning. Spec. Issue Visible Lang. **49**(1–2), 112–127 (2015)
7. Mackenzie-Taylor, M.: Designing for understanding within a context of rapidly changing information. Communication Research Institute. CRI, Melbourne, Australia (1997). http://communication.org.au

8. Napier, P., Wada, T.: Co-designing for healthcare: visual designers as researchers and facilitators. Spec. Issue Visible Lang. **49**(1–2), 128–143 (2015)
9. Passini, R.: Sign-Posting information design. In: Jacobson, R. (ed.) Information Design, pp. 83–98. MIT Press, Cambridge (2000)
10. Sanders, E., Stappers, P.: Probes, toolkits and prototypes: three approaches to making in co-designing. Co-design **10**(1), 5–14 (2014). doi:10.1080/15710882.2014.888183. Accessed 30 January 2016. http://www.tandfonline.com/doi/full/10.1080/15710882.2014.888183
11. Sanoff, H.: Editorial: Special issue on participatory design. Spec. Issue Des. Stud. **28**(3), 213–215 (2007). doi:10.1016/j.destud.2007.02.001. Accessed 30 January 2016. http://www.sciencedirect.com.proxy.lib.wayne.edu/science/article/pii/S0142694X07000178
12. Shiva, V.: Staying Alive: Women, Ecology, and Development. South End Press, Cambridge (2010)
13. Sless, D.: Usable Medicines Information. Communication Research Institute. CRI, Melbourne, Australia (2001). http://communication.org.au
14. Sless, D.: Measuring information design. Inf. Des. J. **16**(3), 250–258 (2008)
15. Stokol, D., Hall, K., Taylor, B., Moser, R.: The science of team science: overview of the field and introduction to the supplement. Am. J. Preventative Med. **35**(2S), S78–S89 (2008). doi:10.1016/j.amepre.2008.05.002. Accessed 1 November 2015. http://ac.els-cdn.com/S074937970800408X/1-s2.0-S074937970800408X-main.pdf?_tid=2eee2b72-c85e-11e5-8854-00000aacb360&acdnat=1454274434_71e00263f10e9753fc1d6e5af981d8eb
16. Taylor, A., French, T., Lennox, J., Keen, J.: Developing a design brief for a virtual hospice using design tools and methods: a preliminary exploration. Spec. Issue Visible Lang. **49**(1–2), 96–111 (2015)
17. Trickett, E., Beehler, S., Deutsch, C., Green, L., Hawe, P., McLeroy, K., Miller, R., Rapkin, B., Schensul, J., Schulz, A., Trimble, J.: Advancing the science of community-level interventions. Am. J. Public Health **101**(8), 1410–1419 (2011). doi:10.2105/AJPH.2010.300113. Accessed 31 October 2015. http://media.proquest.com.proxy.lib.wayne.edu/media/pq/classic/doc/2403
18. Visvanathan, S.: Knowledge, justice, and democracy. In: Leach, M., Scoones, I., Wynne, B. (eds.) Science and Citizens: Globalization and the Challenge of Engagement, pp. 83–94. Zed Books, New York (2007)
19. Wallerstein, N., Duran, B.: Community-Based participatory research contributions to intervention research: the intersection of science and practice to improve health equity. Am. J. Public Health **100**(Suppl. 1), S40–S46 (2010). doi:10.2105/AJPH.2009.184036. Accessed 31 October 2015. http://www.ncbi.nlm.nih.gov/pmc/articles/PMC2837458/?tool=pmcentrez
20. Zender, M., Plate, D.: Designing and evaluating a health program in Africa: Hygiene Matters. Spec. Issue Visible Lang. **49**(1–2), 40–59 (2015)

Gadgile Probing: Supporting Design of Active Mobile Interactions

Susanne Koch Stigberg[✉]

Department of Computer Science,
Østfold University College, 1757 Halden, Norway
susanne.k.stigberg@hiof.no

Abstract. Designing for mobile interactions is a difficult task. Designers must understand the multifaceted nature of the mobile context and require an overview of interaction techniques feasible for that context. We propose gadgile probing as a technique to support the design for mobile interactions. Introducing "off-the-shelf" technology in the inquiry phase enables designers to explore not only *what is* but also *what could be* early in the process. We present an example from running and biking. Our findings demonstrate that gadgile probing can complement contextual inquiries providing a good understanding of the context, listing needs and desires of participants, evaluating alternative interaction techniques, and inspiring designers and users to ideate about future technologies.

Keywords: Probing · Probes · Interaction design · Mobile interactions

1 Introduction

Most mobile systems are "stop-to-interact", designed for interaction only when a user is standing still, paying visual and mental attention to the device [16]. Devices for outdoor sports are no exception, even though the use of mobile devices for self-tracking training sessions is becoming default. Limited attention has been paid to the interaction with these technologies. Lumsden and Brewster [15] requested "a paradigm shift in terms of interaction techniques for mobile technology" already in 2003. Ten years later Marshall and Tennent [16] highlight four challenges designing interactions for mobile devices: cognitive load, physical constraints, terrain and other people. This paper describes a technique, called gadgile probing, for understanding these challenges and supporting system design for mobile interactions. These "interactions in motion" shall enable users to perform meaningful two-way interactions with devices while actively mobile [16].

Probes are means to explore new ideas and include participants in the design process [10]. They have been described as instruments that are "deployed to find out about the unknown" [11] or "collections of evocative tasks meant to elicit inspirational responses from people" [8]. Technology probes [11] are simple, flexible, adaptable technologies with three goals: understanding the needs and desires of users in real-world setting, field-testing the technology, and inspiring users and researchers to think about future technology. Even though technology probes are simple and should be used early in the design process [11], it takes time and effort to create them.

© Springer International Publishing Switzerland 2016
A. Marcus (Ed.): DUXU 2016, Part I, LNCS 9746, pp. 333–343, 2016.
DOI: 10.1007/978-3-319-40409-7_32

Researchers must have an underlying understanding of the context to design and deploy these probes. In contrast gadgile probing is a technique that uses consumer gadgets as probes in the inquiry phase. It strives for the same goals as technology probes without any development effort. In gadgile probing we select from "off-the-shelf" technologies with different interaction styles that can be added to explore the context of active mobile use.

To demonstrate the technique we use an example from running and biking there we got a good understanding of the challenges with mobile interactions in sports and inspiration for designing future technologies for that context. The second chapter covers related work in mobile interaction research, followed by a definition of gadgile probing in Sect. 3. A case study on how we used gadgile probing as technique to support the design for mobile interactions can be found in Sect. 4. We conclude with a discussion on gadgile probing in comparison to traditional contextual inquiry methods [3] and technology probes.

2 Mobile Interactions

In the era of the "selfie", self-tracking training sessions are measured by default. For exercises as well as at competitive levels, a variety of sensing devices are used. Data about the training session is automatically uploaded to online sport diaries to analyze performance and evaluate progress. The impact, on the other hand, of mobile devices on the athlete is poorly researched, in particular interactions with these devices during the workout.

The shift of computing interfaces from a desktop metaphor to the physical environment through mobile computing has been well documented [12]. Unlike the design of interaction techniques for desktop applications, the design of mobile interaction techniques has to address two complex contextual concerns [15]; the users need to maintain focus on navigating in the world around them and the physical context of the surrounding. The latter includes the change in noise levels, temperature or lighting to name a few. Marshall and Tennent [16] have revisited these concerns and highlight four challenges designing interactions for mobile devices: cognitive load, physical constraints, terrain and other people.

Many researchers have explored interaction with mobile devices in distracted contexts, such as driving [1] or walking [17] and noted that there is a trade-off between walking speed and target accuracy for mobile devices [2] as well as manipulating objects using touch is more cognitively demanding than traditional tactile buttons due to increased visual needs [18]. Eyes-free or even hands-free interaction techniques aim to handle these contextual concerns. Experiments in mobile interaction research have demonstrated that novel interaction paradigms based on sound and head gestures [15] or gestures with wearable objects [13] have the potential to address usability issues of interaction with mobile devices in vivacious situations. But such methods must be robust enough to allow inaccuracy in performing a task, and they must provide customized feedback on interaction status so that users can explicitly adjust their actions to compensate for errors [15].

While researchers have noted lower performance in distracted contexts and designed new interaction paradigms for mobile devices, we have not found distinct research connecting these findings to supporting interactions during physical activity such as running or biking.

3 Probing

Probes are not prototypes of new technology, rather they are tools to "find out about the unknown - to hopefully return with useful or interesting data" [11]. They should be used in early stages of projects to investigate new perspectives that can constrain and open future designs [11]. They have been describes as means to collect responses from people, supporting an ongoing dialogue between participants and designers [10]. On the one hand we can interpret probes as data collection tools, complementing contextual inquiries [4]. On the other hand we can interpret probes as participation, supporting reflection by users themselves as part of data acquisition. Participants take responsibility and control of what to do with the probes and what to share with the designers [4]. This combination of contextual and participatory design perspectives is one intriguing aspect of probing.

Since the introduction of cultural probes by Gaver et al. [7] many different types of probing have been developed. Graham and Rouncefield [10] provided an overview over the state of the art of probing. Technology probes are defined by Hutchinson et al. [11] as simple, flexible, adaptable technologies deployed with three goals in mind:

- Understanding the needs and desires of users in real-world setting
- Field-testing the technology
- Inspiring participants and researchers to think about future technology and its use.

Technology probing involves installing a technology into a real use context and observing how this technology is used over a period of time [11]. By this means designers must have an initial idea of what technology would be interesting to probe in the context. In [5] simple step counters are chosen as ready made technology probes to study teenagers motivation for exercising and to find out important lessons for the design of future devices. In [6] a technology probe is applied to measure and assess texting and updating functionality of situated displays. In [19] a mobile technology probe is designed to better understand if and when intimate couples desire to hold hands when apart. In each of these studies designers had assumptions about the design space and preferred technologies. In contrast gadgile probing allows designers to explore several technologies in a context before focusing on one specific technology probe.

3.1 Gadgile Probing

Gadgile probing is not interested in field-testing one technology. It aims to explore how different "off-the-shelf" technologies are used in a context, and how different interaction techniques perform. The outcome is a rich description of technology usage in a specific context providing designers with the needs and desires of users and inspiration for future technologies. Gadgile probing consists of two phases: a technology review phase resulting in a set of available technologies, and a probing phase, there technologies are used in context.

Technology Review. The first step for the designer is to obtain an overview of "off-the-shelf" technologies available for the area of interest. Interviewing area experts, a web search and a visit to the local electronic store can combined provide a good overview. In the second step the designer categorizes these technologies by interaction style. One representative technology for each category is chosen as gadgile probe.

Probing. The gadgile probes need to be integrated in the participants' natural environment. The participants are encouraged to try out the probes during their ordinary activities. An introduction to each probe may be given. Designers collect data during the probing through the logging functionality of the probe and field observations. In-depth interviews with the participants after the probing provide a platform to discuss participants' experiences and ideate about future technologies.

4   Case Study

We implemented gadgile probing to understand mobile technologies for outdoor sports. From the technology review we selected three sport devices with different interaction styles: a sport watch, a mobile phone and a sport visor. We met with a total of 8 participants for a typical training session. During the training the participants used the different technologies. Four of the participants tested the probes during biking and the other four during running. After each training session we conducted a 30 min interview with each participant to get feedback on their experiences with the probes as well as their thoughts on and ideas for mobile technologies. To document the gadgile probing we used activity logging on each probe, observation notes and recordings of the interviews.

4.1   Technology Review

In 2006, Nike introduced the Nike+[1] concept - with a special running app for the IPod[2] and a piezo-electric shoe pod. It was possible to measure pace and distance and transmit this data directly to a web platform [23]. Previously athletes used specially designed sport devices such as sport watches or bike computers for monitoring their training. In recent years the use of mobile phones for physical activity has become popular. In 2014 the fastest growing app category in the Google Play Store[3] has been health and fitness, with 100 000 mobile health apps available for Android. Several research prototypes [14, 20] for mobile devices have been developed for investigating the effects of mobile devices on exercise motivation, obesity prevention, and on users

---

[1]   http://nikeplus.nike.com.

[2]   http://www.apple.com/ipod/.

[3]   https://play.google.com.

overall fitness. These sport applications operate mainly as digital training diaries collecting performance data on the way, using multiple sensors such as GPS, heart-rate monitors, and pedometers. They support four essential training functions: performance feedback, navigational means, competition, and entertainment [14]. Before exercising a sport setting must be chosen in the application. Performance feedback is given visually and as audio [14, 20, 21] directly at the mobile device, forcing the athlete to interact with the device during exercising.

In our case study we explore three different mobile devices: mobile phone, sport watch and sport visor (Fig. 1). We categorized the devices in three different design dimensions; the multi-purpose mobile phone, the traditional and convenient wristwatch, and the fully immersive heads up display.

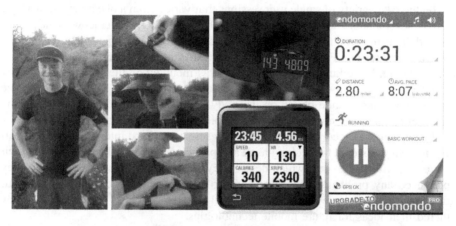

Fig. 1. Placement and interface of sport clock, sport visor and mobile phone

Multi-purpose Mobile Phone. The Sony Ericsson[4] Xperia active is built for an active lifestyle and outdoor sports. It can communicate with sport accessories and is waterproof. Endomondo[5] was chosen as tracking application from a list of most popular sport applications. The user interface presents three fields for workout data, information about workout and sport type and a big button to toggle tracking. In the top bar two more icons for music and volume are visible. During the workout the user needs to toggle the button to start, pause, resume and stop the workout.

Traditional and Convenient Sport Watch. The Motorola Motoactv[6] combines GPS watch, fitness tracker, and music player. The watch has a touch-sensitive screen and connects to several sport accessories. The user interface displays 6 different workout values (time, distance, speed, heart rate, calories and steps). At the bottom four short lines indicate hidden screens. The user can change the interface by swiping or pressing on the

---

[4] http://www.sonymobile.com/.

[5] https://www.endomondo.com.

[6] https://motoactv.com.

screen. To start, pause, resume and stop the workout the user needs to press one of the tactile buttons on the side of the watch or the back button on the bottom of the display.

Fully Immersive Sport Visor. The Osynce Screeneye X[7] sports visor is an innovative heads up display that presents training data in the user's field of vision. It can communicate with sport accessories. The display presents two out of 5 different workout features (time, distance, heart rate, speed or temperature). To change the display feature the user has to press one of three tactile buttons on top of the visor. The other buttons are used to start and stop the workout.

4.2 Deployment

We conducted a variety of single user sessions that varied from a one hour run to a bike ride over several hours, to provide participants the possibility to interact with the probes during their natural training. Participants used the probes an equal amount of time during their exercising. Four of the participants tested the probes during biking and four during running. For biking the mobile phone was mounted on the bike handlebar. For running we provided a mobile phone arm strap, but it was the participants' choice where to place the mobile phone on the body. The sport visor did not fit under the biking helmet and was not evaluated during biking to avoid safety risks.

The probing was accompanied by a 30 min semi-structured interview. The first part of the interview covered the probing itself and participants were asked to report on their experiences with the probes, which device they preferred and why, as well as if they experienced any problems. The second part of the interview focused on their motivation for using mobile devices during physical activity. The third part of the interview gathered their ideas for future mobile technologies.

4.3 Findings

The study was conducted during a two-month period. We recruited participants from local sport clubs in Norway and Sweden. A total of 8 athletes (6 male and 2 female) between the age of 27 and 49 participated in the study. All of them own a mobile phone with a touch sensitive screen that they have used for training at least once before. Table 1 presents an overview of the probing sessions. More than 300 min of interview material were collected and analyzed. The results were categorized in contextual findings, technology evaluation and design inspiration.

Contextual Findings. We conducted gadgile probing in natural training settings. Observations, activity logs and interviews with the participants were analyzed and consolidated using open coding alike contextual inquiry process [3]. Two major themes advanced from the analysis: participants' need for self-tracking technologies, and participants' strategies to minimize interactions with technologies during training sessions.

---

[7] http://www.o-synce.com/.

Table 1. Probing activity per participant

R1	Trail running, switching devices after 4 km lap
R2	Trail running, switching devices after 4 km lap
R3	Long distance run, switching devices after 30 min
R4	Interval run, switching devices after three intervals
C1	Tempo bike ride, switching devices after 10 km lap
C2	Tempo bike ride, switching devices after 10 km lap
C3	2-day long distance bike ride, 100 km per day and device
C4	2-day long distance bike ride, 100 km per day and device

Self-tracking Phenomenon. The possibility for self-tracking provided by many mobile devices creates a need to record many aspects of our lives. This study endorses this need; tracking and analyzing physical activity is as important as performing the activity. 6 out of 8 participants record their training using a mobile device and upload the collected data to online services afterwards. They relive their workout as a track on a map or a diagram presenting different performance aspects. The recorded data becomes an affirmation of their training.

Minimal Interactions. Participants' interaction with the devices during physical activity was very sparse. Mobile devices were used as passive means of logging, with predefined feedback intervals or automatic coaching settings. Even though participants are interested in feedback on demand such as current pace, time, distance and heart rate, they felt that interacting with all three devices were distracting. They had to slow down or even stop to get visual feedback and audio feedback was often misunderstood due to surrounding noise such as wind and traffic.

Technology Evaluation. Participants were eager to try out exercising with sport visor, sport clock and mobile phone. They had no ownership of any of the three devices, allowing them to critique and compare their features more liberally. They reported on functionality, usability and wearability during their workout, supported by previous research [9].

Functionality. All three devices provide similar functionalities such as start, stop, pause and resume a workout recording and getting feedback on time, pace, distance and heart rate. Participants were satisfied with the functionalities and had no problems understanding the different feedback modes.

Usability. All three devices had usability issues. The sport watch was the easiest to use, but the small text on the display was hard to read for some participants. Participants only used the start, stop and lap button on the watch; these interactions needed one tactile button press. During running the phone was setup with automatic audio interval feedback. Participants had to stop running to actively interact with the device and visual feedback was not available due to the placement on the upper arm or in the back pocket. The phone mounted on the handlebar was preferred for biking, providing good visual feedback with a large display and easy access to the touchscreen. The visor gave visual feedback in the field of sight, however participants felt it was hard to see the display when trail running. Changing the display using the buttons on top of the visor was experienced as uncomfortable.

Placement. All participants favored both the visor and the watch placement during running. The mobile phone was experienced as uncomfortable and unreachable for running. For biking the participants preferred the mobile phone placed on the handlebar. The visor did not fit under the helmet and could not be used. The watch on the wrist was hard to interact with during biking.

Design Inspiration. The introduction of the probes enabled participants to think about future technologies. One participant was asking for a voice-controlled small earpiece, a digital coach hidden in his ear. Another participant got inspired by the visor and wanted a similar display integrated into his bicycle helmet. Participants were focused on two main requirements: easier and more reachable input mechanisms and better visual feedback. At the same time the device should not bother during the activity.

The outcome from design inspiration was a simple decision framework with three dimensions: *placement, feedback* and *interaction*. The form factors of the device dictate its placement during the activity. Heavy and large devices should be placed on non-moving parts of the body. Smaller and lighter devices can be placed more freely. Thorough research about placement of wearables can be found in [9]. Visual feedback is preferred by participants, providing information at a glance, but is dependent on device placement. If the device screen is visible, feedback can be given on the device. If the device is placed out of sight during the activity, feedback should be given using a feedback accessory. Interaction is dependent on device placement. If the device is reachable, users can interact directly with the device. If the device is not reachable, an interaction accessory is needed. The use of accessories to enhance device functionality such as heart rate monitor, GPS or foot pod is common in sports. We propose that interaction and feedback with devices could be built on accessories as well.

5   Discussion

Gadgile probing is inspired by and based on contextual inquiry; an interview method to obtain information about the context of use well established in interaction design research. A contextual interviewer observes a user in context as she performs an activity and inquires into the user's actions as they unfold to understand her motivations and strategy. The interviewer and user develop a common understanding of the situation [3]. Active inquiry into the user's world is crucial for the complex nature of mobile context. Contextual inquiry is implemented successfully in numerous workplace situations [22] but there are limitations for mobile context such as outdoor sports.

Observations and inquiries during the activity can be difficult to perform with the user on the move. The interviewer needs to engage in the physical activity and at the same time observe and interview the user. Contextual inquiry enables designers to collect information about the current use situation and associated problems. Visioning possible solutions is detached from the inquiry and depending on the designers' ability to envision future usage. Designing for mobile interaction requires a good understanding of feasible interaction techniques for the context, something that is not explored during the inquiry process.

Probes used as tools for data collection can resolve these challenges and provide a holistic understanding of the context [4]. We designed gadgile probing to enhance the inquiry process. Probes collect usage data on the fly, complementing observations with additional information about use. Gadgile probing introduces different technologies into the inquiry process to collect information about potential new applications and resulting interactions. The findings inform the designer about the feasibility of different interaction techniques. User and designer can compare different technologies and ideate about future solutions, providing valuable input to the visioning process.

Gadgile probing and technology probing have common goals, but are deployed differently. Gadgile probing explores several technologies during an inquiry to compare these technologies and limit the design space. The gadgile probes are "off-the-shelf" technologies selected from a technology review. In contrast, technology probing involves installing one particular technology into a real use context and observing how this technology is used over a period of time [11]. The designer must have an underlying understanding of the context to select which technology to use as a probe and adaption to the context might be necessary. We understand technology probes as a successive step to gadgile probing, a second iteration in the design process to investigate one promising technology in more detail.

6   Conclusion

Designing for mobile interactions is challenging. Designers must understand the multidimensional nature of the mobile context and require an overview of interaction techniques feasible for that context. Established methods in interaction design such as contextual inquiry or technology probing have limitations for mobile context. In this paper we demonstrated gadgile probing as a possible alternative supporting design of active mobile interactions. Introducing "off-the-shelf" technology in the inquiry phase enabled us to explore not only *what is* but also *what could be* early in the design process. We showed an example from running and biking. Our findings demonstrate that gadgile probing can add benefits of probing to traditional contextual inquiry. We generated a good understanding of the context, listed needs and desires of participants, evaluated alternative interaction styles, and inspired designers and participants to ideate about future technologies. Gadgile probing supports a holistic understanding of active mobile interactions. We invite the interaction design community to critically evaluate gadgile probing in future mobile interaction projects.

References

1. Bach, K.M., et al.: You can touch, but you can't look: interacting with in-vehicle systems. In: Proceedings of the SIGCHI Conference on Human Factors in Computing Systems, pp. 1139–1148. ACM, New York (2008)

2. Bergstrom-Lehtovirta, J., et al.: The effects of walking speed on target acquisition on a touchscreen interface. In: Proceedings of the 13th International Conference on Human Computer Interaction with Mobile Devices and Services, pp. 143–146. ACM, New York (2011)
3. Beyer, H., Holtzblatt, K.: Contextual Design: Defining Customer-Centered Systems. Elsevier, Amsterdam (1997)
4. Boehner, K., et al.: How HCI interprets the probes. In: Proceedings of the SIGCHI Conference on Human Factors in Computing Systems, pp. 1077–1086. ACM, New York (2007)
5. Edwards, H.M., et al.: Exploring teenagers' motivation to exercise through technology probes. In: Proceedings of the 25th BCS Conference on Human-Computer Interaction, pp. 104–113. British Computer Society, Swinton (2011)
6. Fitton, D., et al.: Probing technology with technology probes. In: Equator Workshop on Record and Replay Technologies (2004)
7. Gaver, B., et al.: Design: cultural probes. Interactions 6(1), 21–29 (1999)
8. Gaver, W.W., et al.: Cultural probes and the value of uncertainty. Interactions 11(5), 53–56 (2004)
9. Gemperle, F., et al.: Design for wearability. In: Proceedings of the 2nd IEEE International Symposium on Wearable Computers, p. 116. IEEE Computer Society, Washington (1998)
10. Graham, C., Rouncefield, M.: Probes and participation. In: Proceedings of the Tenth Anniversary Conference on Participatory Design 2008, pp. 194–197. Indiana University, Indianapolis (2008)
11. Hutchinson, H., et al.: Technology probes: inspiring design for and with families. In: Proceedings of the SIGCHI Conference on Human Factors in Computing Systems, pp. 17–24. ACM, New York (2003)
12. Ishii, H., Ullmer, B.: Tangible bits: towards seamless interfaces between people, bits and atoms. In: Proceedings of the ACM SIGCHI Conference on Human Factors in Computing Systems, pp. 234–241. ACM, New York (1997)
13. Kim, K., et al.: Wearable-object-based interaction for a mobile audio device. In: CHI 2010 Extended Abstracts on Human Factors in Computing Systems, pp. 3865–3870. ACM, New York (2010)
14. Kurdyukova, E.: Inspire, guide, and entertain: designing a mobile assistant for runners. In: Proceedings of the 11th International Conference on Human-Computer Interaction with Mobile Devices and Services, pp. 75:1–75:2. ACM, New York (2009)
15. Lumsden, J., Brewster, S.: A paradigm shift: alternative interaction techniques for use with mobile & wearable devices. In: Proceedings of the 2003 Conference of the Centre for Advanced Studies on Collaborative Research, pp. 197–210. IBM Press, Toronto (2003)
16. Marshall, J., Tennent, P.: Mobile interaction does not exist. In: CHI 2013 Extended Abstracts on Human Factors in Computing Systems, pp. 2069–2078. ACM, New York (2013)
17. Negulescu, M., et al.: Tap, swipe, or move: attentional demands for distracted smartphone input. In: Proceedings of the International Working Conference on Advanced Visual Interfaces, pp. 173–180. ACM, New York (2012)
18. Noy, Y.I., et al.: Task interruptability and duration as measures of visual distraction. Appl. Ergon. 35(3), 207–213 (2004)
19. O'Brien, S., Mueller, F.: "Floyd": holding hands over a distance: technology probes in an intimate, mobile context. In: Proceedings of the 18th Australia Conference on Computer-Human Interaction: Design: Activities, Artefacts and Environments, pp. 293–296. ACM, New York (2006)

20. De Oliveira, R., Oliver, N.: TripleBeat: enhancing exercise performance with persuasion. In: Proceedings of the 10th International Conference on Human Computer Interaction with Mobile Devices and Services, pp. 255–264. ACM, New York (2008)
21. Preuschl, E., et al.: Mobile motion advisor — a feedback system for physical exercise in schools. Procedia Eng. 2(2), 2741–2747 (2010)
22. Raven, M.E., Flanders, A.: Using contextual inquiry to learn about your audiences. SIGDOC Asterisk J. Comput. Doc. 20(1), 1–13 (1996)
23. Saponas, T.S., et al.: Devices that tell on you: The nike+ipod sport kit (2006)

Building Design Scenarios the Way Life Is Lived: The Contextual-Scenario Toolkit

Eric H. Swanson[✉]

Swanson Research, Wheaton, IL, USA
Eric@DrSwanson.design

Abstract. Designers use two types of fictions to prototype the future: Design Fiction, addressing the long-term future, and design scenarios, addressing the more immediate. Design-Fiction writers ground their work in sophisticated story worlds, where every element is contextually consistent with every other. This paper describes a related model of grounding for design scenarios: building scenarios the way life is lived. In this model, every scenario character becomes grounded within their subjective point of view, their own thoughts and perceptions, accessible only to themselves (and the author). Events occur in chronological order. Scenario authors generate contextual consistency using their inherent human capacity for narrative sense-making. Scenario building would be more turn-based tabletop simulation than writing. We have developed this model into the Contextual Scenario Toolkit (CSTK) system. A validation study demonstrates the CSTK's ability to increase attention to character's subjective worlds, to prevent loss of peripheral characters, and to reduce certain kinds of bias.

Keywords: Scenarios · Scenario-based design · Design fiction · Narrative · Narrative theory · Subjectivity · Contextual-scenario platform

1 Introduction

In design, two types of fictions are used as prototypes of the future: Design Fictions for the long-term future and design scenarios for the more immediate. Design Fictions are carefully constructed narratives, often written more like science fiction than scenarios [1], in which some design idea is addressed as a "diegetic prototype". A diegetic prototype occurs within a narrative that remains truthful to its own story world (its diegesis); it is "situated by proxy" [9, p. 7].

Our ability to tell whether a story is true to itself is a powerful feature of our minds—but one so fundamental it is often also invisible: narrative as a means to make sense of the world [3]. This form is so familiar and ubiquitous "... that it is likely to be overlooked, in much the same way as we suppose that the fish will be the last to discover water" [3, p. 4]. When we see intentional behavior, or behavior we perceive to be intentional, we try to understand it by organizing it into a kind of story [16]. As with design fictions, truthfulness for narrative as sense-making may be judged by verisimilitude [3], whether it "feels" real.

© Springer International Publishing Switzerland 2016
A. Marcus (Ed.): DUXU 2016, Part I, LNCS 9746, pp. 344–355, 2016.
DOI: 10.1007/978-3-319-40409-7_33

1.1 Sense-Making with Narrative—Fictions and Scenarios

The differences between Design Fiction and design scenarios echo the differences between uses of "Narrative". Unlike Design Fictions, according to Blythe [2, p. 4], "most design scenarios are written in the present tense" and "...scenarios do not end, rather, they stop, they are not resolved". These two features could also describe lived experience. Life occurs in present tense. While it has an obvious beginning, life is awash in simultaneous middles, resolutions, and new beginnings. And, like design scenarios, at some point life just stops.

1.2 Situatedness at Multiple Levels

If design scenarios echo the patterns of life, why are they so rarely life-like? Scenario writers rarely give full attention to all the levels at which life is situated. Our lived experience can be considered situated at three levels. Most broadly, it is situated in the world of societies, of governments, of social groups, societal change and geographic boundaries—a special focus of Design Fiction. More narrowly, circumstances situate each person: where they are, who they are with, what they are doing and so on—a world of mostly outside cause and outside effect. Design scenarios often live at this level.

At the third and deepest level, each individual conscious being is situated in their own personal universe. This universe is both subjective and embodied [13]. It is inescapably bound to a point of view [4]. It operates at the pace of human events [3]. It is, phenomenologically, entirely owned by the individual and inaccessible to those outside [13]. It is the realm of skilled crafters of fiction [1] and of Method actors [6,10]. It is life told in first-person.

1.3 Better Scenarios Through Better Situatedness

What could be gained by building scenarios situated in the manner that life is lived? A scenario author could be restricted to the same knowledge and situational limitations as the scenario characters themselves. Such restrictions may force more serious attention to the lived world of their characters.

A second benefit relates to the growing adoption of "Third Paradigm" approaches [8] for design. Such approaches have increased the tools available working with situated experience. Methods like Design Ethnography, Participatory Design and Cultural Probes generate findings at the circumstance and subjectivity levels. However, it has been difficult to integrate findings from these situated methods into design [5]. A focus on situatedness within scenarios could provide hooks to link situated findings with the work of design.

Scenario Challenges. As basic as our ability to understand narrative is, it is difficult to write coherent design stories without methodological support [11]. A fantasized scenario can have the same influence as one that is rigorously built [12]. It is all too easy to tweak the world of the story to promote any feature

[6], or to make bad ideas appear to work [18]. Rigor in construction would keep scenarios sturdy, rather than malleable.

Rigorous attention to characters' point-of-view worlds would limit the creation of thin characters, such as stereotypes [18], or fantasy users, whose needs perfectly match a product offering [12]. Indirect Stakeholders, not directly affected by the object of interest, can become so thin that they disappear [14].

Lastly, authors can fall into habits of bias. One of the most common of biases is that towards the happy design ending—where the technology is used as designed and the users are depicted in a positive light [14]. Such biases can mislead when working with situations with high emotions or major risks.

Personas are an existing approach to situating characters in their worlds at multiple levels. They are hypothetical archetypes of actual users [7], built from a rigorous linkage to original research. Given their potential to situate characters, we have incorporated researched-based personas into our testing protocol.

1.4   Criteria for a System

This research proposes a design-scenario-support tool for building scenarios with profoundly-situated characters. Scenarios would be not so much written as constructed, so that the builder's view of the world becomes limited to that of the scenario's characters. Such a tool should:

- create moments in character-perceived order of occurrence;
- force scenario builders to attend to each character's point-of-view during every moment;
- insulate each character's subjective world from that of every other;
- provide character detail beyond that within the scenario text;
- and provide hooks to integrate findings from situated research methods.

2   The Contextual-Scenario Toolkit (CSTK)

For this study, we developed a working prototype of a system to fulfill these criteria—the *Contextual–Scenario Toolkit (CSTK)*. This extends the prior work of Swanson *et. al.* on the Contextual-Scenario Platform [19–21].

2.1   Mechanisms of the Contextual-Scenario Toolkit

The CSTK employs three Point-of-View (PoV) mechanisms to meet these criteria: *PoV Encoding, PoV Forcing,* and *Dynamic PoV Recall*. All three mechanisms share a semantic structure: the *Situational Index*.

PoV Encoding with the CSTK. In linking findings from situated research to Characters within Scenarios,[1] the CSTK must overcome a clash in levels of abstraction. Empirical findings are generalized, but Scenarios are specific. A research finding would not refer to Neurosurgeon Donna, but rather to the class "Neurosurgeon", while the Scenario would refer to the specific person *Donna*.

The *Situational Index* addresses this clash. A Situational Index specifies a situation from an individual's point of view. For findings, the individual is hypothetical; for Scenarios, the individual is specific. For a Character, a Situational Index enumerates circumstances for *this specific* Character in *this specific* moment of *this specific* Scenario. For research findings, a Situational Index specifies only those features needed for the finding to apply for *to-be-determined* individuals, in *to-be-determined* moments of *to-be-determined* scenarios.

Each Situational Index is an unordered list of situational features—its *Situation Components (SiC)*. A SiC specifies a relationship between an individual and some element of a situation. This empirical finding will serve to demonstrate: *When a Physician is working with an Electronic Medical Record (EMR) while interacting with a patient, the EMR may lure the Physician's attention away from the patient* [15,17].

First, those entities that must be present for the finding to apply are identified. These are *Situation Elements* (Table 1, middle). They are always nouns ('stethoscope'), but not always tangible ('state of sleep deprivation').

Table 1. Elements of a *subjective finding*

Situational Index (aggregated *Situation Components*)

Person-Element Relation	Situation Element	Subjective Attribute
⟨is embodying⟩ Med Provider: Physician		...may direct attention towards the EMR and away from the patient.
⟨is operating⟩ Electronic Medical Record		
⟨is interacting with⟩ Patient		

However, a Situation Element embodies no point of view. To complete the Situation Component, each Situation Element must bear some relationship to the *to-be-determined* individual. In the example, the finding describes a feature of the physician's experience, so the point of view must be a physician's. *Person–Element Relations (PERs)* specify such points of view. A PER is a relationship between an individual and a situation element ('⟨ *is operating* ⟩' [object], '⟨ *is embodying* ⟩' [individual role]) Table 1, left).

Aggregating multiple SiCs generates increasing precision: '⟨ *is embodying* ⟩ Med Provider: Physician' plus '⟨ *is operating* ⟩ Electronic Medical Record' plus '⟨ *is interacting with* ⟩ Patient.' This aggregation becomes the Situational Index.

---

[1] Because 'Scenario' and 'Character' are both data types within the CSTK, both terms will be capitalized where discussed in reference to the software, and uncapitalized in non-specific references.

To complete this encoding of the *Subjective Finding*, the Situational Index is associated with the research finding's point-of-view-related content. This content is the finding's *Subjective Attribute*—its specific change in, or establishment of, human actors' thinking, feeling, perception, or inclination towards action.

PoV Forcing with the CSTK. The CSTK forces builders to attend to point of view through the mechanism of cycles-within-a-cycle. This makes building a Scenario using the CSTK more a turn-based tabletop simulation than an act of writing. Each Scenario Moment is a "turn", and, within each turn, each *Scenario Character* twice has the builder's sole attention. After the opening moment, each turn has three cycles. Most broad is the Moment-to-Moment cycle, which encompasses the other two cycles: one addressing Characters' *Thoughts*; the other, their *Situational Indexes*.

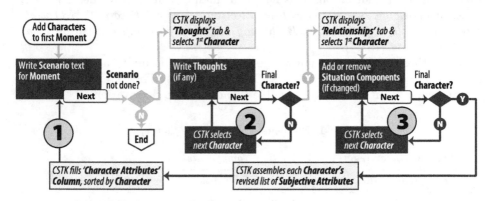

Fig. 1. CSTK Scenario-Building Flow Chart, Showing the Three Cycles: (1) Moment-to-Moment Events (2) Character-by-Character Thoughts and (3) Character-by-Character Situational Indexes.

In the CSTK, the three cycles (Fig. 1, '1', '2' and '3') occur over four stages:

1. Write text for the Scenario's current Moment, based on each Character's Thoughts and CSTK-built attribute lists (start of Cycle 1).
2. Specify the *Thoughts* Character A would have during the event (if any). Repeat for Character B, then C, and so on (Cycle 2).
3. Modify Character A's *Situational Index* based on any changes generated by the event in stage 1. Repeat for Character B, then C, and so on (Cycle 3).
4. Move on to the next Moment (begin new round of Cycle 1).

The first step is the writing of an *Episodic Moment* in the 'What Happened' tab ('1' in Figs. 1 and 2). Each Episodic Moment contains only one change meaningful in the Characters' worlds, though it may contain many sentences. Such changes could include action, shifts in mood, and Characters' entrances or exits.

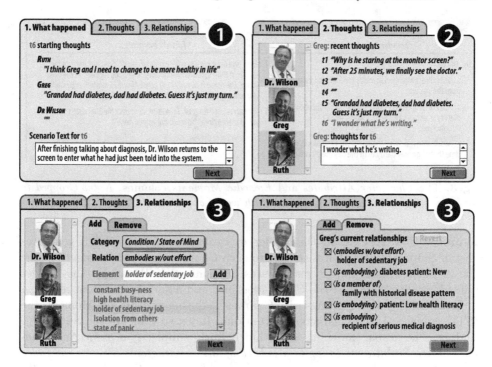

Fig. 2. *What Happened* (1) and *Thoughts* (2) tabs, and both *Relationship* sub-tabs (3). *Note: interfaces simplified for legibility. In the CSTK interface, the "Remove" sub-tab is spacious enough to display a Character's entire set of Situation Components.*

The Episodic Moment text remains visible as the last entry in the CSTK interface's 'Episodic Moments' column (Fig. 3, right).

Clicking *Next* brings up the *Thoughts* tab (Fig. 2, "2"), with the CSTK starting the 'Thoughts' Sub-cycle by selecting the topmost Character of the Character List. The 'Thoughts' tab includes the most recent items from the selected Character's train of thought, forcing the builder to attend to the Character's evolving inner world. Clicking *Next* advances one Character per click, until no untouched Characters remain.

With no untouched Characters left, clicking *Next* advances to the 'Relationships' tab (Fig. 2, bottom left and right). As with 'Thoughts', the CSTK starts the 'Situational Index' Sub-cycle by selecting the topmost Character. Here, the Scenario builder adds new (Fig. 2, bottom left) or removes existing (Fig. 2, bottom right) Situation Components until the Situational Index once again fully describes the Character's situation. This Sub-cycle forces builders to attend to Character's PoV worlds a second time. Again, clicking *Next* advances one Character per click, until no untouched Characters remain.

One last click of *Next* begins a new round of the Moment-to-Moment Cycle. In the split-second before the new Episodic Moment appears, the CSTK hooks empirical findings to Characters through the work of *Dynamic PoV Recall*.

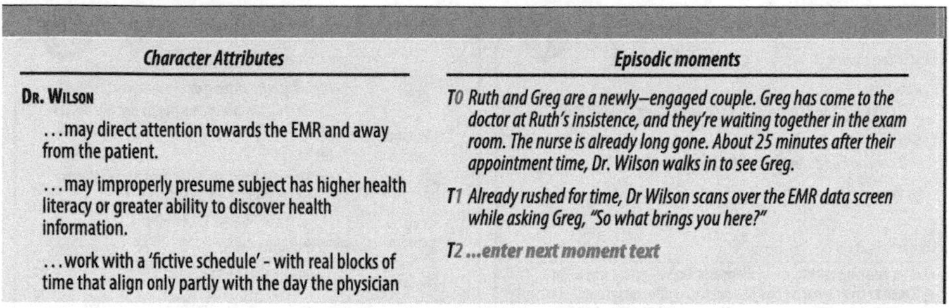

Character Attributes	Episodic moments
DR. WILSON . . . may direct attention towards the EMR and away from the patient. . . . may improperly presume subject has higher health literacy or greater ability to discover health information. . . . work with a 'fictive schedule' - with real blocks of time that align only partly with the day the physician	T0 Ruth and Greg are a newly–engaged couple. Greg has come to the doctor at Ruth's insistence, and they're waiting together in the exam room. The nurse is already long gone. About 25 minutes after their appointment time, Dr. Wilson walks in to see Greg. T1 Already rushed for time, Dr Wilson scans over the EMR data screen while asking Greg, "So what brings you here?" T2 . . . enter next moment text

Fig. 3. The *Character Attributes* and *Episodic Moments* columns. *Note: Cropped to conserve space; attributes for Greg and Ruth would appear in the full-scale interface*

Dynamic PoV Recall. As the builder creates a Scenario, the CSTK generates a list of Subjective Attributes specific to each Character in each moment of time (Fig. 3, left). This is how it instantiates Dynamic PoV Recall; as the builder builds Episodic Moments, the CSTK identifies and associates relevant findings.

To link Subjective Findings with Characters during an Episodic Moment, the CSTK compares each Character's Situational Index to that of each Subjective Finding. The actual matching algorithm is fairly simple: *If a Subjective Finding's entire Situational Index is a subset of this Character's Situational Index during this Episodic Moment, this Finding will apply to this Character in the next Episodic Moment.*

Table 2, below, illustrates how the CSTK matches Subjective Findings to Characters. On the left is a Subjective Finding with its entire Situational Index: three Situation Components. On the right is Dr. Wilson's Situational Index corresponding to Episodic Moment in the example Scenario (T1 in Fig. 3), which includes Situation Components carried over from prior moments. Here, the CSTK has matched every Situation Component from the Subjective Finding with a corresponding one from Dr. Wilson's Situational Index. Thus, the CSTK determined that this Finding will apply to Dr. Wilson at the start of the next Scenario Moment, T2. It adds the Subjective Attribute text from the Finding to Dr. Wilson's portion of the list of Subjective Attributes (Fig. 3, left).

3   The Study

Our validation study using the CSTK tested three hypotheses: (1) The CSTK functions as designed, increasing consistency of attention to PoV experience. (2) The CSTK counters design-scenario weaknesses by improving the consideration of non-central characters. (3) The CSTK counters design-scenario weaknesses by reducing bias in scenario-creation.

3.1   Study Design

This study used a mixed within- and across-subjects design. For within-subject validity, every participant created two scenarios. For the control "Traditional"

Table 2. Applying a subjective finding to a character in an episodic moment

Subjective Finding	Scenario Episodic Moment
. . . *may direct attention towards the EMR and away from the patient.*	*Already rushed for time, Dr. Wilson scans over the EMR data screen while asking Greg, "So what brings you here?"*
	. . . *prior Situation Components. . .*
⟨ is embodying ⟩ Med Provider: Physician =	⟨ is embodying ⟩ Med Provider: Physician
	⟨ embodies w/out effort ⟩ Time pressure
⟨ is operating ⟩ Electronic Medical Record =	⟨ is operating ⟩ Electronic Medical Record
⟨ is interacting with ⟩ Patient =	⟨ is interacting with ⟩ Patient

test, each participant created a scenario using their preferred scenario-building technique. For the experimental "CSTK" test, participants created a Scenario entirely within the CSTK. Both tests were set up identically, with one exception. For the CSTK test, encoded into the CSTK were a set of findings from prior empirical research and a set of features for each persona (which duplicated content of the persona narrative booklets available for all tests). For the control test, the empirical findings were written as natural-language sentences and organized into paper-based tables.

Several items were present for both test conditions: (1) One of two scenario set-ups, consisting of the scenario's opening sentences; (2) persona booklets for each character within the scenario; (3) a master instruction sheet, describing the design-practice situation they were to emulate (writing a realistic scenario to understand how a new tool might work in practice); (4) an illustration of the new tool (an Electronic Medical Record display on highly-flexible iPad mount, to be used in a Physician's exam room); and (5) a Use Case specifying interactions for successful use of the system.

The personas were derived from empirical primary or secondary research. Three characters, Greg, Ruth and Karen, were drawn from primary research which used Design Ethnography and other situated methods. The fourth character, Dr. Wilson, was drawn from secondary research.

For the CSTK and Traditional tests, participants built scenarios starting from two different set-ups: *Alpha* and *Beta*. Both describe the start of a medical visit, in a situation with potential for strong emotional experiences.

Study Procedure. Every session started with a brief presentation exploring subjective experience in relation to design, to counteract the CSTK's structural emphasis on subjectivity.

Half of the participants began by creating a Traditional scenario; the rest, a CSTK Scenario. Likewise, half started with *Alpha*, the rest, *Beta*. This combination produced four patterns: Traditional–Alpha followed by CSTK–Beta; CSTK–Alpha then Traditional–Beta; Traditional–Beta then CSTK–alpha, and

CSTK–Beta then Traditional–Alpha. Eight participants were recruited to ensure coverage of all combinations twice. Participants were drawn from the student population of a Midwestern graduate school of design. They were recruited to two cohorts: a low-experience cohort, with three or fewer years of professional design experience ($n = 4$), and a high-experience cohort, with six or more years of experience ($n = 4$).

Immediately prior to working with the CSTK, participants stepped through a 10- to 15-min tutorial using the CSTK. Upon completion of each scenario, participants filled out a set of Likert scales, then reviewed their scenario with the proctor. The session ended with a semi-structured interview, focused on the participant's comparative experiences with the two scenarios.

3.2 Results

To enable cross-scenario comparison, each participant-generated scenario was divided into "narrative events". A narrative event is a change meaningful to a scenario's characters, and could be one or more sentences. This averaged to more than one narrative event per Traditional paragraph or CSTK Episodic Moment.

Table 3. Frequency-of-Occurrence Tables. *Left:* Narrative Events with Point-of-View content ('P') vs. without ('.'). *Right:* Narrative Events with Ruth ('R') vs. without ('.')

Traditional Method		CSTK	Traditional Method	
.P...P.P...P..P.P..P.PP	*p1*	PP..PPP.PPP.PP.P.	*p1*	.R.RR.........RR.RRRR
.PP...PP..P.P.	*p2*	PP.PPPPP..P	*p4*	.RR..R.......R
.P...P............P..	*p3*	PPP..PP	*p5*	.RR...........
.PP..PP.PP.P.PP	*p4*	.PPPP.PPPPP	*p8*	.RR.R...R.
..P.PP..PPP.PP	*p5*	PPPP.P		
......PPP.P.P..PP	*p6*	.PPPP.P.PP....		*CSTK*
.PPP.PP..	*p8*	PP..PPPP.P.P	*p2*	RR...R..RR..R
....	*p9*	PPP.PP..P.	*p3*	R.R.R.R
			p6	.RRR.RRR...R.
			p9	.RR.R...R

Did Scenario Builders Consistently Attend to PoV Experience? For this, narrative events counted only when a feature was mentioned exclusively from a character's *internal* point-of-view, such as scenario-text descriptions of emotional states, thought bubbles, CSTK Thoughts, and CSTK Situation Components describing internal features.

Test results strongly supported this hypothesis. With the CSTK, Narrative Moments more frequently contained subjective content (69.1 %) than did those of Traditional scenarios (38.8 %, two sample t-test, $p<0.01$). All CSTK Scenarios had subjective content in >50 % of narrative moments (Table 3, left).

Did Builders Give Greater Consideration to Non-Central Characters?
Scenario Set-Up *Alpha* had been written to include an indirect stakeholder, Ruth.
Ruth, the fiancé of Dr. Wilson's patient, Greg, is neither the tool's direct operator
(Dr. Wilson), nor its subject of use (Greg). To quantify the degree of Ruth's
consideration by scenario builders, we measured the relative frequency of her
appearances in narrative moments, whether within the scenario text or through
changes to her state of mind.

Test results support this hypothesis. Narrative moments in CSTK Scenarios
mentioned Ruth more frequently (49.3%, two sample t-test, $p<0.05$) than Traditional ones (30.5%). Additionally, mentions of Ruth in Traditional scenarios
were uneven, clustering towards the start or end (Table 3, subtables on right),
while Ruth's mentions in CSTK Scenarios show greater consistency throughout.

Did Scenario Builders Show a Reduction in Bias? Scenario Set-Up was
written to include an emotional situation with a likely negative outcome. In Beta,
Karen, both a mother and a caregiver to her disabled husband, visits Dr. Wilson
with symptoms of probable skin cancer. Scenarios displaying a positive-outcome
bias would conclude with a happy or neutral ending. Scenarios not displaying

Table 4. Karen end-states *('PR': Problem Resolved; 'AAR': Anxious, Awaiting
Results; 'CI': Confused and Irritated)*

Traditional		
	End	Scenario-end text
p2	PR	She feels relieved at having come to the doctor and found that nothing major was wrong.
p3	AAR	She anxiously waits for results, dismissing [the Doctor's] preachiness. (Searches online for support groups).
p6	CI	[storyboard image] Doctor documenting notes. [Dr. Speech bubble] *"Any questions?"* [Storyboard Image] [Karen thought bubble] *"..."*
p9	PR	[Doctor] comforts her that it is not a major problem.
CSTK		
	End	Scenario-end text
p1	AAR	Karen: *"A biopsy just makes it seem so real. ... I don't want to be here."*
p4	AAR	Karen is feeling completely overwhelmed by her diagnosis and is not sure she understands what Dr. Wilson just told her, feels exceptionally stressed out and wants to leave.
p5	AAR	Karen ⟨ is experiencing ⟩ anxiety. Karen: *"Hopefully I don't have that much to worry about that will take time away from my life."*
p8	AAR	He tries to convince Karen to keep positive until the results come out and explains that he cannot be sure of the likelihood of cancer. Though he'd like to comfort Karen, who appears to be in shock, he has to move on...

positive bias would likely conclude with Karen unhappy, nervous, or scared, and still awaiting testing results.

Test results strongly supported this hypothesis (Table 4). Among users of the Traditional Method, two (p2 and p9) tempered the emotions by simply fixing the medical issue. One (p6) focused on the minor nuisances of Karen's interaction with the software and irritation at the doctor's distraction. Only one (p3) faced Karen's more likely outcome: that she will leave the office anxious with questions unanswered (Table 4, top). Among users of the CSTK, however, all Scenarios (p1, p4, p5, p6) ended with Karen in a state of anxiety and waiting for another appointment. Only one (p5) had a sub-theme of nervous hope, but still retained Karen's anxiety and uncertainty (Table 4, bottom).

4 Conclusion

Section 1.3 asked, "What could be gained by building scenarios situated in the manner that life is lived?" To explore this idea, this research described the Contextual-Scenario Toolkit (CSTK), a tool for crafting design scenarios with profoundly-situated characters. As with Design Fiction, the goal of scenarios generated with the CSTK is a narrative that is true to its own story world. Unlike Design Fiction, the source of truth is not in the text, but in the process of building the scenario.

The study illustrated benefits of such rigor. With the CSTK, builders pay more consistent attention to subjective experience. Characters can retain their sense of self, even when they are only peripheral to the objects at the heart of the scenario. Biases can be fought, and scenario builders can surprise themselves.

There is much still to know. This research does not address feasibility of the CSTK in design practice. User experience with the CSTK needs further research; the study showed dramatically divergent experiences. Some participants felt like the tool was rigid, "like an auditor" (p4), where others found it to be generative, even improvisational: "I can actually imagine the whole thing unfolding in my mind". (p2)

References

1. Bleecker, J.: Design fiction: a short essay on design, science, fact and fiction. Near Future Laboratory 29 (2009)
2. Blythe, M.: Research through design fiction: narrative in real and imaginary abstracts. In: Proceedings of the SIGCHI Conference on Human Factors in Computing Systems, pp. 703–712. ACM (2014)
3. Bruner, J.: The narrative construction of reality. Crit. Inq. **18**(1), 1–21 (1991)
4. Davis, M.: Theoretical foundations for experiential systems design. In: ETP 2003, ACM SIGMM Workshop on Experiential Telepresence, pp. 45–52 (2003)
5. Dourish, P.: Implications for design. In: CHI 2006 Proceedings - Design: Creative & Historical Perspectives, pp. 541–550 (2006)
6. Grudin, J., Pruitt, J.: Personas, participatory design and product development: an infrastructure for engagement. In: Proceedings of PDC, pp. 144–161 (2002)

7. Guo, F.Y., Shamdasani, S., Randall, B.: Creating effective personas for product design: insights from a case study. In: Rau, P.L.P. (ed.) IDGD 2011. LNCS, vol. 6775, pp. 37–46. Springer, Heidelberg (2011)
8. Harrison, S., Tatar, D., Sengers, P.: The three paradigms of HCI. In: Alt. CHI Session at the SIGCHI Conference on Human Factors in Computing Systems. ACM, San Jose, California, USA (2007)
9. Lindley, J.: A pragmatics framework for design fiction. In: Proceedings of the European Academy of Design Conference (2015)
10. Lindley, J., Sharma, D., Potts, R.: Anticipatory ethnography: Design fiction as an input to design ethnography. In: Ethnographic Praxis in Industry Conference Proceedings. vol. 2014, pp. 237–253. Wiley Online Library (2014)
11. Madsen, S., Nielsen, L.: Exploring persona-scenarios - using storytelling to create design ideas. In: Katre, D., Orngreen, R., Yammiyavar, P., Clemmensen, T. (eds.) HWID 2009. IFIP AICT, vol. 316, pp. 57–66. Springer, Heidelberg (2010)
12. McInerney, P., Muller, M.J.: Scenarios in practice: Summary of a CHI 2003 workshop. Technical report RC22931 [W0310-047], IBM (2003)
13. Nagel, T.: What is it like to be a bat? Philos. Rev. **83**(4), 435–450 (1974)
14. Nathan, L.P., Friedman, B., Klasnja, P., Kane, S.K., Miller, J.K.: Envisioning systemic effects on persons and society throughout interactive system design. In: Proceedings of 7th ACM Conference on Designing Interactive Systems, pp. 1–10. ACM (2008)
15. O'Malley, A.S., Cohen, G.R., Grossman, J.M.: Electronic medical records and communication with patients and other clinicians: are we talking less? Issue brief Cent. Stud. Health Syst. Change **131**, 1–4 (2010)
16. Sengers, P.: Narrative intelligence. In: Dautenhahn, K. (ed.) Human Cognition and Social Agent Technology, pp. 1–26. John Benjamins Publishing Company (2000)
17. Shachak, A., Reis, S.: The impact of electronic medical records on patient-doctor communication during consultation: a narrative literature review. J. Eval. Clin. Pract. **15**(4), 641–649 (2009)
18. Suri, J.F., Marsh, M.: Scenario building as an ergonomics method in consumer product design. Appl. Ergon. **31**(2), 151–157 (2000)
19. Swanson, E., Sato, K.: Structuring for subjective experience: the contextual scenario framework. In: 45th Hawaii International Conference on System Science (HICSS), pp. 589–598, January 2012
20. Swanson, E.: The Contextual-Scenario Framework for Representing Subjective Experience. Ph.D. thesis, Institute of Design, Illinois Inst. of Tech., May 2013
21. Swanson, E., Sato, K., Gregory, J.: Exploring cultural context using the contextual scenario framework. In: Aykin, N. (ed.) IDGD 2009. LNCS, vol. 5623, pp. 117–126. Springer, Heidelberg (2009)

Conversion Method for User Experience Design Information and Software Requirement Specification

Ayumi Takeda[⊠] and Yosuke Hatakeyama

Interaction Initiative Inc., Tokyo, Japan
{ayumi.takeda,yosuke.hatakeyama}@interaction-i.co.jp

Abstract. In the era of the Internet of Things, system development is becoming increasingly complex and diverse due to the need for advanced user experience design (UXD) and cross-platform systems. However, current software requirement specification methods have no way to describe UXD. We propose a description method to reflect UXD information, such as user behavior, as UXD requirements.

Keywords: UX design · Software requirement specification · Scenario · UML

1 Introduction

1.1 Changes in System Structure

Obviously, software systems are changing in the current Internet of Things era. In the past, many systems have provided functionality for a single device. Such systems tend to be very simple; they provide basic functions tailored to customer requirements.

At present, a variety of devices such as smart phones and tablets have been invented. In current systems, multiple devices cooperate to provide users with more advanced solutions and experiences. Thus, the structure of such systems is more complex than single device systems, and the system requirements must describe the structure and behavior of the system as well as user experience (UX) design (UXD) information.

1.2 Problems in Current Development

However, system requirement specifications used in current development processes have two problems.

One problem is that current system requirements documents have no method to describe UXD requirements. Essentially, engineers implement a system following only the description in a specifications document, such as a system requirement. However, the UXD process does not connect directly to the system construction process. UX designers research user behavior and consider UXs using customer journey maps, scenarios, and personas, etc. These UX design methods have no common description method; thus, description rules differ for each designer or firm. Consequently, it is

© Springer International Publishing Switzerland 2016
A. Marcus (Ed.): DUXU 2016, Part I, LNCS 9746, pp. 356–364, 2016.
DOI: 10.1007/978-3-319-40409-7_34

difficult to reflect UXD information of a system. However, the importance of UXD information is increasing. Therefore, it is necessary to incorporate UXD information into system requirements to develop solutions that consider UX.

In addition, multi-device systems have problems relative to usability and UX. For a multi-device system, each device typically has access to all application functions. From a UXD perspective, we believe that each device and its functions should have a suitable combination of use cases depending on user circumstance and context, and the division of the function depending on device can reduce the development costs.

1.3 Hypothesis

We have found that there is a significant gap between UX designers and engineers. UX designers design a system by focusing on user behavior in a scenario. On the other hand, engineers focus on the data-flow model. Currently, no unified description method to connect the UX design process and data-flow construction exists. UX information and data-flow appear different; however, both describe the system from different perspectives. Thus, we suspect that UXD information and the system data model can be described using unified expressions, and if they have a common method, it is possible to connect the UX design and data modeling processes.

2 Methodology

2.1 Basic Idea

According to this hypothesis, we consider it necessary to develop a common description method to express and share both types of information throughout the entire development process.

In this paper, we have adopted Unified Modeling Language (UML) as the basis of our method because it is the most common language among software engineers. With the proposed method, UX designers can write UXD information using a definite description method and engineers can receive the information to build the system according to the documentation. In addition, by adopting UML, developers can use pre-established knowledge; thus, they do not need to spend time to study this method from the beginning. UML has definite description rules and simple expressions, which makes it easy to adopt into an actual development process.

2.2 Development of the Description Method

To adopt UML for this method, we first examined UML notation and definitions. The selected diagrams for this method are use case diagrams, activity diagrams, and state machine diagrams. In UML, the use case diagram describes the required usages of a system, the activity diagram shows the flow of execution, and the state machine diagram shows the behavior of a part of the system through state transitions. We considered whether it is possible to describe a system requirement that includes UXD information using these diagrams.

Then, we examined the meaning of each original UML notation. As indicated in Table 1, the meaning of these notations in software requirement specification (UML) can be used as UXD information, such as Scene, Action, and Flow. For example, the round-cornered rectangle expresses one scene, and the text inside the rectangle is a description of the action in the activity diagram. This is interpreted as certain clipped time range. Therefore, it is possible to describe UXD information using UML notation by reading the meaning of the official UML notation. For development of complete solutions with UX, system requirements should have detailed UXD information, such as frequency, importance, and user feeling, for each scene. The UXD information can be converted to actual system requirement design, including GUI design. The expression of these additional notations is extended from the official notation to maintain UML description rules.

Table 1. Correspondence between UXD information and SRS

UML Notation	Software Requirement Specification	UXD information
	Node	Scene: Clipped time range
State*	State	Action: User action in a scene
→*	Transition	Flow: Length of arrow indicates duration
	Additional notation	Frequency: Number of layers is relative to frequency
	Additional notation	Importance: Line width is relative to importance
	Additional notation	Feeling: Complaints and requests about the scene

*Indicates notation except for the grey object

3   UX Description Method

3.1   Proposed Method

The proposed method realizes smooth implementation of UXD information into software requirement specification by developing a description method to describe exhaustive user activities. Thus, we have added scenario to the method.

Generally, there are three types of collaborators in solution development: business owner who build a business model, UX designers who research user behavior and design the UX, and engineers who construct the system model.

After UX modeling, each section of the system is developed, such as the software system, accounting system, and human service. In this paper, we focus on the software system; however, we believe that the proposed method can be applied to other development processes (Fig. 1).

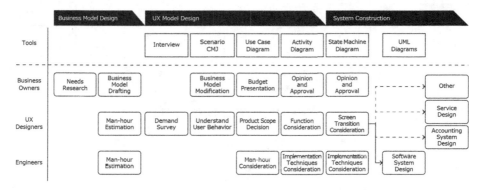

Fig. 1. Solution development process

The proposed method uses four diagrams for the UX design process. First, a scenario is used to determine unknown information about user activities and set the UX goals of the system. Next, a use case diagram is used to determine the scope of the system and its utility. Then, an activity diagram is used to describe the details of the system from the user's perspective. Last, a state machine diagram is used to describe appropriate state transitions for each platform and UXD requirement.

3.2   Scenario

The purpose of the scenario is to understand user behavior, thought and feeling. Exhaustive user information is essential to increase user satisfaction. Our scenario has a matrix structure, and it is possible to organize user information by 5W2H, i.e., when, where, who, what (which), why, how, and how much (Fig. 2), and timeline. Using this matrix structure, it is easy to find unknown user information in the matrix scenario.

In addition, this scenario has UX information, such as frequency, importance, and user feeling. These additional notations can be used to clearly describe the degree of UXD information. For example, the round-cornered rectangle means one scene (clipped time range) in the scenario, and the line-weight indicates the importance of the scene. An expression can be extended using official UML notation (Table 1). Thus, the status of a scene can be determined easily. Such UXD information can be used to determine which user actions should be systemized.

Scenario Basic Information

Title	Wtt a recorded musical disc that is no longer produced at an auction		Precondition	Own a paying member account	Frequency	twice a month
Use Context	Bid at an auction site		Postcondition	Win an auction	Notes	He is correcting the records of a favorite artist. He already has 3 of all records of the artist.

Persona Basic Information — **Prsona Experience Informaiton** — **Persona Character**

Age	50s	Occupation	Manager	Condition	a Bidder	Appearance	Slim
Gender	Male	Workplace	Tokyo Japan	Condition Lv.	Intermediate	Fasion	Sophisticated
Residental Area	Tokyo Japan	Position	Account Section	Motivation to Start	Correcting favorite artist	Possesion	approx. 50 records
Family Structure	Wife, 2 children	Work Environment	20s worker:50%	Purpose	Getting rare records at a low price	Personality	enthusiasm

When	Where	Who	What	(Which)	Why	How	How much	Items
Jan 7 Thu 20 : 00	Home	Mr. Brown	Get home					
			Dinner					
			Watch TV					
Jan 7 Thu 21 : 00	Home -own room		Visit the auction web site			(device) Home PC		
			Search the record		Want to find the item he want to buy	Keep log in		
			Add the record to watch list		Add to the watch list for now. Consider whether bid or not later	Want to do watch list setting with PC		watch list info -item -My maximum bid
	Home		take a shower					

Fig. 2. Sample scenario

3.3 Use Case Diagram

A use case diagram is used to determine the scope of the system using the user information in the scenario. First, an important scene is selected from the scenario. If a scene has user feeling information in the "why" column of the scenario (Fig. 2), such as complaints and requests, the scene can be concerned a new extend function or solution in this process. In the next step, i.e., the activity diagram, user feeling information is transformed to the activity flow of a function or a solution.

Each scenario has one use case diagram because the importance of the scene changes depending on the context of each scenario.

3.4 Activity Diagram

The activity diagram can describe the flow of the solution. The functions in the scope of the system are determined by the use case diagram. Then, the activity diagram shows the detailed steps of each function from a user perspective (Fig. 3).

The scope of a single activity diagram is essentially a single solution, and a solution can potentially contain multiple types of devices. To apply suitable devices for each step in a solution, it is necessary to understand the user's situation and circumstance from the scenario (Fig. 4).

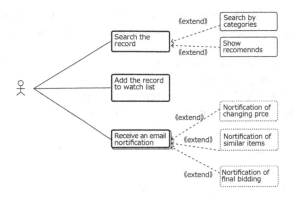

Fig. 3. Sample use case diagram

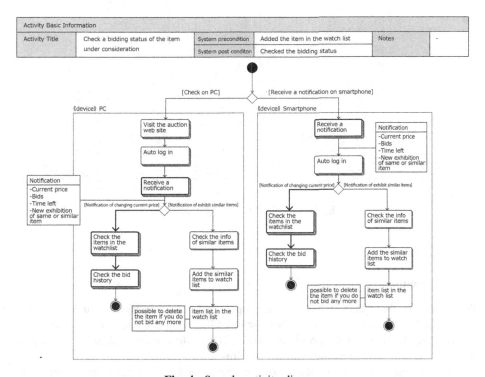

Fig. 4. Sample activity diagram

3.5 State Machine Diagram

The state machine diagram describes state transitions, such as a screen transition diagram for a GUI and its UXD requirements. Note that when the system has two devices, such as PCs and smart phones, two state machine diagrams are required.

UX designers consider a screen transition based on the activity diagram with UXD information to express an appropriate transition and GUI elements. UXD requirements, such as frequency and importance, are already applied to state transitions in a state machine diagram. For example, elements with an expression of very frequently should be accessible from any page; thus, such elements are placed in the main menu of the system. The state machine diagram can precisely describe which elements appear in the window; therefore, there is no confusion for GUI designers and engineers (Fig. 5).

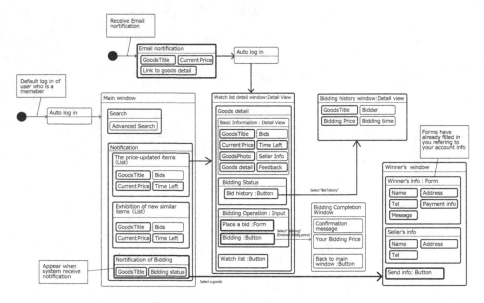

Fig. 5. Sample state machine diagram

4   Case Study

4.1   Preconditions

We examined the effectiveness of the proposed description method and evaluated whether GUI designers could perform actual GUI design using the state machine diagram. As discussed in the previous section, UXD information is already reflected as screen transitions and elements in each window.

In this case study, two GUI designers performed GUI design using the state machine diagram. The theme for the case study is a fictitious exclusive web auction system. The system is described as follows.

System Requirements.

- System: exclusive web auction system
- Devices:
  - PC
  - Smartphone

- Target user age: 20–50
- Target user gender: Male
- Basic functions:
  - Search auction
  - Watch list
  - Bidding
  - Notification

Participants.

- 1 UX designer
- 2 GUI designers

4.2 Process

1. A UX designer receives a system requirement from the business owner and researches auction web sites as a preparatory investigation.
2. The UX designer generates a scenario for the theme by interviewing target users.
3. The UX designer generates a use case diagram and extends the function.
4. The UX designer develops solutions based on user behavior in the scenario and the function(s) in the use case diagram. The UX designer then generates an activity diagram for each solution.
5. The UX designer generates a state machine diagram for each device.
6. The GUI designer receives the state machine diagram from the UX designer to design the layout.
7. Finally, the UX designer receives the layout from the GUI designer and evaluates how well the UXD requirements have been applied to the GUI compared to the UX design intention.

4.3 Case Examples

Here, we show the results and comments from the GUI designers. From the results, we identify limitations of the proposed method. Then, we consider a new solution as the next step.

GUI designer A. Designer A commented about the layout with the state machine diagram received from the UX designer. In particular, the degree of importance of elements was reflected in the layout. Designer A emphasized elements of the importance in various way of GUI layouts. For example, there is a chart that has many elements and text components; therefore, it this chart would occupy a large area of the window. If the chart is less important than other elements, the designer can place the chart in a pop-up window and increase the number of operating procedures that can be used to reach the chart.

GUI designer B. Designer B was also able to design the layout. The state machine expresses the group structure of the elements in the window; thus, the designer could place each element in an appropriate group. However, designer B indicated that the state machine diagram lacked some information about the GUI design, i.e., a detailed explanation of each element, such as functions and data length requirements.

Currently, there is no item to describe detailed element information in the state machine, such as functions and data length requirements. As a result, we have added items to be entered into the diagram or additional documentation.

5   Conclusion

To summarize, using the proposed method, it is possible for UX designers to describe UXD requirements that can be shared with engineers and GUI designers. The effectiveness of the proposed method was verified for software and GUI development.

However, the proposed method has some limitations. First, it is possible that the proposed method could increase development person-hours because it incorporates UXD into system requirements. Current system requirements do not include UXD requirements; therefore, we are concerned that the proposed may incur additional development load. Second, the proposed method describes a system using natural language and diagrams. In this description method, it is difficult to create a prototype, e.g., actual system screens, from the diagrams.

In the future, we will consider the effectiveness of the proposed method for human services other than software systems. Other issues are worth considering. First, this method might incur extra person-hours during development because it incorporates UXD requirements. Next, the proposed method should be examined for the affinity to the iteration of design solutions, including UXD development and verification. In addition, we are considering applying the proposed method to broader components of a service solution, such as interaction among humans.

References

1. Yamazaki, K., et al.: Experience Vision. Maruzen Publishing Co., Ltd., Japan (2012)
2. Gou, K., et al.: Structured scenarios method for human-centered design. In: Proceedings of the Annual Meeting of Japan Ergonomics Society Japan Ergonomics Society 49th Conference, Japan (2011)
3. Kodama, K.: The Essence of UML Modeling. Nikkei Business Publications Inc., Japan (2004)
4. OMG: Unified Modeling Language (OMG UML) Version 1.3, OMG Document number formal-00-03-01, USA (2000)
5. OMG: Unified Modeling Language (OMG UML) Version 2.5, OMG Document number formal-15-03-01, USA (2015)
6. Pilone, D., Pitman, N.: UML 2.0 in a Nutshell. O'Reilly Media Inc., USA (2006)
7. Takeda, A., Hatakeyama, Y.: A Proposal for a Description Method of UX Design Supporting Communication among Developers. Human Interface Society SIG UXSD, Japan (2015)

Enhancing Personas for Well-Being e-Services and Product Service Systems

Sauro Vicini[(⊠)], Adriano Gariglio, Francesco Alberti, Elettra Oleari,
and Alberto Sanna

e-Services for Life and Health, Fondazione Centro San Raffaele, Milan, Italy
vicini.sauro@hsr.it

Abstract. Personas are usually included in listings of standard methods within design. The study at hand explores how the Personas method gets integrated in a User-Centered process in the domain of hospital process re-engineering, health and well-being e-Services. The aim of this paper is to demonstrate how new extensions of the Personas method allow to effectively tackle specific challenges related to the design process, and to support e-Services development since the early stages of a project. The outcomes of our evolution of the Personas method are accurate and valuable Personas profiles that designers, developers and whoever is part of the project team can trust when crafting the user experience (UX), the user interface (UI) and the other components of e-Services.

1 Introduction

The use of various types of visualizations is often held forward as one of the key characteristic of the design field. This paper focuses on *Personas*, "a conceptualization of real users who share common characteristics and needs" [23] exploited throughout the design process. A Personas profile[1] is a single user (significant for the entire segmentation it represents) generally described with a mix of text and images. It highlights the represented user's attitudes, needs, aspirations, behaviors, limits and desires. As it has been documented in literature, the Personas method has several benefits: it helps designers to focus on user goals [24], it allows multidisciplinary teams to incorporate the user needs at an early stage, [19], to introduce users to whom are seeking and designing solutions but have no first hand experience in the environment of use [30], to provide a broad representation of user requirements [30].

This paper contributes to the state-of-the-art both by extending and improving the existing Personas method in order to effectively incorporate user unexploited attributes (such as technology proficiency and privacy behavior), and by identifying the implication of the method within a design methodology (such as the [co]Creation one).

---

[1] We will be distinguishing the Personas *profile* and the Personas *method*, identifying with the former the outcome of the latter.

© Springer International Publishing Switzerland 2016
A. Marcus (Ed.): DUXU 2016, Part I, LNCS 9746, pp. 365–376, 2016.
DOI: 10.1007/978-3-319-40409-7_35

Despite the widespread adoption of the Personas method, we faced several difficulties when exploiting it in highly innovative research domain involving cutting-edge technology. For example the design of an e-Service for securely handling genomic data in un-trusted environments [1]; the design of an e-Service to provide children with Type I Diabetes Mellitus and their families a personalized educational path in order to acquire a correct management of the disease [2]; the development of a smart trolley to be used within a Care Delivery Organization (CDO) [4]; or a Product Service System to set up balanced dietary plans [3]. In these four research domains we based the customization of our Personas method, aiming to effectively dealing complexity.

The contributions of this paper are the description of the improved Personas profile with the implication of its attributes for tackling topics of paramount importance for well-being e-Services and Product Service System (PSS), such as *technology proficiency* and *privacy concerns*, and *health behavior* (Sect. 3), and the specification of our Personas method on the design process (Sect. 4). The paper provides as well an overview of the ^{co}Creation methodology in Sect. 2 and position our Personas profile and method with respect to the state of the art in Sect. 5.

2   The Background: ^{co}Creation Methodology for Well-Being e-Services

Our Personas method has been developed to be exploited within the *^{co}Creation methodology*. The aim of ^{co}Creation methodology is to design, implement, experiment and evaluate e-Services upon an explicit understanding of users, tasks and environments within a Living Lab framework with stakeholders' active participation. The methodology is inspired by two research approaches, i.e., *Living Lab* [27] and *User Centered Design* [15], and it is tailored for contextual-aware, constant-learning, networked digital services (e-Services) evolving in a blend of physical and virtual reality reacting in real time to changes in the environment and patterns of human behavior. Our methodology [6] comprises four phases: ^{co}Design, ^{co}Implementation, ^{co}Experimentation, ^{co}Evaluation. A deeper description of the methodology lies out of the scope of this paper, the interested reader is referred to [29].

3   e-Services for Life and Health Personas Profile

Our Personas profile, showed in Fig. 1, inherits from the state-of-the-art many fields. The fields are organized according to their significance, as to naturally underline the most important ones. Each Personas profile is given a fictitious *name*. The name of our Personas profile exemplifies the main distinguishing trait of the represented user segmentation. The template includes a *picture* and a *quote*. The quote is generally taken from the coding activity performed on the elicitation activity reports. Below the quote, our template displays the *must-do*

Fig. 1. Personas profile visualization template

and *must-never*. Must-do represents a feature that our future e-Service must have, or a task that users consider of central importance in the setting under consideration. The Must-never, instead, identifies a feature that users will never find interesting or useful, independently from how well-designed it is whatsoever.

Under this first block of details, our Personas profile presents an *About* section coupled with a *User's Story*. The About section has demographic data, such as age, sex and nationality, the education and some other specific fields relevant for the investigation domain. The User's Story contextualizes the Personas profile. The remaining fields on the right column point out wishes, needs, opportunities to be pursued by the entire team and the most relevant problems the user segmentation faces in its activities. These are fields and attributes widely adopted in the relevant literature on Personas method. On the left column, instead, we added our distinguishing attributes. Given their importance in our setting, we will detail them below, and conclude here the overview on the more standard fields. These is a pictorial representation of the *Expertise* of the user in relevant fields of the application domain and a list of tools that the user segmentation generally exploit for carrying out its tasks. These may include physical tools, such as a trolley, or intangible tools, such as voice communication. Please go to the following link to check Personas profiles representing segmentations of patients: http://livinglabtools.com/personas-deck.

3.1   New Personas Profile Attributes to Design for Well-Being e-Services

In our working domain, e-Services for well-being, and within the development of PSS by means of the ^{co}Creation methodology described in Sect. 2, we reached the conclusion that three new attributes have to be elicited from the field research and, using already existing segmentation from literature and market analysis, introduced in the Personas profile: *health behavior*, *technology adaption* and *privacy behavior*.

Health behavior highlights the relation of users with their own health status. This is very important along the design of health and well-being e-Services. According with [26] we included five segmentations of users: *Balanced Compensators*, *Live for Todays*, *Unconfident Fatalists*, *Hedonistic Immortals*, and *Health-Conscious Realists*.

Technology adaption highlights the attitude of users towards technology. Technology proficiency of users is extremely heterogeneous and we need to take it into consideration when designing and engineering e-Services. The segmentations to represent these users have been taken from standard literature on marketing strategies (see, e.g., [8]) and are *Innovators*, *Early Adopters*, *Early Majority*, *Late Adopters*, *Laggards*.

Privacy behavior highlights the privacy-awareness. What nowadays is becoming increasingly important, in digital services, is the awareness and the relationship of users with privacy issues. In this case, we found interesting to consider segmentations defined in [17]: *Information Controllers*, *Security Concerned*, *Benefit Seekers*, *Crowd Followers*, and *Organizational Assurance Seekers*.

In the following sections we will describe them more in details, identifying their distinguishing features and pointing out why they play a central role in our working domain.

Health Behavior Segmentation. Given the application domain in which we are working, i.e., well-being and healthcare-oriented e-Services and PSS, we consider of paramount importance the understanding of habits and preferences of the end-users in terms of *Health behavior*. The segmentations offered in [26] provides a good overview of possible classes of uses, widely applicable to our domain. The segmentations are:

- *Balanced Compensators* consider important balancing psychologically and physically status and desire to look good.
- *Live for Todays* are focused on the "here and now" and with chaotic and unstructured tends.
- *Unconfident Fatalists* generally see themselves as stressed and depressed about everyday life.
- *Hedonistic Immortals* consider health more as a mean for achieving a pleasurable and enjoyable lifestyle than as a self-valuable good.
- *Health-Conscious Realists* consider healthy lifestyle as a positive and enjoyable habit to reach results.

Medicine is shifting from a reactive discipline, where diseases are cured when they manifest themselves, to a more preventive one, targeting the overall wellness of individuals, hence trying preventing diseases by suggesting a healthier lifestyle [14]. Being able to characterize users based on their health-related lifestyle is important in order to provide a tailored e-Service meeting their needs and allowing them to achieve their goals, from handling their dietary plans to monitoring their overall health status and correct un-healthier habits.

In the development of a nutritional platform, being able to discriminate the users according to their health behavior is extremely important to meet their expectations. This is what we do in the SmartBreak project [3], where users can take advantage from a personal dietary plan developed based on their preferences, tastes and physicians' recommendations. Understanding user needs and determinants factors is of key importance also in the case of the PAL project [2], where only thanks to a thorough knowledge of the characteristics and wishes of each user we can ensure the delivery of a personalized educational service, that can effectively support them in the management of all the tasks that a disease like type I diabetes requires during the daily life.

Technology Adaption Segmentation. The *technology adaption* level is one of the most relevant trait of today's users. In the healthcare and e-Services for well-being domains, the kinds of end-users spans different generations, hence including both the "digital natives", i.e., those born during or after the rise of digital technologies, and the "digital immigrants", i.e., people born before the advent of digital technologies. It is important to define the end-users into classes identified by their technology adaption in order to tackle the problem of correctly "merging" technological solutions with the right level of technology proficiency.

The five segmentations are those widely adopted in the marketing and economic world (see, e.g., [8]) and are the following:

- *Innovators*, i.e., people willing to experiment new solutions, welcoming new ideas and tolerating the risk of wasting resources due to a e-Service failure.
- *Early Adopters*, i.e., those who welcome new ideas, but need to see a valuable insight in it. They will not spare resources in case of e-Service failure.
- *Early Majority*, i.e., those willing to adopt a new e-Service if positive opinions started to circulate about it.
- *Late Adopters* see the adoption of a new e-Service after the majority of the participants have been already convinced of its benefits.
- *Laggards* do not see added value in innovation and changes. They will be against the introduction of new e-Services in their working routine.

People do exploit technological solutions everyday, but everybody is doing it differently. While some users (that would fall in the *Innovator*) do perceive the novelty and a taste of "experimentation" as an added value of a e-Service, others are extremely reluctant to the changes and struggles in getting through innovations (these are the so-called *Laggards*). However, while everybody could face changes in leisure activities, innovations in the working environment might be stressful and degrade the working performances. It would be, therefore, not only a problem for the single user, but a real issue for the entire division or company. In one of our projects, TAPPS [4], we are developing a smart trolley for nurses. The goal is to reduce therapy errors, help professionals to do their job easier[2], while improving the overall performances of the hospital departments. As everybody can easily imagine, nurses may comprise heterogeneous technology proficiency levels.

The introduction of this new field in our Personas profile achieve another goal: maximize the UX definition. In fact, all the domain experts involved in the design of the e-Service (e.g., engineers, designers, sociologists, etc.) can now sit at the same table and combine efforts towards the best solution which maximize the UI of *all* Personas profiles.

Privacy Behavior Segmentation. Privacy is an old concept (see, e.g., [31]). It became extremely popular in the last years with the increase of importance of personal data, considered always more a fundamental asset by many companies. The entire world of e-Services has to face the challenge of maximizing the benefits of the users while preserving their privacy. Importantly, the concept of privacy still lacks of a precise definition, shifting from "the right to be left alone" [31], to "the right to determine for yourself when, how, and to what extent information about you is communicated to others" [5] until the last definition, which to our opinion best describes the concept of privacy in our domain, i.e., "the right to prevent information to flow from one context to another" [20]. Indeed, in the context of e-Services, personal data of subjects is a fundamental ingredient. Preserving the users' privacy amounts at preventing information leaks.

The segmentations considered are those identified on [17]. We report them here with a brief explanation for the sake of completeness.

---

[2] This may include, for example, a powered trolley able to move autonomously and with sensors to avoid clashes and injuring people on its path.

- *Information Controllers.* They consider the ability to control "their information" a valuable component of an e-Service. They are interested in a granular control of the permissions governing the access and flow of their data.
- *Security Concerned* are those who screens technological solutions adopted by a e-Service, and the compliance with regulations on data protection.
- *Benefit Seekers*, i.e., those for whom the benefits obtained are more valuable than the personal data offered in exchange.
- *Crowd Followers* do not have deep opinion neither on their personal data value compared to the e-Services adopted, nor knowledge on the countermeasures available to protect their privacy.
- *Organizational Assurance Seekers* take in account the countermeasures a company implemented to safeguard their privacy, from the policy and technical perspective integrated in the e-Service.

As follows from this list, despite the segmentation of the end-users, privacy has to be considered when designing a new e-Service. The way privacy is handled is one of the fundamental components of a system nowadays. The envelope in which the technical countermeasures are described and showed to the end-users, the needs of suitable interfaces, etc., are all questions to be answered soon in the design of an e-Service. This is also witnessed by the many privacy-by-design approaches that have been proposed (see, e.g., [10,22]) aiming at forcing thinking about privacy and related solutions in early design stages.

In one of our projects, WITDOM [1], we target the development of a platform for the handling of genomic data. As widely known, genomic data is considered highly sensitive, given the incredible amount of information that can be "extracted" from it. Privacy of end-users, here, does not mean only *anonymity* of the patients, but also *unlinkability* between different genomes of relatives, *confidentiality* in sharing data within the CDO in charge of the analysis, etc. The rapid fall of the DNA sequencing costs [32] allows to imagine a plausible (and not-so-far) scenario in which all the people will have their DNA sequenced and kept secure in some national database, ready to be exploited for personalized treatments or other healthcare treatments. Being able to design a e-Service tailored on the privacy preferences of everybody is much more than challenging. With our Personas profiles we started building tools for devising suitable solutions.

4   Personas Method in the ^{co}Design Sub-process

This section presents our enhanced Personas method throughout the life cycle of the e-Service, with an accent on how the Personas profile are constructed, validated, used and communicated during the ^{co}Design phase.

Personas method plays a central role in the ^{co}Design phase. It is strategically important to know since the beginning of the project if the Personas method is going to be a fundamental driver of the design process. In this phase we aim to tackle the following problems: acceptance of the Personas method as a project driver in the organization, reaching a common agreement on its purposes and uses in various moments with all the project participants; avoid data-poor Personas profile; agree on who are the primary stakeholder.

1. Agree with the project team on the use of Personas method as a project diver, define who will lead the method and set the main purpose of its use
2. Set the research strategy according the Personas and other methods
3. Desk research data collection:
    (a) from existing literature: identify relevant Personas profile attributes
    (b) from demographic/marketing research: identify existing segmentation
    (c) from existing e-Services and PSS: identify users involvement
    (d) from researches done in previous projects: retrieve useful information
4. Field research data collection:
    (a) Identifying possible stakeholders
    (b) Stakeholders prioritization: bring the focus on the most important ones
    (c) Definition and preparation of the elicitation method and type
    (d) Data elicitation with possible users and data transcription

After collecting the data, it is time to analyze and synthesize them. In this sub-process we want to tackle the problem of subjective data analysis, missing connection between demographic/marketing user segmentation checking Personas profiles accuracy and providing communicative Personas profile.

1. Organization of the data collected
2. Analyze finding with analytic and statistical processes
3. Identification of similarities, differences, and patterns
4. Assemble and prioritize a repository of building blocks
5. Users group categorization and refinement process: from a large pool of potential Personas profile to at least one primary Personas profile for each user
6. Visualization of Personas profiles with empirical and fictitious elements
7. Checking accuracy: validate the Personas profile representation

In this sub-process we want to tackle the problem of providing "hermetic" Personas profile and exploit them to interrogate the design. Personas profile need to be used in the e-Service definition phase in order to tackle the problems of communicate across disciplines and take aligned decision in trouble-shooting moments.

1. Dissemination of Personas profiles within the working team
2. Personas profiles as one of the main inputs for the exploration of the solution space and the identification of e-Services concepts and scenarios
3. Screening users for e-Service concepts and scenarios validation
4. Personas profiles to focus on user requirements and to build use cases
5. Personas profiles to define e-Services components
6. Personas profiles to double-check if user requirements have been respected
7. Screening users for e-Service components definition validation

5   Common Background, Differences and Advantages Compared with Other Personas Methods

In order to make sense of our customization of the Personas method, we believe it is important to understand the assumptions and structural character-istics acquired from existing Personas methods in literature. For the purpose of this paper we focused on key aspects of the most well-know methods [9,11,18, 21,23–25].

Personas Method Purpose. We found interesting the role-based perspec-tive [18,23] where the Personas profile communicate the users goal and focuses on behavior. We define the purpose for creating Personas profiles as proposi-tional [12], where the Personas profile want to picture the key characteristics of a segmentation of users to interrogate the design.

Source of the Information. The source of the information in the Personas tends to be one of the variable that causes the most controversy and it is strictly related to the purpose of the Personas method that the designers develop with. As illustrated in [12], two attributes have been identified from the source of information variable, i.e., empirical source of data and fictional components. Our previously mentioned interest in the role-based perspective is also justified by the traditional set of activities to gain users information from qualitative and qualitative research in the Living Lab context in which we operate.

The Process to Build a Personas Profile. As we mentioned before, Personas method impact on the overall ^{co}Creation methodology. For this reason, we had to take the time to dig into the implication of the use of such method in our processes in order to adapt it to our needs, contexts, and resources. Pruitt & Grudin where highly inspiring for their focus on a wide range of data gathering techniques and the process to check the Personas profile representation accuracy; Cooper influenced our proposal with the refinement process where he suggests to create a large pool of initial Personas profile, then refine until one primary Personas profile for each user is defined; and finally Vincent and Nielsen were fundamental for their work of restructuring the overall process paraphrasing and interpreting previously described methods in real working context application.

Personas Profile Visualization and Dissemination. Starting from what it is available in literature, we agree with on using narration as a format to allow communication among people [16]. We think so because the narrative forms provides three essential benefits: (1) to make the Personas profile seem like a real person; (2) to provide a vivid story concerning the needs of the users in the context of the e-Service being designed; (3) to function as a vehicle to communicate user needs and requests to the developers (user requirements) [13]. In our working domain, e-Services for well-being, and within the development of

PSS by means of the ^{co}Creation methodology [7,28] we reached the conclusion that "empirical" and "fictional" elements are most of the time blending together during the composition of Personas profile.

Exploit the Personas Profile. One activity is to create reliable, well-structured, emphatic and useful Personas profiles. An other one is to use them. Because of the strict relation of these two activities, we wanted to follow a reverse engineer approach in the construction of our Personas method. Observing its use documented in literature and comparing it with our previous method application in real project, we listed a series of benefits that our approach has to take into account:

- User focus: a clear picture of users goals, behaviors, needs, and the context
- Research domain fundamental users segmentation: where the user stands in already existing demographic, behavioral and marketing segmentations.
- Problems and requirements prioritization: focus on important issues
- Stakeholders prioritization: bring focus on the most important ones
- Challenge assumptions, prevent self-referential design and create empathy
- Guide validation and support users involvement: facilitate users recruitment
- Support cognitive *walk-through*: assist the generation of scenarios
- Foster communication, collaboration and intuitiveness with natural language
- Support and integrate: shared assets with other methods

6   Conclusions and Future Work

Besides identifying interesting users characterizations and standardizing the method, our paper highlights, as well, valuable future directions. Despite the fact that our enhanced Personas profile works well in our research environment, we are aware that further customizations will be needed whenever it will be applied to other contexts. One of the most significant change, for example, that has to be kept into account is the segmentation to be considered, which varies from application domain to application domain. It would be really interesting to see how our Personas profile and method would change, for instance, in the design of a non-digital service. At the same time, we plan to define range of variability of the content of the newly defined fields, in a continuous investigation of new users segmentations coming from the existing literature.

Acknowledgement. The research presented in this paper has been funded by the projects TAPPS (grant agreements No. 645119 http://www.tapps.eservices4life.org/), WITDOM (grant agreements No. 644371 http://www.witdom.eu/) and PAL (grant agreements No. 643783-RIA http://pal4u.eu/). All of them are part of European Union Horizon 2020 research and innovation programme (H2020-ICT-2014-1). We wish also to warmly thank the healthcare professionals of Ospedale San Raffaele (Milan, Italy) and the people involved in our studies for their precious and constant support.

References

1. empoWering prIvacy and securiTy in non-trusteD envirOnMents (WITDOM). witdom.eu
2. Personal Assistant for a healthy Lifestyle (PAL). pal4u.eu
3. SmartBreak. smartbreak.eservices4life.org
4. Trusted APPs for open CPS (TAPPS). www.tapps.eservices4life.org
5. Alan, F.W.: Privacy and Freedom. Bodley Head, London (1970)
6. Alberti, F., Vicini, S.: Enhancing co-creation with privacy- and security-by-design methodologies. In: ENoLL Research Day Conference Proceedings 2015, pp. 7–15 (2015)
7. Alberti, F., Vicini, S.: Enhancing co-creation with privacy- and security-by-design methodologies. In: ENoLL Conference Proceedings 2015, pp. 7–15 (2015)
8. Arndt, J.: Role of product-related conversations in the diffusion of a new product. J. Mark. Res. **4**, 291–295 (1967)
9. Cooper, A.: The inmates are running the asylum: [Why high-tech products drive us crazy and how to restore the sanity], vol. 261, Sams Indianapolis (1999)
10. Deng, M., Wuyts, K., Scandariato, R., Preneel, B., Joosen, W.: A privacy threat analysis framework: supporting the elicitation and fulfillment of privacy requirements. Requir. Eng. **16**(1), 3–32 (2011)
11. Djajadiningrat, J.P., Gaver, W.W., Fres, J.W.: Interaction relabelling and extreme characters: methods for exploring aesthetic interactions. In: Proceedings of the 3rd Conference on Designing Interactive Systems: Processes, Practices, Methods, and Techniques, pp. 66–71. ACM (2000)
12. Floyd, I.R., Cameron, J.M., Twidale, M.B.: Resolving incommensurable debates: a preliminary identification of persona kinds, attributes, and characteristics. Artifact **2**(1), 12–26 (2008)
13. Hjalmarsson, A., Gustafsson, E., Cronholm, S.: Exploring the use of personas in user-centered design of web-based e-services. In: IConference (2013)
14. Hood, L., Flores, M.: A personal view on systems medicine and the emergence of proactive p4 medicine: predictive, preventive, personalized and participatory. New Biotechnol. **29**(6), 613–624 (2012)
15. ISO. Human-centred design for interactive systems. Ergonomics of human system interaction Part 210 (ISO 9241-210) (2010)
16. Miaskiewicz, T., Kozar, K.A.: Personas and user-centered design: how can personas benefit product design processes? Des. Stud. **32**(5), 417–430 (2011)
17. Morton, A., Sasse, M.A.: Desperately seeking assurances: segmenting users by their information-seeking preferences. In: 2014 Twelfth Annual International Conference on Privacy, Security and Trust (PST), pp. 102–111. IEEE (2014)
18. Nielsen, L.: Personas. https://www.interaction-design.org/literature/book/the-encyclopedia-of-human-computer-interaction-2nd-ed/personas
19. Nieters, J.E., Ivaturi, S., Ahmed, I.: Making personas memorable. In: CHI 2007 Extended Abstracts on Human Factors in Computing Systems, pp. 1817–1824 (2007)
20. Nissenbaum, H.: Privacy in Context: Technology, Policy, and the Integrity of Social Life. Stanford University Press, Redwood City (2009)
21. Norman, D.: Ad-hoc personas & empathetic focus. Jnd. org (2004)
22. Notario, N., Crespo, A., Kung, A., Kroener, I., Le Métayer, D., Troncoso, C., del Álamo, J.M., Martín, Y.-S.: PRIPARE: a new vision on engineering privacy and security by design. In: CSP Forum 2014, pp. 65–76 (2014)

23. Pruitt, J., Adlin, T.: The Persona Lifecycle: Keeping People in Mind Throughout Product Design. Morgan Kaufmann, Massachusetts (2010)
24. Pruitt, J., Grudin, J.: Personas: practice and theory. In: Proceedings of the 2003 Conference on Designing for User Experiences, pp. 1–15. ACM (2003)
25. Sinha, R.: Persona development for information-rich domains. In: CHI 2003 Extended Abstracts on Human Factors in Computing Systems, pp. 830–831 (2003)
26. Smith, A., Humphreys, S., Heslington, L., La Placa, V., McVey, D., MacGregor, E.: The healthy foundations life-stage segmentation. research report no. 2: The qualitative analysis of the motivation segments. Project report, University of Greenwich, London, UK, July 2011
27. Ståhlbröst, A., Holst, M.: The living lab methodology handbook. Published by the SmartIES project, a transnational Nordic Smart City Living Lab Pilot (2012)
28. Vicini, S., Bellini, S., Sanna, A.: The city of the future living lab. Int. J. Autom. Smart Technol. **2**(3), 201–208 (2012)
29. Vicini, S., Bellini, S., Sanna, A.: User-driven service innovation in a smarter city living lab. In: Proceedings of International Conference on Service Science, ICSS, pp. 254–259 (2013)
30. Vincent, C.J., Blandford, A.: The challenges of delivering validated personas for medical equipment design. Appl. Ergon. **45**(4), 1097–1105 (2014)
31. Warren, S.D., Brandeis, L.D.: The right to privacy. Harvard Law Rev. **4**, 193–220 (1890)
32. Wetterstrand, K.A.: DNA Sequencing Costs: Data from the NHGRI Genome Sequencing Program (GSP). www.genome.gov/sequencingcosts. Accessed 12 February 2016

The 100,000 Participant Laboratory - A Crowd-Centered Approach to Design and Evaluate the Usability of Mobile Apps

Ming-Hui Wen[✉]

Department of Commercial Design and Management,
National Taipei University of Business, Taipei, Taiwan
donwen@ntub.edu.tw

Abstract. Mobile apps play important roles in our daily lives. Software developers typically follow the user-centered design (UCD) approach to develop products that optimize usability. However, most usability methodologies require lab experiments or field studies. Usability experiments require higher costs and efforts to prepare related tasks, such as selecting the environmental setting, subject recruiting and conducting the study. Compared to the laboratory experiment of personal computers (PC), mobile usability laboratory settings present greater challenges related to controlling the research context variables.

The purpose of this study is to build an online usability lab by applying Internet and crowdsourcing technologies. The lab allows researchers to invite Internet users to participate in the usability experiment online. This study follows the usability engineering theoretical framework to define mobile usability contextual factors. The clouded-based online usability lab was introduced as a conceptual framework to support both Android and iOS mobile apps. Mobile app developers can upload their apps to the lab system to collect and monitor usability data and track the behavioral data of human-computer interaction. The ultimate goal of this lab was to help researchers conduct usability experiments in real world contexts and develop the dynamic mental model of product users.

Keywords: Mobile usability · Mental model · User experience · Crowdsourcing

1 Introduction

Usability engineering is an important research topic within the study of Human-Computer Interaction and based on the user-center design (UCD) approach. User-centered design seeks to ensure the designers' work meets the users' requirements and ability to conveniently use the design product. Usability engineering applies both qualitative and quantitative research methods to help researchers understand user-product interactions and experiences.

Regardless of the particular method, usability laboratories have played significant roles in the development of the conventional usability process. The process of scientific investigation has allowed researchers to collect user response data and interpret findings to understand user experience quality and product effectiveness (Norman 1988).

© Springer International Publishing Switzerland 2016
A. Marcus (Ed.): DUXU 2016, Part I, LNCS 9746, pp. 377–384, 2016.
DOI: 10.1007/978-3-319-40409-7_36

A usability experiment is composed of four contextual variables, including the user, task, environment and tool (Gould 1988). Usability research should consider these four factors simultaneously to ensure the experimental setting replicates the u. Traditional computer software requires users to sit in front of desks. Conversely, mobile apps are more complex and influenced by many factors, such as multi-tasking, cooperative work, social dynamics and, user interface. The quantity and complexity of contextual variables might affect mobile app use. Therefore, conventional lab-based usability research methods might not be able to provide experimental contexts that highly match real mobile app usage.

Some online services already exist for testing the mobile apps such as Testdroid, Testin, and MonkeyTalk. However, these services only test technical issues, such as operation system compatibility, functional stability, and system stress. These online testing services only ensure that mobile apps operate smoothly online. However, a smooth operating app does not necessarily meet user requirements.

Online survey systems, such as SurveyMonkey, Limesurvey, Google Forms, SurveyGizmo, KwikSurveys, SoSci Survey, Typeform, Client Heartbeat, Gravity Forms, WuFoo, Formsite, and Formassembly, have helped researchers gather data on users' opinions and preferences about mobile apps. However, these tools only allow researchers to develop survey items and analyze data with graphs and tables. These survey tools do not assess the usability experience when the users interacting with the apps.

This study uses the Internet and communication technology to develop an online usability laboratory. The crowdsourcing and social networking mechanism is used to recruit participants. Mobile app developers can upload their products to recruit appropriate candidates. The proposed online lab is expected to allow mobile app developers to collect real usability data (even dynamic data) from real users in a real context.

2   The Influence Variables of Usability Testing

Based on previous literature, the user, tasks, tool and environment are used as a framework for developing the online usability lab. This framework allows Internet users to participate in the usability experiments online. Figure 1 introduces the four contextual factors applied in this study.

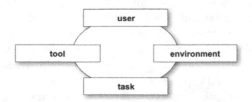

Fig. 1. The four factors of a usability context

2.1   User

Demographics are the most frequently used factors to describe user profiles (Nielsen 1992; Allen et al. 1993; Levanthal et al. 1994). Demographic variable include nationality, race, age, date of birth, blood type, gender, education, income, occupation, family patterns, geographical location, urban living, family life cycle, marital status, and other variables. Demography can be used for basic human classification to help researchers define their user segments.

Lifestyle has also been used to classify user segments (Wansink and Park 2000). This study applied the AIO (Activity, Interest and Opinion) lifestyle rating scale to measure users' intrinsic and extrinsic lifestyles (William and Douglas 1971; Reynolds and Darden 1972). Personality is also commonly applied to psychologically classify users (Christine and Dewit 2001; Devaraj and Easley 2008). Researchers have most commonly used the Big-Five scale to assess personality, which includes five dimensions (Openness, Conscientiousness, Extraversion, Agreeableness, and Neuroticism; McCrae ans Costa 1992, McCrae and Costa 1999).

The online usability lab will provide APIs (Application Programming Interfaces) to allow researchers to add other rating scales or indicators classifying user groups or statuses. One example of which open APIs applies is this addition of related survey items about TAM (Technology Acceptance Model) and Innovation adoption lifecycle.

2.2   Task

Tasks relate to the interactions between users and tools. This study applied activity theory, with three levels (i.e., activity, action, and operation) to describe user motivation and task goals (Leont 1978). Activity analysis allows for the assessment of users motivation and primary objectives related to a particular activity. Engeström (1999) proposed an activity triangle to explain other contextual variables related to user activity. This model includes tool, community, rules, and division of labor factors. These social and culture factors might also affect product usability and interaction design. Researchers need to understand users' motivations, objectives and how they conduct tasks with the tool to achieve their primary objective. Such research may allow mobile app designers to further understand users' mental models and design products accordingly (Norman 1983).

2.3   Tool

The online usability lab uses smartphones and tablets as vehicles to assess mobile app usage. The Android/iOS smartphones and tablets are the most common of such tools. Technical characteristics relating to the tool level include, but are not limited to, brand and model series, CPU number, memory size, operation system, software versions, Internet speed, telecom operators, and screen size. Although different smart devices have different capabilities regarding hardware and software levels, usability experiments should also consider the effects of the tools themselves to ensure experimental quality. Some online services provide a heatmap feature to track operational behaviors step-by-step while the user interacts with the mobile apps (see Fig. 2). Such technologies are very useful for understanding users' activity, actions, and operational level behaviors. In order to promote future development of the online usability lab, the system provides scalable APIs to allow third party technologies. Examples of such technologies include heatmaps, screen video recorders, and mobile eye tracking. Users could operate the mobile app and perform the think-aloud methodology at the same time using the screen recorder. The system can collect this data and remotely send it back to the online usability lab through the Internet. Researchers can then collect usability experiment data from a real usage context. Such information should be very helpful for researchers when conducting large-scale experiments with worldwide samples.

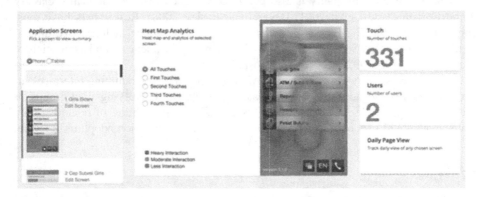

Fig. 2. Head map feature for tracking user operations on a mobile app (Image Source: AppAnalytics.io).

2.4 Environment

Usability experiments should also consider elements of the physical environment that might affect the results of the experiment. Examples of environmental factors include moving state, mobile versus stationary, the noisy degree of illumination, temperature, humidity, vibration, and weather. Physical environmental factors are likely to affect usability during product interaction (Wickens 1992). The mobile app was usually used in the out-door environment and mobile context. The effect of the physical environment in mobile apps is much more complex than the simple PC software context.

To help recreate the physical environment condition of mobile app usage, sensors can be embedded in smart devices to identify pertinent environmental factors. For example, most smart devices are equipped with GPS (Global Positioning System) and Geographic Information Systems (GIS: Geographic Information System). These technologies can be used to indicate users' current locations and relay information back to the online usability lab. Therefore, GPS data can predict user mobility (e.g., standing, walking, running or driving. Computing device speed and direction data from the gravity sensor (G-sensor) and accelerometer of the mobile phone allows for the online lab system to predict possible user activities. The development of the Internet of Things (iOT) has led to the inclusion of temperature, humidity, gas, and pressure sensors to monitor the environment and aid daily life. The online usability lab provides open data APIs to allow researchers to feed data from smart sensors to the system.

3 Motivating Users to Participate in the Online Usability Experiment

The main challenge in realizing the 100,000 participant lab is recruiting thousands of Internet users. The operational model is a platform, meaning we need to grow the number of usability experiment cases and participants. To grow the number of usability experiment cases, the system design SDKs (Software Development Kits) will be used to allow app developers to easily connect to the system and upload cases for testing though APIs. Crowdsourcing social networking technology is also used to recruit more Internet users. The gamification mechanism and associated tangible/intangible rewards system were also added to solicit participation.

Crowdsourcing is an Internet-based technique to facilitate large-scale tasks that are costly or time-consuming with traditional methods (Marzilli et al. 2009). Crowdsourcing has been applied to many Internet services, such as Amazon Mechanical Turk (MTurk), CloudFactory, Clickworker, CloudCrowd, and Fiverr. Research also has proven that crowdsourcing can reduce the cost and time associated with micro human resources tasks online (Kittur and Chi 2008).

Viitamaki (2008) proposed the Focus, Language, Incentives, Rules and Tool (FLIRT) model to guide the crowdsourcing service design. This author also identifies four kinds of peoples (creator, critic, connector, and crowd) who play different roles in the crowdsourcing system. The creator is responsible for generating original solutions for the crowdsourcing tasks. Critics and connectors emphasize their opinions and share information about crowdsourcing tasks to influence a large number of people. Finally, the crowd has a low-level of participation and only activates in some key events (Viitamaki 2008). The FLIRT model can be applied to human-to-human (the four kind of users) and human-to-computer (crowdsourcing tasks) interactions. This study first connects the usability lab to Facebook to assist the registration process. Facebook also allows participants to invite friends and family to participate. Tangible rewards (points) are given to users who invited members of their social network to participate, based on quantity.

Gamification is the process of applying in-game elements to attract and engage people in performing non-game tasks (Deterding and Dixon 2011). Game elements can provide positive experiences and involve people in the game playing process. Some people connect so strongly with games that they become addicted (Hsu and Wen 2009). Gamification has been applied in education (Raymer and Design 2011, Kapp 2012), marketing and sales (Huotari and Hamari 2011) and human resource management (Kumar 2013).

Three gamification features exist, including quests, experience points, challenge unlock and leaderboard access. The quest feature provides detailed information related to app type, function requiring testing, usability goal, testing procedure, expected number of participants, and reward points. Users who were meeting the inclusion criteria will receive the invitation to participate in the online experiment. The number of reward points given by app providers may differ. Users who would like to participate in the quests for reward points should first complete at least 10 basis quests to collect experience points and unlock advanced quests. All testing of participants' achievement across different types of apps (e.g., educational apps, game apps, and tool apps) is calculated and displayed in the leaderboard.

4   The Development of the Usability Laboratory

This study was exploratory, and the author attempted to adapt the traditional laboratory usability experiment to an online environment. The main challenge in this effort was to reconstruct the usability context from offline to online. Therefore, this study applies four human-computer interaction context elements (user, task, tool, and environment) to replicate the usability environment. The use of mobile devices and smart sensors helps increase the efficiency of the usability data collection process.

The system lab supports mobile app developers with SDKs, allowing developers to easily connect their mobile apps to the online lab or upload the Android APK file to the system. The system provides a set of common usability methodologies, such as A/B testing, heuristic evaluation, think aloud, surveys, and open-question interviews. Researchers can easily form an online usability experiment by selecting a usability template from the menu. The computation module will then automatically calculate the related algorithm.

Data can be collected in two ways within this model, including human input and machine-collected data. The platform offers questionnaire design features to collect various forms of human input data. Machine-collected data include that derived from mobile device embedded features (e.g., GPS, GIS, G-sensor), and wireless smart sensors. All usability testing is sent back to the cloud server through APIs. The system can then provide qualitative or quantitative usability indicators as input for the data

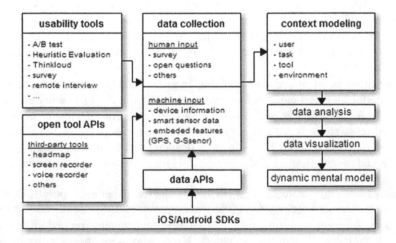

Fig. 3. Conceptual framework of the online usability texting laboratory

visualization model. Finally, the visualized data function was provided with a dynamic update function to allow researchers to easily interpret findings. By building an informative visualization graph with an appropriate algorithm to process the data, researchers can try to build a dynamic mental model of the mobile app indicating its quality. Figure 3 illustrates the lab's conceptual framework.

5 Conclusion

Quality outcomes related to an online, lab-based experiment are very close to those of physical labs. However, the former is timelier and cost-efficient. Additionally, Internet-based experiments allow much easier worldwide participant recruitment (Yen et al. 2013). The ultimate goal of this study is to development an online usability lab that allows hundreds of thousands of people to participate (iOS and Android). Compared to traditional lab experiments, it is easier to collect dynamic usability data and recruit participants in the online version.

The proposed online lab is expected to bring convenience to researchers conducting mobile app usability experiments in three ways. First, this lab prevents the need to replicate the experimental environment because of the mobile nature of the app. Second, this lab makes acquiring the target number of subjects or evaluating cross-cultural effects much easier through crowdsourcing. Finally, this lab allows users' behavioral data when interacting with the mobile app to be sent back to the cloud server. The experimenter can collect data within 24 h, obviating the need for human assistance to support the experiment. The proposed system is expected to help researchers conduct usability experiments in real world contexts and conceptualize the dynamic mental models of product users.

Acknowledgments. The author thank the Ministry of Science and Technology (MOST) in Taiwan for providing financial support under grant MOST 103-2221-E-163 -003 -MY2.

References

Allen, C.D., Ballman, D., Begg, V., Miller-Jacobs, H. H., Muller, M., Nielsen, J., Spool, J.: User involvement in the design process: why, when & how?. In: Proceedings of the INTERACT 1993 and CHI 1993 Conference on Human Factors in Computing Systems, pp. 251–254. ACM (May 1993)

Roy, M.C., Dewit, O., Aubert, B.A.: The impact of interface usability on trust in web retailers. Internet Res. **11**(5), 388–398 (2001)

Costa, P.T., McCrae, R.R.: Four ways five factors are basic. Personality Individ. Differ. **13**(6), 653–665 (1992)

Deterding, S., Dixon, D., Khaled, R., Nacke, L.: From game design elements to gamefulness: defining gamification. In: Proceedings of the 15th International Academic MindTrek Conference: Envisioning Future Media Environments, pp. 9–15. ACM (September 2011)

Devaraj, S., Easley, R.F., Crant, J.M.: Research note-how does personality matter? relating the five-factor model to technology acceptance and use. Inf. Syst. Res. **19**(1), 93–105 (2008)

Engeström, Y.: Activity theory and individual and social transformation. Perspect. Act. Theor., 19–38 (1999)

Gould, J.D.: How to design usable systems. In: Handbook of Human-Computer Interaction, pp. 757–789, Amsterdam (1988)

Hsu, S.H., Wen, M.H., Wu, M.C.: Exploring user experiences as predictors of MMORPG addiction. Comput. Educ. **53**(3), 990–995 (2009)

Huotari, K., Hamari, J.: Gamification" from the perspective of service marketing. In: Proceedings of CHI 2011 Workshop Gamification (May 2011)

Kapp, K.M. The gamification of learning and instruction: game-based methods and strategies for training and education. Wiley. com (2012)

Kittur, A., Chi, E.H., Suh, B.: Crowdsourcing user studies with mechanical turk. In: Proceedings of the SIGCHI Conference on Human Factors in Computing Systems, pp. 453–456. ACM (April 2008)

Kumar, J.: Gamification at work: designing engaging business software. In: Marcus, A. (ed.) DUXU 2013, Part II. LNCS, vol. 8013, pp. 528–537. Springer, Heidelberg (2013)

Leontev, A.N.: Activity, consciousness, and personality. Moscow: Progress (1978)

McCrae, R.R., Costa Jr, P.T.: A five-factor theory of personality. Handb. pers. Theor. Res. **2**, 139–153 (1999)

Levanthal, L., Teasley, B., Stone, D., Lancaster, A.M., Marcus, A., Nardi, B., Nielsen, J., Kurosu, M., Heller, R.: Designing for diverse users: will just a better interface do?. In: Conference Companion on Human Factors in Computing Systems, pp. 191–192. ACM (April 1994)

Nielsen, J.: Finding usability problems through heuristic evaluation. In: Proceedings of the SIGCHI Conference on Human Factors in Computing Systems, pp. 373–380. ACM (June 1992)

Norman, D.A.: Some observations on mental models. In: Mental Models, pp. 7–14 (1983)

Norman, D.A.: The psychology of everyday things. Basic books, New York (1988)

Raymer, R., Design, E.L.: Gamification: using game mechanics to enhance eLearning. Elearn Mag. **2011**(9), 3 (2011)

Reynolds, F.D., Darden, W.R.: Intermarket patronage: a psychographic study of consumer outshoppers. J. Mark. Res. **36**(4), 50–54 (1972)

Viitamaki, S.: The FLIRT model of crowdsourcing: planning and executing collective customer collaboration. Marketing Master Thesis, Helsinki School of Economics, Spring (2008)

Wansink, B., Park, S.B.: Methods and measures that profile heavy users. J. Advertising Res. **40** (2000), 61–72 (2000)

Wickens, C.D.: Computational models of human performance. CSERIAC Gateway **3**, 8–12 (1992)

William, D.W., Douglas, J.T.: Activities, interests and opinions. J. Advertising Res. **11**(4), 27–35 (1971)

Marzilli, M., Yan, T., Holmes, R., Ganesan, D., Corner, M.: mCrowd: a platform for mobile crowdsourcing. In: Proceedings of the 7th ACM Conference on Embedded Networked Sensor Systems, pp. 347–348. ACM (November 2009)

Yen, Y.C., Chu, C.Y., Yeh, S.L., Chu, H.H., Huang, P.: Lab Experiment vs. Crowdsourcing: A Comparative User Study on Skype Call Quality (2013)

Usability and User Experience
Evaluation Methods and Tools

Heuristic Evaluation for Novice Evaluators

André de Lima Salgado$^{(\boxtimes)}$ and Renata Pontin de Mattos Fortes

ICMC University of São Paulo, São Carlos, São Paulo, Brazil
alsalgado@usp.br, renata@icmc.usp.br

Abstract. Adapting the method of Heuristic Evaluation for novice evaluators can capacitate organizations of low monetary power that, usually, do not have conditions to resort to experts. In one of the courses given by the authors, 12 in 15 novice evaluators (80 %) said they had difficulties to distinguish the difference among the traditional usability heuristics. The aim of this study was to explore this affirmation and develop possible adaptations in order to mitigate this problem. Surveys with 13 usability experts and 15 novice evaluators showed that the 3rd and the 7th heuristics, from the traditional set of Nielsen and Molich, are probably more difficult for novices to understand and distinguish between each other. In a third survey, with 7 usability experts, we discussed a new description for heuristics 3 and 7 in order to make them easier for novice evaluators to understand and distinguish. Future studies can validate of the adaptations proposed here.

Keywords: Heuristic Evaluation · Usability heuristics · Novice evaluator

1 Introduction

The Heuristic Evaluation (HE), proposed by Nielsen and Molich in [17], has been widely applied as a low-cost alternative method to evaluate usability of software products [5,8,13]. Our previous study showed that the traditional set of heuristics from Nielsen and Molich were still widely applied even to evaluate new technologies as mobile applications [8,14,17]. Despite its success, the quality of the outcomes of a HE is associated with the knowledge of evaluators [6,14,24].

Participation of usability experts in HEs still represents a high cost for organizations of low monetary power; only a few researches and organizations conduct HEs with the participation of expert evaluator [1,2,7,9,14,15,18,23]. It is intuitive to understand that adapting a popular method of usability evaluator for novice evaluators can empower such organizations. However, an exhaustive literature review can show the existence of only a few evidences about adapting the method of HE for novice evaluators to support practitioners that resort to them to conduct HE. Studies have investigated adaptations for the method of HE for specific profiles of novice evaluators, but their results are not sufficient to generalize to the entire profile of novice evaluators [3,10,11,19,21,22,25].

In order to investigate about the causes that make HE hardly dependent of people who apply it, we started to figure out possible issues related to the

© Springer International Publishing Switzerland 2016
A. Marcus (Ed.): DUXU 2016, Part I, LNCS 9746, pp. 387–398, 2016.
DOI: 10.1007/978-3-319-40409-7_37

characteristics of the HE as a method. Based on the literature of the field, and on our built-up experience teaching Human-Computer Interaction, we believe that one of the possible difficulties of novice evaluators during a HE is to distinguish the difference among the traditional heuristics of Nielsen and Molich [10,21, 25]. During one of the courses taught by the authors, 12 out of 15 participants (80 %) said that they had difficulties to distinguish the difference among the ten heuristics of Nielsen and Molich during a HE - this feedback was the first motivation for this study.

Our goal was to explore situations where novice evaluators could possibly misunderstood different heuristics - regarding the traditional set of heuristics of Nielsen and Molich - as similar and develop adaptations for the heuristics in order to mitigate these misunderstandings. Based on three surveys, the results showed in this paper presented heuristics that are probably misunderstood as similar by novice evaluators. In addition, new descriptions for specific heuristics were made in order to mitigate this problem.

The following presents a review of the literature of the field, the design of this study, the surveys conducted, with its results and discussion, and the conclusions of this paper.

2   Literature Review

2.1   Heuristic Evaluation

The Heuristic Evaluation (HE) method was proposed by Nielsen and Molich [17]. A HE consists in three main sessions: preliminary, evaluation and results [20]. In the preliminary session, the evaluators receive the same instructions on how to conduct the HE from the responsible of organizing the evaluation. In the evaluation session, the evaluators analyze the interface aiming to find discordance between the interface and any of the heuristics. In their study, Nielsen and Molich considered a group of nine heuristics to define the method [17]. Later, Nielsen [14] verified the necessity of adding a tenth heuristic to the group. These ten heuristics have been known as the traditional usability heuristics of Nielsen and Molich. The title of each heuristic is shown as follows:

Heuristic 1 - Visibility of system status.
Heuristic 2 - Match between system and the real world.
Heuristic 3 - User control and freedom.
Heuristic 4 - Consistency and standards.
Heuristic 5 - Error prevention.
Heuristic 6 - Recognition rather than recall.
Heuristic 7 - Flexibility and efficiency of use.
Heuristic 8 - Aesthetic and minimalist design.
Heuristic 9 - Help users recognize, diagnose, and recover from errors.
Heuristic 10 - Help and documentation.

A full description of the heuristics can be retrieved at Nielsen Norman Group website [16].

At the last session of HE, evaluators define a final list of usability problems identified, rating specific severity to each one of them and suggesting solutions [15,20].

2.2 Heuristic Evaluation for Novice Evaluators

In the next subsections, we present the proposed approaches classified in the literature, based on their main goals, that intended to get novice evaluators involved in a HE.

Classifying the Expertise of Evaluators. The literature about classification of expertise on usability evaluations is still reduced. At the best of our knowledge, no schema of classification is widely considered as a standard for classifying expert in usability related area. In this context, we highlighted a few important studies that presented a classification of expertise levels of evaluators in HE.

Regarding the study of Nielsen [14], to be an expert evaluator one needs to have several years of job experience in usability area or a post-graduation degree diploma in usability area. Similarly, those professionals that do not achieve this minimum qualification are classified as novice evaluators.

Slavkovic and Cross [24] studied HE for novice evaluators and, in their study, they qualified *"graduate and undergraduate students in an introductory course on HCI evaluation methods"* as novice evaluators.

At the best of our knowledge, the most structured schema of classification of proficiency in usability evaluation was proposed by Botella et al. [4]. Botella et al. [4] proposed a schema for classifying usability professionals on five different levels:

Novice: Professional without a university degree, but at least a training course on HCI, and few hours of practice in usability evaluation.
Beginner: Professional without a university degree, but several training courses on HCI, and less than 2,500 h of practice in usability evaluation.
Intermediate: Professional with a bachelor degree on usability area, and less than 5,000 h of practice in usability evaluation.
Senior: Professional with master's degree on usability and less than 7,500 h of practice in usability evaluation.
Expert: Professional with at least a master's degree on usability area and more than 10,000 h of practice in usability evaluation.

Nonetheless, the referred classification is still new to the literature and further discussions can be done in order to understand the generalization of these classifications considering different contexts. For the purpose of this study, we advocate that for being an expert in usability area - regarding the Brazilian context - the evaluator should have at least four years of job or research experience in the field of usability.

Adapting HE for Novice Evaluators. Through a literature review, one can see that studies on adapting HE for novice evaluator are still in a reduced number. Adapting a HE implies that it may not lose its main characteristics as a simple method. The need of studies about adaptations to the method of HE was primary shown by Slavkovic et al. [24]. Slavkovic et al. [24] studied HEs conducted by 43 novice evaluators. In their study, they showed that novice evaluators performed superficial analysis of the interface and have difficulties with specific areas of the interface.

A group of studies addressed adaptations of HE to be conducted by specific profiles of novice evaluators, as children and teenagers. A major part of these studies tried to simplify the HE for children as evaluators [10,11,21,22]. These studies showed that children have a better understanding of the children's user profile and, for this reason, they could be considered as evaluators. MacFarlane and Pasiali [10] showed that the following adaptations can be done to HE aiming children as evaluators:

– simplifying heuristic description and;
– changing the severity rating model to a Likert scale using smile faces to represent different degrees of satisfaction.

Results from these studies showed evidences that children can conduct HE adapted for them. Regarding the standard HE, these studies identified that children evaluators can face the following difficulties [22]:

– understand heuristic description
– understand severity ratings, and
– identify similar issues at the result session, if the group needs to generate a unified list of usability issues.

Similarly, Wodike et al. [25] reported a study adapting HE for teenagers as evaluators. Their adaptation used one teenager as a facilitator for a group of teenagers. The role of the facilitator was to instruct his/her group on how to conduct a HE and also motivate them to evaluate the interface. The evaluations occurred in periods of 30 min. After each period, the evaluators had 15 min to free enjoy the interface. The results of this study did not show satisfactory evidences regarding the participation of the facilitator. Nevertheless, Wodike et al. [25] showed a helpful discussion on the theme, according to them the following characteristics of a HE still need adaptations in order to help teenager evaluators:

– set of heuristic,
– severity rating scale, and
– forms for reporting usability problems.

The previous studies about novice evaluators and HE were not sufficient to provide an adaptation of HE for the whole profile of novice evaluators, beside children and teenagers ones, at the best of our knowledge. In this context, a gap remains in the literature on development of adaptations for HE method that can help novice evaluators to qualify their performance.

3   Study Design

The purpose of this study was to adapt HE for novice evaluators. Specifically, we investigated situations in which novice evaluators could possibly misunderstood different heuristics - from the traditional set of heuristics of Nielsen and Molich - as similar in order to adapt them to be better understood by novices. For this reason, we designed three surveys.

Surveys 1 and 2 were planned to obtain data about what is/are the situation(s) that novice evaluators possibly misunderstand different heuristics. Survey 1 was applied with 13 usability experts, and survey 2 with 15 usability novices. Survey 3 was applied with 7 usability experts and planned to find a suggestion of solution for the situation(s) identified in surveys 1 and 2. All participants that took part in the surveys agreed to participate voluntarily. The surveys were limited to the Brazilian context for convenience with the costs.

4   Survey 1

In Survey 1, we aimed to obtain the view from experts about situations in which novice evaluators could possibly misunderstand different heuristics as similar ones. For this reason, we applied this survey with experts with previous experience teaching or coaching (e.g. in software industry context) novice evaluators; it was required in order to ensure that these experts had knowledge about the challenges that novice evaluators may face.

A total of thirteen (13) usability experts took part in this survey. Among them, five (5) respondents were PhD in usability related area, and three (3) were MSc in usability related area. The other five (5) respondents have at least four years of research or job experience in usability related area.

Each respondent was asked to inform whether novice evaluators could possibly misunderstand one specific heuristic with another as similar. The respondents were asked to fill an on-line form containing all the ten heuristics of Nielsen and Molich. For each heuristic, respondents were able to mark another heuristic(s), or option "none", they believed was/were **possibly misunderstood as similar (p.m.a.s.)** by novice evaluators.

4.1   Results and Discussion

Table 1 shows the results of Survey 1. Each column shows one of the heuristics of Nielsen and Molich. Each row shows the number of times possible answer was marked.

Analysing the results showed in Table 1, one can see that some values appear to be much higher than the others for each column (heuristic). However, further analysis need to be done in order to verify the significance of these higher values among the others of the same column. For this reason, we decided to apply a box plot analysis on each column in order to verify the presence of outliers. We understand that analyzing the presence of outliers we could make a filter to focus our study in the most important cases of possible similarities.

Table 1. Results of Survey 1. Number of times that a response (rows) was selected for each heuristic (columns). The initials p.m.a.s. means "possibly misunderstood as similar".

	Heuristics of Nielsen and Molich									
	1	2	3	4	5	6	7	8	9	10
p.m.a.s. to None	2	0	2	2	1	0	3	6	1	4
p.m.a.s. to Heuristic 1	■	4	3	3	7	7	4	3	7	3
p.m.a.s. to Heuristic 2	2	■	1	10	3	8	3	4	1	2
p.m.a.s. to Heuristic 3	3	1	■	2	5	1	8	1	2	1
p.m.a.s. to Heuristic 4	3	7	2	■	3	6	2	4	2	2
p.m.a.s. to Heuristic 5	4	2	4	2	■	1	3	1	6	3
p.m.a.s. to Heuristic 6	3	8	0	5	4	■	3	4	5	4
p.m.a.s. to Heuristic 7	3	1	9	2	3	2	■	1	1	0
p.m.a.s. to Heuristic 8	2	3	1	4	2	1	1	■	2	0
p.m.a.s. to Heuristic 9	7	3	2	4	9	6	3	2	■	6
p.m.a.s. to Heuristic 10	1	3	2	3	5	3	2	1	4	■

The box plot analysis showed the presence of five outliers among all results (see Fig. 1). For each box in Fig. 1 we described which heuristic that its p.m.a.s. value was identified as an outlier. The following outliers were detected:

- The value of p.m.a.s. of heuristic 9 was an outlier among the responses for heuristic 1.
- The value of p.m.a.s. of heuristic 7 was an outlier among the responses for heuristic 3.
- The value of p.m.a.s. of heuristic 2 was an outlier among the responses for heuristic 4.
- The value of p.m.a.s. of heuristic 9 was an outlier among the responses for heuristic 5.
- The value of p.m.a.s. of heuristic 3 was an outlier among the responses for heuristic 7.

Among the outliers detected, the presence of the heuristics 3 and 7 can be highlighted. Heuristic 7 was an outlier among the responses for heuristic 3; and also heuristic 3 was an outlier among the responses of heuristic 7. This kind of reflexivity occurred only between heuristics 3 and 7. For this reason, we believed that we should focus this study on to adapt both heuristics 3 and 7 in order to mitigate the problem of possible misunderstandings. Furthermore, we designed Survey 2 in order to have more insights and possible confirmation about this.

5   Survey 2

Survey 2 was prepared to collect complementary data to the results from Survey 1 in order to help us to define which/what heuristic(s) should be adapted

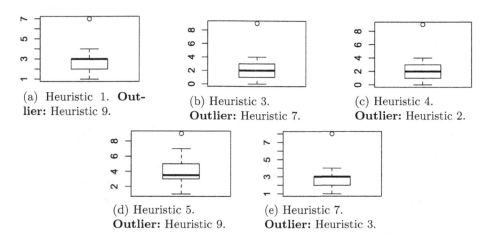

Fig. 1. Box plot showing the presence of outliers among the p.m.a.s values for each heuristic (values of each column in Table 1).

for novice evaluators. In Survey 2, we asked novice about their difficulty for understanding the different heuristics. We did not ask novices for pointing out similarities, as we asked to the experts in Survey 1, because it would be contradictory: if novice evaluators had domain about the misunderstandings they probably perceive when distinguishing the heuristics, they would be capable of distinguishing them as well. We agree and comprehend that each heuristic of Nielsen and Molich is unique and distinguishable from each other, consequently, if novice evaluators understand the heuristic description they would understand its difference from the other heuristics.

A total of 15 novice evaluators took part in this survey. All of them had only an introductory course about Human-Computer Interaction. The respondents were asked to check a level of difficulty of understanding each one of the ten heuristics of Nielsen and Molich. The possible responses were distributed in a 5 options scale varying from "Very Easy" to "Very Difficult" to understand.

5.1 Results and Discussion

The results of Survey 2 are summarized in the graphs of Fig. 2. Each graph shows the responses regarding a specific heuristic. Only one response was possible for each heuristic. Each graph has a five degree scale (horizontal axis) representing the possible responses (levels of understanding easiness): "Very Easy"; "Easy"; "Neutral"; "Diff." (Difficult); and "Very Diff." (Very Difficult). The vertical axis shows the number of times that each response was checked by the novices.

We analyzed the graphs showed in Fig. 2 according to two different regions: easiness region (from option "Very Easy" to "Neutral"); and difficult region (from option "Neutral" to "Very Diff."). Most of the graphs showed most part of responses in the easiness region, what can mean that novice evaluators do

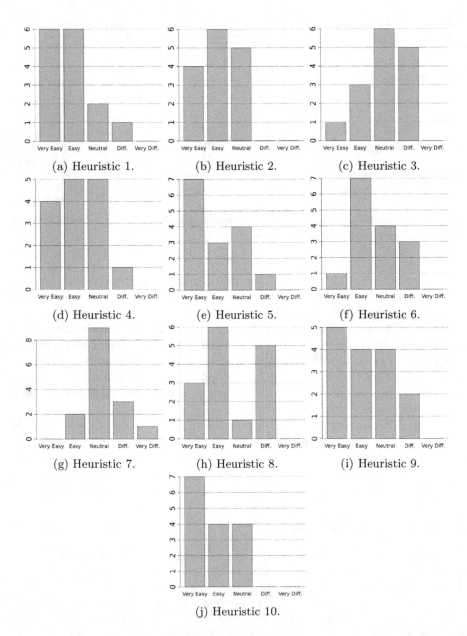

Fig. 2. Number of responses of novice evaluators (vertical axis) that had each level of difficulty (horizontal axis) for understanding each heuristic.

not have many difficulties to understand the heuristics. However, two graphs presented most part of responses in the difficult region: graph (c) and graph (g). These graphs referred to the responses about heuristics 3 and 7, respectively. The characteristic of these graphs were in accordance to the findings of Survey 1 and, for this reason, we believe that both surveys 1 and 2 provided evidences that some kind of clarifying of heuristics 3 and 7 should be made for novice evaluators. In this context, we prepared Survey 3 in order to discuss and develop the adaptations needed for heuristics 3 and 7.

6   Survey 3

Survey 3 was aimed to develop adaptations for heuristics 3 and 7 of the traditional set of usability heuristics of Nielsen and Molich. In this survey, we showed the results of survey 1 and 2 to usability experts, and asked them to suggest adaptations for both heuristics in order to mitigate the difficulty that novices have to understand these heuristics and, also, capacitate novices to distinguish each heuristic from the other. The method for this survey was based on the method used in [12].

A total of seven experts took part in survey 3. Among them, two were PhD in usability related area. All the others had at least four years of experience with heuristic evaluation and teaching novice evaluators about the method. Two usability researchers, the authors of this study, analyzed the suggestions made by the experts in order to synthesize them in a final new description for heuristic 3 and for heuristic 7.

6.1   Results and Discussion

The results of survey 3 showed that the experts preferred to adapt the title of the heuristics, while little changes were made in the descriptions. Two usability researchers compiled the suggestions of the experts with the traditional title and description of the heuristics (retrieved from [16]) to achieve the adaptations aimed by this study. The adapted heuristics are as follows:

Heuristic 3 - Control to undo and redo actions: Users often choose system functions by mistake - e.g. after actions of trial and error - and will need a clearly marked "emergency exit" to leave the unwanted state without having to go through an extended dialogue. Support undo and redo.

Heuristic 7 - Accelerators, shortcuts and efficiency of use: Accelerators (e.g. shortcuts) - unseen by the novice user - may often speed up the interaction for the expert user such that the system can cater to both inexperienced and experienced users. Allow users to tailor frequent actions.

The evidences from this study were not enough to ensure that these adapted heuristics are actually easier for novice evaluators to understand or distinguish them. However, these were initial contributions to this new field about heuristic evaluation for novice evaluators. Further studies are planned in order to explore the generalization of these findings. In addition, we suggest, as future studies, to validate the use of these adapted heuristics in comparison to the use of the traditional heuristics. Future researches can also explore new possibilities of adapting HE for novice evaluators.

7   Conclusions

Heuristic Evaluation (HE) is a popular method of usability inspection. It has many advantages in comparison to other methods. However, it is still dependent on the expertise of evaluators to produce results of quality. The conduction of HEs by novice evaluators is still not well supported.

In this study we investigated reasons and ways to adapt the HE for novice evaluators. The results of this study showed evidences that heuristics 3 and 7 of the traditional set are probably the most difficult for novice evaluators to understand and distinguish from each other. For this reason, we developed adaptations for these two heuristics, based on the knowledge of seven usability experts. The effectiveness of these adaptations in helping novice evaluators still needs to be tested.

Much is still needed in order to have a well-defined adaptation of HE for novice evaluators. This study was limited to a sample in the Brazilian scenario. Future studies can replicate our method with larger samples, also considering contexts from other countries. In addition, further researches can verify the validity of the adapted heuristics and compare the difference of performances among groups of novice evaluators using the traditional set of heuristics, and group of novice evaluators using our new set of heuristics adapted for them.

Acknowledgments. We thank all volunteers that took part in the interview, CAPES and FAPESP for their great support. We also thank the Research Group Intermídia, from USP São Carlos, and ALCANCE, from Federal University of Lavras, for their kindly help. Also, we thank Professor Rudinei Goularte for his great advices at this study.

This study was supported by the grant #2015/09493-5, São Paulo Research Foundation (FAPESP).

References

1. Aljohani, M., Blustein, J.: Heuristic evaluation of university institutional repositories based on DSpace. In: Marcus, A. (ed.) DUXU 2015, Part III. LNCS, vol. 9188, pp. 119–130. Springer, Heidelberg (2015). http://dx.doi.org/10.1007/978-3-319-20889-3_12
2. Borys, M., Laskowski, M.: Expert vs novice evaluators: comparison of heuristic evaluation assessment. In: 16th International Conference on Enterprise Information Systems, ICEIS 2014, vol. 3, pp. 144–149. SciTePress, Institute of Computer Science, Lublin University of Technology, Nadbystrzycka 38D street, Lublin, Poland (27 – 30 April 2014). http://www.scopus.com/inward/record.url?eid=2-s2.0-84902317753&partnerID=40&md5=082b03b8939cb1402c592a0e1a04b4ec

3. Botella, F., Alarcon, E., Peñalver, A.: A new proposal for improving heuristic evaluation reports performed by novice evaluators. In: Proceedings of the 2013 Chilean Conference on Human – Computer Interaction, ChileCHI 2013, pp. 72–75. ACM, New York (2013). http://doi.acm.org/10.1145/2535597.2535601

4. Botella, F., Alarcon, E., Peñalver, A.: How to classify to experts in usability evaluation. In: Proceedings of the XV International Conference on Human Computer Interaction, Interacción 2014, pp. 25:1–25:4. ACM, New York (2014). http://doi.acm.org/10.1145/2662253.2662278

5. Følstad, A., Law, E., Hornbæk, K.: Analysis in practical usability evaluation: a survey study. In: Proceedings of the SIGCHI Conference on Human Factors in Computing Systems, CHI 2012, pp. 2127–2136. ACM, New York (2012). http://doi.acm.org/10.1145/2207676.2208365

6. Hertzum, M., Jacobsen, N.E.: The evaluator effect: a chilling fact about usability evaluation methods. Int. J. Hum. Comput. Interact. **13**(4), 421–443 (2001). http://dx.doi.org/10.1207/S15327590IJHC1304_05

7. Johannessen, G.H.J., Hornbæk, K.: Must evaluation methods be about usability? devising and assessing the utility inspection method. Behav. Inf. Technol. **33**(2), 195–206 (2014)

8. de Lima Salgado, A., Freire, A.P.: Heuristic evaluation of mobile usability: a mapping study. In: Kurosu, M. (ed.) HCII 2014, Part III. LNCS, vol. 8512, pp. 178–188. Springer, Heidelberg (2014). http://dx.doi.org/10.1007/978-3-319-07227-2_18

9. Lowry, P.B., Roberts, T.L., Romano Jr., N.C.: What signal is your inspection team sending to each other? using a shared collaborative interface to improve shared cognition and implicit coordination in error-detection teams. Int. J. Hum. Comput. Stud. **71**(4), 455–474 (2013). http://www.scopus.com/inward/record.url?eid=2-s2.0-84873294809&partnerID=40&md5=f026536f373be4e0af491965aed5e4c7

10. MacFarlane, S., Pasiali, A.: Adapting the heuristic evaluation method for use with children. In: Workshop on Child Computer Interaction: Methodological Research, Interact, pp. 28–31 (2005)

11. MacFarlane, S., Sim, G., Horton, M.: Assessing usability and fun in educational software. In: Proceedings of the 2005 Conference on Interaction Design and Children, pp. 103–109. ACM (2005)

12. Mankoff, J., Dey, A.K., Hsieh, G., Kientz, J., Lederer, S., Ames, M.: Heuristic evaluation of ambient displays. In: Proceedings of the SIGCHI Conference on Human Factors in Computing Systems, CHI 2003, pp. 169–176. ACM, New York (2003). http://doi.acm.org/10.1145/642611.642642

13. Martins, A.I., Queirós, A., Silva, A.G., Rocha, N.P.: Usability evaluation methods: a systematic review. Human Factors in Software Development and Design, p. 250 (2014)

14. Nielsen, J.: Finding usability problems through heuristic evaluation. In: Proceedings of the SIGCHI Conference on Human Factors in Computing Systems, pp. 373–380. ACM (1992)

15. Nielsen, J.: Heuristic evaluation. In: Usability Inspection Methods, vol. 17, pp. 25–62. Wiley & Sons, New York (1994)

16. Nielsen, J.: 10 usability heuristics for user interface design (1995). http://www.nngroup.com/articles/ten-usability-heuristics/

17. Nielsen, J., Molich, R.: Heuristic evaluation of user interfaces. In: Proceedings of the SIGCHI Conference on Human Factors in Computing Systems, pp. 249–256. ACM (1990)

18. Paz, F., Paz, F.A., Pow-Sang, J.A.: Experimental case study of new usability heuristics. In: Marcus, A. (ed.) DUXU 2015, Part I. LNCS, vol. 9186, pp. 212–223. Springer, Heidelberg (2015). http://dx.doi.org/10.1007/978-3-319-20886-2_21

19. Read, J.: Children as participants in design and evaluation. Interactions **22**(2), 64–66 (2015). http://doi.acm.org/10.1145/2735710

20. Preece, J., Sharp, H., Rogers, Y.: Interaction Design: Beyond Human-Computer Interaction, 4th edn. John Wiley & Sons Ltd., Chichester (2015)

21. Salian, K., Sim, G.: Simplifying heuristic evaluation for older children. In: Proceedings of the India HCI 2014 Conference on Human Computer Interaction, IndiaHCI 2014, pp. 26:26–26:34. ACM, New York (2014). http://doi.acm.org/10.1145/2676702.2676704

22. Salian, K., Sim, G., Read, J.C.: Can children perform a heuristic evaluation? In: Proceedings of the 11th Asia Pacific Conference on Computer Human Interaction, APCHI 2013, pp. 137–141. ACM, New York (2013). http://doi.acm.org/10.1145/2525194.2525200

23. Scheller, T., Kühn, E.: Automated measurement of API usability: the API concepts framework. Inf. Softw. Technol. **61**, 145–162 (2015). http://www.sciencedirect.com/science/article/pii/S0950584915000178

24. Slavkovic, A., Cross, K.: Novice heuristic evaluations of a complex interface. In: CHI 1999 Extended Abstracts on Human Factors in Computing Systems, CHI EA 1999, pp. 304–305. ACM, New York (1999). http://doi.acm.org/10.1145/632716.632902

25. Wodike, O.A., Sim, G., Horton, M.: Empowering teenagers to perform a heuristic evaluation of a game. In: Proceedings of the 28th International BCS Human Computer Interaction Conference on HCI 2014-Sand, Sea and Sky-Holiday HCI, pp. 353–358. BCS (2014)

Eye Tracking Usability Testing Enhanced with EEG Analysis

Julia Falkowska[1(✉)], Janusz Sobecki[2], and Martyna Pietrzak[3]

[1] Eyetracking sp. z o.o., Warsaw, Poland
julia.falkowska@wp.pl
[2] Faculty of Computer Science and Management,
Wrocław University of Technology, Wrocław, Poland
Janusz.Sobecki@pwr.edu.pl
[3] Faculty of Cognitive Sciences, University of Warsaw, Warsaw, Poland
martyna.pietrzak@eyetracking.pl

Abstract. We proposed a study evaluating and verifying the validity of the enhancement of eye tracking usability testing with EEG analysis. The aim of our research was to find if there were any regularities and correlations between eye contact characteristics and emotional reaction during task performance. We defined different types of web elements (AOI) for the selected web application and we checked the values of user emotions as generated by EMOTIV EPOC while watching these AOI's.

Keywords: Eye tracking · Tobii X2-60 · EEG · EMOTIV EPOC · Usability testing

1 Introduction

Usability testing with users is now one of the most popular method for website evaluation in user-centered interaction design [1]. There are different ways to conduct usability tests where we can observe user's task performance. Nowadays we can identify over one hundred different usability testing methods [4], for example the experimentation with a moderator in a special usability laboratory [5], or the remote testing in the user's environment [6]. Many methods utilize different equipment such as video recorders, eye trackers, thermal cameras and EEG devices.

In our research we decided to enhance the eye tracking usability testing with EEG metrics analysis in order to enable experts to provide conclusions about usability of web applications, based on the results of the selected SimplyTick web-based system for analysis [11]. Due to the grouping of webpage elements into different sections (i.e. highlight_boxes) it was possible to evaluate whether they were easily noticeable and helped users to complete the task or if they rather distracted their attention. The data we worked with was collected by Tobii X2-60 eye tracker and EMOTIV EPOC EEG devices.

The content of the paper is as follows, the second paragraph presents problem of application of Tobii X2-60 eye tracker in usability testing, the third paragraph introduces Emotiv EPOC application in user emotion determination, the fourth paragraph presents the conducted usability testing experiment of the SimplyTick web-based

A. Marcus (Ed.): DUXU 2016, Part I, LNCS 9746, pp. 399–411, 2016.
DOI: 10.1007/978-3-319-40409-7_38

system with application of eye tracker and EEG analysis, the following two paragraphs discuss the obtained experimental results and further implications.

2 Eye Tracking Testing with Tobii X2-60

Eye tracking is one of the most advanced methods used in usability testing [2]. Gathering the eye tracking data gives us considerably more information about user's behavior than a standard user tests. In our study we aimed to test the usability of the web application – SimplyTick with Tobii hardware X2-60 – a small and portable eye tracker [3] that approximately shows where people are looking using 60 Hz sampling rate. It enables both qualitative and quantitative research using calculations of several metrics.

In order to conduct the usability testing experiments with Tobii X2-60 and analyze the gathered experimental data we had to use Tobii Studio software. With this software it is possible to identify the areas of interest (AOI), which define the areas in the stimulus that are of interest within the scope of the experimental eye tracking analysis [7]. AOIs enables defining and tracking future experimental events, such as dwelling, transitions and AOIs hits. To improve our eye tracking data analysis, we divided each application's subpage into elements with different purposes and then allotted them to main AOI areas.

From the Tobii Studio software package we chose several metrics predefined by the producer, that in our opinion would describe the usability characteristics best. Those were [3]:

- Fixation Count Mean (FCM) – measuring the number of times the participant fixates on an AOI. This metric sets down how many times a user has visited the element (particular AOI) and, following on from this, whether and how much it enchained respondents' attention.
- First Fixation Duration Mean (FFDM) – measuring the duration of the first fixation on an AOI. Owing to this metric, it is possible to indicate 'attractiveness' of an element – whether it seemed interesting to a user or not.
- Fixation Duration Mean (FDM) – measuring the duration of each individual fixation within an AOI. Due to this metric we can calculate the average time of respondent's single look at the particular AOI, so then, whether it is interesting or easy to proceed.
- Time To First Fixation Mean (TTFFM) – measuring how long it takes before a test participant fixates on an active AOI. The measurement of time starts when the AOI is displayed for the first time. This metric allows to describe the catchiness of an element and characterizes what is the most noticeable part of the webpage.
- Visit Duration Mean (VDM) – measuring the duration of each individual visit within an AOI, where the visit is defined as the time interval between the first fixation on the AOI and the end of the last fixation within the same AOI, without outside fixations. Owing to this metric we can investigate the average time that users dedicated to each element, and with regard to this, how long it took them to for example, to find information.

- Visit Count Mean (VCM) – measuring the number of visits within a particular AOI, where the visit is defined as the time interval between the first fixation on the AOI and the end of the last fixation within the same AOI, without outside fixations. This metric calculates how often a user had been visiting an AOI.

By merging values of these metrics the eye tracking experts can provide conclusions about usability of each element [7].

3   EEG Emotion Recognition with EMOTIV EPOC

It is believed that there are many similarities between eye tracking Electroencephalography (EEG), because the sampling frequencies are of the same range and both signals can be investigated as the process is measured [7]. There are many different EEG technologies, which are based on high- and low- impedance, that need different post-processing. Most EEG measurements are non-invasive and are based on the head surface measurements, which must take into account individual variance of the thickness of the skull and scalp. EEG data are usually presented in form of waves that correspond to the activity of the brain. These waves could be manually or automatically interpreted, i.e. it is possible to detect some emotions connected to decision making or reacting to a particular stimulus.

There are many commercial EEG devices available nowadays, i.e. Neurosky, Mindflex, EMOTIV and it is believed that the best low-cost (about 750 USD) device is the last headset – EMOTIV EPOC [8]. It's Software Development Kit for research includes 14 channels based on the international 10–20 electrode location system (plus CMS/DRL references) that use saline sensors and wireless connection as well as quite a large 12 h operating time without external power supply. The impedance of the electrode is decreased by using saline liquid to 10–20 kΩ. It collects neuro data by recording raw brain signals, at a rate of 128 samples per second and then computes them to emotional indicators [10]. No earlier training nor calibration of a user is needed.

The EMOTIV EPOC is provided with a software suite consisting of the following three different detection applications working in real-time: Expressive, Affective and Cognitive. The first interprets the user's facial expressions, the second monitors the user's emotional states and the last enables standard BCI-like control.

EMOTIV EPOC is quite easy to manage and completely non-invasive. The headset is found to cause almost no discomfort whilst installed on the participant's head, so it can be successfully applied to usability testing, where users' comfort during data collection is very important.

The EMOTIV Affective monitors several emotional states, however the company doesn't reveal any exact algorithms for the identification of these emotions. The results are told to have been validated by data collected over recording sessions, and relate to the distribution and correlations in brain networks. The Affective suite monitors the following emotional states [9]:

- Frustration (frst) – described as an unpleasant feeling arousing while a person is not able to perform a task or cannot satisfy their need. The more helpless they feel, the higher the level of frustration score gets.
- Short term excitement (shrt) – is experienced when the subject feels the psychological arousal of positive value. The level of short term excitement rises in response to both surprising or distracting situations.
- Meditation (med) – its score represents a person's composure and calmness. It's level gets higher as a person settles.
- Engagement (eng) – it is experienced when the subject is alert and consciously directs attention towards task-relevant stimuli, the opposite of which is "Boredom". The level of engagement may increase when a person is concentrated, for example during calculating. What decreases the engagement score is closing of the eyes.
- Long term excitement (long) – it reflects a person's general mood (or emotional state), rather than reactions to short surprising stimuli. It is based on the weighted running average of the short-term excitement.

To record EEG data from EMOTIV EPOC and integrate it with Tobii eye tracking, we used the NXRecorder (owned by Eyetracking sp. z o.o.) software, by which it was possible to synchronize the recorded data and the NXWebAnalizer (owned by Eyetracking sp. z o.o.) to visualize the results (see Fig. 1).

4   Experiment Description

In order to conduct the usability testing using eye tracing and EEG analysis we selected the prototype of the SimplyTick [11] web-based application. It serves as the management dashboard for online stores that keep track of business' sales in real-time and finds customers' preferences. The application was developed within the scope of the BIWiSS grant (mentioned in Acknowledgement section). It is planned to be available for common use by the end of March 2016. For the purpose of our study we used the early prototype version with the following subpages: *Basic, Customers* and *Sale* (see Fig. 1).

4.1   Participants

There were 11 people that took part in this experiment – 7 women and 4 men from Warsaw and Wrocław, Poland. All of them were Polish native speakers. Data collected from 10 of them (6 women, 4 men) was included into further investigation. The age of all the participants ranged from 21 to 40 with the mean value equal to 28 years old. 7 participants had a master's or bachelor's degree, 2 own a diploma of Incomplete Higher Education and 1 had finished a secondary school with a maturity diploma. They declared that their knowledge of English is at least at B1 level.

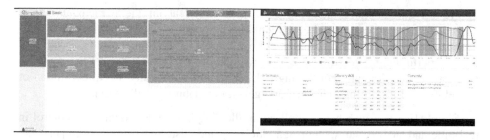

Fig. 1. SimplyTick Basic page with defined AOIs (left), and NXRecorder output with AOIs (right).

4.2 Detailed Experiment Description

The experiment was conducted on December 2nd (Wrocław) and December 3rd (Warsaw). It took place in the Interactive Systems Laboratory at Wrocław University of Technology and in an Eye tracking Laboratory in Warsaw with the attendance of one or two experimenters. The main aim of the study was to enhance the eye tracking usability testing with EEG analysis and to find possible correlations between the eye contact characteristics and emotional reactions during task performance. As it was mentioned before we used Tobii X2-60 eye tracker with Tobii Studio software and the EMOTIV EPOC headset with the Effective software suite.

There were four tasks prepared, each related to testing main the functionalities of the SimplyTick system. Instructions to perform them were given in Polish and participants were to execute all of them, telling the supposed answer out loud. The order of the task was random and it was generated separately for each respondent. There was also a pre-task, conducted to give users the possibility to get acquainted with the webpage and to check if all the devices were connected and worked properly. The results of the pre-task were not given to further analysis. None of the tasks had time a limit and participants were also allowed to ask questions anytime they needed (for example when they had forgotten the instruction). The tasks performed are listed below:

- Provide the difference in the amount of visits to a website between 2014 and 2015.
- Provide the most frequently used source of entering the website.
- Provide information about incomes in 2014 and check users whose operating system had the largest share in these incomes.
- Check in which month of 2015 the smallest number of orders was placed. Next, provide the mean number of all the orders for this month.

The procedure of the experiment was as follows:

1. Participant reception and explanation of main premises of the study.
2. Introduction to the SimplyTick application in the context of its specification. Each participant was given exactly the same information in the form of a short presentation in English – the application's characteristics and a role they were asked to play (an owner of some business).

3. Pre-test questionnaire including basic information about the participant – their gender, age, profession and educational background.
4. Installation of EEG data recorder and eye tracker calibration.
5. Test performing with simultaneous registration of eye tracking and EEG data.
6. Post-test questionnaire concerning task realization – difficulty level, description of helpful and disturbing elements, and general readability of the service.

SimplyTick is a web-based application allowing businesses' owners to control in real-time and analyze sales, campaign efficiency and customers' preferences [11]. We divided its subpages with regard to specific elements and defined 4 AOI groups, which were further divided as shown in Table 1.

Table 1.   SimplyTick elements division

Subpage name	AOI name	AOI group name
Basic	navigation	*operation*
	dates_setup	
	box_revenue	*highlight_boxes*
	box_visit	
	box_order	
	box_bounce	
	box_conversion	
	box_marketing	
Customers	navigation	*operation*
	dates_setup_2	
	source_setup	
	box_revenue_2	*highlights_boxes*
	box_visit_2	
	graph_a	*graphs*
	graph_b	
Sales	navigation	*operation*
	dates_setup_3	
	box_revenue_3	*highlights_boxes*
	box_sessions_3	
	box_visits	
	box_abandoned	
	box_order_3	
	box_avarage_3	
	graph_c	*graphs*
	graph_d	
	graph_e	

By this definition of AOIs and their groups we aimed to evaluate whether specific elements are easily noticeable and help users to complete the task or if they rather distract users' attention.

5 Experimental Results

With regards to the outcomes of the recorded data, our initial hypothesis that there is an emotional reflection in eye tracking usability testing was partially confirmed.

5.1 Eye Tracking Usability Testing

To investigate whether the differences in eye tracking measurements are significant we used the t-student test for each pair of AOIs that was calculated with SPSS software from IBM. In the tables presented below each row highlighted green means that the calculated difference is statistically significant (for example: if Sig. (2-tailed) = 4 it should be understood as 0.004, while the assumed significance level is p = 0.05).

Fixation Count Mean. Table 2 indicates that all the differences between groups of AOI in Fixation Count Mean were statistically significant. As shown in Fig. 2, graphs from all the SimplyTick subpages focused the greatest number of fixations from all the AOI groups, which means that respondents were looking at the graphs most frequently. The bigger the number of fixations, the more attention was paid to the element.

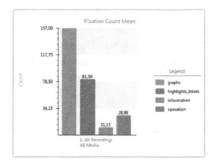

Fig. 2. Fixation Count Mean chart

Table 2. Fixation Count Mean table

Paired Samples Test		Paired Differences					t	df	Sig. (2-tailed)
		Mean	Std. Deviation	Std. Error Mean	95% Confidence Interval of the Difference				
					Lower	Upper			
Pair 1	boxes_FCM - oper_FCM	52.991 667	26 952 303	8 523 066	33 711 151	72 272 185	6 217	9	0
Pair 2	boxes_FCM - inf_FCM	68 750 000	28 845 253	9 615 084	46 577 576	90 922 424	7 150	8	0
Pair 3	boxes_FCM - graph_FCM	-69 416 667	57 033 670	18 035 630	-110 216 096	-28 617 237	-3 849	9	4
Pair 4	oper_FCM - inf_FCM	18.009 259	8 120 880	2 706 960	11 766 998	24 251 520	6 653	8	0
Pair 5	oper_FCM - graph_FCM	-122 408 333	48 653 560	15 385 607	-157 212 994	-87 603 673	-7 956	9	0
Pair 6	inf_FCM - graph_FCM	-143 685 185	48 442 294	16 147 431	-180 921 229	-106 449 142	-8 898	8	0

First Fixation Duration Mean. In Table 3, it is shown that there was a significant difference between 1 out of 6 pairs of AOI only. That was: higlight_boxes vs operation sections. As it can be read from the chart – the longest first fixation concerned the operation AOI, what can mean that respondents needed more time to understand elements from this section or that its elements were the more interesting (than in higlight_boxes).

Table 3. First Fixation Duration Mean table

Paired Samples Test									
		Paired Differences						t	df	Sig. (2-tailed)
		Mean	Std. Deviation	Std. Error Mean	95% Confidence Interval of the Difference				
					Lower	Upper			
Pair 1	boxes_FFDM - oper_FFDM	-42 833	37 249	18 104	-83 787	-1 880	-2 366	9	42
Pair 2	boxes_FFDM - inf_FFDM	8 981	106 323	35 441	-72 745	90 708	253	8	806
Pair 3	boxes_FFDM - graph_FFDM	13	122	39	-74	100	333	9	747
Pair 4	oper_FFDM - inf_FFDM	41 296	95 416	31 805	-32 047	114 639	1 298	8	230
Pair 5	oper_FFDM - graph_FFDM	55 667	97 584	30 859	-14 141	125 474	1 804	9	105
Pair 6	inf_FFDM - graph_FFDM	6 389	97 804	32 601	-68 790	81 568	196	8	850

Fixation Duration Mean. There were statistically significant differences detected in 5 of 6 pairs in Fixation Duration Mean analysis. The longest average time of one fixation related to operation AOI, meaning that respondents probably needed more time to process elements from this section in comparison to elements from other sections (Table 4).

Table 4. Fixation Duration Mean table

Paired Samples Test									
		Paired Differences						t	df	Sig. (2-tailed)
		Mean	Std. Deviation	Std. Error Mean	95% Confidence Interval of the Difference				
					Lower	Upper			
Pair 1	boxes_FDM - oper_FDM	-62 083	77 204	24 414	-117 312	-6 855	-2 543	9	32
Pair 2	boxes_FDM - inf_FDM	38 519	43 035	14 345	5 439	71 598	2 685	8	28
Pair 3	boxes_FDM - graph_FDM	-14 750	42 827	13 543	-45 386	15 886	-1 089	9	304
Pair 4	oper_FDM - inf_FDM	102 222	86 386	28 795	35 820	168 624	3 550	8	8
Pair 5	oper_FDM - graph_FDM	47 333	63 887	20 303	1 631	93 036	2 343	9	44
Pair 6	inf_FDM - graph_FDM	-52 130	56 253	18 751	-95 370	-8 890	-2 780	8	24

Time To First Fixation Mean. In Time To First Fixation Mean parameter, only one pair of AOI had an insignificant difference (0.051, while p = 0.050). From other sections we can conclude, that the most time-consuming element to notice belongs to the information section. That may indicate that this AOI seemed less visually interesting than others (Table 5).

Table 5. Time To First Fixation Mean table

Paired Samples Test		Paired Differences			95% Confidence Interval of the Difference		t	df	Sig. (2-tailed)
		Mean	Std. Deviation	Std. Error Mean	Lower	Upper			
Pair 1	boxes_TTFFM - oper_TTFFM	-2 723 167	2 213 636	700 013	-4 306 706	-1 139 627	-3 890	9	4
Pair 2	boxes_TTFFM - inf_TTFFM	-4 841 759	2 552 806	850 935	-6 804 020	-2 879 499	-5 690	8	0
Pair 3	boxes_TTFFM - graph_TTFFM	-1 580 250	1 660 078	524 963	-2 767 798	-392 702	-3 010	9	15
Pair 4	oper_TTFFM - inf_TTFFM	-2 603 796	3 029 609	1 009 870	-4 932 560	-275 033	-2 578	8	33
Pair 5	oper_TTFFM - graph_TTFFM	1 142 917	1 603 625	507 111	-4 248	2 290 081	2 254	9	51
Pair 6	inf_TTFFM - graph_TTFFM	3 630 648	2 360 448	786 816	1 816 247	5 445 049	4 614	8	2

Visit Duration Mean. For Visit Duration Mean, there were half as many pairs that exhibited a statistically significant difference. All off them concerned graphs AOI, indicating that on average, visits to this section had been longer than in others (Table 6).

Table 6. Visit Duration Mean table

Paired Samples Test		Paired Differences			95% Confidence Interval of the Difference		t	df	Sig. (2-tailed)
		Mean	Std. Deviation	Std. Error Mean	Lower	Upper			
Pair 1	boxes_VDM - oper_VDM	198 750	632 521	200 021	-253 728	651 228	994	9	346
Pair 2	boxes_VDM - inf_VDM	323 426	547 918	182 639	-97 741	744 593	1 771	8	115
Pair 3	boxes_VDM - graph_VDM	-3 160 583	1 643 286	519 653	-4 336 120	-1 985 047	-6 082	9	0
Pair 4	oper_VDM - inf_VDM	154 537	565 499	188 500	-280 144	589 218	820	8	436
Pair 5	oper_VDM - graph_VDM	-3 359 333	1 665 082	526 545	-4 550 461	-2 168 206	-6 380	9	0
Pair 6	inf_VDM - graph_VDM	-3 707 963	1 218 580	406 193	-4 644 646	-2 771 280	-9 129	8	0

Visit Count Mean. Data from Table 7 can both mean that elements from high-light_boxes grabbed participants' attention the most because of their attractiveness or difficulty to process.

Table 7. Visit Count Mean table

Paired Samples Test		Paired Differences			95% Confidence Interval of the Difference		t	df	Sig. (2-tailed)
		Mean	Std. Deviation	Std. Error Mean	Lower	Upper			
Pair 1	boxes_VCM - oper_VCM	12 758 333	6 067 960	1 918 857	8 417 576	17 099 090	6 649	9	0
Pair 2	boxes_VCM - inf_VCM	21 703 704	7 632 750	2 544 250	15 836 653	27 570 755	8 530	8	0
Pair 3	boxes_VCM - graph_VCM	9 441 667	7 043 083	2 227 218	4 403 349	14 479 985	4 239	9	2
Pair 4	oper_VCM - inf_VCM	8 777 778	3 299 305	1 099 768	6 241 707	11 313 848	7 981	8	0
Pair 5	oper_VCM - graph_VCM	-3 316 667	3 566 130	1 127 709	-5 867 722	-765 611	-2 941	9	16
Pair 6	inf_VCM - graph_VCM	-12 212 963	3 629 095	1 209 698	-15 002 532	-9 423 393	-10 096	8	0

5.2   Eye Tracking Enhanced with EEG

We have compared all emotional indicators (x axis in Fig. 8–17) with Tobi Studio parameters (y axis in Fig. 8–17). To check if there were any correlations to be found, we used Pearson product-moment correlation coefficient (R in Fig. 8–17) with p value = 0,1. In MS Excel we created charts presenting 10 detected correlations that turned out to be statistically significant.

Graphs AOI. As shown in Fig. 3, there was positive correlation found between Short Term Excitement and Visit Duration Mean. One visit in a graph AOI lengthens, with the increase of instantaneous excitement.

There was also positive correlation found between Engagement and Time To First Fixation Mean (Fig. 4). This interdependence shows that the more the respondent engages, the longer they need to notice the first element from graphs AOI.

The last correlation detected in graphs AOI was also positive. It was found between Long Term Excitement and Fixation Duration Mean, meaning, that as the Long Term Excitement score increases, fixations while observing graphs AOI lengthens.

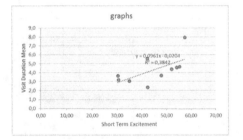 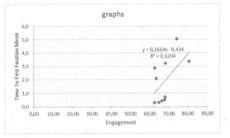

Fig. 3.   shrt-VDM correlation   **Fig. 4.**   eng-TTFFM correlation

Highlight_boxes AOI. In highlight_boxes AOI there were two correlations found, both positive. First of them (Fig. 5) concerned Frustration score and Time To First Fixation Mean. With the increase of frustration, respondents sneeded more time to notice any elements from highlight_boxes AOI. The second positive correlation was found between Long Term Excitement and Visit Duration Mean (Fig. 6). It indicates, that the higher the score of Long Term Excitement, the longer a single visit in high-light_boxes AOI lasts.

Information AOI. The greatest number of correlations was found in information AOI, 4 of them were negative and 1 was positive.

In Fig. 7 a correlation between Frustration and Fixation Count Mean is presented. It suggests that with the increase of frustration, respondents fixate on information AOI elements less often.

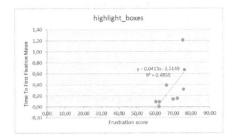

Fig. 5. frst-TTFFM correlation

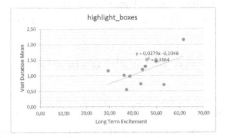

Fig. 6. long-VDM correlation

Another negative correlation was found between Frustration score and Visit Count Mean (Fig. 8). The more frustrated respondents gets, the less they visit an information AOI.

A correlation shown in Fig. 9 is the only positive one found in information AOI. It indicates that as the respondent calms down (the Meditation score gets higher), the duration of a single visit lengthens.

What is interesting, with increasing levels of Meditation, the number of visits in information AOI decreases (Fig. 10). Taking previous correlations into consideration, even though the number of visits decreases, on average, visits last longer.

The last correlation found concerned Short Term Excitement and its influence on Visit Count Mean. In information AOI, the higher the level of Short Term Excitement, the less often the respondents visited an element.

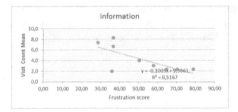

Fig. 7. frst-FCM correlation

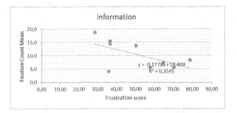

Fig. 8. frst-VCM correlation

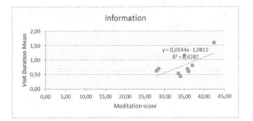

Fig. 9. med-VDM correlation

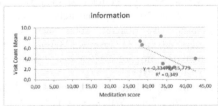

Fig. 10. med-VCM correlation

Operation AOI. There were no significant correlations found between emotional indicators and eye tracking measurements in operation AOI.

6 Discussion and Further Implications

By analyzing the eye tracking data for each AOI on a website, it is possible to provide information about the order of seen elements (gaze plot). With having such an important clue, UX experts are able to scan the exploration path for each visited website and then create an optimal layout.

In our experiment, all examined respondents were Polish. The language of the studied application was English, so there could have appeared a cognitive dissonance in their minds that should be considered as a distracting factor. It would explain the highest levels of EMOTIV indicators – Frustration and Engagement, both connected to concentration and task solving. It could have been frustrating for respondents that all instructions were shown or told in their native language, but the website included foreign-language vocabulary some of which they might not understand. Therefore, to translate the instructions and expressions appearing in the application, they had to pay more attention and as a result increase their engagement level, to find an answer.

If any further searching is conducted, it should consider the differences in both eye tracking and EEG data with regards to the difficulty level of a specific task. All the instructions and applications should be written or said in the same language and more emotional states might be measured with the help of other EEG devices. Moreover, the research group should be increased to around 35 participants.

Acknowledgement. This work was supported by the following grants: ENGINE – http://engine. pwr.edu.pl (Grant Agreement no 316097 of the European Commission under the 7th Framework Programme, Coordination and Support Action) and BiWISS (Grant Agreement no. INNOTECH-K3/IN3/56/225874/NCBR/15 European Union's European Regional Development Fund Third Programme Innotech, IN-TECH).

References

1. Chynał, P., Szymański, J.M., Sobecki, J.: Using eyetracking in a mobile applications usability testing. In: Pan, J.-S., Chen, S.-M., Nguyen, N.T. (eds.) ACIIDS 2012, Part III. LNCS, vol. 7198, pp. 178–186. Springer, Heidelberg (2012)
2. Mohamed, A.O., Perreira Da Silva, M., Courbolay V.: A history of eye gaze tracking (2007), 10 March 2014, http://hal.archivesouvertes.fr/docs/00/21/59/67/PDF/Rapport_interne_1.pdf
3. Studio, User Manual - Tobii. "Ver 3.4.2." Tobii Tecnology AB (2015)
4. Rajeshkumar, S., Omar, R., Mahmud, M.: Taxonomies of User Experience (UX) evaluation methods. In: 3rd International Conference on Research and Innovation in Information Systems (2013)
5. Rubin, J., Chisnell, D.: Handbook of Usability Testing: How to Plan, Design, and Conduct Effective Tests. Wiley, New York (2011)

6. Chynał, P., Sobecki, J.: Statistical verification of remote usability testing method. In: Proceedings of the Mulitimedia, Interaction, Design and Innnovation, p. 12. ACM (2015)
7. Holmquist, K., Nyström, M., Andersson, R., Dewhurst, R., Jarodzka, H., van de Weijer, J.: Eye Tracking: A Comprehensive Guide to Methods and Measures. OUP Oxford, Oxford (2011)
8. Duvinage, M., Castermans, T., Petieau, M., Hoellinger, T., Cheron, G., Dutoit, T.: Performance of the Emotiv Epoc headset for P300-based applications. Biomed. Eng. Online **12**(1), 56 (2013)
9. Emotiv EPOC User Manual, Emotiv 2009
10. Emotiv EPOC Specification, Emotiv 2014, 5 February 2016. https://emotiv.com/product-specs/Emotiv%20EPOC%20Specifications%202014.pdf
11. Simplytick, 5 February 2016. www.simplytick.com

Usability Heuristics for Web Banking

Natali Fierro[1] and Claudia Zapata[2(✉)]

[1] Maestría en Informática, Pontificia Universidad Católica del Perú, Lima, Peru
nfierrod@pucp.pe
[2] Doctorado en Ingeniería, Pontificia Universidad Católica del Perú, Lima, Peru
zapata.cmp@pucp.pe

Abstract. The rapid development of technology has changed the way in which humans and computers interact. This revolution is no stranger to the banking sector, there is a tendency to migrate the services offered by financial institutions face channels to remote channels. This research will focus on the study of the applications of web banking, and through the analysis of the problems it faces, it will seek to establish design guidelines in the form of evaluation methods that allow us to measure the degree of usability of a site, thus contributing to the increase in the degree of user satisfaction by improving the usability of these applications. To achieve this goal, a set of proposed usability heuristics; these also consider issues relating to safety. The proposed heuristic was evaluated in order to compare their effectiveness in contrast to existing heuristics.

Keywords: Usability · Heuristics · Web banking

1 Introduction

The emergence of web banking has been accompanied by a new type of menace for end users: cyber fraud [2, 9, 10]. According to the FFA (Financial Fraud Action), the losses caused by cyber fraud in the UK had an increase of 48 % in 2014 [20]. These events have compromised the user confidence in the web banking, causing the consumers show refusal to conducting their financial operations via online transactions, a phenomenon that is particularly evident in developing countries [5, 6].

In an effort to counter the mistrust associated with the use of web banking, the banks have focused their efforts on developing solutions that deliver high levels of security. However, this emphasis on security has resulted in an increase in the perceived complexity compromising usability [3].

Taking into consideration that several authors argue that characteristics such as quality, perceived safety and usability significantly influence user satisfaction and consequently on the intended use of a site [15, 18], then to promote the adoption of web banking solution is necessary that the increase in the perceived safety goes together with improved usability [1].

Unfortunately most of the time the relationship between security and usability is inversely proportional [9]. Moreover, there are few studies focusing on the importance of the interrelationship of these factors in the field of web banking, and existing work has focused solely on the study of the choice of authentication solutions [1, 3, 9], paying little attention to the usability of the interface as such.

© Springer International Publishing Switzerland 2016
A. Marcus (Ed.): DUXU 2016, Part I, LNCS 9746, pp. 412–423, 2016.
DOI: 10.1007/978-3-319-40409-7_39

It exposed a web banking must be designed and evaluated considering its ease of use and security levels, for which it is required: design guidelines and evaluation methods usability.

2   Heuristic Evaluation and Web Banking

A systematic review of the literature related to usability evaluation was performed on web services, considered as relevant in order to study the work related to the heuristic evaluation usability in e-commerce, transactional services and e-government, and others.

Relevant studies were selected through electronic search in four recognized data bases: Scopus, IEEE Xplore, Science Direct and ACM Digital Library. The keywords used in the search strategy for primary studies were: usability, e-commerce, transactional, e-banking, online, checklist, guidelines, heuristic. The results obtained were filtered based on a review of the title and the abstract; the selected studies are presented below.

2.1   Usability and Transactional Web Services

Paz et al. [14] expose the need for appropriate usability heuristics for evaluating emerging new software products. This premise is verified for transactional web services through a case study. Their work proposes the use of a set of fifteen new usability heuristics for evaluating specific transactional web services.

Meanwhile Garrido et al. [4] studied the problems experienced by users when using electronic processing services offered by their governments. A diagnosis of the state of services electronic procedure is carried out by conducting usability heuristic evaluations sixty transactional services offered by institutional pages of the Chilean government. Their results report usability problems mainly in the following points: (1) user control and freedom, (2) perceived sense of uncertainty (3) absence of user guides. They conclude that usability is an important factor in explaining the slow growth and distrust expressed by users when using a service electronic process variable.

In turn Hughes et al. [7] present a heuristic evaluation tool to assess the usability of financial analysis tools provided in institutional pages from five different countries around the globe. His proposal consists of fourteen heuristics based on the work of Wenham et al. [17].

2.2   Usability and Security

Gonzalez et al. [5] used the approach GQM (Goal Question Metric) and heuristics Johnston et al. [8] to propose a set of metrics to measure the usability and security in e-commerce applications. In addition, they propose a methodology for the design of safe and usable websites [6].

For Nurse et al. [13], usability is one of the most important aspects to consider when designing secure systems because a non-usable system results in improper application of the mechanisms and security policies. With the aim to contribute to obtaining usable and secure applications, consolidate a number of existing general "guidelines" applicable to design usable systems with emphasis on safety.

2.3   Usability and Web Banking

One of the first works on usability in web banking is reported by Wenham and Zaphiris [17], which conducted a review of existing usability evaluation methods and select the most appropriate for assessing implementation of electronic banking. The selected methods are then applied to two case studies and the effectiveness of each method is analyzed. Based on the results propose a set of twelve heuristics to use in evaluating the usability of electronic banking.

Mujinga et al. [11] emphasizes in the vulnerabilities that are exposed web banking users and the necessity to consider usability when designing a secure system. Based on the Nielsen heuristics [12] proposes a heuristic model, consisting of a set of sixteen heuristics, in order to facilitate the design and development of a safe and usable web banking.

3   Methodology

The set of heuristics was obtained using the methodology proposed by Rusu et al. [16], it can be described through six stages (Fig. 1).

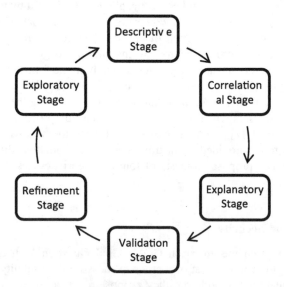

Fig. 1. Methodology

- Exploratory stage: a review of literature related to Internet banking, transactional web services, and security was made.
- Descriptive stage: the most important features of the previously collected information are highlighted, emphasizing aspects related to usability and safety.
- Correlation stage: the main features are identified that a proposal for usability heuristics for web banking should consider, based on Nielsen heuristics.
- Explanatory stage: the set of heuristics proposals formally specified by using a standard template.
- Validation stage: heuristic proposals are validated by performing a heuristic evaluation usability on a previously selected case study, comparing their performance with Nielsen heuristics. In addition, surveys were performed to obtain the appreciations of experts on the proposed heuristics for web banking.
- Refinement stage: were modified some of the heuristics proposals based on feedback obtained from the previous stage.

4 The Proposed Heuristics

Following the methodology described in the previous section has been obtained the set of usability heuristics presented below:

4.1 BIH1 Confidence

Users need to feel a sense of confidence in using the system. Security measures must be visible, user friendly and accessible; you must explain to users how to use the site and the safest way to send alerts when necessary.

Example: Fig. 2 shows a section of the home page of the web banking of Banco de Crédito del Perú (https://www.viabcp.com/wps/portal/viabcpp/personas). The use of the symbol "lock" associated with section "Join your Accounts" transmits the feeling of entering a secure site.

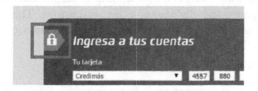

Fig. 2. Example of BIH1 Confidence

4.2 BIH2 Navigability

Navigation of the site must be logically structured and should allow the user to easily move from one place to another. Information should be organized in such a way that the user can easily interact with the system when making a transaction.

4.3   BIH3 Visibility of System Status

Users should be informed of the internal state of the system and state security mechanisms.

Example: Fig. 3 shows the use of iconography to indicate that a security feature of the system is active.

Fig. 3. Example of BIH3 Visibility of System Status

4.4   BIH4 Transaction Status

The system must inform users within a reasonable time, about the success or failure of the transaction.

Example: Fig. 4 shows the use of a notice accompanied by iconography to indicate the status of the execution of a payment transaction.

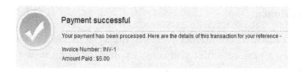

Fig. 4. Example of BIH4 Transaction Status

4.5   BIH5 Familiarity

The system should employ elements, phrases and concepts familiar to the user. They must be used metaphors and dialogues of the real world. The concepts related to security should also be presented in a manner familiar to the user.

4.6   BIH6 Customizing

Users should be free to customize the system interface, including security features, according to their preferences.

Example: Fig. 5 shows the use of customizing of web banking of BBVA Continental (https://www.bbvacontinental.pe). At the top it shows that you can upload a photo.

Fig. 5. Example of BIH6 Customizing

4.7   BIH7 Freedom and User Control

The system must provide support for undo and redo actions. Users could choose a system function by mistake, and they would need a clearly marked exit to leave the undesired state without having to perform many steps.

When possible, it should be allowed users to revoke decisions already taken, including decisions on security measures.

4.8   BIH8 Consistency and Standards

Users should not hesitate if situations, words or different actions mean the same thing. It is very important to maintain a similar design throughout the interface. The website should be consistent not only internally, but consistent with similar sites.

4.9   BIH9 Clarity

The interface should communicate in a simple and concise manner using the language of the user, must transmit the available security features clearly and using appropriate language.

4.10   BIH10 Minimize User Memory Load

The user should not be forced to remember information from a previous state.

System instructions should be easy to remember through highly intuitive interfaces. It could include easy configuration of system security, reduce the number of security decisions that users should take.

4.11   BIH11 Flexibility and Efficiency in Use

The system must provide enough information for novice users, without providing too much information for experienced users.

While novice users may need assistance step by step, expert users should be able to quickly access functionality required by shortcuts.

Example: Fig. 6 shows the correct use of the flexibility and efficiency in use by frequent operations functionality.

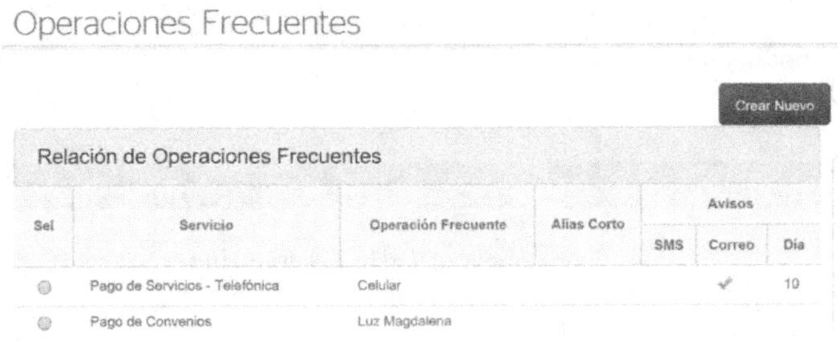

Operaciones Frecuentes

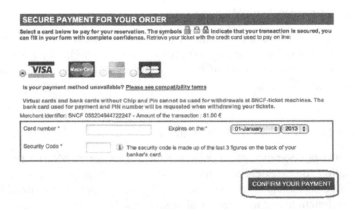

Fig. 6. Example BIH11 Flexibility and Efficiency in Use

4.12 BIH12 Aesthetic and Minimalist Design

Dialogues should not contain information irrelevant or that is rarely used. Every extra unit of information competes with relevant information units and decreases their relative visibility. The interface should contain only relevant for the system or for information security mechanisms. It should not overwhelm the user with information, should reduce the number of settings, passwords to remember.

4.13 BIH13 Error Prevention

Even better than good error handling is a careful design which prevents the occurrence of problems. It is recommended to eliminate error-susceptible conditions or a verification of the same, asking the user for confirmation before performing an action.

Users should know the consequences of any action related to safety, irreversible actions must be clearly marked.

Example: Fig. 7 shows the use of a confirmation button, this mechanism serves to prevent the execution of a payment transaction unwanted.

Fig. 7. Example BIH13 Error Prevention

4.14   BIH14 Helps the User to Recognize, Diagnose and Recover from Mistakes

Error messages should be expressed in clearly language indicating precisely the problem and suggest a solution. If an error occurs should be handled properly.

It should provide users detailed error messages, do not use codes and then allow recovery through simple mechanisms. Care should be taken not to compromise the security of the site to return information about the error occurred.

Example: Fig. 8 shows the correct use of aid the user to recognize, diagnose and recover from errors. It appreciated the use of an informative message about the error produced, it is noteworthy that security is not compromised because no details if the error is in the user or password.

Fig. 8. Example of BIH14 Helps the user to recognize, diagnose and recover from mistakes

4.15   BIH15 Help and Documentation

Although the ideal is that a system can be used without documentation, it is necessary to provide help and documentation. This information should be easy to search, focused on the user's task, list concrete to do and not be too long steps.

Users should be able to easily locate and view online help and documentation system should include documentation of security features. It should also provide recommendations when the user is unsure of a decision and its implications.

5   Validating the Proposal

To validate the usability heuristics, the methodology proposed by Rusu et al. [16], which is to employ two groups working on the same case study on equal terms used.

Usability problems that are identified by each of the groups to be compared using the following criteria:

- P1 - Problems identified by both groups of evaluators
- P2 - Problems identified only by the group using the heuristic proposals
- P3 - Problems identified only by the group using traditional heuristics (Nielsen).

The new usability heuristics work well when:

- P2 includes the highest percentage of usability problems or
- P1 + P2 include the highest percentage of usability problems

  However, if the set P3 includes the highest percentage of usability problems, you must discard the following assumptions:

- H1 - The new heuristics failed to identify many usability problems because they are not properly specified.
- H2 - The evaluators who used the new heuristics ignored subjectively problems.

To validate or reject each of these assumptions will be necessary to make further experiments.

5.1   Case Study

The case study selected to perform the validation of the new set of heuristics was the web banking BBVA Continental (https://www.bbvacontinental.pe/personas/).

The choice of this application as an object of study is justified the participation of BBVA Continental in Peru's banking system, standing at year-end 2014s in loans and deposits and third in economic terms.

Each evaluator is asked to enter the web banking BBVA Continental and perform the following tasks:

- Payment of studies at the Catholic University of Peru
- Consultation savings account balance
- Transfer of funds between accounts
- Querying account credit card

5.2   Evaluation Based on Heuristic Nielsen

Then all the problems associated with each heuristics are presented. It may be observed that the highest percentage of problems (36 %) was associated with heuristics number two "Match between system and the real world" (Table 1).

Table 1. Broken heuristics - Nielsen

ID	Heuristics	Number of problems
NIH1	Visibility of system status	0
NIH2	Coincidence between the system and the real world	8
NIH3	User control and freedom	3
NH4	Consistency and standards	1
NH5	Error prevention	2
NH6	Recognition	2
NH7	Flexibility and efficiency of use	1
NH8	Aesthetic and minimalist design	3
NH9	Helps users recognize, diagnose and recover from mistakes	2
NH10	Help and documentation	0

5.3   Evaluation Based on the New Proposal

Below is all the problems associated with each heuristics are presented. It can be observed that none of them was heuristics associated a percentage significantly higher compared to other problems. Should be noted, the heuristics did not have a counterpart in Nielsen ("BIH1-Confidence", "BIH6- Customizing"), together obtained 12 % (Table 2).

Table 2. Broken heuristics - Proposal

ID	Heuristics	Number of problems
BIH1	Confidence	2
BIH2	Navigability	3
BIH3	Visibility of system status	0
BIH4	Transaction status	0
BIH5	Familiarity	1
BIH6	Customizing	1
BIH7	Freedom and user control	4
BIH8	Consistency and standards	1
BIH9	Clarity	2
BIH10	Minimize user memory load	2
BIH11	Flexibility and efficiency in use	4
BIH12	Aesthetic and minimalist design	2
BIH13	Error prevention	2
BIH14	Helps the user to recognize, diagnose and recover from mistakes	1
BIH15	Help and Documentation	2

5.4   Comparative Analysis

In this section the results of heuristic evaluations by the two groups are listed.

- P1 - Problems identified by both groups of evaluators: 20 %
- P2 - Problems identified only by the group using the heuristic proposed: 46 %
- P3 - Problems identified only by the group using traditional heuristics (Nielsen): 34 %

To compare the detected problems using both proposals, Nielsen heuristics are mapped with the proposals as shown in Fig. 9.

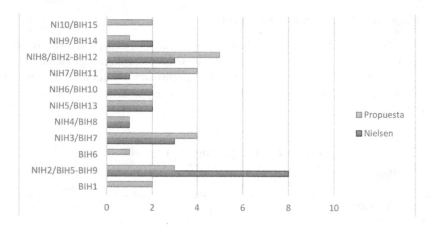

Fig. 9. Problems detected

6 Conclusions and Future Work

The methods, techniques and tools existing for evaluating usability of software applications focus on the characteristics of generic interfaces. However, the web banking has intrinsic to their domain particularities. Therefore, having a specific assessment tool to analyze the usability of these applications is necessary.

This research can develop a theoretical proposal that can integrate security features in usability evaluation of web banking. However, it is important to note that there are certain factors that could influence the data presented in this research, such as the availability of evaluators, the degree of familiarity with the application assessed, among others.

Through the experiments conducted it was determined that the Nielsen heuristics have some limitations when applied to the domain under study, it was observed that most problems identified corresponded to the aesthetic design and the use of metaphors. In contrast, the problems encountered by the proposal concentrated around flexibility and user control. Additionally, it should be noted that the proposal allowed the detection of problems associated with security features, which were not detected by the control group.

Consequently, replication of the experiment in other implementations banking web is necessary. Including implementations made not only by banks but also by financial institutions oriented small businesses, which will allow better analysis of the performance of the proposed heuristics.

References

1. Althobaiti, M.M., Mayhew, P.: Security and usability of authenticating process of online banking: User experience study. In: 2014 International Carnahan Conference on Security Technology (ICCST), pp. 1–6 (2014)

2. Costante, E., et al.: On-line trust perception: What really matters. In: 2011 1st Workshop on Socio-Technical Aspects in Security and Trust (STAST), pp. 52–59 (2011)
3. French, A.M.: A case study on e-banking security-When security becomes too sophisticated for the user to access their information. J. Internet Bank. Commer. **17**(2), 1–14 (2012)
4. Garrido, M. et al.: Usability problems and lines of solutions: an expert evaluation of Chilean online services. In: Proceedings of the 2013 Chilean Conference on Human - Computer Interaction, pp. 76–81. ACM, New York (2013)
5. Gonzalez, R.M. et al.: A measurement model for secure and usable e-commerce websites. In: Canadian Conference on Electrical and Computer Engineering, 2009, CCECE 2009, pp. 77–82 (2009)
6. Gonzalez, R.M. et al.: A pattern methodology to specify usable security in websites. In: 20th International Workshop on Database and Expert Systems Application, 2009, DEXA 2009, pp. 155–159 (2009)
7. Hughes, J., et al.: A heuristic evaluation instrument for e–government online software. Electron. Gov. Int. J. **10**(1), 1–18 (2013)
8. Johnston, J., et al.: Security and human computer interfaces. Comput. Secur. **22**(8), 675–684 (2003)
9. Mockel, C.: Usability and security in EU E-banking systems - towards an integrated evaluation framework. In: 2011 IEEE/IPSJ 11th International Symposium on Applications and the Internet (SAINT), pp. 230–233 (2011)
10. Montazer, G.A., ArabYarmohammadi, S.: Identifying the critical indicators for phishing detection in Iranian e-banking system. In: 2013 5th Conference on Information and Knowledge Technology (IKT), pp. 107–112 (2013)
11. Mujinga, M., et al.: Towards a heuristic model for usable and secure online banking. In: 24th Australasian Conference on Information Systems (ACIS), pp. 1–12. RMIT University (2013)
12. Nielsen, J.: Usability Engineering. Morgan Kaufmann, California (1993)
13. Nurse, J.R.C., et al.: Guidelines for usable cybersecurity: Past and present. In: 2011 Third International Workshop on Cyberspace Safety and Security (CSS), pp. 21–26 (2011)
14. Paz, F., et al.: Usability heuristics for transactional web sites. In: 2014 11th International Conference on Information Technology: New Generations (ITNG), pp. 627–628 (2014)
15. Riffai, M.M.M.A., et al.: Big TAM in Oman: Exploring the promise of on-line banking, its adoption by customers and the challenges of banking in Oman. Int. J. Inf. Manag. **32**(3), 239–250 (2012)
16. Rusu, C., et al.: A methodology to establish usability heuristics. In: ACHI 2011, The Fourth International Conference on Advances in Computer-Human Interactions, pp. 59–62 (2011)
17. Wenham, D., Zaphiris, P.: User interface evaluation methods for internet banking web sites: a review, evaluation and case study. In: Human-Computer Interaction: Theory and Practice, pp. 721–725 (2003)
18. Yoon, H.S., Steege, L.M.B.: Development of a quantitative model of the impact of customers' personality and perceptions on Internet banking use. Comput. Hum. Behav. **29**(3), 1133–1141 (2013)
19. Zhang, H.: The study on evaluation of e-banking web sites from the viewpoint of customers. In: 2010 International Conference on Computer Design and Applications (ICCDA), pp. V2-263–V2-266 (2010)
20. Scams and computer viruses contribute to fraud increases - calls for national awareness campaign. http://www.theukcardsassociation.org.uk/news/EOYFraudFigs2014.asp

A Comprehensive Stylus Evaluation Methodology and Design Guidelines

Kanchan Jahagirdar[1][(✉)], Edward Raleigh[2], Hanan Alnizami[3],
Keith Kao[2], and Philip J. Corriveau[3]

[1] Intel Corporation, Folsom, USA
kanchan.jahagirdar@intel.com
[2] Intel Corporation, Santa Clara, USA
{edward.j.raleigh,Keith.kao}@intel.com
[3] Intel Corporation, Hillsboro, USA
{hanan.alnizami,philip.j.corriveau}@intel.com

Abstract. The stylus is a flexible input device that enables traditional computer interactions and personalization of input. It extends natural and intuitive ways of interacting with computing devices by bringing in the familiar feel of pen on paper. There are two kinds of Styli, Active and Passive. A passive stylus is one that emulates finger touch interactions with no added functionality, while an active stylus is one with added capabilities that could enhance productivity, creativity, and common consumer functions, allowing for a seamless and easy to use computing experience on the go. This paper presents an evaluation methodology for an active stylus. Various factors were considered to provide a set of guidelines and recommendations to enable an optimal stylus experience. Factors identified were based on biomechanics, ergonomics, user preference, human comfort, usability/ease of use, motor control, and performance, all of which collectively impact the experience. The parameters evaluated include overall physical design, adequate palm rejection, productivity usages, efficiency, and convenience. The automated evaluation involves a specific laboratory setup to assess the creative usages of the stylus including accuracy, latency, and pressure sensitivity.

Keywords: Stylus user experience · Stylus evaluation methodology · Design · Quality testing · Electronic pen · Active stylus · Measurement

1 Introduction

The stylus is used across many industries to enhance the productivity and accuracy of interactions. Industrial sectors that have used tablets include retail sales (e.g., assisting customers with product selection), real estate, inventory control, utilities, appliance and machinery repair, design, art, and education. The stylus is also used in the medical industry, and studies have shown that when doctors and nurses used a tablet for simple

---

The original version of this chapter was revised: Figure 4C was removed from the original paper. The Erratum to this chapter is available at DOI: 10.1007/ 978-3-319-40409-7_50

A. Marcus (Ed.): DUXU 2016, Part I, LNCS 9746, pp. 424–433, 2016.
DOI: 10.1007/978-3-319-40409-7_40

tasks, the use of a stylus improved productivity and reduced error when compared to use of a finger [10].

A digital stylus can be used with a tablet computer to improve the experience of human computer interaction and precision of work. The stylus can be used with the tablet in many other settings where mobility is required for note taking, drawing, web browsing, social networking or business applications.

The rapid innovation around input devices has led to a wide variety of styli available for purchase on the internet. The range of styli available vary from Passive to Active stylus. The Passive stylus emulates the finger touch interaction and does not include any electronics in it to provide added functionality. In contrast, the Active stylus has electronics that facilitate communication between the stylus and the device with which it is used. It provides added functionality such as hover capability, scrolling, and palm rejection.

While there is a variety of styli available catering to specific functionalities, and others offering a broader scope of functionalities, there is a lack of research that evaluates user experience holistically when using the stylus as an input modality. Prior literature focuses on writing or drawing with a pen or pencil on paper and touches on issues of psychology [11], motor control [12], biomechanics, preference, legibility, speed, and other factors. The published research begins in the early 1900's and has progressed with technological innovations in research methods. Various studies in the past have provided insights into portions of stylus use and their impact on writing or ergonomics [1, 4, 7, 9, 13]. However, there is no research available that assesses the complete design implementation of a stylus for holistic user experience.

This paper aims to close that gap by presenting a comprehensive stylus evaluation methodology. The methodology is a test suite to characterize the experiences enabled by different stylus implementations. It includes a series of tests for factors that influence a good user experience when using a stylus. The test suite is based on research from various resources including: academic engagements, literature review, user studies, industry recommendations, and online product review sites, from which specific factors important for a good stylus experience were gathered. Factors were identified based on biomechanics, ergonomics, user preference, human comfort, usability/ease of use, motor control, and performance.

The testing suite is split into two main categories: Basic Testing and Advanced Testing. Within each category, there are subsections describing applicable factors and tests for each factor, accompanied by recommendations.

2   Basic Evaluation

The basic testing consists of factors and tests that can be performed manually by a trained evaluator. The basic testing includes four portions, and covers Physical Design Checklist, Palm Rejection, Efficiency & Convenience, and Productivity.

2.1   Physical Design

When considering the design of stylus implementation, the physical affordances are fundamental for using the device as an effective writing/drawing instrument. Pens of different diameters, different cross-sectional shapes, and different weights were tested with college students in Hong Kong as they performed a maze tracing task and a writing task [9]. Another study with employees at Wang tested pens of different diameters and lengths while they drew and wrote on a tablet while watching a monitor [7]. A third study with university students conducted in Taiwan evaluated 12 pens of different lengths and diameter by performing selecting (Fitts' tapping), writing, and drawing tasks on a tablet computer [22, 23]. Online consumer and tech product reviews also indicated the need for a substantial weighted instrument that felt comfortable when writing [19, 20]. Users also liked the option to choose from a variety of colors. Having a variety of colors to choose from is important because a writing instrument is viewed as a personal item [1, 21].

Based on user preference, performance (low error rate), usability, and ergonomics the following set of recommendations for physical design of a stylus were generated.

- Weight: Less than 27 grams [9] but No lighter than 11 grams [19, 20].
- Length: 110–160 mm [7, 22, 23].
- Diameter at grip: 7.5 mm–11 mm [7, 17, 22, 23].
- Cross-sectional shape: Circular [9].
- Grip material: Ribbed grip, matte texture [7].

The tests for the above can be performed by taking physical measurements and making visual observations of the factors mentioned above.

Another aspect related to physical design is palm rejection addressed next since it might impact factors like bezel design which is not addressed in this paper.

2.2   Palm Rejection

Having a robust palm rejection capability in the design implementation of a stylus is another critical consideration when providing a pen or pencil-on-paper-like experience on a digital surface. Being able to comfortably rest the palm on the digital surface while writing is important from both, an ergonomic perspective as well as accuracy. If digital surfaces are to be used on a regular basis, having a robust palm rejection is a must [16]. A stylus would be an ineffective input mechanism if users need to hover their hand over the device surface while using a stylus to avoid unintended actions due to their palm resting on the surface of the device. Since many modern tablets make use of multi-touch recognition, some stylus and app manufacturers have incorporated palm rejection technologies into their products. This works to turn off the multi-touch feature, allowing the palm to rest on the tablet while still recognizing the stylus. A robust palm rejection implementation will enable the users to rest their palm on the touch-screen and use it just as comfortably as using a pen on paper [20].

In order to understand how well the implementation holds up against common writing usages, the researchers looked at various current devices in the market and identified the most common areas of palm rejection errors. When looking at typical right handed stylus usage with a tablet, the researchers found the most errors along the bottom and right edge of the device as the user rested their hand on the screen. Palm rejection errors for left handed users is an area for future exploration. To test for palm

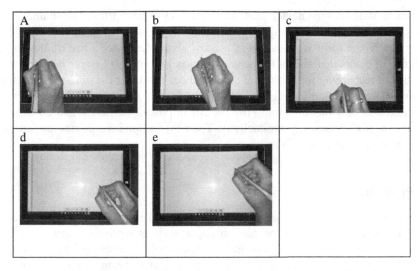

Fig. 1. Palm Rejection Hand Placement: a. Bottom left of the screen, b. Middle of the screen, c. Bottom center edge of the screen, d. Bottom right corner of the screen, e. Middle right edge of the screen.

rejection with left handed usages, scenarios were developed for the following five specific hand placements as shown in Fig. 1a–e. For each of the hand placement positions, the word 'Party' was written and a circle was drawn around the word 'Party'. The word 'Party' was chosen as it included characters that had both descending and ascending parts and a variety of straight and curved parts available in the word [2]. Failures were noted in each run with unintended inking where the hand rested on the screen. Figure 1 above demonstrates the layout of each hand placement position.

In addition to being able to provide a robust palm rejection, there are several other features that can enhance the digital writing and drawing experience.

2.3 Efficiency and Convenience

Additional features, when incorporated into the implementation, provide added convenience and aid efficiency. Many factors were identified as features that users expressed as desirable attributes that would enable the stylus to be used beyond sketching, writing, and selection tasks [19, 20]. The additional features make the stylus multi-functional, providing the user with flexibility, convenience, and increased efficiency during task completion. These features include: (1) An eraser functionality to mimic the traditional pencil on paper experience and leverage existing mental models to quickly erase objects [21], (2) Configurable control buttons so that users can customize the control buttons to perform specific commands [16], (3) A hover capability to provide the same convenience as found in mice to aid in navigation [21], (4) An undo function to be able to quickly revert to previous actions and cut/copy/paste functions to help quick user interactions [8], (5) Auditory feedback to provide confirmation of user actions, (6) Durability of the stylus by providing a protective cover or cap or a way for the stylus to slide into the device shell to protect the stylus tip from any damage [20], (7) Portability of the stylus through a pocket clip, magnetic attachment to the device, or another attachment form as an easy way to stow away the device when on the go [20], (8) Choice of colors that allows for personalization [1], and (9) Longer battery life and easy ways of recharging for additional convenience. The latter list of factors was tested through visual inspection and observation of the feature sets offered.

As noted in previous literature [16, 19, 20] improved efficiency and convenience can lead to a user's increase in productivity. The next section investigates the aspects of a stylus that enhance productivity.

2.4 Productivity

If the stylus was to provide more of a pen-on-paper-like experience, then it needs to support all functions of using the pen on paper such as writing, reviewing, editing, highlighting documents, signing documents, and freehand drawing [8, 14]. Productivity testing included a series of tests based on task analysis to examine the productivity usage of the stylus. It covers writing accuracy, pointing and selecting functionality and collaboration tasks.

When using a stylus, the perception of accuracy during a writing task is impacted by how the inking is rendered on the screen. The perception of stylus accuracy is highly affected by the appearance of broken inking, incomplete or disjointed inking, and/or rugged inking [1]. To uncover the accuracy in writing, two tests were developed. The first test involved writing the following phrase: 'The quick brown fox jumps over the lazy fence' in print using the stylus, as that sentence covers all 26 letters of the alphabet. The second test involved writing a mathematical formula involving symbols with straight and curved strokes. In both cases, failure points were noted in multiple runs of the tests for broken/incomplete inking, non-smooth inking, missing characters or strokes.

In order to understand stylus accuracy when using the device as a pointer and selecting instrument, four user representative tasks involving commonly used Microsoft Office applications were developed. The first one involved using PowerPoint in slide sorter mode to move, delete and add slides. The second task involved moving an image from Word into PowerPoint in multitasking mode. The third task involved watching a YouTube video tutorial on Pivot tables and following along the instructions in multitasking mode while using touch and stylus simultaneously. The final task involved selecting small targets in the system tray of the application (applicable to Windows device only).

To assess how well a stylus could support the collaboration usages, six user tasks involving Microsoft Office Applications and Acrobat PDF were developed. For the first task, the stylus was used to highlight text in PDF, save it and share through available mailing software. The second task involved being able to successfully spell check a Word document. The third task involved editing text of a paragraph in Word. The fourth task involved being able to edit a footnote of a Word document. The fifth task involved being able to highlight and notate a PowerPoint slide in the slideshow mode. The fifth task consisted of playing a video embedded in PowerPoint in the slideshow mode.

The above mentioned tasks were chosen based on task analysis, and are reflective of common productivity tasks across writing, pointing and selecting, and collaboration usages using Microsoft Office applications. Each task was run manually multiple times and was given a score of pass or fail. The usages and tests described in the basic testing section were chosen because they are the most common type of user tasks. The above set of tests were developed to be performed manually by a trained evaluator, and carried out in a manner that is reflective of the user representative task in a reliable manner.

In order to eliminate biases and produce consistent repeatable results, a series of advanced evaluations of the stylus using a robotic arm, Oculus were developed. The advanced testing set up assessed the pen to ink delay, inking accuracy and pressure sensitivity.

3   Advanced Evaluation

The advanced section of the test suite is aimed to evaluate creativity usages of the stylus. A stylus has to enable artistic drawing when using non-touch optimized applications such as graphic design software or a photo editing application [20]. With pressure sensitivity, users also expect their strokes to be rendered smoothly [1]. The tests mentioned in this section were executed by a robotic arm called Oculus, and they cover stroke accuracy, stroke smoothness, and pressure sensitivity.

Fig. 2. The robotic arm drawing straight lines with a stylus on the device under test

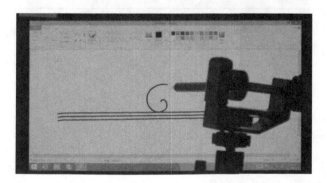

Fig. 3. The robotic arm drawing a spiral with a stylus on the device under test via the high speed camera.

Oculus is a propriety evaluation setup that consists of a 6-axis robotic arm and a high speed camera. The robot can be fitted with multiple end effectors, including one that can grasp the various stylus pens as shown in Figs. 2 and 3 below. The robot is used to execute specific and repeatable actions in a highly controlled manner, including the specification of interaction speed and angle on the device under test, and the interactions are recorded by a high speed camera for later review and extraction of parameters of interest. The entire setup is non-intrusive and device/OS agnostic. In the stylus evaluation described herein, some of the robotic tests also include the use of an angled mirror to determine when initial contact is made by the robot held stylus on the device under test.

When using a stylus, users expects smooth & continuous strokes with no disjointed corners or curves [3]. Also, getting as close to a one-to-one correspondence between the pen and the cursor positions is highly preferred for tablet type devices in order to maintain a perception of accuracy [6].

To check for accuracy, four tests were performed. The first three were done using Oculus as shown in Fig. 4a–c. Oculus was used to draw straight horizontal and diagonal lines as shown in Fig. 4a, spiral lines as shown in Fig. 4b, and a six point star as shown in Fig. 4c. The fourth test was executed manually by a trained evaluator and involved drawing a zigzag line across the screen. The resulting inking was checked for stroke consistency, continuity, and smoothness across all the lines and shapes [2]. In case of the six point star, the angles were evaluated via the ability to produce sharp angles [2]. The six point star has arms of differing lengths (3 mm, 6 mm, 9 mm, 12 mm & 15 mm) to check for accuracy in being able to produce accurate inking of different lengths [1, 2]. The straight lines were checked to ensure they were equidistant to ensure a good mapping.

In order to understand the pressure sensitivity enabled by the implementation, two tests were performed. The first was conducted using Oculus and involved using three specific exerted forces to draw three different lines. The forces used were determined by the range typically used for pencil on paper [18]. The second test involved drawing three different lines manually at three different angles (close to 0 degrees, close to 45 degrees, close to 90 degrees). In both tests, the resulting inking was checked for variation in the stroke thickness across the three lines [1, 20, 21].

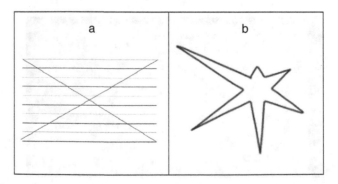

Fig. 4. Images of objects rendered by Oculus: a. straight, diagonal and spiral lines, b. 6-point star.

In addition to checking for accuracy, the Oculus set up was used to calculate latencies. Two types of latencies were calculated: initial latency and average trailing latency. Initial latency is the pen-to-ink delay at the first touch. This latency metric is calculated from when the stylus first touches the screen and the delay in the appearance of the ink on the screen. The trailing latency calculation accounts for the subsequent pen to ink delay of the stylus as it continues to draw the straight lines. It is an average of latencies at the start of the stroke, midpoint and near the end point.

Both initial latency and trailing latency were extracted from the high speed footage by looking through the footage manually in frame-by-frame video editing software. Initial latency was determined by identifying the frame that the stylus makes contact with the device under test with the help of an angled mirror during testing, as well as the frame that ink begins appearing on the device's screen as shown in Fig. 5. These two frame numbers, in addition to the camera frame rate, are used to determine initial latency.

For determining Trailing Latency, a similar process was used. Instead of a contact frame, an initial frame was used, which can be any frame where the robot is in the process of drawing and ink is already showing up on the device. At this point, both the location of where the robot-held stylus tip is on the device under test's screen and the frame number were marked. After the initial markings, the footage was manually stepped through frame by frame until the ink that was being drawn by the robot crossed

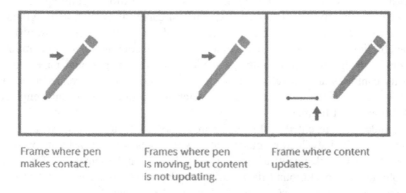

Frame where pen makes contact.   Frames where pen is moving, but content is not updating.   Frame where content updates.

Fig. 5. Frame counting calculation for initial latency

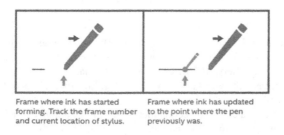

Frame where ink has started forming. Track the frame number and current location of stylus.   Frame where ink has updated to the point where the pen previously was.

Fig. 6. Frame counting calculation for average trailing latency

the threshold passing where the initial mark was placed on the initial frame. See Fig. 6. This frame number was recorded and labeled as the catch frame.

Calculating latency is critical to understanding how well the implementation meets user expectation. Latencies impact the perception of the experience of the device. Delay in inking latencies can cause users to write slower so that they could see what they wrote rather than guess what they wrote [2]. Having lower latencies allows for more efficiency. It has been shown that low latency judgments are made visually. Users use the relative movement between the stylus and ink to be able to make an accurate judgment [1]. Studies have shown that the users can perceive latencies as low approximately two to seven milliseconds for non-inking tasks, and as low as approximately 50 ms for inking tasks [2]. Since latency thresholds have been published, newer technologies have been showing more promise to deliver even lower latencies than 50 ms. While these thresholds can be used to determine how close the implementation is to user expectations, more work is needed to understand how lower latencies impact performance and accuracy of non-inking tasks.

4 Conclusion

With touchscreens becoming more prevalent in phones, tablets, laptops and 2-in-1 s, the stylus becomes an integral part of the computing interaction experience. Styli support a multitude of capabilities in addition to the traditional pointing & selecting functionality. An active stylus provides additional capabilities such as programmable buttons, pressure sensitivity, reduced latency, and eraser functions. However, these new capabilities and technical advancements produce complexity of integration and optimization to the interaction with the device. The use of pen and paper has been around for centuries and, therefore, sets a strong level of end-users expectations when using a stylus. In order to meet these expectations, careful design and engineering considerations must be met.

The guidelines presented in this paper are important factors for stylus design, and represent a detailed evaluation guide with user representative tasks as well as an advanced setup to holistically assess a stylus design implementation. The included methodologies and background data can enable better stylus designs that provides a more robust, flexible, efficient, and enriching user experience.

References

1. Annett, M., Anderson, F., Bischof, W., Gupta, A.: The pen is mightier: understanding stylus behaviour while inking on tablets. In: Graphics Interface Conference, pp. 193–200 (2014)
2. Annett, M., Ng, A., Dietz, P., Bischof, W.F., Gupta, A.: How low should we go? understanding the perception of latency while inking. In: Proceedings of Graphics Interface, pp. 167–174 (2014)
3. Chirag, Y., Fujii, Y., Valera, J.: Direction measurement of friction acting between a ballpoint pen and paper. In: SICE Annual Conference, pp. 1518–1521 (2004)

4. Dong, H., Barr, A., Loomer, P., LaRoche, C., Young, E., Rempel, D.: The effects of periodontal instrument handle design on hand muscle load and pinch force. JADA **137**, 1123–1130 (2006)
5. Digital Trends, http://www.digitaltrends.com/mobile/best-stylus-for-tablets/
6. Forlines, C., Vogel, D., Kong, N., Balakrishnan, R.: Absolute Vs. Relative Pen Input. Mitsubishi Electric Research Laboratries (2006)
7. Francik, E., Akagi, K.: Designing a computer pencil and tablet for handwriting. Proc. Hum. Factors Ergon. Soc. Ann. Meet. **33**, 445–449 (1989)
8. Goldberg, D., Goodisman, A.: Stylus user interfaces for manipulating text. In: ACM User Interface Software and Technology, pp. 127–135 (1991)
9. Goonetilleke, R., Hoffmann, E., Luximon, A.: Effects of pen design on drawing and writing performance. Appl. Ergon. **40**, 292–301 (2009)
10. Holtzinger, A., Holler, M., Schedlbauer, M., Urlesberger, B.: An investigation of finger vs stylus input in medical scenarios. In: Proceedings of ITI 30th Conference on Information Technology Interfaces, pp. 433–438 (2008)
11. Kobayahsi, T.: Some experimental studies on writing behavior. Hiroshima Forum Psychol. **8**, 27–38 (1981)
12. Lacquaniti, F.: Central representations of human limb movement as revealed by studies of drawing and handwriting. Trends Neurosci. **12**(8), 287–291 (1989)
13. Annett, M., Anderson, F.: The pen is mightier: Understanding stylus behaviour while inking on tablets. In: Proceedings of Graphics Interface, pp. 193–200 (2014)
14. Microsoft. (n.d.). Write as fast as you think, https://www.microsoft.com/surface/en-us/accessories/surface-pen
15. Ng, A., Annett, M., Dietz, P., Gupta, A., Bischof, F.W.: In the blink of an eye: investigating latency perception during stylus interaction. In: CHI, pp. 1103–1112 (2014)
16. N-Trig: IHS Technology Interactive Summit Presentation (2013)
17. Pereira, A., Miller, T., Huang, Y., Odell, D., Remple, D.: Holding a tablet computer with one hand: Effect of tablet design featuers on biomechanics and subjective usability among users with small hands. Ergonomics **12**(8), 287–291 (2013)
18. Schomaker, L., Plamondon, R.: The relation between pen force and pen-point kinematics in handwriting. Biolog. Cybern. **63**, 277–289 (1990)
19. The Verge. http://www.theverge.com/2012/4/10/2925937/best-stylus-ipad-review
20. The Verge. http://thewirecutter.com/reviews/best-ipad-stylus/
21. Wacom.: IHS Technology Interactive Summit Presentation (2013)
22. Wu, F., Luo, S.: Performance study on touch-pens size inthree screen tasks. Appl. Ergon. **37**, 149–158 (2006)
23. Wu, F., Luo, S.: Design and evaluation approach for increasing stability and performance of touch pens in screen handwriting tasks. Appl. Ergon. **37**, 319–327 (2006)

A Simple Method to Record Keystrokes on Mobile Phones and Other Devices for Usability Evaluations

Brian T. Lin$^{(\boxtimes)}$ and Paul A. Green

Driver Interface Group, University of Michigan Transportation Research Institute, 2901 Baxter Road, Ann Arbor, MI 48109-2150, USA
{btwlin, pagreen}@umich.edu

Abstract. Task times, sometimes at the keystroke level, as well as the number of keystrokes are often used to assess the usefulness and ease of use of mobile devices. This paper describes a new method to obtain keystroke-level timing of tasks involving Virtual Network Computing (VNC) and Techsmith Morae (commonly used for usability tests). Running VNC, the PC mimics what the mobile device does, which is recorded by Morae running on the PC. To evaluate this configuration, 24 pairs of subjects texted 1,200 messages concerning five topics to each other. Every keystroke was recorded and timed to the nearest 10 ms. As desired, the communications were quite stable, with times of 90 % of the messages on the two recording computers being normally distributed and within ± 100 ms of each other. Others are encouraged to use this method, given its accuracy and low cost, to examine mobile device usability.

Keywords: Keystroke-logging · Usability testing · Mobile devices · Virtual network computing (VNC)

1 Introduction

Mobile devices are widely popular because they are convenient and easy to use. Ease of use can be assessed using many measures and statistics, though the most straightforward measure is task time [1] and number of keystrokes. Previous studies have reported methods to record when and which key is pressed at any given time to determine inter-keystroke intervals for mobile devices [2–4]. However, more specific and easier to implement methods are needed. Until now, usability assessments of these devices have been limited in number because collecting accurate methods to record the desired data is a challenge.

Basically, task time can be determined using (1) a real-time manual timing system operated by an observer, (2) specialized hardware, (3) video records analyzed after the fact (post processed frame by frame), or (4) usability evaluation software embedded in the device being tested (e.g. Remote User Interface, RUI [5], LetterWise [6], Uzilla [7]).

(1) Manual real-time data collection has a long history of use, especially within industrial engineering, typically using stopwatches. However, it is time consuming and events that occur in rapid succession cannot be reliably timed manually. (2) For

© Springer International Publishing Switzerland 2016
A. Marcus (Ed.): DUXU 2016, Part I, LNCS 9746, pp. 434–444, 2016.
DOI: 10.1007/978-3-319-40409-7_41

human-computer interaction, specialized data collection devices inserted between the key and computer (e.g. KeyGhost for PS/2 keyboards, KeyCarbon for USB keyboards) and computer software (Windows APIs, Mac Keylogger by REFOG), can be used to surreptitiously record all keystrokes, mouse actions, and screen updates. By design, most variations of this method will not work for mobile devices. (3) On the surface, post-processing of video records seems to be an easy method to collect the desired data. This approach is not cost effective, and the data analysis is tedious. (4) Finally, one could use specialized evaluation software that runs in parallel with the system being tested. This software may be specifically intended for human-computer interaction evaluations.

Accordingly, tailored approaches for mobile devices have been developed. These approaches involve universal applications such as a small J2ME, a program that can be installed into the device very quickly [8] to log the time of key presses and releases and save them in a file (ASCII, Unicode) on the device. The program is running in the background, independent of other processes. After the data collection phase, the experimenter can export, reduce, and analyze the data. This software may add to the device processor load and memory requirements (leaving insufficient capacity for the applications being assessed), and may affect timing accuracy (adding in variable delays) [9]. Furthermore, these programs often do not provide for some type of independent real time output, in particular a signal that can be used by other software to synchronize related information (e.g. physiological data, other task performance data). Some applications do not encrypt the data, so there may be security concerns.

To overcome mobile device limitations, the mobile device could be emulated on a personal computer, mapping the key/icon assignments (in Flash, JAVA, or XML) to those typical on the PC [6]. The data collection program can be installed in a powerful PC, run in the background [5], and can also combine with other process, such as eye-tracking systems [10]. The PC interface, however, is not what mobile device people use, and the key/icon assignments are device dependent. For example, users will feel odd if they are asked to use a PC numeric keypad instead of the telephone keypad, because the shape, size, layout, and force feedback of the two keypads are very different. Betiol and Cybis [11] clearly indicated that the emulator setup may affect the validity of the usability problems on the device.

Furthermore, these methods can require more software knowledge than those conducting usability evaluations may have, and can exceed their limited budgets and time. Therefore, this paper describes a new method to collect user task times using a remote protocol (Virtual Network Computing, VNC) and usability evaluation software (Morae v.3.2, TechSmith). A sample experiment conducted using this method is described.

2   New Method Description

2.1   Overview of the VNC-Morae Method

A novel method was developed in which VNC (Virtual Network Computing) protocol was installed in a mobile device (a smartphone) that was connected to a PC running the usability evaluation software (Morae v3.2). Because the application involved texting,

Skype was used as the platform for data exchange between mobile devices. Currently, the only limitation of this method is that the mobile device must run on iOS, Android, and BlackBerry operating systems, which constitute the majority of phones sold (94.1 % in Q4 2012, [12]).

By far, Morae is the most popular application for collecting usability data. The software suite consists of a recorder, an observer, and a manager. The Morae Recorder is installed in the subject's computer and records every event (keystroke, mouse action, screen refresh) occurring, along with input from a web-camera (showing the user's face or hands) and a microphone (what the user says). Accuracy can reliably be determined to the nearest 10 ms. Morae Observer, running on another computer connected to the Recorder via a local area network (LAN) or Internet, allows a remote observer to see the user's screen, hear what they say, and see their face as a picture-in-picture (PIP) in real time. Using the Observer software, an experimenter can mark when tasks start and stop, log errors, and enter comments about tasks, and identify segments for highlight clips. The experimenter's inputs are synchronized with subjects' events in the Recorder computer.

Morae Manager shows all recorded data on a single timeline (Fig. 1). In this example (Fig. 1a), the timeline stops at 0h:27m:28s.90 (entire clip duration is 1h:29m:44s.15) that the message "unless that waitress eats them all" was just sent. Two self-triggered markers (triangles, green at the left and red at the right) represent the beginning and end of the task of interest. Corresponding keystrokes are shown (Fig. 1b).

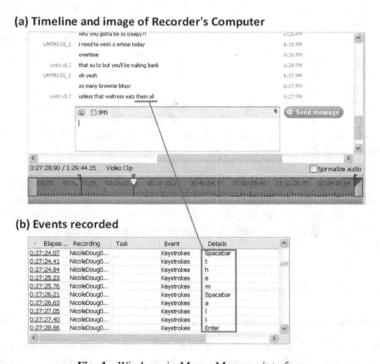

Fig. 1. Windows in Morae Manager interface

2.2   Virtual Network Computing - The Connection Between Mobile Device and Computer

Virtual network computing (VNC) involves using the Remote Frame Buffer (RFB) protocol to remotely control another computer. Color values for pixels on the screen stored in the memory buffer are transferred through RFB. VNC consists of a server, a client (or viewer), and a protocol between them. The machine running the server feeds the signal to the client via RFB protocol, so the client has the same desktop image as the server. As the controller, the client can submit commands and interact with the server.

As a default, the communication uses the TCP port 5900 for connections to the Internet through a broadband connection or LAN. RealVNC, a particular implementation, uses the high-strength AES (Advanced Encryption Standard) data encryption to improve the data transfer security.

2.3   Data Transfer Platform – The Connection Between Computers

Given that user's operations on the smartphone are connected to the computer with VNC server and Morae Recorder running, the data transfer is triggered by the mobile device, but executed by the computer. In other words, the communication between mobile devices can be treated as between computers, which is much easier. The communication can be over a local area network (LAN) or the Internet. Using a LAN eliminates network traffic jams and provides a secure connection.

2.4   Hardware and Software Configuration

Figure 2 shows the configuration used for this test case that supported two smartphone users sending text messages to each other, whose keystrokes and inter-keystroke intervals are recorded. The smartphones were connected to a wireless router via WiFi and connected to the computers with Ethernet, forming two local network areas (left and right halves of Fig. 2) that connected to the Internet via the wireless router. A single router was used in this instance because most of the time data streams exchanged between the two sides did not occur simultaneously. Using one router also reduced the amount of hardware required, but two could be used. The wireless router is very important in the entire process because it establishes the link between the smart phone and computer, and gives the computers access to the Internet.

In summary, what the users see on their smartphone (running the VNC Client) is actually from the PC, which is showing the Skype interaction and running Morae on the background. Most of the computationally intensive software is running on the PC and the smartphone serves as an input device.

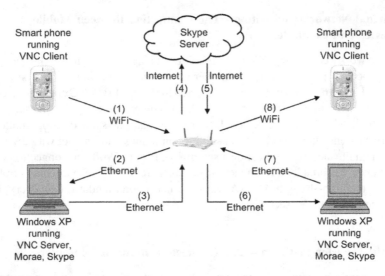

Fig. 2. Manual text entry configuration (The numbers 1–8 represent the steps in each communication cycle).

3 Case Study: Keystroke-Level Accurate Timing of Text Messages Between Smartphones

3.1 Overview

This configuration was used to study users sending text messages to each other [13]. Of interest was both the linguistic content of the message [14] and the keystroke level timing of user inputs. In this experiment, subjects sent text messages on five different topics that were the same for all subjects. About five minutes was spent on each topic, after which the interaction ended and subjects moved on to a new topic. To provide realism of a driving scenario, this experiment took place in a driving simulator. Because texting while driving is illegal, all manual entry by drivers was done with the vehicle parked. The goal of this case study is to examine the protocol of real-time keystroke logging between two smartphones for the usability test, comparing the timelines recorded on the two sides.

3.2 Participants

Twenty-four pairs of young smartphone users who regularly sent text messages to each other participated, an important distinction from other research. Each subject was paid $50 for approximately two hours of his/her time. One subject sat in the driver's seat of the driving simulator (http://www.umich.edu/~driving/facilities/sim.html), and the other subject was elsewhere out of sight of the driver (sitting at desk in an office), as is commonly the case. Subject pairs were equally drawn from two groups, late teens (aged 18–19, mean = 19) and young adults (aged 20–29, mean = 23). Among all drivers, these are the two groups who are most likely to text and drive. Because their relationship could affect their texting interaction, each group of twelve had three male pairs, three female pairs, and six mixed gender pairs. All participants were friends, classmates, or colleagues, but not relatives to avoid relationships that could alter message content.

3.3   Equipment, Materials, and Software

The ideal situation would be for subjects to have used their own phone. Android users used their own phones with the RealVNC Client downloaded (free) and installed from Android Market. Iphone users used two iPhone 4's provided by the UMTRI Driver Interface Group onto which RealVNC had been downloaded before the experiment to save time. To simulate the BlackBerry experience, those users were provided iPhones with an attached hard key QWERTY keyboard (Keyboard Buddy iPhone 4 case, Boxwave Co.). The screen size of the BlackBerry was too small (usually about 2.5 in) to accommodate all the information needed by the VNC Server.

Morae Recorder (version 3.2) running independently on two Windows XP computers that recorded the keys pressed and the inter-keystroke interval to the nearest centisecond. Also, the timestamps of when messages were received were collected. A wireless router (Netgear WNDR3400, N600 wireless dual band, 300 Mbps x 2) was connected to the two mobile devices (via WiFi). One of the WiFi protocols used the band of 2.4 GHz and another used 5.0 GHz, each of which had a bandwidth of 300 Mbps without interference.

3.4   Experiment Design

As mentioned before, subjects then sent text messages to each other, with one subject in the driving simulator and the other in an office. An expressway road scene was presented to the driver, but he/she did not drive. Initially, subjects practiced texting for 10 to 15 min to become familiar with the experimental situation, with the two topics of "I need BBQ" and "I am glad the football season begins." Subjects could either continue the topic assigned, or change to other topics they were more interested in at any time.

Subsequently, subjects participated in five message sequences, each triggered by text provided to the driver by the experimenter on an in-vehicle display. Topics were selected to be statistically representative of those that typically occurred while texting (and not driving) based on a General Motors provided text message corpus collected while not driving [15]. See also Winter et al. [16]. There were 5 topics about human relations, 2 for activities and events, 3 for appointments and schedules, 2 for school and work, 2 for technology, and 1 for emotion. For further information about the design, please refer to Green et al. [13].

3.5   Results

There were 1,200 messages (49,985 keystrokes) sent between the 2 sides, 584 messages from drivers to partners and 616 from partners to drivers. On average, a typical message included 8.5 words (S.D. = 6.2), composed of 41.6 characters (S.D. = 30.7), including 7.5 spaces, 1.2 punctuation marks, and 32.9 letters and numbers. For a detailed analysis of message content, see Hecht et al. [14].

To analyze the inter-keystroke intervals, one needs to have confidence that the timing is accurate. When typing transcripts, the brain is used as a short-term buffer and the typist will load a certain amount of text into the buffer [17]. Text will be grouped into discrete units and entered once [18], so the times between keystrokes can be very short. All too often research is conducted on keying behavior, response times, or eye fixations, but the timing is never checked. This is particularly important when claims are made about millisecond or even centisecond accuracy, but the hardware and software do not support such. The focus of this paper is on how well the method captured the keystrokes and the timing accuracy.

There was no evidence that any of the 49,985 keystrokes were lost or transmitted out of order. Also of interest was if various devices were reporting the same times and the same transmission delays between devices. The issue was addressed in two phases. During the preliminary phase of the development of this method, each smartphone was placed side by side with the PC that was associated with it, and text was entered into the phone. There was no perceptible delay between when keys were pressed, when the text appeared on the smartphone display, and when the text appeared on the associated PC (connected via VNC).

In a subsequent phase, system timing and lags were examined. The time logging started before showing the topic to the driver, continued on the five topics, and did not stop until the texting for all five topics ended. The authors compared the log files on each PC (driver, partner), each with its own timeline and analyzed the effects of message characteristics. In this case, the driver and the partner could not be readily synchronized and compared using a third-party timeline.

The log files included the time a message sent from one device and the time that message received by another device, on different timelines. In this case, a method was conducted to integrate the two timelines, using the first sent/received message as the baseline.

Comparing the adjusted message-sent and -received timelines, the time differences included two parts, the time for Skype to pass messages through the Internet (whose transmission times were variable), and the difference between the Morae timelines running on two non-identical computer to record all the events. (The driver side computer (Intel Core 2 Quad 2.4 GHz + 4 GB of RAM) had more throughput than the other computer (Intel Pentium IV 3.6 GHz + 1 GB of RAM).) These two timelines could not be synchronized without a third-party timeline, which did not exist in this case. Identical hardware for the driver and partner sides was not available, and was initially not thought to be a concern.

Table 1 shows how the data was processed. The first sent/received messages of each subject pair (column A & C) were treated as the baselines for the messages they sent back and forth. Thus, the first message served to zero the timeline, with a log file entry of 0h:00m:00s.00. Using that value, the times for messages being sent and received (columns B and D) could be compared, leading to column E. In column E, the time differences could be positive or negative values, which meant that the time difference was less (if negative) or greater (if positive) than the first sent/received pair.

Table 1. Calculation of the difference between timelines

Msg #	By driver's computer		By partner's computer		(E)
	(A) Sent time	(B) Time based on the first sent message	(C) Received time	(D) Time based on the first received message	Time difference (ms)
0 (First)	0:12:49.52	–	0:11:49.35	–	–
1	0:13:53.85	0:01:04.33	0:12:53.60	0:01:04.25	−80
2	0:14:48.56	0:01:59.04	0:13:48.24	0:01:58.89	−150
3	0:15:49.49	0:02:59.97	0:14:49.35	0:03:00.00	30

During the data collection phase, three messages from the driver to the partner and one from the partner to the driver were delayed by the VNC for greater than five seconds, in which the data stream from VNC Client was not immediately sent to VNC Server. These four messages were removed from further analysis and only 1,196 messages remained.

Further, the time of the first sent/received message of each pair of subjects for both sides did not count because it was the baseline of the time-log adjustment and there was no message sent/received before it. Therefore, 1,148 messages were considered (584 - 24 - 3 = 557 sent from the driver to the partner; 616 - 24 - 1 = 591 from the partner to the driver).

Figure 3 shows the distributions of the time difference that messages were sent from the driver to partner (3a) and vice versa (3b). The white bars at the very right side of Fig. 3a and b represent the relative time difference greater than 300 ms. Times with negative values meant that the processing times for Skype and Morae for a particular message were less than the processing time for the first message sent and received (being assumed as zero).

In Fig. 3a, when the driver sent messages to the partner, the relative time differences were normally distributed, with a mean of 0.70 ms and a standard deviation of 73 ms. Approximately 83 % (463/558) of messages had the relative time differences between $\pm$ 73 ms, the standard deviation, and over 99 % (553/557) between $\pm 3\sigma$. Similar results could be found in Fig. 3b, the messages sent by the partner to the driver. The mean and standard deviation of the relative time differences were 8.2 ms and 73 ms. Time differences between $\pm$ 73 ms were for 77 % (454/591) of messages and over 99 % (589/591) between $\pm 3\sigma$. Thus the mean delay was about 8 ms longer from the partner relative to the first message, but the standard deviation was identical, which is most important. As a reminder, times were determined to the nearest 0.01 s by Morae.

Thus, the message transmission delays due to VNC and Morae were quite stable. However, as long as communication occurred over the Internet, communication delays introduced could not be completely avoided. Certainly using identical hardware for the driver and partner would have led to more consistent time, but the expected differences due to such are likely to be much less than those due to the Internet. However, what is important is that in many situations the inter-keystroke intervals for each device were of sufficient accuracy.

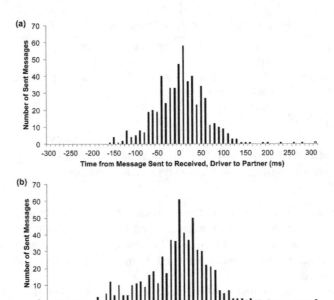

Fig. 3. Histogram of time difference between the driver and partner, based on the first sent/received message.

4   Conclusion

4.1   Strengths of the Method Used

This paper describes in detail a method that easily and accurately collects keystrokes on mobile devices to the nearest centisecond, and provides example performance data collected using this method from a case study. The performance of the configuration was quite good. The data recorded was very stable. Some 83 % (from driver to partner), and 77 % and (from partner to driver) of the messages had the time differences within ± 1σ (73 and 73 ms, respectively), using the first messages as the baselines. When the error tolerance was ± 100 ms, some 93 % (from driver to partner), and 88 % (from partner to driver) were included, respectively. This is excellent, considering that timing was to the nearest 10 ms. Kukreja et al. [5] and Austin et al. [19] report the peak and mean inter-keystroke intervals of 175 ms and 356 ms for typing on a full-size computer keyboard. Therefore, the data-logging configuration in this study was accurate enough to record keystroke timing. The timing was unaffected by the length of the message sent and was fairly stable throughout the experiment.

4.2   Concerns with the Method Used

There are three sources of potential timing errors, (1) the Internet over which the communication occurred, (2) the software (VNC) to exchange messages, and (3) the computers to log the timestamps. The Internet was used in this case for ease of access. There were three outliers in the messages sent from the driver to the partner and one from the partner to the driver. This corresponds to only 0.3 % of all messages, an acceptable low amount. Oddly, three of these cases all occurred in the afternoon, between 1–4 pm, on a particular day, which is why some sort of Internet-related cause is suspected. In theory, a LAN dedicated to an experiment should provide more consistent transmission times because the load is stable and the hardware fixed. However, there are few applications that support LANs and to customizing a LAN information exchange platform is time and cost consuming and the timing will not be as accurate as native programs [20].

Finally, although not considered to be a major source of timing problems, the driver and partner logging computers were different, so their processing time could differ. Using two identical computers is recommended to eliminate any suspicion of a problem.

4.3   Closing Thought

In summary, the method described in this paper provides a simple, low-cost, and accurate method to record and time keystroke-level actions for mobile devices, something which is extremely difficult to do as well using other methods. These data are essential for performing detailed analyses of user actions in applied usability studies and more fundamental analyses of how people interact with mobile devices. The accuracy, using the configurations is good enough for most purposes, but it is not perfect. The next step is to explore (1) using LANs to improve timing, (2) variations in VNC performance as a function of hardware, and (3) recording performance for other input gestures such as swiping and dragging (in particular their path and click locations). Researchers are strongly encouraged to use this method in their research.

References

1. Hornbæk, K., Law, E.L.-C.: Meta-analysis of correlations among usability measures. Paper presented at the CHI 2007 Proceedings, San Jose, CA, USA (2007)
2. Kjeldskov, J., Stage, J.: New techniques for usability evaluation of mobile systems. Int. J. Hum.-Comput. Stud. **60**(5), 599–620 (2004)
3. Klockar, T., Carr, D.A., Hedman, A., Johansson, T., Bengtsson, F.: Usability of mobile phones. Paper presented at the Proceedings of the 19th International Symposium on Human Factors in Telecommunication, Berlin, Germany (2003)
4. Silfverberg, M., MacKenzie, S., Korhonen, P.: Predicting text entry speed on mobile phones. Paper presented at the CHI 2000, The Hague, The Netherlands (2000)
5. Kukreja, U., Stevenson, W.E., Ritter, F.E.: RUI: recording user input from interfaces under Windows and Mac OS X. Behav. Res. Meth. **38**(4), 656–659 (2006)

6. MacKenzie, S., Kober, H., Smith, D., Jones, T., Skepner, E.: LetterWise: prefix-based disambiguation for mobile text input. Paper presented at the Proceedings of the 14th Annual ACM Symposium on User Interface Software and Technology, Orlando, FL, USA (2001)
7. Edmonds, A.: Uzilla: a new tool for web usability testing. Behav. Res. Meth., Instrum. Comput. 35(2), 194–201 (2003)
8. Holleis, P., Otto, F., Hußmann, H., Schmidt, A.: Keystroke-level model for advanced mobile phone interaction. Paper presented at the CHI 2007 Proceedings, San Jose, CA, USA (2007)
9. Keller, F., Gunasekharan, S., Mayo, N., Corley, M.: Timing accuracy of web experiments: a case study using the WebExp software package. Behav. Res. Meth. 41(1), 1–12 (2009)
10. Wengelin, Å., Torrance, M., Holmqvist, K., Simpson, S., Galbraith, D., Johansson, V., Johansson, R.: Combined eyetracking and keystroke-logging methods for studying cognitive processes in text production. Behav. Res. Meth. 41(2), 337–351 (2009)
11. Betiol, A.H., de Abreu Cybis, W.: Usability testing of mobile devices: a comparison of three approaches. In: Costabile, M.F., Paternó, F. (eds.) INTERACT 2005. LNCS, vol. 3585, pp. 470–481. Springer, Heidelberg (2005)
12. Gupta, A., Cozza, R., Milanesi, C., Lu, C.: Market Share Analysis: Mobile Phones, Worldwide, 4Q12 and 2012: Gartner, Inc. (2013)
13. Green, P., Lin, B., Kang, T.-P., Best, A.: Manual and Speech Entry of Text Messages while Driving. University of Michigan Transportation Research Institute (UMTRI), Ann Arbor (2011)
14. Hecht, R.M., Tzirkel, E., Tsimhoni, O.: Language models for text messaging based on driving workload. Paper presented at the 4th International Conference on Applied Human Factors and Ergonomics, San Francisco, CA, USA (2012)
15. Winter, U., Grost, T.J., Tsimhoni, O.: Language pattern aanalysis for automotive natural language speech applications. Paper presented at the Proceedings of the 2nd International Conference on Automotive User Interfaces and Interactive Vehicular Applications, Pittsburgh, PA, USA (2010)
16. Winter, U., Ben-Aharon, R., Chernobrov, D., Hecht, R.M.: Topics as contextual indicators for word choice in sms conversations. Paper presented at the Proceedings of the SIGDIAL 2011: The 12th Annual Meeting of the Special Interest Group on Discourse and Dialogue, Portland, OR, USA (2011)
17. Thomas, E.A.C., Jones, R.G.: A model for subjective grouping in typewriting. Q. J. Exp. Psychol. 22(3), 353–367 (1970)
18. Cooper, W.E.: Cognitive Aspects of Skilled Typewriting. Springer, New York (1983)
19. Austin, D., Jimison, H., Hayes, T., Mattek, N., Kaye, J., Pavel, M.: Measuring motor speed through typing: a surrogate for the finger tapping test. Behav. Res. Meth. 43(4), 903–909 (2011)
20. Eichstaedt, J.: An inaccurate-timing filter for reaction time measurement by JAVA applets implementing internet-based experiments. Behav. Res. Meth. Instrum. Comput. 33(2), 179–186 (2001)

A Systematic Review About
User Experience Evaluation

Camila Loiola Brito Maia[(⊠)] and Elizabeth Sucupira Furtado

University of Fortaleza (Unifor), Fortaleza, CE, Brazil
camila.maia@gmail.com, elizabethsfur@gmail.com

Abstract. The user experience related to a product can determine its success or failure. As a result, companies have invested in research to understand what the user feels when he or she uses a product, but it is not simple to get this information, and many approaches arose through the years. This article presents a systematic review on the user experience evaluation field, based on 25 studies. We found (1) that psychophysiological measures are not yet widely applied in the evaluation of the user experience; (2) researchers prefer qualitative approaches; (3) the evaluations are mostly manual (not real time, therefore), and using ready-made products; and (4) most studies used single measurement, not considering the use of the product over time. This scenario shows an opportunity for UX evaluation methods which consider the use of the product over time and provide real time results.

Keywords: User experience · UX · Evaluation · Measurement

1 Introduction

A product or service that gives good experience to user can offer competitive advantage to companies, since the product could be recommended by satisfied customer. According to Pine and Gilmore [1], a good experience occurs when the user engages in a way that creates a memorable event. This experience is personal, and exists just for that user who got emotional, physical, intellectual and, sometimes, spiritual engagement with a particular product. For companies, if a product or service provides good experiences to users, they can gain competitive advantage, once the satisfied client probably will recommend this product. For this reason, UX is vital to commercial success of the companies [2], and many of these companies already have a team of experts whose focus is to ensure a product that provides a good experience for the users [3].

However, to generate good experiences is necessary to understand how the user feels [4]. In usability tests we usually check efficiency and effectiveness of the product, but not how users feel. If we understand what the user feels while using the product, we can measure and continuously improve his experience. Following this idea, several studies related to the evaluation of user experience have been written and disseminated using qualitative and quantitative analysis.

© Springer International Publishing Switzerland 2016
A. Marcus (Ed.): DUXU 2016, Part I, LNCS 9746, pp. 445–455, 2016.
DOI: 10.1007/978-3-319-40409-7_42

In this way, the purpose of this article is to present results of a systematic review about evaluation of user experience, by investigating how this evaluation of user experience is performed, in terms of moment, used techniques and elements of user experience taken into account.

This paper is organized as follows: Sect. 2 contextualizes the research, Sect. 3 details the systematic review, Sect. 4 presents the analysis of results, and Sect. 5 presents the final considerations.

2 Contextualization

In order to understand and evaluate user experience is essential to collect data from the user. The majority of approaches typically rely on observation [5, 6], psychophysiological measures [7, 8], and questionnaires or surveys [9, 10].

However, it is difficult to measure user experience. First, because several factors influence the user experience, like feelings, culture and communicability [11]. Furthermore, the user experience is multidimensional [2], consisting of various elements, and there is still no consensus among authors about these elements of user experience [2, 3, 12, 13]. There are several proposed models, such as Hassenzahl [14] and Mahlke and Thuring [15], but it seems that the only consensus is that the user experience is composed of pragmatic aspects (utility and usability) and hedonic aspects (emotional) [16].

In addition, as a given product may have users with heterogeneous profiles [17] and each experience is individual [16, 18] the final user experience is likely to have a different value for each user.

Finally, it is not easy to define a criterion to measure user experience because it is subjective and holistic [16].

After measuring user experience, it is important to evaluate this experience, because it provides feedback to those who developed the product, and future improvements can be generated for the user based on his feedback [18]. Moreover, evaluation allows comparisons between different versions of the same product, between different user groups, and in different contexts [18].

According to Machapa and Greunen [19], given the complexity of UX, evaluating an experience and understanding how the user classifies this experience is not a simple task. To evaluate the user experience, we have to collect data related to it. The main instruments used to collect these data are questionnaires and surveys, psychophysiological measures and observation.

In addition, for Kujala and colleagues [20], evaluate a momentary user experience is in most cases not very reliable for predicting the user experience in real life or to evaluate the success of a product. We need information about the long-term user experience because it causes people to continue to use a product and recommend it to others [20]. Furthermore, retrospective evaluations for long term experiments are based on the memory of the user and may be vulnerable [20].

3   Systematic Review

The systematic review was conducted in three phases: planning, execution and analysis of the results, shown below.

3.1   Planning

Objectives, research questions and search strategy were defined in planning phase.

Research Objectives. Based on the scenario described in the contextualization, the general objective of this research is to identify how the user experience is evaluated: the moment of evaluation, what techniques are used, which elements of experience are taken into consideration and the objectives of evaluation.

Research Questions. To meet the objectives of this systematic review, four research questions were formulated, as follows:

Q1.   Do the authors consider a single measurement to assess UX or measurement over time?
Q2.   How is done the UX evaluation (when, how, where and with what resources)?
Q3.   What UX elements are considered when evaluating UX?
Q4.   What are the objectives when evaluating UX?

Search Strategy. The search focused three bases: IEEE Xplore, ACM and Science Direct. The inclusion criteria considered in the systematic review were: articles published from 2008 (analysis of the last eight years), publication in conference or journal, articles available to read (permission to access) and written in English. The search string used was:

("user experience") AND ("evaluate" OR "evaluating")

3.2   Execution

The search yielded the following results: At ACM, 210 studies were found, while 418 studies were found in IEEE Xplore, and 104 in Science Direct, resulting in 732 studies. After the search, there were two phases of exclusion of studies. The first phase consisted of applying the inclusion criteria, and the analysis of titles and abstracts of the studies, excluding 645 of them, and leaving 87 studies for phase 2. The second phase consisted of reading the introduction, the detail of the proposal and conclusions, excluding 62 studies, and leaving 25 studies to collect data about user experience evaluation. The selected studies are presented in Table 1.

Table 1. Selected studies

ID	Year	Reference
1	2015	[21]
2	2015	[22]
3	2015	[23]
4	2014	[10]
5	2014	[24]
6	2014	[25]
7	2014	[26]
8	2013	[27]
9	2013	[28]
10	2013	[29]
11	2013	[5]
12	2013	[30]
13	2012	[31]
14	2012	[32]
15	2012	[33]
16	2012	[34]
17	2012	[35]
18	2011	[36]
19	2011	[20]
20	2011	[2]
21	2011	[19]
22	2010	[37]
23	2010	[38]
24	2010	[39]
25	2010	[40]

4   Analysis of Results

In the final phase of the review, data were collected from the selected studies.

With regards to the question Q1 (*"Do the authors consider a single measurement to assess UX or measurement over time?"*), Fig. 1 shows that 76 % of the studies consider only one measurement for user experience, i.e., only 24 % of the studies measure user experience over use.

To answer the question Q2 (*"How is done the UX evaluation (when, how, where and with what resources)?"*), several information was collected. The first one refers to the time of data collection: most studies consider the best data collection time at the end of the experience (32 %) or during and after it (36 %), as shown in Fig. 2. In addition, 16 % of the studies perform data collection during the experience and 16 % do it before and after.

Regarding the automation of collection of such data, most studies realize data collection manually (80 %), 12 % do it in mixed form (manual and automated) and 8 % do it automatically, as can be seen in Fig. 3.

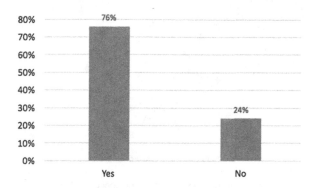

Fig. 1. Single measurement?

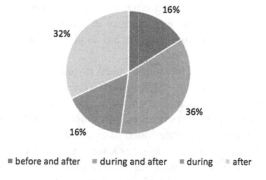

Fig. 2. Moment of data collection

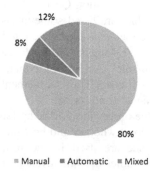

Fig. 3. Automation of user experience's data collection

After collecting user experience data, 84 % of the studies mentioned perform the evaluation of the user experience manually, 8 % do it automatically, 4 % do it in mixed form, and 4 % of the studies did not report how the user experience evaluation is performed. Figure 4 shows this information.

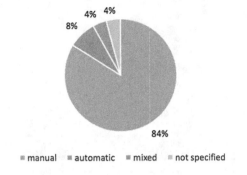

Fig. 4. Automation of user experience evaluation

Most of the studies also provide a controlled environment for experiments with users (44 %), while 36 % run the experiments in the real environment of the user. About 20 % of the studies did not specify what kind of environment carried out the experiments, as shown in Fig. 5.

Figure 6 shows the tools and techniques used to collect the information about the user experience. The majority of the studies (84 %) mentioned questionnaires to assess the user experience. Some of them use only the questionnaire, while others use the questionnaire at the end of the experiments, in conjunction with other tools or techniques. Other tools and techniques mentioned to evaluate user experience are interview, observation, reports, video recording, eye-tracking, among others.

As can be seen in Fig. 7, 72 % of the studies used ready-made products for the experiments, 8 % used prototypes, 16 % used both ready-made products and prototypes, and 4 % of the studies did not specify the product phase.

The graph in Fig. 8 answers the question Q3 (*"What UX elements are considered when evaluating UX?"*). In the chart are listed some facets, according to the model of Peter Morville (2004) plus some elements that were cited and evaluated (but are not cited in this model). The most cited elements were "desirable" and "usable" followed by "attractive (design)" and "valuable". According to that, not all facets are being used on the evaluation of the user experience. The UX element identified and less cited in the studies was "cause engagement" (only once).

The question Q4 addresses the observation made by Law et al. (2014), which states that most of the work does not report whether and how the information collected in the evaluation of the user experience are used in the following development cycles. Figure 9 shows that 56 % of the studies used the evaluation of experience to evaluate a prototype or product (focus on the product, not the user), 28 % categorized or just made records about the methods of evaluation, 8 % evaluated the user experience, 4 % compared user profiles, and 4 % evaluated user satisfaction. Most of the studies, even evaluating the user experience, uses the data to improve the product (in the future), not the user experience.

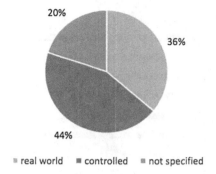

20%

36%

44%

■ real world   ■ controlled   ■ not specified

Fig. 5. Type of environment

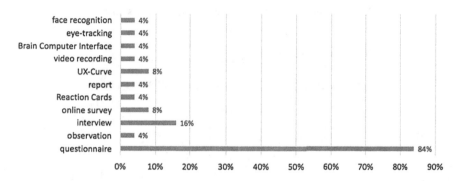

Fig. 6. Tools and techniques used to evaluate user experience

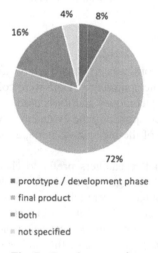

4%   8%

16%

72%

■ prototype / development phase
■ final product
■ both
■ not specified

Fig. 7. Development phase

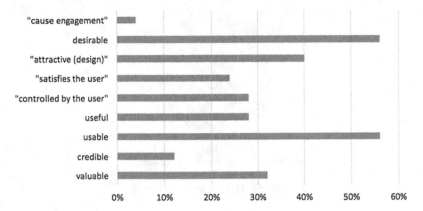

Fig. 8. Elements of user experience cited in the studies

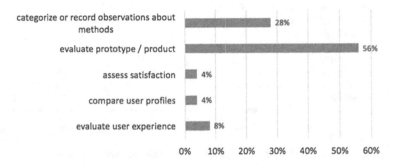

Fig. 9. What was done with the evaluation information?

5 Final Considerations

The main objective of this work was to identify how the user experience is being evaluated so far in the academic community. Data were collected about the moment of measurement and evaluation, techniques and tools used in the evaluation process, and the elements of user experience applied in the evaluation. After searching in the chosen databases and the application of the inclusion criteria, 25 studies were consolidated in this systematic review.

The first conclusion is that researchers prefer to check with participants his/her feeling about the product, even though they used other tools and techniques to evaluate user experience, once questionnaires were administered in 84 % of studies.

Psychophysiological measures, which tells us in real time what the user feels, have been widely used in the HCI area but are not yet being properly applied in evaluation models of the user experience, since 84 % of the studies evaluate the user experience manually.

Most studies cited experiments in controlled environments (44 %), against 36 % in the real user environment. About 20 % of the studies did not report that kind of environment used.

With regards to the development phase when it was used by the user, the product was already complete (developed) in 72 % of the studies. Few evaluation methods of the user experience were cited for product in development.

Despite using an evaluation of user experience, most studies (56 %) used this analysis to evaluate the product, i.e., the focus of the evaluation was the product, not the user.

Moreover, the majority of studies (76 %) utilizes single measurement, not considering the experience over time (during user's day).

Finally, only one of the 25 selected papers performed the evaluation of the user experience in real-time and over time.

Given the analysis above, the conclusion is that more methods for user experience evaluation are needed in a way that the use of the product over time and the information about the user experience in real time are considered. As mentioned earlier, the use of the product over time takes the user to continue using this product and recommend it to others. Moreover, the real time evaluation is important because it avoids relevant information being lost if it is collected after the experiment.

This study has some limitations, like, the use of only three databases for the search, the inclusion of studies from 2008, and the used search string. Although not considered highly relevant, these limitations might be responsible for the exclusion of interesting work and consistent with the theme of this systematic review.

The results of this review will form the basis for future works, since the evaluation of the user experience can provide feedback about the product, enabling improvements in the product and adaptation for the user, among other benefits.

References

1. Pine, B.J., Gilmore, J.H.: Welcome to experience economy. Harvard Bus. Rev. **76**, 97–105 (1998)
2. Kujala, S., Roto, V., Vaananen-Vainio-Mattila, K., Karapanos, E., Sinnela, A.: UX Curve: a method for evaluating long-term user experience. Interact. Comput. **23**(5), 473–483 (2011)
3. Sproll, S., Peissner, M., Sturm, C.: From product concept to user experience- Exploring UX potentials at early product stages. In: Nordic Conference on Human-Computer Interaction, pp. 473–482 (2010)
4. Roto, V., Obrist, M., Vaananen-Vainio-Mattila, K.: User experience evaluation methods in academic and industrial contexts. In: International Conference on Human-Computer Interaction (2009)
5. Makela, S., Bednarik, R., Tukiainen, M.: Evaluating user experience of autistic children through video observation. In: ACM Conference on Human Factors in Computing Systems, Extended Abstracts on Human Factors in Computing Systems, pp. 463–468 (2013)
6. Keskinen, T., Hakulinen, J., Heimoen, T., Turunen, M., Sharma, S., Miettinen, T., Luhtala, M.: Evaluating the experiential user experience of public display applications in the wild. In: International Conference on Mobile and Ubiquitous Multimedia (2013)

7. Foglia, P., Zanda, M.: Towards relating physiological signals to usability metrics: a case study with a web avatar. WSEAS Trans. Comput. **13**, 624–634 (2014)
8. Yao, L., Liu, Y., Li, W., Zhou, L., Ge, Y., Chai, J., Sun, X.: Using physiological measures to evaluate user experience of mobile applications. In: Harris, D. (ed.) EPCE 2014. LNCS, vol. 8532, pp. 301–310. Springer, Heidelberg (2014)
9. Wiebe, E.N., Lamb, A., Hardy, M., Sharek, D.: Measuring engagement in video game-based environments: investigation of the user engagement scale. Comput. Hum. Behav. **32**, 123–132 (2014)
10. Read, J. C.: Evaluating artefacts with children: age and technology effects in the reporting of expected and experienced fun. In: International Conference on Multimodal Interaction, pp. 241–248 (2012)
11. Masip, L., Oliva, M., Granollers, T.: OPEN-HEREDEUX: OPEN HEuristic REsource for Designing and Evaluating User eXperience. In: Campos, P., Graham, N., Jorge, J., Nunes, N., Palanque, P., Winckler, M. (eds.) INTERACT 2011, Part IV. LNCS, vol. 6949, pp. 418–421. Springer, Heidelberg (2011)
12. Mercun, T.: Evaluation of information visualization techniques – analysing user experience with reaction cards. In: Workshop on Beyond Time and Errors: Novel Evaluation Methods for Visualization, pp. 103–109 (2014)
13. Law, E.L., Roto, V., Hassenzahl, M., Vermeeren, A., Kort, J.: Understanding, scoping and defining user experience: a survey approach. In: ACM Conference on Human Factors in Computing Systems, pp. 719–728 (2009)
14. Hassenzahl, M.: The interplay of beauty, goodness, and usability in interactive products. Hum.-Comput. Interac. **19**(4), 319–349 (2004)
15. Mahlke, S., Thuring, M.: Studying antecedents of emotional experiences in interactive contexts. In: ACM Conference on Human Factors in Computing Systems, pp. 915–918 (2007)
16. Roto, V., Rantavuo, H., Vaananen-Vainio-Mattila, K.: Evaluating user experience of early product concepts. In: International Conference on Designing Pleasurable Products and Interfaces, pp. 199–208 (2009)
17. Law, E., Schaik, P., Roto, V.: Attitudes towards user experience (UX) measurement. Int. J. Hum.-Comput. Stud. **72**(6), 526–541 (2014)
18. Robert, J., Lesage, A.: Designing and evaluating user experience. In: Handbook of Human-Machine Interaction (2011)
19. Mashapa, J., van Greunen, D.: User experience evaluation metrics for usable accounting tools. In: Annual Research Conference of the South African Institute of Computer Scientists and Information Technologists, pp. 170–181 (2010)
20. Kujala, S., Roto, V., Vaananen-Vainio-Mattila, K., Sinnela, A.: Identifying hedonic factors in long-term user experience. In: Conference on Designing Pleasurable Products and Interfaces (2011)
21. Nawaz, A., Halbostad, J.L., Chiari, L., Chesani, F., Cattelani, L.: User Experience (UX) of the Fall Risk Assessment Tool (FRAT-up). In: International Symposium on Computer-Based Medical Systems, pp. 19–22 (2015)
22. Carofiglio, V., Ricci, G., Abbattista, F.: User brain-driven evaluation of an educational 3D virtual environment. In: Iberian Conference on Information Systems and Technologies, pp. 1–7 (2015)
23. Lasa, G., Justel, D., Retegi, A.: Eyeface: A new multimethod tool to evaluate the perception of conceptual user experiences. Comput. Hum. Behav. **52**, 359–363 (2015)
24. Walsh, T., Varsaluoma, J., Kujala, S., Nurkka, P., Petrie, H., Power, C.: Axe UX: Exploring long-term user experience with iScale and AttrakDiff. In: International Academic Mindtrek Conference: Media Business, Management, Content & Services, pp. 32–39 (2014)

25. Colombo, L., Landoni, M.: A diary study of children's user experience with EBooks using flow theory as framework. In: Conference on Interaction Design and Children, pp. 135–144 (2014)

26. Santoso, H.B., Isal, R., Yugo K., Basaruddin, T., Sadira, L., Schrepp, M.: Research-in-progress: user experience evaluation of Student Centered E-Learning Environment for computer science program. In: International Conference on User Science and Engineering, pp. 52–55 (2014)

27. Keskinen, T., Hakulinen, J., Heimoen, T., Turunen, M., Sharma, S., Miettinen, T., Luhtala, M.: Evaluating the experiential user experience of public display applications in the wild. In: International Conference on Mobile and Ubiquitous Multimedia (2013)

28. Saarinen, P., Partala, T., Vaananen-Vainio-Mattila, K: Little backpackers: studying children's psychological needs in an interactive exhibition context. In: International Conference on Interaction Design and Children, pp. 415–418 (2013)

29. Sim, G., Cassidy, B.: Investigating the fidelity effect when evaluating game prototypes with children. In: International BCS Human Computer Interaction Conference (2013)

30. Changyuan, G., Shiying, W., Chongran, Z.: Research on user experience evaluation system of information platform based on web environment. In: International Conference on Measurement, Information and Control, vol. 1, pp. 558–562 (2013)

31. Sim, G., Horton, M., Danino, N.: Evaluating game preference using the fun toolkit across cultures. In: Interaction Specialist Group Conference on People and Computers, pp. 386–391 (2012)

32. Sim, G., Horton, M.: Investigating children's opinions of games: Fun Toolkit vs. This or That. In: International Conference on Interaction Design and Children, pp. 70–77 (2012)

33. Staiano, J., Menéndez, M., Battocchi, A., de Angeli, A., Sebe, N.: UX_Mate: from facial expressions to UX evaluation. In: Designing Interactive Systems Conference, pp. 741–750 (2012)

34. Kronbauer, A. H., Santos, C., Vieira, V.: Um Estudo Experimental de Avaliação da Experiência dos Usuários de Aplicativos Móveis a partir da Captura Automática dos Dados Contextuais e de Interação. In: Brazilian Symposium on Human Factors in Computing Systems, pp. 305–314 (2012)

35. Rauschenberger, M., Olachner, S., Cota, M.P., Schrepp, M., Thomasschewski, J.: Measurement of user experience: a Spanish language version of the user experience questionnaire (UEQ). In: Iberian Conference on Information Systems and Technologies (2012)

36. Bach, C., Gauducheau, N., Salembier, P.: Combining interviews and scales in the multidimensional evaluation of user experience: a case study in 3D games. In: Annual European Conference on Cognitive Ergonomics, pp. 157–160 (2011)

37. Schulze, K., Kromker, H.: A framework to measure user experience of interactive online products. In: International Conference on Methods and Techniques in Behavioral Research (2010)

38. Meschtscherjakov, A., Reitberger, W., Tscheligi, M.: MAESTRO: orchestrating user behavior driven and context triggered experience sampling. In: International Conference on Methods and Techniques in Behavioral Research, p. 29 (2010)

39. Korhonen, H., Arrasvuori, J., Vaananen-Vainio-Mattila, K.: Let users tell the story: evaluating user experience with experience reports. In: ACM Conference on Human Factors in Computing Systems, Extended Abstracts, pp. 4051–4056 (2010)

40. Agarwal, A., Meyer, A.: Beyond usability: evaluating emotional response as an integral part of the user experience. In: ACM Conference on Human Factors in Computing Systems, Extended Abstracts, pp. 2919–2930 (2009)

A Process-Based Approach to Test Usability of Multi-platform Mobile Applications

Ingrid do Nascimento Mendes and Arilo Claudio Dias-Neto[✉]

Institute of Computing (IComp),
Federal University of Amazonas (UFAM), Manaus, Brazil
{inm, arilo}@icomp.ufam.edu.br

Abstract. In order to make a mobile application available to a wider audience, developers need to implement different versions on various mobile platforms. As consequence, the application needs to work properly in these platforms considering all quality characteristics. Usability is one of these characteristics that has direct impact on the success or failure of a mobile application. There are many studies that address mobile application tests, however they often do not handle multiplatform tests and also only cover few number of usability attributes used in mobile applications. In this paper, we propose a process-based approach that guides the activities related to usability testing in multiplatform mobile applications. To do that, specific guidelines and templates were proposed to support usability testing in a multiplatform environment. In addition, our approach comprises all seven usability attributes described in the PACMAD (People At the Centre of Mobile Application Development) model. In order to evaluate the proposed approach, a case study using the three current main mobile platforms was performed taking the Flipboard app as the sample mobile application.

Keywords: Usability · Mobile application · Compatibility · Testing

1 Introduction

Since their appearance, applications for mobile platforms, or simply mobile apps, have been constantly evolving in terms of technology and popularity. They are being used in many areas such as retail, media, travel, education, health, finance and others [1]. This large and growing number of mobile apps has challenged software engineers to develop applications with a high level of quality in order to make them more attractive and competitive in this new market. In addition, this platform has introduced some aspects and challenges to be considered during the software development, such as: the need to adapt to the mobile context of use, limited connectivity, small screen size, different video resolutions, limited processing capacity, diversity of data access methods and diversity of platforms [2, 3].

In this context, one of the main challenges to mobile app developers is to keep compatibility of their applications with different mobile platforms. In general, each mobile platform has a particular programming language with its own characteristics and constraints. In order to reach a wider audience, developers need to implement versions of a mobile app on various platforms. These versions must be compatible,

© Springer International Publishing Switzerland 2016
A. Marcus (Ed.): DUXU 2016, Part I, LNCS 9746, pp. 456–468, 2016.
DOI: 10.1007/978-3-319-40409-7_43

considering functional and non-functional requirements despite the specific charac-teristics of each platform. Therefore, a mobile app needs to work properly and similarly on these platforms, considering all quality characteristics, aiming to facilitate its use by different users in case of an exchange platform, as well as minimizing development effort, such as user interface design and tests.

Among the software quality characteristics present on ISO/IEC 25000 [4], Duh et al. [5] claim that usability has a direct impact on the success or failure of a mobile app. A good usability design contributes to increase the operation capacity of mobile device users and, thus, to improve the product quality as a whole. Users tend to choose mobile apps that are easily learned and appear to be more friendly to them [2, 6]. In addition, the compatibility of usability among versions of a multi-platform mobile app is an important requirement to attend users in different platforms.

In this scenario, usability evaluation for these applications becomes an important task to ensure not only their efficiency and user satisfaction, but also the compatibility between the different versions of the same mobile app on different platforms. Usability evaluation in mobile apps is an emerging research field. In recent years, usability analysis and measurement approaches have been proposed and/or evolved in the technical literature [7]. However, they do not support usability testing in multi-platform mobile apps, providing equivalence analysis or reusing of tests among the platforms. Thus, testers have a high effort to design and execute tests in this scenario.

In this paper, we propose an approach that comprises a process, guidelines, artifact templates, and metrics that aims to support usability testing of multi-platform mobile apps. This approach was designed using the PACMAD (*People At the Centre of Mobile Application Development*) usability evaluation model for mobile apps [8]. We applied the proposed approach in a case study that tested a mobile app developed for the three main mobile platforms (Android, iOS and Windows Phone). As a result, we obtained quantitative and qualitative data that provide initial evidences of the feasibility/ applicability of the proposed approach for evaluating the usability of a multi-platform mobile app from the seven usability attributes cited previously.

The paper is organized as follows: Sect. 2 describes concepts of usability testing in mobile apps and related works. Section 3 presents the proposed approach to support usability testing in multi-platform mobile apps, component-by-component. Section 4 reports a case study aiming to describe the feasibility of the proposed approach for usability testing in a multi-platform mobile app. Finally, in Sect. 5, the conclusions of this research and future works are described.

2   Usability Testing in Mobile Applications

Usability testing in mobile apps must take into account the variety of devices with different screen sizes and resolution. Depending on the device platform, its visual elements should follow a guide with the correct patterning of interface elements positions, such as buttons, windows, colors, to not compromise system's functional aspects [3]. Mobile platforms have specificities that affect the development of apps. In mobile apps development, the interface navigation flow design must be provided to support the tester in the software validation according to the specified requirements.

There are several and specific techniques for usability evaluation that can be applied to mobile apps. They can be classified as Empirical (involve the use of participants representing users of the application under test, such as field observations, interviews or focus group) or Non-Empirical (do not use participants and they may be necessary in situations where there may be trouble in finding the target audience or even when there are confidentiality issues, such as expert review, cognitive walkthroughs, heuristic evaluation). These techniques must be combined with approaches that aim to evaluate and measure the usability in mobile apps.

Some works tried to describe experiences on reporting usability testing in multi-platform mobile apps. In [2], the influence of phone complexity and user expertise on performance, ease of use and learnability is analyzed of different mobile phones from different platforms (Nokia, Siemens, Motorola). Nokia's device had the lowest and Motorola, the highest complexity, having Siemens' device ranging between them. The second independent variable was user expertise: 30 novices and 30 experts solved six tasks. Differences among the mobile phones regarding effectiveness, efficiency and learnability were found: Nokia users showed the best performance.

In [3, 6, 9] the authors present studies that evaluated and characterized approaches to support the usability evaluation in mobile apps. From 2004 until 2013, there was a considerable increase in approaches to support usability evaluation in mobile apps, and these assessments cover three types of mobile apps: web, native and hybrid [10]. In those studies, the authors did not map the approaches that deal with usability testing for multi-platform mobile apps.

In this work, we propose an approach that aims to test the compatibility of usability in multi-platform mobile apps comprised of process, guidelines, artifacts templates, and metrics, to be described in Sect. 3.

3   The Process-Based Approach for Compatibility Usability Testing in Multi-platform Mobile Applications

The proposed approach has the purpose of supporting testers of mobile apps in usability testing considering different versions of the same application for different devices/platforms (compatibility testing). It comprises four elements, detailed bellow:

- **Usability Testing Process:** describes four activities (and 16 sub activities), roles, and artifacts to be produced for usability testing in mobile apps. Moreover, these (sub)activities aim to support the analysis and reuse of usability tests considering versions of the same application for multiple mobile platforms. In this paper, we cannot show the complete description of this process due the limited space.
- **Guidelines:** recommend how to perform each activity of the usability testing process in order to test multi-platform mobile apps according to practices extracted and adapted from the technical literature.
- **Artifact Templates:** propose a "skeleton" of the artifacts to be produced when following the proposed process in order to test multi-platform mobile apps.

- **Metrics:** indicates how to measure and evaluate the several usability attributes that need to be analyzed in a mobile app. The attributes were based on the PACMAD model [8] and the metrics were extracted from the technical literature.

3.1   Process to Support Compatibility Usability Testing in Mobile Apps

It is composed of four main activities (Fig. 1), described in the following subsections. This process can be applied to test usability in (multi-platform) mobile apps. However, we introduced sub activities to deal with scenarios in which testers need to evaluate the usability of a mobile app implemented for several mobile platforms/devices.

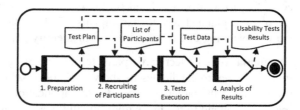

Fig. 1. Graphical representation of the usability testing process

Preparation. To build and prepare all necessary framework for implementing an usability test, starting with an initial study of the mobile app under test to understand its goals/features, target audience identification and specificities for each platform. After this step, we can define the test method, in order to choose the type of evaluation (e.g. field study and/or laboratory experiment), test environment (e.g. device and/or emulators) and mobile platforms in which the mobile app needs to be evaluated. From that, scenarios/tasks and sessions can be structured for the different mobile platforms, we can select attributes and their respective metrics and data collection approaches, the support material is constructed and a pilot test is executed, to try the designed tests. This activity is structured in six sub activities, as presented in Fig. 2.

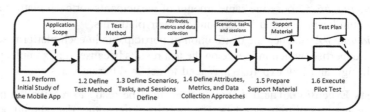

Fig. 2. Graphical representation of the activity *Preparation*

They will be described using guidelines (one of the approach elements) to perform usability testing in multi-platform mobile app.

- *Guideline #1.* The platforms/devices to be tested for a mobile app must be defined at the beginning of the process, since this decision will affect all planning stage.
- *Guideline #2.* In the creation of a task list in a new test instantiated for multiple platforms, we need to identify tasks required for all platforms and tasks not required for one or more platforms. That can be done by an analysis of equivalence among the features provided for all mobile app's versions.
- *Guideline #3.* When you already have a previous test as baseline, we need to identify tasks that will be kept, upgraded or that no longer exist, and if it necessary to create new tasks. Based on these issues, it is possible to reformulate a list of tasks and scenarios instantiated to another platform.
- *Guideline #4.* From this list of tasks and scenarios, we can specify some metrics that can be used to compare results among the selected devices/platforms, such as: possible paths to complete the scenario/task, total of keys or screen to complete the scenario/task, according to what was defined on the previous activity.
- *Guideline #5.* Apply the planned test to participants of all platforms aiming to confirm the good test planning and capture metrics or identify gaps.

Recruiting of Participants. To select participants to perform test on all platforms. Initially, we can apply a survey to candidates to show desirable characteristics of the participants (e.g. if they attend the target audience for the application). After that, we identify the participants that attend to the test's goal. Finally, we need to contact them to schedule the tests. This activity is structured in three sub activities (Fig. 3).

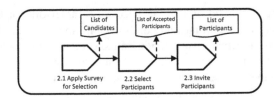

Fig. 3. Graphical representation of the activity *Recruiting of Participants*

The following guidelines describe how this activity is performed in order to support usability testing of multi-platform mobile apps:

- *Guideline #6.* Choose the same amount of participants for each platform under test with similar profile and background in their platforms.
- *Guideline #7.* Balance the distribution of participants in each platform according to their expertise, which influence on the test results because, for example, participants with high and low expertise may tend to act in different ways.

Tests Execution. The test environment must be ready to receive the participants, avoiding any loss of time and data. The tools used to capture data should be initialized and previously checked as well as printing any other support material used during the tests. The test itself must be performed and the data from videos/audios/survey responses should be stored in spreadsheets or other documents. This activity is structured in three sub activities, as presented in Fig. 4.

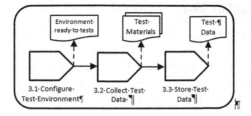

Fig. 4. Graphical representation of the activity *Tests Execution*.

Guidelines to perform this activity in order to support usability testing of multi-platform mobile apps are described below:

- *Guideline #8*. Configure the test environment the same way for each platform, following the test plan, avoiding influence on the results.
- *Guideline #9*. Storing individually the obtained data for each platform under test.

Analysis of Results. To analyze data obtained in tests execution, providing statistics and visual information (graphs). Associating this information to observed usability issues, reporting them to stakeholders. It is structured in three sub activities (Fig. 5).

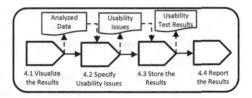

Fig. 5. Graphical representation of the activity *Analysis of Results*.

Some describe guidelines to perform this activity in order to support usability testing of multi-platform mobile apps are:

- *Guideline #10*. Usability issues found in all platforms may mean that this problem is independent of platform structure and it would be more associated with the app.
- *Guideline #11*. In some cases, participants of a mobile platform may have difficult to use a screen or task and the participants of another platform do not have this difficulty. This scenario suggests the usability issue would not be present on both platforms, representing an improvement opportunity in the first platform.

Due to space restriction, it is not possible to show and describe all sub activities that comprise the usability testing process. In the next section, we present the list of metrics, one of the elements that comprise the proposed approach, which can be applied to test usability in mobile apps.

3.2   Metrics for Usability Testing in Multiplatform Mobile Apps

Harrison et al. [8] proposed a usability model called PACMAD (*People At the Centre of Mobile Application Development*). This usability model aims to address some of the shortcomings of existing usability models when applied to mobile apps.

The PACMAD model identifies seven attributes used to define metrics for usability evaluation in mobile apps. Each attribute has an impact on the overall application usability.

- **Effectiveness:** the ability of a user to complete a task in a specified context. To evaluate effectiveness, we suggest the metric *total of (not) completed tasks* [8].
- **Efficiency:** the ability of the user to complete their task with speed and accuracy. It can be evaluated by the *total of attempts*, *keys and time* to complete each task [8].
- **Errors:** how well the user can complete the desired tasks without errors. Errors, as attributed related to effectiveness and efficiency, can be measured by tasks with more problems to be concluded (*attempts*, *time* and/or *total of keys*) [3, 11].
- **Learnability:** the ease with which users can gain proficiency with an application. It can be measured by repeating similar pairs of tasks in each session [2].
- **Memorability:** the ability of a user to retain how to use an application effectively. It can be measured by performing similar tasks into two sections, the second one after a time period of 3 days – default for all participants – in order to verify the performance after a period of inactivity, as described in [2].
- **Cognitive Load:** analyzes the impact that using the mobile device will have on the user's performance. It can be analyzed by several metrics [1]: user experience, level of distractions in the test environment, such as environment with low, medium, and high distraction level, and interface complexity, observed by the screen in which participants reported more problems.
- **Satisfaction:** the perceived level of comfort and pleasantness afforded to the user through the use of the software. It can be measured analyzing the attitudes of participants when using the application. It can be collected by interviews or questionnaires designed during the activity *Preparation*, as suggested by [11].

In the next section, we introduce some new artifacts produced during the usability testing process and propose templates for them, aiming to provide an instrument to support the usability testing process execution. The goal is to minimize the effort to adopt the proposed approach in real software projects.

3.3   New Artifacts to Support Usability Testing in Multi-platform Mobile Apps

The main artifacts to be produced in each activity of the proposed process are presented in Fig. 1. They are traditional artifacts present in usability testing process. Due to space restriction, the template of these artifacts (and others) with an example can be downloaded at https://goo.gl/JDqYcu. In order to support usability testing in multi-platform mobile apps, mainly the Preparation activity, we propose some new artifacts, as described below:

- **Map/Description of Equivalent Elements:** the map shows visually by images the equivalent elements of the application screens on all platforms under test in order to support the identification of key differences. It must be accompanied by a textual detail of the most significant differences present in screens or elements that are part of the tasks already selected. With these artifacts, it is possible to get an overview of the differences among the interface elements in all platforms.
- **Visual Map:** Map describing the flow of application's screens for each platform. It supports the identification of attributes/metrics to be evaluated, such as minimum number of screens or keys for each task.
- **Tasks Flow Graph:** Each screen in the visual map contains an identification. This artifact brings another representation for the flow of screens (described in the visual map), by means of graphs, in which each node is a visual map's screen and each edge indicates a possible transition between screens.

In the next section, we will present the use of the proposed approach (including these new artifacts) to test the usability compatibility of a real mobile app (*Flipboard*) developed for the three main mobile platforms: Android, iOS, and Windows Phone.

4   A Case Study to Test Usability in a Multi-platform Mobile Apps Using the Proposed Approach

We selected *Flibboard* as application to be tested in this case study. It is an aggregator of social networking content with a particular news feed customizable according to the user's interests. There were two reasons for choosing this mobile app: (1) it is easy to find people in the target audience and (2) the existence of the application on three major current mobile platforms (Android, iOS and Windows Phone).

4.1   Preparation and Recruiting of Participants

In Preparation activity, the main concerns are the selection of platforms versions to be tested (in this case, Android, iOS, and Windows Phone – *Guideline #1*) and the definition of sessions, scenarios and tasks for all platforms. We planned two 15 min sessions. The first session aimed to observe the first participant's interaction with the application during the tasks, i.e. the attribute Learnability. The second session was held after a period of inactivity (3 days) in using Flipboard application in order to see if they could perform tasks with varying degrees of proficiency over the first session and, thus, infer a result to the attribute Memorability. Metrics for the seven attributes (effectiveness, efficiency, satisfaction, ease of learning, memorability, errors and cognitive load) that comprise the proposed approach were evaluated (*Guideline #4*).

To support the analysis of equivalence among the platforms a *Map of Equivalent Elements* (partially showed in Fig. 6) has been created. We also created the artifact *Description of Equivalent Elements*, detailing the differences among the platforms, but there is no space to present it in this paper.

Fig. 6. Equivalence Features Map of (Partial View)

From this analysis, we could easily define five scenarios and eight tasks to be followed by the participants (Table 1 – *Guideline* #2). Task T1 is available only in the 1st session and the task T2 is available only in the 2nd session. Moreover, Task T4 has three different descriptions, one for each platform under test, due to their particularities. Task T6 does not exist in Windows Phone's platform (*Guideline* #3).

For each task, we specified possible paths to be followed to complete it using the artifact *Visual Map* (Fig. 7: left) and *Tasks Flow Graph* (Fig. 7: right) for each platform.

From these paths, we calculated total of keys and screens to define an oracle to be used in the results analysis (Table 2). We can observe some cells contain "-", which means that this platform does not have a particular path or task. This information will be used in the analysis of usability metrics that comprises the proposed approach.

We selected 15 participants (5 per platform – *Guideline* #5 and *Guideline* #6) for this study, totaling ten men and five women with average of 22.3 years old (*Guideline* #7). They were selected from a survey conducted with students in UFAM/Brazil.

Table 1. List of tasks to be performed per scenario

Scenarios	Tasks
S1: Start the use.	T1: Create an account in the application
	T2: Log in using your account
S2: Setting feed of news.	T3: Search and add categories of news in the feed
S3: Definition of news to be read later in a private magazine.	T4: [Android] Select some interesting news and flip in the option *read later*; [iOS] Select some interesting News and flip in the option *read later*; [WP] Select some interesting news and flip in any magazine
S4: Organizing Facebook's content in the format of magazine.	T5: Link your Facebook's account to Flipboard (or check it)
	T6: Navigate in the section "Pages" of Facebook by Flipboard.
S5: Additional features.	T7: Create a new public magazine
	T8: Flip in your magazine posts related to it

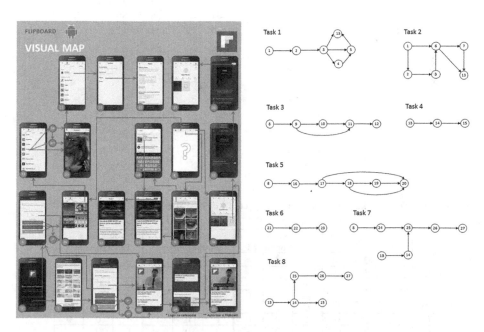

Fig. 7. (left) Visual Map of Tasks and (right) Tasks Flow Graph (Android Platform)

4.2   Tests Executions and Results Analysis

In order to execute tests, a mobile device of each platform under test was used (*Guideline #8*). In Table 3, '-' means that no platform's participant had completed the task in the session/environment, or the task does not exist in the platform/session.

Table 2. Total of keys and screens per path for all Tasks/Scenarios/Platforms

Scenario	Task	Path	Android Key	Android Screen	iOS Key	iOS Screen	WP Key	WP Screen
S1	T1	1	6	4	10	4	10	4
		2	6	6	11	6	11	6
		3	3	5	8	5	8	5
	T2	1	4	3	4	3	4	3
		2	5	4	5	4	5	4
		3	2	3	2	3	2	3
		4	5	5	10	5	10	5
		5	6	6	11	6	11	6
		6	3	5	8	5	8	5
S2	T3	1	4	5	4	5	4	5
		2	3	4	3	4	3	4
		3	4	5	4	5	4	5
		4	–	–	–	–	5	6
		5	–	–	–	–	4	5
		6	–	–	–	–	5	6
S3	T4	1	2	3	2	3	2	3
S4	T5	1	3	4	3	4	5	6
		2	6	5	6	5	8	7
		3	7	6	7	6	9	8
	T6	1	2	3	2	3	–	–
S5	T7	1	5	5	5	5	5	5
		2	5	5	5	5	5	5
	T8	1	2	6	2	3	2	3
		2	5	5	5	5	5	5

Table 3. Total of keys minus total of expected keys per task for all sessions/platforms

	Session 1			Session 2 Environment 1			Session 2 Environment 2			Session 2 Environment 3		
	🤖	🍎	⊞	🤖	🍎	⊞	🤖	🍎	⊞	🤖	🍎	⊞
#1	31	8	0	-	-	-	-	-	-	-	-	-
#2	-	-	-	4	2	0	5	0	0	3	0	0
#3	0	0	4	0	2	0	0	0	1	0	0	0
#4	0	3	3	0	2	4	0	0	6	0	0	7
#5	3	0	0	1	0	0	1	0	1	1	0	0
#6	-	0	-	2	0	-	0	0	-	0	0	-
#7	4	3	4	1	3	3	2	1	4	1	1	5
#8	2	3	8	0	0	3	1	0	4	0	0	5

Table 3 shows the data collected during the tests organized per task/session/platform, reporting the difference between the total of keys obtained with all participants and the total of expected keys. The same analysis was performed with the time and number of attempts required to conclude each task for each session/environment (*Guideline #9*).

The selected metrics could be evaluated based on the data presented in Table 3. From these collected data, all selected metrics could be evaluated in order to analyze the usability quality of the application under test. Due to space restrictions, it is not possible to present the complete tests analysis for each attribute selected during the preparation activity (*Guidelines #10* and *#11*). The goal in this section was to describe how the proposed approach contributed with its process, guidelines, artifacts, and metrics to perform usability testing in multi-platform mobile apps.

5   Conclusions and Future Works

In this work, we described a proposal of approach comprised by process, guidelines, artifacts templates and metrics to support usability compatibility testing in multi-platform mobile apps. This approach has been defined from the instantiation of PACMAD (usability evaluation model for mobile apps).

The application of the process, guidelines, templates and metrics aimed to enhance the results of a usability test instantiated for multiple mobile platforms, with well-defined scope and without reworking in the preparation activity, whereas the proposal aims to support the reuse of tasks and metrics across different platforms.

In order to assess the feasibility of the approach proposed using metrics related to the seven attributes that comprises the PACMAD model, a case study was carried out with the mobile app Flipboard on three mobile platforms (Android, iOS and Windows Phone). Throughout the tests, it was possible to collect information on the number of completed tasks, number of attempts, total of keys and time used for completing tasks. As a result, the approach and its guidelines could be fully applied and it contributed to the identification of problems related to the evaluated attributes.

As future works, we intend to apply and evaluate the approach in the software industry with other mobile apps in order to confirm its feasibility and improve it from the feedback of software engineers with different experience levels in usability testing.

Acknowledgment. The authors thank FAPEAM and INDT for financial support to conduct this research.

References

1. Flood, D., Germanakos, P., Harrison, R., Mc Caffery, F.: Estimating cognitive overload in mobile applications for decision support within the medical domain. In: 14th International Conference on Enterprise Information Systems, Wroclaw, Poland (2012)
2. Ziefle, M.: The influence of user expertise and phone complexity on performance, ease of user and learnability of different mobile phones. Behav. Inf. Technol. **21**, 303–311 (2002)
3. Zhang, D., Adipat, B.: Challenges, methodologies, and issues in the usability testing of mobile applications. Int. J. Hum.-Comput. Interact. **18**(3), 293–308 (2005)

 4. International Organization for Standardization, "ISO/IEC 25000 - Software engineering - Software product Quality Requirements and Evaluation (SQuaRE) - Guide to SQuaRE", ISO/IEC, March 2011
 5. Duh, H., Tan, G., Chen, V.: Usability evaluation for mobile device: a comparison of laboratory and field tests. In: Proceedings of the 8th Conference on Human-Computer Interaction with Mobile Devices and Services (MobileHCI). pp. 181–186 (2006)
 6. Nayebi, F., Desharnais, J.M., Abran, A.: The state of the art of mobile application usability evaluation. In: 25th IEEE Canadian Conference on Electrical Computer Engineering CCECE, pp. 1–4 (2012)
 7. Kjeldskov, J., Stage, J.: New techniques for usability evaluation of mobile systems. Int. J. Hum.-Comput. Stud. **60**(5), 599–620 (2004)
 8. Harrison, R., Flood, D., Duce, D.: Usability of mobile applications: literature review and rationale for a new usability model. J. Interact. Sci. **1**(1), 1–16 (2013)
 9. Kjeldskov, J., Paay, J.: A longitudinal review of Mobile HCI research methods. In: International Conference on Human-Computer Interaction with Mobile Devices and Services (MobileHCI 2012), pp. 69–78. doi:10.1145/2371574.2371586
10. Huy, N.P., VanThanh, D.: Evaluation of mobile app paradigms. In: Proceedings of International Conference on Advances in Mobile Computing & Multimedia (MoMM 2012), Ismail Khalil, pp. 25–30 (2012)
11. Masoodian, M., Lane, N.: An empirical study of textual and graphical travel itinerary visualization using mobile phones. In: Proceedings of the Fourth Australian User Interface Conference on User Interfaces vol. 18, pp. 11–18 (2003)

Extending Empirical Analysis of Usability and Playability to Multimodal Computer Games

David Novick$^{(\boxtimes)}$ and Laura M. Rodriguez

Department of Computer Science, The University of Texas at El Paso,
500 West University Avenue, El Paso, TX 79968-0518, USA
novick@utep.edu, lmrodriguez3@miners.utep.edu

Abstract. The published research examining usability and playability of games is largely theoretical. A prior empirical study of a game with an embodied conversational agent found that most frustration episodes could be understood in terms of both usability and playability, but this study was based on a game in which the interaction by both player and agent were limited to verbal communication. To explore whether these results would hold for a game in which the player and agent communicated with both speech and gesture, we conducted an empirical formative user-experience evaluation of a multimodal game. Our findings strongly confirmed that frustration episodes can be understood as issues of both usability and playability. However, the relative frequencies of the categories of usability and playability issues differed between the speech-only and the speech-and-gesture games. Much of this difference likely arose because higher levels of engagement and rapport between player and agent in the speech-and-gesture game led to the players having greater, and in many cases unfulfilled, expectations for the capabilities of the agent.

Keywords: Embodied conversational agent · User experience · Playability · Usability · Gesture · Engagement · Rapport

1 Introduction

User-experience evaluation typically assesses the effectiveness, efficiency, and user-satisfaction of a system, given its goals [1]. For most user interfaces, the purpose of usability testing is to make the application as easy to use as possible. But for games, the very point of the application is that it not be easy: the application should present the user with interesting challenges. For office applications, user-experience goals center on factors such as task completion, error elimination, and workload reduction; for games, user-experience goals center on factors such as entertainment, the fun of overcoming obstacles, and workload increase [2]. For this reason, the relationship between playability and usability has remained problematic. And as embodied conversational agents (ECAs) [3] become increasingly ubiquitous, developers of ECA-based games, adventures, and other experiences could benefit from an understanding of evaluation methodologies that more clearly explains the relationship between usability and playability.

© Springer International Publishing Switzerland 2016
A. Marcus (Ed.): DUXU 2016, Part I, LNCS 9746, pp. 469–478, 2016.
DOI: 10.1007/978-3-319-40409-7_44

The constructs of usability and playability have been explored with respect to games, but primarily on a theoretical basis. The only known published application of formative empirical evaluation of a computer game evaluated the usability and playability of an ECA-based adventure game [4]. In that study, however, users navigated the application only through relatively simple speech commands. The application's user interface did not enable users to use natural speech or physical gestures as modalities of interaction. In the present study, we address this limitation by reporting on the formative user-experience evaluation of a multimodal ECA-based adventure game in which the player could communicate with the on-screen agent through more natural, unstructured utterances and through upper-body gestures.

In this paper, then, we briefly review the state of the art of user-experience evaluation of video game, explain the challenge for analysis of the relationship between usability and playability, describe the study's methodology, report the results of the formative evaluation, and discuss the implications of these results. We conclude with a contrast of these results with those in [4] and discuss the limitations of our study.

2 Background

Studies of evaluation of the playability and usability video games have, with very limited exceptions, not extended to empirical evaluation of games through user studies. Rather, the research literature of playability and usability has tended to focus on heuristic evaluation of games (e.g., [5–7]), and the research literature on user-centered evaluation of games has tended to remain at the theoretical level (e.g., [1, 8, 9]). In contrast, commercial practice appears to rely largely on empirical usability tests, with little use of heuristic evaluation [10]; unfortunately, the results of the commercial studies tend not to be published. At the same time, the relationship between playability and usability remains unclear. There are evident differences between playability and usability [1, 2]. For example, an office application seeks to make the user's task as easy as possible, while a game seeks to make the user's task interestingly difficult. But from the standpoint of empirical testing of games, the theoretical divisions between playability and usability appear to diminish in practice.

An initial study that assessed playability and usability of a computer game through empirical user testing suggested that the evaluation technique for playability can be the same as for usability: there is really a single technique of empirical testing of the user's experience in computer games, regardless of whether this is called usability testing or playability testing [4]. This paper remains the only published empirical study of user-experience testing of computer games of which we are aware. However, the game that was tested in that study, although it included animated visuals, was entirely verbal in its interaction. The game, called "Escape from the Castle of the Vampire King," although implemented as an immersive game with an ECA, was essentially an immersive version of a text-based adventure game such as Zork [11]. Do these results hold for an immersive game that goes beyond the limitations of verbal interaction to combine verbal interaction with gestural interaction and movement in the virtual world by the human and the agent?

3 Methodology

To address the question of whether the results for relatively simple speech-based interaction hold for more complex, multimodal interaction, we studied the development of an immersive computer game, entitled "Survival on Jungle Island" [12], in which the human user interacted with the ECA through both speech and gesture as the human and the agent moved through the game's virtual world. A brief video of excerpts of the game is available at http://www.cs.utep.edu/novick/jungle.mp4. In the game, each participant partners with the agent to survive on and escape from a deserted jungle island.

The study took place in the Immersion Lab at the University of Texas at El Paso (UTEP). This lab consists of a rectangular room about 14 feet by 17 feet, with the image projected on one of the shorter walls, which is covered with a reflective paint to serve as a screen; the wall is fully covered by the projection. For the jungle game, the lab set-up included artificial plants and other scenery elements that helped make the setting more immersive. The artificial plants were spread out between the player and the projected scene. A camera, placed behind a tree at the lower left corner of the projection wall, recorded the user's experience. The system recognized the player's speech and body gestures via a Microsoft Kinect, which was placed at the bottom center of the projection wall. The person running the experiments was behind the projector at the control table. Figure 1 shows the setup of the room in which experiments took place. Figure 2 shows the interior of lab, including scenery for the Jungle game, with the placement of the projector, Kinect, and camera.

The jungle game, created to study rapport between embodied conversational agents (ECAs) and humans, comprised a series of scenes in which a single user interacts with the ECA through speech and gesture, such as a high-five gesture. The research studied whether users would feel increased rapport with an ECA that elicits and perceives gestures than with one that elicits only speech; inclusion of gestures in the game was essential for achieving the aims of the research.

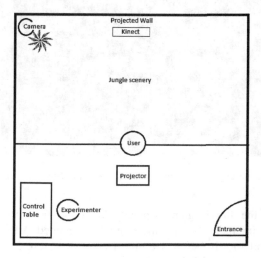

Fig. 1. Experimental setup in UTEP's immersion lab

Fig. 2. Interior of the immersion lab, with scenery for the "Survival on Jungle Island" game

Fig. 3. Adriana, the embodied conversational agent in "Survival on Jungle Island"

A session with the Jungle game typically lasted 40–60 min, depending on the player. The players interacted with a life-sized ECA named Adriana who had been stranded in the island shortly before the player arrived. Figure 3. Depicts Adriana in one of the game's scenes. Adriana would partner with the player to survive on and escape from the deserted island. The participants were video-recorded throughout the game to make note of their reactions. At the game's conclusion, the participants completed a survey in which they communicated their experience with and perceptions of the agent during the game.

For the user-experience evaluation, an experimenter was present in the lab to note the details of the projection at the time of a frustration episode. The experimenter also could step in to troubleshoot, as the system was being evaluated formatively; because it was still in development, the system, on some infrequent occasions, froze.

The formative user evaluation of the Jungle game reported here involved four participants, three male, and one female. As the system uses speech and gesture recognition, it was not practical to use common usability approaches such as think-aloud techniques. We introduced each participant to the game and explained that the session would be recorded for research purposes. Then the experimenter started the game and observed the projection as the game progressed. We considered a frustration episode when the user tried to do something and the system did not respond as the user expected producing observable or expressed reactions of irritability or confusion. After the game, the experimenter asked the participant about specific frustration episodes so that the participant could explain the reasons for frustrations encountered.

4   Results

In the user tests, we observed a total of unique 44 frustration episodes; for the purposes of this analysis, subsequent identical episodes in the same session were not counted. The number of unique frustration episodes per user ranged from 6 to 14, with a mean frequency of 11.0 unique episodes per user. We coded each episode for playability with the six facets of playability developed in [1] (intrinsic, mechanical, interactive, artistic, personal, and social), and coded each episode for usability with the categories developed in [13] for heuristic evaluation (dialog, speaking the user's language, user's memory load, consistency, feedback, clearly marked exits, accelerators, error messages, error prevention, and other). Table 1 summarizes these results.

We found that all of the frustration episodes could be categorized as both a playability issue and a usability issue. For example, an episode where the player became unnerved by the facial expression of the agent as she said words containing the vowel "o" and was smiling because the agent's animation seemed creepy we coded for usability as speaking the user's language and for playability as artistic. An episode where the agent asked the player to not let her fall asleep, but there was no way for the player to keep the agent awake, we coded for usability as consistency and for playability as intrinsic. Table 2 presents four examples of frustration episodes, all in the "dialog" usability category but in three different playability categories.

Overall, of the 34 unique problems identified in the system through the user-experience testing, 18 involved speech production and recognition, 9 involved gesture production and recognition, and 7 involved other factors.

Table 1. Frustration episodes in the Survival in Jungle Island categorized using both usability and playability.

Usability	Playability						
	Intrinsic	Mechanical	Interactive	Artistic	Personal	Social	Total
Dialog	3		3		4		10
Speaking users' lang			14	1			14
User's memory load							0
Consistency	2	1	2	1			5
Feedback	1	2	10				13
Clearly marked exits							0
Accelerators							0
Error messages							0
Error Prevention							0
Other							0
Total	6	3	29	2	4	0	44

Table 2. Example issues and coding into usability and playability categories

Issue	Usability	Playability
Agent's utterance was too fast to understand, so participant did not catch the joke and was confused about why the agent was smiling.	Dialog	Interaction
Agent encouraged participant to not be so quiet in one dialog when in the rest of the game agent talks more than she listens.	Dialog	Intrinsic
Participant complained that agent "doesn't let me talk!"	Dialog	Personal
Participant asked agent about what happened and why she was on the island.	Dialog	Intrinsic

4.1   Frustration Episodes Involving Speech

We encountered several issues regarding the ECA's verbal communication. For example, the agent asked rhetorical questions and did not give the user enough information to know that it was rhetorical or provide time to respond. This upset the players, who felt ignored; some even verbally expressed their complaint to the agent, only to be ignored again, thus compounding the problem and making them even more upset. We coded these frustration episodes for usability as *dialog* and for playability as *personal*.

Players also encountered a problem in an early scene where the agent encouraged the user to talk more. Because the game's designers sought to encourage interaction with the user, they thought that this prompt from the agent would be appropriate. However, the agent's encouragement made the players overconfident about what the agent could understand. As a result, three of the four testers started asking the agent questions in the next scene, but the agent was not designed to answer spontaneous questions from the player; as a result, the agent ignored the players' questions. The testers explained in their post-session interviews that this upset them not only because answering questions was not within the agent's capabilities but because the agent had initially encouraged them to interact more. Because of these problems, most of the testers viewed the agent as a bossy extravert. We coded these frustration episodes for usability as *dialog* and for playability as *intrinsic*.

4.2   Frustration Episodes Involving Gesture

We now turn to playability and usability issues related to gesture. The hardest gestures to perform in the game were spearfishing and starting a fire, and the way these activities are performed depends on their context. Unfortunately, the early version of game evaluated in this study presented little physical context for these activities. Without information on what tool they were using for spearfishing, the testers produced varied gestural responses to the agent's prompts. One of the testers tried to catch fish with his hands.

Similar problems occurred when the agent asked the players to start a fire using two sticks. People who already know how to do this—and possibly people who have merely seen it done—are likely to come up with the way to move their hands to simulate the gesture. The system expected that the players would have both hands in front of their body, close to elbow level, with one hand at an angle striking the other in such a way that one hand lands on top of the other. But in practice, the testers' intuitive gestures for striking two sticks to start a fire in this study were hugely different from this model. One participant tried to strike the two sticks in front of her with her arms perpendicular to the floor. She then tried striking her hands at an angle in which her right hand was on top of the left while both of her hands would come together directly in front of her. Even though the motion was partially right, it was not being performed at the correct angle with respect to the elbows. The participant tried slight variations of this gesture until she got feedback. We coded this frustration episode for usability as *speaking the user's language* and for playability as *interactive*.

Another participant was striking his hands in front of him with a wide and swift arm motion. Each time that he did the gesture and did not get feedback, he would do the motion slower, until eventually he came to a complete stop. We coded this frustration episode for usability as *feedback* and for playability as *interactive*.

Another problem with gestures arose because objects or events to which the agent referred were not accurately depicted in the virtual world in the early version of the game being tested. This confused the testers and distracted them from their task at hand. We coded these frustration episodes for usability as *consistency* and for playability as *interactive*.

5   Conclusion

Our analysis confirmed the findings in [4] that frustration episodes can be viewed as both playability and usability problems. In the current study, all 44 of the episodes could be coded into one of the six facets of playability and could be coded into one of the categories of heuristic usability other than "other."

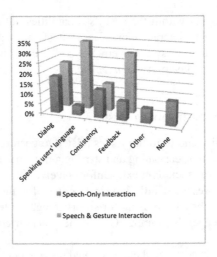

Fig. 4. Comparison with respect to relative frequency of usability issues of speech-only and speech-and-gesture games. (Color figure online)

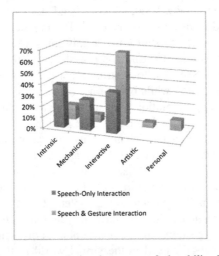

Fig. 5. Comparison with respect to relative frequency of playability issues of speech-only and speech-and-gesture games. (Color figure online)

In terms of playability, we classified 66 % of the frustration episodes as interactive, which is associated with player interaction and videogame user interface development. This contrasts with the results in [4], where only 36 % of the episodes were interactive. In terms of usability, the frustration episodes clustered in the categories of dialog, speaking the user's language, and feedback. This again contrasts with the results in [4], where the frustration episodes clustered in the categories of error prevention and dialog. Figures 4 and 5 contrast the respective playability and usability distributions between [4] and the present study.

This evidence suggests that the modality of games affects the categories of usability and playability issues that users experience. While it may seem paradoxical that the speech-only game had fewer problems with *dialog* and *speaking the user's language* than did the speech-and-gesture game, this effect likely resulted from differences in the way language was used in the two games. The speech-only game, "Escape from the Castle of the Vampire King," was effectively a text-based adventure game with animated pictures. Its speech recognition relied on the players producing highly structured utterances such as "go to lobby" and "pick up castle key," and its agent produced relatively simple utterances. In contrast, the speech-and-gesture game, "Survival on Jungle Island," enabled the players to communicate with unstructured utterances, and the agent's utterances were longer and more conversational. Consequently, the Jungle game had greater opportunity for players to explore the space of speech they produced.

A similar dynamic likely led to the differences in frequency of playability issues. In particular, the speech-only game, with its Zork-like restriction to structured utterances and connected rooms, presented players with greater challenges in their accomplishing goals, thus leading to a greater relative frequency of intrinsic playability issues. In contrast, the speech-and-gesture game, with its promise of apparently free-form spoken interaction, provided greater opportunity for players to reach the limits of the game's natural-language capabilities, thus leading to a relatively higher frequency of interactive usability issues. The Jungle game was not designed so that the agent could answer questions from players. Thus although the game did well making players feel comfortable with the agent, in some of the players this enhanced level of engagement and rapport tended to provoke a sense of curiosity. These users began asking questions of the agent, only to get frustrated at her perceived rudeness. This phenomenon did not appear to occur in the speech-only game, probably because the interaction led to a much lower level of engagement and rapport between player and agent.

6 Postscript

The formative user-experience evaluation reported in this paper enabled the development team to address both the usability and playability issues identified in the user testing. The "Survival on Jungle Island" game went on to receive the award for outstanding demonstration at the 2015 International Conference on Multimodal Interaction [14].

Acknowledgments. The authors acknowledge with gratitude the team, in addition to the authors, that developed Survival on Jungle Island: Ivan Gris, Adriana Camacho, Diego Rivera, Mario Gutierrez, Alex Rayon, Joel Quintana, Anuar Jauregui, Timothy Gonzales, Alfonso Peralta, Victoria Bravo, Jacqueline Brixey, Yahaira Reyes, Paola Gallardo, Chelsey Jurado, Guillaume Adoneth, David Manuel, Brynne Blaugrund, and Nick Farber.

References

1. Sánchez, J.G., Simarro, F.M., Zea, N.P., Vela, F.G.: Playability as extension of quality in use in video games. In: 2nd International Workshop on the Interplay between Usability Evaluation and Software Development (I-USED) (2009)

2. González Sánchez, J.L., Padilla Zea, N., Gutiérrez, F.L.: From usability to playability: introduction to player-centred video game development process. In: Kurosu, M. (ed.) HCD 2009. LNCS, vol. 5619, pp. 65–74. Springer, Heidelberg (2009)
3. Cassell, J.: Embodied Conversational Agents. MIT press, Cambridge (2000)
4. Novick, D., Vicario, J., Santaella, B., Gris, I.: Empirical analysis of playability vs. usability in a computer game. In: Marcus, A. (ed.) DUXU 2014, Part II. LNCS, vol. 8518, pp. 720–731. Springer, Heidelberg (2014)
5. Desurvire, H., Caplan, M., Toth, J.A.: Using heuristics to evaluate the playability of games. In: CHI 2004 Extended Abstracts on Human Factors in Computing Systems, pp. 1509–1512. ACM (2004)
6. Pinelle, D., Wong, N., Stach, T.: Heuristic evaluation for games: usability principles for video game design. In: Proceedings of the SIGCHI Conference on Human Factors in Computing Systems, pp. 1453–1462. ACM (2008)
7. Fierley, R., Engl, S.: User experience methods and games: lessons learned. In: proceedings of the 24th BCS Interaction Specialist Group Conference, pp. 204–210. British Computer Society, Swinton (2010)
8. Nacke, L.: From playability to a hierarchical game usability model. In: 2009 Conference on Future Play on@ GDC Canada, pp. 11–12 (2009)
9. Fabricatore, C., Nussbaum, M., Rosas, R.: Playability in action videogames: a qualitative design model. Hum. Comput. Interact. 17(4), 311–368 (2002)
10. Fabricatore, C., Nussbaum, M., Rosas, R.: Playability in action videogames: a qualitative design model. Hum. Comput. Interact. 17(4), 311–368 (2002)
11. Lebling, P.D., Blank, M.S., Anderson, T.A.: Special feature zork: a computerized fantasy simulation game. Computer 4, 51–59 (1979)
12. Novick, D., Gris, I., Rivera, D.A., Camacho, A., Rayon, A., Gutierrez, M.: The UTEP AGENT System. In: Proceedings of the 17th ACM International Conference on Multimodal Interaction, Seattle, WA, 9–13 November 2015
13. Nielsen, J., Molich, R.: Heuristic evaluation of user interfaces. In: Proceedings of the SIGCHI Conference on Human Factors in Computing Systems, pp. 249–256 (1990)
14. University Communications [of the Univ. Texas at El Paso]: UTEP Computer Science Department develops award-winning interactive agent system, 21 January 2016. http://engineering.utep.edu/announcement012116.htm

Application of the Communicability Evaluation Method to Evaluate the User Interface Design: A Case Study in Web Domain

Freddy Paz[1]($\boxtimes$), Freddy A. Paz[2], and José Antonio Pow-Sang[1]

[1] Pontificia Universidad Católica del Perú, Lima 32, Peru
fpaz@pucp.pe, japowsang@pucp.edu.pe
[2] Universidad Nacional Pedro Ruiz Gallo, Lambayeque, Peru
freddypazsifuentes@yahoo.es

Abstract. According to the Semiotic Engineering, the human-computer interaction is a way of communication between designers and users. The Communicability Evaluation Method (CEM) is a technique to assess this communication and determine the degree in which the designers achieve to convey users their design intents through the system interface. Most case studies that are described in the literature are focused on the evaluation of desktop applications. In this study, we present the results of a communicability evaluation to a transactional Web application. The experimental case was run by three specialists in the field of HCI and involved the participation of four university students from two academic programs in Computing. These users had to perform some tasks that were developed based on the results of a previous work. After an analysis of the interactions, we concluded that the Website can be difficult to use by users with no experience in the use of this type of software. There are certain aspects of the interface design that should be improved.

Keywords: Usability · Communicability evaluation · User interface design · Experimental study · Human-computer interaction

1 Introduction

Nowadays, the use of the Internet has become a critical source of productivity for any company because of its capability to extend the information to many users around the world. Accompanied by the continuous growth and high adoption of this technology, Web software applications have emerged as a means of electronic commerce of products and services.

However, due to a large number of Web sites that daily appear in this competitive market, companies are no longer concerned only with their presence on the Internet. Companies have been forced to change their strategy by focusing on the development of high-quality software products, which meet certain properties related to the quality of use of the systems [4]. One of these properties is the *communicability*, which is defined within the framework of the Semiotic

A. Marcus (Ed.): DUXU 2016, Part I, LNCS 9746, pp. 479–490, 2016.
DOI: 10.1007/978-3-319-40409-7_45

Engineering as the feature of software to effectively and efficiently conveys to users its underlying design intent and interactive principles.

The Communicability Evaluation Method (CEM) is a technique to measure the level of communicability of a software application. The aim of this method is to determine the extent to which users achieve to understand the design of a graphical interface [8]. From the approach of the Semiotic Engineering, the Human-Computer Interaction (HCI) is perceived as a communication between users and designers, given that developers manage to communicate different ways to achieve specific goals through the design of the interface [1,2]. These messages can be both explicit (via texts), or implicit (via icons, symbols, graphics, patterns, frames, and other forms of design). This method allow designers to appreciate how well users are getting the intended messages across the interface by identifying the communication breakdowns that take place during the interaction [9].

This research is the result of an assessment based on the Communicability Evaluation Method (CEM) conducted in the Web domain. The software system that was selected to perform this study was *Booking.com*, a transactional Web site that is used for booking hotels worldwide. As a result, it has been possible to identify the communication breakdowns that could arise during the interaction between the user and the system. This case study has allowed defining the degree of communicability of the software application and the quality of metacommunication between designer and user for future improvements of the Website.

2   Communicability Evaluation Method

In order to conduct an evaluation of the user interface design from the perspective of the Semiotic Engineering, we used the Communicability Evaluation Method (CEM) proposed by de Souza [11]. CEM is a method to determine the degree in which the system designers achieve to communicate users their design intents through the interface design. As well as other theories that were inspired in the Semiotic Engineering, CEM states that the human-computer interaction is a particular type of communication between humans which is mediated through a computer [5]. This interaction involves the participation of both designers and users, and the communication occurs at the time in which users interact with the system interface. If the purpose of each design element is properly communicated, users will be able to achieve their goals through the use of the system [10].

The Communicability Evaluation Method (CEM) is a technique in which a representative number of end users are requested to interact with the software product to be tested. This interaction is guided by a predefined set of tasks that users must perform during the software evaluation. All interactions must be recorded using devices and tools to capture the user's screen and the user's face, in order to subsequently analyze the mouse movements and the facial expressions. This method includes three phases [3]: (1) Tagging, (2) Interpretation and (3) Semiotic Profile. The process of CEM is illustrated in Fig. 1.

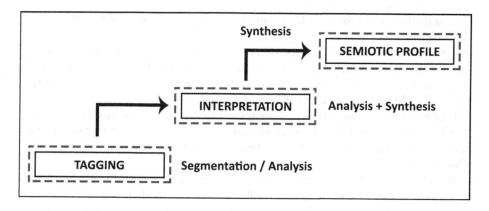

Fig. 1. The three core steps of SEM [11]

In the first phase, the videos, where the interactions were captured, must be analyzed. The purpose is to identify events that are indicative of breakdowns in the communication. There are thirteen expressions of communicative breakdown to classify each event. These tags represent the specialist's interpretation of the user behavior. Once all events are labeled, the evaluators must interpret the meaning of the whole set of communicative breakdowns that were detected. For this phase, the experts should consider the frequency of each tag and identify the design problems that cause these breakdowns. Finally, in the last phase, specialists must elaborate the original message of the designer. The classification of the communicability problems helps specialists to achieve an in-depth characterization of meta-communication, the meaning of the overall designer-to-user message [7].

2.1 Tagging

In this phase, the specialists should use the recordings to analyze the user's reactions and identify communicative breakdowns. Evaluators must relate each evidence of communicative breakdown to 1 of the 13 tags proposed by the Semiotic Engineering. These tags are written in natural language, and they are sometimes expressed verbally by users during the test. According to de Souza [11], this process can be described as *"putting words in the user's mouth"*. The thirteen tags that characterize communicative breakdowns between user and designer are [7]:

- *"I give up."* The user is unable to achieve the proposed goal. There are not enough resources such as time, will, and patience to reach it.
- *"Looks fine to me."* The user is unable to realize that the outcome is not the expected one. The result seems to be fine for the user. However the task has only been partially completed.
- *"Thanks, but no, thanks."* There is enough evidence to ensure that the user knows the design intentions, however, decides to follow a different path.

The user declines designer's invitation to engage in a particular kind of communication.

- *"I can do otherwise."* The user is not aware of the design intentions. Therefore, he does something different from what is expected. The interaction reveals that the user has not received the designer's message about how to use the system in the particular context in which he is.
- *"Where is it?"* The user is looking for a specific functionality of the system, but is unable to find it. The user is expecting certain sign or element in the interface design to carry out a particular strategy, however, can not easily identify it.
- *"What happened?"* The user repeats an operation because he is apparently unable to assign meaning to the result that is provided by the system. The user can not identify the effects caused by their actions (halt for a moment).
- *"What now?"* The user does not know what to do next, and performs a random action. He is clearly looking for a clue that brings him back into the right path to achieve the proposed goals.
- *"Where am I?"* The user performs actions that are inappropriate in the context in which he is. Although the design elements are successfully identified, these are used in a wrong context.
- *"Oops!"* The user chooses certain system functions by mistake and try to leave immediately the unwanted state (commonly via the command 'Undo' or by attempting to restore some previous states of the system).
- *"I can't do it this way."* The user realizes that the sequence of actions he is performing does not lead to the goal. Therefore, he abandons this path of interactions (composed of many steps) and chooses a different one.
- *"What is this?"* The user explores some possibilities of interaction to acquire knowledge about the system functions. He examines the interface design in order to find explanatory tips or clues about the meaning of the elements.
- *"Help!"* The user accesses the help system. He deliberately calls this function by pressing F1 or by reading the manuals that are available. The online support is also considered as a source of help.
- *"Why doesn't it?"* The user performs a series of actions expecting a specific result from the system, however, this scenario is not achieved. Although the outcomes are explicit and clear, these do not match with the user's goals. The user repeats his actions again to determine if he is doing something wrong. He reviews every step carefully because he is sure of the chosen path.

2.2   Interpretation

In this phase, the specialists must analyze the collected data to identify all the problems of the graphical user interface. Each communicative breakdown is related to a specific category of issue [7]: navigation, meaning assignment, task accomplishment and declination/missing of affordance.

2.3 Semiotic Profile

In this final phase, evaluators will be able to identify the meaning of the overall message between users and designers. After an in-depth analysis of the communicative breakdowns, specialists will attempt to retrieve the original designer's metacommunication. They will assume the position of the designers by answering the following questions in first person [7]:

- *Who do I think are the users of the software product I have designed?* The purpose of this question is to identify the main characteristics of users (the listeners of the designer's message).
- *What the users want and need?* This question allows specialists to identify the mismatches between designers and users (the differences between the design intentions and what the user is actually expecting from the design).
- *What are the users' preferences according to what they want and need? Why?* The purpose of this question is to identify the designer's justification for the interface design that was proposed. The answer to this question allows specialists to determine whether the design decisions are consistent with the user expectations.
- *How is the system I have designed for these specific users, and how they should use the system?* The purpose of these questions is to identify the degree in which the expressions and content of the designer's metacommunication are being conveying to users through the interface design.
- *What is my design vision?* Finally, this question allows specialists to identify the degree in which the design is properly understood (and accepted) by the user.

3 Research Design

3.1 Participants

All the participants were students at the National University "Pedro Ruiz Gallo" located in Perú. In order to conduct this experimental case study, four students were randomly chosen from an elective course called "Usability Engineering", that is shared by two academic programs: An Undergraduate and a Master's Program in Computing. They aged between 24 and 41 years old, and three of them had previous experience using the software. We used the following IDs to represent each participant: P1, P2, P3 and P4.

3.2 Description of the Software System

The software system that was evaluated is *Booking.com*, a transactional Web application for hotel booking. The goal of *Booking.com* is to offer the best prices for any type of accommodation, from small, family-run beds and breakfasts to executive apartments and five-star luxury suites [12]. One of the expectations of this trademark is to provide a usable Web site, in which the user easily finds all information regarding hotels. This system should allow travelers to choose from a variety of accommodations around the world in an easy and efficient way.

3.3   Test Design

The communicability evaluation test involved two activities. Participants had to perform these tasks consecutively and in the established order. Moreover, there was a specific time to complete each task. The design of these activities was based on a previous study [6], in which we conducted a heuristic evaluation to a similar software product in order to identify the most critical usability issues of this type of application. The issues that were considered for the development of this test are:

- The lack of visibility of certain important elements of the interface design such as search filters, features and services offered by hotels, and information related to accommodations.
- The lack of certain options of the system, which allow users to make better decisions. For instance, the lack of a tool for comparison among the alternatives of hotel accommodations that are offered by the Web site, and the absence of a feature to sort the results based on user criteria.
- The ambiguity in the meaning of certain icons and symbols that are used as part of the interface design, and the confusion these representations can cause among the users of the system.
- The lack of a cultural perspective for the development of the interface design. Given that a Web site is used worldwide, some cultural aspects that should be considered such as language, currency, date formats, writing direction, special characters, calendars, symbols, colors, etc.

Given that the purpose of this test is not to verify the usability of the Web site but the communicative breakdowns between the user and the designer, the number of usability issues that were considered for the test design are appropriate. Attempts were made to develop a realistic scenario, a real situation with possible conditions that could arise when users book a hotel. The scenario that was considered for the test of communicability is described as follows:

"You have decided to spend your summer vacation in Europe with your best friend. After a long talk with your partner, you agreed to be responsible for all costs of accommodation. However, you only have S/.2400.00 (local currency of Perú) for this purpose. Also, you have considered that a three-star hotel is acceptable for both. Given these conditions, please complete the activity, considering that the accommodation date is from February 4 to February 10, 2016."

In the second part of the test, the users were requested to search for a particular hotel. The following scenario was proposed to evaluate the ease with which the users manages to determine if given a specific hotel name, they achieve to conclude if it meets their preferences. Both activities are described in Table 1.

"Some friends have recommended you the following hotel located in Paris (France): Jean Gabriel. For this reason, you will review its services, features and rates to determine whether it meets the above conditions."

Table 1. Description of tasks of the communicability evaluation

Activity	Description
Task N.1	**Purpose:** The user must identify, by using the Website *Booking.com*, a hotel in Paris (France) that meets the conditions of the proposed scenario. **Specific Tasks:** 1. Enter the Website *Booking.com*. 2. Select "Spanish" in the language settings. 3. Perform a search to display hotels available in Paris (France) for two people during the dates that were specified in the scenario. 4. Identify a hotel which meets all requirements of the scenario and whose total cost does not exceed the budget is available according to the test. 5. Once the hotel is identified, the user must specify the name of the hotel, the rate per night, the total price and the room type is being considered for the calculation of the total amount including taxes.
Task N.2	**Purpose:** The user must perform a new search on the Website *Booking.com* to find a specific hotel. After a review of the services, features and rates, the user must determine whether it meets the conditions of the proposed scenario. **Specific Tasks:** 1. Perform a new search on *Booking.com* to find the "Jean Gabriel" hotel located in Paris (France). 2. Select this hotel and review 3. Answer successfully the following questions regarding the hotel: – Does this hotel meet the proposed conditions? – According to the case study, do you have enough money to book this hotel for you and your friend considering the established dates? – Is it a three-star hotel? 4. Identify three services that are offered by this hotel. 5. Identify the room type that was considered for the calculation of the total amount.

3.4   Test Environment

The communicability evaluation of *Booking.com* was performed on January 23th, 2016. This study was conducted in a computer lab at the National University "Pedro Ruiz Gallo". We used the following electronic devices and software:

- A *webcam* to record all gestures and facial expressions of the users.
- *Cam Studio Open Source*, a free streaming video software to record the interaction between user and system.
- *TeamViewer*, a software package for remote control and desktop sharing.

4   Data Analysis and Results

4.1   Tagging

After an analysis of the interaction between user and system during the test and a study of the recorded videos, we identified the communicative breakdowns. The results show that no events were registered for the following communicative breakdowns: **What happened?**, **What now?**, **Where am I?**, **Oops!** and **Help!** The events for the remaining tags are described as follows:

I Give up.

- After several attempts to display the rate per night of the hotel room, P1 gave up this activity. After a brief interview, he said he was spending a lot of time and chose to continue with the other activities.

Looks Fine to Me.

- P2 and P4 tried to find quickly the hotel that meets the proposed conditions by using the search filter. However, this tool was used in a wrong way. Nevertheless, the results of these actions seem to be fine for them. Instead of helping them, these actions complicated the search, and they had to spend more time than the other participants.

Thanks, but No, Thanks.

- The system displayed a calendar in which P2 could specify the check-in and check-out dates. However, he decided to use another functionality (implemented by a combo box) to establish these dates. He is aware that both choices lead to the same result, but prefers to leave the current workflow to use a different option.
- There is an option in the interface to search by hotel name. However, P4 decided to use search filters to identify the hotel that was requested in the test.

I Can Do It Otherwise.

– There is not an option in the system to display the room rate per night, only the total price. Therefore, P2, P3 and P4 decided to use the calculator of Microsoft Windows to perform this estimation.

Where Is It?

– P2 tries to locate an option that allows displaying only those hotels whose total price ranges from a certain amount of money to the available budget.
– P2 tries to find a functionality that allows sorting the search results by room rate from the cheapest to the most expensive hotels.
– P3 tries to find a link to visualize the services that are offered by the hotels.
– P2 and P4 try to find an option that allows them to view the room rates per night of the selected hotels.
– P1 tries to locate the option that allows performing a search by hotel name.

I Can't Do It This Way.

– P2 and P4 selected some search filters to find a hotel that meets the proposed conditions of the activity. However, this action delayed the search process instead of simplifying it. Users concluded it was not the proper way to perform the activity. Therefore, they stop the current sequence of actions to choose a different path.

What Is This?

– P1, P2, P3 and P4 tried to find out how the search filters should be used. They tried to determine if these tools are useful and appropriate to achieve the goals of the task.
– P2 and P4 examined some system options to sort the search results. Users tried to determine if these options were appropriate to display the list of hotels in a specific order.
– P1, P2 and P3 tried to discover the purpose of some elements of the interface randomly. After a brief interview with the participants, they stated the system provides many options whose intention is unclear.
– P1 tried to find out how to use the system options that allow users to view images and videos about the hotels.
– P2 examined some system options that allow users to modify the room type of a hotel booking, in an attempt to determine if there was a possibility to cover all the expenses with the proposed budget.

Why Doesn't It?

– P1 tries to perform a search using an element that was designed for another purpose. The results are not the expected by the user who is confused.

4.2 Interpretation

Given that the results show a small amount of communicative breakdowns, we can conclude that the level of communicability of *Booking.com* is acceptable. However, it is important to consider that three participants of this evaluation had experience using this software. Additionally, the test design was based on usability issues that were identified in a similar system. Although the test is valid, the tasks that were requested only addressed overall aspects.

The communicative breakdowns with the highest occurrence were: *I can do otherwise*, *Where is it?*, and *What is this?* These results establish that the system provides several options for users to identify immediately a hotel that meets their preferences. However, there are elements that are not visible enough and whose design intents are not explicit. The Website has been designed for users with experience in the use of this type of software applications. Novice users are forced to examine the interface continuously (*What is this?*) and determine how to use the system. Several times, they tried to find the location of certain options to achieve their goal (*Where is it?*) and performed a different path of actions to the proposed one by the designers (*I can do otherwise*).

4.3 Semiotic Profile

Who Do I Think Are the Users of the Software Product I Have Designed? Users are people who have experience in the use of software systems. They manage to become quickly familiar with my system. I should consider that they have different needs to choose a hotel. They have different types of perceptions and are from different cultures.

What the Users Want and Need? Users want to make a hotel reservation. However, for users to make a decision, they need to be informed properly about the hotel services, room facilities and rates. I am aware that users have different perspectives, and therefore, they could have different search criteria.

What Are the Users' Preferences According to What They Want and Need? Why? Users need to find quickly a hotel that meets their needs. I believe that most users are looking for an affordable hotel, that is visually appealing and offers the essential services. However, I am also aware that all users have not the same preferences. Some of them might be considering specific criteria, such as if the hotel is near to a particular location, if the room rates are affordable or if the star rating is appropriate.

How Is the System I Have Designed for These Specific Users, and How They Should Use the System? The system I have designed offers all the information you need to book a hotel that meets your preferences. The software is flexible and implements multiple search filters. The search results will include a summary of the most relevant information about each hotel.

The system will display photos and videos of the hotels for you to make a better decision. All information will be displayed in your language, and the rates will be in your local currency. You can sort the search results according to your preferences. Additionally, there will be an interactive map, in which you will be able to see the specific location of the hotels. I know that your opinion matters, and for that reason, I have designed a section where you can register your opinion as feedback for other users. Finally, I guarantee your privacy by establishing user accounts to register all your personal information.

What Is My Design Vision? *Booking.com* does not consider novice users. Many system options are not visible or explicit. Users who are not familiar with the software application are forced to discover how the system should be used. The level of communicability is acceptable, but there are still elements of the design that should be improved. Users do not follow the normal workflow that was proposed by the designers. However, the Website can be very useful for experienced users in the use of this type of applications. This technological tool offers multiple search options and provides the required information about each hotel. In this way, all users can make a decision according to what they are considering.

5   Conclusions and Future Works

This paper establishes the results of a case study, in which the Communicability Evaluation Method (CEM) was applied to a transactional Web application for hotel reservations (*Booking.com*). This inspection, whose purpose was essentially academic, involved the participation of four university students. The purpose of this assessment was to determine the degree in which the designers achieve to communicate users their design intents through the system interface. An analysis of the results allowed specialists to conclude that the level of communicability of this software application is acceptable.

Through the Communicability Evaluation Method (CEM) is possible to identify important aspects of the metacommunication between designers and users of a software product. In this study, we determined some communicative breakdowns in the interaction that delay the execution of specific tasks. The results of this research showed that the level of communicability of *Booking.com* is quite acceptable due to the small number of communication breakdowns that were identified. However, certain aspects need to be improved as the visibility and location of some design elements. The system should be more explicit with certain options since that users are continuously exploring the system to determine the result of certain features.

Most case studies that have been conducted in this area are focused on the evaluation of desktop applications. It is important to determine the results of the Communicability Evaluation Method (CEM) in other contexts such as mobile applications, video games, augmented reality applications and virtual worlds. Specialists should determine if it is necessary a change in the methodology to obtain accuracy results when a new category of software product is evaluated.

References

1. de A. Maués, R., Barbosa, S.D.J.: Cross-communicability: evaluating the meta-communication of cross-platform applications. In: Kotzé, P., Marsden, G., Lindgaard, G., Wesson, J., Winckler, M. (eds.) INTERACT 2013, Part III. LNCS, vol. 8119, pp. 241–258. Springer, Heidelberg (2013)
2. Alarcon, C., Medina, F., Villarroel, R.: Finding usability and communicability problems for transactional web applications. IEEE Latin Am. Trans. **12**(1), 23–28 (2014)
3. Bim, S.A., Leitão, C.F., de Souza, C.S.: Can the teaching of hci contribute for the learning of computer science the case of semiotic engineering methods. In: Proceedings of the 11th Brazilian Symposium on Human Factors in Computing Systems, pp. 185–194. IHC 2012. Brazilian Computer Society, Porto Alegre, Brazil (2012)
4. Lee, S., Koubek, R.J.: The effects of usability and web design attributes on user preference for e-commerce web sites. Comput. Ind. **61**(4), 329–341 (2010)
5. Pascual, A., Ribera, M., Granollers, T.: Comunicability of two web 2.0 accessibility evaluation tools. In: 2015 10th Computing Colombian Conference (10CCC), pp. 269–272, September 2015
6. Paz, F., Paz, F.A., Villanueva, D., Pow-Sang, J.A.: Heuristic evaluation as a complement to usability testing: a case study in web domain. In: 2015 12th International Conference on Information Technology - New Generations (ITNG), pp. 546–551, April 2015
7. Prates, R.O., Barbosa, S.D.J., de Souza, C.S.: A case study for evaluating interface design through communicability. In: Proceedings of the 3rd Conference on Designing Interactive Systems: Processes, Practices, Methods, and Techniques, DIS 2000, NY, USA, pp. 308–316. ACM, New York (2000)
8. Reis, S., Prates, R.: An initial analysis of communicability evaluation methods through a case study. In: CHI 2012 Extended Abstracts on Human Factors in Computing Systems, CHI EA 2012, NY, USA, pp. 2615–2620. ACM, New York (2012)
9. Segura, V., Simões, F., Sotero, G., Barbosa, S.D.J.: Multi-level communicability evaluation of a prototyping tool. In: Kurosu, M. (ed.) HCII/HCI 2013, Part I. LNCS, vol. 8004, pp. 460–469. Springer, Heidelberg (2013)
10. da Alves, A.S., Ferreira, S.B.L., de Oliveira, V.S., da Silva, D.S.: Evaluation of potential communication breakdowns in the interaction of the deaf in corporate information systems on the web. Procedia Comput. Sci. **14**, 234–244 (2012). Proceedings of the 4th International Conference on Software Development for Enhancing Accessibility and Fighting Info-exclusion (DSAI 2012) (2012)
11. de Souza, C.S., Leitão, C.F.: Semiotic Engineering Methods for Scientific Research in HCI. Morgan & Claypool Publishers, Pennsylvania State University, PA, USA (2009)
12. The Priceline Group: Overview about booking.com (2012). http://www.booking.com/content/about.html. Accessed on 10 Feb 2016

Validating Mobile Designs with Agile Testing in China: Based on Baidu Map for Mobile

Jia Qu and Jing Zhang[✉]

Financial Design Center, Baidu, Beijing, China
{qujia, zhangjing03}@baidu.com

Abstract. The mobile market in China has boomed recently. In using UCD methods in enterprises, however, Chinese practitioners are faced with challenges in both design and research, given the fast iterative pace and an inflating number of features in applications. In this context, the article aims to present an agile, solid and integrated approach to valid mobile designs, integrating online experimentation, survey and usability testing. It will also present an empirical example using the methodology to push forward an innovative design in Baidu Map for Mobile. The example described how we understand major influences of the new designs through a series of studies over half-a-month, and moved forward to improve and finally realize the designs. The article also summarizes some insights we gained in the practice.

Keywords: Enterprise · Empirical study · User-centered design · Map for mobile

1 Introduction

The mobile market in China has boomed recently. By the end of 2014, the total number of mobile internet users in China reached 0.56 billion, 85.8 % of internet users in all [1]. The applications in the Apple App Store and Google Play added up to 2.64 million by January 2015 [2]. Many practitioners in large internet enterprises in China have endeavored to adopt User-Centered Design (UCD) methodologies, emphasizing specialized methods of end-user research before the product is made. Methods typically used in mobile user experience research include lab-based usability studies, interviews, focus groups, lab experiments, log analysis, as well as observational and ethnographic research [3]. However, with the boom come challenges for application design and experience research, as designs of potentially complex applications need to be produced and updated at a fast pace. In many design programs, the above methods need to be combined to obtain solid results in a short period.

In this paper we will describe a typical practice using the UCD process for minimal cost to ensure user experience in fast iterative development, in which we combined several methods with the aim to overcome some of their limitations when used in isolation. We report key findings, and highlight the methodological insights we gained in our practice.

© Springer International Publishing Switzerland 2016
A. Marcus (Ed.): DUXU 2016, Part I, LNCS 9746, pp. 491–498, 2016.
DOI: 10.1007/978-3-319-40409-7_46

2 Baidu Map for Mobile (BMM)

The studies we are reporting investigated the user experience of Baidu Maps for Mobile (current version available for download at wuxian.baidu.com/map) [4]. Baidu (Nasdaq: BIDU) was a Chinese internet search service provider founded in 2000 by Robin Li, providing users with many channels to find and share information via its core web search engine and many more services [5]. BMM allows users to access the full set of maps (including street maps and satellite images) with traffic information available via Baidu Map [6], as well as Baidu's local search index (i.e. businesses and services, landmarks, facilities, etc.). Additional features include speech navigation for driving and walking, on-the-road sharing and chatting, and favorites, among others. By June 2015, its market share in China exceeded 70 % [7].

The Location-Based Service User Experience (LBS UE) Group has been dedicated to building user interface standards and promoting consistent brand experience for BMM from 2014. As BMM is part of a rapidly growing class of mobile mapping, navigation and location-based service applications, its designing balances navigation tools and shopping services, and requires consideration of multiple use scenarios. It also calls for cross-cultural thinking to design for other Asian countries (e.g.: Japan, Korea, Singapore, and Thailand). By the end of 2015, the LBS UE Group is a team of over 50 based in both Beijing and Shenzhen, China, consisting experts in areas of user interface design, interaction design, and user experience research.

3 Case Study: An Innovation of Simpler Interface with More Flexibility

3.1 The Design

Before 2015, Baidu Map for Mobile (BMM) utilized the popular interaction architecture for map applications in China, with a search box at the top and other major features (i.e.: Local, Route, Car Navigation, and Mine) listed side by side at the bottom of the homepage. However, after local services were enriched and prioritized, the previous interaction design faced major challenges. The first challenge was to emphasize local services as a strategic focus, which was hard since too many buttons and tools attracted attention on the homepage. Second, each time a local service (e.g.: the Chauffeured Car service) needed traffic diversion, a new shortcut icon had to be added to the homepage, undermining the interaction standardization. Hence we decided to make improvements on the product design.

Figure 1 illustrates the old design and the design solution for test after several rounds of feature carding and brainstorming among the team. An outstanding achievement in the new design was reduction of numbers of buttons and colors applied. Only two round buttons were present at the bottom, the Local (marked 1 in Fig. 1) and the Navigation buttons (marked 2 in Fig. 1), to highlight the importance of the Local feature. The feature Mine was moved to the left of the Search Box, represented with an image icon (marked 3 in Fig. 1). Car Navigation was shrunk under Travel, as listed below the Route feature on a semi-screen layer triggered when the Travel button was

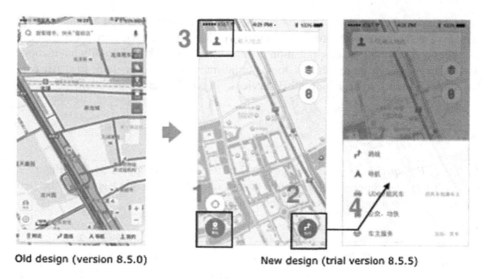

Old design (version 8.5.0)   **New design (trial version 8.5.5)**

Fig. 1. Homepages of BMM version 8.5.0 (the old) and version 8.5.5 (the new for trial), with major changes marked in numbers.

clicked (marked 4 in Fig. 1). Other travel services were also listed on the layer, such as the chauffeured car services, and services for drivers like fueling and washing. They were listed vertically, instead of in a matrix, to allow more space to display promotional activities. Colors for the two buttons were selected in consistency with the Baidu logo, with red indicating life and consumption, and blue indicating tool and efficiency. The design was also inspired by the current trend to simplize mobile user interfaces, as evident in many applications including Google Maps for Mobile (e.g.: version 4.14.74645), but the process to earn executive votes proved to be challenging given the many features in BMM.

3.2   Study Method

We wanted to evaluate the overall user experience of the new design. A trial version (version 8.5.5, 8.5.0 as the official version available) was developed for the study. We then ran online A/B experiments to quantify its acceptance and learning cost in real-life contexts, and conducted an online survey and usability tests as well to understand user's behaviors and opinions. The entire process lasted for half a month.

For the online A/B experiment, we sampled 1.5 million random Android called user identification numbers (CUIDs) as well as all users of Android version 8.4 of BMM, and sent upgrade tips of trial version 8.5.5 to them via in-app pop-up notice and app pushes over a 5-day period. After the number of daily active user (DAU) stabilized, we started the experiment and monitored online log data for 5 days.

For the survey, we posted an online questionnaire with a banner in a third-tier menu in trial version 8.5.5, asking participants to rate their attitudes to the trial version. For the usability tests, a total of 8 participants were recruited to try our trial version for typical tasks and interviewed after in our lab. The participants consisted of 5 male and 3 female. 5 participants were frequent users of BMM, while 2 used Amap for Mobile, another popular mobile map application in China, and 1 used both for daily navigation. 4 participants drove more while 4 took public transport more in daily life. All participants were used to searching local services via mobile map application.

3.3   Results

Online A/B Experiment. The average DAU of the trial version was 54,224. Figure 2 shows the click-through rate (CTR) and search rate of each major feature on the two versions in percentage of DAU over the treatment period.

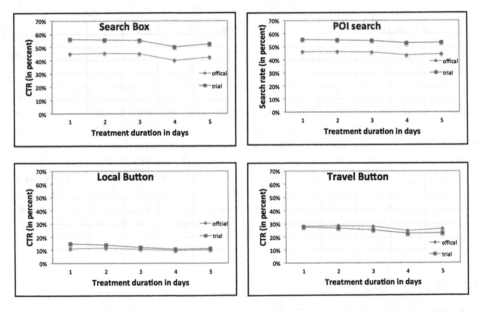

Fig. 2. CTR in percent of the search box, the local button and the travel button, as well as the search rate in percent of Point-of-Interest (POI) in both versions.

On the trial version, the average CTR of the Search box was 54.06 %, much higher than the 43.61 % on the official version. The actual search rate was also higher on the trial version. This suggests that compared with the previous version, user tended to search more because of the new design.

The CTR of the Local button on the trial version averaged 12.45 %, while that on the official (control) version was 10.66 %. Difference between the two versions narrowed as the experiment went on, which indicates that simply enhancing the visual importance of the button had little effect on its actual usage.

CTR of the Travel button averaged 24.9 % on the trial version, while that on the control version averaged 27 % (CTR on the control version equaled CTR sum-up of the Route button and the Car Navigation button). On the trial version, CTR of Travel button didn't differ much from that on the control version in the beginning, but slipped a little later. On the fifth day, the difference between the two versions reached 3.28 %. These results suggest that cutting out the Car Navigation button caused small but limited effect on the usage of the feature.

We went on to investigate the entire usages of Route Search and Car Navigation in the two versions. Figure 3 illustrates CTR of Route and Car Navigation on the homepage versus the actual search rates regarding the two features. While CTR of both Route and Car Navigation via the Travel button dropped, compared with the control version, the actual search rates increased instead. This suggests that although the new design altered users' click flows– instead of using the two features directly on the homepage, slightly more users were led to type in the destination before searching route or using speech navigation through the box– it didn't shrink their actual navigation demands.

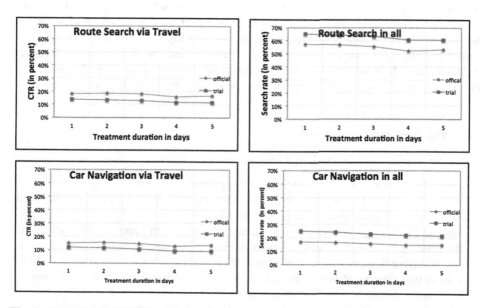

Fig. 3. Rates in percent in both versions throughout the treatment period, including CTR of route Search via the travel button versus actual search rate of routes (above), and CTR of car navigation via the travel button versus actual use of car navigation (below).

Survey and Usability Tests. We collected 4331 valid questionnaires from our channel in the trial version. Among them, 78.3 % agreed or strongly agreed that they were supportive of the version update. When asked about their preference between the previous and the new version, 50.2 % participants favored the new one. These results suggest obvious preference for the new design among the test users (Fig. 4).

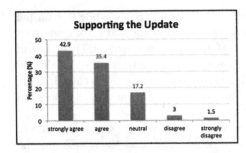
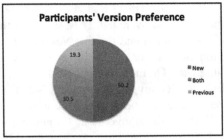

Fig. 4. Participants' attitude towards in trial version (left), and preference between the two versions (right). (Color figure online)

Face-to-face tests and interviews were conducted at the same time to investigate the usability of the new design. We focused on the most distinct change in the new design, which was the integration of the Route and the Car Navigation buttons into the Travel button. All participants understood the "Travel" button and clicked it when they needed to search routes or start speech navigation. The extra steps that it required to use the two features were still within their acceptance. However, participants found it weird to see services such as fuel charging on the semi-screen layer triggered by clicking the Travel button. A few participants tried several times to find the Mine icon, and found it unlike a clickable button and inconvenient for one-hand operation. Generally speaking, the participants found the trial version "awesome" and felt "a thicker taste of design".

3.4 Findings and Improvements

The main results from the study were summarized as follows:

- Most users preferred the new design to the previous version.
- Due to reduction of buttons, users tended to use the Search box more in the trial version v8.5.5 compared to the official one v8.5.0.
- Instead of clicking the buttons on the homepage to search routes or use speech car navigation, more users search destinations first in the new design. This alternation in interactive flow, however, didn't cause the actual search rates to fall down, which means that despite of button reduction, the trial version could still satisfy users' navigation demands, only in a new way.
- The alignment of fueling services with route search was not comprehensible.
- The icon of Mine was not imagic enough for BMM's users.

We moved on to improve the design based on the study results, and the final interfaces were shown in Fig. 5. These were also the final designs that we released in version 9.0.0. Major improvements included:

- The Mine button was changed into users' personal avatar to be more conspicuous (marked 1 in Fig. 5).
- The Local button was adjusted into a small bar to the bottom edge (marked 2 in Fig. 5), which could be swiped up into a semi-screen layer listing all services

provided in BMM, including food, drink and entertainment, services for drivers like fuel charging, and so on (marked 4 in Fig. 5). This layer could be further pressed and dragged to cover the entire screen, showing the full spectrum of services. This design reduced the interaction steps needed to use local services, and left the right of the bar a fixed place to expose promotion activities on the homepage.

- When clicked, the Travel button switched into a new page instead of a semi-screen layer, where users could flick horizontally to change the navigation as wanted at the top (e.g.: bus route, driving route, bicycle route, Chauffeured Car service, etc.) (marked 3 in Fig. 5). And the button was redesigned to incorporate the previous icon for Car Navigation.
- The beginner's guide was presented in semi-transparent layers whenever a new design was triggered in real-life use, so that users could better understand the brand new interface.

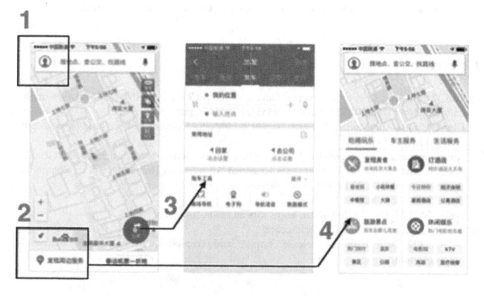

Fig. 5. Improved and released interface designs based on the study results

4 Discussion and Conclusion

The paper described an agile testing methodology, integrating online experimentation, survey and usability testing, to validate mobile designs in Chinese enterprises. An empirical case was presented of the methodology validating and improving the innovative design of Baidu Mobile Map (BMM). It is evident that this methodology produced quick and persuading results to push forward design innovations in the enterprise.

Our experience with the application has also resulted in a number of lessons learnt. These could be considered by organizations planning for similar design innovation.

- Reduction of first-tire buttons doesn't necessarily result in usage decline, as long as the alternative path is natural and convenient enough for application users. Thus it is strongly recommended to re-consider application interfaces and flows facing inflating features under changes in technology and business models.
- In the mobile context, convenience is especially important given the usually short time span that users could spare for each application. Half-screen draggable layers could shorten interaction paths, and have been proved to be acceptable for users in our experience. As handset screens increase in size, which is a trend witnessed in Asia, this design will probably become more popular.
- It is advisable to leave space for exposure of promotional activities in mobile application designing, especially when the application is facing an intensive competitive market or in the process of introducing new features.

Acknowledgements. The authors are grateful to Ye Bian, Yu Kang, Yanan Liu, Chunjin Zhao and many other colleagues for their dedicated work in the studies mentioned in this paper.

References

1. The 35th Statistical Report on Internet Development in China by CNNIC. https://www.cnnic.cn/hlwfzyj/hlwxzbg/201502/P020150203551802054676.pdf
2. China Mobile App Market Research Report by iiMedia Research Group. http://www.docin.com/p-1353331543.html
3. Riegelsberger, J., Nakhimovsky, Y.: Seeing the bigger picture: a multi-method field trial of google maps for mobile. In: CHI 2008 Extended Abstracts on Human factors in Computing Systems, pp. 2221–2228 (2008)
4. The Baidu Story. http://ir.baidu.com/
5. Baidu Map Mobile for download. http://wuxian.baidu.com/map/
6. Baidu Map for PC. http://map.baidu.com/
7. BIDU- Q2 2015 Earnings Release. http://ir.baidu.com/phoenix.zhtml?c=188488&p=irol-reportsAnnual

Assessing the Customer eXperience Based on Quantitative Data: Virtual Travel Agencies

Virginica Rusu[1], Cristian Rusu[2], Daniel Guzmán[2], Diego Espinoza[2],
Daniel Rojas[2], Silvana Roncagliolo[2], and Daniela Quiñones[2(✉)]

[1] Universidad de Playa Ancha de Ciencias de la Educación, Valparaíso, Chile
virginica.rusu@upla.cl
[2] Pontificia Universidad Católica de Valparaíso, Valparaíso, Chile
{cristian.rusu, silvana}@ucv.cl,
daniel.e.guzman.s@gmail.com,
diego.espinoza.rios@gmail.com,
drrvdrojas@gmail.com, danielacqo@gmail.com

Abstract. Usability is a key concept that refers not only to software systems, but also to products and services. User eXperience (UX) extends the usability concept. The broader concept of Customer eXperience (CX) is emerging. There are well established usability evaluation methods, but evaluating UX is more challenging. UX evaluation methods are also able to evaluate some CX aspects; some others require specific methods. The paper analyzes quantitative data on customers' opinion, freely available at two virtual travel agencies' websites.

Keywords: Customer experience · User experience · Usability · Customer experience evaluation · Virtual travel agencies

1 Introduction

Usability is a key concept in Human – Computer Interaction. It was discussed for decades, but its definition is still evolving. A widely accepted definition is the one provided by the ISO 9241-210 "the extent to which a system, product or service can be used by specified users to achieve specified goals with effectiveness, efficiency and satisfaction in a specified context of use" [1]. It highlights that usability refers not only to software systems, but also to products and services.

User eXperience (UX) goes beyond the three generally accepted usability's dimensions: effectiveness, efficiency and satisfaction. The ISO 9241-210 standard defines UX as a "person's perceptions and responses resulting from the use and/or anticipated use of a product, system or service" [1]. Again, UX does not limit to software systems; it applies to products and services as well.

A broader concept of Customer eXperience (CX) is emerging. It addresses the growing emphasis on service design and the service science as discipline [2]. Service science is an interdisciplinary area of study focused on systematic innovation in service.

There are well established usability evaluation methods. Evaluating UX is more challenging and arguably overwhelming for newcomers. As CX is a wider concept, assessing CX is even more challenging than assessing UX. If usability is a subset of

© Springer International Publishing Switzerland 2016
A. Marcus (Ed.): DUXU 2016, Part I, LNCS 9746, pp. 499–508, 2016.
DOI: 10.1007/978-3-319-40409-7_47

UX, and UX is a subset of CX, that means usability evaluation methods and UX evaluation methods are also able to evaluate some CX aspects. But how can we evaluate other (uncovered) CX aspects?

Web mining techniques offer valuable outcomes on CX. A common research approach nowadays is the opinion mining. It analyzes customers' opinion (sentiment analysis), based on their (qualitative) feedback. An alternative approach is the web content mining, which may also offer interesting (complementary) results, based on quantitative data.

The paper analyzes quantitative data on customers' opinion, freely available at virtual travel agencies' websites. Two websites were used as case studies: www. tripadvisor.cl and www.hotelclub.com. Section 2 reviews the concepts of usability, UX, and CX. Section 3 presents the experimental results. Data relationships are identified and interpreted as CX outcomes. Section 4 points out conclusions and future work.

2 Evaluating eXperiences

The current ISO 9241 defines usability as "the extent to which a system, product or service can be used by specified users to achieve specified goals with effectiveness, efficiency and satisfaction in a specified context of use" [1]. It makes clear that usability refers not only to software systems, but also to products and services. The ISO/IEC 20000 1 standard define a service as "means of delivering value for the customer by facilitating results the customer wants to achieve" [3]. The use of the term "customer" does not necessarily imply a financial relationship.

Literature refers to usability dimensions as "attributes", "factors" or "goals". Several aspects are recurrent in all usability definitions, as well as in ISO standards: effectiveness, efficiency, satisfaction, and context of use. As Bevan, Carter and Harker highlight, the ISO 9241 current approach directly relates usability to user and business requirements: effectiveness means success in achieving goals, efficiency means not wasting time and satisfaction means willingness to use the system. The standard is currently under review, and three main lessons have been learned since its first version, back in 1998: (1) the importance of understanding UX, (2) the "measurement-based" usability approach is not enough, (3) the need to explain how to take account negative outcomes that could arise from inadequate usability [4].

UX goes beyond the three generally accepted usability's dimensions: effectiveness, efficiency and satisfaction. The ISO 9241-210 standard defines UX as a "person's perceptions and responses resulting from the use and/or anticipated use of a product, system or service" [1]. Again, UX does not limit to software systems; it applies to products and services as well.

Even if most authors consider UX as an extension of the usability concept, some are still using the terms usability and UX indistinctly. There is a tendency to move from usability to UX; even the former "Usability Professionals Association" (UPA) was renamed as "User Experience Professionals Association" (UXPA) [5].

A broader concept of CX is emerging. It addresses the growing emphasis on service design and the service science as discipline [2]. Service science is an interdisciplinary area of study focused on systematic innovation in service. A compelling CX leads to enhanced customer attraction and retention. As UX extends the usability concept, CX extends the UX concept. Service science and CX may benefit from the adoption of lessons learned in usability engineering and UX design.

The concept of CX is not (yet) well understood and has no clear and consistent definition. CX is increasingly discussed, but is rarely defined [6]. Laming and Mason define CX as: "the physical and emotional experiences occurring through the interactions with the product and/or service offering of a brand from point of first direct, conscious contact, through the total journey to the post-consumption stage" [7].

CX includes a series of interactions between the customer and the company (or companies) that offer the product and/or service, called customer "touch-points". Joshi resumes CX management as "the concentrated efforts made by an organization to improve the quality of the interactions between customer and the organization at various touch-points in a manner that is consistent and effective" [6]. He points out that CX management may lead to differential advantage for service organizations.

Gentile, Spiller and Noci consider CX as an evolution of the concept of relationship between the company and the customer [8]. They identify several CX dimensions: sensorial, emotional, cognitive, pragmatic, lifestyle, and relational. Nambisan and Watt also identify CX dimensions: pragmatic, hedonic, sociability, and usability [9].

Obviously, CX impacts the future relation that between the customer and the service/product's provider. That is why is surprising that the CX is a relatively new concept; the academic research on CX is limited yet, and its application in marketing theory is quite recent [7]. Schmitt proposes experiential marketing as a new approach to traditional marketing [10]. Experiential marketers perceive customers not only as rational, concerned about functional features and benefits, but also as emotional human beings, concerned with achieving pleasurable experiences. Schmitt points out four key features of experiential marketing: (1) it focuses on CX, (2) it focuses on consumption as a holistic experience, (3) it considers customers as emotionally and rationally driven, and (4) it requires eclectic methods and tools.

Usability evaluation methods are usually classified as: (1) empirical usability testing, based on users' participation [11], and (2) inspection methods, based on experts' judgment [12]. Evaluating UX is more challenging and arguably overwhelming for newcomers. More than 80 UX evaluation methods are described by Allaboutux.org [13].

As CX is a wider concept, assessing CX is even more challenging than assessing UX. If we consider usability as a subset of UX, and UX as a subset of CX, that means usability evaluation methods and UX evaluation methods are also evaluating some CX aspects. Evaluating other CX aspects requires specific methods. A key indicator is the customer satisfaction. But CX is much more than one overall satisfaction score [7]; it should be assessed at least at each "touch-point" (instance of interaction between the customer and the product/service).

Web mining techniques offer valuable outcomes on CX. A common research approach nowadays is the opinion mining. It analyzes customers' opinion (sentiment analysis), based on their (qualitative) feedback. An alternative approach is the web content mining, which may also offer interesting (complementary) results.

Chiou, Lin and Perng advocate for a "strategic evaluation" of virtual travel agencies' websites [14]. Kim, Kim and Han study several virtual travel agencies' websites, analyzing the attributes that determine users' preferences for a particular website [15]; they identify as the most critical attribute finding low fares, followed by security. The study of Bernardo, Marimon and Alonso-Almeida shows that both functional quality and hedonic quality contribute to the perceived value of a virtual travel agency, but functional quality is more relevant than hedonics [16]. All three above mentioned studies use the term "online travel agency".

Our research interest in virtual travel agencies initially focused on usability. We proposed a methodology to evaluate transactional websites [17]. We also developed a set of usability heuristics for transactional web applications [18]. Most of the case studies that we used were virtual travel agencies. We are also evaluating virtual travel agencies websites' usability on a regular basis, with our undergraduate and graduate students; it gives us an important feedback for both researching and teaching. Later on we extended our research to UX, and recently to CX.

First we thought customers' opinions available on virtual travel agencies' websites could complement our previous findings on usability and UX. But we quickly realized that very few comments refer to the user interaction with the virtual travel agency's website; instead they refer to the quality of the services acquired through the website. As researches usually focus on qualitative customers' comments, we decided to take an alternative approach, focusing on quantitative data.

3   Experiments: Virtual Travel Agencies

Two virtual travel agencies were used as case studies: www.tripadvisor.cl and www. hotelclub.com. Customers' opinions are freely available at both websites. Quantitative and qualitative data are available. Customers' quantitative perceptions on several dimensions, as well as their overall satisfaction, are given in a 1 (negative perception) to 5 (positive perception) scale.

The present study analyzes quantitative data on hotels located in Viña del Mar, one of the most popular tourist destinations in Chile. Data were extracted in November, 2015. As observations' scale is ordinal, and no assumption of normality could be made, data were analyzed using nonparametric statistics tests.

3.1   Case Study: www.tripadvisor.cl

TripAdvisor is a popular platform that shares customers' reviews and compares prices. It offers links to several virtual travel agencies. Travelers' reviews are both qualitative (comments) and quantitative (numeric evaluation). Quantitative evaluation is made on the following dimensions:

- D0 – *Overall rating,*
- D1 – *Location,*
- D2 – *Sleep quality,*
- D3 – *Rooms,*
- D4 – *Service,*
- D5 – *Value,*
- D6 – *Cleanliness.*

Travelers are using for the 6 dimensions, as well as for the overall rating, a 5 points scale:

- 1 – *Terrible*,
- 2 – *Poor*,
- 3 – *Average*,
- 4 – *Very good*,
- 5 – *Excellent*.

We analyzed the Chilean version of *TripAdvisor*, specifically the "Hotels" section: www.tripadvisor.cl/Hotels. We found data on 44 hotels located in Viña del Mar, Chile. A total of 3097 reviews were extracted. Most of the reviews do not rate all dimensions, therefore reviews were filtered. We selected only the reviews that evaluate the overall satisfaction and all 6 above mentioned dimensions. 865 reviews met the criteria and were analyzed.

The *Spearman* ρ test was performed to check the hypothesis:

- H_0: $\rho = 0$, the dimensions D_m and D_n are independent,
- H_1: $\rho \neq 0$, the dimensions D_m and D_n are dependent.

Table 1. *Spearman* ρ test for the overall satisfaction (D0) and dimensions D1, D2, D3, D4, D5, D6 (case study: *TripAdvisor*)

	D0: Overall rating	D1: Location	D2: Sleep quality	D3: Rooms	D4: Service	D5: Value	D6: Cleanliness
D0	1	0.508	0.768	0.828	0.792	0.793	0.753
D1		1	0.481	0.492	0.445	0.474	0.520
D2			1	0.764	0.656	0.662	0.709
D3				1	0.686	0.708	0.759
D4					1	0.714	0.708
D5						1	0.673
D6							1

As Table 1 shows, there are positive correlations between all dimensions. In all cases, the correlations are significant, because the p-value is less than the chosen significance level ($\alpha = 0.05$). Correlations are moderate to very strong.

- The overall rating (D0) is very strongly correlated with D3 (*Rooms*), is strongly correlated with D2 (*Sleep quality*), D4 (*Service*), D5 (*Value*), D6 (*Cleanliness*), and is moderately correlated with D1 (*Location*); we could assume that location influences less than other dimensions when assigning the overall rating.
- *Location* (D1) is moderately correlated with all other dimensions: D2 (*Sleep quality*), D3 (*Rooms*), D4 (*Service*), D5 (*Value*), and D6 (*Cleanliness*).
- Dimensions D2 (*Sleep quality*), D3 (*Rooms*), D4 (*Service*), D5 (*Value*), and D6 (*Cleanliness*) are strongly correlated.

Travelers are classified by *TripAdvisor* in 5 types, described below; the number of analyzed reviews associated to each type is also indicated:

- *Families* (230 reviews),
- *Couples* (452 reviews),
- *Solo* (34 reviews),
- *Business* (73 reviews),
- *Friends* (76 reviews).

The *Kruskal–Wallis H* test was performed to check the hypothesis:

- H_0: there are no significant differences between the opinions of different type of travelers,
- H_1: there are significant differences between the opinions of different type of travelers.

We used p-value ≤ 0.05 as decision rule.

Table 2. Kruskal–Wallis *H* test for types of traveleres, by dimensions (case study: *TripAdvisor*)

	D0: Overall rating	D1: Location	D2: Sleep quality	D3: Rooms	D4: Service	D5: Value	D6: Cleanliness
p-value	0.064	0.061	0.325	0.112	0.176	0.063	**0.024**

The *Kruskal–Wallis H* test results (Table 2) indicate that there are significant differences between the opinions of different types of travelers only concerning dimension D6 (*Cleanliness*).

3.2   Case Study: www.hotelclub.com

HotelClub is a virtual travel agency oriented to hotels/accommodations. As in the case of *TripAdvisor*, travelers' reviews are both qualitative (comments) and quantitative (numeric evaluation). Quantitative evaluation is made using a 5 points scale, from 1 (worst) to 5 (best), on the following dimensions:

- D0 – *Overall rating*,
- D1 – *Amenities*,
- D2 – *Cleanliness*,
- D3 – *Hotel staff*,
- D4 – *Comfort*,
- D5 – *Location*,
- D6 – *Value*.

HotelClub is less popular in Chile. Only 3 hotels in Viña del Mar have got more than 5 reviews, and were therefore selected for our study. A total of 27 reviews were extracted. All reviews include overall evaluations (D0) and rates on all dimensions (D1, D2, D3, D4, D5, and D6).

The *Spearman ρ* test was performed to check the hypothesis:

- H_0: $\rho = 0$, the dimensions D_m and D_n are independent,
- H_1: $\rho \neq 0$, the dimensions D_m and D_n are dependent.

As decision rule we used $p \leq 0.05$.

Table 3. *Spearman ρ* test for the overall satisfaction (D0) and dimensions D1, D2, D3, D4, D5, D6 (case study: *HotelClub*)

	D0: Overall rating	D1: Amenities	D2: Cleanliness	D3: Hotel staff	D4: Comfort	D5: Location	D6: Value
D0	1	0.659*	0.183	0.178	0.311	-0.067	0.470*
D1		1	0.333	0.313	0.418*	0.280	0.589*
D2			1	0.708*	0.684*	0.476*	0.560*
D3				1	0.501*	0.347	0.344
D4					1	0.629	0.641*
D5						1	0.433*
D6							1

Table 3 shows the correlations between all dimensions. Only correlations marked with (*) are significant at level $\alpha = 0.05$, and will be interpreted.

- The overall rating (D0) is strongly correlated with dimension D1 (*Amenities*), and is moderately correlated with dimension D6 (*Value*).
- *Amenities* (D1) is moderately correlated with dimensions D4 (*Comfort*) and D6 (*Value*).
- *Cleanliness* (D2) is strongly correlated with dimensions D3 (*Hotel staff*) and D4 (*Comfort*), and is moderately correlated with dimensions D5 (*Location*) and D6 (*Value*).
- *Hotel staff* (D3) is moderately correlated with dimension D4 (*Comfort*).
- *Comfort* (D4) is strongly correlated with dimension D6 (*Value*).
- *Location* (D5) is moderately correlated with dimension D6 (*Value*).

Travelers are classified by *HotelClub* in 6 types, described below. The number of analyzed reviews associated to each type is also indicated; 7 travelers did not specify the group they belong to:

- *Business* (no reviews),
- *Couples* (13 reviews),
- *Families* (4 reviews),
- *Friends* (no reviews),
- *Singles* (3 reviews),
- *LGBT* (no reviews).

The *Kruskal–Wallis H* test was performed to check the hypothesis:

- H_0: there are no significant differences between the opinions of different type of travelers,
- H_1: there are significant differences between the opinions of different type of travelers.

As three types of travelers have no associated reviews, the hypothesis may be checked only for the types *Couples*, *Families* and *Singles*. We used $p \leq 0.05$ as decision rule.

Table 4. *Kruskal–Wallis H* test for types of traveleres, by dimensions (case study: *HotelClub*)

	D0: Overall rating	D1: Amenities	D2: Cleanliness	D3: Hotel staff	D4: Comfort	D5: Location	D6: Value
p-value	0.848	0.996	0.202	0.129	0.253	0.966	0.713

The *Kruskal–Wallis H* test results (Table 4) indicate that there are no significant differences between the opinions of different the three indicated types of travelers (*Couples*, *Families* and *Singles*).

4 Conclusions

CX extends the UX concept beyond the use of interactive software systems, services or products. It focuses on service science as interdisciplinary area of study. Service science and CX may benefit from the adoption of lessons learned in usability engineering and UX design. Assessing CX is more challenging than assessing UX. CX is more than an overall customer satisfaction score; it should be assessed at least at each "touch-point" (instance of interaction between the customer and the product/service).

Our research interest in virtual travel agencies initially focused on usability. Later on we extended our research to UX, and recently to CX. Web mining techniques offer valuable outcomes on CX. As researches usually focus on qualitative customers' comments, we decided to take an alternative approach, focusing on quantitative data.

We analyzed quantitative data on hotels located in Viña del Mar, one of the most popular tourist destinations in Chile. Two virtual travel agencies were used as case studies: www.tripadvisor.cl and www.hotelclub.com. Travelers' quantitative perceptions on several dimensions, as well as their overall satisfaction, are freely available at both websites. Travelers give their opinion in a 1 (negative perception) to 5 (positive perception) scale. 865 reviews were extracted from www.tripadvisor.cl, but only 27 reviews were extracted from www.hotelclub.com.

The *Kruskal–Wallis H* test indicates that in the case of *TripAdvisor* there are significant differences between the opinions of different types of travelers only concerning dimension *Cleanliness*. There are no significant differences in the case of *HotelClub*.

The *Spearman ρ* test indicates that in the case of *TripAdvisor* there are positive correlations between all dimensions; correlations are moderate to very strong. It seems that travelers tend to evaluate uniformly all dimensions. Results are similar in the case of *HotelClub*, but only approximately half of the correlations are significant at level $\alpha = 0.05$.

As future work, we will extend the study. We will first analyze travelers' perception on hotels from other regions of Chile and Latin America. We intend to check if the preliminary conclusions are also valid in new contexts. We will then extend the research targeting other regions. We also intend to analyze data available at other virtual travel agencies' websites.

References

1. ISO 9241-210: Ergonomics of human-system interaction — Part 210: Human-centred design for interactive systems. International Organization for Standardization, Geneva (2010)
2. Lewis, J.: Usability: lessons learned… and yet to be learned. Int. J. Hum Comput Interact. **30** (9), 663–684 (2014)
3. ISO/IEC 20000 1: Information technology – Service management – Part 1: Service management system requirements. International Organization for Standardization, Geneva (2011)
4. Bevan, N., Carter, J., Harker, S.: ISO 9241-11 revised: what have we learnt about usability since 1998? In: Kurosu, M. (ed.) Human-Computer Interaction. LNCS, vol. 9169, pp. 143–151. Springer, Heidelberg (2015)
5. Rusu, C., Rusu, V., Roncagliolo, S., Apablaza, J., Rusu, V.Z.: User experience evaluations: challenges for newcomers. In: Marcus, A. (ed.) DUXU 2015. LNCS, vol. 9186, pp. 237–246. Springer, Heidelberg (2015)
6. Joshi, S.: Customer experience management: an exploratory study on the parameters affecting customer experience for cellular mobile services of a telecom company. Procedia – Soc. Behav. Sci. **133**, 392–399 (2014)
7. Laming, C., Mason, K.: Customer experience – an analysis of the concept and its performance in airline brands. Res. Transp. Bus. Manage. **10**, 15–25 (2014)
8. Gentile, C., Spiller, N., Noci, G.: How to sustain the customer experience: an overview of experience components that co-create value with the customer. Eur. Manage. J. **25**(5), 395–410 (2007)
9. Nambisan, P., Watt, J.H.: Managing customer experiences in online product communities. J. Bus. Res. **64**, 889–895 (2011)
10. Schmitt, B.: Experiential marketing. J. Mark. Manage. **15**(1–3), 53–67 (1999)
11. Dumas, J., Fox, J.: Usability testing: current practice and future directions. In: Sears, A., Jacko, J. (eds.) The Human – Computer Interaction Handbook: Fundamentals, Evolving Technologies and Emerging Applications, pp. 1129–1149. Taylor & Francis, New York (2008)
12. Cockton, G., Woolrych, A., Lavery, D.: Inspection – based evaluations. In: Sears, A., Jacko, J. (eds.) The Human – Computer Interaction Handbook: Fundamentals, Evolving Technologies and Emerging Applications, pp. 1171–1189. Taylor & Francis, New York (2008)
13. Allaboutux.org: All About UX. http://www.allaboutux.org/. Accessed 7 January 2016
14. Chiou, W.-C., Lin, C.-C., Perng, C.: A strategic website evaluation of online travel agencies. Tour. Manag. **32**, 1463–1473 (2011)

15. Kim, D.J., Kim, W.G., Han, J.S.: A perceptual mapping of online travel agencies and preference attributes. Tourism Manage. **28**, 591–603 (2007)
16. Bernardo, M., Marimon, F., Alonso-Almeida, M.: Functional quality and hedonic quality: a study of the dimensions of e-service quality in online travel agencies. Inf. Manage. **49**, 342–347 (2012)
17. Otaiza, R., Rusu, C., Roncagliolo, S.: Evaluating the usability of transactional web sites. In: Advances in Computer-Human Interaction, ACHI 2010, pp. 32–37. IEEE Computer Society Press (2010)
18. Quiñones, D., Rusu, C., Roncagliolo, S.: Redefining usability heuristics for transactional web applications. In: 11th International Conference on Information Technology: New Generations, ITNG2014, pp. 260–265. IEEE Computer Society Press (2014)

An Analysis of Data Collection Methods for User Participatory Design for and with People with Autism Spectrum Disorders

Debra Satterfield[1](✉), Sunghyun Kang[2], Christopher Lepage[3], and Nora Ladjahasan[4]

[1] California State University Long Beach, Long Beach, USA
debrasatterfield@gmail.com
[2] Iowa State University, Ames, IA, USA
[3] Sutter Neuroscience Institute, Sacramento, CA, USA
[4] Institute for Design Research and Outreach,
Iowa State University, Ames, IA, USA

Abstract. User participatory design is considered to be one of the best methods for understanding the needs of a target audience and creating high quality, well designed solutions to meet their needs. However, for many persons with autism traditional forms of user input and participation are either severely limited or impossible. Without this input, well-targeted designs for persons with autism may be limited in their effectiveness for this audience. Therefore, there is a critical need to identify user participatory processes that allow all persons with autism to be involved in user participatory design in appropriate and meaningful ways. This paper will identify and discuss methods of user participatory design that can engage all persons across the autism spectrum. It will also discuss the significance of four different types of data collection with regard to informing the design process. The ethical considerations involved with each of the methods will also be discussed.

Keywords: User participatory design · Autism · Design research methods

1 Introduction

User participatory design (UP) is known as a design method in the area of computer based technology [1]. User participatory design is considered to be one of the best methods for understanding the needs of a target audience, however the participants' ability to contribute is key to being successful in the process [1]. Therefore, there is a critical need to create high quality, well-designed user participatory methods to meet the needs of persons with all levels of autism. For many persons on the autism spectrum with severe language and cognitive disabilities, traditional forms of user input and participation are either extremely limited or impossible. And without their input, well-targeted designs may be equally limited with regard to their appropriateness. Therefore, there is a critical need to develop a method that allows designers to select appropriate user participatory processes or instruments for including all target audiences regardless of cognitive ability.

© Springer International Publishing Switzerland 2016
A. Marcus (Ed.): DUXU 2016, Part I, LNCS 9746, pp. 509–516, 2016.
DOI: 10.1007/978-3-319-40409-7_48

Similar to UP methods, direct observation and the recording [2] of behaviors are methods of data collection that are commonly used in autism to understand persons with autism spectrum disorders (ASD) and to model new behaviors. Therefore, these common strategies of data collection can be used for UP for persons with ASD. The following are examples of UP with persons with autism:

- an anonymous on-line survey of qualitative open ended questions (Putnam and Chong) was given to parents, caregivers, and persons with autism. Open ended questions framed as "in a perfect world describe." were used to identify trends of software and technology use for persons with autism and preferences in the design of new software or technology products for autism. The findings provided a preliminary understanding of user goals and concerns for the design of software and technologies. The study found no meaningful correlations between gender, verbal ability, diagnosis or age. However 19 percent (22 responders) responded that software be designed with fun as a goal. The study also reported that this disproportionately represented parents of children with autism over those with ADD-NOS and Aspergers [3].
- In a 2009 study using participatory design with adolescents on the autism spectrum, Madsen et al. identify the issues of cognitive impairments, including memory problems and low reading ability; complications associated with atypical sensory processing; and fine and gross motor difficulties as impacting the ability of persons with autism to participate fully in user participatory design. And for those reasons the researchers chose to use an iterative participatory design process for their research [4].
- In the blog, UX Matters, Zsombor Varnagy-Toth, identifies verbal difficulties with think-aloud protocols as difficult for persons with autism due to language and communication issues associated with non-verbalness and echolalia. Non-verbal communication was identified as being effective due to the more pronounced use of strong emotion or body language by some persons with autism. Specifically signs of excitement through repetitive behaviors, hand-flapping, rocking and vocalizing were associated with excitement or possible discomfort; signs of focus identified through complete silence and lack of physical movement; and signs of joy in success as interpreted through jumping and laughing out loud. As a conclusion, it is noted that usability testing is critical to the success of products and understanding the atypical responses is important to interpreting the usability test outcomes [5].

1.1   Hypothesis

There is a need for design research that identifies the best practices for collecting meaningful data for persons with autism from one or more protected human subject categories based on effective inclusion criteria strategies in ways that maintain a strict ethical code of conduct. Therefore, the following three areas should be addressed:

1. Research methods vary in their ability to be used by persons with differing cognitive levels in autism and familiar methods from other disciplines may be appropriated.

2. Data collections methods can be combined between quantitative and qualitative to form a richer set of information than either single method can produce for autism.
3. Robust strategies for inclusion criteria need to be part of the research methodology to categorize participants with autism in meaningful ways.

2 Methodology

Four methods of user participatory data collection are discussed: (1) an online survey completed by college students both with ASD and their typical peers; (2) a focus group survey of caregivers and teachers; (3) data collection via an on-site observation of persons with varying levels of ASD; (4) and a user participatory case study of two subjects one with ASD with severe language and cognitive disabilities and a neurologically typical peer. The following four research data collection methods will be discussed with regard to survey instruments, inclusion criteria for participants, implementation and outcomes working with persons with autism from a variety of age and cognitive ability levels.

Online Survey: An online survey was used with university students to compare course content and delivery preferences between neurologically typical students and students with high functioning autism. To be included in the study all participants had to have the ability to independently answer questions using the RAADS-R autism assessment tool as an online survey. The survey was administered in Fall 2014, at Iowa State University. It was sent via e-mail to 33,241 students ages 18-years and older for possible inclusion in this study. The students were from all eight colleges in the university and one academic degree-granting unit. Both undergraduate and graduate students were included in the survey. The responding students provided basic demographic information, completed the Ritvo Autism Aspergers Diagnostic Scale-Revised (RAADS-R) test questions, and answered questions with regard to preferences in course content delivery methods and course evaluation methods. Full approval for this survey was obtained from the Iowa State University Institutional Review Board (IRB). Of the students contacted, 653 responses (226 males, 420 females) were collected. The data was evaluated according to colleges, gender, and RAADS-R scores. A score of 65 and above on the RAADS-R test indicates the presence of ASD. For males who responded to this survey, the mean score on the RAADS-R was 74.8 and for females the mean score was 61.2. All RAADS-R scores across all nine academic units ranged from a low of 4 to a high of 215 with a standard deviation of 37.9 and a mode of 57 [6].

The ethical considerations for this online study were mainly focused on the possible stress of answering symptomatic questions and concerns that might arise in participants with regard to a possible autism condition. Participants were all over 18 years old and were given an informed consent statement with options to discontinue participation at any time. No significant risks or benefits to participants were identified and there were no significant ethical implications.

Focus Group: A Spring 2013 study using qualitative and quantitative data collection methods was given to parents, caregivers and teachers. It included 66 parents and 66 teachers through invitation and snowball effect. It measured their perceptions of the importance of social skills, communication and behavior for children with neurodevelopmental disorders. Each of these three areas as measured by scales were determined to be highly important to these children based on criteria outlined in the Diagnostic and Statistical Manual of Mental Disorders, Fifth Edition (DSM-5) [7]. The DSM-5 uses three severity specifiers to describe the level of symptomology in the two domains of social communication and restricted/repetitive behaviors. These levels and domains were used to inform the content of this survey. The parent, caregiver and teacher survey that was developed used a series of 5 focus groups to determine the most relevant questions for the development of the mixed method online survey tool. The online survey examined within each of the DSM-5 scale criteria the most important skills for children with autism in higher functioning levels compared to children in low functioning levels as answered by familiar people identified as being part of one of the categories of either parents, caregivers, siblings or teachers. Respondents were asked to rate the importance of social skills (6 questions), communication skills (7 questions), and behavioral skills (7 questions) in performing their roles in taking care of child(ren) with neurodevelopmental disabilities. These issues or measures were formatted using a 1 to 5-likert scale (1 being not very important, 3 as uncertain and 5 as very important). Each of those three skills were subjected to factor analysis. Cronbach's alpha was also computed to assess the internal consistency of the derived factors [8].

The ethical considerations for the focus group and survey participants were mainly focused on the possible stress of answering questions of a personal nature. Participants were all over 18 years old and were given an informed consent statement with options to discontinue participation at any time. No significant risks or benefits were identified for participants. The most significant factor in this study was to make distinctions between the participants with regard to their relationship to the person with ASD. This gives more accurate interpretations of the responses and allows for analysis of the data to look for patterns based on these respondent categories.

Ethnographic Observation: A data collection tool to observe the natural environment and activities of children with ASD was created and data was collected at a therapy provider site to understand persons in the differing cognitive/developmental levels. Students in the provider programs were divided into groups according to their cognitive and language abilities. For the data collection, an "Activities Observation Sheet" was designed based on the Connectivity Model [9], a research model that uses scales to measure a target audience's verbal and non-verbal communication in social, emotional, behavioral and physical realms. Through interviews and focus group studies qualitative data sets were collected and combined with quantitative data from survey tools. The qualitative data provides designers with very specific information that allows them to accurately interpret the social and emotional UP data from their target audiences. A series of four on-site ethnographic observations across different weeks were conducted using the Activities Observation Sheet. A team of observers that included designers and autism specialists used the sheets to record social, communication, behavioral and physical verbal and non-verbal data. Demographic data with regard to age, gender, and number of children in the facility was also recorded. The data was used to design educational workshops that were later conducted on the same site with the children from the observations.

The ethical considerations for the ethnographic observations were mainly focused on the possible stress on children in the observation and possible identifying information. The research team was coached on how to create minimal impact on the children by not initiating direct contact while observing and how to give the minimally appropriate verbal responses when directly engaged a child-initiated conversation. Prior to the observations, a letter of support was provided by the collaborating children's therapy site in support of the research. Because the children were not being directly engaged or interviewed, no specific directions were given to the children being observed. Parents were provided with information and consent/assent forms for their child's participation.

Case Study: The Play IT Observation method was designed for use in user participatory ethnographic observations in small case study environments. This method was designed to be used with all DSM-5 levels of autism. This specific case study observation used the appropriate DSM-5 level of fascilitated support as indicated by the child's language and cognitive levels for a child with severe autism. The case being analyzed was the study of an educational software app being used by two children, a 12-year-old boy with severe autism and cognitive disabilities and a neurologically typical 8-year-old female peer. The observations were conducted with a facilitator present during the study. Both verbal and non-verbal data were collected and an autism UP talk aloud protocol with verbal and hand-over-hand prompts was also used because of its familiarity to the child with autism. The data on the use of the product was analyzed with regard to the Play•IT protocols [10]. Play•IT is a UP methodology that incorporates ethnographic research strategies from autism behavioral training and the social, emotional, behavioral and physical scales of the Connectivity Model. This case study collected comparative data on the skills of child with severe language and cognitive disabilities and on the neurologically typical peer. This allowed comparisons to be analyzed between the two children using the device. This data was then used in enhancing the product design for both types of users. The Play•IT method allows social interactions and social rehearsal to take place between target audiences in ways that are natural because it examines the use object being studied in the context of appropriately facilitated interactions between participants. The data is collected by observing and coding interactions based on the Play•IT criteria that involve multiple participants such as a person with autism, their caregiver, and a peer as they interact together with a product in a more natural situation. It also allows for the evaluation of a product within the appropriate level of support and physical assistance as indicated by the DSM-5 for that specific user. This is particularly important in situations where the level of ASD indicates that completely independent functioning is not possible because of language or cognitive limitations.

The ethical considerations for the ethnographic observations were on the possible stress on the children in the observation environment. The research team was coached on how to create minimal impact on the children while observing them interacting with the software app. The researchers were also instructed with regard to how to give appropriate verbal and non-verbal or hand-over-hand prompts that are common in autism behavioral training to facilitate the case study. Because the children were not being directly assessed but rather the software was under review, no specific directions were given to the children. Parental consent for their children's participation was given.

3 Discussion

In UP for autism, there are three types of participants; (1) persons familar with autism or closely associated to those persons, (2) persons with ASD who have severe limitations in language and cognitive abilities, and (3) persons with ASD who have social issues that may impact their daily lives differently than neurologically typical persons but do not inhibit their ability to function cognitively in a mostly independent way and to use language as their primary form of communication. Research strategies in UP vary with their ability to be used effectively with each of these groups.

When collecting data from respondents who do not have ASD, there is a critical need to accurately assess and categorize them with regard to their relationship to the person with ASD. In studies such as the focus groups conducted with parents, caregivers, siblings and teachers, there was a high degree of correlation between responses. The only points of difference dealt with questions specific to a role such as questions about classroom habits as responded by teachers or daily living questions as responded by persons who are involved in that aspect of the autistic person's life. Therefore clearly categorizing respondent data with regard to relationships will allow more accurate interpretations to be drawn.

For persons with autism of a severity that significantly limits verbal and cognitive ability, using the DSM-5 levels and domains to inform research categories for inclusion in studies will make the data more accurate and will make the research group more homogenous. Using strategies such as the Connectivity Model and Play•IT aligns the research to the diagnostic criteria and ability levels associated with the target audience. These methods when applied to UP in autism do not imply a diagnosis but rather link evaluation criteria to specific types of persons with ASD. By using DSM-5 criteria to make the UP research participants more homogenous, the data collection strategies can be applied more uniformly and the data analysis outcomes have greater implications for similarly categorized persons with autism.

The Connectivity Model and Play•IT focus on collecting and analyzing important and highly informative non-verbal data for persons with autism with severe cognitive and language impairments. In these research method, data collection through observation of natural environments and third party reporting via focus groups and survey tools are combined to form a more accurate assessment. It is important that observations be done by persons trained in autism. In addition, multiple observations done over a period of time may be more accurate and give a clearer picture of the range of performances and skills typical of the UP group. It is important to acknowledge and respect the DSM-5 levels in each domain for the person or groups being studied. If assessed levels are consistent with a level of required support, researchers should test with this level of support as part of the research design. For example, if a test subject is typically not capable of performing a task due to cognitive or physical constraints, it is not appropriate to expect the test subjects to perform a research task without this required level of support.

For persons with ASD who can function independently to read and answer a survey, using standard autism tools such as the RAADS-R or other tools to categorize levels or sub-groups of social ability is more reliable than a subjec's self-reported level of autism. In addition, it does not specifically require a participant to divulge medically sensitive information that may be HIPPA protected. The outcomes of the assessment tool are not made known to the participant and therefore any ethical implications of diagnosis are avoided. The RAADS-R tool can be used to give very reliable numerical assessments of participants and clearly indicates both ASD or non-ASD levels.

In addition, with regard to ethical guidelines, researchers need to be trained in how to demonstrate or communicate using an appropriate cognitive and language level the expectations of the person in the study with regard to the tasks that they are to complete. For instance if a test subject is non-verbal, the test situation may need to be exactly communicated visually through several iterations prior to the data collection phase of testing. In addition, researchers must be well informed with regard to signs of non-compliance, agitation, boredom, or frustration from the test subject as indications that they no longer wish to participate in the research activity. Non-verbal communications must be respected as a sign to discontinue the study and disregard the data collected as directed in the IRB compliance agreements.

Ethical considerations involved with each of the four methods vary with regard to informed consent procedures. They also vary with regard to how the study expectations are communicated for user groups that involve children and persons with cognitive impairments. In addition, signs of refusing consent or rescinding consent are based on verbal communication for high functioning populations and based on non-verbal communication indicators for children and persons with cognitive impairments. In each case, the strategies for obtaining consent and plans for ethical discontinuance must be identified and all members of the research team coached in identifying these communications. In cases with children and persons with cognitive disabilities, it is always important to protect the identity and sensitive information collected and to have a plan for destruction of information and identifiers when the study concludes.

4 Conclusions

The findings of this research indicate that methods do vary in their ability to be used by persons with differing cognitive levels in autism. It was also found that familiar UP methods from autism may be appropriated especially those methods for ethnographic observation that are designed for engaging people with autism with a higher severity level as indicated by the DSM-5. For persons with a low level of severity in both DSM-5 domains, the RAADS-R is a highly effective tool for use with both neurologically typical people and high functioning persons with autism who require no support. The RAADS-R effectively identifies two groups of respondents; those with response patterns that are indicative of symptomatic autism and non-symptomatic persons. For persons who lack the ability to read and independently respond to questions, the DSM-5 is an effective tool to provide criteria for designing ethnographic research strategies and observation methods. The DSM-5 can also be used to indicate levels of symptoms in the two domains of social communication and restricted, repetitive behavior. The levels are requiring support, requiring substantial support and requiring very substantial support. It can also indicate that no support is needed and the subject can perform in that domain independently. The leveled support categories can be used to determine if the UX tool should be used or observed independently with the person with autism or if the observation or data collection should be used with the indicated level of support that is indicative of the autism participant.

Inclusion criteria must be clearly defined and the DSM-V is an effective tool for use as a method of discussing autism types with regard to levels of support needed and the ability to function appropriately in the domains of social communication and restricted, repetitive behaviors. Using the DSM-5 will align research outcomes to the diagnosis criteria of the target audience in a meaningful and useful way.

When involving persons with autism in the design process, cognitive ability and communication levels will determine the types of involvement that are possible. Observational data can be very informative and can often be used with persons from any cognitive or communication level. Researcher training is also a critical part of involving persons with autism into the research process. Researchers should also be made familiar with how to appropriately use verbal prompts or physical assists during research collection that involves direct contact or interaction with persons with autism.

References

1. Kensing, F., Bromberg, J.: Participatory design: issues and concerns. Comput. Support. Netw. **7**(3), 167–185 (1998)
2. Hailpern, J., Karahalios, K., Halle, J., DeThorne, L.S. Coletto, M.: A3 coding guideline for HCI + Autism research using video annotation. In: Proceedings of the 10th International ACM SIGACCESS Conference on Computers and Accessibility, ASSETS 2008, pp. 11–18 (2008)
3. Putnam, C., Chong, L.: Software and technologies designed for people with autism: what do users want? In: Proceedings of the ACM SIGACCESS Conference on Computers and Accessibility, pp. 3–10, New York. ACM (2008)
4. Madsen, Miriam et al.: Lessons from participatory design with adolescents on the autism spectrum. In: Proceedings of the 27th International Conference Extended Abstracts on Human Factors in Computing Systems, pp. 3835–3840, Boston. ACM (2009)
5. Varbagy-Toth, Z.: Usability testing with people on the autism spectrum: what to expect. UX Matters, 5 October 2015. www.uxmatters.com/mt/archives/2015/10/usability-testing-with-people-on-the-autism-spectrum-what-to-expect.php. Accessed 1 February 2016
6. Satterfield, D., Lepage, C., Ladjahasan, N.: Preferences for online course delivery in higher education among students with autism. In: 6th International Conference on Applied Human Factors and Ergonomics (AHFE), 26–30 July, Las Vegas (2015)
7. Diagnostic and Statistical Manual of Mental Disorders, 5th ed. American Psychiatric Association, Arlington (2013)
8. Satterfield, D., Lepage, C., Ladjahasan, N.: Children with neurodevelopmental disorders: comparison of parent and teacher perceptions. In: A poster presented at the 12th Annual Meeting for the International Society for Autism Research (INSAR) International Meeting for Autism Research (IMFAR), 2–4 May, Donastia/San Sebastian (2013)
9. Kang, S., Satterfield, D.: Connectivity model: design methods for diverse users. In: Ji, Y.G (ed.) Advanced in Affective and Pleasurable Design, pp. 32–40. CRC Press (2013)
10. Satterfield, D.: Play•IT: a methodology for designing and evaluating educational play experiences for children with cognitive disabilities. In: 7th International Conference on Design & Emotion, 4–7 October, Chicago (2010)

Research Trends in Web Site Usability: A Systematic Review

Tuba Ugras[1(✉)], Sevinç Gülseçen[2], Ceren Çubukçu[3],
İpek İli Erdoğmuş[4], Vala Gashi[2], and Merve Bedir[2]

[1] Yildiz Technical University, Istanbul, Turkey
tugras@yildiz.edu.tr
[2] Istanbul University, Istanbul, Turkey
gulsecen@istanbul.edu.tr, valagashi@ogr.iu.edu.tr,
mervebed@gmail.com
[3] Maltepe University, Istanbul, Turkey
cerencubukcu@maltepe.edu.tr
[4] Kadir Has University, Istanbul, Turkey
ipekili@khas.edu.tr

Abstract. The present study aims to review systematically all the studies of web site usability conducted in the years from 2005 to 2014, in order to present the research trends in usability issues of web sites. Regarding the inclusion criteria, 199 studies in total were included in the study. The major findings include that the most frequently addressed usability issue is navigation (excluding general usability issues), most of the studies used user-based Usability Evaluation Methods (UEMs), the most frequently used user-based methods are questionnaire and usability testing, and user experience of special user groups was not taken into consideration much. This comprehensive research on the usability issues of web sites provides important implications for future research by presenting the research trends. Also, it has the importance of being a reference for the reviewing process with the analysis structure of research questions, especially with the proposed classification for UEMs.

Keywords: Usability · User experience · Web site · Systematic review · Research trends · Web design

1 Introduction

Usability has been receiving increased attention among both designers and researchers. Besides the criteria of effectiveness and efficiency, thanks to user's satisfaction and pleasure -being one of the strongest determinants, recently- usability of web sites has become more important. Usability issues in web sites have been examined in academic literature. Previous studies have provided important insights into web site usability.

Systematic review is important to evaluate the work done in a specific area, compare the obtained results, find out the focused topics and the issues left missing, and explore further research topics that shall be done. Starting from this point, the present study takes a systematic review in order to examine the research trends in web

© Springer International Publishing Switzerland 2016
A. Marcus (Ed.): DUXU 2016, Part I, LNCS 9746, pp. 517–528, 2016.
DOI: 10.1007/978-3-319-40409-7_49

site usability. The study aims to review systematically all the studies of web site usability conducted in the last decade, in order to present the research trends in usability issues of web sites. To summarize, this comprehensive research on the usability issues of web sites presents the research trends with various trending topics and thus, provide important implications for future research.

2   Theoretical Background

There are various definitions of usability. According to United States Department of Health and Human Services, "usability refers to the quality of a user's experience when interacting with products or systems, including web sites, software, devices, or applications. Usability is about effectiveness, efficiency and the overall satisfaction of the user" [1]. Nielsen [2] explains usability with regards to five attributes: learnability, efficiency, memorability, errors and satisfaction. Usability is also defined as "the degree to which people (users) can perform a set of required tasks" [3]. Similar to this defi-nition, Dumas and Redish [4] states "usability means that the people who use the product can do so quickly and easily to accomplish their own tasks". Rubin and Chisnell [5] mention that a product or a service can be accepted as usable if the user can accomplish what s/he wants to do without having any problems or without asking for help. However, the most widely used definition of usability is the one indicated by ISO 9241. The ISO standard 9241-11, defines usability as "the extent to which a product can be used by specified users to achieve specific goals with effectiveness, efficiency and satisfaction in a specified context of use" [6].

When we considered the research on usability issues for web sites, we found out that the first study[1] was published in 1995. The question of "What are the usability issues examined in the publications throughout the years?" comes into mind. It is possible to find some answers to this question by looking at the systematic review studies. There is not any systematic review study related to web site usability, pub-lished before 2008. It is considered that the field of usability has become more important in the literature and the increasing number of studies on web site usability also increased the number of systematic reviews since 2008. We could reach a limited number of systematic review studies on web site usability published after 2008. These studies focus especially on web site usability evaluation methods (UEMs).

Insfran and Fernandez [7] designed a systematic review study. They indicate that theirs is the first systematic review study related to usability evaluation. They searched for *"usability AND web AND development AND (evaluation OR experiment OR study OR testing)"* query in IEEExplore and ACM digital libraries and reached to 410 studies published between 1998 and 2008. According to inclusion criteria, an article should contain the website UEMs, be related to web applications, and be a full text. On the other hand, as the exclusion criteria, the articles those aim to review the literature on the principles or recommendations for web design, use a combination of methods for

---

[1] The search criteria (the search string) for determining the first publication on usability issues for web sites is the same for the publications reviewed in the present study. The search results are also limited to the accessible publications through the online library of Istanbul University.

measuring usability, use usability metrics, published in a special issue, written in non-English, or published in conference proceedings are not included in the research. Finally, the number of articles reviewed as a part of the study declined to 51.

Fernandez et al. [8] designed a systematic mapping for the studies including web UEMs and published between 1996 and 2009. The studies were scanned by using IEEEXplore, ACM Digital Library, Springer Link and Science Direct databases. Additionally, conference papers and journals were scanned manually. *"Web (web OR website OR internet OR www) AND Usability (usability OR usable) AND Evaluation (evalu*/OR assess*/OR measur*/OR experiment/OR stud*/OR test*/OR method*/OR techni*/OR approach*)"* query was used for the search. As the inclusion criteria, the studies should related to web applications and report the employment of the current methods on the web. On the other hand, the studies that were not related to web, suggestions for web design, evaluated the usability features and their measurement, emphasized only accessibility, mentioned how to integrate UEMs, or reported on the functionality were not included in the research. Additionally, introductory studies, iterative, or non-English articles were removed from the list. Finally, 206 of 2703 studies were included in the research.

Nawaz and Clemmensen [9] prepared a general evaluation for the studies on website usability published between 2001 and 2011. They searched for "website" and "usability" words and selected the studies for only Asia, which is the first author's country. They eliminated the iterative studies and included studies in English. They expected the studies would be related to cultural differences, UEMs, website design methods, religious and public websites, and would include quantitative research and rural users. They used ACM Digital Library, Scopus, Web of Science (SSCI), and Science Direct for the search. They included 60 studies according to inclusion criteria.

Table 1 presents the highlighted results from these three systematic reviews.

It's possible in this paper to cite many other studies related to website usability. The fact is that there are some common research questions in the usability review studies which are mostly related to UEMs used and usability issues focused. However, some other questions are still missing in most of the review studies and needs to be answered. These questions are related to web design life cycle stages, suggestions offered, number of publications per year, countries of origin, website contents, user profiles, and numbers of users. On the other hand, there is always a need for systematic review studies because there are always new publications in a specific theme every year. Therefore, the present review study aims to be comprehensive and to present up-to-date information by examining the last ten years' publications.

3 Methodology

A systematic review is "a review of a clearly formulated question that uses systematic and explicit methods to identify, select, and critically appraise relevant research, and to collect and analyze data from the studies that are included in the review" [10]. As Torgerson [11] states, "A systematic review differs from a traditional narrative review in that its methods are explicit and open to scrutiny. It seeks to identify all the available evidence with respect to a given theme." In other words, systematic reviews allow

Table 1. Highlighted results from systematic reviews on website usability

Systematic review	Review highlights
[7]	• New (i.e. specifically crafted for the Web) UEMs were reviewed in 45 % of the studies
	• The most frequently used UEM was user testing which was reviewed in 41 % of the studies. (A method is classified as user testing if it reports an evaluation that involves the user's participation.)
	• 20 % of the studies reported inspections, whereas 39 % reported other UEMs. (Inspections indicate an evaluation based on expert opinion and other methods indicate the use of other methods such as focus group, web usage analysis, paper prototype, remote user testing, and survey.)
	• The usability evaluations were performed at the implementation stage in 68 % of the studies, at the intermediate artifacts stage in 27 %, and at the requirements specification stage in only 5 %
	• 69 % of the studies reported that the evaluation was performed manually whereas 31 % reported automatically
	• 71 % of the studies emphasized usability problems but no feedback on the design artifacts, only 29 % offered suggestions for design changes
[8]	• 39 % of the studies used the new methods, which are developed for the web usability. 61 % used existing methods for usability evaluation, such as cognitive walkthroughs, heuristic evaluations, questionnaires or remote user testing
	• Most of the studies applied user tests (59 %) for the usability evaluation
	• 56 % of the studies did not run any empirical validation for the usability testing. 44 % of them implemented empirical validation by surveys (12 %), case study (16 %) and controlled experiment (17 %)
	• 82 % of the studies used their own usability definition while 18 % used the standard definition
	• Automatic evaluation was employed in 31 % of the studies and manual in 69 % of the studies
	• 90 % of the studies employed UEMs in implementation stage, 26 % in design stage, and only 3 % in requirement stage
	• 68 % of the studies were associated with usability problems and only 32 % gave suggestions
[9]	• The beginning of the studies was 2003 and the number of studies increased after 2007
	• Most of the studies were from China (15 articles) and the least of them were from Singapore (1 article). There were some studies also from Japan, Malaysia, and Taiwan
	• The studies were related to behavioral intention (5 articles), learning (5 articles), cognitive theories (5 articles), and cultural theories (5 articles)
	• In contrast to the expected results, there was only 1 study on a religious website. Most studies examined academic, touristic, and e-commerce websites

(Continued)

Table 1. (*Continued*)

Systematic review	Review highlights
	• Most studies (62 %) contained users as university students and academicians in contrast to the expectation of rural users
	• The number of users was varied between 3 and 54 in experimental studies, and between 77 and 250 in observational studies

researchers to compare the results of all reports in a specific research theme. Through systematic review, it is possible to see what the trend is, what the studies are generally focused on, and what they are missing.

The present study takes a systematic review approach based on the theoretical framework by Kitchenham [12]. This framework performs a systematic review identified in three main phases. In the first phase, which is called *Planning the Review*, we first identified the need for a review through the following research questions:

1. What is the distribution of the number of publications per year?
2. What is the distribution of web site contents in usability studies?
3. What is the user profile distribution in usability studies?
4. What are the most frequently used methods in usability studies?
5. What are the most frequently addressed usability issues in usability studies?
6. Which are the most cited studies?

Then, we developed a review protocol as follows. The search was undertaken through the online library collection of Istanbul University in 2015. Searches were restricted to peer-reviewed articles, written in English, and published between 2005 and 2014. The search string used was: *((usability OR hci OR "human computer interaction" OR ux OR "user experience" OR "user test" OR "user tests") AND ("web site" OR "web page" OR "web sites" OR "web pages") AND (user OR users))*. The only contextual criterion for a publication to be included in the systematic review was that the publication should aim to examine the usability of a web site(s).

In the second phase which is *Conducting the Review*, the search process was completed through the following steps:

- Publications that include the keyword set within their abstract and published in the years between 2005 and 2014 were listed. This search yielded to 1047 results in total.
- Publications listed in the above search results were checked, if their full text were downloadable through the online library of Istanbul University. Then, 450 of them were downloaded as full text articles.
- These full texts were checked if they were (i) published as an article in a peer-reviewed journal or as a conference paper published in the proceedings book and (ii) whether they were written in English. Multiple copies were also excluded. Then, 233 full texts were left to be checked whether their context match the aim of our study.

- Finally, we checked these full texts to see if they were suitable for our systematic review study in terms of their research objectives. Publications (i) which aim to examine the usability issues but not the usability of a web site, or (ii) which examine a web site but not in terms of the usability issues were excluded. Therefore, at the end of the systematic search process, 199 full texts were included into this study for reviewing.

Then, the selected publications were analyzed and synthesized according to above research questions. Finally, the research report was written as stated by *Reporting the Review* phase which is the third phase.

4   Results

We detailed the results of the systematic review analysis based on our six research questions, as follows.

4.1   What is the Distribution of the Numbers of Publications Per Year?

It can be seen through Fig. 1 that 2005 (28 studies) and 2006 (26 studies) are the years with the highest publication number and 2013 (13 studies) with the lowest.

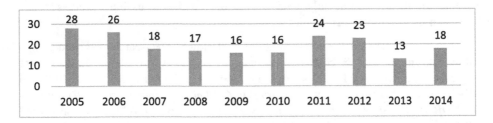

Fig. 1. Distribution of the publication years of the studies

However, the number of studies issued in the other years are pretty close to each other and within the average range (Avg=20; SD=5).

4.2   What is the Distribution of Web Site Contents in Usability Studies?

Regarding the context of web sites which were tested in the studies, five main categories were formed: Education, Business, Health, Socio-cultural, and Civil services. The distribution of classification of web sites tested in the studies is presented in Fig. 2, except the studies whose contexts were not specified (24.1 %). There is also a category of Multi-context, which indicates the studies with more than one context. Among the studies under the education category (71 studies; 35.7 %), library web sites draw the attention alone with the highest ratio (47 studies; 23.6 %), which is higher than all others.

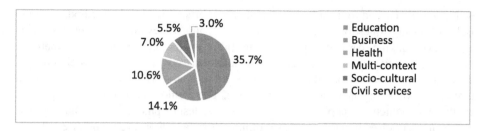

Fig. 2. Distribution of web site contents (Color figure online)

4.3   What is the User Profile Distribution in Usability Studies?

It is possible to classify the special user groups in usability studies as listed by Rızvanoğlu [13]. We modified that list with the addition of the special user group of individual differences, such as spatial visualization ability. Excluding studies in which the web sites were tested without any user participation (29.1 %), the rest of the participant profile distribution in the studies is as below Fig. 3. Also, the web sites were tested with more than one special user group in six of all the studies. Although the studies with non-special user groups (43.7 %) consist the majority, there are some studies with various special user groups. Among those, the highest rate belongs to the studies with disabled users (7.5 %).

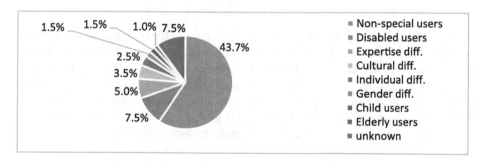

Fig. 3. User profile distribution (Color figure online)

On the other hand, it is remarkable that the term "accessibility" was mentioned at least once in 14 (out of 15) studies with disabled users whereas it was mentioned only in 10 (out of 30) studies with the other kind of special user groups. In spite of the fact that accessibility is a concept that is related to universal design [13], i.e. any kind of user groups, that term was associated mostly with the disabled user group regarding the studies reviewed in the present study.

4.4   What are the Most Frequently Used Methods in Usability Studies?

We propose to classify UEMs under five main categories: User-based, Expert-based, Data-driven, Design process, Literature review. Users directly participate to the usability evaluation in user-based methods whereas in expert-based methods, usability evaluation is carried out only by usability experts. User-based methods include usability testing, questionnaire, interview, prototyping (if evaluated by users), focus group, eye tracking, card sorting, remote usability testing, etc. Expert-based methods consist of expert evaluation, Heuristic evaluation, cognitive/barrier walkthrough. Data-driven methods are based on stored data and its analysis by various methods, such as Web analytics, log analysis, data mining, etc. The methods related to design process are the ones which are applied mostly during the design phase, without any participation of users directly, such as user profiling, storyboarding, prototyping, etc. Literature review is the method of only reviewing the literature, without any usability test. Figure 4 shows the distribution of UEMs according to these five categories.

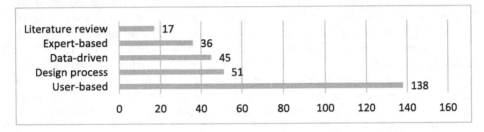

Fig. 4. Methods used in usability studies

Most of the studies (138 out of 199) used user-based UEMs so that we detailed this category as in Fig. 5. "Others" category consisted of diary, participatory design, guerilla testing, 5-Second test, and EMG. Also, in some of the studies, remote usability testing (1), card sorting (1), and usability testing (19) were accompanied by "think aloud" protocol. The most frequently used methods are questionnaire (98) and usability testing (81). On the other hand, it is remarkable that eye tracking was used only in seven studies, in spite of its attractiveness thanks to its technology.

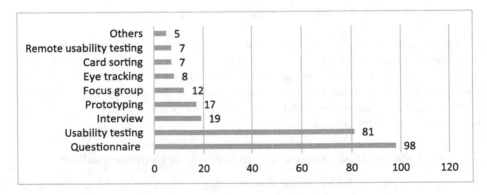

Fig. 5. Methods used in usability studies

4.5   What are the Most Frequently Addressed Usability Issues in Usability Studies?

Regarding the usability issues, studies were reviewed by paying attention to each study's own terminology. Figure 6 shows the distribution of usability issues. If no specific usability issue or only a common usability factor -such as effectiveness- was mentioned in a study, then we classified it under general usability issues category. Methodological issues category consists of the studies on which either how to evaluate, research, redesign, test the tool, apply the method (29) or how to design (12). "Others" category indicates the issues (icon design, color, personalization, etc.) which were addressed in less than 10 studies, in total.

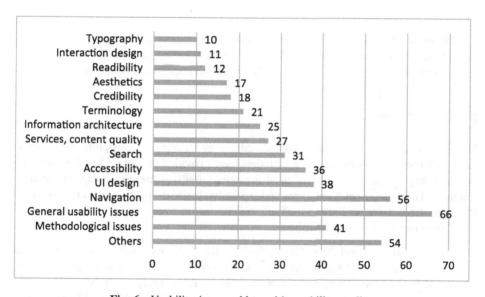

Fig. 6. Usability issues addressed in usability studies

Excluding general usability issues, the most frequently addressed usability issue is navigation (56) and it is followed by methodological issues (41), UI design (38), and accessibility (36).

4.6   Which are the Most Cited Studies?

It would be useful to catch the key points in studies by assessing them according to how many times they were cited. Therefore, citation numbers listed in Web of Science were reported for each study by March, 2016. Three of the studies have been cited more than 50 times, 13 studies 20–49 times, 26 studies 10–19 times, and 70 studies 1–9 times whereas 18 studies haven't been cited yet and the other 69 studies have no citation record in Web of Science. The top 3 studies are summarized in Table 2.

Table 2. Summary of the most cited studies

Study	#	Year	Content	User profile	Methods	Usability issues
[14]	101	2006	unknown	N/A	Literature Review	General usability issues, How to evaluate
[15]	80	2006	Business	Non special	Questionnaire	General usability issues
[16]	53	2008	Business	Non special	Questionnaire, 5-Second Test	UI design, Credibility

The most cited study (101 citations) is a literature review on general usability issues and proposes a new model of usability measurement called Quality in Use Integrated Measurement (QUIM). Thus, it is possible to see the importance of theoretical studies.

5 Conclusion

Usability evaluation is widely considered as necessary for designing web sites. Although previous systematic review studies have provided important insights into web site usability studies, there is still need for comprehensive and up-to-date research in the field. The present study analyzes and reports web site usability studies published in the years from 2005 to 2014, which are 199 studies in total.

The major findings are as follows.

- 2005 (28 studies) and 2006 (26 studies) are the years with the highest publication number and 2013 (13 studies) with the lowest. However, the number of studies issued in the other years are within the average range (Avg = 20; SD = 5).
- The top 3 content of web sites were education (71 studies, including 47 library web sites), business (28 studies), and lastly, health (21 studies).
- User experience of special user groups was not taken into consideration much (disabled users in 15 studies, expertise differences in 10, cultural differences in 7, individual differences in 5, gender differences in 3, child users in 3, and elderly users in 2).
- Most of the studies (138 out of 199) used user-based UEMs. The most frequently used user-based methods are questionnaire (98) and usability testing (81).
- Excluding general usability issues, the most frequently addressed usability issue is navigation (56) and it is followed by methodological issues (41), UI design (38), and accessibility (36).
- The most cited study (101 citations) is a literature review on general usability issues and proposes a new evaluation model.

This systematic review provides useful insights for researchers and practitioners based on a systematic investigation of web site usability studies. First of all, the study is important that it represents a collection to see the overall picture as well as the present research trends and missing points in the usability studies. By doing so, this study also helps enrich researchers' understanding of usability research design perceptions as it reviews both the methodology and the target user profiles in the studies. In addition, the study expands the usability literature by summarizing the related studies. Also, it has the importance of being a reference for the reviewing process with the analysis structure of research questions, especially with the proposed classification for UEMs.

Future studies can be conducted by extending the research questions of the present study to discover the trends by other elements, such as various other characteristics of the target user group, or various environments on which the web sites are being published. In order to utilize from the results of this systematic review, a relational analysis on the data set, comparisons across the research questions are also required for future work. Also generalizing the results to all web site usability studies may require some confirmatory studies with the use of additional keywords (i.e. "redesign" or "website") while searching with an extended publication date range. Moreover, there is also need for systematic review studies on usability issues for other online products, such as mobile applications.

In conclusion, this comprehensive systematic review study presents the research trends between 2005 and 2014 on the usability issues of web sites. The inclination of research design in web site usability in the last ten years also provides important implications for future research.

Acknowledgements. This work was supported by Scientific Research Projects Coordination Unit of Istanbul University. Project number 40421.

References

1. Usability.gov (2015). Usability Evaluation Basics. http://www.usability.gov/what-and-why/usability-evaluation.html. Accessed 15 December 2015
2. Nielsen, J.: Usability Engineering. Academic Press, Boston (1993)
3. Brinck, T., Gergle, D., Wood, S.: Designing Web Sites that Work. Morgan Kaufmann Publishers, San Francisco (2002)
4. Dumas, J., Redish, J.: A Practical Guide to Usability Testing. Ablex Pub. Corp, Norwood (1993)
5. Rubin, J., Chisnell, D.: Handbook of Usability Testing. Wiley, Indianapolis (2008)
6. Iso.org (2015). https://www.iso.org/obp/ui/#iso:std:iso:9241:-11:dis:ed-2:v1:en. Accessed 15 December 2015
7. Insfran, E., Fernandez, A.: A systematic review of usability evaluation in web development. In: Hartmann, S., Zhou, X., Kirchberg, M. (eds.) WISE 2008. LNCS, vol. 5176, pp. 81–91. Springer, Heidelberg (2008)
8. Fernandez, A., Insfran, E., Abrahão, S.: Usability evaluation methods for the web: A systematic mapping study. Inf. Softw. Technol. **53**(8), 789–817 (2011)
9. Nawaz, A., Clemmensen, T.: Website usability in Asia "from within": an overview of a decade of literature. Int. J. Hum. Comput. Interact. **29**(4), 256–273 (2013)

10. Cochrane Community Archive: Frequently Asked Questions - General: What is the difference between a protocol and a review? (2015). http://community-archive.cochrane.org/faq/general#t86n544. Accessed 8 February 2016
11. Torgerson, C.: Systematic Reviews. Bloomsbury Publishing, London (2003)
12. Kitchenham, B.: Procedures for performing systematic reviews. Keele, UK, Keele Univ. 33 (2004), 1–26 (2004)
13. Rızvanoğlu, K.: Başka Türlü bir İletişim Mümkün II: Herkes için Web: Evrensel Kullanılabilirlik ve Tasarım. Punto Yayınları, İstanbul (2009). 9789750110399
14. Seffah, A., Donyaee, M., Kline, R.B., Padda, H.K.: Usability measurement and metrics: A consolidated model. Software Qual. J. 14(2), 159–178 (2006)
15. Zviran, M., Glezer, C., Avni, I.: User satisfaction from commercial web sites: The effect of design and use. Inf. Manag. 43(2), 157–178 (2006)
16. Kim, H., Fesenmaier, D.R.: Persuasive design of destination web sites: An analysis of first impression. J. Travel Res. 47, 3–13 (2008)

Erratum to: A Comprehensive Stylus Evaluation Methodology and Design Guidelines

Kanchan Jahagirdar[1(✉)], Edward Raleigh[2], Hanan Alnizami[3],
Keith Kao[2], and Philip J. Corriveau[3]

[1] Intel Corporation, Folsom, USA
kanchan.jahagirdar@intel.com
[2] Intel Corporation, Santa Clara, USA
{edward.j.raleigh,Keith.kao}@intel.com
[3] Intel Corporation, Hillsboro, USA
{hanan.alnizami,philip.j.corriveau}@intel.com

Erratum to:
Chapter 40 in: A. Marcus (Ed.)
Design, User Experience, and Usability
DOI: 10.1007/978-3-319-40409-7_40

Figure 4c on page 430 of the paper "A Comprehensive Stylus Evaluation Methodology and Design Guidelines", authored by Kanchan Jahagirdar, Edward Raleigh, Hanan Alnizami, Keith Kao, and Philip J. Corriveau, has been retracted as it was used without permission.

The updated original online version for this chapter can be found at
DOI: 10.1007/978-3-319-40409-7_40

A. Marcus (Ed.): DUXU 2016, Part I, LNCS 9746, p. E1, 2016.
DOI: 10.1007/978-3-319-40409-7_50

Author Index

Printed in the United States
By Bookmasters